Māmaka Kaiao

Māmaka Kaiao
A Modern Hawaiian Vocabulary

A compilation of Hawaiian words
that have been created, collected, and approved
by the Hawaiian Lexicon Committee
from 1987 through 2000

Kōmike Hua'ōlelo
Hale Kuamo'o • 'Aha Pūnana Leo

University of Hawai'i Press
Honolulu

Pa'i 'ia ma 'Amelika Hui Pū 'ia
Printed in the United States of America

08 07 06 05   6 5 4 3 2

Library of Congress Cataloging-in-Publication Data
Mamaka kaiao: a modern Hawaiian vocabulary : a compilation of Hawaiian words that have been created, collected, and approved by the Hawaiian Lexicon Committee from 1987 through 2000 / Komike Hua'olelo, Hale Kuamo'o, 'Aha Punana leo.
    p. cm.
    ISBN 0-8248-2786-4 (cloth : alk. paper) — ISBN 0-8248-2803-8 (pbk. : alk. paper)
    1. Hawaiian language—Dictionaries—English. 2. English language—Dictionaries—Hawaiian. 3. Hawaiian language—New words—Dictionaries—English. I. 'Aha Punana Leo. II. Komike Hua'olelo. III. University of Hawaii at Hilo. Hale Kuamo'o.

    PL6446.M36 2003
    499'.42321—dc21

                                            2003050726

Pa'i 'ia nā puke a ka Hale Pa'i o ke Kulanui O Hawai'i ma ka pepa 'akika 'ole me ka ho'okō pū i nā ana ho'okele ho'opa'a puke a ka 'Aha Kumuwaiwai Hale Waihona Puke.
University of Hawai'i Press books are printed on acid-free paper and meet the guidelines for permanence and durability of the Council on Library Resources.

KA LAU 'ILI PUKE: 'O ka moena makaloa i hō'ike 'ia ma ka 'ili puke, he māhele ia o kekahi moena i ulana 'ia ma ke kaila pāwehe o Ni'ihau e kekahi wahine Ni'ihau 'o Kala'i kōna inoa a me kāna kāne i mea e ho'opi'i ai i ka Mō'ī 'o Lunalilo e "ho'ololi i ka 'auhau ma luna o nā holoholona." I ka hala 'ana na'e o Lunalilo ma mua o ka pa'a 'ana o ka moena, ua hā'awi 'ia i ka Mō'ī 'o Kalākaua i ka lā 27 o 'Apelila MH 1874. Aia ka moena ma ka Hale Hō'ike'ike O Kamehameha.
COVER DESIGN: The makaloa mat shown on the cover is a portion of a mat woven in the Ni'ihau pāwehe style by a Ni'ihau weaver named Kala'i and her husband as an appeal to King Lunalilo to "amend the tax on animals." As Lunalilo died before the mat was completed, however, it was presented to King Kalākaua on April 27, 1874. The mat is located in the Bishop Museum.

Hakulau 'ia na Hōkūlani Cleeland
Designed by Hōkūlani Cleeland

Papa Kuhikuhi   *Contents*

ʻŌlelo Mua

Māmaka Kaiao:
I mea e māmaka ai i ka ʻōlelo a puka he kaiao hou

I kō kākou hōʻea ʻana i ke kekeke o nā makahiki 1980, aia kā kākou ʻōlelo e kāpekepeke ana ma kaʻe o ka lua o ka make loa. Ma muli naʻe o ke kū ʻana o kō nā mokupuni me ka ʻauamo like i ka ukana nui he aloha i ka ʻōlelo, aia nō ke ʻīnana hou mai nei. Pēlā i kupu mai ai ʻo *Māmaka Kaiao* nei he wahi hua o kō kākou māmaka like ʻana i ka ʻōlelo o ka ʻāina a puka he kaiao hou o Hawaiʻi nei.

Eia nō ke paneʻe aku nei ke Kōmike Huaʻōlelo i kēia pukana ʻekolu o *Māmaka Kaiao* me ka manaʻolana e paʻi hou ʻia ana nā puke hou i kēia mua aku me kōna mau pākuʻina papa huaʻōlelo hou no ia wā. No kēia pākuʻina, ua helu ʻia he hoʻokahi kaukani ʻikamu Hawaiʻi hou a piha iho nei ka huina pau loa o kēia paʻi ʻana he ʻeono kaukani ʻelima haneli ʻikamu Hawaiʻi. Eia ke Kōmike ke kāmau nei nō i luna o kekahi mau papa huaʻōlelo hou e waiho nei.

Ke lele mai nei nā ʻike hou o kēlā me kēia ʻano me ka ʻimo o ka maka ma o nā ʻenehana hou o kēia au. Ua hala ia mau lā o ka hali ʻia ʻana mai o nā mea hou i luna o nā moku holo moana. No laila, mau nō ka paipai a nei Kōmike i kō ʻoukou makaʻala ʻana i ke ola o kā kākou ʻōlelo ma nā manawa e pupū ai ka ʻōlelo i ka loaʻa ʻole o kekahi huaʻōlelo Hawaiʻi kūpono. ʻApo i ia manaʻo hou ma ka ʻōlelo Hawaiʻi ʻana a e kāʻana mai i ia ʻōlelo no ka pono o nā hoa ʻōlelo Hawaiʻi a pau.

I loaʻa hoʻi kēia pukana hou o *Māmaka Kaiao* ma muli o nā ʻohana ʻo Hoʻohana ʻŌlelo mā. Inā ʻaʻole ʻōlelo ʻia ka ʻōlelo Hawaiʻi e ia ʻano ʻohana ma nā wā a pau a i nā wahi a pau, inā ua emi loa ka pākēneka o ka hui ʻana he alo a he alo me Manaʻo Hou mā. Ua pau ia mau lā o ka hoʻohana wale ʻana nō i loko o kekahi lumi papa aʻo ʻōlelo, a i ke kani ʻana o ka hola, ʻo ka pau ia o ka ʻōlelo Hawaiʻi ʻana. ʻO nā kānaka e hoʻohana nei i ka ʻōlelo ma nā pōʻaiapili like ʻole ma nā minuke a pau o ka lā, ʻo ia nā koa o ka ʻōlelo e ʻike maoli nei i ka hana e hōʻīnana ai i kā kākou ʻōlelo no ke au e neʻe nei. ʻO nā ʻohana hoʻohana ʻōlelo ka poʻe nōna ka mahalo o kēia paʻi hou ʻia ʻana o kekahi *Māmaka Kaiao* hou.

E hōʻīnana ʻia kā kākou ʻōlelo.

Nā Hua‘ōlelo

He loli mau nā ‘ōlelo ola a pau o ka honua nei, a pēlā pū ka ‘ōlelo Hawai‘i.
No laila, i mea e kōkua ai i ka po‘e ‘ōlelo Hawai‘i a pau o kēia au, ke pa‘i hou
‘ia nei ‘o *Māmaka Kaiao* ma ke ‘ano he hoa like o ka puke wehewehe ‘ōlelo
Hawai‘i a Pūku‘i mā.

No nā haumāna ‘ōlelo Hawai‘i, ‘a‘ole lawa ho‘okahi wale nō puke wehewehe
‘ōlelo i kēia manawa, no ka mea, he ‘oko‘a ke ‘ano o kēia mau puke ‘elua. He
mea nui ka puke a Pūku‘i mā no ka wehewehe ‘ana e pili ana i nā hua‘ōlelo
kahiko a hiki mai i kēia wā hou o kākou. Na *Māmaka Kaiao* ho‘i ka hana
ko‘iko‘i o ka ho‘olaha ‘ana i ka lehulehu i nā hua‘ōlelo hou e haku ‘ia nei e
ke Kōmike Hua‘ōlelo.

Hālāwai nā lālā o ke Kōmike Hua‘ōlelo ma waena o ‘ehā a me ‘eono manawa
o ka makahiki no ke kūkākūkā ‘ana e pili ana i nā hua‘ōlelo e ‘āpono ai. ‘O
ka hapa nui o nā hua‘ōlelo e hāpai ‘ia, ‘o ia nā hua‘ōlelo i nele i loko o ka
puke wehewehe ‘ōlelo Hawai‘i i ka wā i haku a unuhi ‘ia ai paha kekahi
ha‘awina, mo‘olelo, puke, a i ‘ole kekahi ‘ano palapala ‘ē a‘e ma ka ‘ōlelo
Hawai‘i.

Komo nui nā ha‘awina kula o kēia au i loko o nā mana‘o hou i nele i kekahi
hua‘ōlelo Hawai‘i ma nā puke wehewehe ‘ōlelo. No laila, ma muli o ka
ho‘omohala papa ha‘awina ho‘olu‘u ‘ōlelo Hawai‘i o kēia au i puka ma‘amau
mai ai nā hua‘ōlelo hou no ka ‘ike hou o kēia wā. Na ke kanaka haku a
unuhi paha ka mea ma‘amau nāna e hāpai i kāna mau hua‘ōlelo i hana ai a i
mua o ke Kōmike no ka ‘āpono a ho‘omalele ‘ana.

Inā pili kekahi papa hua‘ōlelo i ke kumuhana e pono ai ka ‘ike a kekahi po‘e
loea i ia kumuhana, kono ‘ia ia ‘ano po‘e a hele pū i ka hālāwai. Inā ua hiki
ke loa‘a ka ‘ike kūpono mai nā puke wehewehe ‘ōlelo, nā puke kumuhana, a
me ka ‘ike o nā lālā, a laila, ho‘ohana ‘ia ia mau mea no ke kōkua ‘ana i
mōakāka loa ka mana‘o ma mua o ka ho‘oholo ‘ana i ka hua‘ōlelo Hawai‘i
kūpono.

Aia ma lalo iho nei kekahi mau kulekele e hahai ai ke Kōmike i ka haku
hua‘ōlelo ‘ana. ‘A‘ole kūhāiki ‘ia ka haku hua‘ōlelo ‘ana i kēia mau kulekele
wale nō, akā na‘e, pēlā nō ka haku ‘ia ‘ana o ka hapa nui o nā hua‘ōlelo hou.

1. E ho‘ololi iki i ka pela ‘ana o kekahi hua‘ōlelo i pa‘i ‘ia ma ka puke
wehewehe ‘ōlelo. ‘O nā loli ma‘amau, ‘o ia ka ho‘okomo a wehe ‘ana paha i
kekahi kahakō, a i ‘ole, ka ho‘ohui a ho‘oka‘awale ‘ana paha i kekahi mau
māhele o ka hua‘ōlelo a māpuna ‘ōlelo paha. Ua ho‘ohana ‘ia ke kahakō ma
nā hua‘ōlelo e like me "hāpaina" (*carrier*) a me "kāka‘ikahi" (*few*), a ua

ho'oka'awale 'ia ka pela 'ana i nā hua'ōlelo e like me "a pau" (all) a me "me he" (as if).

2. E ho'opa'a i kekahi hua'ōlelo i lohe 'ia mai ka mānaleo mai i pa'a 'ole na'e i loko o ka puke wehewehe 'ōlelo, a i 'ole, i pa'a 'ole ia mana'o a ka mānaleo ma ka puke wehewehe 'ōlelo. 'O "ho'ohūpō" (feign ignorance), "kāka'ahi" (deal, as cards), a me "'alo'ahia" (stress) kekahi o nā hua'ōlelo a nā mānaleo i loa'a 'ole i loko o ka puke wehewehe 'ōlelo, a 'o "huka" (zipper), "maka'aha" (screen), a me "nemonemo" (bald, as a tire) kekahi mua hua'ōlelo i wala'au 'ia e ka po'e mānaleo me ka mana'o 'oko'a i kēlā i hō'ike 'ia i loko o ka puke wehewehe 'ōlelo.

3. E ho'opālua i kekahi hua'ōlelo a hapa hua'ōlelo paha ma ke kaila ma'amau o ka 'ōlelo Hawai'i. Pēlā i loa'a ai kekahi mau hua'ōlelo e like me "ūlialia" (coincidence) mai ka hua'ōlelo 'o "ulia," "hohoki" (neutral) mai ka hua'ōlelo 'o "hoki," a me "monamona" (dessert) mai ka hua'ōlelo 'o "momona" i ho'opōkole mua 'ia, a laila, ua ho'opālua 'ia ma hope.

4. E pāku'i i kekahi pāku'ina kau mua a kau hope paha i kekahi hua'ōlelo. 'O kēia nō ho'i kekahi hana ma'amau ma ka 'ōlelo Hawai'i, a ua ho'ohana 'ia nā pāku'ina kahiko me ka haku pū i kekahi mau pāku'ina hou. No ka loa'a 'ana o ka mana'o concentrated, ua pāku'i 'ia 'o "-hia" i ka hua'ōlelo 'o "pa'apū" (pa'apūhia), a laila, i mea e loa'a ai ka mana'o to concentrate, make less dilute, ua pāku'i 'ia 'o "ho'o-" i kēia hua'ōlelo ho'okahi (ho'opa'apūhia). Ua ho'ohana 'ia ho'i ka pāku'ina kau hope 'o "-na" ma kekahi mau hua'ōlelo no ka ho'ololi 'ana i kekahi hamani paha a i kikino, e like me "pāku'ina" (affix; pāku'i + -na) a me "koina" (requirement; koi + -na). Ua lilo ka hua'ōlelo 'o "kālai" i pāku'ina kau mua hou no ka hō'ike 'ana i ka mana'o -ology, the scientific study of. Pēlā i loa'a ai nā hua'ōlelo hou e like me "kālaiaopaku" (physical science) a me "kālaianiau" (climatology).

5. E wehewehe i ka mana'o o kekahi hua'ōlelo a māpuna 'ōlelo paha ma o nā hua'ōlelo Hawai'i. Ua ho'ohana nui 'ia kēia kulekele, no ka mea, inā lohe a heluhelu 'ia paha kekahi māpuna 'ōlelo "hou" i haku 'ia me kēia, e maopopo koke ana paha ka mana'o i ka mea lohe a heluhelu paha. Eia kekahi mau māpuna 'ōlelo i haku 'ia me kēia kulekele: "ala mōlehu" (crepuscular), "uila māhu pele" (geothermal electricity), "kuhi hewa o ka maka" (optical illusion), a me "'ōlelo kuhi lima 'Amelika" (American Sign Language).

6. E haku i kekahi hua'ōlelo i ka ho'oku'i 'ana i nā hua'ōlelo Hawai'i. 'Ano like kēia kulekele me ke kulekele helu 5 o luna nei, aia nō na'e, 'a'ole paha e 'apo koke 'ia ka mana'o ke lohe mua 'ia ma muli paha o ke ahuwale 'ole o ka mana'o ke 'ike 'ia nā māhele o ka hua'ōlelo hou. Pēlā nō paha no nā hua'ōlelo 'o "hamulau" (herbivore), "ka'a'ike" (communication), "kōpia" (carbohydrate), a me "poelele" (satellite).

7. E hoʻopōkole i kekahi huaʻōlelo a mau huaʻōlelo Hawaiʻi paha. ʻOiai ua hoʻohana nui ʻia kēia kulekele no nā huaʻōlelo makemakika a ʻepekema, haku ʻia nō hoʻi nā ʻano huaʻōlelo like ʻole ma o kēia kulekele. Eia kekahi mau huaʻōlelo i haku ʻia ma o kēia ʻano hana: "analahi" (*regular, as in shape*; ana + maʻalahi), "ikehu" (*energy*; ika + ehu), "lāhulu" (*species*; lāhui + hulu), a me "moʻolako" (*inventory*; moʻolelo + lako).

8. E hoʻākea i ka manaʻo o kekahi huaʻōlelo i paʻa mua i loko o ka puke wehewehe ʻōlelo, a i ʻole, e hāʻawi i kekahi manaʻo hou. Ua hoʻākea wale ʻia nō ka manaʻo o nā huaʻōlelo e like me "eaea" (*aerated*), "haumia" (*pollution*), "kaulua" (*double, in math*), a me "lakolako" (*computer accessories*), a ua hāʻawi ʻia kekahi manaʻo hou i nā huaʻōlelo e like me "oho" (*capillary*), "muku" (*tight end, in football*), a me "palaholo" (*gel*).

9. E hoʻohana i kekahi huaʻōlelo a hapa huaʻōlelo Polenekia paha me kōna manaʻo piha, a i ʻole, me ka hoʻololi iki ʻia. ʻO "pounamu" (*jade*) kekahi huaʻōlelo Māori i lawekahiki ʻia mai me ka pela ʻana a me ka manaʻo Māori. Ua hoʻohana ʻia ka huaʻōlelo Lalokona ʻo "maʻaka" (nui) ma ka māpuna ʻōlelo ʻo "hua maʻaka" (*capital letter*), a me ka huaʻōlelo Polapola ʻo "naʻinaʻi" (liʻiliʻi) ma ka māpuna ʻōlelo ʻo "hua naʻinaʻi" (*lower-case letter*). I kekahi manawa, lawekahiki ʻia ka manaʻo o kekahi huaʻōlelo Polenekia me ka hoʻololi iki a hoʻohawaiʻi ʻia paha o ka pela ʻana, e like me "kōkaha" (*condensation*) mai ka huaʻōleolo Māori ʻo "tōtā," a me "haʻuki" (*sport*) mai ka huaʻōlelo Polapola ʻo "haʻuti." Ua hoʻokuʻi ʻia nō hoʻi kekahi mau huaʻōlelo Hawaiʻi me ka huaʻōlelo o kekahi ʻāina Polenekia, e like me "hakuika" (*mollusk*) i hana ʻia i ka hoʻokuʻi ʻana iā "haku" (pōhaku) a me ka huaʻōlelo ʻo "kuita" (heʻe) mai ka Poroto ʻOseania Hikina. ʻO "makahiʻo" (*explore*) kekahi huaʻōlelo i haku ʻia i ka hoʻokuʻi ʻana iā "maka" me ka huaʻōlelo Polapola ʻo "hiʻo" (nānā).

10. E hoʻohawaiʻi i ka pela ʻana o kekahi huaʻōlelo lāhui ʻē. ʻOiai hoʻohawaiʻi nui ʻia nā huaʻōlelo Pelekānia e like me "naelona" (*nylon*), "ʻakika tanika" (*tannic acid*), "ʻokikene" (*oxygen*), a pēlā aku, ua hoʻohawaiʻi ʻia nō hoʻi nā huaʻōlelo mai nā ʻōlelo ʻē like ʻole ʻē aʻe ke noʻonoʻo ʻia he kūpono, e like me "kaimine" (*saimin*) mai ka ʻōlelo Kepanī mai, "kokeiʻa" (toceyʻa, *prairie dog*) mai ka ʻōlelo Ute mai, "lalinoka" (rahleenos, *hieroglyph*) mai ka ʻōlelo ʻAsuria mai, a me "ʻōmā" (homard, *Maine lobster*) mai ka ʻōlelo Palani mai.

Eia kekahi, ʻaʻole nā huaʻōlelo wale nō i haku ʻia e ke Kōmike ma o nā kulekele o luna nei kai hoʻokomo ʻia i loko o kēia puke. Ua loaʻa pū kekahi mau huaʻōlelo i ʻano laha paha ma waena o ka poʻe ʻōlelo Hawaiʻi, no laila, ua loaʻa pū kekahi o kēia mua huaʻōlelo i loko o ka puke wehewehe ʻōlelo Hawaiʻi a Pūkuʻi mā, a i ʻole, ma kekahi puke wehewehe ʻōlelo Hawaiʻi ʻē aʻe paha.

He mau kumu no ka hoʻokomo ʻia ʻana o kēia mau huaʻōlelo ma loko nei. ʻO ke kumu nui o ka loaʻa ʻana o kēia ʻano huaʻōlelo, ʻo ia ka nānā ʻana o ke Kōmike i kekahi papa huaʻōlelo e pili ana i kekahi kumuhana, a ʻoiai ua pono e haku ʻia ka hapa nui paha o nā huaʻōlelo, ua loaʻa mua kekahi i laha i ka hoʻohana ʻia, a ua hoʻokomo pū ʻia i mea e kōkua ai i ka mea huli huaʻōlelo e pili ana i ia kumuhana. Eia hou kekahi kumu no ka hoʻokomo ʻana i ia ʻano huaʻōlelo: I kekahi manawa, ua laha kekahi mau huaʻōlelo i like ka manaʻo, a ua noʻonoʻo ke Kōmike he kūpono ka hoʻohana ʻia ʻana o kekahi huaʻōlelo kikoʻī ma ia pōʻaiapili.

ʻOiai ʻaʻole kēia he hana maʻamau, ua loaʻa pū kekahi mau huaʻōlelo ʻano kākaʻikahi i haku ʻia e ke Kōmike i loko nō o ka loaʻa mua ʻana o kekahi huaʻōlelo i loko o ka puke wehewehe ʻōlelo me ka manaʻo hoʻokahi. No kēia ʻano huaʻōlelo, ua noʻonoʻo ke Kōmike ʻaʻole i laha loa ka hoʻohana ʻia ʻana o ia huaʻōlelo o loko o ka puke wehewehe ʻōlelo i kēia wā, a ua ʻano hemahema nō hoʻi ma muli o ke kūpono ʻole paha o ka manaʻo ma loko o nā pōʻaiapuni hou o kēia wā. No laila, ua makemake ke Kōmike e hāpai i kekahi koho me ka manaʻolana ua ʻoi aku ke kūpono o ka huaʻōlelo hou.

No ka wehewehe ʻana i ka manaʻo o kekahi huaʻōlelo, hōʻike ʻia ma ka Māhele ʻŌlelo Hawaiʻi kōna ʻano he kikino ʻoe, he hamani ʻoe, he hehele ʻoe, he ʻaʻano ʻoe, a i ʻole, he iʻoa ʻoe. A laila, ma hope pono o ka wehewehe ʻana i ka manaʻo ma ka ʻōlelo Haole, ua hōʻike ʻia ka molekumu i mea e maopopo ai ka mea heluhelu no hea mai ia huaʻōlelo, a i ʻole, ke ʻano o ka haku ʻia ʻana o ia huaʻōlelo a māpuna ʻōlelo paha e ke Kōmike Huaʻōlelo.

He nui a hewahewa nā hola i lilo aku nei i ke kūkākūkā ʻana e pili ana i nā huaʻōlelo a pau i loko o *Māmaka Kaiao*, ʻaʻohe huaʻōlelo i ʻāpono wale ʻia, a i mea e hōʻoiaʻiʻo ai ʻo kēlā me kēia huaʻōlelo a māpuna ʻōlelo paha ʻo ia ka huaʻōlelo maikaʻi loa i hiki ke noʻonoʻo ʻia e ke Kōmike, ʻāpono ʻia nā huaʻōlelo a pau ʻelua manawa ma ʻelua hālāwai ʻokoʻa.

Ua maopopo leʻa i nā lālā pākahi o ke Kōmike ʻaʻole hiki ke hemolele nā huaʻōlelo a pau i ʻāpono ʻia, a i ka hala ʻana o kekahi manawa, ʻano piʻi ka ʻiʻini i loko o nā lālā e nānā hou i nā huaʻōlelo i ʻapono mua ʻia i ʻoi aku ka maikaʻi. Ma muli naʻe o ka nui ʻino o nā huaʻōlelo i koe e kali nei i ka haku ʻia, hoʻololi ʻia kekahi huaʻōlelo i ka manawa wale nō i loaʻa ai kekahi ʻike hou a ua noʻonoʻo ʻia ua hewa a hemahema paha ka huaʻōlelo i ʻāpono mua ʻia.

Hoʻāʻo mau nō naʻe ke Kōmike e ʻāpono i nā huaʻōlelo wale nō e kōkua ana i ka māmaka ʻana i ka ʻōlelo makuahine o nēia ʻāina aloha o kākou a i kaiao hou i loko o kēia kenekulia hou.

Ke Kaʻina Pīʻāpā Hawaiʻi

Ua hoʻokaʻina ʻia nā ʻikamu a pau ma loko o ka māhele mua o *Māmaka Kaiao*, ʻo ia hoʻi ka Māhele ʻŌlelo Hawaiʻi, ma o ka pīʻāpā Hawaiʻi. Penei ke kaʻina o nā huapalapala ma ka pīʻāpā Hawaiʻi:

a   e   i   o   u   h   k   l   m   n   p   w   ʻ

No laila, inā aia nō ʻoe ke huli aʻe nei i ka huaʻōlelo ʻo "ulahi" ma ka Māhele ʻŌlelo Hawaiʻi, pono e huli ma mua loa, ma hope pono o ka *a, e, i* me ka *o*, akā, ma mua o ka *h*.

E akahele nō naʻe, no ka mea, nui nō nā huaʻōlelo Hawaiʻi e hoʻomaka ana me ka ʻokina, no laila, ʻoiai aia ʻo "ulahi" ma mua o ka *h*, aia ʻo "ʻūomo" ma hope o ka *w*, no ka mea, he ʻokina ka huapalapala mua o ka huaʻōlelo ʻo "ʻūomo."

Inā hoʻomaka kekahi huaʻōlelo me kekahi huapalapala Paipala, ʻo ia hoʻi kekahi huapalapala i loaʻa ʻole i loko o ka pīʻāpā Hawaiʻi maʻamau, aia ia mau huaʻōlelo ma hope o ka ʻokina i loko o ka Māhele ʻŌlelo Hawaiʻi. Penei ke kaʻina o nā huapalapala Paipala:

b   c   d   f   g   j   q   r   s   t   v   x   y   z

ʻO ka mea nui, mai poina ua nānā ʻia nā huapalapala a pau o kekahi huaʻōlelo no ka hoʻokaʻina pīʻāpā ʻana, ʻaʻole ka huapalapala mua wale nō. No laila, aia ka huaʻōlelo ʻo "kūʻaiemi" ma hope o ka huaʻōlelo ʻo "kūwaho," no ka mea, nānā ʻia ka huapalapala ʻekolu o kēia mau huaʻōlelo, ʻo ia hoʻi ka *w* me ka ʻ, a aia ka ʻokina (ʻ) ma hope o ka *w*.

ʻO ka mea wale nō i nānā ʻole ʻia no ke kaʻina pīʻāpā Hawaiʻi, ʻo ia ke kahakō, koe naʻe, inā ʻo ia wale nō ka ʻokoʻa o ka pela ʻana o kekahi huaʻōlelo i kekahi. Inā pēlā, aia ka huaʻōlelo kahakō ʻole ma mua o ka huaʻōlelo mea kahakō, e like me "mika," "mīka," a me "mīkā."

No laila, e akahele mau i ka huli ʻana aku i kekahi huaʻōlelo ma ka Māhele ʻŌlelo Hawaiʻi, no ka mea, inā ʻaʻole pololei kāu wahi e nānā ana, e noʻonoʻo ana ʻoe ʻaʻole loaʻa ka huaʻōlelo i loko o ka puke, a ua loaʻa nō paha.

Ke Kōmike Hua'ōlelo

Ua ho'okumu 'ia ke Kōmike Hua'ōlelo mua loa i ka makahiki 1987 no ka haku 'ana i nā hua'ōlelo no nā mea hou o kēia au i 'ike 'ole 'ia ho'i e nā kūpuna o ka wā ma mua.

Aia ma ia kōmike mua loa nā kūpuna a me nā mānaleo Hawai'i i 'ike i ka waiwai nui o ia hana, 'o ia ho'i 'o Elama Kanahele, Lani Kapuni, Albert Like, Josephine Lindsey, Joseph Maka'ai, Sarah Nākoa, a me Helen Wahineokai, me ke kōkua o Kalani Akana, Kana'i Kapeliela, Haunani Makuakāne-Drechsel, a me Leinani Raffipiy.

Ke moe maila kekahi o ia mau kōmike i ka moe kau a ho'oilo, a 'oiai ua ho'i akula ke kai i waho, aia nō ke koe hūlalilali maila nā momi waiwai i uka. Mahalo nui loa 'ia nā kōmike mua loa pākahi a pau.

I kēia manawa, ke haku a hō'ili'ili hua'ōlelo nei ke Kōmike e kū nei, 'o ia ho'i 'o Larry Kimura (Luna Ho'omalu; Ka Haka 'Ula O Ke'elikōlani ma Hilo), Hōkūlani Cleeland (Luna Kāhuakomo; Ke Kula Ni'ihau O Kekaha ma Kaua'i), Kamaui Aiona (he 'elele no ke kaiaulu o Maui), Lōkahi Antonio (Ke Kulanui Kaiaulu O Maui), Keoni Kelekolio (Ka Haka 'Ula O Ke'elikōlani), Kaliko Trapp (Ke Kula 'O Nāwahīokalani'ōpu'u ma Kea'au), a me Ipo Wong lāua 'o Laiana Wong (Ke Kulanui O Hawai'i ma Mānoa).

He mahalo nui nō ho'i i nā lālā 'ē a'e i lawelawe ma ke Kōmike no ka pono o ka 'ōlelo i nā makahiki i hala aku nei, 'o ia ho'i 'o Keao NeSmith lāua 'o No'eau Warner (Ke Kulanui O Hawai'i ma Mānoa), Kalena Silva lāua 'o William H. Wilson (Ka Haka 'Ula O Ke'elikōlani), a me Kamoa'e Walk (Ke Kulanui 'O Brigham Young ma Lā'ie), me ke kōkua pū a 'elua lālā kūikawā, 'o ia ho'i 'o Hiapo Perreira (Ka Haka 'Ula O Ke'elikōlani) lāua 'o Kaleionālani Shintani (Ke Kula Ni'ihau O Kekaha).

He manawale'a wale 'ia ho'i nā hola he nui e lilo mau ana i ia hana a nā lālā o ke Kōmike Hua'ōlelo, a me ke aloha nui i ka 'ōlelo Hawai'i i hā'awi 'ia ai ia mau hola a pau me ka mana'olana e 'ōlelo hou 'ia ana i nā manawa a pau a ma nā wahi a pau.

Kōmike Hua'ōlelo
Hale Kuamo'o–Kikowaena 'Ōlelo Hawai'i
Ke Kulanui O Hawai'i ma Hilo
200 West Kāwili Street
Hilo, Hawai'i 96720-4091

mamaka@leoki.uhh.hawaii.edu

The Words

Living languages throughout the world are in a state of constant change and growth, and so it is with the Hawaiian language. Therefore, in order to provide assistance to all Hawaiian-language speakers in this new era, *Māmaka Kaiao* is once again being printed to serve as a companion to the *Hawaiian Dictionary* by Pūkuʻi and Elbert.

For Hawaiian-language students, one dictionary is no longer sufficient because these two volumes serve different purposes. The *Hawaiian Dictionary* provides invaluable information about Hawaiian vocabulary from the earliest days of recording the language up to the 1980s, but it is the task of *Māmaka Kaiao* to make available to the general public the new vocabulary that is being created by the Hawaiian Lexicon Committee.

Members of the Lexicon Committee generally meet from four to six times each year to discuss new vocabulary for the Hawaiian language. Most of the words that are brought up for discussion are words which are not found in the *Hawaiian Dictionary* but are needed when writing or translating a lesson, a story or article, a book, or any other document in the Hawaiian language.

Because today's educational curricula involve many new concepts which lack equivalent Hawaiian terms in the *Hawaiian Dictionary*, development of the Hawaiian-immersion curriculum has resulted in the emergence of many new terms related to new fields of knowledge. The creators or translators of educational materials are generally the ones who bring the new words they have created before the Committee for discussion, approval, and dissemination.

If a particular vocabulary list concerns a subject which requires the knowledge of an expert in the field, such experts are invited to the meeting. If sufficient information is available in dictionaries or other resource materials, or is within the scope of knowledge of members of the Committee, then these resources are utilized so that the concept or meaning of the terms will be clearly understood before decisions are made concerning what Hawaiian word or term is most suitable.

Listed below are guidelines which are commonly used by the Committee to create the new words which are included in *Māmaka Kaiao*. Although the creation of new words is not limited to these guidelines, they do describe how most of the new words have been created.

1. Make minor changes to a word which already appears in the dictionary. The most common changes are to either insert or delete a *kahakō*, or to join or separate parts of a word or term. A *kahakō* has been added to words like

hāpaina (carrier) and *kāka'ikahi* (few), while terms like *a pau* (all) and *me he* (as if) have been written as two words instead of one.

2. Record a word which is used by native speakers but is not found in the dictionary, or one which appears in the dictionary but is used by native speakers with a meaning which is different from that listed in the dictionary. Words like *ho'ohūpō* (feign ignorance), *kāka'ahi* (deal, as cards), and *'alo'ahia* (stress) have been used by native speakers but are not found in the dictionary, while the words *huka* (zipper), *maka'aha* (screen), and *nemonemo* (bald, as a tire) appear in the dictionary but without the particular meanings used by native speakers being included.

3. Use reduplication of an existing word in order to alter or extend the meaning. This is a common practice in Hawaiian vocabulary development and has been done to create words like *ūlialia* (coincidence) from *ulia*, *hohoki* (neutral) from *hoki*, and *monamona* (dessert) from first shortening *momona* and then expanding it through reduplication.

4. Add either a prefix or a suffix to an existing word. This, too, is a common way of forming new words in Hawaiian, and traditional affixes have been used by the Committee as well as new ones created to fill specific needs. In order to create a word which means "concentrated," the traditional suffix *-hia* was added to the word *pa'apū*, and then, in order to arrive at the meaning "to concentrate, make less dilute," the traditional prefix *ho'o-* was added to form the word *ho'opa'apūhia*. The traditional suffix *-na* has also been used to change verbs to nouns, such as adding it to *pāku'i* (append) to form the word *pāku'ina* (affix, in grammar), and to *koi* (require) to form the word *koina* (requirement). The word *kālai* (intellectual policy) has been transformed into a prefix meaning "-ology, the scientific study of." With this meaning, it has been used to form new words such as *kālaiaopaku* (physical science) and *kālaianiau* (climatology).

5. Explain the meaning of a word or term by using Hawaiian words. This guideline has been used rather extensively because when the "new" term is encountered by a speaker of Hawaiian, its meaning should be rather easily grasped even if the reader or listener is not familiar with the English word or term. The following are some terms which have been created using this guideline: *ala mōlehu* (crepuscular), *uila māhu pele* (geothermal electricity), *kuhi hewa o ka maka* (optical illusion), and *'ōlelo kuhi lima 'Amelika* (American Sign Language).

6. Combine Hawaiian words to create a new word. This guideline is somewhat similar to the previous one with the main difference being that the meaning will probably not be immediately apparent to a speaker of Hawaiian because it may not be obvious even when recognizing the separate parts of the word. Examples of words formed using this guideline are

hamulau (herbivore), *ka'a'ike* (communication), *kōpia* (carbohydrate), and *poelele* (satellite).

7. Combine Hawaiian words while shortening at least one of the words. Although this guideline has been used for a number of math and science terms, it is also used for new words in a variety of other areas. Some words that have been created in this way include: *analahi* (regular, as in shape) which was formed by adding *ana* to a shortened *ma'alahi*; *ikehu* (energy) which was formed by combining *ika* and *ehu*; *lāhulu* (species) which comes from a shortened *lāhui* plus *hulu*; and *mo'olako* (inventory) which comes from *mo'olelo* and *lako*.

8. Extend the meaning of a word which is already found in the dictionary, or give an existing word a new meaning. Words whose meanings have been extended to create new terms include *eaea* (aerated), *haumia* (pollution), *kaulua* (double, in math), and *lakolako* (computer accessories), while new meanings have been given to the words *oho* (capillary), *muku* (tight end, in football), and *palaholo* (gel).

9. Use a word or part of a word from another Polynesian language with its meaning intact or slightly changed. The word *pounamu* (jade) is a Māori word which has been borrowed without changing its spelling or meaning. The Rarotongan word *ma'aka*, meaning "big," is used in the term *hua ma'aka* (capital letter), while the Tahitian word *na'ina'i*, meaning "small," is used in the term *hua na'ina'i* (lower-case letter). Sometimes words from other Polynesian languages are borrowed with changes in spelling to better fit Hawaiian orthography, such as *kōkaha* (condensation) from the Māori word *tōtā*, and *ha'uki* (sport) from the Tahitian word *ha'uti*. Hawaiian words are also sometimes combined with other Polynesian words, such as *hakuika* (mollusk) from the Hawaiian word *haku* (*pōhaku*) and *kuita*, a Proto Eastern Oceanic word meaning "squid." The word *makahi'o* (explore) was created by combining the Hawaiian word *maka* (eye) with the Tahitian word *hi'o* (look).

10. Hawaiianize the orthography of a word or term from a non-Polynesian language. Many English words have been Hawaiianized since earliest contact with the English language, and the Committee continues this practice with words such as *naelona* (nylon), *'akika tanika* (tannic acid), and *'okikene* (oxygen). Lexical borrowing is not limited to English, however. Hawaiianization also extends to words from a variety of other languages such as *kaimine* from the Japanese word *saimin*, *kokei'a* (prairie dog) from the Ute word *tocey'a*, *lalinoka* (hieroglyph) from the Assyrian word *rahleenos*, and *'ōmā* (Maine lobster) from the French word *homard*.

Not all of the words and terms included in *Māmaka Kaiao* have been created by the Committee, however. There are also words which are already established Hawaiian vocabulary, and therefore may also be found in the *Hawaiian Dictionary*.

There are several reasons for having included these words. Perhaps the primary reason is that when the Committee looks at a vocabulary list developed for a particular subject, although most of the terms may require the creation of new Hawaiian vocabulary, some words already exist and may be included merely as an aid to anyone using *Māmaka Kaiao* to find vocabulary related to this particular subject. Another reason for including vocabulary that can be found in another dictionary is that there may be more than one word with the same or a similar meaning, and the Committee feels that a certain word would be most appropriate for use in a particular context.

Although not a common occurrence, there are also a few words which have been created by the Committee in spite of the fact that Hawaiian words with the same meaning already exist in the dictionary. In most cases, the Committee felt that the dictionary words are not in general use today and other words could be created by the Committee which would more accurately reflect contemporary concepts being described, thus providing Hawaiian-language speakers with additional vocabulary choices.

For each entry in the first section of the vocabulary, words are classified as *hamani* (transitive verb), *hehele* (intransitive verb), *'a'ano* (stative verb), *kikino* (common noun), or *i'oa* (proper noun), and following the definition of the word in English, the derivation or origin of the word is indicated. This etymology not only gives the reader a better understanding of where the word came from or how it was created, but it may also help to give a better understanding of its meaning.

Innumerable hours have been spent discussing all of the words which appear in *Māmaka Kaiao*. No single word has been approved without first being discussed, often extensively, and in order to ensure that the word or term is the best one that the Committee is able to create, each word or term must be approved and reapproved at two different Committee meetings.

Members of the Committee realize, however, that every approved word cannot be a perfect choice, and as time passes the desire to revisit previously approved words frequently arises in order to try to find an even better choice. But because of the seemingly endless number of words and terms still waiting for Hawaiian equivalents to be created, changes are usually approved only when new information shows that a previously approved word or term may be inaccurate.

So the Hawaiian Lexicon Committee continues to meet several times each year in its attempt to provide new Hawaiian words and terms which will truly help to carry (*māmaka*) the Hawaiian language into a new dawn (*kaiao*) in the twenty-first century.

Hawaiian Alphabetical Order

Entries in the first section of *Māmaka Kaiao*, i.e. the Hawaiian-English section, have been arranged according to the Hawaiian alphabet, and it is important to understand this alphabetization in order to facilitate finding words in this section. The following is the standard order of the Hawaiian alphabet:

a   e   i   o   u   h   k   l   m   n   p   w   '

So if you are looking for the word *ulahi*, for example, you must look in the beginning of the section directly following *a*, *e*, *i*, and *o*, but before *h*.

Be careful, however, because there are many Hawaiian words which begin with the *'okina* ('), so although *ulahi* is found toward the beginning of the Hawaiian-English section before *h*, *'ūomo* is found at the back of the section following *w* since the first letter of *'ūomo* is the *'okina*.

Words beginning with letters of the English alphabet which are not in the standard Hawaiian alphabet will be found after the *'okina* at the end of the Hawaiian-English section in the following order:

b   c   d   f   g   j   q   r   s   t   v   x   y   z

Another important thing to remember is that all of the letters of a word are considered when alphabetizing a word, not just the first letter. Therefore, the word *kū'aiemi* will be found after the word *kūwaho* since the third letter of *kū'aiemi* is the *'okina* while the third letter of *kūwaho* is *w*, and the *'okina* follows *w* in the Hawaiian alphabet.

Only the *kahakō* is generally not considered in Hawaiian alphabetization except when the presence or lack of a *kahakō* is the only difference in the spelling of two words. If that is the case, then the word without the *kahakō* precedes the word with the *kahakō*, as in *mika*, *mīka*, and *mīkā*.

So until you become accustomed to finding words listed according to Hawaiian alphabetical order, be careful not to jump to the conclusion that a word is not included in *Māmaka Kaiao* when it may be that you are simply not looking in the correct location for the particular word.

The Hawaiian Lexicon Committee

The first Hawaiian Lexicon Committee (Kōmike Hua'ōlelo) was established in 1987 to create words for concepts and material culture unknown to our ancestors. Committee members were native speakers of Hawaiian, most of them elderly, who saw the value in and the need for creating new Hawaiian words. Elama Kanahele, Lani Kapuni, Albert Like, Josephine Lindsey, Joseph Maka'ai, Sarah Nākoa, and Helen Wahineokai were assisted by recorders Kalani Akana, Kana'i Kapeliela, Haunani Makuakāne-Drechsel, and Leinani Raffipiy.

Although some of these first committee members have passed on, the fruits of their labor form the foundation upon which the present committee's work is based.

Present committee members include Larry Kimura (committee chair; Ka Haka 'Ula O Ke'elikōlani at Hilo), Hōkūlani Cleeland (*Māmaka Kaiao* editor; Ke Kula Ni'ihau O Kekaha on Kaua'i), Kamaui Aiona (representing the Maui community), Lōkahi Antonio (Maui Community College), Keoni Kelekolio (Ka Haka 'Ula O Ke'elikōlani), Kaliko Trapp (Ke Kula 'O Nāwahīokalani-'ōpu'u in Kea'au), as well as Ipo Wong and Laiana Wong (University of Hawai'i at Mānoa).

Gratitude is also due to past members who have served on the committee for the benefit of the Hawaiian language: Keao NeSmith and No'eau Warner (University of Hawai'i at Mānoa), Kalena Silva and William H. Wilson (Ka Haka 'Ula O Ke'elikōlani), and Kamoa'e Walk (Brigham Young University at Lā'ie), and two pro tem members, Hiapo Perreira (Ka Haka 'Ula O Ke'elikōlani) and Kaleionālani Shintani (Ke Kula Ni'ihau O Kekaha).

All of these members of the Hawaiian Lexicon Committee, both past and present, have unselfishly donated their time and effort because of their deep love and concern for the Hawaiian language and a desire to see it once again spoken at all times in all places.

Kōmike Hua'ōlelo (Hawaiian Lexicon Committee)
Hale Kuamo'o–Kikowaena 'Ōlelo Hawai'i
Ke Kulanui O Hawai'i ma Hilo
200 West Kāwili Street
Hilo, Hawai'i 96720-4091

mamaka@leoki.uhh.hawaii.edu

Nā Hua Hōʻailona *Abbreviations*

abb.	abbreviation
Bib.	Bible
cf.	compare
comb.	combined form
dic.	dictionary definition
e.g.	for example
Eng.	English
ext. mng.	extended meaning
i.e.	that is
inv.	invention
Japn.	Japanese
lit.	literally
mān.	*mānaleo* (native speaker)
new mng.	new meaning
PPN	Proto Polynesian
redup.	reduplication
sh.	shortened form
sp. var.	spelling variation
Tah.	Tahitian
trad.	traditional literary sources
var.	variation
ham	*hamani* (transitive verb)
heh	*hehele* (intransitive verb)
ʻaʻ	*ʻaʻano* (stative verb)
kik	*kikino* (common noun)
iʻoa	*iʻoa* (proper noun)

Nā Mānaleo i Hōʻike ʻia

EK	Elama Kanahele
HA	Henry Auwae
HHLH	Helen Haleola Lee Hong
HKM	Harry Kunihi Mitchell
JPM	Joseph Puipui Makaai
KKK	Kaui Keola Keamoai
LK	Louise Keliihoomalu
MMLH	Martha Manoanoa Lum Ho
MW	Minnie Whitford

Nā Palapala i Hōʻike ʻia

Anatomia	Judd, Gerrit P. *Anatomia*
Bihopa	Bihopa, E. A. *Haawina Mua o ka Hoailona Helu*
Bounty	*He Moolelo no na Luina Kipi o ka Moku Bounty*
Legendre	Legendre, A. M. *Ke Anahonua*
Judd	Judd et al. *Hawaiian Language Imprints, 1822-1899*
Pakaa	Nakuina, Moses K. *Pakaa a me Ku-a-Pakaa*
Wilcox	Wilcox, Robert

Māhele ʻŌlelo Hawaiʻi
Hawaiian-English

A

a And, when, until, to, etc. *Dic., sp. var.*

ā A word used only at the end of a sentence or phrase, with meanings such as: I told you so; don't you forget it; you should know; you dummy. *Ua hoʻomaka ka papa i ka hola ʻehiku, ā.* The class started at seven o'clock, you dummy. *Niʻihau.*

ā *Iwi ā.* Jawbone, mandible.

aeʻo·lele *kik* Pogo stick. *Lit.,* stilt (for) jumping.

ai *Maʻi lele ai.* Sexually transmitted disease (STD).

aia *Aia i loko o ka papa.* To take a class. *Aia wau i loko o ka papa ʻōlelo Hawaiʻi i kēia kau kula.* I'm taking a Hawaiian language class this semester. *Cf. komo.*

ai pale·kana *heh* Safe sex; to practice safe sex. *E ai palekana ʻoe; e komo i ka pāpalekimo.* Practice safe sex; wear a condom. *Lit.,* safe coition. See *maʻi lele ai. Ai palekana ʻole.* Unprotected sex; to practice unprotected sex.

ao *kik* Cloud, general term. *Dic.* See entries below and *lālahilewa, loa, ʻōpua. Hōkelo ao.* Cloud chamber, i.e. a scientific device which detects nuclear particles through the formation of cloud tracks.

ao *Ala ao.* Diurnal, i.e. active during the daytime. *Mea ao ʻē.* Extraterrestrial, space alien.

ā·ohi·ohi *ham* Resistance, i.e. opposition to the flow of electricity, or any opposition that slows down or prevents movement of electrons through a conductor. *Sh. kāohiohi. Āohiohi ea.* Air resistance, i.e. the force of air against a moving object. *Lima āohiohi.* Resistance arm, i.e. the distance from the fulcrum to the resistance force in a lever. *Manehu āohiohi.* Resistance force.

ao kū·lohe·lohe *kik* Nature. *Lit.,* natural world. *Puni ao kūlohelohe.* Naturalist. Also *kanaka puni ao kūlohelohe.*

Ao·tea·roa *iʻoa* New Zealand. *I ka hiki ʻana o ke kanaka mua ʻo Kupe i ka ʻāina ʻo Aotearoa, ʻike akula ʻo ia he ao keʻokeʻo lōʻihi ma luna o ia ʻāina.* When the first man, Kupe, arrived in New Zealand, he saw a long, white cloud over the land. *Māori.* Also *Nukilani.*

au *kik* Age, epoch, era, period. *Dic.* See *Au Palaʻo, au paʻahau. Ke au haku kūlohelohe.* Eolithic age, in anthropology. *Ke au haku kā pahi.* Paleolithic age. *Ke au haku kā nahau.* Mesolithic age. *Ke au haku ʻānai.* Neolithic age. *Ke au haku keleaweʻula.* Aeneolithic age. *Ke au keleawekini.* Bronze age.

au *kik* Mood. *ʻO ka hoʻāeae, he au pilialoha kōna.* The hoʻāeae (style of chanting) has a romantic mood. *Naue ka manawa i ke au o ka puolo.* The time moves to the mood of the music. *Dic., ext. mng.* See *au manaʻo.*

au *kik* Current. *Dic.* See entries below. *Au uila.* Electic current.

au emi *kik* Recession, i.e. a period of reduced economic activity. *Ma muli o ka hopohopo nui o ka lehulehu i ka nele i ka hana, ua hoʻomaka ka hoʻokele waiwai e komo i ke au emi.* Because of great public concern about unemployment, the economy entered into a recession. *Lit.,* receding period.

au·kahi *heh* Direct current (DC). *Dic., ext. mng. Cf. au māʻaloʻalo. Uila aukahi.* Direct current electricity. *Mālamalama aukahi.* Coherent light, i.e. light in which all the waves vibrate in a single plane with the crests and troughs all aligned.

au kā·ʻei pō·ʻai waena honua *kik* Equatorial current, in oceanography. *Lit.,* equator zone current.

au kikī *kik* Stream current, in oceanography. *Lit.*, swiftly flowing current.

au makani kikī *kik* Jet stream. *Lit.*, swift wind current.

au manaʻo *kik* Tone, as of a literary work. *Lit.*, mood (of the) meaning. See *au.*

au mā·ʻalo·ʻalo *kik* Alternating current (AC). *Lit.*, current passing back and forth. Cf. *aukahi. Uila au māʻalo-ʻalo.* Alternating current electricity.

Au Palaʻo *kik* Kingdom, in Egyptology. *Lit.*, age (of) Pharoahs. See entries below.

Au Palaʻo Kū·hou *kik* New Kingdom, in Egyptology, 1574-1085 BC. *Ua noho Palaʻo ke keiki ʻo Tutankha-men i ke Au Palaʻo Kūhou o ʻAikupita.* The boy Tutankhamen ruled as Pharaoh over Egypt during the New Kingdom.

Au Palaʻo Kū·kahiko *kik* Old Kingdom, in Egyptology, 2780-2280 BC. *Kaulana ke Au Palaʻo Kūkahiko o ʻAikupita i ka mohala hikiwawe ʻana o ka ʻoihana kuhikuhipuʻuone.* The Old Kingdom is marked by rapid mastery of stone architecture.

Au Palaʻo Kū·waena *kik* Middle Kingdom, in Egyptology, 2133-1780 BC. *Ua hoʻokumu ʻia ʻo Tebesa i kikowaena o ka hoʻomana ma ʻAikupita i ke Au Palaʻo Kūwaena.* Thebes became established as the religious center of Egypt during the Middle Kingdom.

au·pana *kik* Rhythm, in linguistics. Comb. *au + pana.* Cf. *papana.*

au paʻa·hau *kik* Ice age. *Nui ka nūnē ʻana a ka poʻe ʻepekema no ke kumu o ke au paʻahau, ʻo ia hoʻi ka wā i paʻa ai ka honua holoʻokoʻa i ka hau.* There is much speculation among scientists as to how the ice age began when the whole world was frozen in ice. *Lit.*, frozen age.

au·puni *kik* Government; national. *Dic.* Cf. *kaumokuʻāina, kauʻāina, māhele ʻāina, mokuʻāina, pekelala.* See entries below. *Paimana aupuni.* Communism. *Pāka aupuni.* National park. *ʻAha Aupuni Hui Pū ʻia.* United Nations (UN). *ʻAha kūkā poʻo aupuni.* Summit, i.e. a conference of highest-level officials, as heads of government. *ʻOihana Pāka Aupuni.* National Park Service.

au·puni kā·nā·wai na ka lehu·lehu *kik* Direct democracy, i.e. a government in which laws are made directly by the citizens. *Lit.*, government (of) laws by the people. Cf. *aupuni na ka lehulehu.*

au·puni kiwi·kā *kik* Municipality, i.e. a city or town having its own incorporated government for local affairs. *Lit.*, municipal government. See *kānāwai kūloko.*

au·puni mana kē·nā kahi *kik* Dictatorship. *Lit.*, government (with) one power to command.

Au·puni Mō·ʻī Hui Pū ʻia *iʻoa* United Kingdom.

Au·puni Mō·ʻī ʻo Tonga *iʻoa* Kingdom of Tonga.

au·puni na ka lehu·lehu *kik* Democracy. *ʻO ka nui o nā ʻāina o ʻEulopa, he mau ʻāina aupuni na ka lehulehu ia, no ka mea, na ka lehulehu nō e koho pāloka i nā luna aupuni.* Most European countries are democracies since the public elects the government leaders. *Lit.*, government by the people. Cf. *aupuni kānāwai na ka lehulehu.*

au·puni ʻao·ʻao ʻelua *kik* Two-party system of government. *ʻOiai ua loaʻa he mau ʻaoʻao kālaiʻāina ma ke aupuni o ʻAmelika Hui pū ʻia, ʻōlelo wale ʻia nō he aupuni ʻaoʻao ʻelua ia no ka nānā nui ʻia o ʻelua wale nō ʻaoʻao.* Although there are a number of political parties in the U.S., it is generally said that it is a two-party system since only two parties are considered by most. *Lit.*, two-party government. Cf. *ʻelua hale.*

au·puni ‘eme·pela *kik* Empire.
*Wahi a ka ‘ōlelo kahiko, " ‘A‘ohe
napo‘o ‘ana o ka lā ma luna o ke aupuni
‘emepela Beretānia."* As the old saying
goes, "The sun never sets on the British
empire." *Lit.,* emperor kingdom.

au·puni ‘emila *kik* Emirate. *Lit.,*
emir government. Also *aupuni ‘emira.*
See entry below.

**Au·puni ‘Emira ‘Ala·pia Hui Pū
‘ia** *i‘oa* United Arab Emirates.

au ‘ae‘a *kik* Drift current, in
oceanography. *Lit.,* wandering current.

ahe·ahe *kik/‘a‘* Gentle breeze; dust
raised and small branches move, in
meteorology. *Dic.* See *makani.*

ahi *Pale ahi.* Flame retardant.

ahi·ho‘o·le‘a·le‘a *kik* Fireworks.
Lit., fire (for) amusement. See *ahikao,
ihoihokī, hōkūpa‘alima, lūpahū,
pahūpahū.*

ahi·kao *kik* Rocket, as space or
fireworks. *Dic., ext. mng.* See
*ahiho‘ole‘ale‘a, kelena moku ahikao.
Ahikao hā‘awe.* Manned Maneuvering
Unit, as for a space flight. *Moku ahikao.*
Spaceship, rocket ship.

Ahi·wela *i‘oa* Fomalhaut, a star.
Mān. (HA).

aho ‘ea *kik* Monofilament. *Mān.
(KKK).*

ahu ea *kik* Air mass, as in weather.
Lit., mass (of) air.

ahu·oi *kik/ham* Clue; to give a clue
about. *Comb. a + huoi.*

ahu ho‘o·koe *kik* Cache, as in
computer program. *Lit.,* cache pile. See
ho‘okoe.

ahu kā·loa‘a *kik* Capital, i.e. anything
produced in an economy that is
accumulated or used to produce other
goods and services. *Ke pi‘i pa‘a mau
mai nei ka nui ahu kāloa‘a o ka pā‘oihana a Kale ma ke kumuloa‘a a me ka
lako.* Kale's business has been steadily
increasing its capital in profits as well as

equipment. *Lit.,* business collection. See
paikāloa‘a.

ahu·papa *kik* Composite, as volcanic
cone. *Lit.,* mound (of) strata. *Pu‘u
ahupapa.* Composite cone.

ahu·wale See *ho‘oku‘ia ahuwale.
Hopena ahuwale.* Predictable, as the
ending of a story. *Mo‘olelo hopena
ahuwale.* Predictable story.

aka ‘a‘ Shadowed, as on computer or in
typesetting. *Dic., ext. mng.* See *ho‘āka.*

aka ani·ani *kik* Reflection, in math.
Lit., mirror reflection. See *‘ālikelike
aka.*

aka·ki‘i *kik* Photo negative. *Dic.*

ake *kik* Liver. *Dic.*

ā·kea ‘a‘ Width or breadth, in math.
Dic. Also *ana ākea.* See *laulā.* Cf. *loa,
lō‘ihi, hohonu, ki‘eki‘e.*

ake·aka·mai *kik* Science. *Dic.* Also
‘epekema.

ake·loa *kik* Spleen. *Dic.*

ake·mā·mā *kik* Lung. *Dic. A‘a kino
akemāmā.* Pulmonary vein. *A‘a
pu‘uwai akemāmā.* Pulmonary artery.

akua *Ho‘omana akua kahi.*
Monotheism; monotheistic. *Ho‘omana
akua lehulehu.* Polytheism; polytheistic.

ala *kik* Aisle, as in a supermarket.
Dic., ext. mng. Also *alakaha.* See entries
below.

ala *kik* Lane, as on a highway or in a
bowling alley. *Dic., ext. mng.*

ala ao *‘a‘* Diurnal, i.e. active during the
daytime. *Lawe ‘ia mai nei ka manakuke
i Hawai‘i nei no ke kāohi i ka ‘iole, akā,
he ala ao ka manakuke a he ala pō ka
‘iole, no laila, ‘a‘ohe i kō ka makemake.*
The mongoose was brought to Hawai‘i to
control the rat population, but the
mongoose is diurnal and the rat is
nocturnal, so the objective was not
achieved. *Lit.,* awake (during) daylight.
Cf. *ala pō, ala mōlehu.*

ala hā·nuku *kik* Alley, alleyway. *Lit.,* road (with) narrow passageway. *See hānuku.*

ala hei·hei kī·ke'e·ke'e *kik* Slalom course. *Lit.,* zigzag race path.

ala hekehi *kik* Hiking trail.

ala·hiō *kik* Ramp. *Lit.,* inclined path.

ala·kau *kik* Mode of transportation, as motor vehicle, space vehicle, etc. *Comb. ala + kau.*

ala·kaha *kik* Aisle, as in a supermarket. *Lit.,* way (to) pass by. *Also ala.*

ala·kalaiwa *kik* Driveway.

ala·ka'i *Kumu alaka'i.* Precedent, i.e. something done or said that may act as an example to justify it being done again. *Leo alaka'i.* One who sings the melody of a song. *Puke alaka'i.* Teacher's guide, manual.

ala·kō *ham* To drag, as in computer program. *E alakō i ka 'iole, a kuhikuhi i ke ki'iona.* Drag the mouse, and point at the icon. *Dic., ext. mng. Also ki'i a alakō. Alakō ma luna o.* To drag onto. *Also alakō a kau ma luna o.*

ala ku'u moku·lele *kik* Runway. *See ku'u, ala lele mokulele.*

ala lele moku·lele *kik* Flight corridor. *Lit.,* path (of) airplane flight.

ala mō·lehu *'a* Crepuscular, i.e. appearing or flying in the twilight. *He lele kekahi mau 'ano 'ōpe'ape'a i nā hola mōlehulehu o ke ahiahi, no ka mea, he ala mōlehu ia mau 'ano holoholona.* Some kinds of bats fly only in the twilight hours of the evening because they are crepuscular creatures. *Lit.,* awake (during) twilight. *Cf. ala ao, ala pō.*

ala nu'u·kia *kik* Mission, as in the mission statement of an organization. *Lit.,* vision path. *See nu'ukia. 'Ōlelo ala nu'ukia.* Mission statement.

ala pili·pā *kik* Parallel, as of a computer port. *Lit.,* parallel path. *See ala pūka'ina. Awa ala pilipā.* Parallel port.

ala·pine *kik* Frequency, in math. *Dic., ext. mng.*

ala·pī·pā *kik* Sidewalk. *Lit.,* sidewalk path.

ala·pi'i mele *kik* Musical scale: *pā, kō, lī, hā, nō, lā, mī, pā. Dic. Also pākōlī.*

ala pō *'a* Nocturnal. *Lit.,* awake (at) night. *Cf. ala ao, ala mōlehu.*

ala pū·ka'ina *kik* Serial, as of a computer port. *Lit.,* series path. *See ala pilipā.*

alelo *kik* Tongue. *Dic. Kū'au alelo.* Back of the tongue. *Lau alelo.* Blade. *Mole alelo.* Root. *Waena alelo.* Central portion. *Wēlau alelo.* Tip.

alelo·mo'o *kik* Party favor. *Lit.,* lizard tongue.

ā·lia·lia *kik* Marsh, with salt or brackish water and no trees. *Dic., ext. mng. See nāele, 'olokele. Ālialia nono.* Anchialine pool. *Ālialia wai maoli.* Fresh-water marsh.

alo *kik* Face, as one side of a space figure, in math. *Dic., ext. mng. See kā'ei alo, pale alo* and entries under *'ōpaka. 'Ao'ao huli alo.* Opposite leg or side of a right triangle.

alo ua *kik* Rainy side, as of a mountain.

aloha *Kinipōpō aloha.* Aloha ball, in volleyball.

aloha 'āina *kik* Nationalism, patriotism. *Na ka po'e aloha 'āina Hawai'i i kāko'o ka mō'ī.* Hawaiian patriots supported their king. *Dic., ext. mng.*

alo 'ū·hā See *mākala 'ūhā.*

alu *kik/heh* Drive, as for cans; to conduct a drive. *Dic., ext. mng. Alu hō'ili'ili nūpepa.* Newspaper drive. *Alu ho'oma'ema'e pā kula.* School clean-up drive.

a.m. Ante meridium, a.m. (pronounced 'āmū). *Eng.* See *p.m.*

AM *kik* AM, amplitude modulation (pronounced 'āmū). *Eng.* Cf. *FM.* See *'anini laulā hawewe.*

ama *kik* Port or left side of a double-hulled canoe or a ship when looking forward. *Lit.,* outrigger float. Cf. *'ākea, muku.*

amo hao *ham* Weight lifting; to lift weights. *Lit.,* lift iron. Also *hāpai hao.*

ana *kik/ham* Measurement; dimension, in math. *'Ehia ke ana o kēia lumi?* What are the dimensions of this room? *Dic., ext. mng.* Also *nui.* See entries below. *Ana ākea, ana laulā.* Width. *Ana hohonu, ana ki'eki'e.* Height. *Ana loa, ana lō'ihi.* Length.

ana au uila *kik* Ammeter, an instrument used to measure the amount of electric current in a circuit. *Lit.,* electric current gauge.

ana·alike *Kaha anaalike.* Directrix, as a line which divides a parabola into two equal areas, in math. Cf. *kaha kau.*

ana ikehu kā·'oko'a *kik* Calorimeter, an instrument used to measure changes in thermal energy. *Lit.,* thermal energy gauge.

ana ō·la'i *kik* Seismograph. Also *mīkini ana ōla'i.*

ana hele wā·wae *kik* Pedometer. *Lit.,* gauge (for) walking.

ana·honua *kik* Geometry. *Dic.* Also *moleanahonua. Papakui anahonua.* Geoboard.

ana ho'o·hā·like *kik* Standard, i.e. an established model or example. *Lit.,* standard (for) comparison. *Ho'opa'a i ke ana ho'ohālike.* To set the standard.

ana huina *kik* Protractor. *Lit.,* angle measurement. *Ana huina kūpono.* Right angle protractor.

ana kau·maha wai *kik* Hydrometer. *Lit.,* water weight gauge. Cf. *ana kawaūea.*

ana kahe pele *kik* Lava tube. *Lit.,* cave (where) lava flows.

ana·kahi *kik* Unit of measurement. *Dic.* Cf. *kūana helu. Anakahi mekalika.* Metric unit of measure. *Anakahi 'Amelika.* US standard or customary unit of measurement. *Anakahi nuipa'a 'ātoma.* Atomic mass unit. See *nuipa'a 'ātoma. Hakina anakahi.* Unit fraction.

ana·kahi uila *kik* Volt, in electricity. *'O ka 7,200 anakahi uila ka 'awelika o ka nui o ke anakahi uila o nā uea o nā pou kelepona o ka'e o nā alanui.* 7,200 volts is the average voltage contained in the utility lines alongside roads. *Lit.,* electric unit of measurement. Cf. *'ome.*

ana kawa·ū·ea *kik* Hygrometer. *Lit.,* humidity gauge. Cf. *ana kaumaha wai. Ana kawaūea 'ōpu'u pulu a malo'o.* Wet-and-dry-bulb hygrometer. *Ana kawaūea kūlua.* Psychrometer. *Ma'a ana kawaūea kūlua.* Sling psychrometer.

ana kilo lani *kik* Sextant. *Lit.,* gauge (for) astronomy.

ana ki'e·ki'ena *kik* Altimeter. *Lit.,* altitude gauge.

ana·konu *kik* Equilibrium. *Ke kaulike 'elua manehu i ka pahu 'ana o kekahi i kekahi, pa'a maila ke anakonu.* When two opposing forces are equal, equilibrium is achieved. (Sāmoan *agatonu* [equal].) *Mīkā anakonu.* Isostasy, i.e. the equilibrium of the earth's crust, in geology.

ana·kuhi *kik* Template. Comb. *ana + kuhi. Anakuhi mahaka.* Stencil. *Pepa anakuhi lālani.* Linear unit paper, in math.

ana·lahi *'a* Regular, as in shape. Sh. *ana + ma'alahi.* Cf. *laukua. Huinalehu- lehu analahi.* Regular polygon. *Kinona analahi.* Regular shape.

ana lama hanu *kik* Breathalyzer. *Lit.,* gauge (to measure) intoxicating drink (in) breath. Cf. *nui lama koko.*

ana·like ʻaʻ Isometric. Comb. *ana* + *like*. *Pepa kiko analike.* Isometric dot paper.

ana·lula *kik* Pattern, as a word or sentence pattern in Hawaiian grammar. Comb. *ana* + *lula*. Cf. *lauana*. *Puke aʻo analula.* Pattern book, as for teaching grammatical patterns in reading.

ana mā·mā makani *kik* Anemometer. *Lit.,* wind speed gauge.

ana·manaʻo *kik/ham* Opinion survey, poll; to conduct an opinion survey or poll. Comb. *ana* + *manaʻo.* See entry below.

ana·manaʻo pā·loka *ham* To canvass, i.e. go door to door handing out political information and asking people which candidate they support. *Manaʻo aku ka meia he pono ke mālama ʻia he anamanaʻo pāloka ma ke kaona e ʻike ai i ka papaha o kōna lanakila ʻana ma ka holo moho hou ʻana.* The mayor felt it was necessary to canvass the town to see what his chances would be of winning a re-election bid. *Lit.,* ballot poll.

ana mī·kā ea *kik* Barometer. *Lit.,* air pressure gauge. *Ana mīkā ea kuhikuhi.* Aneroid barometer.

anana ʻē·heu *kik* Wingspan. *Lit.,* distance between wing tips.

ana·paona *kik* Scales, as used for weighing something. *Dic. Anapaona home.* Bathroom scales. Usu. *anapaona. Anapaona kaulike.* Balance scales. *Anapaona pilina.* Spring scales.

ana piʻi wela *ham* Specific heat, in physics. *Lit.,* measurement (of) heat increase.

ana·poʻo *heh* To set, as the sun. *Niʻihau.* Usu. *napoʻo.*

ana·puni *kik* Circumference, in math; perimeter. *Dic. Lākiō anapuni.* Constant of proportionality.

ana·waena *kik* Diameter, in math. *Dic.*

ana wela *kik/ham* Thermometer; to take the temperature of. *Dic./lit.,* measure heat. See *anu, mahana, mehana, wela, kēkelē.*

ana ʻakika *ham* Acid indicator. *Lit.,* measure acid. *Pepa ana ʻakika.* Litmus paper.

ana ʻome *kik* Ohmmeter. *Lit.,* Ohm gauge. See *ʻome.*

ane koʻe *kik* Mealworm. Comb. *ane* + *koʻe.* Cf. *ane ʻuku.*

ane ʻuku *kik* Mealy bug. *Dic., sp. var.*

ani·au *kik* Climate. *Lit.,* air movement (over) time. Cf. *anilā. Aniau hāiki.* Microclimate. *Lit.,* restricted climate.

ani·ani *kik* Mirror. *Dic.* Also *aniani nānā, aniani kilohi, aniani kilo.* See entries below. *Aniani ʻeʻele.* Concave mirror. *Aniani ʻeʻemu.* Convex mirror.

ani·ani awe *kik* Fiberglass. *Lit.,* thread glass. Cf. *aniani ʻea.*

ani·ani hoʻo·nui ʻike *kik* Magnifying glass, hand lens. *Dic.* Cf. *aniani kaulona.*

ani·ani kau·lona *kik* Lens, as for a camera or microscope. *Lit.,* glass (for) observing closely. Cf. *aniani hoʻonui ʻike. Aniani kaulona ʻeʻele.* Concave lens. *Aniani kaulona ʻeʻemu.* Convex lens.

ani·ani kau·paneʻe *kik* Slide, as for a microscope. Usu. *aniani. Lit.,* glass for placing and pushing along. See *paepae aniani kaupaneʻe.*

ani·ani kilohi kaʻa *kik* Rear-view mirror for a car. Also *aniani kaʻa.*

ani·ani kilohi pai·kikala *kik* Rear-view mirror for a bicycle. Also *aniani kilo paikikala, aniani paikikala.*

ani·ani kū *kik* Full-length mirror. *Dic.*

ani·ani pāiki *kik* Small mirror kept in a purse. Also *aniani liʻiliʻi.*

ani·ani paʻa lima *kik* Hand mirror. *Dic.* Also *aniani lima.*

ani·ani ʻea *kik* Plexiglass. *Lit.*, plastic glass. Cf. *aniani awe.*

ani·lā *kik* Weather. *Lit,* air movement (during the) day. Cf. *aniau.*

anu *ʻa* Temperature, when weather considered cold. *ʻEhia ke anu o kēia lā?* How cold is it today? *Lit.*, cold. Cf. *mahana, mehana, wela.* See *kēkelē.*

Ā·nui *iʻoa* Perseus, a constellation. *Māori.*

anp Abbreviation for *anapuni* (perimeter).

anw Abbreviation for *anawaena* (diameter).

a pau All, entirely. *Dic., sp. var.*

apo laho·lio *kik* Rubber band.

apo lohe *kik* Headphone, headset. *Lit.*, band (for) hearing. See *pihi lohe.*

apo po·o *kik* Hairband. *Niʻihau.*

apo ʻili kuapo *kik* Belt loop, as on a pair of pants. *Ua hala iaʻu kekahi apo ʻili kuapo i koʻu komo ʻana i koʻu ʻili kuapo.* I missed a belt loop when I put on my belt.

apu·apu *kik* Rasp (tool). *Dic.* Cf. *waiehu.*

awa *kik* Port, as in a computer. *Dic., ext. mng. Awa ala pilipā.* Parallel port. *Awa ala pūkaʻina.* Serial port.

awāwa uma *kik* U-shaped valley. *Lit.*, curve valley.

awāwa kū·hō·hō *kik* Canyon. *Lit.*, deep valley. See *Hakaʻama.*

awāwa mā·wae *kik* Rift valley. *Lit.*, fissure valley. *Pae awāwa māwae.* Series of rift valleys.

awe ō·ewe *kik* Chromosome. *Lit.*, gene thread.

awe uholo uila *kik* Brush, i.e. a contact that supplies electric current to a commutator. *Lit.*, strand (through which) electricity runs. Cf. *mea uholo uila.* See *ʻūkake uila.*

awe pale ahi *kik* Asbestos. *Lit.*, thread (which) resists fire.

aʻa·haʻa·pupū *kik* Arteriolosclerosis, in medicine. *ʻO ke aʻahaʻapupū, ʻo ia ka paʻa ʻana ʻo loko o ka ʻili o ke aʻa koko puʻuwai a hoʻēmi ʻia ke kahe o ke koko.* Arteriosclerosis is the hardening of the inner walls of the arteries slowing blood flow. *Comb. aʻa + haʻapupū.* Cf. *aʻalāʻau.*

aʻa kino *kik* Vein. *Sh. aʻa koko kino.* Also *aʻa koko kino.* Cf. *aʻa puʻuwai.* See entries below.

aʻa kino ake·mā·mā *kik* Pulmonary vein. *Lit.*, lung vein.

aʻa kino haku·ʻala *kik* Renal vein. *Lit.*, kidney vein.

aʻa kino hilo *kik* Femoral vein. *Sh. aʻa kino + iwi hilo.*

aʻa kino kā *kik* Iliac vein. *Lit.*, pelvic-bone vein.

aʻa kino kū wā·wae *kik* Tibial vein. *Sh. aʻa kino + iwi kū wāwae.*

aʻa kino wena·kawa See *wenakawa.*

aʻa kino ʻā·ī *kik* Jugular vein. *Lit.*, neck vein.

aʻa koko kino *kik* Vein. *Comb. aʻa koko + kino.* Also *aʻa kino.* Cf. *aʻa koko puʻuwai.*

aʻa koko puʻu·wai *kik* Artery. *Comb. aʻa koko + puʻuwai.* Also *aʻa puʻuwai.* Cf. *aʻa koko kino.*

aʻa·lā·ʻau *kik* Arteriosclerosis, atherosclerosis, hardening of the arteries, in medicine. *Comb. aʻa + lāʻau.* Cf. *aʻahaʻapupū.*

aʻa·lolo *kik* Nerve. *Dic.*

aʻa·lonoa *kik* Receptor, as of nerve endings in the body, in biology. *ʻO ke aʻalonoa o ke aʻalolo ke ʻike mua i ke kūlale.* The receptors of the nerves are the first to sense stimuli. *Comb. aʻa + lonoa. Aʻalonoa mīkā.* Pressure receptor. *Aʻalonoa ʻono.* Taste receptor.

aʻa puʻu·wai *kik* Artery. *Sh. aʻa koko puʻuwai.* Also *aʻa koko puʻuwai.* Cf. *aʻa kino.* See entries below.

aʻa puʻu·wai ake·mā·mā *kik* Pulmonary artery. *Lit.,* lung artery.

aʻa puʻu·wai haku·ʻala *kik* Renal artery. *Lit.,* kidney artery.

aʻa puʻu·wai hilo *kik* Femoral artery. Sh. *aʻa puʻuwai + iwi hilo.*

aʻa puʻu·wai kā *kik* Iliac artery. *Lit.,* pelvic-bone artery.

aʻa puʻu·wai kū wā·wae *kik* Tibial artery. Sh. *aʻa puʻuwai + iwi kū wāwae.*

aʻa puʻu·wai ʻā·ʻī *kik* Carotid artery. *Lit.,* neck artery.

aʻi·a·ʻi *ʻa* Transparent. *Dic., ext. mng.*

aʻi·a·ʻi hau·ʻoki *ʻa* Opaque. *Lit.,* frosty clear.

aʻo *Kiʻina aʻo.* Pedagogy, i.e. the art of teaching. *Pahu aʻo.* Dialog box, in computer program.

aʻo·ā·kumu *ham* Student teacher; to student teach. *Lit.,* teach until (becoming a) teacher. *Luna aʻoākumu.* Student teacher field service supervisor.

aʻo hou *ham* To reteach. *Lit.,* teach again. *Puke aʻo hou.* Reteaching book.

aʻo kahua lawena *ham* Performance-based learning, kinesthetic-based learning. *Lit.,* learning (with a) behavior base.

aʻo kahua ʻike kuʻuna *ham* Traditional knowledge-based learning. *Lit.,* learning (with a) traditional knowledge base.

aʻo kahua ʻō·lelo *ham* Language-based learning. *Lit.,* learning (with a) language base.

aʻo kahua ʻuhane *ham* Spiritually-based learning. *Lit.,* learning (with a) spiritual base.

aʻo launa kanaka *ham* Socialization; to socialize, i.e. fit, teach or train (someone) for a social environment or to associate sociably with others. *Lit.,* teach (to) associate (with) people.

E

ē A word used only at the end of a sentence or phrase, with meanings such as: Yeah; right; isn't that so? (Commonly pronounced the same as the French *hein* which carries the same meaning.) *Paʻakikī loa kēlā haʻawina, ē?* That was a really hard lesson, yeah? *Mān.*

ea *kik* Fume. *Dic.* Also *ea puka.* *Āohiohi ea.* Air resistance, i.e. the force of air against a moving object. *Ana mīkā ea.* Barometer. *Pōhaku puka ea.* Air stone, i.e. the porous rock in an aquarium that creates tiny bubbles at the surface of the water to facilitate the exchange of gases. *Pūnuku ea make.* Gas mask, as used during World War II.

ea·ea *ʻa* Aerated; aerobic, i.e. living, active, or occurring only in the presence of oxygen. *Dic., ext. mng.* See *hōʻeaea.* *Ka hoʻohāpopo eaea ʻana.* Aerobic decomposition. *Ka hoʻohāpopo eaea ʻole ʻana.* Anaerobic decomposition.

ea puka *kik* Fume. *Lit.,* emitting fume. Also *ea.*

eo (i/iā) *ʻa* To lose. *Ua eo ʻo Punahou iā Kamehameha.* Punahou lost to Kamehameha. *Ua eo iaʻu kāu mau kinikini.* I won your Pogs. *Ua lilo iaʻu ke eo.* I won. *Dic.* See *hāʻule.*

ē·ulu *kik* Top of a tree or plant. *Dic.*

ehu *kik* Pollen. *Dic.* See entries below and *hoʻēhu pua.* *Ehu pua.* Flower pollen. *Waiū ehu.* Powdered milk. Also *waiū pauka.*

ehu·ehu *kik/ʻa* Animated, violent. *Dic. Kiʻiʻoniʻoni ehuehu.* Action movie.

ehu·ō *kik* Inertia. Comb. *ehu + ō.*

ehu·ola *kik* Vigor. *Ke mālama pono ʻia ke olakino, he ehuola ke kino no ka wā lōʻihi o ke ola ʻana.* When you keep your health in good condition, your body will have vigor for a long time in your lifetime. Sh. *ehuehu + ola.* Cf. *hāʻehuola.*

ehu kī·kina *kik* Visible airborne particles, as from a spray can. Comb. *ehu + kīkina.* See *kīkina.*

ehu lepo *kik* Dust. *Dic.* Also *ehu.*

ehu poho *kik* Chalk dust. Cf. *ehu lepo.*

emi *'a'* Depleted, as a species. *Dic., ext. mng. Lāhui emi.* Depleted species. Also *lāhulu emi.*

emi See entries below and *woela emi. Au emi.* Recession, i.e. a period of reduced economic activity. *'Ōnaehana mīkā emi.* Low-pressure system, in meteorology. Cf. *'ōnaehana mīkā pi'i.*

emi iho *'a'* Less than, in math. Also *'oi aku ke emi.* Cf. *nui a'e.*

emi ha·a·ha'a loa *'a'* Greatest decrease, in math. *Lit.,* lowest decrease. Cf. *pi'i ki'eki'e loa.*

emi ka mā·mā holo *'a'* To decelerate; decelerated. *Lit.,* the running speed decreases. Cf. *emi māmā holo, ho'ēmi i ka māmā holo.* See also *pi'i ka māmā holo, ho'opi'i i ka māmā holo.*

emi mā·mā holo *kik* Deceleration. *Lit.,* decrease (of) progress. Cf. *emi ka māmā holo, pi'i māmā holo.*

ewe o lalo *kik* Abdominal aorta. *Lit.,* lower aorta *(dic., sp. var.).* Cf. *ewe o luna.*

ewe o luna *kik* Aorta. *Lit.,* upper aorta. Cf. *ewe o lalo.*

I

Iā·maika *i'oa* Jamaica; Jamaican. *Dic., sp. var.* Also *Iāmeka.*

Iā·meka *i'oa* Jamaica; Jamaican. *Dic.* Also *Iāmaika.*

Ian. Abbreviation for *Ianuali* (January).

Ianu·ali *i'oa* January. *Dic., sp. var.* Abb. *Ian.*

Iā·pana *i'oa* Japan. *Dic. Ke kai 'o Iāpana.* Sea of Japan.

Iape·tusa *i'oa* Iapetus, a moon of Saturn. *Eng.*

iā·pona *kik* Jabong, a type of citrus. *Japn.* See *pomelo.*

Iawa *i'oa* Java. *Eng. Ke kai 'o Iawa.* Java Sea.

Ie·mene Hema *i'oa* South Yemen; South Yemenite, South Yemeni. Comb. Eng. + *hema.*

Ie·mene 'Ā·kau *i'oa* North Yemen; North Yemenite, North Yemeni. Comb, Eng. + *'ākau.*

Ie·rese *i'oa* Jersey. *Eng. Ka mokupuni 'o Ierese.* Jersey Island.

ioio *kik* Yoyo. *Eng.*

Iowi·ana *i'oa* Jovian, in astronomy. *Eng. Hōkūhele Iowiana.* Jovian planet.

Iore·dāne *i'oa* Jordan; Jordanian. *Trad.*

Iose·mite *i'oa* Yosemite. *Ka Pāka Aupuni 'o Iosemite.* Yosemite National Park.

Iul. Abbreviation for *Iulai* (July).

Iu·lai *i'oa* July. *Dic.* Abb. *Iul.*

Iun. Abbreviation for *Iune* (June).

Iune *i'oa* June. *Dic.* Abb. *Iun.*

iuni·pela *kik* Juniper. *Dic.*

Iugo·sola·wia *i'oa* Yugoslavia; Yugoslavian. *Eng.*

ihi *ham* To peel, as an orange or taro. *Dic.* Cf. *uhole.*

iho *kik* Battery. *Dic.* Also *pakalē.* See entries below and *'ōmole iho uila. Iho poke.* Battery for flashlight, radio, etc. *Iho 'eono.* Six-volt battery. *Iho 'umikūmālua.* Twelve-volt battery. *Iho pihi.* Button-shape battery.

iho *kik* Axle, i.e. a shaft on which a wheel turns. *Dic.* Also *paepae komo huila.*

iho *kik* Axis, in math. *Dic. Nā iho kuhikuhina.* Coordinate axes, i.e. two intersecting perpendicular number lines used for graphing ordered number pairs in math. See *kuhikuhina.*

iho *kik* Nucleus of a syllable, in linguistics. *Dic., ext. mng.*

iho·iho·kī *kik* Roman candle (fireworks). *Lit.,* shooting candle. See *ahihoʻoleʻaleʻa.*

ihu *kik* Bow, of a boat. *Dic.*

ikaika hawewe kani *kik* Amplitude, i.e. the amount of energy in a sound wave. See *hawewe kani.*

ika·kani *kik* Decibel. *Lit.,* sound strength.

ikehu *kik* Energy, power. Sh. *ika + ehu.* See entries below. *Pālākiō ikehu ōlaʻi.* Richter scale.

ikehu uila *kik* Charge, as electric. *Lit.,* electric energy. *Ikehu uila hohoki.* Neutral charge. Also *ikehu hohoki.* See *hohoki, hoʻoikehu. Ikehu uila puhi wāwahie.* Thermoelectric power. *Ikehu uila wai kahe.* Hydroelectric power.

ikehu kā·ʻokoʻa *kik* Thermal energy, i.e. the total energy of all the particles in an object. *Lit.,* complete energy. *Ana ikehu kāʻokoʻa.* Calorimeter, an instrument used to measure changes in thermal energy.

ikehu kemi·kala *kik* Chemical energy. *Hana ʻia ka ikehu kemikala ke hoʻohuihui pū ʻia kekahi mau ʻano kemikala.* Chemical energy is produced when certain chemicals are mixed together.

ikehu lā *Hawewe ikehu lā.* Solar energy wave.

ikehu neʻe *kik* Kinetic energy. *Lit.,* moving energy.

ikehu noho *kik* Potential energy. *Lit.,* possessed energy.

ikehu nuke·lea *kik* Nuclear energy.

ikehu·ʻā *kik* Calorie. *Lit.,* burning energy. *Ikehuʻā pākaukani.* Kilocalorie. Abb. *ikpk.*

iki *ʻaʻ* Little, small. *Dic. Manamana iki.* Little finger. Also *manamana liʻiliʻi.*

-iku Suffix in chemical compounds and terms: -ic.

ikpk Abbreviation for *ikehuʻā pākaukani* (kilocalorie).

ili *ʻaʻ* Transplanted. *Dic., ext. mng.* Cf. *hoʻoili. Puʻuwai ili.* Transplanted heart.

ili *heh* Distribution or to be distributed, as data on a graph, in math and science. Sh. *hoʻoili.* Cf. *kākuhi, waiho, ʻanopili hoʻoili.* See entry below. *Ili haiakonu.* Normal distribution. *Ka ili o ka ua.* Rain distribution. *Ka ili o ka ʻikepili.* Data distribution.

ili pū·ʻuo *heh* Population distribution, in geography. *Ua loli ka ili pūʻuo kanaka i loko o nā makahiki 100 i hala aʻe nei mai ka noho nui ʻana ma kahi kuaʻāina a ka neʻe nui ʻana i kahi o nā kūlanakauhale.* Human population distribution in the last 100 years has changed from people mostly living in rural areas to people moving and mostly inhabiting areas near the cities. Also *ili pūʻuo kanaka.*

ilo *heh* To germinate, sprout; maggot. *Dic.* See *hoʻoilo. Ilo ʻakaʻakai.* Onion maggot.

Ilo·ano *iʻoa* Libra, a constellation. *Mān. (HA).*

inoa *kik* Title, as of a book or story. *Dic.* Also *poʻo inoa.* Name, as of file in computer program. *ʻO wai (ka inoa o) ka palapala?* What is the name of the document? *Inoa o ke pihi.* Name of key. *Hāpai inoa.* To nominate. Also *waiho inoa* (dic.). *Kālaikapa inoa.* Taxonomy, the science of classifying plants and animals. *Kelepona inoa.* Person-to-person call; to make such a call.

inu *ham* To take, as medicine or a pill. *Niʻihau.* Cf. *ʻai. Inu i ka huaale.* To take a pill. *Inu i ka lāʻau.* To take (liquid) medicine.

ipu *kik* Squash, general term. *Dic., ext mng.* See *palaʻai.*

ipu·hao hana kai *kik* Sauce pan. *Lit.,* pan (for) making sauce.

ipu·leo *kik* Microphone. *Lit.*, voice vessel. Also *mea hoʻolele leo* (dic.). *Mea kīkoʻo ipuleo.* Boom operator, as for movie or video production.

ipu lua *kik* Toilet bowl. Cf. *ipu mimi, noho lua.*

ipu mimi *kik* Urinal, bedpan. *Dic., ext. mng.* Cf. *ipu lua.* See *mīana.*

ipu·ʻala *kik* Cantaloupe. *Dic.* See *meleni.*

iwi *kik* Side of a sporting field or court. *Lit.*, stones or earth ridge marking land boundary. Also *ʻaoʻao.* Cf. *poʻo.* See entries below and *haʻihaʻi iwi, kimeki iwi, palaku iwi. Laina iwi.* Side line. Also *laina ʻaoʻao. Laina iwi kī.* Side line of the key on a basketball court.

iwi *kik* Bone. *Dic.* See entries below. *Niniki wahī iwi.* Periosteum, i.e. the tough membrane adhering tightly to a bone.

iwi ā *kik* Jawbone, mandible. *Dic.*

iwi ule *kik* Baculum, i.e. a slender bone reinforcing the penis in many mammals. *Lit.*, penis bone.

iwi uluna *kik* Humerus, i.e. the long bone of the upper arm. *Dic.*

iwi hilo *kik* Femur, i.e. the long bone of the thigh. *Dic.*

iwi kā *kik* Hip bone, pelvis. *Dic., ext. mng. Iwi kā o luna.* Ilium, i.e. the upper portion of the pelvis. *Iwi kā o lalo.* Ischium, i.e. the lower portion of the pelvis.

iwi kamumu *kik* Cartilage. *Dic.*

iwi kua·moʻo *kik* Backbone, spine; vertebrate. *Dic., sp. var., ext. mng.* See *iwi kuamoʻo ʻole. Holoholona iwi kuamoʻo.* Vertebrate animal. *Paukū iwi kuamoʻo.* Vertebra, i.e. a segment of the backbone.

iwi kua·moʻo ʻole *kik* Invertebrate. *Lit.*, without (a) backbone. See *iwi kuamoʻo. Holoholona iwi kuamoʻo ʻole.* Invertebrate animal.

iwi kū lima *kik* Ulna, i.e. the longer and thinner of the two bones of the forearm on the side opposite the thumb. *Dic., sp. var., ext. mng. + lima.* Cf. *iwi pili lima.* See *iwi kū wāwae.*

iwi kū·loko *kik* Endoskeleton. *Lit.*, internal bones. Cf. *iwi kūwaho.*

iwi kū·waho *kik* Exoskeleton. *Lit.*, external bones. Cf. *iwi kūloko.*

iwi kū wā·wae *kik* Tibia, i.e. the inner bone of the lower leg. *Dic., sp. var. + wāwae.* Cf. *iwi pili wāwae.* See *iwi kū lima.*

iwi kuʻe ʻamo *kik* Coccyx, i.e. the terminus of the spinal column; tailbone. *Sh. iwi + kuʻekuʻe + ʻamo.* Also *kuʻe ʻamo.*

iwi lei *kik* Clavicle, collarbone. *Dic., sp. var.*

iwi mana·mana lima *kik* Phalanx (*plural* phalanges), i.e. the bones of the fingers. *Lit.*, finger bone.

iwi mana·mana wā·wae *kik* Phalanx (*plural* phalanges), i.e. the bones of the toes. *Lit.*, toe bone.

iwi pā·ʻani *kik* Domino. *Lit.*, playing bone. See *pāʻani iwi.*

iwi pili lima *kik* Radius, i.e. the shorter and thicker of the two bones of the forearm on the same side as the thumb. *Dic. + lima.* Cf. *iwi kū lima.* See *iwi pili wāwae.*

iwi pili wā·wae *kik* Fibula, i.e. the outer and thinner bone of the lower leg. *Dic. + wāwae.* Cf. *iwi kū wāwae.* See *iwi pili lima.*

iwi poli wā·wae *kik* Metatarsus, i.e. one of the five bones of the foot immediately proximal to the phalanges. *Lit.*, bone (of the) instep.

iwi poʻo *kik* Skull. *Dic.*

iwi·puhi *kik* Herringbone weave. *Dic.* Also *maka puhi.*

iwi pū·lima *kik* Any one of the eight carpal bones of the wrist. *Lit.*, wrist bone.

iwi wili·wili *kik* Bonemeal. *Trad.* Cf. *'i'o wiliwili.*

iwi 'alā *kik* Cortical bone. *Lit.*, bone (like) hard lava. Cf. *iwi 'ana.*

iwi 'ana *kik* Cancellous bone. *Lit.*, pumice bone. Cf. *iwi 'alā.*

i'a *kik* Fish or any marine animal. *Dic.* See entries below. *Kini i'a.* Canned fish. *Mahi i'a.* Aquaculture. *Manamana i'a.* Fish stick. *'Oihana I'a me ka Holoholona Lōhiu o 'Amelika.* US Fish and Wildlife Service.

i'a·uli *kik* Bluefish. Comb. *i'a + uli.*

i'a kai *kik* Marine animal. *Dic.* + *kai.*

i'a kapi *kik* Guppy. Comb. *i'a* + Eng.

i'a·kea *kik* Whitefish. Comb. *i'a + kea.*

i'a makika *kik* Mosquito fish, medaka.

i'a moli *kik* Molly. Comb. *i'a* + Eng.

i'a puna·kea *kik* Trout. *Lit.*, rainbow fish.

O
―――――

o *Ma o.* In terms of, in math.

ō *Waihona ō.* Endowment fund. *Lit.*, fund (which) endures. Also *waihona kālā kūmau.*

oe·oe *kik* Alarm bell, as on a clock or fire alarm. *Dic., ext. mng.* Also *pele.* See *oeoe uahi.*

oe·oe uahi *kik* Smoke alarm. *Lit.*, smoke siren.

ō·ewe *kik* Gene; genetic. Comb. *ō + ēwe.* Cf. *welo.* See *awe ōewe, ho'oliliu-ewe, kālaiōewe.*

oho *kik* Capillary, i.e. one of the minute blood vessels between the arteries and the veins. *No ka li'ili'i loa o kekahi mau oho, pono e nānā 'ia me ka 'ohe ho'onui 'ike.* Since some capillaries are so small, they must be observed using a microscope. *Dic., new mng.*

Ohta-san See *'ukulele Ohta-san.*

oka lā·'au *kik* Sawdust. *Dic.*

ola *Pō'aiapuni ola.* Life cycle.

ola·kino *kik* Health. *Dic. Kūlana olakino.* Health status. *Kāko'o 'oihana olakino.* Allied health professional. *'Inikua olakino.* Medical insurance. *Helu 'inikua olakino.* Medical coverage number.

ola lā *kik* Per diem, i.e. a daily allowance for living expenses while traveling in connection with one's work. *Sh. uku ola lā.* Also *uku ola lā.*

ola mehana *heh* Mesophilic, i.e. midtemperature-loving. *Lit.*, live (in) warmth. Cf. *ola wela. Ko'ohune ola mehana.* Mesophilic bacteria.

ola wela *heh* Thermophilic, i.e. heat-loving. *Lit.*, live (in) heat. Cf. *ola mehana. Ko'ohune ola wela.* Thermophilic bacteria.

ō·la'i *kik* Earthquake. *Dic. Kiko ōla'i.* Epicenter. *Manunu muli ōla'i.* Aftershock, i.e. a minor shock following an earthquake. *Pālākiō ikehu ōla'i.* Richter scale.

olo·ea *kik* Aerophone, i.e. a musical instrument whose sound is produced by air passing through it. Comb. *olo + ea.*

olo·olo·nā *kik* Ligament. *Dic.*

olo·kaula *kik* Chordophone, i.e. a musical instrument whose sound is produced by plucking, strumming, striking, or bowing strings. Comb. *olo + kaula.*

olo·kino *kik* Idiophone, i.e. a musical instrument whose sound is dependent upon the nature of the material from which it is made. Comb. *olo + kino.*

olo·pī *kik* Bead. Comb. *olo* + Eng.

olo·'ili *kik* Membranophone, i.e. a musical instrument whose sound is produced by striking a membrane or skin of the instrument. Comb. *olo + 'ili.*

omo *ham* To give an electric shock. *Mān.* Also *miki.* Cf. *'ūmi'i.*

omo *ham* To absorb. *Dic.* See *'ūomo.* Cf. *omowaho.* See *kaupokupoku omo.*

omo·ā·ea *heh* To evaporate. *Lit.*, evaporate into air.

omo·ola *kik/heh* Parasite; to live as a parasite. Comb. *omo + ola.* See *kauomolia, koʻe omoola.*

omo hoʻo·kulu *kik* Dropper (eyedropper, etc.). *Lit.,* suction tube (for) dropping liquid.

omo·waho *ham* To adsorb. Comb. *omo + waho.* Cf. *omo. ʻAe omowaho.* Solvent front, i.e. the leading edge of a moving solvent as in a developing chromatogram.

omo wela *ham* Endothermic, i.e. absorbs heat. Cf. *kuʻu wela.*

one *Lalo one.* Subsand.

one ʻā *kik* Volcanic cinder. *Dic.* See *ʻākeke.*

ono See *pihi wili ono.*

ō·puhe *kik* Finch, general term. *Kaulana ka pae moku ʻo Galapagosa no ka nui a me ka laulā o nā ʻano manu ōpuhe o ia wahi.* The Galapagos Islands are famous for the many and varied types of finches that are found there. Metathesis of *hōpue* See English entries under finch. *Ōpuhe pao lāʻau.* Woodpecker finch.

ō·puna *kik* Calcite. Sh. *one + puna.*

oʻi·oʻina lewa lipo *kik* Space station. *Lit.,* resting place for travelers (in) space.

oʻo *Pae oʻo.* Varsity, as a league of sports at school.

U

ua *kik* Rainfall. *Lit.,* rain. See *kualā. Alo ua.* Rainy side, as of a mountain. *Ua pili pali.* Orographic rainfall. *Ka ili o ka ua.* Rain distribution. *Palapala ʻāina ua.* Rainfall map. *Wai ua.* Rain water.

uai *heh* To slide, as a door. *Dic. Laka uai.* Sliding latch. *Puka uai.* Sliding door. Also *ʻīpuka uai.*

ua oki Cut! i.e. a command to stop the filming of a movie or video scene (pronounced *uoki*). *Dic., ext. mng.*

ua·ua *kik* Tendon. *Mān.* Also *lohi.*

uahi See *puka uahi.*

ua·keʻe *kik* Curve or turn, as in a road or on a trail. *Dic. Uakeʻe hiō.* Banked curve, as on a race track.

uaki *ham* To time. *Dic., ext. mng.* Also *uāki.* Cf. *helu manawa.* See *uaki helu manawa. Helu uaki.* To tell time. Also *helu uāki.*

uaki helu manawa *kik* Stopwatch. *Lit.,* watch (to) compute time. Also *uāki helu manawa.* See *helu manawa.*

uaki hoʻāla *kik* Alarm clock. *Lit.,* clock (for) waking. Also *uāki hoʻāla.*

uaki kiko·hoʻe *kik* Digital watch or clock. *Lit.,* watch (with) digits. Also *uāki kikohoʻe.* Cf. *uaki lima kuhikuhi.*

uaki lima kuhi·kuhi *kik* Analog watch or clock, i.e. a watch or clock with hands. Also *uāki lima kuhikuhi.* Cf. *uaki kikohoʻe.*

uate *kik* Watt. *Eng.* Abb. *uat.* See *kilouate.*

uea Wire. *Dic.* See entries below and *kaula uea. Uea nikoroma.* Nichrome wire.

uea kau lole *kik* Hanger. *Lit.,* wire (for) placing clothes. See *lāʻau kau lole, mea kau lole, ʻea kau lole.*

uea makika *kik* Screen, as for windows. *Lit.,* mosquito wire. Also *makaʻaha.*

uea nā·kiʻi *kik* Twist tie, as used with plastic bags. *Lit.,* tying wire.

uea peleki *kik* Brake cable, as on a bicycle. *Niʻihau.*

Uēki ʻAi·lana *iʻoa* Wake Island. *Eng.*

uepa *kik* Wax. *Dic., ext. mng.* Also *pīlali.* Cf. *uepa ihoiho, ʻōihoiho.*

uepa iho·iho *kik* Paraffin. *Lit.,* candle wax seal.

uila *kik* Electricity. *Dic.* See entries below and *ana au uila, anakahi uila, awe uholo uila, lapaʻau hoʻomiki uila, luna uila, mea uholo uila, puka uila, puni uila, ʻōmole iho uila, ʻuiki uila, ʻūkake uila, ʻūʻōki puni uila.*

uila auˈkahi *kik* Direct current (DC) electricity. *Lit.,* electricity flowing together. Cf. *uila au māˈaloʻalo.*

uila au māˈaloˈalo *kik* Alternating current (AC) electricity. *Lit.,* electricity (with) current passing back and forth. Cf. *uila aukahi.*

uila huila makani *kik* Wind-generated electricity. *Lit.,* electricity (from) windmill. See *uila māhu pele, uila puhi wāwahie, uila wai kahe.*

uila māhu pele *kik* Geothermal electricity. *Lit.,* electricity (from) volcanic steam. See *uila huila makani, uila puhi wāwahie, uila wai kahe.*

uila puhi wāˈwahie *kik* Thermoelectricity; thermoelectric. *Lit.,* electricity (from) burning fuel. See *uila huila makani, uila māhu pele, uila wai kahe. Ikehu uila puhi wāwahie.* Thermoelectric power.

uila wai kahe *kik* Hydroelectricity; hydroelectric. *Lit.,* electricity (from) flowing water. See *uila huila makani, uila māhu pele, uila puhi wāwahie. Ikehu uila wai kahe.* Hydroelectric power.

uiniˈhapa ʻakoˈpie *kik* Adobe block. *Lit.,* adobe brick.

uipoˈuila *kik* Whippoorwill. *Eng.* Also *manu uipouila.*

uhi *Lepo uhi.* Topsoil. Cf. *lalo lepo.*

uhiˈmoe *kik* Bedspread. *Dic.*

uhole *ham.* To peel or strip, as a banana. *Dic.* Cf. *ihi.*

uholo uila See *awe uholo uila, mea uholo uila.*

ukali *kik* Satellite. *Dic., ext. mng.* Also *poelele.* Cf. *hōkū ukali.*

Ukaliˈaliʻi *iʻoa* Mercury (the planet). *Dic.*

uku ola lā *kik* Per diem, i.e. a daily allowance for living expenses while traveling in connection with one's work. *Na ke keʻena i hoʻolako mai ka uku ola lā iaʻu ma ka ʻaha kūkā i ka ʻāina ʻē.* The department provided me with per diem while I was away at the convention overseas. *Lit.,* pay (for) means of support (for the) day. Also *ola lā.*

uku hoˈoˈmau *kik* Pension. *Ua lawe au i ka uku hoʻomau i loko o Iune.* I drew my pension in June. *Dic.*

uku leka *kik* Postage. *Lit.,* letter fee.

uku pāˈnaʻi *kik/ham* Compensation, as to make amends for loss or damage; payment for services. *Ke hoʻāʻo nei wau e loaʻa iaʻu ka uku pānaʻi no ka ʻinoʻino o koʻu kaʻa.* I am seeking compensation for the damage to my car. *Dic., ext. mng.*

uku paneˈe *kik* Interest, as on principal when borrowing money. *Dic.* See *kumupaʻa. Pākēneka uku paneʻe.* Rate of interest.

ukuˈwai *kik* Portion of a canoe between forward and aft outrigger booms. *Dic.*

uku ʻāˈkena See *uku ʻēkena.*

uku ʻēˈkena *kik* Commission, i.e. a fee paid to an agent for transacting business or performing a service. *Lit.,* agent pay. Also *uku ʻākena.* See *komikina.*

uku ʻiniˈkua *kik* Insurance premium. *Dic.*

ulahi *kik* Flake. Sh. *unahi + lahi. Ulahi iʻa.* Fish flake. *Ulahi meaʻai iʻa.* Fish food flake. *Ulahi hau.* Snowflake. *Ulahi ʻokamila.* Oatmeal flake.

ula kahi See *kapuahi ula kahi.*

ula pāˈpapa *kik* Slipper lobster. *Dic., new mng.* Also *ula ʻāpapapa.* Cf. *ʻōmā.*

ula ʻāˈpapapa *kik* Slipper lobster. *Niʻihau.* Also *ula pāpapa.* Cf. *ʻōmā.*

ule *Iwi ule*. Baculum, i.e. a slender bone reinforcing the penis in many mammals.

ulele *heh* To take off, as a bird or plane taking flight. *Trad.* See *kīloi ulele, pa'i ulele*.

ulele hua *ham* To set type, as for video captions. Comb. *ulele + hua*. *Mea ulele hua*. Character operator.

ulele kikī *heh* Fast break, as in basketball; to make a fast break. *'Āha'i akula ka ho'okūkū iā Lāhainā Luna no kō lākou ma'alea aku i kō lākou hoa paio i ka ulele kikī*. Lāhainā Luna really took the game due to their outwitting their opponent in the fast break. *Lit.*, leap swiftly into action. *Cf. kīloi ulele kikī*. See *kuemi*.

ule'o *kik* Pendulum. *Sh. uleule + 'olo*. See *'ukē*.

ulia *kik* Accident. *Dic. Ulia ka'a*. Car accident, automobile accident.

ū·lia·lia *kik* Coincidence. *Ma ka ūlialia, ua hui akula wau me ka'u kanaka e huli ana*. By coincidence, I ran into the guy I was looking for. Redup. of *ulia*. See *ūlialia pōmaika'i*.

ū·lia·lia pō·mai·ka'i *kik* Serendipity, i.e making a fortunate discovery by accident. *He ūlialia pōmaika'i ka loa'a 'ana ia'u he pūnāwai ma ko'u pā hale i ko'u 'ō'ō 'ana ma ka māla*. It was serendipity that I discovered a spring in my yard while I was digging in the garden. *Lit.*, fortunate coincidence.

ulu *heh* To grow. *Dic.* See entries below. *Ulu papakū*. To grow vertically. *Ulu papamoe*. To grow horizontally. *Palena ulu*. Grow limit.

ulu *kik* Compression, i.e. the most dense concentration of wave particles in a compressional wave. *Dic., new mng. Cf. wele*. See *hawewe papamoe*.

ulu·ā·hewa *'a'* To grow wild and lush. *Dic. Cf. ulu wale*.

ulu·ō *kik* Momentum. Comb. *ulu + ō. Loli uluō*. Impulse, i.e. the change in momentum produced by a force, in physics.

Ulu·kou 'Ai·lana *i'oa* Howland Island. Comb. dic. + *'ailana*.

ulu·lā·'au *kik* Forest. *Dic., sp. var. Ho'oneo 'āina ululā'au*. Deforestation; to deforest. *Mahi ululā'au*. Agroforestry.

ulūlu *heh* Strong, as wind; large branches in motion and whistling heard in wires between utility poles, in meteorology. *Dic., ext. mng.* See *makani*.

uluna *kik* Pillow. *Dic. Pale uluna*. Pillowcase. *Iwi uluna*. Humerus, i.e. the long bone of the upper arm.

ulu wale *heh* To grow wild, as weeds. *Dic. Cf. uluāhewa*. See entry below.

ulu wale *heh* Impromptu, spontaneous. *Ha'i'ōlelo ulu wale maila ka pelekikena i kōna 'ō'ili 'ana mai i ka 'aha kūkā*. The president made an impromptu speech when he made his appearance at the conference. *Dic., ext. mng. Kākau ulu wale*. Extemporaneous writing; to freewrite, as writing about anything one chooses.

uma *kik* Curve, as on a graph or as a geometric curve. *Dic., ext. mng.* See *awāwa uma, uma kī. Mākala uma iki*. Pectoralis minor muscle of the upper chest. *Mākala uma nui*. Pectoralis major muscle of the upper chest.

umauma *'Au umauma*. Breast stroke; to swim the breast stroke. See *kīloi umauma*.

umauma moa *kik* Chicken breast.

uma kī *kik* Top of the key on a basketball court. *Lit.*, key curve. Also *uma, pōheo*. See *pukakī*.

uma pala·pola *kik* Parabolic curve. Comb. *uma + Eng.*

umu·ko'a *kik* Artificial reef. Comb. *umu + ko'a*.

unahi·one *kik* Paper shell (*foraminiferans*). Comb. *unahi + one*.

una honua *kik* Plate, as in geology. *Lit.*, earth shell. *Ka Una Honua Kokosa.* Cocos Plate. *Ka Una Honua Naseka.* Nazca Plate. *Ka Una Honua ʻEulāsia.* Eurasian Plate. *Ka Una Honua ʻĪnionūhōlani.* Indo-Australian Plate. *Kuʻina una honua.* Plate techtonics.

une *ham* Lever; to pry, as with a lever. *Dic.*

une kini *kik* Tab, as on soda cans. *Lit.*, can lever. *Une kini koloaka.* Soda can tab.

une kukui *kik* Light controls, as for stage productions. *Lit.*, lever (for) lights.

unu *kik* Chip, as in computer hardware. *Dic., ext. mng.* See *unu lawelawe.*

unuhi kū·ana *ham* Expanded form, in math; to expand. *E unuhi kūana i ka helu 395.* Expand the number 395 *[395 = 300 + 90 + 5].* *Lit.*, interrupt place value. *Helu unuhi kūana.* Expanded numeral.

unu·kā *kik* Asphalt. *Sh. unu + kā.* See *hoʻūnukā.*

unu lawe·lawe *kik* Processor, as in computer hardware. *Lit.*, chip (to) perform. See *unu.*

H

hā *kik* Fa, the fourth note on the musical scale. *Dic.* See *pākōlī.*

hai *Kū i ka hai.* Freelance.

haia·hū *kik* Deviation, in math. Comb. *haia + hū.* Cf. *haiakonu. Haiahū kūmau.* Standard deviation.

haia·konu *ʻa* Normal, in math and science. Sh. *haia + waenakonu.* Cf. *haiahū. Ili haiakonu.* Normal distribution.

haia·mui *kik* Caucus, i.e. a meeting of political party leaders to determine policy, choose candidates, etc. *Hālāwai nā ʻaoʻao kālaiʻāina ma kahi kaʻawale ma ka haiamui no ka hoʻoholo ʻana ʻo wai ana lā nā luna o ia mau ʻaoʻao no kēia makahiki.* Political parties meet separately in caucus to decide who will be their party leaders for the year. Comb. *hai- + a + mui.*

hāiki *Pahuhopu hāiki.* Objective.

haiko·kene *kik* Hydrogen. *Eng. Haikokene lua ʻokikene lua.* Hydrogen peroxide (H_2O_2).

hai·lawe *ham* To barter. *Ma mua o ka hoʻopaʻa ʻana i ka ʻōnaehana kālā, ʻo ka hailawe ʻana ka hana maʻamau a ka poʻe o Hawaiʻi nei.* Before establishing the cash system, the barter system was prevalent among those living here in Hawaiʻi. *Dic. Ka hailawe ʻana.* Barter system.

Hai·peli·ona *iʻoa* Hyperion, a moon of Saturn. *Eng.*

hai·pili·kia *kik* Pest, as any plant or animal detrimental to humans or their interests. Sh. *hailepo + pilikia.*

hai·doro·kolo·riku Hydrochloric. *Eng. ʻAkika haidorokoloriku.* Hydrochloric acid.

hao *kik* Rim of basket, in basketball. *E ʻāhaʻi a ka hao.* Take it to the rim. *Dic., ext. mng.* Also *kuku.* See entries below and *hīnaʻi, hupa.*

hao hoʻo·kani *kik* Tuning fork. *Niʻihau.* Also *ʻō hoʻokani* (preceded by *ke*).

hao kau lole *kik* Clothes rack, as on wheels in a clothing store. *Niʻihau.* Also *haka lole.*

hao keko *kik* Monkey bars, a kind of playground equipment. *Lit.*, monkey iron. Cf. *hao pīnana.*

hao kope *kik* Garden rake. *Lit.*, metal tool (for) raking. See *kope.*

hao pela *kik* Bedframe. *Lit.*, mattress iron. See *kūmoe.*

hao pī·nana *kik* Jungle gym, a kind of playground equipment. *Lit.*, iron for climbing. Cf. *hao keko.*

hā·ʻo·o *ʻa* Cured, i.e. prepared by chemical or physical processing for keeping or use. Comb. *hā- + ʻoʻo.* See *hoʻohāʻoʻo.*

Hau·hoa *i'oa* Zuben Elgenubi, a star. *Mān.* (HA).

hau·kōhi *kik* Shave ice, snow cone. *Mān.*

hau·kona *kik* Hawthorne. *Eng. Pī'ai haukona.* Hawthorne berry.

hau·lāpa *kik* Balsa. *Lit.,* raft hau.

hau·māna *Haumāna mua puka.* Undergraduate student. *Haumāna muli puka.* Graduate student. *Ho'ona'auao haumāna lololo.* Gifted education, as a school program. *Loiloi holomua haumāna.* Student assessment.

hau·mia *kik* Pollution. *Dic., ext. mng. Haumia ea.* Air pollution.

hau·naele kū·loko *kik* Civil unrest. *Ho'āla 'ia a'ela he haunaele kūloko ma ke kūlanakauhale no ka nui loa o nā hihia ma waena o ka po'e e noho ana ma ia wahi.* Civil unrest was created in the city due to the tremendous amound of tension between the people who live in the area. *Trad.*

hau·naku *kik* Defensive middle guard, nose guard, nose tackle, in football. *Dic., new mng.*

hau·nene'e *kik* Glacier. *Lit.,* creeping ice. *Ka haunene'e 'ana.* Glaciation. *I ka haunene'e 'ana, pa'apū nā kuahiwi a me ka 'āina i ka hau no nā makahiki he nui ka lō'ihi.* In glaciation, the mountains and land become covered with ice for a period of many years. *Ka Pāka Aupuni 'o Haunene'e.* Glacier National Park.

hau·waiū·tepe *kik* Frozen yogurt. *Lit.,* ice yogurt. *Cf. haukalima* (dic.). See *waiūtepe.*

haha *heh* To pant, as a dog. *Dic.*

hā hā *kik* Four-by-four. *Papa hā hā.* Four-by-four board or lumber. See *lua hā.*

hahai holo·holona *Ho'omalu lawai'a a me ka hahai holoholona.* Fish and game management; to manage fish and game.

hahaina *kik* Function, in math. Comb. *hahai + -na.* Cf. *hana, lawelawe hana. Hahaina lālani.* Linear function. *Hahaina pāho'onui lua.* Quadratic function. See *ha'ihelu pāho'onui lua. Ho'okūkū hahaina.* Curve-fitting, in math.

hahai 'ō·kuhi *ham* To follow directions. See *'ōkuhi.*

hahī *kik* Fricative, in linguistics. *Onomatopoeia.*

hahili poloka *kik* Antennariv Commersonil, a kind of fish. *Lit.,* frog fish.

haka *kik* Heart, i.e. the shape. *Dic., ext. mng.*

haka ihu *kik* Nasal cavity. *Lit.,* nose open space.

haka·haka See *ka'ele, pani hakahaka, pa'i hakahaka.*

haka·haka pā *kik* Disk space, as on computer hard drive or floppy disk. *Ua lawa kūpono ka hakahaka pā o kēia pā malule.* There is just enough disk space on this floppy disk. *Lit.,* disk vacant space.

haka kau *kik* Shelf. *Dic. Haka kau puke.* Bookshelf.

haka kau·la'i pā *kik* Dish rack. *Lit.,* rack (for) drying dishes.

haka·kino *kik* Structure, as of a molecule. Comb. *haka + kino.*

haka·lama *kik* Syllabary. Comb. *hā + kā + lā + mā.* See *huahakalama.*

haka lole *kik* Clothes rack, as on wheels in a clothing store. Also *hao kau lole.*

haka moni *kik* Pharynx, in anatomy. *Lit.,* open space (for) swallowing. *Haka moni o lalo.* Laryngopharynx, i.e. the lower part of the pharynx adjacent to the larynx. *Haka moni o luna.* Nasopharynx, i.e. the portion of the pharynx behind the nasal cavity and above the soft palate. *Haka moni o waena.* Oropharynx, i.e. the lower part of the pharynx contiguous to the mouth.

haka moʻoni *kik* Cochlea, i.e. inner ear cavity. *Lit.,* spiral open space.

haka pā·ʻā·lua *kik* Code style, as in computer program. *Lit.,* code rack.

haka waha *kik* Oral cavity. *Lit.,* mouth open space. Cf. *puka niho.*

Haka·ʻama *iʻoa* Grand Canyon. (*Hualapai* elder river.) Also *ke awāwa kūhōhō nui ʻo Hakaʻama. Ka muliwai ʻo Hakaʻama.* Colorado River. See *Kololako.*

haki *kik* Crease, as on a pair of pants. *Niʻihau.* Also *ʻopi.*

hakina *kik* Fraction, in math. *Dic. Hakina anakahi.* Unit fraction. *Hakina heluna like.* Equivalent fraction. *Hakina lapa.* Improper fraction. *Hakina palena haʻahaʻa loa.* Lowest-terms fraction.

hakina·heʻe *kik* Geologic fault, as San Andreas Fault. *Lit.,* slipping break.

haki wale *heh* Fragile, easily broken. *Dic.* Cf. *nahā wale, pāloli.*

haku *kik* Sponge-like material in a sprouting coconut. *Dic.* Cf. *niu haku.* See entries below and *lumi moe haku, pepeke haku.*

haku *ham* To make, as a test; to write, as a computer program. *Dic., ext. mng.* Cf. *hana i ka hōʻike, kākau i ka hōʻike. Haku i ka hōʻike.* To make a test. *Haku kōmi ʻōkuhi.* To write a (computer) script. *Haku polokalamu.* To write a program, as for a computer.

haku·ahua *ham/ʻa* To synthesize, as compounds; synthetic. *Comb. haku + a + hua. Nā pūhui i hakuahua ʻia.* Synthesized compounds.

haku·ika *kik* Mollusk. *Sh. pōhaku + kuita* (*Proto Eastern Oceanic,* squid).

haku·hia *ʻa* Invented. *Ua hakuhia iā ia kekahi mīkini hou.* A new machine was invented by him/her. *Comb. haku + -hia.* Cf. *hoʻohakuhia.*

haku·hune *kik* Tuff, i.e. a rock composed of finer kinds of detritus, usually more or less stratified and in various states of consolidation, in geology. *Sh. pōhaku + hune. Puʻu hakuhune.* Tuff cone.

haku kā nahau *kik* Mesolithic, in anthropology. *Lit.,* stone (for) striking arrows. See *au. Ke au haku kā nahau.* Mesolithic age, period.

haku kā pahi *kik* Paleolithic, in anthropology. *Lit.,* stone (for) striking knives. See *au. Ke au haku kā pahi.* Paleolithic age, period.

haku kele·awe·ʻula *kik* Aeneolithic, in anthropology. *Lit.,* copper stone. See *au. Ke au haku keleaweʻula.* Aeneolithic age, period.

haku·kuleke *kik* Turquoise, i.e. the mineral. *Comb. haku + Kuleke.*

haku kū·lohe·lohe *kik* Eolithic, in anthropology. *Lit.,* natural stone. See *au. Ke au haku kūlohelohe.* Eolithic age, period.

haku·lau *ham* To design. *Lit.,* arrange (a) design.

haku·lau kahua *ham* To design sets, as for movie or video production. *Mea hakulau kahua.* Set designer.

haku·leʻi *ʻa* Nonfiction. *Sh. haku + pololeʻi.* Cf. *hakupuni. Puke hakuleʻi.* Nonfiction book.

haku·loli *ham* To adapt, as a written document by shortening or lengthening, or by changing the form or style. *Comb. haku + loli.* See *hōʻano hou.*

haku mele *ham* Composer; to compose songs or chants. *Dic.*

haku·puni *ʻa* Fiction; fictitious. *Comb. haku + puni.* Cf. *hakuleʻi.* See *mōhihiʻo. Hakupuni kohu ʻoiaʻiʻo.* Realistic fiction. *Hakupuni mōʻaukala.* Historical fiction. *Puke hakupuni.* Fiction book.

haku·ʻala *kik* Kidney. *Niʻihau. Aʻa kino hakuʻala.* Renal vein. *Aʻa puʻuwai hakuʻala.* Renal artery.

haku ʻā·nai *kik* Neolithic, in anthropology. *Lit.,* stone (for) grinding. See *au. Ke au haku ʻānai.* Neolithic age, period.

haku·ʻili *kik* Gravel. Sh. *pōhaku* + *ʻiliʻili.*

hala akula i waho Out, in volleyball. *Niʻihau.* Cf. *ʻauka.*

hala·hī *Kī halahī.* Air ball, missed shot, in basketball; to make such a shot. Also *kī halahū.*

hala·hū *Kī halahū.* Air ball, missed shot, in basketball; to make such a shot. Also *kī halahī.*

hala kahiki *kik* Pineapple. *Dic.* Also *painaʻāpala.*

hala ka pā·lulu *ʻa* To pass through the block, in volleyball. *Niʻihau.*

hā·lana See *wai hālana.*

hala·pohe *ʻa* Extinct. Comb. *hala* + *pohe* (Tah., dead). Also *make loa, nalo-wale loa. ʻAne halapohe.* Endangered. See *Kānāwai Lāhulu ʻAne Halapohe.*

hā·lā·wai hoʻo·lohe *kik* Hearing, i.e. a time for presenting official testimony or argument. *Lit.,* meeting (for) listening. Also *ʻaha hoʻolohe.*

hā·lā·wai hoʻo·na·ʻau·ao *kik* Workshop. *Lit.,* meeting (for) educating.

hā·lā·wai malū *kik* Subconference, in telecommunications. *Lit.,* secret meeting.

Hale *kik* House, as a legislative assembly; short for House of Representatives. *Ua hoʻopuka ʻia ka pila e kō ka ʻAha Kenekoa a ke hele nei i ka Hale no ka ʻāpono ʻana.* The bill has been passed by the Senate and is now making its way to the House for ratification. *Dic., ext. mng.* See entries below and *lāʻau hoʻomaʻemaʻe hale, ʻelua hale.*

hale aʻo kilo hō·kū *kik* Planetarium. *Lit.,* building (for) teaching astronomy. Cf. *hale kilo hōkū.*

hale hana kiʻi·ʻoni·ʻoni *kik* Movie studio, i.e. the building itself. *Lit.,* building (for) making movies. Cf. *keʻena hana kiʻiʻoniʻoni.*

hale ha·ʻuki *kik* Gymnasium. *Lit.,* sports building. Cf. *hale hoʻoikaika kino.*

hale hoʻo·ikaika kino *kik* Athletic club, fitness center. *Lit.,* building (for) strengthening (the) body. Cf. *hale haʻuki.*

hale hoʻo·ulu mea·kanu *kik* Greenhouse. *Dic.*

hale hoʻo·malu ma·ʻi *kik* Quarantine station. Comb. dic. + *maʻi.*

hale kau lā·ʻau *kik* Treehouse. *Trad.*

hale kā·pi·ʻo *kik* Lean-to shelter. *Dic.*

hale kiaʻi ulu·lā·ʻau *kik* Ranger watchtower, esp. one used for watching for forest fires. *Lit.,* building (for) guarding forests. See *lanakia.*

hale kilo hō·kū *kik* Observatory. *Lit.,* astronomy building. Cf. *hale aʻo kilo hōkū.*

hale kū·ʻai *kik* Store. *Dic. Hale kūʻai mahi māla.* Garden store, gardening store.

hale lio *kik* Stable. *Dic.*

hale mā·lama ʻī·lio *kik* Kennel, an establishment for boarding or breeding dogs. *Lit.,* building (for) taking care of dogs. Cf. *pene halihali, pene ʻīlio.*

hale moe *kik* Dormitory. *Dic.* Cf. *hale noho haumāna.*

hale noho *kik* Residence. *Dic.* Also *wahi noho.*

hale noho hau·māna *kik* Residence hall, dormitory, as at a school. *Lit.,* house where students live. Cf. *hale moe.*

hale·pe·ʻa *kik* Tent. *Dic., sp. var. Pine halepeʻa.* Tent stake.

hale ʻaina *kik* Restaurant. *Dic. Hale ʻaina meaʻai hikiwawe.* Fast-food restaurant. *ʻO ka maʻalahi o ka hale ʻaina meaʻai hikiwawe, ʻo ia hoʻi ka loaʻa koke, akā, ʻaʻole ia ka meaʻai paiola loa o ke ʻano.* The convenience of fast food restaurants is that they are easy to find, however, the food there is not the most nutritious.

hale ʻī·lio *kik* Doghouse. See *hale mālama ʻīlio.*

hali·lele *ham* Airmail; to send by airmail. Comb. *hali + lele. Leka halilele.* Airmail letter. *Poʻoleka halilele.* Airmail stamp.

hā·lino *ʻa* Fluorescent, as colors. Sh. *hāweo + lino.* Cf. *hāweo. ʻĀkala hālino.* Fluorescent pink.

hā·liʻi moe *kik* Bedsheet. *Dic.* Also *hāliʻi pela.*

hā·liʻi papa·hele *kik* Rug, as for living room or any large room. Also *moena.* See *moena weleweka, pale papahele.*

hā·liʻi ʻea *kik* Plastic sheeting, general term. *Lit.,* plastic spread. See *ʻea painaʻāpala.*

hā·loko·loko *kik* Puddle. *Dic.*

halo ʻā·pika·pika *kik* Suction cup fin, as beneath the stomach of an *ʻoʻopu. Lit.,* fin (with) suction cups.

hā·mau *ʻa* Silence; silent. *Dic. E hāmau (kō ke kahua)!* Quiet (on the set)!

hā·mama *ʻa* Wide open. See *hemo.*

hā·meʻa *kik* Device, doohickey, gadget, gizmo, thingamajig, i.e. something made or used for a particular purpose. *Loaʻa kekahi hāmeʻa no ka hoʻāwīwī ʻana i ke paʻi ʻana.* There's a device for speeding up the printing. Comb. *hā- + meʻa* (Tongan for *mea*). See entries below and *maomeka, mauhaʻa, mea hana. Hāmeʻa huakomo.* Input device, as on a computer. *Hāmeʻa huapuka.* Output device.

hā·meʻa hana kino·ea *kik* Gas generator, i.e. a device used for producing gases as in a chemistry lab. *Lit.,* device (for) making gas.

hā·meʻa poka·kaʻa *kik* Block and tackle, an arrangement of pulleys and rope or cable used to lift or haul. *Lit.,* pulley device.

hā·meʻe *kik* Character, as in a story; role, as in a play or movie. Comb. *hā- + meʻe.*

hā·meʻa hoʻā·ʻo *kik* Tester, as a battery tester. *Lit.,* device (for) testing. Cf. *mīkini hoʻāʻo. Hāmeʻa hoʻāʻo iho.* Battery tester (not a machine).

hamu·iʻa *ham* Carnivore; carnivorous. Comb. *hamu + iʻa.* See entries below. *ʻEnuhe hamuiʻa.* Carnivorous caterpillar (Eupithecia spp).

hamu·hika *ham* Cannibal, among animals, insects, etc. *Nui nā ʻano holoholona ʻāhiu he hamuhika ke ʻano, a pēlā e hoʻēmi ʻia ka nui o kā lākou mau keiki ponoʻī e ola a hiki i ka piha ʻana o ke ola ʻana.* Many types of animals in the wild are cannibalistic by nature, and the number of their own young who achieve a full life is diminished in this way. Comb. *hamu + hika-.* Cf. *ʻai kanaka* (dic.). *Homeka hamuhika.*

hamu·lau *ham* Herbivore; herbivorous. Comb. *hamu + lau. Hamulau lāʻau.* Browser, i.e. an animal that eats twigs and leaves. *Hamulau mauʻu.* Grazer, i.e. an animal that eats grass.

hamu·pela *ham* Scavenger; to scavenge. Comb. *hamu + pela.*

hamu·ʻakoʻa *ham* Omnivore; omnivorous. Comb. *hamu + ʻakoʻa* (var. of *ʻokoʻa*).

hamu·ʻelala *ham* Insectivore, insectivorous. Comb. *hamu + ʻelala.*

hana *kik* Errand. *Dic. Nui kaʻu mau hana e hana ai i ke kaona i kēia lā.* I have a lot of errands to do/run in town today. Also *ʻāpana hana.*

hana *kik* Function, as on a calculator or computer keyboard. *Dic., ext. mng.* Cf. *hahaina, lawelawe hana.* See *hana hoʻomākalakala. Pihi hana* (preceded by *ke*). Function key.

hana *ham* To take, as a test. *Dic., ext. mng.* Also *kākau.* Cf. *haku i ka hōʻike. Hana i ka hōʻike.* To take a test.

hā·nā *kik* Wood shavings. *Dic.*

hana a loaʻa ka hāʻina To solve. *E hana a loaʻa ka hāʻina o ka polopolema helu ʻekolu.* Solve problem three. *Lit.,* do until gotten. Also *hoʻomākalakala.*

hā·nai *ham* To feed, as paper into a printer or copy machine. *Dic., ext. mng. Hānai kaʻe.* To edge feed. *Hānai waena.* To center feed. *Hānai ʻakomi.* To auto feed. *Ua hoʻopaʻa ʻia ka mīkini paʻi ma ka hānai ʻakomi.* The printer has been set to auto feed.

hā·nai *ham* To feed, assist, as in basketball and most team sports except baseball. *Iā Magic Johnson ka nui loa o nā hānai o ka NBA holoʻokoʻa.* Magic Johnson has the most assists in the entire NBA. *Dic., ext.mng.* See entries below and *hāʻawi.* To serve, in volleyball; to set or set up (the ball), as from number 2 to number 3. *Niʻihau.* Cf. *hānai puʻupuʻu, paʻi ulele. Mea hānai, hānai.* Setter.

hānai·ahuhu *kik* Pet. *Dic. Hale kūʻai hānaiahuhu.* Pet shop.

hā·nai i hope To make a back set, in volleyball. *Lit.,* set back Also *hānai kīkala.*

hā·nai kī·kala *ham* To make a back set, in volleyball. *Niʻihau.* Also *hānai i hope.*

hā·nai lō·ʻihi *ham* To make an outside set, in volleyball. *Niʻihau.*

hā·nai pō·kole *ham* To make a short set, in volleyball. *Niʻihau.*

Hā·nai·pono *iʻoa* Mirphack, a star. *Mān. (HA).*

hā·nai puʻu·puʻu *ham* To serve underhand, in volleyball. *Niʻihau.* Cf. *kuʻi puʻupuʻu.*

hā·nau *Kaupalena hānau.* Family planning, planned parenthood, population control. See *paihānau, paikoho. Kuleana hānau.* Natural or inalienable rights, i.e. rights that people are born with and that a government should not attempt to deny.

hana hoʻo·mā·kala·kala *kik* Operation, in math. *Lit.,* solving activity. *Hana hoʻomākalakala huli hope.* Inverse operation.

hana hoʻo·nanea *ʻOihana o nā Pāka a me nā Hana Hoʻonanea.* Department of Parks and Recreation.

hana keaka *ham* To act, as in a play, movie or video production; to act out, as a math problem. *Dic., ext. mng.* See *ʻōhua, hāmeʻe. Mea hana keaka.* Actor. *Moʻolelo hana keaka.* Script.

hana kolohe *heh* To fake or hit, in volleyball. *Niʻihau.* Also *mīʻoi wale.*

hana komo pae *kik* Rite of passage, initiation. See *komo pae, hoʻokomo pae.*

hana kope *ham* To copy, make a copy.

hana maʻa·lahi *ham* User friendly, as a computer program. *Ua lohe aku nei wau he hana maʻalahi ka Macintosh.* I've heard that the Macintosh is user friendly. *Lit.,* do easily.

hanana *kik* Event, as in math; also as a happening in a story. *Dic., ext. mng.*

hana ʻia ma kau·hale Homemade. *Lit.,* made at home.

haneli *kik* Hundred. *Mān.* See *hapa haneli. Hoʻokahi haneli.* One hundred. *Moena helu hapa haneli.* Hundredths square, in math.

hano *kik* Cylinder; thermos. *Dic., ext. mng.* See *hano hoʻokolohua, paukū ʻolokaʻa. Hano ana.* Graduated cylinder.

hano *Me ke kau i ka hano.* Cum laude, with distinction, with honors, as in academics. *Me ke kau i ka hano hoʻonani.* Magna cum laude, with high honors. *Me ke kau i ka hano hāweo.* Summa cum laude, with highest honors.

hano·hano *'a* Distinction. *Dic.* Cf. *ho'omaika'i.* See English entry. *Me ka hanohano.* With distinction, as when graduating from a college or university.

hano ho'o·kolo·hua *kik* Test tube. *Lit.,* experiment container. *Kū hano ho'okolohua.* Ring stand.

hano kā·nuku *kik* Beaker. *Lit.,* beaker container.

hano kui *kik* Syringe. *Lit.,* needle syringe.

hano 'ohi *kik* Collection tube, e.g. a test tube used to collect gas generated in an experiment.

hanu *heh* Respiration; respiratory. *Dic., ext. mng.* See *lā'au make hanu, paipu hanu. 'Ōnaehana hanu.* Respiratory system. *Ana lama hanu.* Breathalyzer. Cf. *nui lama koko.*

hā·nuku *kik* Narrow passageway, as in a canyon. Comb. *hā + nuku.* Cf. *ala hānuku.*

hanu'u *heh* To fluctuate, as the tide. *Dic.*

hāpa *kik* Harp, the musical instrument. *Dic.* See *nī'aukani. Pila hāpa.* Autoharp. Also *hāpa pa'a lima.*

hā·pai *ham* To lift, make a double hit, in volleyball. *Ni'ihau.* See entries below and *'a'ena pa'i lua. 'A'ena hāpai.* Carrying violation.

hā·pai *Mea hāpai pila.* Sponsor, i.e. a legislator who presents and/or assumes responsibility for the passing of a bill.

hā·pai inoa *ham* To nominate. *'Ehā kanaka i hāpai 'ia ai kō lākou inoa.* Four people were nominated. *Lit.,* raise (a) name. Also *waiho inoa* (dic.).

hā·pai hao *ham* Weight lifting; to lift weights. *Lit.,* lift iron. Also *amo hao.*

hā·pai kā·nā·wai *ham* Initiative, i.e. the procedure enabling citizens to propose a law and submit it to the legislature for approval. *Hāpai 'ia ka pila e nā kupa o ke kaiaulu no ka 'āpono 'ana i kānāwai.* The bill was initiated by the citizens of the community for ratification into law. *Lit.,* raise (a) law.

hā·paina *kik* Carrier, as of a radio-wave signal. *Dic., sp. var.*

hapa·hā *kik* Quarter, i.e. the coin. *Dic. 'Āpana hapahā.* Quadrant.

hapa haneli *kik* Hundredths; centi-, a prefix meaning one hundredth (c). *Dic., ext. mng., sp. var.* Abb. *hhn.* Also *keni-. Moena helu hapa haneli.* Hundredths square, in math.

hapa kau·kani *kik* Milli-, a prefix meaning one thousandth (m). Comb. *hapa + kaukani.* Abb. *hkk. Hapa kaukani kekona.* Millisecond, in math.

hapa kili·ona *kik* Pico-, a prefix meaning one trillionth (p). Comb. *hapa + kiliona.* Abb. *hkl.*

hapa kolona *kik* Semicolon. *Lit.,* half colon. See *kolona.*

hā·pale *kik* Trowel, as used for digging. *Dic.*

hapa·lua kā·lā *kik* Half dollar. *Dic.* Also *hapalua.*

hapa·lua kā·lani *kik* Half gallon.

hapa·malu See *papa hapamalu.*

hapa mili·ona *kik* Micro-, a prefix meaning one millionth (u). Comb. *hapa + miliona.* Abb. *hml. Hapa miliona kekona.* Microsecond, in math.

hapa moe·ā *Helu hapa moeā.* Complex number, in math. Cf. *helu maoli, helu moeā.*

hapa mo'a *'a* Medium rare, as meat. *Makemake wau i ka'u pipi kō'ala he hapa mo'a.* I like my grilled steak medium rare. *Lit.,* partial cooked. Also *mo'a hapa.*

hapa mua *kik* Front-end, in math. *Lit.,* front part. *Kikoho'e hapa mua.* Front-end digit. *Koho hapa mua.* Front-end estimation.

hā·pana *kik* Sample, as a small part of a larger whole. *Sh. hapa + ʻāpana.* Cf. *laʻana. Hāpana pono koho.* Random sample. *Nā kiʻina ʻohi hāpana.* Sampling methods.

hā·pane *kik* Response, as to a stimulus. *Comb. hā- + pane.*

hapa nui *ʻAoʻao hapa nui.* Majority party, in politics.

hapa pili·ona *kik* Nano-, a prefix meaning one billionth (n). *Comb. hapa + piliona. Abb. hpl.*

hapa ʻumi *kik* Tenths; deci-, a prefix meaning one tenth (d). *Dic., ext. mng., sp. var. Abb. hʻm.* Also *keki-.* Cf. *hapaʻumi. ʻAukā helu hapa ʻumi.* Tenth strip, in math.

hapa·ʻumi *kik* Nickel, i.e. five cents. *Dic.* Cf. *nikala.*

hā·pa·ʻu·pa·ʻu *ʻa* Dull, not shiny. *Dic., ext. mng.*

hapa ʻu·ʻuku *Kākoʻo hapa ʻuʻuku.* Affirmative action. *ʻAoʻao hapa ʻuʻuku.* Minority party, in politics.

Hā·pela *iʻoa* Hubble. *Eng. Ka ʻohenānā lewa lipo ʻo Hāpela.* Hubble space telescope.

hā·popopo *ʻa* Decomposed, putrefied. *Comb. hā- + popopo.* See *hoʻohāpopopo.*

hapū *kik* Clan, subtribe. *Māori.* Cf. *ʻalaea, nāki.*

Hawaiʻi *iʻoa* Hawaiʻi; Hawaiian. *Dic. Keʻena Kuleana Hawaiʻi.* Office of Hawaiian Affairs (OHA). *Kula kaiapuni Hawaiʻi.* Hawaiian-medium school. *Papa kaiapuni Hawaiʻi.* Hawaiian-medium class.

hā·weo *ʻa* Glowing, as in the dark; phosphorescent. *Dic., ext. mng.* Cf. *hālino.* See entry below. *Kukui hāweo.* Fluorescent light.

hā·weo *Me ke kau i ka hano hāweo.* Summa cum laude, with highest honors, as in academics.

hawewe Wave, in scientific usage. *Dic., ext. mng.* See entries below and *hoʻolaulā hawewe, laulā hawewe, ʻanini laulā hawewe.*

hawewe ikehu lā *kik* Solar energy wave.

hawewe kani *kik* Sound waves, as used in measuring ocean depths. *Lit.,* sound vibration. See *hoʻopapā hohonu. Ikaika hawewe kani.* Amplitude, i.e. the amount of energy in a sound wave. *Kōā hawewe kani.* Sound wavelength.

hawewe papa·moe *kik* Compressional wave, i.e. a wave in which matter vibrates in the same direction as the wave moves. *Lit.,* horizontal wave. Cf. *hawewe ʻaleʻale.* See *ulu, wele.*

hawewe ʻale·ʻale *kik* Transverse wave, i.e. a wave in which matter vibrates at right angles to the direction in which the wave moves. *Lit.,* undulating wave. Cf. *hawewe papamoe.*

haʻa·a·ʻe Sideward *Comb. haʻa- + aʻe.* See *haʻalalo, haʻaluna. ʻEhia ʻaoʻao haʻaaʻe?* Pages across, as in computer program.

hā·ʻae *kik* Saliva; salivary. *Dic. Lōkuʻu hāʻae.* Salivary gland.

haʻa·ha·ʻa See *woela haʻahaʻa.*

haʻa·kipu *ham* To breed animals or propagate plants. (Māori *whakatipu*.) Cf. *hoʻēhu pua, hoʻopiʻi* (dic.).

haʻa·kupu ʻaila·kele *kik/ʻa* Adipogenesis, i.e. the formation of fat or fatty tissue in a body; adipogenetic. *Comb. haʻa- + kupu + ʻailakele.* See *ʻailakele, ʻaʻa hunaola ʻailakele.*

haʻa·lalo Downward. *Comb. haʻa- + lalo.* Cf. *haʻaaʻe, haʻaluna.* See *kolikoli. Ehia ʻaoʻao haʻalalo?* Pages down, as in computer program.

haʻa·lele *ham* To evacuate, as a building. *Dic.* Cf. *hoʻohaʻalele.*

haʻa·lele *ham* To quit, as a computer program. *Dic., ext. mng.*

ha·a·liu *ham* To process. *'O ka nui o
nā mea'ai i kū'ai 'ia ma loko o ke kini,
he mea'ai ia i ha'aliu 'ia.* Most food sold
in cans is processed food. *Comb. ha'a-* +
liu (Sāmoan, alter, change). *Waiūpa'a i
ha'aliu 'ia.* Process(ed) cheese.

ha·a·loko Inward. *Comb. ha'a-* +
loko. Cf. ha'awaho.

ha·a·luna Upward. *Comb. ha'a-* +
luna. Cf. ha'aa'e, ha'alalo. See *kolikoli.*

Ha·a·moa *i'oa* Sāmoa; Sāmoan. *Dic.*
Also *Kāmoa. Ha'amoa 'Amelika.*
American Sāmoa; American Sāmoan.
Also *Kāmoa 'Amelika.*

ha·a·pupū See *a'aha'apupū. Pu'u
ha'apupū.* Speed bump, as on a road or
in a parking lot.

ha·a·waho Outward. *Comb. ha'a-* +
waho. Cf. ha'aloko.

hā·awi *ham* To set or set up (the ball),
in volleyball. *Ni'ihau.* Also *hānai.
Hā'awi i ke kinipōpō i kekahi 'ao'ao.* Side
out. Also *ka'a pa'i ulele, ka'a. 'Ai
hā'awi wale.* Ace, in volleyball. Also
'eki.

hā·awi·aholo *ham* To give and go,
in basketball. *Ma ka hā'awiaholo 'ia aku
o ke kinipōpō iā ia i 'āha'i ai 'o Limanui
a hiki loa i ka hīna'i.* Limanui took off
with the ball on the give and go all the
way to the basket. *Lit.,* give and run.

ha·a·wina Hawai'i *Māhele
ha'awina Hawai'i.* Hawaiian studies
department, as at a university or
community college.

ha·a·wina ho·i·ho·i *kik* Homework.
*Pono wau e hana mua i ka'u mau
ha'awina ho'iho'i, a laila, hiki ia'u ke
pā'ani.* I have to do my homework first,
then I can play. *Lit.,* lesson (to) return.

ha·a·wina kā·lā hele kula *kik*
Scholarship. *Lit.,* monetary grant (for)
going to school. Also *ha'awina kālā.
Ha'awina kālā 'ālapa.* Athletic
scholarship.

ha·a·wina 'ai *kik* Serving of food.
Lit., food portion.

hā··a·a 'ai *kik* Fiber, as referring to
diet. *He mea nui ka hā'a'a 'ai ma ka
papa'ai, no ka mea, he kōkua ma ka
wāwahi 'ai 'ana.* Fiber is an important
part of the diet since it helps in the
digestion of food. *Lit.,* edible fibrous.

hā··ehu·ola *kik* Healthful, healthy,
wholesome, i.e. promoting physical
health. *Comb. hā-* + *ehuola.* See
ehuola. Mea'ai hā'ehuola. Health food.

ha·i *kik* Expression, in math. *Dic., ext.
mng.* See entries below and *ha'ihelu,
ha'ilula. Ha'i hō'ailona helu.* Algebraic
expression.

ha·i *Kelepona kāki iā ha'i.* Third-party
call; to make such a call.

ha·i·ha·i iwi *ham* Osteopathy; to
practice osteopathy. *Dic., ext. mng.
Kauka ha'iha'i iwi.* Osteopath.

ha·i·ha·i kā·nā·wai *ham* To break
the law. *Dic.* Also *'a'e kānāwai. Cf. pale
kānāwai.*

ha·i·helu *kik* Numerical problem (as
2+3); equation (as 2+3=5). *Comb. ha'i* +
helu. See *ha'i, ha'ilula. Ha'ihelu
ho'oili.* Chi-squared distribution, in
math. *Ha'ihelu kemikala.* Chemical
equation. *Ha'ihelu kemikala kaulike.*
Balanced chemical equation. *Ha'ihelu
lālani.* Linear equation. *Ha'ihelu
pāho'onui lua.* Quadratic equation. See
hahaina pāho'onui lua.

ha·i heluna like *kik* Equivalent
expression, in math. *Lit.,* equal amount
expression.

ha·i hou ma kekahi 'ano *ham* To
paraphrase orally. *E Mānai, e ha'i hou
mai i ka mo'olelo i ha'i 'ia a'e nei ma
kekahi 'ano 'oko'a.* Mānai, retell the story
that was just told another way. *Lit.,* retell
in another way. See *kākau hou ma
kekahi 'ano.*

ha·i ho·o·kō *kik* Operator, as a sign in
a computer mathematical operation.
Lit., tell (to) carry out. *Cf. pākō.*

ha'i hui·huina *kik* Combinatorial coefficient, in math. *Lit.,* combination expression.

ha'i kake ka'ina *kik* Permutatorial coefficient, in math. *Lit.,* permutation expression.

ha'i·lono *'Oihana ha'ilono.* Journalism.

ha'i·lula *kik* Formula, in math and science. Comb. *ha'i + lula.* See *ha'i, ha'ihelu. Ha'ilula kemikala.* Chemical formula.

ha'i·mau·lia *kik* Matrix, i.e. a rectangular array of numbers, symbols or functions which are often added or multiplied according to certain rules. Sh. *ha'ihelu + ho'omaulia.*

ha'i mua *'Ōlelo ha'i mua.* Foreword, preface, as in a book. Also *'ōlelo mua.* Cf. *'ōlelo ho'ākāka.*

hā·'ina *kik* Solution, answer to a problem. *Dic., sp. var.* See *'imi hā'ina. Hana a loa'a ka hā'ina.* To solve.

ha'i·nole *ham* To stimulate, as with a drug. *Dic., ext. mng.* Cf. *kūlale. Lā'au ha'inole.* Stimulant.

ha'i waha *ham* Oral. *Dic.* Cf. *palapala.* See *mo'olelo ha'i waha. Hō'ike ha'i waha.* Oral report. *Ka'a'ike ha'i waha.* Oral communication. *Mo'okalaleo ha'i waha.* Oral literature.

ha'i·ō·lelo *kik* Speech. *Dic.* See *hō'ike ha'i waha, mikolololehua. Ha'i'ōlelo hō'ike.* Oral report, presented as a speech. *Ha'i'ōlelo ho'ohuli mana'o.* Persuasive speech. *Ha'i'ōlelo kūhaha'i.* Narrative speech. *Ha'i'ōlelo mikolololehua.* Expressive speech, speech to entertain.

hā·'oi *kik* Baritone. Sh. *'ehā + 'oi. 'Ukulele hā'oi.* Baritone 'ukulele.

ha'uki *kik* Sport. (Tah. *ha'uti.*) See *'uao ha'uki. Hale ha'uki.* Gymnasium.

ha'uki Helene *kik* Track and field. *Lit.,* Greek sport. *Nā ha'uki Helene.* Track and field events.

hā·'ule *heh* To lose, as in sports. *Dic.* Cf. *eo. Māhele hā'ule.* Consolation bracket, as in a sports tournament.

hā·'ule·ā·pa'a *kik* Deadfall, a kind of animal trap. *Lit.,* fall until secure.

hā·'ule·lau *kik* Autumn, fall. *Dic., sp. var.* See *māuiili.*

ha'u·poho *kik* Parachute. Sh. *puha'u + poho.*

-hate Suffix in chemical compounds and terms: -ate.

hei *'a'* Addiction; addicted. *Ua hei 'o ia i ka paka.* S/he was addicted to cigarettes. *Dic., ext. mng.*

hei·hei ho'o·ili *kik* Relay race. Also *kūkini ho'oili.* See *maile ho'oili.*

Heiti *i'oa* Haiti; Haitian. *Eng.*

heona *'a'* Artistic, i.e. esthetically appealing or having artistic talent. *Ua heona kāu mau ki'i; he kanaka heona maoli 'oe.* Your pictures are esthetically pleasing; you're really an artistic person. *Lit.,* an attraction. Cf. *ho'oheona, pāheona.*

hehelo pā·pā·lina *kik* Rouge, blush, as makeup. *Lit.,* cheek reddishness.

hehena *Ma'i hehena.* Maniacal delirium.

hehe'e *heh* To melt. *Dic. Kēkelē hehe'e.* Melting point.

hehu *kik* Seedling, as of *'ilima* plants. *Dic.* See *kauwowo.*

hekau pepa *kik* Paperweight. *Ho'okau 'ia ka hekau pepa i luna o ka pu'u pepa i 'ole e puehu i ka makani.* The paperweight was put onto the stack of papers so that they wouldn't scatter in the wind. *Lit.,* anchor (for) paper.

hekehi *heh* Hike; to go on a hike. Sh. *hele + ke'ehi,* also metathesis of *ke'ehi.* Cf. *holoholo wāwae. Ala hekehi.* Hiking trail. *Kāma'a hekehi.* Hiking shoe. *Mea hekehi.* Hiker.

heke·kale *kik* Hectare, a metric unit of land measurement. *Eng.* Also *heketare.* Abb. *ht.*

hē·kī *kik* Jet. *Sh. hele + kikī. Mokulele hēkī.* Jet airplane.

hekili See *manu hekili.*

heko- Hecto-, i.e. a prefix meaning hundred. *Eng.* Also *pāhaneli.* See entries below.

heko·kalame *kik* Hectogram. *Eng.* Abb. *hkkal.*

heko·lika *kik* Hectoliter. *Eng.* Abb. *hkl.*

heko·mika *kik* Hectometer. *Eng.* Abb. *hkm.*

hele·uī *kik* Halloween. *Eng.* Also *lā ho'omāka'uka'u. Pū heleuī.* Jack-o'-lantern. Also *pala'ai heleuī.*

hele·kona *kik* Walkathon. Comb. *hele* + Eng.

hele·kopa *kik* Helicopter. *Ni'ihau.* Also *mokulele helekopa.*

hele lana·kila *heh* To go freely, i.e. to have freedom to go wherever one pleases, to "have the run of the place." *He hele lanakila wale nō mākou i kō mākou noho 'ana i ke kākela o ke keiki ali'i.* We were given the run of the house while we stayed at the castle of the prince. *Trad. (20,000 Lekue ma Lalo o ke Kai).* Cf. *noa (dic.).*

hele lewa lipo *heh* Spacewalk. *Lit.,* walk (in) space.

Helene *i'oa* Greece; Greek, Grecian. *Dic.* See *ha'uki Helene.*

hele wale *Kinipōpō hele wale.* Kill, in volleyball.

Hele·'ekela *i'oa* Uranus. *Dic., sp. var.*

Hēli *i'oa* Halley. *Eng. Ka hōkū puhipaka 'o Hēli.* Halley's comet.

helu *kik* Amount. *Dic., ext. mng. Eia 'elua pū'ulu helu 'elua.* Here are two groups of twos. *Dic., ext. mng.* Also *heluna.* See entries below and *mīkini helu. Waiwai helu.* Numerical value.

helu *kik* Size, as of clothes. *Mān.*

helu uaki *ham* To tell time. Also *helu uāki.* Cf. *helu manawa.*

helu hapa moe·ā *kik* Complex number, in math. *Lit.,* part-imaginary number. Cf. *helu maoli, helu moeā.*

helu·ha'a *kik* Lower division, as a course at a college or university. *'O ka mea ma'amau, komo nā haumāna i loko o nā papa heluha'a ma ke kau mua i ke kulanui.* Students usually take lower-division courses in their first semester of college. Comb. *helu + ha'a.* Cf. *heluki'e. Papa heluha'a.* Lower-division course.

helu heluna *kik* Cardinal number. *Lit.,* amount number. Cf. *helu ka'ina.*

helu·helu pā See *mīkini heluhelu pā.*

helu·helu pā·kā·kā *ham* To skim read. Comb. *heluhelu* + redup. of *pākā. Ka heluhelu pākākā 'ana.* Skim reading.

helu ho'o·hana *kik* Constant, in math. *Lit.,* number (for) use.

helu ho'o·hui *kik* Addend, in math. *Lit.,* number (for) adding.

helu ho'o·nui *kik* Factor, in math. *Lit.,* number (for) multiplying. See *helu ho'onui kemikala. Helu ho'onui like.* Common factor. *Helu ho'onui like ki'eki'e loa.* Greatest common factor. *Papa helu ho'onui kumu.* Factor tree.

helu ho'o·nui kemi·kala *kik* Coefficient, i.e. a number placed in front of a chemical symbol or formula in order to balance the chemical equation. *Lit.,* number (to) add to (a) chemical.

helu kau·like *kik* Even number. *Dic.* See *helu kau'ewa.*

helu kau·'ewa *kik* Odd number. *Lit.,* number placed unevenly. See *helu kaulike.*

helu kaha *ham* Tally; to tally. *Lit.,* count (with) marks.

helu kanaka *ham* Census, a periodic official enumeration of a population and its characteristics. *Ma 'Amelika Hui Pū 'ia, mālama 'ia ka helu kanaka i kēlā me* *kēia 'umi makahiki.* In the United States, the census is conducted every ten years. *Dic.*

helu ka'ina *kik* Ordinal number. *Lit.,* number (that shows) sequence. Cf. *helu heluna.*

helu·ki'e *kik* Upper division, as a course at a college or university. *Pono nā haumāna e hele nei no ka kēkelē laepua e komo i loko o nā papa heluki'e.* Students pursuing a bachelor's degree must take upper-division courses. Comb. *helu + ki'e.* Cf. *heluha'a. Papa heluki'e.* Upper-division course.

helu kohu pai *kik* Transcendental number, in math. *Lit.,* number resembling pi.

helu komo *kik* Divisor, in math. *Dic.*

helu kū·ana *ham* Counting on, a strategy used in mental math. E.g., 83 + 30 = 113: add 3 tens; think 83, 93, 103, 113. *Lit.,* place value counting.

helu kuhi *kik* Zip code. *Lit.,* pointing number. See entry below.

helu kuhi puke *kik* Call number, as for a library book. *Lit.,* number pointing (to) book. *Kāleka helu kuhi puke.* Catalog card, as in a library. See *pahu kāleka kuhi puke.*

helu kumu *kik* Prime number, in math. *Lit.,* base number. *Helu kumu kūlua.* Twin primes. *Hua helu kumu.* Counting number.

helu laka *kik* Combination, as for a lock. *Lit.,* lock number. Cf. *laka helu.*

helu lele *ham* To skip count, in math. *Lit.,* jump count.

helu lele pine·pine *kik* Frequent-flyer number, as used in airline promotions. *Inā e ho'opihapiha 'oe i ka pepa no ka helu lele pinepine, hiki iā 'oe ke 'ohi i nā mile a loa'a kahi kikiki manuahi.* If you fill out the frequent-flyer number form, you can accrue miles until you get a free ticket. *Lit.,* number (for) frequent flying.

helu Loma *kik* Roman numeral.

helu maoli *kik* Real number, in math.

helu mā·hoe *kik* Double number, same number used twice, in math. *Lit.,* twin number. Cf. *kaulua.*

helu mā·hua *kik* Multiple, in math. *Lit.,* multiplied number. Also *māhua. Helu māhua like.* Common multiple. *Helu māhua like ha'aha'a loa.* Least common multiple.

helu maka·hiki kala·pona *kik* Carbon dating, radiocarbon date. *Ma ka helu makahiki kalapona 'ana, hiki ke 'ike 'ia ka wā i pa'a mai ai kekahi pōhaku a i 'ole ka wā i hana 'ia ai kekahi mea koehana.* By carbon dating, the time a rock was formed or the time an artifact was made can be determined. *Lit.,* number (of) carbon years.

helu manawa *kik/ham* Time, recorded duration; to time, as speed, duration, etc. *He aha kou helu manawa ma ka holo kikī haneli 'īā?* What was your time on the hundred-yard dash? *Lit.,* count time. Cf. *helu uaki.* See *uaki.*

helu moe·ā *kik* Imaginary number, in math. Cf. *helu hapa moeā, helu maoli.*

heluna *kik* Amount. *Dic.* Also *helu.* See *helu heluna.*

heluna huna 'āne *kik* Atomic number. *Lit.,* proton amount. See *huna 'āne.*

heluna make·make *kik* Demand, i.e. a desired commodity within the consumer's ability to pay. *Lit.,* quantity desired. *Ho'olako me ka heluna makemake.* Supply and demand.

helu na'au *ham* Mental math. *Lit.,* mind counting. Also *makemakika na'au.*

helu pana pu'u·wai *kik* Heart rate, pulse rate. *Lit.,* heart pulse count.

helu piha *kik* Whole number or integer, in math. *Lit.,* complete number. *Helu piha 'i'o.* Positive integer. *Helu piha 'i'o 'ole.* Negative integer.

helu puka *kik* Quotient. *Dic.*

helu pu'u·naue koena *kik* Irrational number, in math. *Lit.,* indivisible number. *Helu pu'unaue koena 'ole.* Rational number.

helu pu'u·naue lua *kik* Composite number.

helu wawe *kik* Hotline. *Lit.,* fast number. *Helu wawe maluō.* Conservation hotline.

helu·wawe *ham* To speed read. Sh. *heluhelu + wawe.* Cf. *kāwawe. Ka heluwawe 'ana.* Speed reading.

helu·'ai *kik* Score, as in sports or games. *Dic., ext. mng.* See *'ai. Papa helu'ai.* Scoreboard.

helu 'ini·kua ola·kino *kik* Medical coverage number. *Lit.,* health insurance number. See *'inikua olakino.*

helu 'i'o *kik* Positive number. *Lit.,* number (with) substance. Cf. *helu 'i'o 'ole.*

helu 'i'o 'ole *kik* Negative number. *Lit.,* number without substance. Cf. *helu 'i'o. 'Ekolu 'i'o 'ole.* Negative three (-3).

helu 'ō·lapa *ham* To count down, as in launching a rocket; countdown. *Lit.,* lift-off count.

helu 'ō·'ā *kik* Mixed number, in math, as 3 3/4. *Lit.,* mixed number.

hema *kik* South. *Dic.* Abb. *Hm. Kō'ai hema.* Counterclockwise. *Poepoe hapa hema.* Southern hemisphere.

hema·laka *kik* Hemlock. *Eng.*

hemo *'a'* Open, as for business; unlocked; ajar. See entry below and *hāmama.*

hemo *'a'* To be open, as for a play in basketball. *'Oiai ua hemo kekahi hoa kime ma lalo pono o ka hīna'i, kī pa'ewa wale akula 'o Mānea.* Even though one of his teammates was open right under the basket, Mānea went ahead and made a bad shot. *Dic., ext. mng.* See *ho'ohemo.*

hene moku·honua *kik* Continental slope. *Lit.,* continent slope. Cf. *holopapa mokuhonua.*

henua *Pilina henua.* Relative location, in geography. Cf. *kuhikuhina.*

hewa See entry below and *ho'oholo i ke kū i ka hewa, kaha pela hewa, ke'ehi hewa, palena 'āluna o ka hewa.*

hewa kū·pili *kik* Logic error, as a message on a calculator display that shows an operation is not logical.

he'e *kik* Squid (local definition); octopus (Haole definition). *Dic.* Cf. *mūhe'e.*

he'e *ham* To skim, as milk. *Dic. Waiū he'e.* Skim milk.

he'e·aholo *heh* To leach, i.e. the action of liquid percolating through layers of soil thus removing nutrients from the soil. *Comb. he'e + a + holo.* Cf. *ho'ohe'eaholo.*

he'e hau *heh* To ski, in snow. *Lit.,* slide (on) snow. See *he'e wai. He'e hau pe'a 'āina.* To cross-country ski.

he'e·na *kik* Ramp, as for skateboarding. *Comb. he'e + -na.* Cf. *alahiō. He'ena papa huila.* Skateboard ramp.

he'e wai *heh* To water ski. *Lit.,* slide (on) water. See *he'e hau.*

hero·ina *kik* Heroin. *Ua waiho aku 'o Marvin i loko o ka haukapila no ka lapa'au 'ana i kōna hei i ka heroina.* Marvin was laid up in the hospital for treatment for his heroin addiction. *Eng.*

Hese·gowina *i'oa* Herzogovina. *Eng. Bosenia me Hesegowina.* Bosnia and Herzogovina.

hese *kik* Witch. *German. Nananana hese 'ele'ele.* Black widow, a kind of spider. Also *nanana hese 'ele'ele.*

hia·moe pono *heh* To sleep well. *E hiamoe pono 'oe.* Good night; sleep well. Also *e hiamoe maika'i 'oe; a hui hou i kakahiaka.*

Hiapo *i'oa* Equatorial Countercurrent, in oceanography. *Mān. (HA).*

hia·ʻume *ʻa* To have an affinity for (something). Comb. *hia-* (to be disposed to) + *ʻume.*

hiō *ʻa* Italic. *Lit.,* slanting. Also *hua hiō.* See entry below and *uakeʻe hiō, hoʻohiō.*

hiō *Mākala kū hiō o loko.* Internal abdominus oblique muscle. *Mākala kū hiō o waho.* External abdominus oblique muscle.

hiu *kik* Chip, as used in poker, checkers, counting, etc. *Dic. ext. mng.*

hihi *Pāma hihi.* Rattan.

hihia *kik* Problem or difficulty, as in the plot of a story. *Dic.* See *hopena holo.*

hī·hī·kai *kik* Glaucus. *Sh. hīhīwai + kai.*

hika- A prefix meaning self- or auto-. *PPN kita* (one, the indefinite pronoun). See entries below.

hika·pili·olana Comb. *hika-* + *piliolana.* Autobiography; autobiographical. *Moʻolelo hikapiliolana.* Autobiography, autobiographical story.

hiki *Kelepona kāki hiki.* Collect call; to make such a call. *ʻOhi hiki.* COD, cash on delivery.

hiki·ā·loa *ʻa* Long-range, long-term. Comb. *hiki + ā + loa. Papa hoʻolālā hikiāloa.* Long-range plan, long-term plan. See *papa hoʻolālā. I ka hikiāloa.* In the long run.

hiki·ā·lō·pū *ʻa* Medium-range, medium-term. Comb. *hiki + ā + lōpū. Papa hoʻolālā hikiālōpū.* Medium-range plan, medium-term plan. See *papa hoʻolālā.*

hiki·ā·poko *ʻa* Short-range, short-term. Comb. *hiki + ā + poko. Papa hoʻolālā hikiāpoko.* Short-range plan, short-term plan. See *papa hoʻolālā.*

hiki·ā·pua·ane·ane *ʻa* Life-long. Comb. *hiki + ā + puaaneane.*

hiki hope *heh* Late, as registration for a conference. *Lit.,* arriving after. See *hiki mua. Kāinoa hiki hope.* Late registration.

hiki mua *heh* Pre-, early, beforehand, as registration for a conference. *Dic., ext. mng.* See *hiki hope. Kāinoa hiki mua.* Preregistration.

hikina *kik* East. *Dic. Abb. Hk. Poepoe hapa hikina.* Eastern hemisphere.

Hikina Waena *iʻoa* Middle East; Middle Eastern.

hiki·wawe *Meaʻai hikiwawe.* Fast food. *Hale ʻaina meaʻai hikiwawe.* Fast-food restaurant.

Hiki·wawe *iʻoa* Sadr, a star. *Mān. (HA).*

hiku *ham* To pick, as an ʻukulele or guitar. *Mān.* Also *panapana.*

hili *ham* To spike (the ball), in volleyball. *Niʻihau.* Also *pākī.* See *kuʻi puʻupuʻu, pākī, paʻi pālahalaha, ʻai hele wale. Hili laina.* Line spike. *Hili ʻaoʻao.* Angle spike. *Manawa hili.* At bat, up (to bat), in baseball.

hili·uma *kik* Helium. *Eng.*

hilo *Aʻa kino hilo.* Femoral vein. *Aʻa puʻuwai hilo.* Femoral artery. *Iwi hilo.* Femur, i.e. the long bone of the thigh.

hī·meni kū·launa like *ham* To sing in harmony.

hī·nā·lea nā·ʻuke *kik* Cleaner wrasse (labroides Phthirophegus), a kind of fish. *Lit.,* wrasse (which) searches for lice.

Hina·lua *iʻoa* Achernar, a star. *Mān. (HA).*

hī·naʻi *kik* Basket, in basketball; basketball net. *Komo mau kāna mau kī ʻana i ka hīnaʻi.* His shots always make it into the basket. *Dic., ext. mng.* See *hao, hupa, kuku, pōhīnaʻi. Papa hīnaʻi.* Backboard. *ʻAi hīnaʻi.* Basket (score). *ʻAi hīnaʻi kolu.* Three pointer.

hinu·kele *kik* Grease, as used in machines or for tools with moving parts. Comb. *hinu* + *kele*.

hipo·pō·kamu *kik* Hippopotamus. *Dic., sp. var.*

hī·pu'u *kik* Knot. *Dic.* See entry below.

hī·pu'u pewa *kik* Bow, as ribbon or string. *Lit.*, fishtail knot. Cf. *lei 'ā'ī pewa.*

hi'o·hia *'a'* Discovered, existence revealed. *Ua hi'ohia 'o Hawai'i nei no kō nā 'āina 'ē iā Kāpena Kuke.* Hawai'i was discovered for foreigners by Captain Cook. Comb. *hi'o* (*Tah.*, look) + *-hia.* Cf. *kaunānā. Mea hi'ohia.* Find, as an archeological find.

hi'o·hi'ona *kik* Effects, as in special effects. *Dic., ext. mng. Hi'ohi'ona na'iau.* Special effects. See *kani keaka. Luna hi'ohi'ona na'iau.* Special effects coordinator, as for movie or video production. *Hi'ohi'ona pa'i.* Printer effects, as on a computer printer. *Ho'ona'iau (i ka hi'ohi'ona).* To add special effects.

hi'ona *kik* General appearance, impression; feature. *Dic.* Cf. *hi'onaina.* See entries below. *Hi'ona na ke kanaka.* Man-made topographical feature.

hi'o·naina *kik* Landscape. *Sh. hi'ona* + *'āina.* Cf. *hi'ona.* See *kāhi'onaina.*

hi'ona kaha *kik* Cross section, in math. *Lit.*, appearance (when) cut open.

hi'ona·pā·'ili *kik* Texture. *Lit.*, features (when) touched.

hi'ona wai *kik* Body of water; water form or feature, as a lake, pond, river, etc., in geography. *'O ka hi'ona wai, he muliwai, he loko wai, he kahawai, he wailele, a pēlā aku nō.* A water feature can be a river, lake, stream, waterfall, and the like. *Lit.*, water feature. Cf. *hi'ona 'āina.*

hi'ona 'āina *kik* Contour, as the elevations of a particular place; land feature, as a mountain, valley, etc.; topography. *Palapala hi'ona 'āina.* Topographic map.

hi'u *kik* Tails, as in coin toss. *Dic., ext. mng.* Also *'ao'ao hi'u.* See entry below and *pana ho'olei, po'o.*

hi'u *kik* Tip of a leaf, as hala. *Mān. (MW).* Also *welelau.* Cf. *po'o.*

-hite Suffix in chemical compounds and terms: -ite.

hoa helu ho'o·nui like kahi *kik* Relatively prime numbers, i.e. numbers which share one factor between them, and that factor is 1, in math. *Lit.*, companion common factor (of) one.

hoaka See entries below. *Pae moku hoaka.* Island arc.

hoa kaia·home *kik* Neighbor, not necessarily next door. See *kaiahome.*

hoaka kī·kolu *kik* Three-point arc, in basketball. *Lit.*, three-shot arch.

hoaka kū *kik* Arch, as the Arch of Triumph in Paris. *Lit.*, standing arch.

hoa kupa *Kiule hoa kupa.* Jury of peers, as in court trials.

hoa like *kik* Like term, in math. *Lit.*, like companion. Cf. *paukū, hua pa'a.*

hoa mā·hu'i *kik* Emulation, as in a computer printer. *Lit.*, imitating companion.

hoa paio *kik* Opponent, as in a sporting event. *'O Punahou ka hoa paio o Kamehameha i kēia ho'okūkū nei.* Punahou is the opponent of Kamehameha in this game. *Dic.*

hoe·hoena o ke kai *kik* Tide. *Lit.*, breathing of the sea.

hou See *puka kikī hou.*

hou loa *'a'* Brand new. *Lit.*, very new.

houpo *kik* Diaphragm. *Dic.*

hohoki *'a'* Neutral, as particles in an atom. Redup. of *hoki.* See *ikehu uila hohoki.* See also *'ane, 'ine. Huna hohoki.* Neutron.

hohonu *ʻa* Height or depth, in math. *Dic., ext. mng. ʻEhia ʻīniha ka loa, ka laulā a me ka hohonu o kēnā pahu?* How many inches is the length, width and height of that box? Also *ana hohonu*. Cf. *ākea, laulā, loa, lōʻihi.* See *kiʻekiʻe.*

hō·kē *kik* Hockey. *French. Hōkē alanui.* Street hockey.

hō·keo *kik* Kit, as of equipment needed for a particular activity. *Dic., ext. mng.* Cf. *kini lapaʻau, kini poho ea, poho lāʻau pōulia.* See entries below. *Hōkeo kūmau hoʻāʻo lepo.* Standard soil-testing kit.

hō·keo hoʻāhu *kik* Library, i.e. a temporary buffer for storage of codes or information in a computer program. *Lit.,* container (for) laying away.

hō·keo ʻike·pili *kik* Database, as in a computer program; data bank, an organized collection of information, in math. *Lit.,* data container. See *ʻikepili. Polokalamu hōkeo ʻikepili.* Database program.

hō·kele mū·hune See *huila mūhune.*

hō·kelo *kik* Container, general term. *Dic., ext. mng.* See entries below.

hō·kelo ao *kik* Cloud chamber, i.e. a scientific device which detects nuclear particles through the formation of cloud tracks. *Lit.,* cloud container.

hō·kelo huʻa *kik* Bubble chamber, in chemistry. *Lit.,* bubble container.

hokona *ham* To market (something), i.e. to make available and promote the sale of a product. *Comb. hoko (Māori,* buy, sell*) + -na.*

hō·kū *Hua hōkū.* Starfruit.

hokua *kik* Crest of a wave. *Dic.* Also *hokua o ka nalu, hokua o ka ʻale.* Cf. *honua.*

hō·kū ukali *kik* Satellite star. *Dic.* Cf. *ukali, poelele.*

hō·kū·hele *kik* Planet. *Dic., sp. var. Hōkūhele Iowiana.* Jovian planet. *Hōkūhele o waho loa.* Outer planet.

hō·kū kai *kik* Starfish. *Dic.*

hō·kū·kimo *kik* Jack, as used in the game of jacks. See *kimo.*

Hō·kū·loa *iʻoa* Venus. *Dic.*

hō·kū·naʻi *kik* Asteroid. *Sh. hōkū + naʻinaʻi (Tah.,* small*). Kāʻei hōkūnaʻi.* Asteroid belt.

hō·kū·paʻa·lima *kik* Sparkler, as fireworks. *Lit.,* hand-held star. See *ahihoʻoleʻaleʻa.*

hō·kū puhi·paka *kik* Comet. *Dic.* Cf. *hōkū welowelo. Ka hōkū puhipaka ʻo Hēli.* Halley's comet.

hō·kū welo·welo *kik* Shooting star. *Dic.* Cf. *hōkū puhipaka.*

Hō·kū·ʻula *iʻoa* Mars. *Dic.* Also *Hōkūʻulapīnaʻau.*

Hō·kū·ʻula·pī·na·ʻau *iʻoa* Mars. *Sh. Hōkūʻula + Holoholopīnaʻau* (to differentiate from other stars called Hōkūʻula). Also *Hōkūʻula.*

hola *kik* Hour. *Dic. Abb. hl.* See *palena pau.*

hola kū·pono On time. *ʻAʻole ʻo ia i hōʻea mai i ka hola kūpono; ua lohi ʻo ia.* S/he didn't arrive on time; s/he was late.

hō·lapu See *mū hōlapu pale ʻea pau.*

holo *kik/heh* Run. See *holoē, māmā holo, ʻai holo. Holo ʻekolu haneli ʻīā.* Three hundred-yard run.

holo a lele loloa *kik/heh* Running long jump.

holo·ē *kik* Hallway. *Eng.* Also *holo.*

holoi *ham* To delete or clear, as in computer program. *E holoi i ka ʻikepili e kū nei.* Clear the existing data. *Dic., ext. mng. Holoi i hope.* To backspace, as on an IBM computer; to delete, as with delete key on a Macintosh computer.

holoi *Mīkini holoi pā.* Dishwasher. *Kopa mīkini holoi pā.* Dishwasher soap. *Pena holoi.* Primer for PVC pipe cement.

Holo·ika·uaua *iʻoa* Pearl and Hermes Reef. *Lit.*, (Hawaiian monk seal that) swims in the rough.

holo hau *heh* To ice skate. *Lit.*, run (on) ice. *Kāmaʻa holo hau.* Ice skate.

holo·holo *heh* Traveling, in basketball; to travel. *Ua lilo ke kinipōpō iā Waiākea no ka holoholo ʻana a ke kūkahi o Hilo.* The ball was turned over to Waiākea after the point guard for Hilo traveled. *Dic., ext. mng.*

holo·holona See entries below and *hoʻomalu lawaiʻa a me ka hahai holoholona. Hoʻomalu holoholona lōhiu.* State wildlife official. Also *luna hoʻomalu holoholona lōhiu. Loea holoholona lōhiu.* Wildlife expert. *ʻĀina Hoʻomalu Holoholona Lōhiu o Hawaiʻi.* Hawaiian Islands National Wildlife Refuge. *ʻAhahui Makaʻala Holoholona.* Humane Society. *ʻOihana Iʻa me ka Holoholona Lōhiu o ʻAmelika.* US Fish and Wildlife Service.

holo·holona iwi kua·moʻo *kik* Vertebrate animal. *Lit.*, animal (with) backbone. See *holoholona iwi kuamoʻo ʻole.*

holo·holona iwi kua·moʻo ʻole *kik* Invertebrate animal. *Lit.*, animal without backbone. See *holoholona iwi kuamoʻo.*

holo·holona lō·hiu *kik* Wildlife. *Lit.*, naturally wild animals.

holo·holona ʻai waiū *kik* Mammal. *Lit.*, animal (which) suckles. Also *māmela.*

holo·holo wā·wae *heh* Stroll; to go for a stroll. *Lit.*, stroll (by) foot. Cf. *hekehi.*

holo hoʻo·ili *kik/heh* Shuttle run. *Lit.*, transfer run. Cf. *kūkini hoʻoili.*

holo·kahi *heh* One-way, as a street or trip. *E makaʻala i nā alanui holokahi o ke kaona ke kalaiwa ʻoe ma ia wahi.* Be careful of the one-way streets in town when driving through there. *Lit.*, one ride. Cf. *holo puni.*

holo kā·maʻa huila *heh* To roller skate. *Lit.*, run (on) wheeled shoes. See *kāmaʻa huila.*

holo kele wai *kik* Runoff, as water running from the land into the sea. *Lit.*, muddy flow.

holo kikī *kik/heh* Dash, sprint. *Lit.*, swift run. *Holo kikī haneli mika.* Hundred-meter dash.

holo lapa huila *heh* To skate with rollerblades. *Lit.*, run (on) wheeled ridges. See *kāmaʻa lapa huila.*

holo·leʻa *kik* A ride, as at a carnival or amusement park. Sh. *holo + leʻaleʻa.*

holo lola *kik* Film movement, as in a movie or video camera. *Lit.*, cassette running.

holo·mua *heh* To improve. *Dic. He mau manaʻo e holomua ai ka hana.* Suggested improvements. *Loiloi holomua haumāna.* Student assessment. *ʻAukā holomua.* Fill bar, in computer program.

holona kaʻa *kik* Drive-through, as at a restaurant or bank. Comb. *holo + -na + kaʻa.* Cf. *holona makani.*

holona makani *kik* Breezeway, as an open area between buildings. Comb. *holo + -na + makani.* Cf. *holona kaʻa.*

holo·papa moku·honua *kik* Continental shelf. *Lit.*, continent ledge. Cf. *hene mokuhonua.*

holo papa peʻa *heh* To windsurf. See *papa peʻa.*

holo peki *kik/heh* Jogging; to jog. *Lit.*, jog running.

holo puni *heh* To run a lap, take a lap; to circulate, as blood; round trip. *Dic., ext. mng.*

hō·loʻa *ham* To dispense, provide in measured quantities. Sh. *hō + loaʻa,* also Tah. *hōroʻa* [to give]. See *ʻūhōloʻa.*

holo ʻā·puʻu·puʻu *Kaʻa holo ʻāpuʻupuʻu.* Any off-road vehicle, e.g., ATV, 4x4, dirt bike, etc. Also *kaʻa ʻāpuʻu.*

hō·lua hau *kik* Sled, for snow. *Lit.,* snow sled.

home *Mākau nohona home.* Home economics, as a course at school.

homeka *kik* Land snail. *Dic. Homeka hamuhika.* Cannibal snail. *'Ai ka homeka hamuhika i kōna 'ano lāhui pono'ī o ka homeka.* Cannibal snails eat their own species of snail.

home lula *kik* Home rule, i.e. self-government or limited autonomy, as in a city or county. *Ua loa'a ka 'Ao'ao Home Lula ma Hawai'i nei a pa'a akula 'o Kūhiō ma ka 'oihana 'elele no ka 'Aha'ōlelo Lāhui.* The Home Rule Party existed in Hawai'i until Kūhiō took the office of delegate to Congress. *Dic., ext. mng.*

hō·mona *kik* Hormone. *Eng. Hōmona ho'ā'a.* Rooting hormone. Also *hōmona ho'oa'a. 'Ōnaehana hōmona.* Endocrine system, in biology.

hona *kik* Grosbeak finch (chloridops kona). *Lit.,* name of a tree frequented by this finch. Cf. *hōpue* (dic.). See *nuku 'ekue, 'ainohu Kauō, 'ainohu Nīhoa.*

hone *kik* Syrup. *Ni'ihau.* Also *malakeke.*

Hono·durasa *i'oa* Honduras; Honduran. *Eng.*

honu See *honu lū'au, honu pahu.*

honua *kik* Trough of a wave. *Dic.* Also *honua o ka nalu, honua o ka 'ale.* Cf. *hokua.* See *mekala honua 'ākilikai. Ke Kai Waena Honua.* Mediterranean Sea. *Pūnaewele Puni Honua.* World Wide Web (www), as on the Internet.

Honua *i'oa* Earth, i.e. the planet. *Ua ha'alele ka moku ahikao iā Honua i nehinei.* The rocket ship left Earth yesterday. *Dic.* See *pāpa'a honua, 'ikoi honua.*

Honua·iā·kea *i'oa* Palmyra island. *Lit.,* name of Pele's canoe when travelling to Hawai'i.

honu lū·'au *kik* Green sea turtle. *Lit.,* turtle (with) greenish meat. Also *honu.*

honu pahu *kik* Box turtle.

hope alo 'ū·hā See *mākala 'ūhā.*

hope hō·'ulu·'ulu palapala *kik* Subsummary, as in a computer program. *Lit.,* behind document summary.

hope kahua *kik* Subfield, as in a computer program. *Lit.,* behind field. See *kahua.*

hopena *kik* Conclusion; effect. *Dic.* See entries below and *kumu. Ho'oholo i hopena.* To draw a conclusion. *Palapala Hō'ike Hopena Kaiapuni.* Environmental Impact Statement (EIS).

hopena *kik* Outcome; a possible result in a probability experiment, in math. *Dic., ext. mng.* See *'ōpa'a hopena.*

hopena ahu·wale *ham* Predictable, as the ending of a story. *Lit.,* obvious ending. *Mo'olelo hopena ahuwale.* Predictable story.

hopena holo *kik* Resolution or solution, as of a problem in a story. *Lit.,* determined solution. See *hihia.*

hopena kau·konu *kik* Ideal result, in math. *Lit.,* center-placed (*kau* + -*konu*) result.

hopena pā·heu *kik* Allergic reaction. *Lit.,* allergy effect. See *pāheu.*

hope wai·hona 'ike *kik* Virtual memory, as in computer program. *Lit.,* substitute memory.

hopo hala·pohe *'a* Threatened, as rare plants or animals. *Lit.,* anxious (lest) extinct. Also *hopo make loa, hopo nalowale loa.* Cf. *'ane halapohe.*

hopu See *'ai hopu. Kaha hopu.* A line written from the end of one paragraph to the beginning of the next paragraph to indicate that the two paragraphs should be combined, in proofreading. *Palapala hopu.* Arrest warrant, warrant for arrest, i.e. a document issued by a magistrate authorizing an officer to make an arrest.

Hopu·hopu *i'oa* Rasalhague, a star. *Mān. (HA).*

hopuna·helu *kik* Math sentence, number sentence. Comb. *hopuna* + *helu*. Cf. *hopunaʻōlelo*.

hopuna·ʻō·lelo *kik* Sentence, as a grammatical unit. *Mān. Hopunaʻōlelo wehe kumuhana*. Topic sentence, as of a paragraph. Cf. *hoʻomaka*.

hoʻā *ham* To turn on, as a light, radio, TV, etc. *Mān.* Cf. *hoʻopio*.

hō·ʻae *heh* To yield, as in traffic. *Dic., ext. mng. Hōʻailona hōʻae*. Yield sign.

hō·ʻai·lona *kik* Sign, as traffic signs. *Dic., ext. mng.* Cf. *papa hoʻolaha*. See entries below. *Hōʻailona hōʻae*. Yield sign. *Hōʻailona hoʻokū*. Stop sign.

hō·ʻai·lona *kik/ham* Symbol, sign, as in math. *Dic.* To symbolize, stand for. *"Inā hoʻi he huahelu ʻokoʻa ka mea i hōʻailona ʻia e ka A, e like nō hoʻi ka hana ʻana."* Even if A symbolizes a different number, the process is the same. *Trad.* (Bihopa). See entry below and *pihi hōʻailona*.

hō·ʻai·lona helu *kik* Algebra. *Dic. Haʻi hōʻailona helu*. Algebraic expression.

hō·ʻai·lona mele *kik* Clef, in music. *Lit.*, song sign. *Hōʻailona mele leo kāne*. Bass clef. Also *leo kāne. Hōʻailona mele leo wahine*. Treble clef. Also *leo wahine*.

hō·ʻaiʻē *Kumu hōʻaiʻē*. Credit, as at a bank or store.

hō·ʻaui·kala *kik* Chromatography. *Lit.*, deviate color. See *palaholo silaka g. Hōʻauikala papa lahilahi*. Thin-layer chromatography. *Hōʻauikala pepa*. Paper chromatography. *Kiʻi hōʻauikala*. Chromatograph. *Pepa hōʻauikala*. Chromatographic paper.

hō·ʻauka *ham* To tag or strike out, in baseball. Comb. *hō-* + *ʻauka*. Cf. *ʻauka*.

hoʻā·hewa *ham* To impeach, i.e. formally accuse (a public official) of misconduct in office. *He mea koʻikoʻi maoli ka hana hewa a ka pelekikena e*

pono ai ke kū ʻo ia i ka mea i hoʻāhewa ʻia ai. The misdeeds of the president must have been very serious if he was found guilty of the things he is being impeached for. *Trad.* Cf. *kīpaku luna kālaiʻāina*.

hoʻāhu *ham* To lay away, store away, accumulate. *Dic. Waihona hoʻāhu kālā*. Savings account, as in a bank. See *lumi hoʻāhu, waihona hoʻāhu, waihona kālā. Hōkeo hoʻāhu*. Library, i.e. a temporary buffer for storage of codes or information in a computer program.

hoʻā·hua kua·hene *ham* Shield building; to build a shield (volcano). *Lit.*, pile up shields.

hoʻāka *ham* To shadow, as on computer or in typesetting. Comb. *hoʻ-* + *aka*. See *aka*.

hoʻā·kāka *ham* To explain, clarify. *Dic., sp. var.* See *ʻaoʻao hoʻākāka. ʻŌlelo hoʻākāka*. Introduction, as in a book. Cf. *ʻōlelo haʻi mua*.

hoʻā·kea *ham* To extend, as text in computer word processing. *Dic., ext. mng.* Cf. *hoʻohāiki*.

hoʻāla *ham* To format, initialize, as a computer disk. *Dic., ext. mng.* Cf. *hoʻonohonoho. Hoʻāla hou*. To reformat.

hō·ʻalo *ham* To alternate, as in computer program. *Dic., ext. mng. Pihi hōʻalo* (preceded by *ke*). Alternate key.

hoʻā·mana *ham* To let, as in math problems; to assign a value or power. *E hoʻāmana ʻia ke K he 15 kōna waiwai*. Let K equal 15. *Dic., ext. mng.*

hoʻāna·kahi *ham* To unitize, in math. Comb. *hoʻ-* + *anakahi*.

hoʻāni *ham* To wave something. *Dic., ext. mng.*

hō·ʻano hou *ham* To modernize a written document using modern spelling and punctuation standards. *Lit.*, cause new style. See *hakuloli*.

hō·ʻano hou *ham* To update, as a computer program; to refresh, as a computer screen. Cf. *hoʻopuka hou loa*.

hō·ʻanuʻu *ham* To dump, in volleyball. *Niʻihau.*

hoʻā·ʻa *ham* To enable to develop roots. Comb. *hoʻ-* + *aʻa.* Also *hoʻoaʻa. Hōmona hoʻāʻa.* Rooting hormone.

hoʻā·ʻo *ham* To test (for something), as in a scientific experiment. *Dic.* Cf. *hoʻāʻoamaka.* See *hāmeʻa hoʻāʻo, mīkini hoʻāʻo.*

hoʻā·ʻo·amaka *kik* Trial, as a test in a probability experiment, in math. Comb. *hoʻāʻo* + *a* + *maka.* Cf. *hoʻāʻo.*

hoʻā·ʻo·a·ʻo *ham* Trial and error; to do something by trial and error. Redup. of *hoʻāʻo.*

hoʻā·ʻo mua See *hōʻike hoʻāʻo mua.*

hō·ʻea·ea *ham* To aerate. Comb. *hoʻ-* + *eaea.* See *eaea.*

hoʻēhu pua *ham* To pollinate. *Lit.,* cause flower pollen. Cf. *hoʻopiʻi kaʻakepa.* See *ehu. Hōʻehu pua kaʻakepa.* To cross-pollinate.

hō·ʻeleu mō·ʻaui *ham* Catalyst, i.e. a substance which increases the rate of a chemical reaction without being permanently changed itself. *Lit.,* animate reaction. Also *ʻūmōʻauiwawe.*

hoʻēmi *ham* Discount; to discount, as a price for merchandise. *Ke loaʻa kēia kūpona iā ʻoe, he loaʻa mai ka hoʻēmi iā ʻoe ma ka hale kūʻai.* If you have this coupon you can get a discount at the store. *ʻEhia ka hoʻēmi o kēia uaki?* What's the discount on this watch? *Dic.*

hoʻēmi·emi *Kūkā hoʻēmiemi.* Plea bargain, as in the negotiation of an agreement between a prosecutor and a defendant.

hoʻēmi i ka mā·mā holo *ham* To decelerate. *Lit.,* cause to decelerate. Cf. *emi ka māmā holo.* See also *piʻi ka māmā holo, hoʻopiʻi i ka māmā holo.*

hoʻēmi kino *ham* To diet, reduce. *Dic.* See *papaʻai.*

hoʻēmi woela *kik* Vowel reduction, in linguistics. *Lit.,* reduce vowels. See *pua woela* and entries under *woela.*

hoʻi *heh* To revert, as in computer program. *Dic., ext. mng. Hoʻi i ka mālama.* To revert to previous save.

hō·ʻio·kine *ham* To iodize. Comb. *hō-* + *ʻiokine.* See *ʻiokine.*

hoʻi·hoʻi *ham* To save, in volleyball. *Niʻihau.* Also *lou. Haʻawina hoʻihoʻi.* Homework.

hoʻi·hoʻi mai *ham* To undo, as in computer program. *Lit.,* return. Cf. *hoʻokaʻawale, hoʻōki.*

hō·ʻike *kik* Display, as on computer screen. *Dic., ext. mng.* See entries below.

hō·ʻike *ham* To report. *Dic.* Cf. *hōʻike haʻi waha, hōʻike palapala. Haʻiʻōlelo hōʻike.* Oral report, presented as a speech. *Haku i ka hōʻike.* To make a test. *Hana i ka hōʻike.* To take a test. Also *kākau i ka hōʻike.*

hō·ʻike haʻi waha *kik* Oral report. Also *ʻōlelo hōʻike.* Cf. *hōʻike palapala.*

hō·ʻike honua *kik* Geography. *Dic. Nā kuhikuhina hōʻike honua.* Geographical coordinates.

hō·ʻike hua pihi *kik* Key caps, on computer program. *Lit.,* show key letters.

hō·ʻike manaʻo *ham* To prewrite, as part of the writing process, i.e. introducing the topic through brainstorming, discussion, presentations, etc. *Lit.,* show ideas. See *kūkā ma ka pūʻulu.*

hō·ʻike mua aʻo *kik* Pretest. *Lit.,* first-try test. Cf. *hōʻike muli aʻo.*

hō·ʻike muli aʻo *kik* Posttest. *Lit.,* after-teaching test. Cf. *hōʻike mua aʻo.*

hō·ʻike pala·pala *kik* Written report. *Lit.,* report (by) writing. Cf. *hōʻike haʻi waha.*

hō·ʻike ʻia Given, as in a math problem. *Lit.,* indicated.

hō·ʻike·ʻike *kik* Fair. *Dic.* Also *fea.* See entry below and *papa hōʻikeʻike. Hōʻikeʻike ʻepekema.* Science fair. *Hōʻikeʻike kalana.* County fair. *Hōʻikeʻike mokuʻāina.* State fair.

hō·‘ike·‘ike *ham* To show and tell, as in a preschool or elementary school class. *Dic., ext. mng.*

hō·‘ili·‘ili *ham* To collect. *Dic.* See *hō‘ili‘ilina.*

hō·‘ili·‘ilina *kik* Collection. Comb. *hō‘ili‘ili* + *-na.* *Hō‘ili‘ilina po‘oleka.* Stamp collection.

hō·‘ī·pale *ham* To insulate. Comb. *hō-* + *‘ipale.* See *‘ipale.*

ho‘o·a·‘a *ham* To enable to develop roots. *Dic.* Also *ho‘ā‘a.* *Hōmona ho‘oa‘a.* Rooting hormone.

hō·‘oia *ham* To verify, check, give proof, as for a math problem. *Dic., ext. mng.* *Kūkulu hō‘oia.* Proof, in math.

ho‘o·ikaika kumu *ham* Inservice teacher training. *Lit.*, strengthen teacher. Cf. *ho‘omākaukau kumu.*

ho‘o·ikaika pu‘u·wai *ham* Aerobic. *Lit.*, strengthen heart. Cf. *eaea.* See *‘onilele.* *Hana ho‘oikaika pu‘uwai.* Aerobic activity. *‘Ai ho‘oikaika pu‘uwai.* Aerobic point.

ho‘o·ikehu *ham* To charge, as a battery. Comb. *ho‘o-* + *ikehu.*

ho‘o·ili *ham* To transfer, as funds in a bank account. *Dic.* See entries below.

ho‘o·ili *ham* Distribution, to distribute, distributive, in math. *Dic., ext. mng.* *Ha‘ihelu ho‘oili.* Chi-squared distribution, in math. *Kānāwai ho‘oili.* Distributive law. *‘Anopili ho‘oili* (preceded by *ke*). Distributive property.

ho‘o·ili *ham* To transplant. *Dic., ext. mng.* Cf. *ili.* See *‘anopili ho‘oili.* *Ho‘oili pu‘uwai.* To transplant a heart.

ho‘o·ili *ham* To download, as in computer program. *Dic., ext. mng.* Cf. *ho‘ouka.* See *mīkini ho‘oili ki‘i.*

ho‘o·ili *ham* To hand off (the ball), in football. *Ua ho‘oili aku nei ‘o ia i ke kinipōpō i ka helu 42.* He handed off the ball to number 42. *Dic., ext. mng.*

ho‘o·ilo *kik* Winter. *Dic.* See entry below and *māuiki‘iki‘i.*

ho‘o·ilo *ham* To cause to germinate, sprout. *Dic.* See *ilo, pī‘ai ho‘oilo.*

hō·‘oi·‘ene·hana *ham* To industrialize; developing, as a Third World Country. *I ka wā hō‘oi‘enehana o nā ‘āina o ‘Eulopa, kūkulu nui ‘ia nā hale wili like ‘ole he nui.* In the industrialization period of the European nations, many factories of various types were built. Comb. *hō-* + *‘oi‘enehana.* Cf. *‘oi‘enehana.* *‘Āina hō‘oi‘enehana.* Developing country; Third World Country.

ho‘o·uahi *ham* To smoke, as meat or fish. *Dic.*

ho‘o·uka *ham* To load, as a computer program; to install, as software. *E ho‘ouka ana wau i ka waihona ma ka PLH i hiki iā ‘oe ke ho‘oili ma kāu kamepiula.* I'm going to load the file on the BBS so that you can download it onto your computer. *Dic., ext. mng.* Cf. *ho‘oili.* See entry below.

ho‘o·uka *kik/ham* Attack, raid. *Dic.* *Ho‘ouka pāna‘i.* Counterattack. *Pū‘ali ho‘ouka kaua.* Marine corps.

ho‘o·ulu See entry below and *kāmāhuaola, pahu ho‘oulu meakanu.*

ho‘o·ulu pā·ku‘i *ham* To grow by grafting. *Nui nā kala like ‘ole o nā pua mēlia e pua nei ma ke kumu mēlia ho‘okahi a ko‘u hoa noho ma muli o kāna ho‘oulu pāku‘i ‘ana mai nā kumulā‘au like ‘ole mai.* Many different colored plumeria flowers are blooming on one plumeria tree that belongs to my neighbor; he accomplished this by grafting from different trees. *Dic.* See *pāku‘i.*

ho‘o·una *ham/i‘oa* To send or enter data into a computer database or calculator after it has been typed; enter, as the enter key by the number pad on an extended computer keyboard. *E kōmi iā ho‘ouna.* Press enter. *Lit.*, send. See *kāho‘i, kāhuakomo.* *Pihi ho‘ouna.* Enter key (preceded by *ke*).

hoʻo·u·ʻi·u·ʻi *ham* To put on makeup. *Niʻihau. Aia ʻo Tita ke noho nei i mua o ke aniani me ka hoʻouʻiuʻi pū.* Tita's sitting in front of the mirror putting on makeup. Also *hoʻonaninani.*

hoʻo·hāiki *ham* To condense, as text in computer document. *Dic., ext. mng.* Cf. *hoʻākea.*

hoʻo·hā·o·ʻo *ham* To cure, i.e. to prepare by chemical or physical processing for keeping or use. Comb. *hoʻo-* + *hāoʻo.* See *hāoʻo.*

hoʻo·hau·mia See *kumu hoʻohaumia.*

hoʻo·haku·hia *ham* To invent. See *hakuhia.*

hoʻo·hali·ʻa maka·hiki See *puke hoʻohaliʻa makahiki.*

hoʻo·hana See entry below and *helu hoʻohana, wā hoʻohana.*

hoʻo·hana ʻāina *ham* Land use, in geography. *Lit.*, use land. *Komikina Hoʻohana ʻĀina o ka Mokuʻāina.* State Land Use Commission.

hoʻo·hani *ham* To hint at, give a hint. *Dic. ʻŌlelo hoʻohani.* Hint.

hoʻo·hanini *ham* To dump. *Dic., ext. mng. Kalaka hoʻohanini.* Dump truck.

hoʻo·hā·popopo *ham* To decompose, putrefy. Comb. *hoʻo-* + *hāpopopo.* See *hāpopopo. Ka hoʻohāpopo eaea ʻana.* Aerobic decomposition/putrefaction. *Ka hoʻohāpopo eaea ʻole ʻana.* Anaerobic decomposition/putrefaction.

hoʻo·haʻa·lele *ham* To evacuate, as people from a building. Comb. *hoʻo-* + *haʻalele.* Cf. *haʻalele.*

hoʻo·heona *ham* To make artistic, decorate artistically. See *heona.*

hoʻo·hehe·ʻe *ham* To dissolve (something). *Dic.* See entry below.

hoʻo·hehe·ʻe mea·ʻai *ham* To digest food. *Trad.* See *hoʻowali ʻai, hoʻonapele* (dic.). *ʻŌnaehana hoʻoheheʻe meaʻai.* Digestive system.

hoʻo·hele moe·ā *ham* To utilize guided imagery. *Lit.*, cause to imagine.

hoʻo·hemo *ham* To disconnect, as in computer program. *Dic., ext. mng.* Cf. *hoʻokuʻi.* See entry below.

hoʻo·hemo *ham* To get oneself open, as for a play in basketball. *Kīloi mau ʻia ke kinipōpō iā Kaina, no ka mea, ʻeleu ʻo ia i ka hoʻohemo.* The ball always gets passed to Kaina since he's so quick to make himself open. *Dic., ext. mng.* See *hemo.*

hoʻo·he·ʻe·aholo *ham* To leach, i.e. subject to the action of percolating liquid. Comb. *hoʻo-* + *heʻeaholo.* See *heʻeaholo.*

hoʻo·hiō *ham* To tip or tilt, as a glass containing water. *Dic., ext. mng.* See entry below.

hoʻo·hiō *ham* To italicize. *E aho nō kēia huaʻōlelo ke hoʻohiō ʻia.* It would be better if this word were italicized. *Lit.*, cause to slant. See *hiō.*

hoʻo·hiki See *palapala hoʻohiki.*

hoʻo·hilu·hilu *ham* Fancy, elegant. *Dic., ext. mng.*

hoʻo·hina *ham* To tackle (someone), in football. *Dic., ext. mng.* Also *kulaʻi.* Cf. *kūlua.*

hoʻo·hinu·hinu *Kīkina hoʻohinu-hinu.* Spray wax. *Mea hoʻohinuhinu.* Polish, i.e. a substance used to give smoothness or shine. *ʻAila hoʻohinu-hinu.* Wax, as for polishing a car.

hoʻōho *ham* To exclaim. *Dic. ʻŌlelo hoʻōho.* Exclamatory statement; to make such a statement.

Hoʻo·hoku·ika·lani *iʻoa* Daughter of Wākea and Papa. *Dic.*

hoʻo·holo *ham* To start, as a machine; to play, as a film or tape. *Dic., ext. mng.* See *hoʻokuʻu.*

hoʻo·holo *ham* To control, as in a computer program. *Dic., ext. mng. Hoʻoholo laulā.* General controls. *Papa hoʻoholo.* Control panel. *Pihi hoʻoholo* (preceded by *ke*). Control key.

ho'o·holo i hopena *ham* To draw a conclusion. *Lit.*, determine a conclusion.

ho'o·holo i ke kū i ka hewa *ham* To convict, i.e. to find or prove to be guilty. *Na ke kiule i ho'oholo i kōna kū i ka hewa i ka pepehi kanaka.* The jury convicted him of murder. *Lit.*, determine to be in error.

ho'o·holo mana'o *Mākau ho'oholo mana'o.* Decision-making skill.

ho'o·holo pili la'ana *kik/ham* Inductive reasoning, i.e. generalizing from examples, in math. *Lit.*, decide concerning examples.

ho'o·holu·nape *ham* Blowing of the wind; palm fronds and tree branches sway, and whitecaps form on the ocean, in meteorology. *Comb. ho'o-* + *holu nape.* See *makani.*

ho'o·hua *'Ōnaehana ho'ohua.* Reproductive system, in biology.

ho'o·hui *ham* To add, in math; to connect, as dots, etc. *Dic.* Cf. *hō'ulu- 'ulu. Helu ho'ohui.* Addend. *Kumu ho'ohui pālima.* Base five, in math. Also *kumu pālima. Kōkua helu kumu ho'ohui pālima.* Base-five counting piece. *Pepa maka'aha kumu ho'ohui pā'umi.* Base-ten grid paper.

ho'o·huli *ham* To flip, as to turn a figure to its reverse side, in math. *Dic., ext. mng.* Cf. *ho'one'e.*

ho'o·huli mana'o *ham* To induce change of opinion, persuade. *Dic., ext. mng. Ha'i'ōlelo ho'ohuli mana'o.* Persuasive speech. See *ha'i'ōlelo.*

ho'o·hūpō *heh* To feign ignorance, "act dumb." *Mān.* Also *ho'opalō.*

ho'o·hu'u *ham* To imply. *Ke ho'ohu'u mai nei 'oe na'u i hana?* Are you implying that I did it? (Tongan *fakahu'u.*) See *hu'u.*

ho'o·kae *ham* Discrimination, prejudice; to discriminate or be prejudiced against. *Ho'opi'i 'ia ka pā'oihana e kekahi limahana no ka ho'okae 'ana.* The business was sued by an employee for discrimination. *He pā'ewa'ewa a he ho'okae kōna mana'o ho'oholo ma muli o kōna mana'o 'ino i ka lāhui o ke kanaka.* His decision was biased and prejudiced because of his negative opinion of the man's race. *Dic., ext. mng.* See entries below and *paiha'akei 'ili.*

ho'o·kae kanaka *ham* Misanthropy, hatred of mankind. *'O ke kanaka ho'okae kanaka, 'a'ohe ōna hilina'i a he inaina ho'i i nā kānaka.* Someone who is misanthropic is distrustful and has malice toward mankind. *Lit.*, despise mankind.

ho'o·kae kāne *ham* Misandry, hatred of males. *Lit.*, despise men.

ho'o·kae keka *ham* Sexism. *'Ike 'ia ka ho'okae keka ma waena o nā keka 'elua i kekahi manawa; aia nō i ka pā'ewa'ewa o ka mana'o o kekahi pū'ulu keka i kekahi.* Sexism exists among both sexes at times; it all depends on the bias a group of one sex has toward the other sex. *Lit.*, despise (because of) gender.

ho'o·kae wahine *ham* Misogyny, hatred of women. *Lit.*, despise women.

ho'o·kai·aka *ham* To dilute. *Comb. ho'o-* + *kaiaka.* Cf. *pa'ipa'i.*

ho'o·kā·inoa *ham* To register (someone for something). *Comb. ho'o-* + *kāinoa.* See *kāinoa. Ho'okāinoa po'e koho pāloka.* To register voters for an election.

ho'o·kau·alewa *ham* To balance something. *Hiki iā 'oe ke ho'okaualewa i kēnā peni ma kou manamana lima?* Can you balance that pen on your finger? *Comb. ho'o-* + *kaualewa.* Cf. *kaualewa.*

ho'o·kau·apono *heh* To compensate, counterbalance. *Comb. ho'o-* + *kauapono.* Cf. *uku pāna'i.* See *kauapono. 'Ōnaehana ho'okauapono.* Balancing mechanism, in biology.

ho'o·kau·lihi *ham* To justify, as type in printing. Comb. *ho'okau + lihi.* Cf. *ho'okauwaena, kaulihi.* Ho'okaulihi *hema.* To justify left. *Ho'okaulihi 'ākau.* To justify right. *Ho'okaulihi like.* To justify full. *Kaha ho'okaulihi.* Two vertical lines written to the left of lines of print to indicate that the left margin should be justified, in proofreading.

ho'o·kau·waena *ham* To center justify. *Ua ho'okauwaena 'ia ka 'ao'ao mua o kēia palapala.* The first page of this document is center justified. Comb. *ho'o- + kauwaena.* Cf. *ho'okaulihi, kauwaena.*

ho'o·kau·weli *ham* Horror, as stories or movies. Comb. *ho'okau + weli. Ki'i'oni'oni ho'okauweli.* Horror movie.

ho'o·kahe wai *ham* To irrigate. *Lit.,* to irrigate (with) water.

ho'o·kahua *Lauana ho'okahua.* Settlement pattern, in geography.

ho'o·kahuli au·puni *ham* Revolution, as against a government. *Dic. Kaua ho'okahuli aupuni.* Revolutionary war.

ho'o·kake ka'ina *ham* To mix up the order, jumble. *Lit.,* disturb (the) order.

ho'o·kala·kala *ham* To unsmooth, as in computer program. *Lit.,* cause (to be) rough. Cf. *ho'olaumania.*

ho'o·kala·kupua *ham* Magic, as supernatural or enchanted. *Dic.* Cf. *pāha'ohuna.*

ho'o·kala pā·'ā·lua *ham* To unencrypt, as a code or computer data. *Lit.,* undo (a) code. See *ho'opā'ālua, pā'ālua.*

ho'okani See *hao ho'okani, mīkini ho'okani pāleo, mīkini lola.*

ho'o·kā·wai·hia *ham* To hydrolyze. Comb. *ho'o- + kā + wai + -hia. Ka ho'okāwaihia 'ana.* Hydrolysis.

ho'o·kā·wā·holo *ham* To tab, as on a computer or typewriter. Comb. *ho'o- + kāwāholo.* Cf. *kīpo'o.* See *kāwāholo.*

ho'o·ka'a·hua *Kaha ho'oka'ahua.* A "straight" Z-shaped line written to indicate where two words written as one should be separated, in proofreading. Also *kaha ho'okōā.* Cf. *kaha ka'ahua.*

ho'o·ka'a·wale *ham* To segregate, separate. *He ho'oka'awale 'ia ka noho 'ana o ka lāhui Pā'ele ma ka 'ao'ao hema o 'Amelika ma mua o nā makahiki kanaono.* Blacks in the South lived segregated before the sixties. *Dic. Ka ho'oka'awale 'ana.* Segregation. *Pale ho'oka'awale.* Buffer.

ho'o·ka'a·wale *ham* To put away, as in a computer program. *Dic., ext. mng.* Cf. *ho'iho'i mai, ho'ōki.*

ho'o·ka'a·wale i ka manawa *ham* To take the time (to do something). *Lit.,* set aside time. Also *ho'olilo i ka manawa.*

ho'o·ka'a·wale 'ao·'ao *ham* Page break, as in computer program. *E ho'oka'awale i ka 'ao'ao ma hope o kēia paukū.* Insert a page break after this paragraph. *Lit.,* cause a page division.

ho'o·ka'a·'ike *ham* To communicate. Comb. *ho'o- + ka'a'ike.* See *ka'a'ike. Mākau ho'oka'a'ike.* Communication skill.

ho'o·kā·'ele *ham* To bold, set in boldface type. Comb. *ho'o- + kā'ele.* See *kā'ele.*

ho'o·ka'ina *ham* To put in order, sequence. Comb. *ho'o- + ka'ina.* Cf. *ho'olauka'i.* See entries below. *Ho'o-ka'ina pī'āpā.* To alphabetize, put in alphabetical order.

ho'o·ka'ina maka·koho *ham* To prioritize, set priorities. Cf. *ho'omaka-koho.* See *makakoho.*

ho'o·ka'ina mana'o *ham* To sequence ideas, as in a composition.

ho'o·ka'ina pae *ham* To rank, as from small to large. *Lit.,* put ranks in sequence. See *pae.*

ho'o·ka'o·hau *ham* To freeze dry. Comb. *ho'o- + ka'ohau.* See *ka'ohau.*

ho‘o·kē To blow one's nose. *Dic.* Also *hūkē.*

ho‘o·kele See entries below and *luna ho‘okele, pahu ho‘okele.*

ho‘o·kele wai·wai *ham* Economy. *Ikaika ka ho‘okele waiwai ‘ana o ka ‘āina.* The country's economy is strong. *Lit.,* conduct financial business. *Cf. ho‘omohala waiwai, kālaiho‘okele waiwai.* See entries below.

ho‘o·kele wai·wai kū lana·kila *ham* Free-market economy, i.e. the economy of a country wherein buying and selling can take place without government restrictions. *Lit.,* economy (that) exists freely. *Cf. ho‘okele waiwai mana kahi.*

ho‘o·kele wai·wai mana kahi *ham* Command economy, i.e. an economic system in which the government controls the factors of production and makes the basic economic decisions. *Lit.,* economy (with) one authority. *Cf. ho‘okele waiwai kū lanakila.*

ho‘o·kele wa‘a *ham* Wayfinding; to wayfind. *Lit.,* sail (a) canoe. Also *kele moana.*

ho‘o·kemua *ham* To assimilate. *He ho‘okemua ka nui o ka po‘e komone‘e o kekahi ‘āina iā lākou iho i ka noho ‘ana o kō ia ‘āina.* Most immigrants to a country assimilate themselves into the lifestyle of that counrty. *Comb. ho‘o-* + *kemua.* See *kemua.*

ho‘ōki *ham* To cancel, as a computer function. *E ho‘ōki i ke pa‘i ‘ana.* Cancel the print job. *Dic., ext. mng. Cf. ho‘iho‘i mai, ho‘oka‘awale. ‘Aelike ho‘ōki.* Cloture, i.e. a method of ending debate and causing an immediate vote to be taken, as in a legislature.

ho‘o·kī·ki‘i *ham* To cause to tilt, as the camera when filming a movie or video production. *Dic., ext. mng.*

ho‘o·kipa See *lumi ho‘okipa.*

ho‘o·kiwi·kā *ham* To urbanize. See *kiwikā.*

ho‘o·kō See *palapala ho‘okō. Ha‘i ho‘okō.* Operator, as a sign in a computer mathematical operation. *Cf. pākō. Māhele mana ho‘okō.* Executive branch (of a government).

ho‘o·kō·ā *Kaha ho‘okōā.* A "straight" Z-shaped line written to indicate where two words written as one should be separated, in proofreading. Also *kaha ho‘oka‘ahua. Pihi ho‘okōā.* Space bar, on typewriter or computer keyboard, variant term (preceded by *ke*). Also *pihi ka‘ahua.*

ho‘o·koana *ham* To set spacing, as single- or double-space on a typewriter. *Comb. ho‘o-* + *koana.* See *koana, ka‘ahua.*

ho‘o·koe *ham* To cache, as a computer function. *Ua ho‘okoe ‘ia kēia pā.* This disk has been cached. *Eng., ext. mng.* See *ahu ho‘okoe. Ho‘okoe pā.* To cache disks.

ho‘o·kohu a like *ham* To dither, i.e. approximate the appearance of a graphic image from another computer operating system. *Lit.,* assume a likeness until similar.

ho‘o·kokoke *ham* To cluster, i.e. find addends or factors that are nearly alike, in math. *Dic., ext. mng.* See entry below.

ho‘o·kokoke *ham* To zoom in, as with a movie or video camera. *Dic., ext. mng. Cf. ho‘olaulā.*

ho‘o·kolamu *ham* To line up vertically, place in columns. *E ho‘okolamu i kēia palapala no ka nūpepa e puka ana.* Make this document into column format for the newspaper that's coming out. *Comb. ho‘o-* + *kolamu.*

ho‘o·kolo·hua *kik/ham* Experiment; to experiment, as in a laboratory. *Comb. ho‘okolo* + *hua.* See *pahiki ho‘okolohua. Ho‘okolohua no.* To experiment on. *Ho‘okolohua me.* To experiment with.

ho‘o·kolo·kolo *Māhele ‘aha ho‘okolokolo.* Judicial branch (of a government). *Mana ho‘okolokolo.* Appellate jurisdiction, i.e. a court's authority to hear an appeal of a decision made by another court. *Mana ho‘okolokolo maka mua.* Original jurisdiction, in law.

ho‘o·kolo·naio *ham* To colonize, particularly from the perspective of a people who have been colonized by a dominant culture or political entity. Comb. *ho‘o- + kolonaio.* Cf. *ho‘opanalā‘au.* See *kolonaio.*

ho‘o·komo *ham* To file, as files in a file cabinet. *Ho‘okomo ‘ia aku nei kōna waihona ma kōna inoa hope.* His file was filed under his last name. *Dic., ext. mng.* Also *waiho.* See entries below.

ho‘o·komo *ham* To insert, put in, as a disk into a computer. *Dic. Kālā ho‘okomo.* Deposit, as money placed into a bank account. *Kaha ho‘okomo.* Caret (^, ˇ), a mark used to show where something is to be inserted, in proofreading. *Lina ho‘okomo.* A circle around a period, colon, or semicolon to show that it has been inserted.

ho‘okomo i ke kinipōpō *ham* To sink (make) a basket, in basketball. *Dic., ext. mng.*

ho‘o·komo pae *ham* To initiate. Comb. *ho‘o- + komo pae.* See *komo pae, hana komo pae.*

ho‘o·konu·konu *ham* To regulate, i.e. to fix the time, amount, degree, or rate of something by making adjustments. (Tongan *fakatonutonu.*) *Lōku‘u ho‘okonukonu pūnao.* Thyroid gland.

ho‘o·kuene *kik/ham* Setup; to set up, as in a computer program. *Lit.,* lay out, arrange. *Ho‘okuene ‘ao‘ao.* Page setup.

ho‘o·kuene ‘ike·pili *ham* To browse, as in a database program having the capability to rearrange data. *Lit.,* set up data. Cf. *māka‘ika‘i, kele.*

ho‘o·kū·o‘o *heh* To act serious, "get serious." Comb. *ho‘o- + kūo‘o.*

ho‘o·kū·kohu·kohu *ham* To simulate. Comb. *ho‘o- + kū + kohukohu.* Cf. *ho‘omeamea.*

ho‘o·kū·konu *heh* To take a neutral position. Comb. *ho‘o- + kūkonu.* Cf. *kūkonu.*

ho‘o·kū·kū *ham* To compare. *E ho‘okūkū ‘oe i kēia mau pū‘olo manakō. ‘O ka pū‘olo hea ka mea i ‘oi aku kōna kaumaha?* Compare these bags of mango. Which bag is heavier? *Dic.*

ho‘o·kū·kū *kik/heh* Tournament, in sports. *Ni‘ihau.* Also *ho‘okūkū moho.* See entries below. *Ho‘okūkū pōpa‘ipa‘i.* Volleyball tournament.

ho‘o·kū·kū hahaina *kik* Curve-fitting, in math. *Lit.,* compare functions.

ho‘o·kū·kū hana pani·olo *kik* Rodeo. *Lit.,* contest (of) cowboy activities.

ho‘o·kū·kū kahu·lui *kik* Championship, in sports. *Lit.,* championship match. See *ho‘okūkū kio, ho‘okūkū moho.*

ho‘o·kū·kū kio *kik* Scrimmage, as for sports. *Lit.,* mock warfare match. See *ho‘okūkū kahului, ho‘okūkū moho.*

ho‘o·kū·kū moho *kik* Tournament, as for sports; playoff or finals, as in sporting events. *Lit.,* champion match. Also *ho‘okūkū.* See *ho‘okūkū kio, ho‘okūkū kahului.*

ho‘o·kū·kū pā puni *ham* Round-robin, as in sports. *Lit.,* tournament touching round.

ho‘o·kū·launa *ham* To harmonize. *E ho‘okūlauna kākou i kēia hīmeni.* Let's harmonize this song. Comb. *ho‘o- + kūlauna.* See *kūlauna.*

ho‘o·kulu *ham* To dink, i.e. to mishit or clip (the ball), in volleyball. *Ni‘ihau.* Also *pa‘i lihi.* See *‘ai hele wale.*

ho‘o·kū·lua *ham* To pair off. Comb. *ho‘o- + kūlua.* Cf. *kūlua* (dic.).

ho'o·kumu *Palapala ho'okumu.*
Charter, a document defining the
organization of a city, colony, or corporate
body.

ho'o·kū·pa'i *ham* To stack, as
windows in computer program. *Comb.*
ho'o- + *kūpa'i. Ho'okūpa'i pukaaniani.*
To stack windows.

ho'o·kū·pī *ham* To reflect, as light,
heat, or sound. *Ho'okūpī 'ia ka*
mālamalama ma ke aniani. The light is
reflected in the mirror. *Comb. ho'o-* +
kūpī. See *kūpī.*

ho'o·ku'e·maka *heh* To frown. *Dic.*
Cf. *pūtē.*

ho'o·ku'i *ham* To crash, as cars; to
bump or bang into. *Dic.* See entries
below.

ho'o·ku'i *ham* To open or complete,
as an electric circuit. *Dic., ext. mng.* See
'oki.

ho'o·ku'i *ham* To connect, as in a
computer program. *E 'olu'olu e ho'o-*
ku'i i ka mōkema me ke kamepiula.
Please connect the modem to the
computer. *Dic., ext. mng.* Cf.
ho'ohemo. See *ku'ina.*

ho'o·ku'i *Kaha ho'oku'i.* A curved
line (or lines) linking two letters or words
to indicate that the letters or words
should be joined, in proofreading.

ho'o·ku·ia *ham* To foul deliberately,
in team sports such as basketball. *'A'ole*
'o ia i 'ūpo'i i ke kinipōpō; ho'oku'ia
ahuwale 'ē 'ia 'o ia e ke kūpale. He didn't
get a chance to dunk the ball; he was
intentionally fouled by the defender.
Dic., ext. mng. Cf. *ku'ia.* See entry below.
Ho'oku'ia ahuwale. To commit an
intentional foul. *Ho'oku'ia kīpaku.* To
commit a flagrant foul.

ho'o·ku·ia *ham* Checks and balances,
as in government. *Ho'okumu 'ia ka*
ho'oku'ia ma waena o nā māhele nui
'ekolu o ke aupuni pekelala o 'Amelika
i mea e maka'ala ai i ka ho'okō 'ia o ka
mana o kēlā me kēia māhele. The system

of checks and balances between the three
divisions of the federal government of
the United States was set up so that the
exercise of power among each division
could be checked. *Dic.*

ho'o·ku'i helu wahi *kik/ham* Mail
merge, as in a computer program. *Lit.,*
splice addresses. Cf. *ho'oku'i pū.*

ho'o·ku'i·kahi *'Aha ho'oku'ikahi.*
Convention, i.e. an assembly of people
who meet for a common purpose, in
politics.

ho'o·ku'i·ku'i *ham* To splice, as film
or video segments for movie or video
production. *Dic., ext. mng. Luna*
ho'oku'iku'i. Assemble editor.

ho'o·ku'i pū *ham* To merge, as in a
computer program. *Lit.,* join together.
Cf. *ho'oku'i helu wahi.*

ho'o·ku'u *Ho'oku'u i ka wai o ka lua.*
To flush a toilet. *Ni'ihau. Also ho'o-*
holo i ka wai. Dic. 'Au ho'oku'u wai o
ka lua. Toilet handle (preceded by *ke*).

ho'o·ku'u hua·'ine *ham* To ovulate.
Lit., release ovum. See *hua'ine.*

ho'o·ku'u no ka manawa *ham*
Suspension, as from school; to suspend.
Ua ho'oku'u 'ia 'o Kalani no ka manawa
i ho'opa'i nōna. Kalani was suspended
from school as his punishment. *Lit.,*
expel temporarily. Cf. *ho'opa'i 'au'a.*

ho'o·ku'u 'ae·like *ham* To cede, as
land or territory. *Ho'oku'u 'aelike 'ia ka*
'āina o Tekasa iā 'Amelika Hui Pū 'ia
ma hope o ke kaua me Mekiko. Texas
was ceded to the United States after the
war with Mexico. *Lit.,* release (by)
agreement.

ho'o·lau·ka'i *ham* To coordinate, put
in order. *Comb. ho'o-* + *lauka'i.* See
ho'oka'ina, lauka'i.

ho'o·lau·lā *ham* To generalize; to
zoom out, as with a movie or video
camera. *Dic., ext. mng.* Cf. *ho'okokoke.*
See *ho'olaulā hawewe.*

ho'o·lau·laha *ham* To publicize.
Dic. Mea ho'olaulaha. Publicist.

ho‘o·lau·lā hawewe *ham* To amplify, i.e. increase the amplitude of a wave. *Lit.,* widen waves. See *laulā hawewe.*

ho‘o·lau·mania *ham* To smooth, as in a computer program. *Dic., ext. mng.* Cf. *ho‘okalakala.*

ho‘o·launa *ham* To handshake, as in a computer program. *Dic., ext. mng.*

ho‘o·laha See *papa ho‘olaha, Papa Lawelawe Ho‘olaha.*

ho‘o·laha kū·‘ai *kik* Advertisement, ad; commercial. *Dic., ext. mng.*

ho‘o·lako *Ho‘olako me ka heluna makemake.* Supply and demand. See *heluna makemake.*

ho‘o·lako ‘ai·‘ē *ham* To lend, as money lent at interest. Comb. *ho‘o-* + *lako ‘ai‘ē.* Cf. *lawe ‘ai‘ē, ‘ae.* See *lako ‘ai‘ē.*

ho‘o·lālā See *papa ho‘olālā. Mākau ho‘olālā.* Planning skill. *Ke‘ena Ho‘olālā o ke Kalana.* County Planning Department. *‘Oihana Ho‘olālā a me ka Ho‘omohala Waiwai o ka Moku‘āina ‘o Hawai‘i.* Hawai‘i State Department of Planning and Economic Development.

hō·‘ola·lau mana‘o *ham* To cause hallucination. Comb. *hō-* + *‘olalau* + *mana‘o.* Cf. *mana‘o ‘olalau* (dic.). *Mea hō‘olalau mana‘o.* Hallucinogen.

ho‘o·lā·lani *ham* To align, as type in a computer program. *E ho‘olālani i nā kinona ma ‘ekolu kolamu a me ‘ekolu lālani.* Align the shapes in three columns and three rows. *Dic., ext. mng. Kaha ho‘olālani.* Horizontal lines written above and below a word or words to indicate that they should be written or printed straight, in proofreading.

ho‘o·lana *Manehu ho‘olana.* Buoyant force, i.e. the upward force of a fluid on an object in it.

ho‘ō·lapa *ham* To cause to blast off, as a rocket; to launch, as a spaceship. Comb. *ho-* + *‘ōlapa.* Cf. *‘ōlapa.* See *helu ‘ōlapa. Kahua ho‘ōlapa.* Launch pad.

ho‘o·lawe *ham* Subtraction; to subtract, in math. *Dic.* Cf. *lawe.*

hō·‘ole *La‘ana hō‘ole.* Counterexample.

ho‘o·lei See *pana ho‘olei.*

ho‘o·lei·alewa *ham* To juggle. *Lit.,* toss as floating.

ho‘o·lele See *mīkini ho‘olele ki‘iaka, mīkini ho‘olele ki‘i‘oni‘oni, pākū ho‘olele ki‘i, pahu ho‘olele leo.*

ho‘o·like *ham* Associative, in math. *Dic., ext. mng. ‘Anopili ho‘olike.* Associative property (preceded by *ke*).

ho‘o·like·like *ham* To match, as in the game of concentration. *Dic., ext. mng.*

ho‘o·liliu·ewe *ham* To engineer genetically. Comb. *ho‘o-* + *liliuewe.* See *liliuewe. Ka ho‘oliliuewe ‘ana.* Genetic engineering.

ho‘o·liliu·welo *heh* To adapt biologically. Comb. *ho‘o-* + *liliuwelo.* See *liliuwelo. Malele ho‘oliliuwelo.* Adaptive radiation.

ho‘o·lilo *ham* To change something into a different form or product. *Ua ho‘olilo ke keiki i ka ‘ili lā‘au i pepa.* The child changed the bark into paper. *Dic., ext. mng. Kānāwai ho‘olilo moku‘āina.* Admission act, statehood act.

ho‘o·lilo i ka manawa *ham.* To take the time (to do something). *Lit.,* spend time. Also *ho‘oka‘awale i ka manawa.*

ho‘o·lilo pā·keu *ham* Deficit spending. *Lit.,* spend excessively. See *lilo pākeu.*

ho‘o·lohe *Hālāwai ho‘olohe.* Hearing, i.e. a time for presenting official testimony or argument. Also *‘aha ho‘olohe.*

hō·‘olo·ke·a *ham* To outline, as a summary of topics and subtopics using letters and numbers in headings. Comb. *hō-* + *‘oloke‘a.* See *‘oloke‘a.*

ho‘o·lo·li *ham* To edit, as on a computer. *Dic., ext. mng.* See *pākuʻi ho‘ololi* and entries under *ho‘oponopono. Palapala noi ho‘ololi kānāwai.* Constitutional initiative, i.e. a process by which one can propose an amendment by gathering signatures on a petition.

hō·‘olu ea See *mīkini hō‘olu ea.*

ho‘o·lulu See *lumi ho‘olulu.*

ho‘o·lū·maua *ham* To fertilize, as an egg. *Ho‘olūmaua ‘ia nā kowaū a ka ‘o‘opu wahine e ke kāne.* The female ‘o‘opu's eggs are fertilized by a male. Comb. *ho‘o-* + *lūmaua.* See *lūmaua.*

ho‘o·lu·‘u *Palai ho‘olu‘u.* To deep-fry.

ho‘o·mai·ka·‘i *ham* To praise. *Dic.* Cf. *hanohano.* See English entry *honors. Me ka ho‘omaika‘i.* With honors, as when graduating from a college or university. *Me ka ho‘omaika‘i nui.* With high honors.

ho‘o·mao·popo *He mea ho‘omaopopo kēia.* For your information. Also *i maopopo iā ‘oe, i mea e maopopo ai ‘oe.*

ho‘o·mau·lia *ham* To calculate. Comb. *ho‘omau* (make secure) + *-lia.* Also *huli a loaʻa, huli.*

ho‘o·maha *kik* Intermission. *Dic., ext. mng.* See entries below. *Ho‘omaha hapalua.* Halftime, as in sports or games. *Manawa ho‘omaha.* Time out, in team sports such as volleyball.

ho‘o·maha *kik* Rest, in music. *Dic.* See entries below.

ho‘o·maha hapa·hā *kik* Quarter rest, in music.

ho‘o·maha hapa kana·kolu·kū·mā·lua *kik* Thirty-second rest, in music.

ho‘o·maha hapa·lua *kik* Half rest, in music.

ho‘o·maha hapa·walu *kik* Eighth rest, in music.

ho‘o·maha hapa ‘umi·kū·mā·ono *kik* Sixteenth rest, in music.

ho‘o·mahaka *ham* To trace, as a picture. *Niʻihau,* from *māka.*

ho‘o·maha ‘oko‘a *kik* Whole rest, in music.

ho‘o·mā·hele *ham* To build, in math. *E ho‘omāhele i kēia ha‘i hō‘ailona helu.* Build this algebraic expression (i.e. by showing its separate steps). *Dic., ext. mng.* Cf. *ho‘omakala.*

ho‘o·mahola *ham* To expand or explode, as a file in a computer program; to extend, as a math problem which can be extended into other similar problems or situations. *E ho‘omahola i kēia waihona.* Expand this file. *E ho‘omahola a‘e i kēia polopolema ma ka haku ‘ana i kekahi mau polopolema ‘ano like.* Extend this problem by making up some similar problems. Comb. *ho‘o-* + *mahola.* See *mahola, ‘opi, ‘opihia.*

ho‘o·maka *ham* To begin, start, as a computer program. *Dic.* See *ha‘alele; hopuna‘ōlelo wehe kumuhana, kino, pau. Ka ho‘omaka ‘ana.* Opening, as of a story.

ho‘o·mā·kau·kau kumu *ham* Preservice teacher training. *Lit.,* prepare teacher. Cf. *ho‘oikaika kumu.*

ho‘o·maka·koho *ham* To make something a priority. Comb. *ho‘o-* + *makakoho.* Cf. *ho‘oka‘ina makakoho.* See *makakoho.*

ho‘o·makala *ham* To undo, in math. *Ho‘omakala nā hana ho‘omākalakala huli hope kekahi i kekahi.* Inverse operations undo each other. *Lit.,* cause to undo. Cf. *ho‘omāhele.*

ho‘o·mā·kala·kala *ham* To solve; to decode. *Dic., new mng.* Also *hana a loaʻa ka hā‘ina.* Cf. *ho‘oponopono pilikia.* See *mākalakala. Ho‘omākalakala i ka polopolema.* To solve a problem. *Hana ho‘omākalakala.* Operation. *Hana ho‘omākalakala huli hope.* Inverse operation. *Ka‘ina ho‘omākalakala.* Order of operations.

ho‘o·maka·ʻāi·nana *ham* To naturalize, i.e. admit to citizenship of a country. Comb. *ho‘o-* + *maka‘āinana.* *Ka ho‘omaka‘āinana ‘ana.* Naturalization.

ho‘o·make·ʻaka Funny, humorous, witty. *Dic., ext. mng., sp. var. Puke ho‘omake‘aka.* Humorous book, in literature.

ho‘o·mā·lama·lama *ham* To light, as a set for a movie or video production. *Luna ho‘omālamalama.* Lighting director.

ho‘o·malele *ham* To distribute, as in delivering or making publications available to the public. *Dic., ext. mng.* Cf. *kāka‘ahi.*

ho‘o·mā·lō *ham* To stretch, as for warming up before exercise. *E aho ‘oe e ho‘omālō ma mua o ka ho‘okūkū i ‘ole ai e huki ke a‘a.* You'd better stretch before the game so that you don't pull a muscle. *Dic., ext. mng. Ho‘omālō ‘ā‘ī.* Neck stretches, i.e. a warm-up exercise for sports such as volleyball; also to do this exercise. *Wili ho‘omālō.* Banding tool, as for putting metal bands on boxes, water tanks, etc. See *kalapu hao.*

ho‘o·malu See entries below and *‘āina ho‘omalu. Wā ho‘omalu.* Probation, in law. *Luna wā ho‘omalu.* Probation officer. *‘Āina Ho‘omalu Holoholona Lōhiu o Hawai‘i.* Hawaiian Islands National Wildlife Refuge. *‘Aha Ho‘omalu Lawai‘a o ka Pākīpika Komohana.* Western Pacific Fishery Management Council. *‘Ōnaehana Ho‘omalu ‘Āina Kūlohelohe.* Natural Areas Reserves System (NARS).

ho‘o·mālū *Lā‘au ho‘omālū.* Barbiturate.

ho‘o·malu·ō *ham* To conserve, i.e. to use or manage wisely, as natural resources. See *maluō.*

ho‘o·malu holo·holona lō·hiu *kik* State wildlife official. *Lit.,* protect wildlife. Also *luna ho‘omalu holoholona lōhiu.*

ho‘o·malu lawai‘a a me ka hahai holo·holona *ham* Fish and game management; to manage fish and game. *Lit.,* protect fishing and animal hunting.

ho‘o·malule *heh* To molt, as a crab its shell. *Dic.* Cf. *māunu.*

ho‘o·malu ma‘i *ham* To quarantine. *Ho‘omalu ma‘i ‘ia nā holoholona i lawe ‘ia mai i Hawai‘i nei mai nā ‘āina ‘ē mai no kekahi kōā o ka manawa.* Animals brought to Hawai‘i from other lands are put in quarantine for a period of time. *Dic. Hale ho‘omalu ma‘i.* Quarantine station.

ho‘o·mana akua kahi *kik* Monotheism; monotheistic. *Ho‘okumu ‘ia nā ho‘omana Mohameka, Iudaio, a me ke Kalikiano ma luna o ke kumu a‘o o ka ho‘omana akua kahi.* The Muslim, Jewish, and Christian religions are based upon the principle of monotheism. *Lit.,* religion (with) only one god. Cf. *ho‘omana akua lehulehu.*

ho‘o·mana akua lehu·lehu *kik* Polytheism; polytheistic. *Ma ka ho‘omana akua lehulehu o ka nui o nā lāhui Polenekia, mālama nui ‘ia kekahi akua ma mua o kekahi.* In the polytheistic religions among most Polynesian people, some gods are venerated more so than other gods. *Lit.,* religion (with) numerous gods. Cf. *ho‘omana akua kahi.*

ho‘o·mā·nalo wai kai *kik* To desalinate, desalinize salty water. *Lit.,* remove saltiness (of) sea water.

ho‘o·mā·neʻo·neʻo *ham* To tickle. *Dic.*

ho‘o·ma‘a *ham* To adapt to. *Dic.* See *ma‘a.*

ho‘o·ma‘aka *ham* To capitalize (a letter of the alphabet). Comb. *ho‘o-* + *ma‘aka.* See *ho‘ona‘ina‘i. Kaha ho‘oma‘aka.* Three lines drawn under a letter to indicate that the letter is to be capitalized, in proofreading.

ho‘o·ma·a·lahi *ham* To simplify, as in a math problem. Comb. *ho‘o-* + *ma‘alahi.*

ho‘o·ma·a·ma·a *ham* To practice. *Dic. Puke ho‘oma‘ama‘a ha‘awina.* Practice book. Also *puke ho‘oma‘ama‘a.*

ho‘o·ma·e·ma·e hale See *lā‘au ho‘oma‘ema‘e hale.*

ho‘o·mā·‘e·ele *ham* To anesthetize. Redup. of *ho‘omā‘ele. Lā‘au ho‘omā-‘e‘ele.* Anesthetic.

ho‘o·mea·mea *kik/ham* Simulation, in math. *Dic., ext. mng.* Cf. *ho‘okūkohukohu.*

ho‘o·mehana Honua *ham* Global warming, greenhouse effect. *Lit.,* warm Earth.

ho‘o·meheu *ham* To outline, as type on computer or in typesetting. Comb. *ho‘o-* + *meheu.* Cf. *mahaka.* See *meheu.*

ho‘o·mī·kā *ham* To pressurize. Comb. *ho‘o-* + *mīkā. Ho‘omīkā ‘ia.* Pressurized.

ho‘o·miki uila *Lapa‘au ho‘omiki uila.* Shock therapy.

ho‘o·moana *heh* To camp. *Dic.* Cf. *‘āpo‘e. Kahua ho‘omoana.* Campground. *Ka‘a ho‘omoana.* Camper; camping vehicle.

ho‘o·moe *ham* To incubate, hatch (eggs). *Ni‘ihau. Mīkini ho‘omoe hua.* Incubator (for eggs). See *kanaka ho‘omoe paipu.*

ho‘o·moe·ā *ham* To imagine deliberately. *E ho‘ā‘o ‘oe e ho‘omoeā he tika ‘oe.* Try to imagine that you're a tiger. Cf. *moeā.*

ho‘o·mohala mana‘o *Mākau ho‘omohala mana‘o.* Productive-thinking skill. *Nīnau ho‘omohala mana‘o.* Open-ended question.

ho‘o·mohala wai·wai *ham* Economic development. *I ka wā o ka pupū o ka mohala ‘ana o ka ho‘okele waiwai o ka Moku‘āina, pono e ‘imi i nā ‘ano like ‘ole o ka ho‘omohala waiwai ‘ana.* Whenever the State's economic growth is weak, other types of economic development must be sought. *Lit.,* develop wealth. *‘Oihana Ho‘olālā a me ka Ho‘omohala Waiwai o ka Moku‘āina ‘o Hawai‘i.* Hawai‘i State Department of Planning and Economic Development.

ho‘o·momona *ham* To fertilize. *Dic.* Cf. *kīpulu. Mea ho‘omomona lepo.* Fertilizer. *Mea ho‘omomona lepo kā‘oko‘a.* Complete fertilizer, i.e. fertilizer which contains the six necessary elements for plant growth.

hō·‘omo·‘omo *ham* To model, mold, or shape, as clay. *Dic., ext. mng.*

ho‘o·nā *ham* To settle, as a claim. *Dic. ‘Aha ho‘onā ‘āina.* Land court. *‘Ōnaehana ho‘onā ‘āina.* Land registration system.

ho‘o·nalo·pe‘e *ham* To camouflage. Comb. *ho‘o-* + *nalo* + *pe‘e.* See *nalope‘e.*

ho‘o·nanā *heh* To act cocky, strut about looking for a fight. *Ua ho‘onanā hele ke keiki ma ka pā pā‘ani.* The boy went strutting around the playground looking for a fight. *Ni‘ihau. Lele ho‘onanā.* Aggression, as a threat of attack by one country upon another. Cf. *lele kaua.*

ho‘o·nanea *‘Oihana o nā Pāka a me nā Hana Ho‘onanea.* Department of Parks and Recreation.

ho‘o·nani *Me ke kau i ka hano ho‘onani.* Magna cum laude, with high honors, as in academics.

ho‘o·nani·nani *ham* To put on makeup. *Ni‘ihau.* Also *ho‘ou‘iu‘i.*

hoʻo·na·ʻau·ao hau·mā·na lololo
ham Gifted education, as a school
program. *Lit.,* educate deep-thinking
children.

hoʻo·na·ʻau·ao ka·ʻa·ʻoko·ʻa *kik*
Alternative education, as a school
program. *Lit.,* educate separate.

hoʻo·na·ʻi·au *ham* To add special
effects. Comb. *hoʻo-* + *naʻiau.* Usu.
hoʻonaʻiau i ka hiʻohiʻona. See *naʻiau,
hiʻohiʻona naʻiau.*

hoʻo·na·ʻi·na·ʻi *ham* To change (a
letter of the alphabet) from capital to
lower case. Comb. *hoʻo-* + *naʻinaʻi.* See
hoʻomaʻaka. Kaha hoʻonaʻinaʻi. A line
drawn diagonally through a capital letter
to indicate that the letter is to be written
in lower case, in proofreading.

hoʻo·neo ʻāina ulu·lā·ʻau *ham*
Deforestation; to deforest.

hoʻo·ne·ʻe *ham* To move, as files in
computer program. *Dic.* See entry below.
Kaha hoʻoneʻe. A circle around a word or
words with an arrow going from the
words to the place where they are to be
moved, in proofreading.

hoʻo·ne·ʻe *ham* To slide, without flipping or turning, as a geometric figure, in
math. *Dic., ext. mng.* Cf. *hoʻohuli.*

hoʻo·noho *ham* To set up, as printer
specifications for a computer. *Dic., ext.
mng.*

hoʻo·noho kū·ana helu *ham* To
rename, in math. *Lit.,* arrange place
value.

hoʻo·noho·noho *ham* To format, as
a document in a computer program.
Dic., ext. mng. Cf. *hoʻonohonohona,
hoʻāla.*

hoʻo·noho·nohona *kik* Format, as in
a computer program. Comb. *hoʻonohonoho* + *-na.* Cf. *hoʻonohonoho.
Hoʻonohonohona pilikino.* Custom
format.

hoʻo·nonia·kahi *ham* To integrate,
i.e. incorporate (parts) into a whole. *He
noniakahi kekahi mau polokalamu
kamepiula ma ka hoʻononiakahi pū
ʻana i nā hana kikokiko palapala me ka
hōkeo ʻikepili, a me kekahi mau ʻano o
ka lako polokalamu pū kekahi.* Some
computer programs are integrated by
integrating word processing functions
together with database and other software
functions. Comb. *hoʻo-* + *noniakahi.*
See *noniakahi.*

hō·ʻono·ʻono *ham* To make tasty.
Dic. Mea hōʻonoʻono. Flavoring.

hoʻo·nui *ham* Multiplication; to
multiply. *Dic.* See entries below and
helu hoʻonui kemikala. Kaha hoʻonui.
Multiplication sign. *ʻAnopili ʻole o ka
hoʻonui.* Zero property of multiplication
(preceded by *ke*).

hoʻo·nui leo See *pahu hoʻonui leo.*

hoʻo·nui pau·kū pā·kahi *ham.* To
multiply through, in math. *Lit.,* multiply
each term.

hoʻo·nui pā·ʻanu·u *ham* Factorial,
in math. Comb. *hoʻonui* + *pā* + *ʻanuʻu.
ʻEono hoʻonui pāʻanuʻu.* Six factorial (6!).

hoʻo·nui ʻike *ham* Enrichment; to
enrich, i.e. to increase knowledge. *Lit.,*
increase knowledge. *Puke hoʻonui ʻike.*
Enrichment book, challenge book.

hoʻo·pai·ola *ham* To enrich, i.e. to
improve the nutritive value of
something. Comb. *hoʻo-* + *paiola.
Hoʻopaiola ʻia.* Enriched.

hoʻo·pai·pai *ham* To lobby, i.e. to
conduct activities aimed at influencing
public officials or legislation. *Hoʻāhewa
nui ʻia nā luna aupuni no ka lawelawe
ʻana no ka poʻe hoʻopaipai.* Political
leaders are often accused of catering to
lobbyists. *Dic., ext. mng. Mea
hoʻopaipai.* Lobbyist.

hoʻo·pā uila *ham* To utilize the
process of electrolysis. See *pā uila.*

ho·ʻo·pau·pili·kia See *lumi ho'opaupilikia.*

ho·ʻo·pahemo *ham* To take off line, as a computer system. *Na ka luna pūnaewele i ho'opahemo i ka 'ōnaehana i hiki iā ia ke ho'ouka i kekahi mau lako polokalamu hou ma luna o ka pūnaewele.* The system was taken off-line so that the network supervisor could install some new software onto the network. Comb. *ho'o-* + *pahemo.* Cf. *ho'opa'e'e.* See *pahemo.*

ho·ʻo·pahe·ʻe See *kele ho'opahe'e.*

ho·ʻo·pā·hi·ʻa *ham* Touch pass, in basketball; to make such a pass. *Ho'opāhi'a 'ia aku nei ke kinipōpō e Nalu iā Piko, a laila, iā Kekua.* The ball was touch passed by Nalu to Piko, and then to Kekua. Comb. *ho'o-* + *pāhi'a.*

ho·ʻo·pakele *Papa Hana Ho'opakele Sila.* Seal Recovery Program.

ho·ʻo·palai See *kīloi ho'opalai.*

ho·ʻo·pale kā·kau *ham* To write protect, as a computer file or disk. *Ua ho'opale kākau 'ia kēia pā e a'u.* This disk has been write protected by me. *Lit.,* ward off writing. *Ho'opale kākau 'ia.* Write protected.

ho·ʻo·palō *heh* To feign ignorance, "act dumb." *Dic.* Also *ho'ohūpō.*

ho·ʻo·pana·lā·ʻau *ham* To colonize, as a land by either people, animals, or plants. Comb. *ho'o-* + *panalā'au.* Cf. *ho'okolonaio.*

ho·ʻo·panoa *heh* Desertification, i.e. the processes by which an area becomes a desert, in geography. *Dic., ext. mng.*

ho·ʻo·papā hohonu *ham* To measure depth, as in the ocean. *Lit.,* cause echoes in depths. See *hawewe kani.*

ho·ʻo·papa·kū *ham* To make vertical. Comb. *ho'o-* + *papakū.* See *papakū.*

ho·ʻo·papa·ʻa *ham* To backup, as a file in a computer program. *E ho'opapa'a i kēia waihona.* Backup this file. Comb. *ho'o-* + *papa'a.*

ho·ʻo·pa·ʻa *ham* To set, as margins or tabs on a computer file or typewriter. *E ho'opa'a i nā kāwāholo ma kēlā me kēia 'umi ka'ahua.* Set the tabs every ten spaces. *Dic., ext. mng.* See entries below. *Ho'opa'a i nā lihi.* To set the margins. *Ho'opa'a i nā kāwāholo.* To set the tabs.

ho·ʻo·pa·ʻa *ham* To record, as on a cassette. *Dic.* Also *'oki. Mīkini ho'opa'a leo.* Tape recorder.

ho·ʻo·pa·ʻa *ham* To turn off, as water. *Mān. Ho'opa'a i ke kī wai.* To turn off the water.

ho·ʻo·pa·ʻa·hau *ham* To freeze (something). *Sh. ho'opa'a i ka hau.* Cf. *pa'ahau.*

ho·ʻo·pā··ā·lua *ham* To encode, encrypt, as computer data. Comb. *ho'o-* + *pā'ālua.* See *ho'okala pā'ālua, pā'ālua.*

ho·ʻo·pa·ʻa mo·ʻo·helu kā·lā To make a budget. *E ho'opa'a kākou i mo'ohelu kālā no ka pā'ina Kalikimaka.* Let's make a budget for the Christmas party. *Lit.,* fix (a) budget.

ho·ʻo·pa·ʻa·pū·hia *ham* To concentrate, i.e. make less dilute. Cf. *ho'okaiaka.* See *pa'apūhia.*

ho·ʻo·pa·ʻe·ʻe To bring on line, as a computer system. *Ua ho'opa'e'e 'ia maila ka 'ōnaehana ma hope o ka ho'oponopono 'ia e ka luna pūnaewele.* The system was brought on line after the network supervisor fixed the problem. Comb. *ho'o-* + *pa'e'e.* Cf. *ho'opahemo.* See *pa'e'e.*

ho·ʻo·pa·ʻi ʻau·ʻa *ham* Detention, as punishment at school. *Ua pono nā keiki kolohe e holoi i ka lumi lua i ho'opa'i 'au'a.* The rascal kids had to clean the bathroom for detention. *Lit.,* punish (by) detaining. Cf. *ho'oku'u no ka manawa. Ho'opa'i 'au'a i ka wā kula.* In-school detention. *Ho'opa'i 'au'a muli kula.* After-school detention.

ho·ʻo·pio *ham* To turn off, as a light, radio, TV, etc. *Mān.* Cf. *ho'ā.*

ho‘o·piha *kik* Washer, as used in plumbing. *Ni‘ihau.* Also *pihi ho‘opiha.* See entries below.

ho‘o·piha kaha *ham* To supplement, as angles, in math. *Lit.,* fill (a) line. Cf. *ho‘opiha kūpono. Nā huina ho‘opiha kaha.* Supplementary angles, i.e. two angles whose measures have a sum of 180°.

ho‘o·piha kū·pono *ham* T o complement, as angles, in math. *Lit.,* fill right (angle). Cf. *ho‘opiha kaha. Nā huina ho‘opiha kūpono.* Complementary angles, i.e. two angles whose measures have a sum of 90°.

ho‘o·pī·ka‘o *ham* To dehydrate (something). *Ho‘opīka‘o ‘ia nā ‘āpana mai‘a ma loko o ka mīkini ho‘opīka‘o.* Banana pieces are dehydrated in the dehydrating machine. Comb. *ho‘o-* + *pīka‘o.* See *pīka‘o.*

ho‘o·pili *ham* To match, as one thing to its counterpart by drawing a line. *Dic., ext. mng.*

ho‘o·pili·pili *ham* Imitation. *Waiū ho‘opilipili.* Imitation milk.

ho‘o·pili pū *ham* To aggregate, i.e. bind together *Lit.,* cause to unite.

ho‘o·pi‘i *ham* To breed, impregnate. *Dic.* Cf. *ha‘akipu.* See entries below and *pākēneka ho‘opi‘i.*

ho‘o·pi‘i *Kumu ho‘opi‘i.* Complaint, i.e. a legal document that charges someone with having caused harm. *Loio ho‘opi‘i.* Prosecutor, prosecuting attorney, plaintiff attorney. *Mea ho‘opi‘i.* Plaintiff. *‘Ao‘ao ho‘opi‘i.* Prosecution, i.e. the prosecuting party in a court case. *‘Aha pane ho‘opi‘i.* Arraignment, i.e. a court hearing in which a defendant is formally charged with a crime and enters a plea of guilty or not guilty. *‘Alo ho‘opi‘i ‘elua.* Double jeopardy, i.e. to be tried in court twice for the same offense.

ho‘o·pi‘i i ka māmā holo *ham* To accelerate. *Lit.,* cause to accelerate. Cf. *pi‘i ka māmā holo.* See *emi ka māmā holo, ho‘ēmi i ka māmā holo.*

ho‘o·pi‘i i ke koi pohō *ham* To make a claim for damages, as to an insurance company. See *koi pohō.*

ho‘o·pi‘i kaha *ham* Bonus, extra credit, as a class assignment or question on a quiz. *Lit.,* raise grade. Also *‘ai keu. Nīnau ho‘opi‘i kaha.* Bonus question, extra-credit question. Also *nīnau ‘ai keu.*

ho‘o·pi‘i ka‘a·kepa *ham* T o crossbreed. *Lit.,* breed diagonally. Cf. *ho‘ēhu pua ka‘akepa.*

ho‘o·pi‘i kū·helu *ham* Indictment; to indict. *Ho‘opi‘i kūhelu ‘ia ke kanaka no ka ‘aihue.* The man was indicted on charges of theft. *Lit.,* officially accuse in court.

ho‘o·pi‘i kū·ē *ham* To appeal, i.e. ask a higher court to review a decision made by a lower court. *Ua ho‘opane‘e ‘ia ka mana‘o ho‘oholo a ka luna ho‘okolokolo ma kahi o ka ho‘opi‘i kū‘ē ‘ia mai o kōna mana‘o e ka mea i ho‘āhewa ‘ia.* The judge's decision is suspended pending an appeal of his decision by the accused. *Lit.,* appeal (in) opposition. See *‘aha pane ho‘opi‘i.*

ho‘o·polo·lei *Pihi ho‘opololei.* Adjuster, as on triple-beam balance scales.

ho‘o·pono·pono See entries below. *Pukaaniani ho‘oponopono.* Edit screen, in a computer program.

ho‘o·pono·pono kahua *ham* T o decorate sets, as for a movie or video production. *Mea ho‘oponopono kahua.* Set decorator.

ho‘o·pono·pono kani *ham* To edit sound, as for a movie or video production. Cf. *kani keaka. Luna ho‘oponopono kani.* Sound editor.

ho·'o·pono·pono   ki·i·'oni·'oni
ham To edit, as movies or movie
productions. *Lit.,* edit movies. See
*ho'oponopono kani, ho'oponopono
wikiō. Hale ho'oponopono ki'i'oni'oni.*
Editing facility (for movies).

ho·'o·pono·pono   lau·oho *ham* T o
style hair, as for a play, movie, or video
production. *Mea ho'oponopono
lauoho.* Hair stylist.

ho·'o·pono·pono   pili·kia   *h a m* To
solve a problem, i.e. resolve a difficulty.
Cf. *huli hā'ina, 'imi hā'ina.* See
ho'omākalakala.

ho·'o·pono·pono   wiki·ō *ham* T o
edit, as videos or video productions.
Lit., edit videos. See *ho'oponopono
kani, ho'oponopono ki'i'oni'oni. Hale
ho'oponopono wikiō.* Editing facility (for
videos).

ho·'o·pō·'ai·apuni   *h a m*   To recycle.
Comb. *ho'o-* + *pō'aiapuni.* See *pō'aiapuni.*

ho·'o·pū·hala·lū   *h a m*   To inflate, fill
with air. *Dic.* Also *puhi a piha.* See
'ananu'u.

ho·'o·puka *Lako ho'opuka.* Factors of
production, in economics.

ho·'o·puka *ham* To produce, as a
movie or video production. *Dic., ext.
mng.* See *kuhikuhi, manakia ho'o-
puka, luna 'enehana. Luna ho'opuka.*
Producer. *Luna ho'opuka papahana.*
Project producer.

ho·'o·puka *ham* To publish, as in a
computer program. *Dic., ext. mng.* Cf.
loulou. See *ho'opuka hou loa,
ho'opuka ho'oponopono 'ia.*

ho·'o·puka hou loa *kik/ham* A n
update, as of a computer program. *Lit.,*
newest issue. Cf. *ho'opuka ho'oponopono 'ia, hō'ano hou.*

ho·'o·puka   ho·'o·pono·pono   'ia
kik/ham Interim or maintenance
release, as of a computer program. *Lit.,*
cause regulated emergence.

ho·'o·puka·puka *ham* To invest.
Dic. Kea ho'opukapuka. Stock, as in the
stock market. *Mea ho'opukapuka kālā.*
Investment. Also *ho'opukapuka.*

ho·'o·pule·lehua *ham*   To filibuster,
i.e. make a long speech in order to
prevent action on a legislative bill.
*Ho'opulelehua aku nei ke kenekoa he
'ehiku hola me ka mana'olana e hala ka
wā no ke koho pāloka.* The senator
filibustered for seven hours in hopes that
the time would lapse for the vote to take
place. *Dic., ext. mng.*

ho·'o·pū·nana *heh* To nest. *Dic.
Kau ho'opūnana.* Nesting season.

ho·'o·pū·'ulu   *h a m*   To group, in
math; to form or break into groups.
Dic., ext. mng. See *pū'ulu. 'Anopili
ho'opū'ulu.* Grouping property (preceded
by *ke*).

ho·'o·wela wai See *pahu ho'owela
wai.*

ho·'o·weli·weli *ham* To terrorize.
*Ke hopu 'ia nei ka mea i ho'ohuoi 'ia no
ka ho'oweliweli 'ana i nā 'ōhua ma luna
o ka moku.* The suspect is being detained
for terrorizing the passengers on the ship.
Dic., ext. mng.

hō·'ulu·'ulu   *kik/ham*   Addition, in
math. *Dic.* Cf. *ho'ohui.*

hō·'ulu·'ulu   mana'o   *kik/ham*
Summary; to summarize. *Dic.*

hō·'ulu·'ulu   pala·pala *kik*
Document summary, as in computer
program. *E hō'ike 'ia ka mea nāna i
kikokiko ma ka hō'ulu'ulu palapala.* The
typist will be shown in the document
summary. See *hope hō'ulu'ulu
palapala.*

ho·'ūnu·kā *ham* To pave with asphalt.
See *unukā, kīpapa* (dic.).

hū *kik* Yeast; baking powder. *Dic.;
mān.* See *pauka koka.*

hū *kik* Overflow error, as on a
calculator display. *Lit.,* overflow.

hū See *manu hū.*

hua *kik* Corm, as of taro. *Trad.* See entries below and *ʻauhua.*

hua *kik* Sound segment, in linguistics. *Dic., ext. mng.*

hua·aka *kik* Palindrome, a word or sentence that reads the same backward as forward. *Lit.,* reflection word.

hua·ale *Inu i ka huaale.* To take a pill. Also *ʻai i ka huaale.* See *inu, ʻai.*

hua·aʻa *kik* Tuber. Comb. *hua + aʻa.*

hua inoa *kik* Initial. *Lit.,* name letter. Cf. *hua hōʻailona.* See *pūlima hua.*

hua·haka·lama *kik* Syllabary symbol, in linguistics. Comb. *hua + hakalama.* See *hakalama.*

hua·hana *kik* Product, i.e. something that has been produced or manufactured. *Lit.,* fruit (of) labor. *Luna huahana.* Product manager.

hua·helu *kik* Figure or number (the character), numeral. *Dic.* See *helu Loma, kino huahelu.*

hua helu kumu *kik* Counting number, in math. *Lit.,* basic number.

hua hō·kū *kik* Starfruit.

hua hope hā·ule *kik* Apocope, in linguistics. *Lit.,* drop word ending.

hua hō·ʻai·lona *kik* Abbreviation. *Dic.* Cf. *hua inoa.*

hua·kani *kik* Tone, in music. *Dic., sp. var.*

hua kanu *kik* Bulb, as of a lily or tulip. *Dic. ʻŌmaka hua kanu.* Bulb tip.

hua·ka·ʻi maka·hi·o *kik/heh* Excursion, field trip. *Lit.,* trip (for) exploring. Also *huakaʻi.*

hua·kō *kik* Fructose. *He mea hoʻomomona ka huakō ma loko o ka wai meli a me nā ʻano huaʻai he nui nō.* Fructose is a sweetener found in honey and many kinds of fruits. Comb. *hua + kō.* Cf. *monakō.*

hua komo *kik* Epenthetic sound, in linguistics. *Lit.,* sound (which) enters.

hua·komo *kik* Input, as in a computer program. Comb. *hua + komo.* Cf. *huapuka.* See *kāhuakomo. Hāmeʻa huakomo.* Input device, as on a computer.

hua kumu ʻoka *kik* Acorn. *Lit.,* oak tree seed. Also *ʻēkona.*

hua·kū·ʻai *kik* Commodity, i.e. anything bought or sold. *He kuapo huakūʻai kaʻu ʻoihana.* I'm in the commodities exchange business. Comb. *hua + kūʻai.*

hua·lau *kik* Variable, a symbol that can stand for any quantitative value, in math. *Lit.,* many numbers.

hua·leo *kik* Phoneme, in linguistics. *Lit.,* language segment. See *puana hualeo, puanaleo.*

hua·loaʻa *kik* Product, in multi-plication. *Dic. Hualoaʻa kaupeʻa.* Cross product.

hua lou·lou *kik* Edition, as in a computer program. *Lit.,* linking result.

hua maʻaka *kik* Upper case (capital) letter. Comb. *hua + maʻaka.* Cf. *hua naʻinaʻi.*

hua mele *kik* Note, in music or on music staff. *Dic.* See entries below and *kī, kōkua hua mele. Hua mele laina.* Line note. *Laina o ke kōkua hua mele.* Horizontal line on a musical staff. Also *laina o ke kōkua. Wā o ke kōkua hua mele.* Space between horizontal lines on a musical staff. Also *wā o ke kōkua.*

hua mele hapa·hā *kik* Quarter note, in music.

hua mele hapa·hā kiko *kik* Dotted quarter note, in music.

hua mele hapa·lua *kik* Half note, in music.

hua mele hapa·lua kiko *kik* Dotted half note, in music.

hua mele hapa·walu *kik* Eighth note, in music.

hua mele hapa ʻumi·kū·mā·ono *kik* Sixteenth note, in music.

hua mele ʻokoʻa *kik* Whole note, in music.

hua naʻi·naʻi *kik* Lower case (small) letter. Comb. *hua* + *naʻinaʻi* (*Tah.*, small). Cf. *hua maʻaka.*

Huana·denowa *iʻoa* Juan De Nova. *Eng. Ka mokupuni ʻo Huanadenowa.* Juan De Nova Island.

hua·neʻe *kik* Anagram. Comb. *hua* + *neʻe.*

hua·pala·pala *kik* Letter (of the alphabet). *Dic., sp. var.*

hua paʻa *kik* Constant term, in math. *Lit.*, fixed result. Cf. *hoa like, paukū.*

hua paʻi *kik* Character, as of type in a computer program. Usu. *hua.* *ʻAʻole paʻi kēia mīkini paʻi i kekahi mau hua paʻi.* This printer doesn't print certain characters. *Lit.*, print letter.

hua·puka *kik* Output, as in a computer program. Comb. *hua* + *puka.* Cf. *huakomo.* See *kāhuapuka.*

hua waina maloʻo *kik* Raisin. *Lit.*, dry grape.

hua·ʻai kiwi *kik* Kiwi fruit. Also *lahomāpū.*

hua·ʻāne *kik* Spermatozoon, sperm, in biology. Comb. *hua* + *-ʻāne.* Cf. *huaʻine.* See *keakea* (dic.).

hua·ʻi *ham* To open, as an imu. *Dic. Huaʻi i ka imu.* To open an imu. Cf. *kuʻi i ka imu.*

hua·ʻine *kik* Ovum, in biology. Comb. *hua* + *-ʻine.* Cf. *huaʻāne.* *Hoʻokuʻu huaʻine.* To ovulate. *Lōkino huaʻine.* Ovary.

hua·ʻō·lelo *kik* Word. *Dic., sp. var.* See entries below. *Mākau huaʻōlelo.* Word skill.

hua·ʻō·lelo manaʻo like *kik* Synonym. *Lit.*, word (with) same meaning.

hua·ʻō·lelo manaʻo ʻē·koʻa *kik* Antonym. *Lit.*, word (with) opposite meaning.

hua·ʻō·lelo puana like *kik* Homonym. *Lit.*, word (with) same pronunciation.

hū·ea *kik* Gas, as in the digestive system. *E nui ka hūea o ka ʻōpū ma muli o kekahi mau ʻano meaʻai.* You can get a lot of gas in your stomach from certain foods. Comb. *hū* (*Tah.*, flatulence) + *ea.* Cf. *kinoea.*

huelo·pō·poki *kik* Cattail.

huē·woela *kik* Diphthong. Comb. *hue* + *woela.*

hui *heh* To intersect, as lines on a grid, in math. *Dic., ext. mng.* See entries below and *kaha huina.*

hui *kik* Conference, in sports. *Dic., ext. mng.* Cf. *ʻaha kūkā.* See *Hui Pōpeku Aupuni, Hui Pōpeku ʻAmelika, kuʻikahi.*

hui *Nā Hui Nui ʻElima.* The Big Five, i.e. the five corporations that controlled most of the sugar industry in Hawaiʻi.

hui·hui hō·kū *kik* Constellation. *Lit.*, star constellation.

hui·huina *kik* Combination, mixture; composite. *ʻEhia huihuina o kēia mau waihoʻoluʻu i hiki ke loaʻa?* How many possible combinations do these colors have? Comb. *huihui* + *-na. Hāpana huihuina.* Composite sample. *Haʻi huihuina.* Combinatorial coefficient.

huika *kik* Wheat. *Dic.* See entries under *palaoa. Huika piha.* Whole wheat. *Pua huika.* Straw.

hui·kaina *kik* Set, i.e. a collection of like items or elements. Comb. *hui* + *kaina* (kind). Cf. *ʻopaʻa.*

hui kau·peʻa *kik/heh* The intersection of two or more lines, all of which go through the intersection point, in math; to intersect thus. *Lit.*, crossed meeting. Cf. *hui poʻo.*

hui kea See *waihoʻoluʻu hui kea.*

hui·kuʻi *ʻa* Integrated, as computer software. Comb. *hui* + *kuʻi.*

hui kuʻi·kahi *kik/heh*   Alliance, i.e. a group of nations that have agreed to help or protect each other; to form such an alliance. *Ke komo nei nā aupuni o Palani a me ʻEnelani i ka hui kuʻikahi e hoʻopau ai i ke kaua ma ka Hikina Waena.* France and England are joining the alliance to end the war in the Middle East. *Lit.,* alliance (formed by) treaty.

huila *kik* Wheel. *Dic.* See entry below and *paepae komo huila. Huila paiki-kala.* Bicycle wheel.

huila makani *kik* Windmill. *Niʻihau. Uila huila makani.* Wind-generated electricity.

huila mū·hune *kik* Biofilter for a fish tank, in aquaculture. *Lit.,* germ wheel. Also *hōkele mūhune* (slang).

huina *kik* Angle, in math. *Dic.* See entries below and *hoʻopiha kaha, hoʻopiha kūpono, kaha huina. Huina peleleu.* Obtuse angle. *Huina ʻoi.* Acute angle. *Pakuhi huina ʻikepili.* Cross-tab graph.

huina·iwa *kik* Nonagon, i.e. a nine-sided polygon. *Comb. huina + iwa.*

huina·ono *kik* Hexagon. *Dic.*

huina·hā *kik* Quadrilateral. *Dic.* See entries below.

huina·hā hiō like *kik* Rhombus. *Dic. + like.* Cf. *huinahā like.*

huina·hā like *kik* Square, i.e. the geometric shape. *Dic.* See *huinahā hiō like.*

huina·hā lō·ʻihi *kik* Rectangle. *Lit.,* long quadrilateral. *Huinahā lōʻihi kula.* Golden rectangle, i.e. a rectangle in which the ratio of the width to the length is the same as that of the length to the sum of the width plus the length. *Lau huinahā lōʻihi.* Rectangular array. *ʻŌpaka huinahā lōʻihi.* Rectangular prism.

huina·hā paʻa pili·pā *kik* Trapezoid. *Lit.,* quadrilateral (with one) pair (of) parallel (sides). Cf. *huinahā pilipā.*

huina·hā pili·pā *kik* Parallelogram. *Lit.,* parallel quadrilateral. Cf. *huinahā paʻa pilipā.*

huina·hiku *kik* Heptagon, i.e. a seven-sided polygon. *Dic.*

huina kaha *kik* Straight angle, i.e. an angle that has a measure of 180°, in math. *Lit.,* line angle.

huina keʻa *kik* Intersection of two lines on a grid. *Lit.,* cross junction. Also *huina.* Cf. *kiko huina. Nā kaha huina.* Intersecting lines.

huina kiko·waena *kik* Central angle, i.e. an angle that has its vertex at the center of a circle, in math. *Lit.,* center angle.

huina·kolu *kik* Triangle. *Dic. Huinakolu like.* Equilateral triangle. *Huinakolu peleleu.* Obtuse triangle. *Huinakolu ʻelua ʻaoʻao like.* Isosceles triangle. *Huinakolu ʻaoʻao like ʻole.* Scalene triangle. *Huinakolu ʻoi.* Acute triangle.

huina kū·pī *kik* Angle of reflection, i.e. the angle between a reflected wave and the normal to the barrier from which it is reflected. *Lit.,* reflecting angle. Cf. *huina papā.*

huina kū·pono *kik* Right angle. *Lit.,* perpendicular angle. *Ana huina kūpono.* Right-angle protractor.

huina kū·waho *kik* Exterior angle, in math. *Lit.,* external angle.

huina launa *kik* Corresponding angle, of a triangle. *Lit.,* associated angle. Cf. *ʻaoʻao launa.*

huina·lehu·lehu *kik* Polygon. *Lit.,* many angles. *Huinalehulehu analahi.* Regular polygon.

huina·lima *kik* Pentagon. *Dic.*

huina·nui *kik* Sum, total. *Lit.,* grand total. See entries below.

huina·nui hapa *kik* Subtotal. *Lit.,* partial total. See *huinanui pau loa.*

huina·nui pau loa *kik* Grand total. See *huinanui hapa.*

huina pā *kik* Intercept, in math. *Lit.,* intersection (by) touching. *Huina pā X.* X-intercept.

huina papā *kik* Angle of incidence, i.e. the angle made between a wave striking a barrier and the normal to the surface. *Lit.,* echo angle. Cf. *huina kūpī.*

huina·walu *kik* Octagon. *Dic.*

huina ʻike·pili *Pakuhi huina ʻikepili.* Cross-tab graph, in math.

huina ʻoi *kik* Acute angle.

huina ʻumi *kik* Decagon, i.e. a ten-sided polygon. Comb. *huina + ʻumi.*

huipa *Kalima huipa.* Whipped cream.

Hui Pō·peku Au·puni *kik* National Football Conference (NFC).

Hui Pō·peku ʻAme·lika *kik* American Football Conference. (AFC).

hui poʻo *kik/heh* The intersection of two lines wherein one or both lines do not continue beyond the point of intersection, in math; to intersect thus. *Lit.,* end meeting. Cf. *hui kaupeʻa.*

hui pū ʻia United. *Dic. Aupuni Mōʻī Hui Pū ʻia.* United Kingdom. *Lepupalika Hui Pū ʻia ʻo Tanazania.* United Republic of Tanzania. *ʻAha Aupuni Hui Pū ʻia.* United Nations (UN). *ʻAmelika Hui Pū ʻia.* United States of America. *ʻEmira ʻAlapia Hui Pū ʻia.* United Arab Emirates.

hui ʻāina *kik* Union, as of states or countries into one political entity. *Lit.,* union (of) lands.

huo·huoi *Maʻi huohuoi.* Schizophrenia. *Maʻi huki huohuoi.* Schizophrenic convulsion.

huhu·pao *kik* Borer, a kind of insect. Comb. *huhu + pao.*

huka *kik* Zipper. *Niʻihau.*

hū·ka·a *kik* Resin, for musical instrument strings. *Dic., ext. mng. Hūkaʻa ʻea.* Acrylic.

hū·kē *ham* To blow one's nose. *Dic.* Also *hoʻokē.*

huki *Maʻi huki.* Convulsion. *Maʻi huki huohuoi.* Schizophrenic convulsion.

huki·alewa *heh* Chin-up, pull-up. *Lit.,* pull when hanging. See *pohoalo, pohokua. Hukialewa pohoalo.* Pull-up. *Hukialewa pohokua.* Chin-up.

huki pō·pō *kik/ham* Center, in football; to hike (the ball). *Lit.,* pull (the) ball. Also *huki i ka pōpō, huki i ke kinipōpō (ham.).* Cf. *kūlima.*

huku ʻou pele *kik* Dike, a geological formation. *Lit.,* projection (of) protruding lava.

hula·hula·kona *kik* Dance-a-thon. Comb. *hulahula + Eng.*

hule·hulei *heh* To seesaw, teeter-totter. *Dic.* See *papa hulei.*

huli- Scientific study of, -ology, with no specific intent to influence change. *Dic., ext. mng.* Cf. *kālai-, kilo.*

huli *kik* Direction. *Ua loli ka huli o ka makani i ka pō.* The direction of the wind changed during the night. *Dic., new mng.* See entries below.

huli *ham* To find, search for, as in a computer program. *Dic. Huli a kuapo.* To find and change, search and replace, in a computer program.

huli *ham* To evaluate, i.e. to find the number that an algebraic expression names, in math. *Dic., ext. mng.* See *huli a loaʻa.*

huli alo *ʻAoʻao huli alo.* Opposite leg or side of a right triangle. See *ʻaoʻao.*

huli a loaʻa *ham* To find, calculate, in math. Also *huli. Dic.* Cf. *hoʻomaulia.*

huli hā·ʻina *ham* To solve a problem, i.e. look for a solution. Also *huli i ka hāʻina.* Cf. *hoʻoponopono pilikia, ʻimi hāʻina.*

huli helu hoʻo·nui kumu *ham* Prime factorization, in math. *Lit.,* search for base multiplication number. See *helu kumu.*

huli·hia *'a'* Upside down. *Dic.* See *lolea.*

huli·honua *kik* Geology. *Dic., sp. var. Kahua hulihonua.* Geological site.

huli hope *'a'* Inverse, in math. *Dic. Hana ho'omākalakala huli hope.* Inverse operation.

huli·kanaka *kik* Anthropology. *Dic., sp. var.*

huli·koe·hana *kik* Archaeology. Comb. *huli-* + *koehana.* See *koehana. Kahua hulikoehana.* Archaeological site. *Kanaka hulikoehana.* Archaeologist. Also *mea hulikoehana.*

huli kumu·kū·'ai *ham* Cost analysis. *Ma ka huli kumukū'ai 'ana, huli 'ia ke kumukū'ai e pono ai kekahi huahana e kū'ai 'ia ana ma ka mākeke.* In cost analysis, an appropriate price is sought for certain products to be sold at the market. *Lit.,* study price.

hulili *Kahena hulili.* Riffle, as in a stream.

hū·lili *kik* Railing support, balluster. *Mān.* Also *'ūlili.* Cf. *paehumu.*

huli lole·lole *ham* To scan search, as with audio or video equipment. *Lit.,* search (by) skimming through.

huli·mō·'ali·haku *kik* Paleontology. Comb. *huli-* + *mō'alihaku. Kanaka hulimō'alihaku.* Paleontologist. Also *mea hulimō'alihaku.*

hulu *kik* Wool. *Dic.* See entries below. *Hulu aniani.* Glass wool.

hulu *kik* Format, as of a computer file. *Dic., new mng. Hulu waihona.* File format.

hulu·heu *kik* Cilium, cilia. Comb. *hulu* + *heu.*

hulu·hulu a'a *kik* Root hairs. *Lit.,* rootlet fur.

hulu koko *kik* Blood type. *Ke huli 'ia nei ka po'e i like ka hulu koko me ke keiki i loa'a i ka ma'i no ka hā'awi mai i ke koko nōna.* Blood donors are being sought who have the same blood type as

the child who is inflicted with the disease. *Lit.,* blood kind.

hulu māpa *kik* Mop head. *Lit.,* mop plumage.

hulu pena *kik* Paint brush. *Lit.,* paint plumage. Cf. *lola pena, pena lola.*

hulu·pō·'ē·'ē *kik* Sphagnum. Comb. *hulu* + *po'ē'ē.* Also *mākōpi'i hulupō-'ē'ē.* See *mākōpi'i.*

huna *kik* Ceiling. *Ni'ihau.* Also *kilina.* See entries below and *lumi huna.*

huna *kik* Particle, as in an atom. *Dic., ext. mng.* See *huna hohoki, huna 'āne, huna 'ine, huna 'ālepa, huna beta.*

huna *kik* Bit, i.e. a computer unit of information. *'Ewalu huna o ka 'ai.* There are eight bits to a byte. *Dic., ext. mng.* See *'ai.*

huna·ola *kik* Biological cell. Comb. *huna* + *ola.* See entries below. *'A'a'a hunaola.* Tissue, as structural material of a plant or animal. *'A'a'a hunaola 'ailakele.* Adipose tissue, i.e. animal tissue in which fat is stored.

huna·ola kahi *kik* One cell, single cell; one-celled, single-celled.

huna·ola koko *kik* Blood cell. *Hunaola koko ke'oke'o.* White blood cell. *Hunaola koko 'ula'ula.* Red blood cell.

huna hohoki *kik* Neutron. *Lit.,* neutral particle. See *huna 'āne, huna 'ine.*

huna·huna See entries below and *puke hunahuna, 'ōmole 'apo hunahuna.*

huna·huna palaoa *kik* Bread crumbs.

huna·huna 'ike *kik* Trivia. *Lit.,* bits (of) information.

huna kau·kala *kik* Pigment grain, in biology.

Huna·kalia *i'oa* Hungary; Hungarian. *Dic.* Also *Hunagaria.*

huna ʻā·lepa *kik* Alpha particle, i.e. a positively charged particle made up of two protons and two neutrons. See *huna beta.*

huna ʻāne *kik* Proton. *Lit.,* positive particle. See *huna ʻine, huna hohoki.*

huna ʻine *kik* Electron. *Lit.,* negative particle. See *huna ʻāne, huna hohoki.*

huna beta *kik* Beta particle, i.e. a negatively charged electron moving at high speed. See *huna ʻālepa.*

Huna·garia *iʻoa* Hungary; Hungarian. *Dic.* Also *Hunakalia.*

hune hulili *kik* Glitter. *Lit.,* tiny sparkles.

hune·hune ʻū·pī *kik* Vermiculite. *Lit.,* very fine sponge.

hupa *kik* Basket, in basketball. *Dic., ext. mng.* Also *hīnaʻi.* Cf. *ʻai hīnaʻi.* See *hao, kuku. Papa hupa.* Backboard. Also *papa hīnaʻi.*

huʻa *Hōkelo huʻa.* Bubble chamber, in chemistry.

huʻa·huʻa *Kokoleka me ka waiū huʻahuʻa.* Chocolate with frothed milk.

huʻa·kai *kik* Sponge, the aquatic animal. *Dic.* Cf. *ʻūpī* (dic.).

huʻe·a·o *kik* Intern, i.e. one who works as an apprentice. *Sh. huʻelepo + aʻo.*

huʻi·huʻi *ʻa* Cold. *Dic.* See *kuʻina. Kuʻina huʻihuʻi.* Cold front, as of weather.

huʻu *ham* To infer. *Sh. hoʻohuʻu.* See *hoʻohuʻu.*

hhn Abbreviation for *hapa haneli* (centi-).

Hk Abbreviation for *hikina* (east).

hkk Abbreviation for *hapa kaukani* (milli-).

hkkal Abbreviation for *hekokalame* (hectogram).

hkl Abbreviation for *hapa kiliona* (pico-) and *hekolika* (hectoliter).

hkm Abbreviation for *hekomika* (hectometer).

hl Abbreviation for *hola* (hour).

Hm Abbreviation for *hema* (south).

hml Abbreviation for *hapa miliona* (micro-).

hpl Abbreviation for *hapa piliona* (nano-).

hʻm Abbreviation for *hapa ʻumi* (deci-).

ht Abbreviation for *hekekale, heketare* (hectare).

K

k Abbreviation for *kana* (ton).

K Abbreviation for *koena* (difference, remainder).

kā- A prefix indicating a process. *Dic., ext. mng.* See entries below.

kā *kik* Tar. *Dic.* Also *tā.* See *kēpau kā.*

kā *Aʻa kino kā.* Iliac vein. *Aʻa puʻuwai kā.* Iliac artery. *Iwi kā.* Hip bone, pelvis. *Iwi kā o luna.* Ilium, i.e. the upper portion of the pelvis. *Iwi kā o lalo.* Ischium, i.e. the lower portion of the pelvis.

kaea *kik* Tire. *Eng.* Also *taea. Kaea paikikala.* Bicycle tire.

kā·ehu·ehu *ham* To dust, i.e. brush or apply lightly a thin coat, such as sulphur to a plant. *Comb. kā- + ʻehuehu.*

kae·kene *kik* Sewage sludge. *Sh. kae + kukene* (Niʻihau). See *kāemikala. Kaekene maka.* Raw sewage.

kā·emi·kala *ham* To treat chemically, as sewage. *Sh. kā- + emi + kemikala. Ke kaekene i kāemikala ʻia.* Treated sewage. See *kaekene.*

kai *kik* Sea; aquatic, marine. *Dic., ext. mng. ʻOihana Lawaiʻa Kai Pekelala.* National Marine Fisheries Service.

kaia- A prefix which indicates a clustering together. See entries below.

kaia·ola *kik* Ecosystem. *Comb. kaia- + ola.* See *kālaikaiaola.*

kaia·ulu *kik* Community. *Dic., sp. var.* Cf. *kaiahale, kaiahome.* See *ʻōnae-hana olakino kaiaulu. Kulanui kaiaulu.* Community college. *Kulanui*

Kaiaulu o ʻEwa. Leeward Community College.

kaia·ulu ʻā·ha·ʻi *kik* Climax community, in biology. *Lit.*, winning community.

kaia·hale *kik* Housing development, subdivision. Comb. *kaia-* + *hale.* Cf. *kaiaulu, kaiahome.*

kaia·home *kik* Neighborhood. Comb. *kaia-* + *home.* Cf. *kaiaulu, kaiahale.*

kai·aka *ʻaʻ* Diluted. *Dic.* See *hoʻokaiaka, waʻa kaiaka.*

kaia·mea·ola *kik* Biological community, as in science. Comb. *kaia-* + *meaola. Kaiameaola kūlohelohe.* Natural biological community.

kai·ana·side *kik* Cyanide. *Eng. Potasiuma kaianaside.* Potassium cyanide.

kaia·noho *kik* Habitat. Comb. *kaia-* + *noho.*

kaia·pili *kik* Society, i.e. an enduring social group. Comb. *kaia-* + *pili.*

kaia·puni *kik* Environment; medium. Comb. *kaia-* + *puni.* See entry below. *Kaiapuni aʻo.* Learning environment. *Kula kaiapuni Hawaiʻi.* Hawaiian-medium school. *Papa kaiapuni Hawaiʻi.* Hawaiian-medium class. *Palapala Hōʻike Hopena Kaiapuni.* Environmental Impact Statement (EIS).

kaia·puni hoʻōla piha *kik* Total healing environment. *Lit.*, complete healing environment.

kaia·wao *kik* Biome. Comb. *kaia-* + *wao.*

Kai·kana *iʻoa* Titan, a moon of Saturn. *Eng.*

Kaiki·kana *iʻoa* Kyrgyzstan. *Eng.*

kai·kona *kik* Daikon. *Japn.*

kaila hou *kik* Modern. *Lit.*, new style.

kaila hua *kik* Print style or attribute, as italic or bold, in printing or computer program. *Lit.*, letter style.

kai·mana pō·hili *kik* Baseball diamond, infield. *Lit.*, baseball diamond. Cf. *kahua pōhili.*

Kai Mele·mele *iʻoa* Yellow Sea.

kai·mine *kik* Saimin. *Japn.*

kā·inoa *kik/ham* Registration; to register, as for a class; to borrow or check out something by signing for it. *Ua kāinoa ʻoe i kēnā puke?* Did you check out that book? Comb. *kā* + *inoa.* See entries below and *palapala kāinoa.*

kā·inoa hiki hope *kik* Late registration. *Lit.*, registration arriving after. Cf. *kāinoa hiki mua.*

kā·inoa hiki mua *kik* Preregistration, early registration. *Lit.*, registration beforehand. Cf. *kāinoa hiki hope.*

kā·inoa komo *ham* To register or check in, as at a conference or hotel. Also *kāinoa.* Cf. *kāinoa puka. Palapala kāinoa.* Registration form.

kā·inoa puka *ham* To check out, as of a hotel. Cf. *kāinoa komo.*

Kai Waena Honua *Ke Kai Waena Honua.* Mediterranean Sea. *Dic., sp. var.*

Kai ʻĀ·kau *iʻoa* North Sea.

Kai ʻEle *iʻoa* Black Sea.

Kai ʻUla *iʻoa* Red Sea.

kāohi *ham* To control. *Kāohi ʻia ka maʻi ma ka ʻai ʻana i ka lāʻau.* Sickness is controlled by taking medication. *Dic.* See entries below. *Kulekele kāohi.* Containment, as a government policy of preventing the expansion of a hostile power or ideology.

kāohi mea·ola *ham* Biological control. *ʻO ke kāohi meaola kekahi mea e noʻonoʻo ʻia nei no ke kāohi ʻana i nā lāʻau a me nā holoholona malihini e hoʻopilikia nei i nā kaiapuni ʻōiwi o Hawaiʻi.* Biological control is one method being considered to control introduced plants and animals that are damaging native environments in Hawaiʻi. *Lit.*, control living things.

kāohi wai hā·lana *ham* Flood control. *Lit.*, control floods.

kaola kā·wele *kik* Towel rack. *Lit.*, towel bar.

kao lele *kik* Missile. *Dic., ext. mng. Kao lele pahū.* Missile bomb.

kaomi *kik/ham* Click; to click, press or depress, as in a computer program. *Dic., ext. mng.* Also *kōmi.* See *paʻina.*

kaona *kik* Downtown. *Dic., ext. mng.* Cf. *kiwikā, kūlanakauhale, ʻāpana pāʻoihana kauwaena. Kaona ukali.* Suburb.

kao wā·wahie kino·paʻa *kik* Solid rocket booster. *Lit.*, solid fuel rocket. Also *kao wāwahie paʻa.*

kau- A prefix meaning complex, as referring to vitamins. *Dic., ext. mng. Kauwikamina B.* B-complex vitamin.

kau *kik* Season. *Dic. Kau hoʻopūnana.* Nesting season.

kau *ʻĀlikelike kau.* Translation symmetry, in math. See *kaha kau, ʻaoʻao kau, ʻālikelike. ʻŌmaka kau peʻa.* Universal fitting, for putting pipes together.

kau *Me ke kau i ka hano.* Cum laude, with distinction, with honors, as in academics. *Me ke kau i ka hano hoʻonani.* Magna cum laude, with high honors. *Me ke kau i ka hano hāweo.* Summa cum laude, with highest honors.

kaua See entry below and *pale kaua. Lele kaua.* Aggression, as an attack by one country upon another. Cf. *lele hoʻonanā. Pūʻali kaua lewa.* Air force. *Pūʻali kaua moana.* Navy. Also *ʻau moku kaua, ʻoihana moku. Kahua pūʻali kaua moana.* Navy base. *Pūʻali hoʻouka kaua.* Marine corps.

kaua koʻe·koʻe *kik* Cold war, i.e. intense rivalry between nations but without military combat. *He kanahā makahiki i paʻa ai ke kaua koʻekoʻe ma waena o Wakinekona a me Mokekao.*

The cold war between Washington and Moscow lasted for forty years. *Lit.*, chilled war.

kau·alewa *ʻa* Balanced, as equal distribution of weight. Comb. *kau + a + lewa.* Cf. *hoʻokaualewa, kaulike.*

kau·ana·kahi *kik/ham* Calibration; to calibrate. Comb. *kau + anakahi.*

Kau·ano *iʻoa* Alnilam, a star. *Inv.*

kau·apono *kik* Compensation, i.e. something that constitutes an equivalent. Sh. *kaualewa + hoʻoponopono.* Cf. *uku pānaʻi.* See *hoʻokauapono.*

kau·ō *ham* To tow. *Dic.* See entries below. *Kalaka kauō.* Tow truck.

kau·ō *kik* Egg white or yolk. *Dic. Kauō keʻokeʻo.* Egg white. *Kauō melemele.* Egg yolk.

Kau·ō *iʻoa* Laysan, the island. *Lit.*, yolk or white of an egg. *ʻAinohu Kauō.* Laysan finch (telespiza cantanc).

kau·omo·lia *kik* Host, as of a parasite. Comb. *kau + omo + -lia.* See *omoola.*

kau·haʻa *kik/ham* Subscript, as in computer program or printing. Comb. *kau + haʻa.* Cf. *kaupiʻi.*

kau·helu *kik* Notation, in math and science. Comb. *kau + helu. Kauhelu pāhoʻonui.* Exponential notation. *Kauhelu ʻepekema.* Scientific notation.

kau·hope See *woela kauhope.*

kauka *kik* Doctorate, as a degree at a university. *Dic., ext. mng.* Also *laeʻula.* See *laeʻula.*

Kauka *kik* Doctor, for use as a title before a person's name. See entries below. *ʻO Kauka Halenui ke kauka nāna i lapaʻau mai iaʻu.* Doctor Halenui is the doctor who treated me. *Dic.* Abb. *Kk.*

kauka haʻi·haʻi iwi *kik* Osteopath. *Lit.*, osteopathy doctor. See *haʻihaʻi iwi.*

kauka hoʻo·polo·lei niho *kik* Orthodontist. *Lit.*, doctor (who) straightens teeth.

kau·kala *kik* Pigment. Comb. *kau + kala*. *Huna kaukala*. Pigment grain, in biology.

kaukani See *hapa kaukani*.

kauka pālomi *kik* Chiropractor. *Lit.,* chiropractic doctor.

kau·kaʻi *Kumuloli kaukaʻi*. Dependent variable.

kau·koma *kik* Glaucoma. *Ke hāpōpō mālie mai nei ka ʻike ʻana o koʻu kupuna kāne no kōna loaʻa i ke kaukoma*. My grandfather's vision is gradually getting cloudy because he has glaucoma. *Eng.*

kau·konu *Hopena kaukonu*. Ideal result, in math.

kaula *kik* String, as on an ʻukulele or guitar. *Mān.* See entries below and *ʻukulele, ʻukulele ʻewalu kaula*. Names of strings on an ʻukulele: *ke kaula o luna loa* (G), *ke kaula ʻelua*, (C), *ke kaula ʻekolu* (E), *ke kaula ʻehā* (A).

kaula uea *kik* Cable. *Dic.* Also *uea*.

kaula·hao *kik* Chain. *Dic.* *Kaulahao paikikala*. Bicycle chain.

kaula hō·ʻike piʻo *kik* Chord, of an arc, in math. *Legendre.*

kaula kau·laʻi lole *kik* Clothesline. *Dic.*

kaula kaʻi *kik* Leash. *Lit.,* rope (for) leading.

kaula lele *kik* Jump rope. *Cf. lele kaula*.

kau lalo *kik* Footer, as in computer documents. *Lit.,* placed below. *Cf. kau luna*.

kaula piko *kik* Safety line, as in a spacecraft. *Lit.,* navel string.

kau lā·ʻau *ʻa* Arborial. *Lit.,* set (on a) tree. *Hale kau lāʻau*. Treehouse. *Poloka kau lāʻau ʻalani*. Orange tree frog.

kau·lele *ʻa* Overtime. *Dic.* *Uku kaulele*. Overtime pay. *Hana kaulele*. Overtime (work). *Hola kaulele*. Overtime (hours).

kau·lihi *ʻa* Justified, as type in printing. Comb. *kau + lihi*. See *hoʻokaulihi, hoʻokauwaena, kauwaena*. *Kaulihi hema*. Left justified. *Kaulihi ʻākau*. Right justified. *Kaulihi like*. Full justified.

kau·like *ʻa* Balanced, evenly balanced, in science; even, in math; fair, just, equitable. *Dic., ext. mng.* Cf. *kaualewa*. *Haʻihelu kemikala kaulike*. Balanced chemical equation. *Helu kaulike*. Even number. See *kauʻewa*. *Manehu kaulike*. Balanced force. *Pāʻani kaulike*. A fair game, as one in which each player has the same chance of winning. *Pono kaulike*. Justice, i.e. the quality of being impartial or fair.

kau·like ʻole *ʻa* Inequality, in math. *Lit.,* not equal. *ʻŌlelo no ke kaulike ʻole*. Inequality statement.

kau lole See *uea kau lole*.

kau·lona See *aniani kaulona*.

kau·lua *kik* Double, in math. *ʻO ka 8 ke kaulua o ka 4*. Eight is the double of four. *Dic., ext. mng.* Cf. *helu māhoe*. *Lima kaulua*. Ambidextrous.

kau luna *kik* Header, as in computer documents. *Lit.,* placed above. *Cf. kau lalo*.

kau·maha *ʻa* Weight, in math. *Dic.* *Ana kaumaha wai*. Hydrometer.

kau·mī·kini *kik* Compound machine. Comb. *kau + mīkini* (cf. *kauhale*/dic.).

kau·moku·ʻāina *kik* Country, nation-state; national. Comb. *kau* (plural marker) + *mokuʻāina*. Cf. *aupuni, kauʻāina, māhele ʻāina, mokuʻāina, pekelala*. See entry below. *Kupa kaumokuʻāina pālua*. Dual citizen. Also *makaʻāinana kaumokuʻāina pālua*. *ʻAhahui kaumokuʻāina*. National organization.

kau·moku·ʻāina muli pana·lā·ʻau *kik* Postcolonial country. *Lit.,* after colony country. Also *ʻāina muli panalāʻau*.

kau·mua See *woela kaumua.*

kau·nā·nā *ham* To discover. *Dic.* Cf. *hiʻohia.*

kauna palaki niho *kik* Toothbrush holder. *Lit.,* toothbrush placement.

kau·noʻo *kik* Learning center. *Sh. kau + noʻonoʻo.*

kau·paku See *kaʻa kaupaku pelu, lumi kaupaku.*

kau·pale *ham* To defend against, as an opponent in sports. *Me he nalo mumulu ʻo Ewing ma ke kaupale ʻana iā Olajuwon.* Ewing was like a fly all over Olajuwon while defending him. *Lit.,* thrust aside. Cf. *kūpale, pale.*

kau·palena *ham* To set a deadline. *Dic.* See *palena pau.*

kau·palena hā·nau *kik* Family planning, planned parenthood, population control. *He noʻonoʻo kō kekahi mau mākua i ke kaupalena hānau ma muli o nā kumu hoʻokele waiwai.* Some parents consider family planning due to economic reasons. *Lit.,* limit birth. See *paihānau, paikoho.*

kau·pē *Mākala kaupē.* Deltoid muscle of the upper arm.

kau·peʻa See *hui kaupeʻa.*

kau pipi *ʻAlekuʻu kau pipi.* Cattle egret.

kau·piʻi *kik/ham* Superscript, as in a computer program or printing. *Comb. kau + piʻi.* Cf. *kauhaʻa.*

kau·poku See *papa kaupoku. ʻIole kaupoku.* Roof rat.

kau·poku·lani *kik* Outdoor. *Comb. kaupoku + lani.* See *maluhale. Haʻuki kaupokulani.* Outdoor sport. *Mākeke kaupokulani.* Outdoor market. *ʻAha mele kaupokulani.* Outdoor concert.

kau·poku·poku omo *kik* Hood, as an exhaust hood above a stove. Redup. of *kaupoku + omo.* Also *kaupokupoku.*

kau·waena *ham* To center, as type on printed page. *Comb. kau + waena.* See *hoʻokauwaena, hoʻokaulihi, kaulihi, woela kauwaena. ʻApana pāʻoihana*

kauwaena. Central business district. Cf. *kaona.*

kau·wela *kik* Summer. *Dic., sp. var.* See *māuikiʻikiʻi.*

kau·wika·mina B *kik* B-complex vitamin. *Comb. kau- + wikamina + B.*

kau·wowo *kik* Shoot from root of a plant. *Dic.* Also *kawowo, kā, ʻelia (mān., J. Nākoa), ilo (mān., Kawaʻa, Kapuni).* See *hehu, kawowo.*

kau·ʻāina *kik* International. *Comb. kau + ʻāina.* See *kaumokuʻāina.*

kau·ʻewa *Helu kauʻewa.* Odd number. See *helu kaulike.*

kaha *heh* To drive, in basketball. *Ua kaha palamimo ʻo Ioredāne ma waena o nā kūpale ʻehā.* Jordan slyly cut right through the four defenders. *Dic., ext. mng. Kīloi kaha.* Lead pass; to throw such a pass.

kaha *kik* Line. *Dic.* Also *kaha laina.* See entries below and *huina kaha. ʻApana kaha.* Line segment. *Helu kaha.* To tally.

kaha ana *kik* Benchmark, in math. *Lit.,* mark (for) measuring.

kaha ana·alike *kik* Directrix, as a line which divides a parabola into two equal areas, in math. *Lit.,* line (which) measures until the same. See *kaha kau.*

kaha·apo *kik* Parenthesis. *Dic.* See *kahaapo kihikihi. Kahaapo wehe.* Open parenthesis. *Kahaapo pani.* Close parenthesis.

kaha·apo kihi·kihi *kik* Bracket, in punctuation. *Lit.,* angular parenthesis. *Kahaapo kihikihi wehe.* Open bracket. *Kahaapo kihikihi pani.* Close bracket.

kā·hā·inu *kik* Water dispenser, as in a bird cage. *Comb. kā- + hāinu.* Cf. *kāhānai.*

kaha·hā·nai *kik* Radius of a circle. *Dic.*

kaha hiō *kik* Slash, in printing (/). *Lit.,* mark (that) leans up. Also *kaha hiō piʻi. Kaha hiō iho.* Backslash (\).

kaha hopu *kik* A line written from the end of one paragraph to the beginning of the next paragraph to indicate that the two paragraphs should be combined, in proofreading. *Lit.,* mark (for) grasping.

kaha ho·o·kau·lihi *kik* Two vertical lines written to the left of lines of print to indicate that the left margin should be justified, in proofreading. *Lit.,* mark (for) justifying.

kaha ho·o·ka·a·hua *kik* A "straight" Z-shaped line written to indicate where two words written as one should be separated, in proofreading. Comb. *kaha + ho'o- + ka'ahua.* Also *kaha ho'okōā.* Cf. *kaha ka'ahua.*

kaha ho·o·kō·ā *kik* A "straight" Z-shaped line written to indicate where two words written as one should be separated, in proofreading. *Lit.,* mark (for) separating by a space. Also *kaha ho'oka'ahua.* Cf. *kaha ka'ahua.*

kaha ho·o·komo *kik* Caret (^, ˇ), a mark used to show where something is to be inserted, in proofreading. *Lit.,* mark (for) inserting. Cf. *lina ho'okomo.*

kaha ho·o·ku'i *kik* A curved line (or lines) linking two letters or words to indicate that the letters or words should be joined, in proofreading. *Lit.,* mark (for) connecting.

kaha ho·o·lā·lani *kik* Horizontal lines written above and below a word or words to indicate that they should be written or printed straight, in proofreading. *Lit.,* mark (for) placing in rows.

kaha ho·o·lawe *kik* Minus sign. *Dic.* Cf. *kaha 'i'o 'ole.*

kaha ho·o·ma·aka *kik* Three lines drawn under a letter to indicate that the letter is to be capitalized, in proofreading. *Lit.,* mark (for) capitalizing. Cf. *kaha ho'ona'ina'i.*

kaha ho·o·na·i·na·i *kik* A line drawn diagonally through a capital letter to indicate that the letter is not to be capitalized, in proofreading. *Lit.,* mark (for) writing in lower case. Cf. *kaha ho'oma'aka.*

kaha ho·o·ne·e *kik* A circle around a word or words with an arrow going from the words to the place where they are to be moved, in proofreading. *Lit.,* mark (for) moving.

kaha ho·o·nui *kik* Multiplication sign. *Dic.*

kaha hui *kik* Plus sign. *Dic.*

kaha huina *kik* Intersecting line.

kaha kau *kik* Directrix, as a line from which a curve can be made by taking all equidistant points of a conic section, in math. *Lit.,* placed line. See *kaha anaalike.*

kaha·kaha kolohe *kik* Graffiti. *'O ka hō'ea maila nō ia o nā māka'i i ka manawa kūpono no ka hopu 'ana i ka po'e keiki ma ke kahakaha kolohe 'ana.* The police arrived just in time to catch the kids in the act of drawing graffiti. *Lit.,* destructive markings.

kaha kā·lā *kik* Dollar sign ($). Cf. *kaha kēneka.*

kaha kā·pae *kik* A line used to indicate that something is to be deleted, in proofreading. *Lit.,* mark (for) deleting.

kaha ka·a·hua *kik* A pound sign (#) used to indicate that a space should be inserted, in proofreading; a superscript number written next to the symbol indicates the number of spaces if more than one (#²). *Lit.,* space mark. Cf. *kaha ho'oka'ahua.*

kaha kē·neka *kik* Cent sign (¢). Cf. *kaha kālā.*

kaha kiko *kik/ham* Punctuation mark; to punctuate. Comb. *kaha + kiko.*

kaha kinona *ham* To complete, as a geometric figure, in math. *E kaha kinona iā DXCH no ka hana ʻana i ka huinakolu DXC.* Complete DXCH to form triangle DXC. *Lit.,* draw (a) geometric figure.

kaha kiʻi kū·kulu *ham* To draft, as blueprints; draftsman, drafter. *Lit.,* draw blueprints.

kaha koe *ham* To etch. *Lit.,* draw (by) scratching. *Kiʻi kaha koe.* Etching.

kaha kuapo *kik* A curved line written over a word or letter and then under the adjoining word or letter to indicate that the order of the words or letters should be reversed, in proofreading. *Lit.,* mark (for) exchanging.

kaha laina *kik* Line, in math. Also *kaha.*

kaha lala *kik* Diagonal, a segment other than a side connecting two vertices of a polygon, in math. *Lit.,* diagonal line.

kaha·lalo *ham* To underline. *E kahalalo i kēia lālani kikokikona.* Underline this line of text. Comb. *kaha + lalo.* Cf. *kahalina, kahapeʻa, kahawaena.*

kaha like *kik* Equal sign.

kaha·lina *ham* To circle, draw a circle around. *Lit.,* draw (a) ring. Cf. *kahalalo, kahapeʻa, kahawaena.*

kaha maha *kik* Dash, in punctuation. *Dic.* Cf. *kaha moe.*

kaha·makau *kik* Check mark. *Lit.,* fishhook mark.

kaha moe *kik/ham* Hyphen; to hyphenate. *E kaha moe i ka huaʻōlelo i loaʻa ai ke kaha moe ma hope o ka huapalapala a.* Hyphenate the word so that the hyphen appears after the letter a. *Dic., ext. mng.* Cf. *kaha maha.*

kaha moʻo·lelo See *moʻolelo kaha.*

kā·hā·nai *kik* Feeder, as for birds. Comb. *kā- + hānai.* Cf. *kāhāinu.*

kahana lonoa *ham* Lateral line, i.e. a linear series of sensory pores and tubes along the side of a fish, in biology. *Lit.,* drawing (a) line (of) senses.

kaha nuku muli·wai *kik* Delta (of a river). *Ma ke kaha nuku muliwai o ka muliwai ʻo Nile i ʻAikupita kahi o nā kahua kauhale kanaka kahiko loa a puni ka honua.* The delta of the Nile river in Egypt is where some of the most ancient human settlements are found. *Lit.,* place (of the) river mouth.

kaha pā·ka·ʻa·wili *ham* To draw a spiralateral. See *pākaʻawili.*

kaha pala·pala ʻāina *ham* To field map a site. *Lit.,* draw (a) map.

kaha pā lihi *kik* Tangent, i.e. a line which touches a circle at one point, in math. *Lit.,* line barely touching (a circle).

kaha pela hewa *kik* A circle around a misspelled word with the letters ph (*pela hewa*) written above the word, in proofreading. *Lit.,* spelling error mark.

kaha·peʻa *ham* To cross out. Comb. *kaha + peʻa.* Cf. *kahalina, kahalalo, kahawaena.*

kaha puana·ʻī *kik* Quotation mark. See *puanaʻī. Kaha puanaʻī pākahi wehe.* Single open quote; printer's symbol for the ʻokina. *Kaha puanaʻī pālua pani.* Double close quote.

kaha puʻu·naue *kik* Division sign. *Dic.*

kaha·waena *ham* To strike through or line out, as on a typewriter or computer; also used to indicate that the letters or words lined out are to be deleted and replaced by those written above, in proofreading. Cf. *kahalalo, kahaluna, kahapeʻa.*

kaha·wai *Koʻana kahawai.* Stream sediment. *ʻAumana kahawai.* Stream tributary.

kaha waiho *kik* A series of dots written under a word or words which have been lined out to show that no

kaha·'imo *kik* Cursor, I-bar, or insertion point in computer program. *Lit.*, blinking mark. Cf. *nahau 'iole.*

kaha 'i'o 'ole *kik* Negative sign, in math (-). Cf. *kaha ho'olawe.*

kaha 'oki hapa·lua *kik* Bisector, in math. *Lit.*, line (for) bisecting. See *'oki hapalua. Kaha 'oki hapalua kūpono.* Perpendicular bisector.

kaha 'oki pō·'ai *kik* Secant, i.e. a line which intersects a circle at two points, in math. *Lit.*, line (which) cuts (a) circle.

kaha 'oki·'oki *kik* Transversal, i.e. a line that intersects two given lines, in math. *Lit.*, cutting line.

change should be made from the original, in proofreading; stet. *Lit.*, mark (for) leaving (as is).

kahe See *uila wai kahe.*

kā·hea See *pahu kāhea.*

kahe·aholo *kik* Traffic, especially the movement of. *Pa'apū ke kaheaholo ka'a i kēia lā.* Traffic is congested today. Comb./sh. *kaheāwai + holo. Kaheaholo ka'a.* Highway traffic. *Kaheaholo mokulele.* Air traffic.

kā·hela See *pa'i kāhela.*

kahena hulili *kik* Riffle, as in a stream. *Lit.*, undulating flowing.

kahena koko *kik* Bloodstream. *Lit.*, flowing (of) blood.

kahena wai *kik* Stream bed. *Dic.* Also *papakū kahawai, papakū.*

kahi See *ho'omana akua kahi, 'ūlau kahi. Hunaola kahi.* One cell, single cell; one-celled, single-celled.

kahi·ā·uli *ham* To shade, as with a pencil; to block or highlight text, as in a computer program. Comb. *kahi + a + uli.*

kahiko *Puka kahiko.* Anus, i.e. the posterior opening of the alimentary canal. Also *puka 'amo.*

kā·hili·hili *ham* To dust, as with a duster. *Dic., ext. mng.* Cf. *kāwele. Mea kāhilihili.* Duster.

kā·hi'o·naina *ham* To landscape, as a yard. Comb. *kā + hi'onaina.* See *hi'onaina.*

kahi 'ū·mi'i lau·oho *kik* Folding hairclip with teeth. *Ni'ihau.*

kā·ho'i *ham/i'oa* To use the enter or return key on a computer or typewriter keyboard in order to return the cursor or carriage to the left margin on a new line; enter or return, as the key just above the shift key on a computer keyboard. *E kōmi iā kāho'i.* Press enter or return. Comb. *kā + ho'i.* See *ho'ouna, kāhua-komo. Pihi kāho'i.* Return key (preceded by *ke*).

kahu *kik* Controller, administrator, as for a computer network. *E hō'ike i ka pilikia i ke kahu pūnaewele.* Report the problem to the network administrator. *Dic., ext. mng. Kahu pūnaewele.* Network controller, network administrator.

kahua *kik* Site. *Dic.* See entries below and entries beginning with *a'o kahua. Kahua hulihonua.* Geological site. *Kahua hulikoehana.* Archaelogical site. *Kelepona kahua.* Station-to-station call; to make such a call.

kahua *kik* Base. *Dic. Kahua pū'ali koa.* Military base. *Kahua pū'ali kaua moana.* Navy base.

kahua *kik* Court, as for basketball or volleyball; field, as for baseball or football. *E ho'oholo 'ia nō ia ma ke kahua pōhīna'i.* Let's settle this on the basketball court. *Dic., ext. mng.* See entries below.

kahua *kik* Field, as in a database. *Dic., ext. mng. Hope kahua.* Subfield.

kahua *kik* Set, as for movie or video production. *Dic., ext. mng.* See *pono kahua. Mea kūkulu kahua.* Stagehand, grip. *Luna kūkulu kahua.* Stage manager, key grip. *Mea hakulau kahua.* Set designer. *Mea ho'oponopono kahua.* Set decorator.

kahua hamo·hamo holo·holona
kik Petting zoo. *Lit.*, site (for) petting
animals.

kahua hana *kik* Principle, as an
accepted rule of action. *Dic.* Also
kulehana. See *kulehana.*

kahua ho'o·moana *kik* Campground.
Dic. See *'āpo'e.*

kahua kā·lai·'āina *kik* Platform, i.e.
a declaration of principles and policies
adopted by a political party or candidate.
*'O ke kōkua nele ke kahua kālai'āina o
kōna paipai kālai'āina i kia'āina.* Welfare
was the platform of his campaign for
governor. *Lit.*, political platform.

kā·hua·komo *ham* To enter or input,
as typing data into a computer database or
a calculator. Comb. *kā + huakomo.* Cf.
kāhuapuka. See *ho'ouna, huakomo,
kāho'i. Kāhuakomo 'ikepili.* To input
data.

kahua pa'a *kik* Home screen, in a
computer program. *Dic., ext. mng.* See
papa kuhikuhi kahua pa'a.

kahua pō·hili *kik* Baseball field. Cf.
kaimana pōhili.

kahua pō·hī·na'i *kik* Basketball
court.

kahua pō·pa'i·pa'i *kik* Volleyball
court. Also *pahu.*

kahua pō·peku *kik* Football field.
Also *kahua.*

kā·hua·puka *ham* To output, as data
in a computer program. Comb. *kā +
huapuka.* Cf. *kāhuakomo.* See
huapuka. Kāhuapuka 'ikepili. To output
data.

kahu·lui *Ho'okūkū kahului.* Championship, in sports. See *ho'okūkū kio,
ho'okūkū moho.*

kahu pāka *kik* Park keeper.

kā·kai *kik* Handle for lifting, as of
bucket or suitcase. *Dic.* Cf. *pōheo, 'au.
Kākai pahu 'ukulele.* 'Ukulele case
handle.

kā·kau *ham* To take, as a test. *Dic.,
ext. mng.* Also *hana.* Cf. *haku i ka
hō'ike. Kākau i ka hō'ike.* To take a test.

kā·kau i memo *ham* To take a
message; to write a memo. *Lit.*, write a
memo.

kā·kau ulu wale *ham* Extemporaneous writing; to freewrite, as writing
about anything one chooses. *Lit.*, write
spontaneously.

kā·kau hou ma kekahi 'ano *ham*
To paraphrase, in writing. *E kākau i nā
'ōlelo a ka mea ha'i'ōlelo ma kekahi
'ano.* Paraphrase on paper what the
speaker said. *Lit.*, rewrite in another way.
See *ha'i hou ma kekahi 'ano.*

kā·kau maoli *ham* Script; to write in
script. *Ni'ihau.* Cf. *kākau pākahikahi.*
See *limahiō.*

kā·kau maka·kū *ham* Creative
writing. *Lit.*, write (with) creative
imagination.

kā·kau mo'o·lelo ki'i·'oni·'oni
ham To write a screenplay. Also *kākau
mo'olelo. Mea kākau mo'olelo
ki'i'oni'oni.* Screenwriter. Also *mea
kākau ki'i'oni'oni.*

kā·kau pā·kahi·kahi *ham* Print; to
print, as in handwriting. *Ni'ihau.* Cf.
kākau maoli. See *limahakahaka.*

kā·kau 'ō·lelo *kik* Secretary; scribe.
*Na ke kākau 'ōlelo e ho'onohonoho
pono i nā hana o ke ke'ena me ka
maiau.* The secretary will keep the office
organized and operating efficiently. *Dic.*

kakaha *kik/ham* Notes, as taken
during a lecture, etc.; to take such notes;
to make a note (of something). *'A'ole
wau i kakaha i ka ha'i'ōlelo o nehinei.* I
didn't take notes on yesterday's lecture.
E kakaha wau. I'll make a note of that.
Also *na'u e kakaha. Dic., ext. mng.* Cf.
memo.

kaka·lina *'Ūhōlo'a kakalina.*
Carburetor, as in an internal combustion
engine.

kakani *'a'* Crunchy, as fresh potato chips. *Dic., ext. mng.* Also *nakeke*. See *kamumu, nakekeke*.

kā·ka'ahi *ham* To dole out or deal, as cards; to distribute or pass out, as papers in a class. *Ni'ihau*. Cf. *ho'omalele*. See *kakekake*.

kā·ka'i·kahi *'a'* Few, sparse; seldom, rarely. *Ua kāka'ikahi wale nō ka hua 'ulu o kā mākou kumu 'ulu i kēia kau*. There were only a few breadfruit on our breadfruit tree this season. *Dic., sp. var.* See *kaka'ikahi* (dic.).

kake *ham* To shift, as on a computer or typewriter keyboard. *Dic., ext. mng. Pihi kake*. Shift key (preceded by *ke*).

kake·kake *ham* To shuffle, as cards. *Dic.* See *kāka'ahi*.

kake·ka'i *ham* To collate. *Lit.* mix (into) order.

kake ka'ina *kik/ham* Permutation, i.e. a selection of objects from a set in a particular order, in math; to permute. *Lit.*, mixing (in) order. *Ha'i kake ka'ina*. Permutatorial coefficient, in math.

kā·kele *heh* Transform, i.e. sliding in plate techtonics, in geology. *Dic., ext. mng.* Cf. *ku'i, ne'e 'oā. Palena kākele*. Transform boundary.

kakena *kik* Disk drive, as on a computer. *Comb. kake + -na. Kakena pa'aloko*. Hard drive. *Kakena kūloko*. Internal drive. *Kakena kūwaho*. External drive.

kāki *ham* To charge. *Dic.* See entries below and *mo'okāki, waihona*. *Waihona kāki*. Charge account, credit account, as in a bank.

kāki iā ha'i *Kelepona kāki iā ha'i*. Third-party call; to make such a call.

kāki hiki *Kelepona kāki hiki*. Collect call; to make such a call.

kā·kiko *ham* To bitmap, a style of printing a graphic image as on a computer printer. *Comb. kā + kiko*. Cf. *ki'i kiko. Kākiko miomio*. Precision bitmapping.

kāki koho *kik* Estimated cost or charge, as for services. Cf. *kumukū'ai koho*. See *koho*.

kāki kū·'ai·emi *kik* Sale price. *Lit.*, sale charge. Cf. *kāki koho*.

kā·kino·ea *ham* Gasification; also to gasify, i.e. convert into gas. *Comb. kā- + kinoea. Kākinoea lānahu*. Coal gasification, i.e. the process in which steam and hot coal produce hydrocarbons.

kāki 'ole *'a'* Toll free. *Lit.*, no charge. *Helu kelepona kāki 'ole*. Toll-free number.

Kakoka Hema *i'oa* South Dakota; South Dakotan. *Dic.* Also *Dakota Hema*.

Kakoka 'Ā·kau *i'oa* North Dakota; North Dakotan. *Dic.* Also *Dakota 'Ākau*.

kā·komo *ham* To import; also as in a computer program. *Hiki ke kākomo 'ia ka 'ikepili mai kekahi hōkeo 'ikepili a i kekahi*. Data can be imported from one database to another. *Comb. kā- + komo*. Cf. *kāpuka*.

kako·pone *kik* Saxophone. *Eng.* Also *pū kakopone*.

kā·ko'o *Mana'o kāko'o*. Supporting idea, as in a composition.

kā·ko'o hapa 'u·uku *ham* Affirmative action. *Ua loa'a kekahi mau 'ano ha'awina kālā hele kula ma ke 'ano he kāko'o hapa 'u'uku*. Some scholarships are available in support of affirmative action. *Lit.*, support (the) minority.

kā·ko'o ho'o·na'au·ao *kik* Education support staff. *Lit.*, support (for) educating.

kā·ko'o 'oi·hana ola·kino *kik* Allied health professional. *Lit.*, health occupation support.

kaku·ana *kik* Takuwan. *Japn.*

kā·kuhi *ham* To chart, make a chart, graph; to distribute, as data on a graph. *E kākuhi ʻoe i ka nui o ka ua o Waiʻaleʻale no hoʻokahi makahiki.* Chart the rainfall on Waiʻaleʻale for one year. *Sh. kākau + kuhi- kuhi. Cf. ili, waiho.* See *pakuhi kaʻina. Kākuhi kaʻina.* To make a flow chart. *Kākuhi i ke kiko.* To graph the point. *Mīkini kākuhi.* Graphing calculator.

kā·kuna *kik* Cartoon. *Eng.* Also *kātuna, kākuni.*

kā·kuni See *kākuna.*

kal Abbreviation for *kalame* (gram).

kala *kik* Crayon. *Eng.* Also *peni kala. Niʻihau. Kala meaʻai.* Food coloring. *Laulā kala.* Tint, as of a television screen.

kala *kik* Collar. *Dic.* Also *ʻāʻī, ʻāʻī lole, ʻāʻī kala.*

kala *ʻa* Into the net, in volleyball. *Niʻihau (from the name of the fish).*

kā·lā *kik* Cash, currency, dollar, money. *Dic.* See *kumupaʻa, mīkini ʻohi kālā, manu kālā. Kālā heleleʻi.* Loose change. *Niʻihau. Cf. kenikeni. Kālā keʻokeʻo.* Silver dollar. *Dic. Kālā kini.* Petty cash. *Niʻihau. Cf. kini kālā. Kālā kūʻike.* Cash. *Kālā mālama.* Savings, as money saved on a sale item. *Kaha kālā.* Dollar sign. *ʻOihana Kālā o ka Mokuʻāina ʻo Hawaiʻi.* Hawaiʻi State Department of Finance.

kā·lai- Scientific study of, -ology. *Dic., ext. mng. Cf. huli-, kilo.* See entries below.

kā·lai *ham* To hoe. *Dic.* Also *hō.* See *koʻi kālai.*

kā·lai·ao·paku *kik* Physical science. *Sh. kālai- + ao + pōhaku.*

kā·lai·ani·au *kik* Climatology. *Hoʻāʻo ka poʻe kālaianiau e koho i ke kumu o kekahi mau mea i hana ʻia ma ke aniau.* Climatologists try to determine the source of certain climatic phenomena. *Comb. kālai- + aniau. Cf. kālaianilā. Kanaka kālaianiau.* Climatologist. Also *mea kālaianiau.*

kā·lai·ani·lā *kik* Meteorology. *Comb. kālai- + anilā. Cf. kālaianiau.*

kā·lai·ō·ewe *kik* Genetics. *Comb. kālai- + ōewe.* See *ōewe.*

kā·lai·honua *kik* Geophysics. *Comb. kālai- + honua. Cf. hulihonua.*

kā·lai·hoʻo·kele wai·wai *kik* Economics. *Ma kā mākou papa kālaihoʻokele waiwai, aʻo mākou i nā ʻōnaehana hoʻokele waiwai like ʻole o nā ʻāina like ʻole.* In our economics class, we learn about the different economic systems of different countries. *Sh. kālai- + hoʻokele waiwai.*

kā·lai·kaia·ola *kik* Ecology. *Comb. kālai- + kaiaola.* See *kaiaola.*

kā·lai·kalaima *kik* Criminology, i.e. the study of crime and criminals. *Comb. kālai- + kalaima. Cf. kālaimeheu kalaima. Kanaka kālaikalaima.* Criminologist. Also *mea kālaikalaima.*

kā·lai·kani *kik* Science of acoustics. *Comb. kālai- + kani.*

kā·lai·kanu *kik* Horticulture. *Comb. kālai- + kanu. Mea kālaikanu.* Horticulturist.

kā·lai·kapa inoa *kik* Taxonomy, the science of classifying plants and animals. *Comb. kālai- + kapa inoa.*

kalaiki·kala *kik* Tricycle. *Eng. Cf. paikikala.*

kalaiki·kala lawe ʻō·hua *kik* Pedicab. *Lit.,* tricycle (for) taking passengers.

Kalai·kona *iʻoa* Triton, a moon of Neptune. *Eng.*

kā·lai·kū·lohea *kik* Physics. *Sh. kālai- + ao kūlohelohe + -a.*

kā·lai·kupa·paʻu *kik* Autopsy, necropsy. *Comb. kālai- + kupapaʻu.*

kā·lai·lai *ham* To analyze. Redup. of *kālai-.* See *kālai-.*

kā·lai·lau nahele *kik* Botany. *Comb. kālai- + lau nahele.*

kā·lai·launa kanaka *kik* Sociology. *Comb. kālai- + launa + kanaka.*

kā·lai·lawena *kik* Behavioral science. *Ma ke kālailawena, noiʻi ka poʻe noʻeau i ke kumu o ka lawena o kekahi poʻe.* In behavioral science, experts examine why people behave the way they do. Comb. *kālai- + lawena.*

kā·lai·leo *kik* Phonology, in linguistics. Comb. *kālai- + leo.*

kā·lai·lepo·mahi *kik* Agronomy. Comb. *kālai- + lepo + mahi.*

kalaima See *kālaimeheu kalaima, meheu kalaima. Kānāwai kalaima.* Criminal law, i.e. the law of crimes and their punishments.

kā·lai·manaʻo *kik* Philosophy. Comb. *kālai- + manaʻo.*

kā·lai·mea·ola *kik* Biology. Comb. *kālai- + meaola.* See *kālaimeaolahune. Kanaka kālaimeaola.* Biologist. Also *mea kālaimeaola. ʻOhana kālaimeaola.* Biological family.

kā·lai·mea·ola·hune *kik* Microbiology. Comb. *kālaimeaola + hune.*

kā·lai·meheu kalaima *kik* Criminalistics, i.e. the scientific study of physical evidence in the commission of crimes. Comb. *kālai- + meheu kalaima.* Cf. *kālaikalaima. Kanaka kālaimeheu kalaima.* Criminalist. Also *mea kālaimeheu kalaima.*

kā·lai·puolo *kik* Musicology. Comb. *kālai- + puolo. Kālaipuolo lāhui.* Ethnomusicology. *Kanaka kālaipuolo.* Musicologist. Also *mea kālaipuolo.*

kā·lai·wai *kik* Hydrology. *Ma ke kālaiwai, nānā ʻia ke ʻano a me ka pōʻaiapuni ʻana o ka wai ma luna a ma lalo hoʻi o ka ʻili o ka honua.* In hydrology, the nature and cycles of water are examined both above and below the earth's surface. Comb. *kālai- + wai. Kanaka kālaiwai.* Hydrologist. Also *mea kālaiwai.*

kalaiwa paiki·kala *kik* Handlebars, on a bicycle. Niʻihau. Also *ʻau paikikala* (preceded by *ke*).

kā·lai·ʻāina *Kahua kālaiʻāina.* Platform, i.e. a declaration of principles and policies adopted by a political party or candidate. *Kīpaku luna kālaiʻāina.* Recall, i.e. the right or procedure by which an elected official may be removed from office. Also *kīpeku luna kālaiʻaina. ʻAoʻao kālaiʻāina.* Political party.

kā·lai·ʻike *kik* Academics; academic. *He wahi kālaiʻike ke kulanui.* The university is an academic institution. Comb. *kālai- + ʻike.*

kā·lai·ʻō·lelo *kik* Linguistics. Comb. *kālai- + ʻōlelo.*

kalaona *kik* Clown. *Eng.*

kā·lā hoʻo·komo *kik* Deposit, as money placed into a bank account. *Ua hoʻokomo wau i ke kālā i loko o kaʻu waihona kālā panakō i nehinei.* I made a deposit into my bank account yesterday. *Lit.,* money (to) deposit.

kala·kala *ʻa* Low-quality print resolution, as on a computer printer. *Dic., ext. mng.* Cf. *miomio.*

kala·kuhi *kik/ham* Color code; to color code (something). Comb. *kala + kuhi.*

kā·lā kū·mau *Waihona kālā kūmau.* Endowment fund. Also *waihona ō.*

kalame *kik* Gram. *Eng.* Abb. *kal.* See *māikikalame.*

kala·mela *kik* Caramel. *Eng. Kanakē kalamela.* Caramel candy.

kala·mena *kik* Salamander. *Eng.* Also *salamena. Kalamena kuaʻula.* Red-backed salamander.

kalana *kik* County. *Dic. Hōʻikeʻike kalana.* County fair. See *fea.*

kā·lana kā·kau *kik* Notebook, tablet. *Dic.* Cf. *puke lina kui.*

kala·nakula *kik* Tarantula. *Eng.* Also *nananana kalanakula, nanana kalanakula.*

kā·lani *kik* Gallon. *Dic. Abb. kln. Hapalua kālani.* Half gallon. *ʻŌmole kālani.* Gallon jar, gallon jug.

kala·paike *kik* Graphite. *Eng.*

kala paipu *kik* Pipe wrench. *Niʻihau.*

kala·pepelo *kik* Propaganda. *I ka wā kaua, nui ke kalapepelo e hoʻopuka ʻia e ke aupuni.* In time of war, a lot of propaganda is put out by the government. *Comb. kala + pepelo.*

kala·pona *kik* Carbon. *Eng.* Also *karabona.* Cf. *ʻōpaʻu.* See entry below. *Helu makahiki kalapona.* Carbon dating, radiocarbon date. *ʻAkika kalapona.* Carbonic acid. *ʻAkika pūhui kalapona.* Carboxylic acid.

kala·pona ʻoki·kene lua *kik* Carbon dioxide. *Lit.,* two-oxygen carbon. Also *karabona diokesaside. Pōʻaiapuni ʻokikene kalapona ʻokikene lua.* Oxygen-carbon dioxide cycle.

kalapu hao *kik* Metal band, as for banding around metal boxes, water tanks, etc. *Niʻihau.* See *wili hoʻomālō.*

kala·puna *kik* Seagull. (Maori *tarā-punga.*)

kalapu wā·wae See *ʻili kalapu wāwae.*

kala·wake *kik* Cravat. *Eng. Lei ʻāʻī kalawake.* Necktie. Also *lei kalawake.*

Kale *iʻoa* Charles. *Eng. Ke kānāwai a Kale.* Charles' law, in science, i.e. the volume of a gas increases as its temperature increases if the pressure remains constant.

kalē *kik* Modeling clay. *Eng.* Cf. *palēkō, pālolo.*

kaleila *kik* Trailer. *Eng.* Cf. *pāki-huila.*

Kaleiwa·hana *kik* A nickname for ClarisWorks, the computer program. *Niʻihau.*

kā·leka *kik* Card. *Eng.* See entries below. *Kāleka aloha.* Greeting card. *Kāleka lā hānau.* Birthday card. *Kāleka*

piha makahiki. Birthday or anniversary card. *Kāleka puka kula.* Graduation card. Also *kāleka hemo kula.*

kā·leka aʻo *kik* Flash card. *Lit.,* teaching card.

kā·leka ola·kino *kik* Fitness card, as for sports or physical education. *He hōʻike kāna kāleka olakino he ahuahu wale nō kōna olakino.* Her fitness card showed that she was in good health. *Lit.,* health card.

kā·leka helu kuhi puke *kik* Catalog card, as in a library. *Lit.,* call-number card. See *helu kuhi puke.*

kā·leka kāki *kik* Charge card. Also *ʻea kāki.*

Kale·kale *iʻoa* Southern Equatorial Current, in oceanography. *Mān. (HA).*

kā·leka pahu *kik* Index card. *Lit.,* box card.

kā·leka poʻo·leka *kik* Postcard. *Lit.,* postage-stamp card.

kale·kona *kik* Dragon, as in fairy tales. *Dic.* Also *kelekona.*

kā·lele *kik/ham* Accent or stress, in linguistics. *Dic., ext. mng.*

kale palaoa *kik* Batter, as when making pancakes. *Mān.*

Kale·piana *iʻoa* Caribbean. *Dic.* Also *Karebiana.*

Kale·poni *iʻoa* California; Californian. *Dic. Mauʻu Kaleponi.* California grass.

kale ʻai *kik* Residue of poi after pounding, or of milk after beating. *Dic., ext. mng.*

kā·liki *kik* Brace, as for body parts. *Dic., ext. mng. Kāliki pūlima.* Wrist brace.

Kali·leo *iʻoa* Galileo, Galilean. *Eng. Nā mahina ʻo Kalileo.* Galilean moons.

kalima huipa *kik* Whipped cream. *Kokoleka me ke kalima huipa.* Chocolate with whipped cream.

kalina *kik* Fungus, general term. PPN *taringa* (ear).

kalina paʻu *kik* Smut, a kind of plant disease or the fungus which causes it. *Lit.*, soot fungus. *Kalina paʻu kūlina.* Corn smut.

kā·lino *ham* To weave, as on a loom. *Sh. kāmola + lino.*

kā·lī pahū·pahū *kik* String of firecrackers. See *ahihoʻoleʻaleʻa.*

kali·palaoa *kik* Cauliflower. *Dic.*

kali·puna *kik* Calcium *Sh. Eng. + puna.*

kali·puna ʻokesa·ili·hate *kik* Calcium oxilate.

Kalito *iʻoa* Callisto, a moon of Jupiter. *Eng.*

kalo *Kipi kalo.* Taro chip.

kā·loaʻa *kik* Business, i.e. purchase and sale of goods and services. *Comb. kā- + loaʻa. Cf. ʻoihana, pāʻoihana.* See *ahu kāloaʻa, paikāloaʻa. Pōʻaiapuni kāloaʻa.* Business cycle, i.e. a repeated series of economic growth and recession.

kalo kala·koa *kik* Caladium. *Dic.*

Kalo·laina *iʻoa* Carolina; Caroline. *Dic. Kalolaina Hema.* South Carolina; South Carolinean. *Kalolaina ʻĀkau.* North Carolina; North Carolinean. *Ka pae moku ʻo Kalolaina.* Caroline Isles. Also *ka pae moku ʻo Karolaina.*

Kā·lona *iʻoa* Charon, a moon of Pluto. *Eng.*

kalo Pā·kē *kik* Lotus. *Lit.*, Chinese taro. Also *līkao.*

Kalua·koke *iʻoa* Bellatrix, a star. *Mān. (HA).*

kalu·hā *kik* Papyrus. *Dic.*

kaluli *kik* Slurry, a viscous solution of liquid and a solid. *Eng.*

kā·luʻu See *palekona kāluʻu.*

kā·mahaka *ham* To make a rubbing, as of petroglyphs. *Comb. kā- + mahaka (māka).* See *mahaka.*

kā·mā·hua·ola *kik* Hydroponics, i.e. the growing of plants in a nutrient solution. *Comb. kā- + māhuaola. Hoʻoulu kāmāhuaola wai.* To grow hydroponically in water. *Hoʻoulu kāmāhuaola one.* To grow hydroponically in sand. *Hoʻoulu kāmāhuaola hunehune ʻūpī.* To grow hydroponically in vermiculite. *Māʻōʻāna kāmāhuaola.* Hydroponic solution.

kā maka·wela *ham* To slash and burn, a method of land cultivation. *Lit.*, turn the soil (of) land cleared by burning.

kama·kū·aka *kik* Kumquat. *Eng.*

kā·mala *kik* Booth, as at a carnival. *Dic.*

kama·loli *kik* Slug, a gastropod closely related to land snails. *Dic.*

Kama·pia *iʻoa* Gambia. *Eng.*

kama·poko *kik* Fish cake, kamaboko. *Japn.*

kā·maʻa hekehi *kik* Hiking shoe.

kā·maʻa hele hau *kik* Snow shoe. *Lit.*, shoe (for) walking (on) snow.

kā·maʻa holo hau *kik* Ice skate. See *holo hau.*

kā·maʻa huila *kik* Roller skate. See *holo kāmaʻa huila.*

kā·maʻa lapa huila *kik* Rollerblade. See *holo lapa huila.*

kā·maʻa lole *kik* Sneaker, tennis shoe. *Lit.*, cloth shoe.

kā·maʻa poho·pū *kik* Loafer, slip-on style shoe. *Lit.*, pouch together shoe.

kā·maʻa puki heʻe hau *kik* Ski boot. See *heʻe hau.*

kā·maʻa ʻili helei *kik* Oxford, saddle shoe. *Lit.*, shoe (with) straddling strap.

Kama·bodia *iʻoa* Cambodia; Cambodian. *Eng.*

Kameha·meha *Pulelehua Kamehameha.* Kamehameha butterfly.

kame·piula *kik* Computer. *Eng.* Also *lolouila, mīkini hoʻonohonoho ʻikena. Kamepiula lawelima.* Laptop computer. Also *lolouila lawelima.*

Kame·runa *iʻoa* Cameroon, Cameroun; Cameroonian, Camerounian. *Eng.*

Kā·moa *iʻoa* Sāmoa; Sāmoan. *Dic.* Also *Haʻamoa. Kāmoa ʻAmelika.* American Sāmoa; American Sāmoan. Also *Haʻamoa ʻAmelika.*

kā·mua *kik/ham* Draft, i.e. a preliminary version; to prepare a draft. Sh. *kākau/kaha + mua. Kāmua ʻekahi.* First draft. *Kāmua ʻelua.* Second draft.

kamumu *ʻa* Crunchy, general term, but especially for *loli, ʻopihi,* etc. *Dic.* See *kakani, nakeke, nakekeke.*

kana *kik* Ton. *Dic.* Abb. *k.*

kana·uika *kik* Sandwich. *Eng.*

kā nahau *Haku kā nahau.* Mesolithic, in anthropology. *Ke au haku kā nahau.* Mesolithic age, period.

Kana Helena *Mauna Kana Helena.* Mount Saint Helens. Also *Mauna Sana Helena.*

kanaka See entries below and *aʻo launa kanaka. Hoʻokae kanaka.* Misanthropy, hatred of mankind. See *hoʻokae. Noʻonoʻo kanaka.* Common sense; to use common sense.

Kanaka *ʻAilana Kanaka.* Isle of Man.

Kana·kā *iʻoa* Canada; Canadian. *Dic., sp. var.*

kanaka iwi *kik* Skeleton, as for Halloween. *Lit.,* bone man. Also *kelekona.* Cf. *kinanahiwi.*

kanaka hau *kik* Snowman.

kanaka hana uila *kik* Electrician. *Niʻihau.*

kanaka hoʻo·moe paipu *kik* Plumber. *Niʻihau.* Also *wilipaipu.*

kanaka huli·honua *kik* Geologist. See *hulihonua.*

kanaka kino liona *kik* Sphinx, a mythological monster with the head of a woman and the body of a lion. *Loaʻa nō nā moʻolelo Helene kahiko e pili ana i ke kanaka kino liona.* There are ancient Greek stories about sphinxes. *Lit.,* man (with) lion body. Cf. *Sapenika Liona.*

kanaka luʻu kai *kik* Scuba diver. *Lit.,* person (who) dives (in the) sea.

kanaka maka·ʻala ʻupena *kik* Referee, in volleyball. *Niʻihau.* See *ʻuao.*

kanaka puni ao kū·lohe·lohe *kik* Naturalist. *Lit.,* person (who is) fond (of) nature. Also *puni ao kūlohelohe.*

Kana·kawia *iʻoa* Scandanavia; Scandanavian. *Eng.*

kanaka ʻea *kik* Mannequin. *Kāhiko ʻia ke kanaka ʻea no ka hōʻikeʻike ʻana i ke ʻano o nā paikini hou o ka hale kūʻai.* The mannequins are dressed up to display the new fashions that the store has to offer. *Niʻihau.*

kanaka ʻepe·kema *kik* Scientist. Also *kanaka akeakamai.*

kana·kē *kik* Candy. *Dic. Kanakē kalamela.* Caramel candy. *Kanakē koʻokoʻo.* Candy cane. *Kanakē ʻau.* Lollipop, sucker. Also *kō omōmo.*

kā·nā·wai *kik* Act, as a law, decree or edict, in government. *Ua kākoʻo ʻia ka Papahana Kula Kaiapuni Hawaiʻi ma o ke Kānāwai Hoʻonaʻauao ʻŌiwi Hawaiʻi o ʻAmelika Hui Pū ʻia.* The Hawaiian Language Immersion Program has been supported through the United States Native Hawaiian Education Act. *Dic.* See entries below and *haʻihaʻi kānāwai, pale kānāwai, ʻaʻe kānāwai.* See also *Kale, Poila. Kānāwai Lāhulu ʻAne Halapohe.* Endangered Species Act. *Mana kaukānāwai.* Legislative powers. *Pae kānāwai.* Legal alien; to arrive as a legal alien. Cf. *pae malū. Papa kānāwai.* Code, i.e. a systematic collection of existing laws. *Papa kānāwai wai o ka moku-ʻāina.* State water code. *ʻAʻa kānāwai.* Civil disobedience, i.e. breaking a law because it goes against personal morals.

kā·nā·wai *kik* Legislation, in politics. *Dic., ext. mng.* See entries below and *mokuna, poʻo kānāwai. Aupuni kānāwai na ka lehulehu.* Direct democracy, i.e. a government in which laws are made directly by the citizens. *Hāpai kānāwai.* Initiative, i.e. the procedure enabling citizens to propose a law and submit it to the legislature for approval. *Kū i ke kaʻina kānāwai.* Due process of law, i.e. the process by which the government must treat accused persons fairly according to rules established by law. *Palapala noi hoʻololi kānāwai.* Constitutional initiative, i.e. a process by which one can propose an amendment by gathering signatures on a petition. *ʻAelike mālama kānāwai.* Compact, i.e. a written agreement to make and obey laws for the welfare of the group.

kā·nā·wai ho·ʻo·ili *kik* Distributive law, in math. *Lit.,* transferring law. Cf. *ʻanopili hoʻoili.*

kā·nā·wai ho·ʻo·lilo moku·ʻāina *kik* Admission act, statehood act. *Lilo ʻo Hawaiʻi he mokuʻāina ma ke kānāwai hoʻolilo mokuʻāina o 1959.* Hawaiʻi became a state by the statehood act of 1959. *Lit.,* law to make (into a) state.

kā·nā·wai kalaima *kik* Criminal law, i.e. the law of crimes and their punishments. *E hoʻopaʻa ana wau i ke kānāwai kalaima ma ke kula i hiki ai iaʻu ke lilo i loio.* I am going to study criminal law so I can become a lawyer.

kā·nā·wai kī·wila *kik* Civil law. *Pili ke kānāwai kīwila i nā pono o ke kanaka, ʻaʻole naʻe ka hana kalaima ʻana.* Civil law has to do with the rights of individuals, not necessarily the committing of crimes. *Dic.* Also *kānāwai sīwila.*

kā·nā·wai kū·loko *kik* Ordinance, i.e. a municipal regulation. *Ma ke kānāwai kūloko o ke kūlanakauhale, ua pāpā ʻia ke kīloi ʻana i ka ʻōpala ma kēia wahi.* City ordinances prohibit the throwing of trash in this area. *Lit.,* local law. See *kānāwai.*

kā·nā·wai kumu *kik* Common law. *Trad.* See other entries in dictionary.

Kā·nā·wai Mā·mela Kai *kik* Marine Mammals Act.

kā·nā·wai ʻaha·ʻō·lelo *kik* Statute, i.e. a law enacted by the legislative branch of a government. *Lit.,* legislature law. See *kānāwai.*

kāne *Hoʻokae kāne.* Misandry, hatred of males. See *hoʻokae.*

kā·nela *kik* Channel, station, as on radio or television. *Eng.*

Kāne·milo·haʻi *iʻoa* French Frigate Shoals. *Lit.,* name of Pele's brother left as an outguard on northwestern shoal as they travelled from Tahiti to Hawaiʻi.

Kane·sasa *iʻoa* Kansas; Kansan. *Dic.*

kani *kik* Sound effects, as on a computer. *Dic., ext. mng.* See *kani keaka, pīpa.*

kani See *māmā kani, palena holo kani.*

kani·olo See *pū kaniolo.*

kani keaka *kik* Sound effects, as for a play, movie, or video production. *Lit.,* theater sounds. *Luna kani keaka.* Sound effects coordinator. Cf. *luna hoʻopono-pono kani, mea ʻenehana kani.*

kani·kela *kik* Consul. *Hoʻokohu ʻia ke kanikela e ke aupuni e noho ʻelele ma kekahi ʻāina no ka mālama ʻana i nā hana pāʻoihana a me nā hana ʻē aʻe o kōna aupuni ma ia ʻāina ʻo ia e noho ʻelele nei.* The consul is appointed by the government to live in another country as a representative of the government to protect the economic and other interests of his government in the country he is appointed to reside in. *Dic. Kanikela nui.* Ambassador, i.e. an official representative to a foreign country.

kani ko'ele *kik/heh* To tick, as a clock. *Ko'ele maila ke kani a ka uaki.* The clock ticked. *Lit.,* ticking sound.

Kani·meki *i'oa* Ganymede, a moon of Jupiter. *Eng.*

kāni·wala See *pāka kāniwala.*

kani 'ā *kik* Dial tone, on a telephone. *Lit.,* turned-on sound.

kani·'ā·'ī *kik* Larynx. *Dic.* Also *paipu hanu o luna.*

kā·nono *heh* To infiltrate, i.e. pass through by filtering or permeating, in science. *Comb. kā-* + *nono.*

kanu *kik/ham* Crop or planting, i.e. the number of plantings of a particular plant. *'Ekolu kanu laiki 'ana o kēia lo'i o ka makahiki.* This paddy produces three crops of rice per year. *Cf. meaulu.*

kā·nuku *kik* Funnel; hopper. *Dic.; dic., ext. mng. Ka'a kānuku.* Hopper car, as on a train.

kapa *kik* Blanket. *Dic.* Also *kapa moe. Kapa uila.* Electric blanket. *Kapa huluhulu.* Heavy or woolen blanket. Also *huluhulu. Kapa kuiki.* Quilt.

kā pā·ani·ani *ham* To knit. *Lit.,* knit yarn. See *pāaniani.*

kā·pae *Kaha kāpae.* A line used to indicate that something is to be deleted, in proofreading.

kapa·uli *kik* Ground cover. *Comb. kapa* + *uli.*

kā pahi *Haku kā pahi.* Paleolithic, in anthropology. *Ke au haku kā pahi.* Paleolithic age, period.

kapa kai See entry below. *Pū'ali pale kapa kai.* Coast guard.

Kapa Kai Palaoa *i'oa* Ivory Coast; Ivorian.

kā·pala *ham* To print, i.e. impress or stamp something in or on something else. *Dic.* See entry below. *Lau kāpala.* A print.

kā·pala *ham* To fingerprint, i.e. take the fingerprints of (someone). *Dic., ext. mng.* Also *kāpala i ka meheu manamana lima (māka manamana lima, ki'i manamana lima). Cf. 'ohi.*

kā·pala·pala *ham* To draft or draw up documents. *Kanaka kāpalapala.* A person who draws up documents.

kā·pana *kik* Syllable. *Sh. kālele* + *pana.*

Kapa·nui *i'oa* Dipha, a star. *Mān. (HA).*

Kapela *i'oa* Ankaa, a star. *Mān. (HA).*

kapi *kik* Cubby hole. *Eng.*

kā·piki meo·neki *kik* Cole slaw. *Lit.,* mayonnaise cabbage.

kā·piki ponī *kik* Skunk cabbage.

Kapiko·owā·kea *i'oa* Equator. *Ua 'a'e wale 'ia akula 'o Kapikoowākea e Hōkūle'a i kōna holo 'ana mai Hawai'i a Tahiti.* The equator was crossed by the Hōkūle'a as it sailed from Hawai'i to Tahiti. *Dic., sp. var.* Also *pō'ai waena honua.*

kā·pili *ham* To build, put together. *Dic. Kāpili kūkohu mokulele.* To build a model airplane. *Hana kāpili.* To manufacture. *Hui hana kāpili.* Manufacturer. Also *kanaka hana kāpili. 'Oihana kāpili.* Manufacturing industry. Also *'oi'enehana kāpili.*

kā·pi'o *Hale kāpi'o.* Lean-to shelter. *Dic.*

kā·pi'o·kaha *kik/ham* Construction; to construct, as in making a surveying figure with the use of only a compass and a straightedge, in geometry. *Comb. kā* + *pi'o* + *kaha.*

Kapona *i'oa* Gabon; Gabonese. *Eng.* Also *Gabona.*

kā·pō·'ai See *'ūpā kāpō'ai.*

Kapo'e *i'oa* Alpha Tuscanae, a star. *Mān. (HA).*

kapu *Kā'ei kapu.* Domain, as on the Internet.

kapu·ahi See entries below. *Pā kapuahi.* Burner, as on a stove.

kapu·ahi ula kahi *kik* Bunsen burner. *Lit.,* burner (with) single flame.

kapu·ahi ho‘o·pume·hana *kik* Fireplace. *Lit.,* stove (for) warming.

kapu·ahi Mika *kik* Meeker burner. Comb. *kapuahi* + Eng.

kapu·ahi papa·kau *kik* Hot plate. *Lit.,* counter stove. Cf. *pā kapuahi.*

kapu·ahi puka·puka *kik* Fisher burner. *Lit.,* burner (with) many holes.

kapu·a‘i *kik* Foot, a unit of measurement. *Dic.* Abb. *kp.*

kapu·a‘i kuea *kik* Square foot, lay term. Cf. *kapua‘i pāho‘onui lua.*

kapu·a‘i pā·ho‘o·nui lua *kik* Square foot, in math. Abb. *kp ph²* . Cf. *kapua‘i kuea.*

kapu·hau See *pāpale kapuhau.*

kā·puka *ham* To export. Comb. *kā-* + *puka.* See *kākomo.*

kā·puka ‘ai *kik/ham* Producer, i.e. an organism that can make its own food, such as green plants. *Lit.,* export food.

kapu·kino *kik* Cappuccino, i.e. espresso coffee and steamed milk. *Italian.*

kapu ‘au·‘au *kik* Bathtub. *Dic.* See *kililau.*

kā·wā *kik* Discrepancy. *‘Ehia ke kāwā o ke koho?* How much is the discrepancy of the estimate? *Dic., ext. mng.*

kā·wā *kik* Space, as in tab settings on a computer or typewriter. *Dic., ext. mng.* See *kāwāholo, ka‘ahua, koana.*

kā·wā ola *kik* Life span. *Lit.,* life's length of time.

kawa·ū *‘a* Damp or moist with fog or dew, wet from cold. *Dic.* See *kawaūea.*

kawa·ū·ea *kik* Humidity. Comb. *kawaū* + *ea. Pā kawaūea.* Relative humidity. *Ana kawaūea.* Hygrometer.

kā·wā·holo *kik* Tab, as on a computer or typewriter. Comb. *kāwā* + *holo.* See *ho‘okāwāholo, kāwā, kake. Pihi kāwāholo.* Tab key (preceded by *ke*).

kā·wawe *kik/ham* Any document which has been written using speed writing; to speed write. Comb. *kā-* + *wawe.* Cf. *heluwawe.*

kā·wele *ham* To dust or wipe with a cloth. *Dic.* Cf. *kāhilihili. Kāwele malo‘o.* To dust with a dry cloth. *Kāwele ma‘ū.* To dust with a damp cloth.

kā·wī *ham* To extract. *Dic., ext. mng.* See *kāwina.*

kawia See *‘iole kawia.*

kā·wina *kik* Extract. Comb. *kāwī* + *-na.* See *kāwī. Kāwina wanila.* Vanilla extract.

kawowo *kik* Sprout. *Dic., ext. mng.* See *hehu, kauwowo. Kawowo pāpapa.* Bean sprout. *Kawowo ‘alapapa.* Alfalfa sprout.

ka‘a *kik* Ground vehicle with wheels or runners. *Dic.* See entries below.

ka‘a·ahi kau lewa *kik* Elevated train, as the Japan monorail. *Lit.,* suspended train.

ka‘ao *kik* A traditional tale, especially one relating to a particular culture; folktale. *Dic.* Also *mo‘oka‘ao.* See entries below.

ka‘ao kele moana *kik* A traditional tale describing ocean travels, such as those of Kila, Mō‘īkeha, or Pā‘ao.

ka‘ao kupua *kik* A traditional tale whose primary character is a demigod, such as Kamapua‘a, Māui, Pele, or ‘Aukelenuia‘īkū. *Lit.,* demigod tale.

ka‘ao me‘e *kik* A traditional tale which describes the adventures of a particular character, such as Kawelo or Punia. *Lit.,* hero tale.

ka‘a hau *kik* Snowmobile.

ka‘a hali·hali *kik* Shuttle. *Lit.,* vehicle (for) transporting.

ka'ahi hewa *heh* Over the line, in volleyball. *Ni'ihau.* Also *ke'ehi hewa.*

ka'a holo one *kik* Dune buggy. *Lit.,* vehicle (for) traveling (on) sand.

ka'a holo mahina *kik* Lunar rover. *Lit.,* vehicle (for) traveling (on the) moon.

ka'a holo 'ā·pu'u·pu'u *kik* Any off-road vehicle, e.g., ATV, dirt bike, 4x4, etc. *Lit.,* vehicle (that) travels (on) rough (terrain). Also *ka'a 'āpu'u.* Cf. *mokohuilahā.*

ka'a·hope *'a* Elapsed, as of time. *Dic., ext. mng. Hola ka'ahope.* Elapsed time.

ka'a ho'o·moana *kik* Camper; camping vehicle. *Lit.,* camping car.

ka'a·hua *kik* Space, as between words when typing on a computer or typewriter. *Sh. ka'awale + hua'ōlelo.* Cf. *kāwā, koana. Kaha ka'ahua.* A pound sign (#) used to indicate·that a space should be inserted, in proofreading; a superscript number written next to the symbol indicates the number of spaces if more than one (#²). *Pihi ka'ahua.* Space bar (preceded by *ke*).

ka'a huki palau *kik* Tractor. *Lit.,* vehicle (for) pulling (a) plow. Also *ka'a palau.*

ka'a kau·paku pelu *kik* Convertible, i.e. a car with a top that can be lowered or removed. *Lit.,* car (with) folding roof. Also *ka'a kaupoku pelu, ka'a kaupuku pelu.*

ka'a·kā·lai *kik* Strategy or approach, as in solving a math problem. *E koho 'oe i ke ka'akālai kūpono no keia polopolema.* Choose the appropriate strategy for this problem. *Sh. ka'a kaua + kālaimana'o* (dic.).

ka'a·ka'a *'a* Open, as a frame in a computer program. *Dic., ext. mng.* Cf. *pa'a. Mōlina ka'aka'a.* Open frame.

ka'a·kepa *heh* To warp, as in Nintendo games (not as wood). *Dic., ext. mng.* See *pihi pīna'i, ho'opi'i ka'akepa. Kā'ei ka'akepa.* Warp zone.

ka'a·kepa *Mākala ka'akepa 'ūhā.* Sartorius muscle crossing the anterior portion of the upper leg.

ka'a·konelo *kik* Subway, the train. *Lit.,* tunnel vehicle. *Ala ka'akonelo.* Subway, the tunnel. *Kahua ka'akonelo.* Subway station.

ka'a·kuene *ham* To map, as a computer keyboard. *Comb. ka'a + kuene.* Cf. *'ōkuene. Ka'akuene papa pihi.* Keyboard mapping.

ka'a launa See *mea ka'a launa.*

ka'a·lehia *kik* Gymnastics; gymnast. *Lit.,* skilled twisting and turning.

ka'a·lilo *kik* Monopoly, i.e. exclusive possession or control of a commodity or service in a market. *Sh. ka'a + a + lilo. Pā'oihana ka'alilo.* A business or company which has a monopoly.

ka'a limo *kik* Limousine. *Comb. ka'a + Eng.*

ka'a lola *kik* Roller coaster. *Lit.,* roller vehicle.

ka'a mā·keke *kik* Shopping cart. *Lit.,* market cart.

kā·'ama·wāhi·wai *kik* Photolysis. *Comb. kā + 'ama + wāhi + wai.* Cf. *kā'ama'ai.*

kā·'ama·'ai *kik* Photosynthesis. *Comb. kā + 'ama + 'ai* (create edible light).

ka'a mio *kik* Sports car. *Lit.,* streamlined car.

ka'a·ne'e *ham* Play, as a particular maneuver in a sporting event; to execute a play. *Ua lapuwale kēlā ka'ane'e; ua lilo ho'i ke kinipōpō i kekahi 'ao'ao.* That was a pretty dumb play; they lost the ball to the other side. *Sh. ka'akālai + ne'e.*

ka'a pahu *kik* Pushcart.

ka'a·pahu *kik* Boxcar, as of train.

ka'a palau See *ka'a huki palau.*

ka‘a pa‘i ulele *kik/‘a‘* Side out, in volleyball. *Ka‘a koke ke pa‘i ulele iā lākou.* They are good at siding out. *Lit.,* transferred service. Also *ka‘a, hā‘awi i ke kinipōpō i kekahi ‘ao‘ao.*

ka‘a·pē·pē *kik* Baby carriage.

ka‘a·wale *Paikū ka‘awale.* Isolationism. *Paimana ka‘awale.* Federalism, i.e. the principle of division of power between the state and national governments. *Pūhui naikokene ka‘awale.* Free nitrogen compund.

kā·‘awe *kik* Strap. *Mān.* See *lole wāwae kā‘awe, pala‘ili kā‘awe, pale‘ili kā‘awe. Kā‘awe kalipa.* Slipper strap.

Ka‘ā·wela *i‘oa* Jupiter. *Dic.*

Ka‘a·wili *i‘oa* Mintaka, a star. *Mān. (HA).*

ka‘a·wili·wili See *makani ka‘awiliwili.*

ka‘a·‘au·huki *kik* Child's wagon. *Lit.,* wagon (with) handle (for) pulling.

ka‘a ‘ā·pu‘u See *ka‘a holo ‘āpu‘upu‘u.*

ka‘a·‘ike *kik* Communication. *‘A‘ohe ka‘a‘ike ma waena o ke kamepiula a me ka mīkini pa‘i.* There's no communication between the computer and the printer. *Lit.,* transferred knowledge. See *ho‘oka‘a‘ike, keleka‘a‘ike, leaka‘a‘ike. Ka‘a‘ike ha‘i waha.* Oral communication. Also *ka‘a‘ike waha. Ka‘a‘ike pāna‘i.* Intercommunication, two-way communication.

ka‘a·‘oko‘a *Ho‘ona‘auao ka‘a‘oko‘a.* Alternative education, as a school program.

ka‘e *kik* Edge, as of a three-dimensional geometric figure. *Dic., ext. mng.* See *ka‘e pololei.*

kā·‘ei *kik* Zone. *Dic.* See entries below and *ka‘akepa, pale kā‘ei. Kā‘ei hola.* Time zone, as Pacific or Rocky Mountain. *Kā‘ei māwae.* Rift zone. *Palapala kā‘ei meakanu.* Vegetation zonation sheet.

kā·‘ei alo *kik* Foreground, as in a photo, movie, or video scene. *Lit.,* front zone. Cf. *kā‘ei kua.*

kā·‘ei iki *kik* Subzone. *‘O kahi o ka ‘o‘ole‘a loa o ka mālama ‘ia, ‘o ia ke kā‘ei iki mālama.* The preservation subzone within the conservation district is the most restrictive. *Lit.,* small zone.

kā·‘ei hō·kū·na‘i *kik* Asteroid belt.

kā·‘ei kau lā *kik* Solar constant. *Lit.,* zone (where) sun shines.

kā·‘ei kapu *kik* Domain, as on the Internet. *Lit.,* forbidden zone.

kā·‘ei ki‘i kā·lai *kik* Frieze. *Lit.,* sash of carved images.

kā·‘ei kopi·kala *kik* The tropics. *Lit.,* tropical zone. See *kā‘ei ku‘ina kopikala.*

kā·‘ei kua *kik* Background, as in a photo, movie, or video scene, or on a computer screen. *E holo ana kekahi polokalamu ma ke kā‘ei kua.* The other program is running in the background. *Lit.,* back zone. Cf. *kā‘ei alo.*

kā·‘ei ku‘ina kopi·kala *kik* Intertropical convergent zone (ITCZ). *Lit.,* tropical junction zone. *Abb. KKK.*

kā·‘ei manehu uila *kik* Electrical force field. *Lit.,* electrical force zone.

kā·‘ei ‘ā·‘ī *kik* Scarf. *Lit.,* neck sash.

ka‘ele *‘a‘* Empty, as a bowl. *Dic.* Usu. *hakahaka.*

kā·‘ele *‘a‘* Bold, on a computer or in typesetting; boldface. *Dic., ext. mng.* See *ho‘okā‘ele.*

ka‘elo *kik* Ciguatera, i.e. poisoning caused by eating fish with accumulated toxic substance in its flesh. *‘O ke ka‘elo, he ‘ano ma‘i ia i hiki ke loa‘a ma ka ‘ai ‘ana i kekahi i‘a i loa‘a i kēia ‘ano ma‘i.* Ciguatera is a kind of sickness one can get by eating fish contaminated with this kind of sickness. (*Tah. ta‘ero.*)

ka‘e polo·lei *kik* Straightedge.

ka'i *kik/ham* Coach; to train (someone), as for sports. *Dic., ext. mng. Ka'i hana keaka.* Drama coach. *Ka'i ha'uki.* Sports trainer. *Ka'i pu'ukani.* Vocal coach. *Ka'i 'ālapa.* Coach for sports or physical education.

ka'i *kik* Onset of a syllable, in linguistics. *Lit.,* lead.

ka'i·lau *kik* Coefficient, in math. Comb. *ka'i + lau. Ka'ilau o ke X.* Coefficient of X.

kā·'ili *Mana kā'ili o ke aupuni.* Eminent domain, i.e. the right of the government to take, or to authorize taking, the private property of a citizen for public use with just compensation being given to the citizen whose property has been taken.

ka'ina *kik* Order, sequence. *Dic.* See entries below and *ha'i kake ka'ina, ho'oka'ina, kake ka'ina, pakuhi ka'ina.*

ka'ina hana *kik* Procedure, process to follow. *Lit.,* sequence (of) tasks.

ka'ina ho'i hope See *'anopili ka'ina ho'i hope.*

ka'ina ho'o·mā·kala·kala *kik* Order of operations, in math problems. *Lit.,* solving order.

ka'ina kā·nā·wai *Kū i ke ka'ina kānāwai.* Due process of law, i.e. the process by which the government must treat accused persons fairly according to rules established by law.

ka'ina pī·'ā·pā *kik* Alphabetical order. *Lit.,* alphabet order. See *ho'oka'ina pī'āpā.*

ka'ina wā·wae *kik* Steps, as in a dance or routine. *Lit.,* foot sequence. Cf. *ki'ina.*

ka'ina 'ē·ko·'a *kik* Vice versa. *Lit.,* opposite order. Also *ka'ina 'oko'a.*

ka'i wā·wae *kik/heh* Stride; to stride. *'Ehia 'īniha ka lō'ihi o kōna ka'i wāwae?* How many inches is the length of his stride? *Lit.,* step (by) foot.

ka'o·hau *'a* Freeze-dried. Comb. *ka'o + hau.* See *ho'oka'ohau.*

kā·'oki·kene *'a* To oxidize; oxidized. Comb. *kā + 'okikene.*

ka'oko *'a* Dormant. (Tah., *sleep.*)

kā·'oko'a *'a* Complete. *Dic., ext. mng.* See *ikehu kā'oko'a. Kumuloa'a kā'oko'a.* Gross national product (GNP), i.e. the total monetary value of all goods and services produced in a country in a year. *Mea ho'omomona lepo kā'oko'a.* Complete fertilizer, i.e. fertilizer which contains the six necessary elements for plant growth.

ka'u·ka'u *kik* Delay, as in computer program. *Nui ke ka'uka'u ma waena o ke kōmi 'ana i ke pihi a me ka hana.* There is a long delay between pressing the key and the action. *Dic., ext. mng.*

ka'ū·mana *Pua ka'ūmana.* Azalea.

Kada *i'oa* Chad; Chadian. *Eng.*

kara·bona·hate *kik* Carbonate. *Eng. Kupuriku karabonahate.* Cupric carbonate. *Ferousa karabonahate.* Ferrous carbonate.

kara·bona mono·kesa·side *kik* Carbon monoxide. *Eng.*

kara·bona dio·kesa·side *kik* Carbon dioxide. *Eng.* Also *kalapona 'okikene lua.*

kara·bona disuli·faside *kik* Carbon disulfide. *Eng.*

Kare·biana *i'oa* Caribbean. *Dic.* Also *Kalepiana.*

Karo·laina See *Kalolaina.*

Kasa·kana *i'oa* Kazakhstan. *Eng.*

Kase·piana *i'oa* Caspian. *Eng. Ke kai 'o Kasepiana.* Caspian Sea.

Kata·kila *i'oa* Catskills, a mountain range. *Eng.*

Katala *i'oa* Qatar. *Eng.*

kā·tuna *kik* Cartoon. *Eng.* Also *kākuna, kākuni. Puke kātuna.* Comic book.

kea See *kea ho'opukapuka.*

Keao·pō *i'oa* Alphekka, a star in the constellation Corona Borealis. *Mān. (HA).*

kea hoʻo·puka·puka *kik* Stock, as in the stock market. *Lit.,* stock (for) speculating. Also *kea.*

keaka·ika·ʻā·wai *kik* Jack-in-the-pulpit, a kind of flower.

keaka·pahu *kik* Jack-in-the-box. *Lit.,* jack box.

keiki lawe·hala *kik* Juvenile delinquent. *Lit.,* delinquent child. Cf. *lawehala ʻōpiopio.*

Kei·moka *iʻoa* Deimos, a moon of Mars. *Eng.*

Keo·kia *iʻoa* Georgia; Georgian. *Dic.*

Keola *kik* Name of Hawaiian language version of Bingo.

keu *ʻa* Extended, as of computer memory; enhanced or expanded, as a computer keyboard. *ʻOi aku ka nui o nā pihi ma ka papa pihi keu.* There are more keys on the expanded keyboard. *Dic., ext. mng.* Cf. *māhuahua. Waihona ʻike keu.* Extended memory. *Papa pihi keu.* Enhanced keyboard, expanded keyboard.

keu See *ʻai keu. Pono keu.* Fringe benefit, i.e. any employee benefit other than salary, such as medical insurance, etc.

kē·uli *kik* Blue jay. *Usu. manu kēuli.* Comb. *Eng. + uli.*

keu pono *kik* Advantage. *Ua ahuwale ke keu pono o Kuʻulei ma mua o Kuʻuhoni.* The advantage of Kuʻulei over Kuʻuhoni was obvious. *Lit.,* extra benefit.

Kehoʻo·ea *iʻoa* Lyra, a constellation. *Dic.*

kek Abbreviation for *kekamika* (decameter).

Kek. Abbreviation for *Kekemapa* (December). See *Dekemapa.*

keka- Deca-, i.e. a prefix meaning ten. *Eng.* Also *pāʻumi.* See entries below.

keka *kik* Cheddar. *Eng.* See entry below. *Waiūpaʻa keka.* Cheddar cheese.

keka *Hoʻokae keka.* Sexism. See *hoʻokae.*

keka·kalame *kik* Decagram. *Eng.* Abb. *kekal.*

kekal Abbreviation for *kekakalame* (decagram).

keka·lika *kik* Decaliter. *Eng.* Abb. *kel.*

keka·mika *kik* Decameter. *Eng.* Abb. *kek.*

Kekeka *iʻoa* Texas; Texan. *Dic.* Also *Tekasa, Teseta.*

kekeke *kik* Decade. *Eng.*

kē·kelē Degree. *Dic., sp. var. Kēkelē laeoʻo.* Master's degree. Also *palapala laeoʻo. Kēkelē laepua.* Bachelor's degree. Also *palapala laepua. Kēkelē laeʻula.* Doctorate degree. Also *palapala laeʻula.*

kē·kelē *kik* Degree, as referring to temperature. *Dic., sp. var.* See entries below. *He ʻumi kēkelē Kelekia.* Ten degrees Celsius. *ʻElima kēkelē Palanaheika.* Five degrees Fahrenheit. *ʻEhia kēkelē Ph ke anu [ka mahana, ka mehana, ka wela] o ka Poʻahā?* How many degrees Fahrenheit was the temperature on Thursday?

kē·kelē heheʻe *kik* Melting point. *Lit.,* degree (for) melting.

kē·kelē paila *kik* Boiling point. *Lit.,* degree (for) boiling.

kē·kelē paʻa·hau *kik* Freezing point. *Lit.,* degree (for) freezing.

Keke·mapa *iʻoa* December. *Dic., sp. var.* Abb. *Kek.* Also *Dekemapa.*

keki- Deci-, i.e. a prefix meaning one tenth. *Eng.* Also *hapa ʻumi.* See entries below.

keki·kalame *kik* Decigram. *Eng.* Abb. *kkkal.*

keki·lika *kik* Deciliter. *Eng.* Abb. *kkl.*

keki·mala *kik* Decimal. *Dic. Kiko kekimala.* Decimal point. *Kekimala pani.* Terminating decimal. *Kekimala pīna'i.* Repeating decimal. *Kekimala 'ō'ā.* Mixed decimal. *Kuana kekimala.* Decimal place. *'Ōnaehana kekimala.* Decimal system.

keki·mika *kik* Decimeter. *Eng. Abb. kkm.*

keko See entries below and *palaoa keko.*

keko·hala *kik/ham* Sexual harassment; to subject to sexual harassment. *Japn.*

Keko·kia *i'oa* Scotland; Scot, Scots, Scottish. *Dic.* Also *Sekotia.*

keko lekuka *kik* Rhesus monkey. Comb. *keko* + Eng.

kekona *kik* Second. *Dic. Abb. kkn.*

keko pueo *kik* Owl monkey.

kel Abbreviation for *kekalika* (decaliter).

Kela·uea *i'oa* Delaware; Delawarean. *Dic., sp. var.* Also *Delauea.*

kelaka See *manu kelaka.*

kela·lani *kik* Astronaut. *Lit.,* sky sailor.

kela·wini *kik* Gale. *Dic.* Also *makani kelawini.*

kele *heh* To "surf," as the Internet. *Dic., ext. mng. Cf. māka'ika'i.*

kele ama kā·moe *heh* Beam reach on the port side, i.e. sailing at a 90° angle from the direction of the wind, with the port side windward. *Lit.,* sail straight port. Cf. *kele 'ākea kāmoe.*

kele ama ka'a·kepa *heh* Broad reach on the port side, i.e. sailing downwind at an angle between 90° and directly downwind, with the port side windward. *Lit.,* sail diagonal port. Cf. *kele 'ākea ka'akepa.*

kele ama kū·nihi *heh* Close hauled on the port side, i.e. sailing into the wind at the closest angle possible, generally 67°, with the port side windward. *Lit.,* sail sideways port. Cf. *kele 'ākea kūnihi.*

kele·awe *kik* Brass. *Dic. Cf. kele-awekini, keleawe'ula.*

kele·awe·kini *kik* Bronze. *Lit.,* tin brass. *Ke au keleawekini.* Bronze age, period. See *au.*

kele·awe·'ula *kik* Copper. Comb. *keleawe* + *'ula. Haku keleawe'ula.* Aeneolithic, in anthropology. *Ke au haku keleawe'ula.* Aeneolithinic age, period.

kele ho'o·pahe'e *kik* Vaseline, petrolatum. *Lit.,* lubricating jelly.

kele ka'a·lalo *heh* To sail directly downwind. *Lit.,* sail (to) leeward.

kele·ka'a·'ike *kik* Telecommunication. Comb. *kele-* [Eng.] + *ka'a'ike.*

Keleke *i'oa* Crete; Cretan. *Dic.* Also *Kerete.*

Kele·kia *kik* Celsius. *Eng. Abb. Klk.* See *kēkelē.*

kele·kona *kik* Dragon, as in fairy tales. *Dic.* Also *kalekona.* See entry below.

kele·kona *kik* Skeleton, as for Halloween. *Eng.* Also *kanaka iwi. Cf. kinanahiwi.*

keleku *kik* Circus. *Eng.*

Kele·mā·nia *i'oa* Germany; German. *Dic.*

kele moana *heh* Wayfinding; to wayfind. *Lit.,* sail (the) ocean. Also *ho'okele wa'a.* See *ka'ao kele moana.*

kelena moku ahi·kao *kik* Space capsule. Comb. *kele* + *-na* + *moku ahikao.*

kele pahē *kik* Jam. *Lit.,* jelly (with) pulp.

kele·pa'i *ham* To fax. Sh. *kelepona* + *pa'i. Mīkini kelepa'i.* Fax machine.

kele·pona See entries below and *'apo kelepona.*

kele·pona inoa *kik/ham* Person-to-person call; to make such a call. *Lit.,* phone (to) name. Cf. *kelepona kahua.*

kele·pona kahua *kik/ham*
Station-to-station call; to make such a
call. *Lit.*, phone (to) site. Cf. *kelepona
inoa*.

kele·pona kāki iā haʻi *kik/ham*
Third-party call; to make such a call.
Lit., phone (by) charging someone else.

kele·pona kāki hiki *kik/ham* Collect
call; to make such a call. *Lit.*, phone (by)
charging (on) arrival.

kele·pona kū·loko *kik/ham* Local
call; to make such a call. *Lit.*, phone
internally.

kele·pona kū·waho *kik/ham*
Long-distance call; to make such a call.
Lit., phone externally.

kele·pona pili·ʻāina *kik/ham*
Interisland call; to make such a call. *Lit.*,
phone interisland.

kele·pona ʻāina ʻē *kik/ham*
International call; to make such a call.
Lit., phone internationally.

kele·wī *kik* Abbreviation for *kelewikiona* (television). *Dic.* Also *kīwī*.

kele·wiki·ona *kik* Television. *Dic.*
Abb. *kelewī, kīwī*.

Kele·wine *iʻoa* Kelvin. *Eng.* ʻOle
Kelewine. Zero degrees K (Kelvin);
absolute zero, i.e. a hypothetical
temperature characterized by complete
absence of heat.

kele ʻā·kea kā·moe *heh* Beam reach
on the starboard side, i.e. sailing at a 90°
angle from the direction of the wind,
with the starboard side windward. *Lit.*,
sail straight starboard. Cf. *kele ama
kāmoe*.

kele ʻā·kea kaʻa·kepa *heh* Broad
reach on the starboard side, i.e. sailing
downwind at an angle between 90° and
directly downwind, with the starboard
side windward. *Lit.*, sail diagonal
starboard. Cf. *kele ama kaʻakepa*.

kele ʻā·kea kū·nihi *heh* Close
hauled on the starboard side, i.e. sailing
into the wind at the closest angle possible,
generally 67°, with the starboard side
windward. *Lit.*, sail sideways starboard.
Cf. *kele ama kūnihi*.

keli *kik* Cherry. *Eng.*

kē·lia *kik* Terrier. (Latin *terrarius*.)
Also *ʻīlio kēlia*.

keluka *kik* Thrush. *Dic.* Also *manu
keluka*. *Manu keluka ululāʻau*. Wood
thrush.

kelu·lose *kik* Cellulose. *Eng.*

keme·pale *ʻaʻ* Temperate, in science.
Eng. Cf. *kopikala*. *Nahele kemepale*.
Temperate forest.

kemika *kik* Chemistry. *Eng.* *Kemika
meaola*. Biochemistry.

kemi·kala Chemical. *Eng.* See
kāemikala. *Ikehu kemikala*. Chemical
energy. *Haʻihelu kemikala*. Chemical
equation. *Haʻihelu kemikala kaulike*.
Balanced chemical equation. *Haʻilula
kemikala*. Chemical formula. *Helu
hoʻonui kemikala*. Coefficient. *Loli
kemikala*. Chemical change. *Māʻōʻāna
kemikala*. Chemical solution. *Mōʻaui
kemikala*. Chemical activity. *ʻAnopili
kemikala*. Chemical property (preceded
by *ke*). *ʻŌʻā kemikala ʻia*. Chemically
combined.

kemo·kalaka *Lepupalika
Kemokalaka ʻo Konokō*. Democratic
Republic of the Congo.

kemu *ham* To consume, i.e. to use a
commodity or service. *ʻO ka poʻe kauka
ka poʻe kemu nui i nā pono lapaʻau*.
Doctors are the major consumers of
medical supplies. *Dic., ext. mng.* *Mea
kemu*. Consumer, i.e. a person who uses
a commodity or service.

kēmu *kik* Board game, as checkers.
Eng. *Papa kēmu*. Game board.

kemua ʻaʻ To be assimilated. *Ua kemua maoli ka poʻe komoneʻe o nā ʻāina ʻEulopa i ka noho ʻana o kō ʻAmelika ma hope o ke komoneʻe ʻana i ʻAmelika.* European immigrants assimilated well into the lifestyle of Americans after immigrating to America. Comb. *kemu + -a.* See *hoʻokemua.*

kē·nā kahi *Aupuni mana kēnā kahi.* Dictatorship.

kena·kena ʻaʻ To experience a suffocating sensation. *Dic., ext. mng.*

kē·neka *kik* Cent. *Dic. Kaha kēneka.* Cent sign.

Kene·kī *iʻoa* Tennessee; Tennessean. *Dic.* Also *Tenesī.*

Kene·kuke *iʻoa* Kentucky; Kentuckian. *Dic.* Also *Kenetuke.*

Kenele *Ka pae moku ʻo Kenele.* Canary Isles.

Kene·maka *iʻoa* Denmark; Dane; Danish. *Dic.* Also *Denemaka.*

Kene·tuke *iʻoa* Kentucky; Kentuckian. *Dic.* Also *Kenekuke.*

keni- Centi-, i.e. a prefix meaning one hundredth. *Eng.* Also *hapa haneli.* See entries below.

Kenia *iʻoa* Kenya; Kenyan. *Eng.*

keni·kalame *kik* Centigram. *Eng.* Abb. *kkal.*

kenika manu *kik* Badminton. *Lit.,* bird tennis.

kenika pā·kau·kau *kik* Ping-pong, table tennis.

keni·keni *kik* Dime, loose change. *Dic.* Cf. *kālā heleleʻi.*

keni·lika *kik* Centiliter. *Eng.* Abb. *kl.*

keni·mika *kik* Centimeter. *Eng.* Abb. *knm.*

Kep. Abbreviation for *Kepakemapa* (September).

kepa *kik/ham* Spur; to spur; to gore with a tusk. Var. of *kēpā.* See *palaka kepa. Niho kepa.* Boar's tusk.

kepa *ham* To contract labor. *Dic.*

kē·pau *kik* Lead; leaden. *Dic.*

kē·pau kā *kik* Asphalt compound, i.e. a brown or black tar-like substance, a variety of distilled tar (bitumen) found in a natural state or obtained by evaporating petroleum; pitch. *Lit.,* tar pitch. See *kā.*

Kepa·kemapa *iʻoa* September. *Dic.* Abb. *Kep.*

Kepa·nia *iʻoa* Spain. *Dic.* Also *Sepania.*

kepela *kik* Zebrina, a kind of flower. Usu. *pua kepela. Lit.,* zebra.

kepila See *ʻiole kepila.*

kē·puka *kik/ham* Trick, prank; to play such tricks, usually with malicious intent. *Dic., ext. mng.* Cf. *nalea, pāhaʻohuna.*

kewe ʻaʻ Wraparound, as a window or eyeglasses. *Dic., ext. mng. Pukaaniani kewe.* Wraparound window.

kewe kopa·lā *kik* Steam shovel. *Lit.,* crane shovel.

keʻa·haka *Mākala keʻahaka.* Rectus abdominus muscle of the anterior torso.

keʻehi hewa *heh* Over the line, in volleyball. *Niʻihau.* Also *kaʻahi hewa.*

keʻe·lelena *kik* Trampoline. Sh. *keʻehi + lele + -na.*

keʻena *kik* Chamber, i.e. a generalized term for any of the chambers of the heart. *Dic., ext. mng.* See *pona puʻuwai, ʻōpū puʻuwai.*

keʻena *kik* Department, office. *Dic., ext. mng.* Also *ʻoihana.* Cf. *māhele.* See entries below. *Leka kūloko keʻena.* Office mail.

keʻena hana kiʻi·ʻoni·ʻoni *kik* Movie studio, i.e. the company responsible for making movies. *Lit.,* studio (for) making movies. Cf. *hale hana kiʻiʻoniʻoni. Kumu keʻena hana kiʻiʻoniʻoni.* Studio teacher.

keʻena hoʻo·kolo·hua *kik* Laboratory. *Lit.,* room (for) experiments.

Keʻena Hoʻo·lā·lā o ke Kalana *kik* County Planning Department.

Ke'ena Ho'o·noho·noho Ha'a·wina *kik* Office of Instructional Services (OIS). *Lit.*, office (for) organizing lessons.

ke'ena kili·lau *kik* Shower stall. See *kililau*.

Ke'ena Kule·ana Hawai'i *kik* Office of Hawaiian Affairs (OHA). *Na ke Ke'ena Kuleana Hawai'i i ho'olako ke kālā no ka papahana.* The Office of Hawaiian Affairs financed the project. *Lit.*, office (of) Hawaiian rights.

ke'ena mā·lama pō·ulia *kik* Emergency facility, emergency room. *Lit.*, room (to) take care of emergencies.

ke'ena pū·lumi *kik* Broom closet.

ke·o·ke'o *Kope ke'oke'o.* Café au lait, i.e. hot coffee served with an equal amount of hot or scalded milk. *Palaoa ke'oke'o.* White bread. See entries under *palaoa. Papa ke'oke'o.* White board, dry erase board. Also *papa peni kuni.*

Kerete *i'oa* Crete; Cretan. *Dic.* Also *Keleke.*

kesa·'ō *kik* Tic-tac-toe. Comb. *kesa + 'ō (XO).*

kī See entries below and *puna kī.*

kī *kik/ham* Shot; to shoot, as in basketball. *Dic., ext. mng.* See entries below and *komohia, kuhō, pākī.*

kī *kik/ham* Key, in music; peg, as for tuning stringed instruments; to tune, as a stringed instrument. *Dic.; Ni'ihau.* See *hua mele, ki'eleo.*

kī *ham* To tune up, as an engine. *Ua kī 'o ia i ka 'enekini o kōna ka'a.* He tuned up his car's engine. *Dic., ext. mng.*

kia *kik* Gear, as in machinery. *Eng.* See *kia pihi.*

kia·hai *kik* Trophy. *Sh. kia + 'āhai. Cf. pāhai.*

kia·ho'o·mana'o *kik* Monument. *Dic.* See *Kūkā'oko'a Kiaho'omana'o. Pāka kiaho'omana'o aupuni.* National monument, a park administered by the government.

kiaka *kik* Teak, a kind of wood. *Eng.*

kia lō *kik* Roe deer. Comb. *kia + Eng.*

Kiana *i'oa* Guiana. *Eng. Kiana Palani.* French Guiana.

kia pihi *ham* Remote control; to control by remote control. *Lit.*, button steering. See *lima kia pihi.*

kia'i *kik* Security guard. Also *kia'i pō; māka'i kia'i (pō). Ni'ihau.*

kielo *kik* Jello. *Eng.*

kio *Ho'okūkū kio.* Scrimmage, as for sports. See *ho'okūkū kahului, ho'okūkū moho.*

kioia See *pānini kioia.*

kiola *ham* To throw underhand. *Dic., ext. mng. Cf. nou.*

Kione *i'oa* Dione, a moon of Saturn. *Eng.*

kiu *kik* Cue, as in the game of pool. *Eng. Kiu pahupahu.* Pool cue.

kiule hoa kupa *kik* Jury of peers, as in court trials. *He kuleana kō ka mea i ho'āhewa 'ia e ho'okolokolo 'ia e ke kiule o nā hoa kupa.* The accused has the right to be judged by a jury of his peers. *Lit.*, jury (of) fellow citizens.

kiu·lela *kik* Squirrel. *Dic. Kiulela 'Ālika.* Arctic ground squirrel. *Kiulela 'akuiki.* Chipmonk. Also *'akuiki.*

kiuna *kik* Oriental-style scroll, usually decorative. (Cantonese *gyun.*)

kiupe *kik* Tube. *Eng.*

kiupe ho'o·lohe *kik* Stethoscope. *Lit.*, tube (for) listening. Also *'ili ho'olohe pu'uwai.*

kī hala·hī *ham* Air ball, missed shot, in basketball; to make such a shot. *He kī halahī wale nō kāna.* He made a bad shot. *Lit.*, shot (that) passes. Also *kī halahū.*

kī hala·hū *ham* Air ball, missed shot, in basketball; to make such a shot. *Lit.*, shot (that) misses. Also *kī halahī.*

kīhei *kik* Light blanket, shawl. *Dic.* Also *kīhei pili.*

kihi *kik* Corner, particularly an outside corner. *Dic.* Cf. *kū'ono, po'opo'o.*

kihi·kihi *kik* Brim, of a hat. *Mān.* (MW). Also *pekekeu.* Cf. *laulau.*

kihi·'aki *kik* Vertex, in math. *Legendre.*

kī·hoe *kik* Nomad. *'A'ohe noho pa'a ka po'e kīhoe ma kahi ho'okahi no ka wā lō'ihi, no ka mea, pono lākou e huli mau i kahi kūpono e lako ai ka noho 'ana.* Nomads do not stay very long in one place since they must constantly search for places with enough to sustain themselves. *Dic., ext. mng.*

kī·kā *kik* Guitar; cigar. *Dic.* For guitar parts, see *'ukulele.* See also *'ukulele pahu kīkā.*

kika·kī See *manu kikakī.*

kī·kala *Hānai kīkala.* To make a back set, in volleyball. Also *hānai i hope.*

kī·kē·kē *'Elelū kīkēkē.* American cockroach (Periplaneta americana).

kī·kē·koa *kik* Maui parrotbill (pseudonestor xanthophrys). Comb. *kīkē + koa.*

kikī See *puka kikī hou.*

kī·kī *ham* To spray. *Dic., ext. mng.* Cf. *kīkina.*

kikihi *kik* Doorframe. *Dic.*

kikiki *ham* To cheat. *Dic.*

kī kī·ko'o *ham* Lay-up, in basketball; to make such a shot. Lit., extending shot. Also *kī pai.*

kī·kina *kik* Substance, as sprayed from an aerosal can. Comb. *kīkī + -na.* See *ehu kīkina, pena kīkina. Kīkina ho'ohinuhinu.* Spray wax.

kiki'u·wai *kik* Xylem. Redup. of *ki'u* [rootlet] + *wai.* Cf. *kiki'u'ai.*

kiki'u·'ai *kik* Phloem. Redup. of *ki'u* [rootlet] + *'ai.* Cf. *kiki'uwai.*

kiko *kik* Point, in math. *Dic., ext. mng.* See entries below. *Kiko kekimala.* Decimal point. *Pepa kiko analike.* Isometric dot paper.

kiko *kik* Point, a unit of measurement for type size. *He 'umikūmālua ka nui ma'amau o kēlā kinona hua.* Twelve point is the standard size for that font. *Dic., ext. mng.* No abbreviation.

kiko ō·la·'i *kik* Epicenter. *Lit.,* earthquake point.

kiko·ho'e *kik* Digit, in math. *'Ehia kikoho'e o ka helu 327? 'Ekolu ōna kikoho'e.* How many digits are in the number 327? It has three digits. Comb. *kiko + ho'e* (Tah., one). *Kikoho'e hapa mua.* Front-end digit.

kiko ho'o·maha *kik* Comma. *Dic.* Also *kiko koma.*

kiko huina *kik* Dot on a grid. *Lit.,* point (on a) junction. Cf. *huina ke'a.*

kiko kau *kik* Focus point. *Lit.,* placed dot.

kiko kau·waena *kik* Midpoint, in math. *Lit.,* centered point.

kiko·kiko *ham* To type. *Dic.* Also *pa'i hakahaka.* See *pakuhi kikokiko.*

kiko·kikona *kik* Text of a document, as in a computer program. Comb. *kikokiko + -na. Kikokikona kīpuni.* Text wrap, as in a word-processing document.

kiko kolu *kik* Ellipsis, in punctuation. *Lit.,* three punctuation marks.

kiko koma *kik* Comma. *Dic., new mng.* Also *kiko ho'omaha.*

kiko kuhia *kik* Reference point, in math; reference object, as in science. *Lit.,* referent point. See *kuhia.*

kiko lā *kik* Sunspot. Cf. *lapa ahi lā, puapua'i lā, 'ale ahi lā.*

kī·kolu *Hoaka kīkolu.* Three-point arc, in basketball.

kiko nī·nau *kik* Question mark. *Dic.*

kiko pau *kik* Period, in punctuation. *Lit.,* ending punctuation mark.

kiko pū·'iwa *kik* Exclamation point. *Dic.*

kiko·wā *'a'* Synchronic, in linguistics. *Comb. kiko + wā.* Cf. *kōāwā. Lula kikowā.* Synchronic rule.

kiko·waena *kik* Center of a circle. *Dic.* See entries below and *huina kikowaena.*

kiko·waena kahi *kik* Concentric. *Lit.,* one center. *Nā pō'ai kikowaena kahi.* Concentric circles.

kiko·waena kilo ani·lā *kik* Weather station. *Lit.,* center (for) forecasting weather.

kiko·waena kū·'ai *kik* Shopping center, mall.

kiko·waena pā·nā·nā *kik* Field station, as used when mapping a certain area. *Lit.,* compass center.

kiko·waena pū·nae·wele *kik* Network server, as for a computer network. *Lit.,* network central.

kiko·waena wili *kik* Turn center, in math.

kiko·'ī *'a'* Specific. *Sh. ke kiko o ka 'ī. Mea kiko'ī, mea li'ili'i kiko'ī, mea li'ili'i.* Detail.

kī·ko'o *ham* To draw or withdraw money from the bank. *Dic.* See *kī kīko'o, pila kīko'o, waihona kālā. Waihona kīko'o.* Checking account, as a in bank.

kī·ko'o ipu·leo *ham* To operate a boom, as for movie or video production. *Lit.,* extend microphone. *Mea kīko'o ipuleo.* Boom operator.

kī·ko'u *ham* Cultivator; to cultivate. *Dic., ext. mng. Kīko'u pa'a lima.* Hand cultivator.

kī kū *ham* Set shot, in basketball; to make such a shot. *Holo akula 'o ia, a laila, kū ihola a kī kū 'o ia.* He ran and then stopped, and made a set shot. *Lit.,* standing shot.

kila *kik* Chisel. *Ni'ihau/dic.*

kila·okolo·mona *kik* Seal-of-Solomon, a kind of flower. *Eng.*

kī·lau·ea See *lua kīlauea. Pāka Aupuni 'o Kīlauea.* Hawai'i Volcanoes National Park.

kila pao *kik* Chisel. *Dic.*

kile *kik* Tile. *Eng. Kile lāmeka.* Ceramic tile. *Kile papahele.* Floor tile. Also *kile 'ili, moena 'ili 'āpanapana.* See *moena 'ili.*

Kile *i'oa* Chile; Chilean. *Dic.* Also *Kili.*

kī·leo See *palaku kīleo.*

kī lele *ham* Jump shot, in basketball; to make such a shot. *'Eleu wale nō 'o Muggsy Bogues ma ke kī lele.* Muggsy Bogues is a great jump shooter.

kī·lepa·lepa *kik* Pompom. *Dic., ext. mng.* Also *pōpō kīlepalepa.*

kili *kik* Chili. *Eng.*

Kili *i'oa* Chile; Chilean. *Dic.* Also *Kile.*

kili·ala *kik* Cereal. *Eng.* Also *siriala.*

kili·ona See *hapa kiliona.*

kī·like·like *kik* Assimilation, in linguistics. *Comb. kī + redup. of like.*

kiliki o lapu Trick or treat. *Lit.,* treat or else (be) haunted.

kili·lau *kik* Shower, for bathing. *Lit.,* many raindrops. *Kililau lima.* Hand-held shower. See *ke'ena kililau, pale kililau, pāpale kililau, po'o kililau, 'au'au kililau.*

kilina *kik* Ceiling. *Dic.* Also *huna.*

Kili·paki *i'oa* Kiribati. *Dic. Ka Lepupalika 'o Kilipaki.* Republic of Kiribati.

kilo- Kilo-, i.e. a prefix meaning thousand. *Eng.* Also *pākaukani.* See entries below.

kilo *kik* Kilo. *Dic. Abb. kl.*

kilo *ham* To study (i.e. examine, observe) something. *Dic., ext. mng.* Cf. *huli, kālai-.*

kī·loi *ham* To empty trash, as in a computer program. *Dic., sp. var., ext. mng.*

kī·loi *ham* To pass, in basketball. *E maka'ala mau i ke kanaka hemo e kīloi ai i ke kinipōpō.* Always keep an eye out for the open man to pass the ball to. *Dic., ext. mng.* See entries below.

kī·loi ulele *ham* Inbound pass, in basketball; to throw such a pass. *Kīloi ulele akula 'o Shawn Kemp iā Gary Payton ma lalo o ka hīna'i, a komo ihola ka 'ai lua.* Shawn Kemp made an inbound pass to Gary Payton under the basket, and he made it in for two. *Lit., pass into action.*

kī·loi ulele kikī *ham* Lead pass, in basketball; to throw such a pass. *He kīloi ulele kikī ke kīloi 'ana i ke kinipōpō i mua o ka hoa kime e holo ala i ka hīna'i.* A lead pass is when the ball is passed ahead of a teammate as he makes a run for the basket. *Lit., swift inbound pass. Also kīloi kaha. Cf. ulele kikī.*

kī·loi umauma *ham* Chest pass, in basketball; to throw such a pass. *Inā makemake 'oe e kīloi 'āwīwī i ke kinipōpō, e kīloi umauma 'oe.* If you want to make a quick pass, you make it a chest pass.

kī·loi ho'o·palai *ham* Blind pass, no-look pass, in basketball; to throw such a pass. *He kīloi ma'alea ke kīloi ho'opalai.* The blind pass is meant to be sneaky. *Lit., pass (with) face turned away.*

kī·loi kaha *ham* Lead pass, in basketball; to throw such a pass. *Lit., drive pass. Also kīloi ulele kikī.*

kī·loi kua *ham* Behind-the-back pass, in basketball; to throw such a pass. *Inā ke hiki mai nei ke kūpale mai mua mai ou, e kīloi kua i kou hoa kime ma ka 'ao'ao ou.* If the defender is coming at you from ahead, you can make a behind-the-back pass to your teammate on the side of you. *Lit., back pass.*

kī·loi palemo *ham* Back-door pass, in basketball; to throw such a pass. *He ka'ane'e kūlele 'e'epa maika'i ke kīloi palemo e lanakila ai.* The back-door pass is a clever offensive play for scoring. *Lit., slip-away pass.*

kī·loi papa·hele *ham* Bounce pass, in basketball; to throw such a pass. *Kīloi papahele 'o Moano ma waena o nā wāwae o Kahu a hiki iā Pono.* Moano made a bounce pass between the legs of Kahu and over to Pono. *Lit., floor pass.*

kī·loi papa'i *ham* Tip pass, in basketball; to throw such a pass. *Kīko'o akula 'o Kā'eo i kona lima e kīloi papa'i i ke kinipōpō iā Lā'au.* Kā'eo reached out his hand to tip pass the ball to Lā'au. *Lit., slapping pass. Cf. kī papa'i.*

kī·loi pa'ewa *ham* To throw away (the ball), in basketball. *Eo ihola mākou iā Leilehua ma muli o ke kīloi pa'ewa 'ana o Nānuha i ke kinipōpō i waho.* We lost the game to Leilehua because Nānuha threw the ball away. *Lit., throw wrong.*

kī·loi pi'o *ham* Lob pass, in basketball; to throw such a pass. *He ki'eki'e ke kīloi pi'o i 'ole e 'apo 'ia ke kinipōpō e ka hoa paio.* A lob pass is high so that the ball doesn't get caught by the opponents. *Lit., arched pass. Cf. kī pi'o.*

kī·loi 'ao·'ao *ham* Hook pass, in basketball; to throw such a pass. *'O ke kīloi 'ao'ao wale akula nō ia o ka helu 4 ma luna o ka mea e kaupale ana iā ia.* Number 4 made a hook pass right over the one who was defending him. *Lit., side pass.*

kilo·uate *kik* Kilowatt. *Eng. Abb. klt.* See *uate.*

kilo·kalame *kik* Kilogram. *Eng. Abb. klkal.*

kilo lani *Ana kilo lani.* Sextant.

kilo·lika *kik* Kiloliter. *Eng. Abb. kll.*

kilo·mika *kik* Kilometer. *Eng. Abb. klm.*

kima·lola *kik* Steamroller. *Dic.* See *lola*.

kimeki iwi *kik* Cast, as for a broken arm. Comb. Niʻihau + *iwi.* Also *puna.*

kimo *kik* Jacks, the game. *Dic.* See *hōkūkimo.*

kimu *kik* Precipitation. Samoan *timu* (rain).

Kina *iʻoa* China; Chinese. *Dic.* See *Pākē, ʻĀina Pākē. Ke kai ʻo Kina Hema.* South China Sea. *Ke kai ʻo Kina Hikina.* East China Sea.

kina·mona *kik* Cinnamon. *Dic.*

kinamu *kik* Gingham. *Dic.*

kinana·hiwi *kik* Skeleton. Comb. *tinana* (Maori, body) + *hiwi.* Cf. *kanaka iwi, kelekona.*

Kī·naʻu *iʻoa* Avior, a star. *Mān.* (HA).

kini See entries below. *Une kini.* Tab, as on soda cans. *Une kini koloaka.* Soda can tab.

Kini *iʻoa* Guinea. *Eng.* See *Kini ʻEkuakolia, Kinibisau.*

kini ea luʻu kai *kik* Scuba tank. Usu. *kini ea. Lit.,* air can (for) diving (in the) sea. Cf. *luʻu kini ea.*

kini iʻa *kik* Canned fish.

kini hoʻo·pio ahi *kik* Fire extinguisher. Also *kini kinai ahi.*

kini hoʻo·pulu mea·kanu *kik* Watering can.

kini hue·wai *kik* Canteen. *Lit.,* water gourd can.

kinika *kik* Sink, as in a bathroom or kitchen. *Eng.*

kini kā·lā *kik* Cashbox. *Lit.,* money can. Cf. *kālā kini.*

kiniki *kik* Zinc. *Eng.*

kini kī·kī *kik* Aerosol can. *Lit.,* can (which) sprays.

kini·kila See *lāpaki kinikila.*

kini kinai ahi *kik* Fire extinguisher. Also *kini hoʻopio ahi.*

kini·kona *kik* Quinine. *Eng. (from cinchona, the tree from which quinine is made).*

kini lapa·ʻau *kik* First aid kit. *Lit.,* medical can. Also *poho lāʻau pōulia.*

kini·pai *kik* Pot pie. Comb. *kini + pai.*

kini paipu ahi *kik* Muffler, as on a car. *Niʻihau.* Cf. *paipu ahi.*

kini pipi *kik* Can of corned beef; canned corned beef. *Mān.* Cf. *pipi kini.*

kini poho ea *kik* Repair kit, for tires. *Niʻihau.*

kini·pō·pō *kik* Ball. *Dic.* See entries below.

kini·pō·pō aloha *kik* Aloha ball, in volleyball. *Niʻihau.*

kini·pō·pō hele wale *kik* Kill, in volleyball. *Niʻihau.*

kini·pō·pō pō·hili *kik* Baseball, the ball. See *pōhili.*

kini·pō·pō pō·hī·naʻi *kik* Basketball, the ball. See *pōhīnaʻi.*

kini·pō·pō pō·peku *kik* Football, the ball. See *pōpeku.*

kini·pō·pō pō·wā·wae *kik* Soccer ball. See *pōwāwae.*

kini ʻai·ō *kik* Lunch pail. *Niʻihau.* Also *kini ʻai.*

Kini ʻEkua·kolia *iʻoa* Equatorial Guinea. *Eng.*

kini ʻoki·kene *kik* Oxygen tank.

Kini·bisau *iʻoa* Guinea-Bissau. *Eng.*

kini tuna *kik* Can of tuna.

kino *kik* Body, as of a composition or text. *Dic., ext. mng.* See *hoʻomaka, pau.*

kī noa *ham* Free throw, in basketball; to make such a shot. *He 65% ʻo John Stockton ma ka laina kī noa.* John Stockton is 65% at the free-throw line. See *laina kī noa. Kī noa pākahi.* Single free throw. *Kī noa kī hou.* One-and-one free throw. *Kī noa pālua.* Two-shot free throw.

kino·ea *kik* Gas, gaseous, as opposed to solid or liquid. Comb. *kino + ea.* Cf. *huea, kinopaʻa, kinowai.* See *hāmeʻa hana kinoea.*

kino·hapa *kik* Numerator, in math. *Lit.,* partial body. Cf. *kinopiha.*

kino hua·helu *kik* Standard form, as for numbers. *ʻO ke kino huahelu o ke kanakolu, penei nō ia: 30.* This is the standard form of thirty: 30. *Lit.,* number form.

kino lā·toma *kik* Allotrope, i.e. a different molecular form of an element, in science. *Lit.,* molecule body.

kino liona *Kanaka kino liona.* Sphinx, a mythological monster with the head of a woman and the body of a lion.

kinona *kik* Shape; geometric figure. Comb. *kino + -na.* See entries below. *Kinona analahi.* Regular shape.

kinona hua *kik* Font, typeface, as in printing or a computer program. *E hoʻololi i ke kinona hua.* Change the font. *Lit.,* letter shape. *Pāpahu kinona hua.* Font cartridge.

kinona like *kik* Image, in math. *Lit.,* same shape. *Kinona aka like o kekahi ʻaoʻao.* Reflection image. *Kinona like o kekahi ʻaoʻao.* Rotation image. *Kinona like kau.* Translation image. *Kinona like wili.* Turn image. *Kinona like wili hapalua.* Half-turn image. *Kinona like wili hapahā.* Quarter-turn image. Also *kinona like wili 1/4.*

kinona papa *kik* Plane figure, a figure that lies on a flat surface, in math. *Lit.,* flat-surface shape.

kinona paʻa *kik* Solid figure, in math. *Lit.,* solid shape.

kinona pihana·haka *kik* Space figure, in math. *Lit.,* volume figure.

kinona ʻano like *kik* Similar figure, in math.

kino·paʻa *kik* Solid, as opposed to liquid or gas. Comb. *kino + paʻa.* Also *paʻa.* Cf. *kinoea, kinowai. Kao wāwahie kinopaʻa.* Sold rocket booster.

kino·piha *kik* Denominator, in math. *Lit.,* complete body. Cf. *kinohapa. Kinopiha haʻahaʻa loa.* Least common denominator.

kino·wai *kik* Liquid, as opposed to solid or gas. Comb. *kino + wai.* Cf. *kinoea, kinopaʻa.*

kī pai *ham* Lay-up, in basketball; to make such a shot. *Kupanaha maoli ka lele ʻana o Koʻi ma luna o ka pūʻulu kūpale no ke kī pai ʻana a komo.* That was an amazing leap Koʻi made over the herd of defenders to make the layup shot. *Lit.,* raising shot. Also *kī kīkoʻo.*

kī·paku *ham* To expel, as from a school or institution. *Hiki nō ke kīpaku ʻia ʻoe ke hana ʻino hou ʻoe.* You can be expelled if you commit another offense. *Dic., sp. var.* Also *kīpeku.* See *hoʻokuʻia kīpaku.*

kī·paku luna kā·lai·ʻāina *ham* Recall, i.e. the right or procedure by which an elected official may be removed from office. *Ua kīpaku ʻia ka meia ma muli o ka lilo malū o kekahi puʻu kālā o ke kalana.* The mayor was recalled due to the illegal expenditure of county funds. *Lit.,* expel (a) political leader. Also *kīpeku luna kālaiʻāina.* Cf. *hoʻāhewa.*

kī papa *ham* Bank shot, in basketball; to make such a shot. *He ʻupena wale nō ke kī mua, a laila, he kī papa ka lua.* The first shot was all net, then the second one was a bank shot. *Lit.,* backboard shot.

kī·pā·pali *kik* Small cliffs; hilly. *Dic.*

kī·papa puka·ani·ani *kik* Tile windows, as in a computer program. *Lit.,* window pavement.

kī papaʻi *ham* Tip-in, as a basket in basketball; to make such a shot. *ʻEono āna ʻai ma ke kī papaʻi ʻana.* He has six points by tip-ins. *Lit.,* slapping shot. Cf. *kīloi papaʻi.*

kī·pehi *ham* To hit, as with a racket. *Dic., ext. mng. Kīpehi pohoalo.* To hit forehand. *Kīpehi pohokua.* To hit backhand.

kī·peku *ham* To eject, as a disk from a computer or a video cassette from a VCR. *E kīpeku i ke pā mai ke kakena.* Eject the disk from the drive. *Ni'ihau, ext. mng.*

kī·peku *ham* To expel, as from a school or institution. *Ni'ihau.* Also *kīpaku.* See *kīpaku luna kālai'āina.*

kipi *kik* Chip, as a potato chip. *Eng. Kipi 'uala kahiki.* Potato chip. *Kipi kalo.* Taro chip.

kī pi'o *ham* Hook shot, in basketball; to make such a shot. *He kīloi pi'o nui 'o Kareem Abdul Jabar, no ka mea, mio wale nō 'o ia ma ia hana.* Kareem Abdul Jabar does a lot of hook shots because he is so good at it. *Lit.,* arched shot. *Cf. kīloi pi'o.*

kī·poka *kik* Porcupine. *Dic.*

kipola *kik* Tiple, a musical instrument with ten strings. *Eng.*

kī·po'i *ham* Pocket veto, i.e. a way in which the President can veto a bill by holding onto the bill for ten days, during which time Congress ends its session. *Ua mana'o ka Pelekikena e hā'ule ana kāna wiko 'ana i ka pila, no laila, kīpo'i 'o ia i ka pila a hala ka wā noho o ka 'Aha'ōlelo Lāhui.* The President thought his veto would not stand, so he pocket vetoed the bill until the time of the Congressional session passed. *Dic., ext. mng. Cf. wiko (dic.).*

kī·po'o *ham* To indent, as the first line of a paragraph. *E kīpo'o i ka laina mua o ka paukū 'elima ka'ahua mai ka lihi hema mai.* Indent the first line of the paragraph five spaces from the left margin. *Sh. kīpo'opo'o + po'o hou. Cf. ho'okāwāholo.*

kī·po'o·po'o See *palaoa kīpo'opo'o.*

kī·pulu *kik/ham* Compost; to compost. *Dic., ext. mng. Cf. ho'omomona. Hana kīpulu.* To make compost.

kī·puni *'a* Hygroscopic. *Dic., ext. mng. Wai kīpuni.* Hygroscopic water.

kī·puni *Kikokikona kīpuni.* Text wrap, as in a word-processing document.

kī wai *kik* Faucet. *Mān. 'Au kī wai.* Faucet handle (preceded by *ke*).

kī·wī *kik* Abbreviation for *kelewikiona* (television); TV. *Dic.* Also *kelewī.* See *'ohe kīwī. Papakaumaka kīwī.* TV screen. *Pahu papakaumaka kīwī.* TV monitor.

kiwi·kā *kik* City, urban area; municipal (note that in Hawai'i most things are county rather than municipal). (Latin *civicus.*) See *ho'okiwikā, kānāwai kūloko. Cf. kaona, kūlanakauhale. Aupuni kiwikā.* Municipality, i.e. a city or town having its own incorporated government for local affairs. *Kahua pā'ani kolepa kiwikā.* Municipal golf course. *'Āina kumu wai kiwikā.* Municipal watershed.

kī·wī·kona *kik* Telethon. *Comb. kīwī* + Eng.

kī·wila *Kānāwai kīwila.* Civil law. Also *kānāwai sīwila.*

kī 'ai kolu *ham* Three-point shot, in basketball; to attempt such a shot. *He kī 'ai kolu kekahi hapalua o kāna mau 'ai.* Half of his points are three-pointers. *Cf. 'ai kolu.*

kī·'aha *kik* Cup, as a unit of measurement. *Dic., ext. mng. Abb. kh. Kī'aha ana.* Measuring cup.

ki'e Abbreviation for *ki'eki'e* (height).

ki'ei *ham* To peer, i.e. look narrowly or searchingly at something. *Dic.* Also *'ōwī.*

ki'e·ki'e *'a* Height. *Dic. Abb. ki'e.* Also *ana ki'eki'e. Cf. ākea, laulā, loa, lō'ihi.* See *hohonu, ki'eki'ena, lele ki'eki'e, woela ki'eki'e.*

ki'e·ki'ena *kik* Altitude, elevation. *Dic.* See *ki'eki'e. Ana ki'eki'ena.* Altimeter. *Ki'eki'ena nalu, ki'eki'ena 'ale, ki'eki'ena.* Height, as of a wave. See *kōā.*

ki'e kū·pono *kik* Altitude of a triangle. *Lit.,* perpendicular altitude. Cf. *ki'eki'e, ki'eki'ena.*

ki'e·leo *kik* Pitch, in linguistics and music. Sh. *ki'eki'e o ka leo. Ki'eleo ha'aha'a.* Low pitch. *Ki'eleo ki'eki'e.* High pitch.

ki'ena·o'a *kik* Skyscraper. Sh. *ki'eki'ena + o'a.* Cf. *nu'uo'a.*

ki'i *kik* Figure, as an illustration in a textbook; graphics. *Ua komolike 'o ki'i A a me ki'i E.* Figures A and E are congruent. *Dic., ext. mng.* See entries below and *pakuhi ki'i. Loulou ki'i.* To subscribe, as in a computer program. *Mea 'enehana ki'i.* Graphics technician, as for movie or video production. *Pakuhi ki'i.* Pictogram, pictograph, as in a computer program.

ki'i *ham* To receive a serve, in volleyball; also first pass. *Ni'ihau.*

ki'i a ala·kō *ham* To drag, as in a computer program. *Lit.,* fetch and drag. Also *alakō. Alakō ma luna o.* To drag onto. Also *alakō a kau ma luna o.*

ki'i·aka *kik* Slide, i.e. a photographic transparency. Comb. *ki'i + aka.* See *pākū ho'olele ki'i. Mīkini ho'olele ki'iaka.* Slide projector. *Mōlina ki'iaka.* Slide mount.

ki'i·ona *kik* Icon, as in a computer program. Sh. *ki'i* + Eng.

ki'i hō·'aui·kala *kik* Chromatograph. *Lit.,* chromatography diagram. See *hō'auikala.*

ki'i ho'o·maka'u manu *kik* Scarecrow. *Lit.,* image (for) frightening birds.

ki'i kaha koe *kik* Etching. *Lit.,* etched picture. Cf. *ki'i māio.* See *kaha koe.*

ki'i kiko *kik* Bitmap; a bitmapped graphic image. *Ua kākiko 'ia kēia ki'i kiko ma kēnā mīkini pa'i.* This bitmapped graphic image was bitmapped on that printer. *Lit.,* dot picture. Cf. *kākiko.*

ki'i kū *Puke ki'i kū.* Pop-up book, as for children's stories.

ki'i·kuhi *kik* Diagram, schematic drawing. Sh. *ki'i + kuhikuhi. Ki'ikuhi pahiki.* Tree diagram, in math. *Ki'ikuhi Wene.* Venn diagram, i.e. a diagram using overlapping circles to show relationship of data.

ki'i kū·kulu *kik* Blueprint. *Lit.,* diagram (for) building. Also *ki'i kūkulu hale.*

ki'i ku'i·kepa *kik* Sculpture. *Dic.*

ki'i lima *kik* Puppet. *Lit.,* hand doll. Also *pāpeka, pāpeta.* See *pāpeka kaula.*

ki'i·lou *ham* To save, in basketball. *Lele po'o wale 'o Kekoa ma waena o ke anaina nānā iā ia e ki'ilou ana i ke kinipōpō.* Kekoa just dove headlong right into the crowd when he went to save the ball. Comb. *ki'i + lou.*

ki'i māio *kik* Lithograph. *Lit.,* grooved picture. Cf. *ki'i kaha koe.*

ki'i mana·mana lima *kik* Fingerprint. *Lit.,* finger picture. Also *māka manamana lima, meheu manamana lima.* See *kāpala, māioio manamana lima. 'Ohi i ke ki'i manamana lima.* To collect fingerprints.

ki'ina *kik* Movements, as in dancing. *Dic., ext. mng.* Cf. *ka'ina wāwae.* See entries below. *Ki'ina lima.* Hand movements. *Ki'ina wāwae.* Foot movements.

ki'ina a'o *kik* Pedagogy, i.e. the art of teaching. *Lit.,* teaching method.

ki'ina hana *kik* Method, technique. Comb. *ki'ina + hana.* Also *ki'ina. Nā ki'ina 'ohi hāpana.* Sampling methods.

ki'ina leo *kik* Intonation. *Dic.*

ki'i·pā *heh* To vamp, as in hula or singing. *Dic.*

ki'i pā·lā·kiō *kik* Scale drawing, in math.

ki'i pa'i *kik* Photograph, shot. Cf. *pa'i ki'i.*

ki'i·'oni·'oni See *mīkini ho'olele ki'i'oni'oni, mo'olelo ki'i'oni'oni, pākū ho'olele ki'i*. *Ki'i'oni'oni ehuehu.* Action movie. *Ki'i'oni'oni kohu pa'a.* 3D movie.

kī·'ō·ko'a·ko'a *kik* Dissimilation, in linguistics. Comb. *kī* + redup. of *'oko'a*.

ki'o wai *kik* Pool of water, as in a stream. *Dic.* See *ki'o wai wailele*.

kī·'o'e *ham* To skim; to ladle, scoop. *Dic.* See *puna kī'o'e, 'o'e.*

kita·rahate *kik* Citrate. *Eng. Sodiuma kitarahate.* Sodium citrate.

ki'o wai wai·lele *kik* Plunge pool. *Lit.*, waterfall pool.

kō Of. *Dic.* Also *ko.*

kō *kik* Re, the second note on the musical scale. *Dic.* See *pākōlī.*

kō *Mimi kō.* Diabetes. Also *ma'i kōpa'a.*

koa *Kahua pū'ali koa.* Military base. *Pū'ali koa.* Army; military service. *Pū'ali koa kūikawā.* Militia.

kō·ā *kik* Crack or space, as between fence boards. *Dic., ext. mng.* Cf. *'oā.*

kō·ā *kik* Length, as of a wave; wavelength. *Dic., ext. mng., sp. var.* Also *kōā nalu, kōā 'ale.* See *ki'eki'ena. Kōā hawewe kani.* Sound wavelength.

koali lele·pinao *kik* Trapeze. *Dic., ext. mng.* See *lelepinao.*

koana *kik* Spacing, as lines in a printed document. *Dic., ext. mng.* Cf. *ka'ahua.* See *ho'okoana. Koana pākahi.* Single space, single-line spacing. *Koana pākahi me ka hapalua.* One and one-half space, One and one-half-line spacing. *Koana pālua.* Double space, double-line spacing.

kō·ā·wā *'a'* Diachronic, in lingustics. Comb. *kōā* + *wā.* Cf. *kikowā. Lula kōāwā.* Diachronic rule.

koe *ham* To strike, as a match. *Dic.* Cf. *koekoe.* See *kaha koe.*

koea a mania *'a'* Eroded smooth. *Dic.*

koe·hana *kik* Artifact. Comb. *koe* + *hana.* See *hulikoehana.*

koe·koe *ham* To strum, as an 'ukulele or guitar. *Dic.* Cf. *koe.*

koena *kik* Remainder, difference, in math. *Dic.* Abb. *K.*

koena *kik* Change, as from a purchase. *Dic., ext. mng.* Cf. *kālā helele'i.*

koi *'Aha koi pohō 'u'uku.* Small-claims court, small-debts court.

kō·ī *Wai kōī.* Cataract, i.e. steep rapids in a large river.

koi·ū *kik* Shoyu, soy sauce. *Dic. Pāpapa koiū.* Soybean.

koi·hā *kik* Weight, as for scales, etc. *Tah.*

koina *kik* Requirement; required. Comb. *koi* + *-na.* See *koho. Papa ha'awina koina.* Required curriculum or coursework. *Papa koina.* Required class or course. *'Ai koina.* Required credit, as for a school course.

koi pohō *kik* Claim for damages, as to an insurance company. *Dic. Ho'opi'i i ke koi pohō.* To make a claim for damages.

kō omōmo *kik* Lollipop, sucker. *Dic., ext. mng.* Also *kanakē 'au.*

koho *kik/ham* Elective. *Dic., ext. mng.* See *koina. Papa ha'awina koho.* Elective curriculum or coursework. *Papa koho.* Elective class or course. *'Ai koho.* Elective credit, as for a school course.

koho *ham* To choose, as in a computer program; choice; option, as on a computer keyboard. *Dic., ext. mng.* See entries below. *Pihi koho.* Option key (preceded by *ke*). *Papa koho.* Menu bar.

koho *kik/ham* Guess, estimate; to guess, estimate. *Dic.* See *kohoemi, koho'oi. Koho hapa mua.* Front-end estimation, in math. *'Āmana koho.* Dichotomous key.

koho·emi *ham* To underestimate. Comb. *koho* + *emi.* See *kohoʻoi.*

koho·koho *kik* Multiple-choice. *Dic., ext. mng.* Also *pane kohokoho.* *Nīnau kohokoho.* Multiple-choice question.

koho·lā kua·piʻo *kik* Humpback whale. *Lit.,* arched-back whale.

koho pā·lā·kiō *kik* Scale selection, as in a computer program.

koho pā·loka See entries below. *Kuleana koho pāloka.* Suffrage, i.e. the right to vote.

koho pā·loka lau·lā *kik* General election, in politics. *Lit.,* publicly (held) election. Cf. *koho pāloka wae moho.*

koho pā·loka wae moho *kik* Primary, primary election, i.e. a preliminary election to nominate candidates for office. Comb. dic. + *pāloka.* Also *wae moho.* See *wae moho.*

koho·ʻoi *ham* To overestimate. Comb. *koho* + *ʻoi.* See *kohoemi.*

kohu *kik* Sap. *Dic.*

kō hua mele *kik* Duration, in music. *Lit.,* hold (a) note in music.

kohu pai *Helu kohu pai.* Transcendental number, in math.

kohu pa·ʻa *ʻa* Three-dimensional or 3D, as a picture or movie. *Lit.,* like three-dimensional. Cf. *paʻa.* *Kiʻiʻoniʻoni kohu paʻa.* 3D movie.

kohu ʻoia·ʻi·ʻo *ʻa* Realistic. *Lit.,* resembling truth. *Hakupuni kohu ʻoiaʻiʻo.* Realistic fiction.

koka *kik* Cord, a unit for measuring firewood. *Dic.*

kō·kaha *kik/heh* Condensation; to condense, as gas to liquid. (Māori *tōtā.*).

Koka Rika *iʻoa* Costa Rica; Costa Rican. *Eng.*

kō·keina *kik* Cocaine. *Eng.*

kokeiʻa *kik* Prairie dog. (Ute *toceyʻa.*)

koke·kau *kik/ʻa* Approximation; approximate. *He kokekau wale nō kēia hāʻina ma muli o ka loaʻa ʻole mai o ka ʻikepili ʻauliliʻi.* This answer is only an approximation because of a lack of precise data. *E koho i ka huapalapala nōna ka ʻili kokekau o kēia huinakolu.* Choose the letter with the approximate area of this triangle.

koki·kone *kik* Cortisone, a hormone used in the treatment of arthritis. *Eng.* *Kokikone wai.* Hydrocortisone.

koko *kik* Blood. *Dic. Hulu koko.* Blood type. *Hunaola koko.* Blood cell. *Hunaola koko keʻokeʻo.* White blood cell. *Hunaola koko ʻulaʻula.* Red blood cell. *Kahena koko.* Bloodstream. *Koko huʻihuʻi.* Cold-blooded, as an animal. *Koko mehana.* Warm-blooded. *Lapa koko.* Blood clot. *Monakō koko.* Blood glucose. *Nui lama koko.* Blood alcohol level. Cf. *ana lama hanu. Pākela koko piʻi.* Hypertension, i.e. abnormally high arterial blood pressure.

koko *kik* Rare, as meat. *Dic., ext. mng.* Also *kokoko.*

kokoke *ʻa* Close, near. *Dic.* See *laulā, lōpū. Paʻi kokoke.* Close-up, as of a photograph or in movie or video production (preceded by *ke*). *Paʻi a kokoke.* To take a close-up. *Paʻi kokoke loa.* Extreme close-up. *Paʻi a kokoke loa.* To take an extreme close-up.

kokoko *ʻa* Rare, as meat. *Dic.* Also *koko.*

koko·leka *kik* Chocolate, hot chocolate. *Dic., ext. mng. Kokoleka me ka waiū huʻahuʻa.* Chocolate with frothed milk. *Kokoleka me ka waiū māhu.* Chocolate with steamed milk. *Kokoleka me ke kalima huipa.* Chocolate with whipped cream.

koko·leka pā·hoe·hoe *kik* Fudge. *Lit., pāhoehoe*-like chocolate.

Kō·ko·ʻo·lua *iʻoa* Mirach, a star. *Mān. (HA).*

Kokosa *i'oa* Cocos. *Eng. Ka Una Honua Kokosa.* Cocos Plate.

kō·kua See entries below. *Lawelawe kōkua.* Social services. *Mākala kū kōkua.* Striated muscle.

kō·kua helu *Mea kōkua helu.* Counter, as beans or bottle caps to help with a math problem. *Moena kōkua helu.* Counting mat, flat or stripmat, in math. *Pa'a'iliono kōkua helu.* Counting cube. *'Aukā kōkua helu.* Counting rod or strip.

kō·kua helu kumu ho'o·hui pā·lima *kik* Base-five counting piece, in math. *Lit.,* base five (to) help count.

kō·kua hua mele *kik* Musical staff. *Makua Laiana.* Also *ko'oko'o, kumu 'ākōlī. Laina o ke kōkua hua mele.* Horizontal line on a musical staff. Also *laina o ke kōkua. Wā o ke kōkua hua mele.* Space between horizontal lines on a musical staff. Also *wā o ke kōkua.*

kō·kua nele *kik/ham* Welfare, i.e. public financial assistance for needy persons. *Kūkulu 'ia nā papahana kōkua nele e ke aupuni no ke kōkua 'ana i ka lehulehu ma nā pono ma kahi o ka loa'a 'ole o ka hana, ka lawa 'ole o ke kālā, a me ka uku ho'omau no ka wā rītaia.* Government welfare programs were set up to provide public aid for those who are in need of unemployment benefits, financial assistance, and pensions. *Lit.,* help needy (persons).

kō·kua 'āina 'ē *kik* Foreign aid, as a government policy. *Ma ke kōkua 'āina 'ē i kōkua 'ia ai ka 'āina o Nikalakua ma hope o ka makani pāhili i ho'opō'ino i kēlā 'āina.* By way of foreign aid the country of Nicaragua was given help in the wake of the hurricane that devastated that land. *Lit.,* aid (to) foreign land. *Cf. kulekele 'āina 'ē.*

kolamu *kik* Column. *Dic.* See *ho'okolamu. Pukaaniani kolamu 'ikepili.* List editor screen, in a computer program.

Kō·lea Hema *i'oa* South Korea; South Korean. *Dic.* Also *Kōrea Hema.*

Kō·lea 'Ā·kau *i'oa* North Korea; North Korean. *Dic.* Also *Kōrea 'Ākau.*

koleke *kik* College, as a division or department within a university. *Eng. Koleke mahi'ai.* College of agriculture. *Koleke pāheona me ka 'epekema.* College of arts and sciences.

kolepa *kik* Golf. *Dic. Kahua pā'ani kolepa kiwikā.* Municipal golf course. *'Ūhili kolepa.* Golf club.

koli *kik* Meteor. *Dic.*

koli·koli *ham* To round off, in math. *Dic., new mng.* See *'uala kahiki kolikoli. Kolikoli ha'alalo.* To round down. *Kolikoli ha'aluna.* To round up.

kolo *'Au kolo.* Free-style or crawl, in swimming; to swim using this style.

Koloa·tia *i'oa* Croatia. *Eng.*

kolohe *Hana kolohe.* To fake or hit, in volleyball. *Kahakaha kolohe.* Graffiti.

Kolo·lako *i'oa* Colorado; Coloradan. *Dic.* Also *Kolorado.* See *Haka'ama. Ka muliwai 'o Kololako.* Colorado River.

Kolome·pia *i'oa* Colombia; Colombian. *Eng.* Also *Kolomebia.*

Kolome·bia *i'oa* Colombia; Colombian. *Eng.* Also *Kolomepia.*

kolona *kik* Colon, in punctuation. *Dic.* See *hapa kolona.*

kolo·naio *'a'* Colonized, particularly from the perspective of a people who have been colonized by a dominant culture or political entity. *Eng.* See *ho'okolonaio, ho'opanalā'au.*

kolo·nahe *heh* Blowing softly, as a gentle breeze; leaves in constant motion, in meteorology. *Dic.* See *makani.*

kolo·palake *kik* Chloroplast. *Eng.*

kolo·pila *kik* Chlorophyll. *Eng.* See *palasika.*

kolo·poma *kik* Chloroform. *Eng.*

Kolo·rado *i'oa* Colorado; Coloradan. *Dic.* Also *Kololako.*

kolo·rine *kik* Chlorine. *Eng.*

kolori·side *kik* Chloride. *Eng.*
Kobalata koloriside. Cobalt chloride.
Satanousa koloriside. Stannous chloride.

koloro·dane *kik* Chlorodane. *Eng.*

koloro·foloro·kala·pona *kik* Chlorofluorocarbon. *Hoʻohewa nui ʻia ke kolorofolorokalapona no ka hoʻopilikia ʻana i ke kāʻei ʻokikene kolu o ka lewapuni.* Chlorofluorocarbons are often blamed for damaging the ozone layer of our atmosphere. *Eng.*

kolū·kalaiwa *kik* Screwdriver. *Mān.* See *kui nao.*

koma *Kiko koma.* Comma. Also *kiko hoʻomaha.*

koma luna *kik* Apostrophe. *Dic.*

kōmi *ham* Click; to click, press or depress, as in a computer program. *E kōmi pālua i ka ʻiole ma luna o ke kiʻiona.* Double click the mouse on the icon. *Niʻihau; dic., ext. mng.* Also *kaomi.* See *kōmi ʻōkuhi, paʻina.*

komi·kina *kik* Commission. *Dic.* See *uku ʻēkena. Komikina Hoʻohana ʻĀina o ka Mokuʻāina.* State Land Use Commission. *Komikina Māmela Kai.* Marine Mammal Commission. *Komikina wai.* Water commission.

Komi·nika *iʻoa* Dominican. *Dic. Lepupalika Kominika.* Dominican Republic.

kōmi ʻō·kuhi *kik* Macro, as in a computer program; script, i.e. a set of computer codes programmed to run consecutively in a computer system. *Lit.,* press directions. *Haku kōmi ʻōkuhi.* To write a (computer) script; scripting.

komo *kik* Ring. *Dic.* See *helu komo. Manamana komo.* Ring finger. Also *manamana pili.*

komo *Komo i loko o ka papa.* To take a class. *Ua komo wau i loko o ka papa ʻōlelo Hawaiʻi i kēlā makahiki aku nei.* I took a Hawaiian language class last year. Also *komo i ka papa.* Cf. *aia.*

komo (i loko o) *heh* To access, as in computer program. *E komo i loko o ka polokalamu ma ke kōmi ʻana iā ʻOia.* Access the program by clicking on OK. *Dic., ext. mng.*

komo·hana *kik* West. *Dic. Abb. Km. Poepoe hapa komohana.* Western hemisphere.

komo·hia *ʻa* Made a basket, in basketball. *Komohia (ka hīnaʻi) iā ʻoe!* You made a basket! *Dic., ext. mng.* Cf. *hoʻokomo i ke kinipōpō.* See *kī.*

komo·like *heh* Congruent. *Comb. komo + like. Huinakolu komolike.* Congruent triangle. *Kinona komolike.* Congruent figure.

komo·ne·ʻe *heh* To immigrate. *Ua komoneʻe lākou i loko o Hawaiʻi nei.* They immigrated to Hawaiʻi. *Comb. komo + neʻe.* Cf. *pukaneʻe.*

komo pae *heh* Passage, initiation, as into a group. *Lit.,* enter (a) group. See *hoʻokomo pae. Hana komo pae.* Rite of passage, initiation.

komo pū *heh* Included. *Lit.,* include together with. *ʻAuhau komo pū.* Tax included. *He ʻeono kālā ʻauhau komo pū o kēia palaʻili.* This T-shirt is six dollars, tax included.

Komo·rosa *iʻoa* Comoros. *Eng.*

komosa *kik* Cosmos, a kind of flower. *Eng.*

-kona -thon. *Eng.* See *helekona, hulahulakona, kīwīkona,* etc.

kōna His, her, hers, its. *Dic.* Also *kona.*

kone ala·nui *kik* Cone used as a traffic marker. *Lit.,* street cone. See *papale kone.*

koneka *kik* Consonant. *Eng.*

Kone·kikuka *iʻoa* Connecticut. *Dic.* Also *Konetikuta.*

kō·nelo *kik* Tunnel. *Niʻihau (Eng.).*

kone ʻai·kalima *kik* Ice cream cone.

Kone·tikuta *iʻoa* Connecticut. *Dic.* Also *Konekikuka.*

Kono·kō *iʻoa* Congo; Congolese. *Eng.*
Lepupalika Kemokalaka ʻo Konokō.
Democratic Republic of the Congo.

kopa *kik* Soap. *Dic. Kopa kahi
ʻumiʻumi.* Shaving soap. *Usu. kopa
ʻumiʻumi. Kopa lauoho.* Shampoo.
Kopa mīkini holoi pā. Dishwasher soap.
Pā kopa. Soap dish (preceded by *ke*).

kopa·laka *kik* Cobalt. *Eng.* Also
kobalata.

kopa·lā lima *kik* Garden trowel.
Lit., hand shovel.

kopa·lā liʻi·liʻi *kik* Small spade, as a
garden tool. *Lit.,* small shovel.

kō·pa·a *Maʻi kōpaʻa.* Diabetes. Also
mimi kō.

kope *kik* Copy, as of a document. *Dic.*
See *papaʻa. Hana kope.* To copy, make a
copy. *Kope kumu.* Original or master
copy, i.e. a master used for making
additional copies.

kope *ham* To rake. *Dic.* Also *kopekope, pūlumi. Hao kope.* Garden rake.
Kope ʻōpala. Rake, as for leaves.

kope·ika *kik* Espresso, i.e. strong black
coffee prepared by forcing steam under
pressure through ground dark-roast
coffee beans. *Comb. kope + ika.* See
kope keʻokeʻo.

kope keʻo·keʻo *kik* Café au lait, i.e.
hot coffee served with an equal amount
of hot or scalded milk. *Lit.,* white coffee.
See *kopeika.*

kō·pia *kik* Carbohydrate. *Comb. kō +
pia.*

kopi·ana *kik* Scorpion. *Dic.* See other
entries in dictionary.

kō·pia·ʻā *kik/heh* Respiration; to
respire. *Lit.,* burning carbohydrates.

kopi·kala *ʻa* Tropic; tropical. *ʻAʻohe
ōna wahi ulu, koe wale nō ma nā ʻāina
kopikala.* It only grows in tropic lands.
Eng. Cf. kemepale. Kāʻei kopikala. The
tropics. *Kāʻei kuʻina kopikala.*
Intertropical convergent zone (ITCZ).
Lalo kopikala. Subtropical. *ʻIno
kopikala.* Tropical storm.

kō·pū mea·ola *kik* Biomass. *Comb.*
kōpū (sh. *tōpūtanga* [*Māori*, mass]) +
meaola.

koʻa *Limu koʻa.* Coraline algae.

kō·ʻai hema *ham* Counterclockwise.
E kīloi i ke kinipōpō ma ke kōʻai hema.
Throw the ball counterclockwise. *Lit.,* stir
(to the) left. *Cf. kōʻai ʻākau.*

kō·ʻai ʻā·kau *ham* Clockwise. *E
holo a puni ka hale ma ke kōʻai ʻākau.*
Run around the house clockwise. *Lit.,*
stir (to the) right. *Cf. kōʻai hema.*

koʻa·ko·ana *kik* Precipitate, i.e. a
substance separated from a solution or
suspension by chemical or physical
change. *Redup. of koʻana.*

kō·ʻala See *ʻoma kōʻala.*

koʻana *kik* Sediment. *Dic. Koʻana
kai.* Marine sediment. *Koʻana kahawai.*
Stream sediment.

Koʻana·ko·a *iʻoa* Maro Reef. *Lit.,*
settling (of) coral.

koʻe *kik* Worm. *Dic.* See entries below.

koʻe omo·ola *kik* Parasitic worm, e.g.
heartworm, nematode, roundworm,
tapeworm, etc. *Lit.,* parasite worm.

koʻe honua *kik* Earthworm.

koʻe·koʻe *Kaua koʻekoʻe.* Cold war, i.e.
intense rivalry between nations but
without military combat.

koʻe·lau *kik* Fluke. *Comb. koʻe + lau.*
Koʻelau ake. Liver fluke.

koʻe moe·ʻalā *kik* Polychaete worm, a
kind of worm found underneath stream
rocks. Also *moeʻalā.*

koʻe pā·kiʻi *kik* Planaria. *Lit.,* flat
worm.

koʻe pā·laha·laha *kik* Flatworm. *Cf.*
koʻe poepoe.

koʻe poe·poe *kik* Roundworm. *Cf.*
koʻe pālahalaha.

koʻe puʻu·wai *kik* Heartworm.

koʻe ʻele·muku *kik* Nematode.
Comb. koʻe + elemutu (*Tokelau*, worm).

koʻe ʻula *kik* Tubifex. *Lit.,* red worm.

ko'i *kik* Axe. *Dic.* Also *ko'i lipi. Mān.* See *ko'i kālai.*

kō·'ie·'ie *Wai kō'ie'ie.* Run, as in a stream.

ko'i kā·lai *kik* Hoe. *Lit,* adze (for) hoeing. Also *hō, 'ō'ō kālai.* See *kālai.*

ko'o *Ku'ina ko'o.* Plug-in, as in a computer program. *Paipu ko'o.* Pipe used to hold up clear plastic sheeting over an aquaculture tank.

ko'o·hune *kik* Bacteria. *Lit.,* small staff (from Greek). *Ko'ohune ola mehana.* Mesophilic bacteria. *Ko'ohune ola wela.* Thermophilic bacteria. *Ko'ohune naikokene.* Azobacter, a type of bacteria containing nitrogen.

ko'o·ko'o See *kōkua hua mele.*

ko'o lele *kik* Pole vault. *Lit.,* pole (for) jumping. See *lele ko'o.*

ko'o lima *kik/heh* Pushup; to do pushups. *Dic.*

ko'o puka *kik* Doorstop. *Lit.,* door prop. Also *ko'o 'īpuka.*

ko'u *ham* To jab with fingertips, in volleyball. *Ni'ihau.*

koba·lata kolori·side *kik* Cobalt chloride. *Eng.*

Kō·rea Hema *i'oa* South Korea; South Korean. *Dic., sp. var.* Also *Kōlea Hema.*

Kō·rea 'Ā·kau *i'oa* North Korea; North Korean. *Dic., sp. var.* Also *Kōlea 'Ākau.*

kū *kik* Stand. *Ni'ihau (Eng. calque).* See *kī kū, kukui kū. Kū ko'okolu.* Tripod. *Kū pena ki'i.* Easel.

kua *'Au kua.* Back stroke, in swimming; to swim the back stroke. *Lit.,* swim (on the) back. See entries below and *kā'ei kua, kīloi kua.*

kua uma *kik* Beam, of a boat. *Lit.,* stern beam.

kua hao paiki·kala *kik* Crossbar (on a bicycle). *Ni'ihau.*

kua·hene *kik* Shield, as in volcanoes. Comb. *kua-* + *hene.* Cf. *pale kaua. Ho'āhua kuahene.* Shield building; to build a shield (volcano). *Lua pele kuahene.* Shield volcano. *Lua pele kuahene kuamua.* Primary shield volcano.

kua·hope Final or terminal, as last in time, order, or importance. Comb. *kua* + *hope.* See *kuamua, kualua, kuakolu. 'Āmanapu'u kuahope.* Terminal bronchiole, in anatomy.

kuaka *kik* Quart. *Dic.* Abb. *kk.*

kū·ā·kea *'a'* Open, as a primary election. *Dic., ext. mng., sp. var.* Cf. *kūloko. Wae moho kūākea.* Open primary.

Kuake·mala *i'oa* Guatemala; Guatemalan. *Dic.*

kua·kolu Tertiary, as third in time, order, or importance. *Dic., ext. mng.* See *kuamua, kualua, kuahope. 'Āmanapu'u kuakolu.* Tertiary bronchus, segmental bronchus, in anatomy.

kua·lā *kik* Dorsal fin, of a fish, nonscientific term. *Dic.* See entry below. *Kualā laukua.* Dorsal fin, of a fish, scientific term. *Kualā laumua.* Anterior dorsal fin. *Kualā lauhope.* Posterior dorsal fin.

kua·lā *kik* Rain, in a small area while sun is shining, sometimes considered an omen of misfortune. *Mān. (HHLH).* Also *ua kualā.*

kua·lapa waena moana *kik* Mid-ocean ridge. *Lit.,* ocean-middle ridge.

kū·aloli *'a'* Metamorphosis. *He kūaloli ka 'enuhe ke puka 'o ia mai loko mai o kōna wili'ōka'i ma ke 'ano he pulelehua.* The catepillar experiences a metamorphosis when it emerges from the cocoon as a butterfly. Comb. *kū* + *a* + *loli. Kūaloli kino.* Morphological metamorphosis.

kua·lua Secondary, as second in time, order, or importance. *Dic., ext. mng.* See *kuamua, kuakolu, kuahope.* *'Ā kualua.* Secondary activity, of a volano. *'Āmanapu'u kualua.* Secondary bronchus, lobar bronchus, in anatomy.

kua·manawa *kik* Prehistoric. *Lit.,* back (of) time.

Kua·manō *i'oa* La Pérouse Rock. *Lit.,* shark's back.

kua·mo'o See *iwi kuamo'o.*

kua·mua Primary, as first in time, order, or importance. Comb. *kua + mua.* See *kualua, kuakolu, kuahope.* *Hū pele kuamua.* Primary volcanic activity. *Lua pele kuahene kuamua.* Primary shield volcano. *'Āmanapu'u kuamua.* Primary bronchus, in anatomy.

kū·ana *kik* Place value, usually in compound terms. Comb. *kū + ana.* See entries below and *unuhi kūana, helu kūana.*

kū·ana haneli *kik* Hundreds, as place value, in math.

kū·ana helu *kik* Unit of counting; place value of a number. *Lit.,* number place value. Cf. *anakahi.* See *helu kūana.*

kū·ana kā·lā *kik* Monetary denomination.

kū·ana keki·mala *kik* Decimal place. See *kiko kekimala.*

kua·naki *kik* Quota. (Māori *kua nawhi.*)

kuana kū See *kuana pepa.*

kuana moe See *kuana pepa.*

kuana pepa *kik* Orientation, as of a page in a computer program. *Lit.,* paper position. *Kuana kū.* Portrait orientation. *Kuana moe.* Landscape orientation.

kū·ana 'ekahi *kik* Ones, as place value, in math.

kuana·'ike *kik* Perspective. *Lit.,* position (of) sight or knowledge.

kū·ana 'umi *kik* Tens, as place value, in math.

kua noho *kik* Seat back.

kua·papa *kik* -base. *He kinowai kuapapa wai i kapa 'ia he koko.* A water-base fluid called blood. (Māori *tūāpapa* [foundation].) *Pena kuapapa wai.* Water-base paint. *'Anahaidaraside kuapapa.* Basic anhydride, a metallic oxide that forms a base when added to water.

kua·pele *kik* Volcanic mountain. Comb. *kua- + pele.*

kua·pi'o *Koholā kuapi'o.* Humpback whale.

kuapo *ham* To exchange, as of gases in the body; to trade, in math; to change or replace, as in a search-and-replace feature in a computer program. *Dic., ext. mng. Huli a kuapo.* To find and change, search and replace.

kuapo *heh* To rotate, in volleyball; also to switch sides. *Ni'ihau.*

kuapo *Kaha kuapo.* A curved line written over a word or letter and then under the adjoining word or letter to indicate that the order of the words or letters should be reversed, in proofreading.

kuapo hao *kik* Rim of a wheel. *Ni'ihau.*

kū·awa *kik* Guava. *Mān./dic., sp. var.*

kua·wehi *'a'* Ultraviolet. *Dic., ext. mng. Kukuna kuawehi.* Ultraviolet ray.

kua'i *ham* To remove, as an opihi from its shell. *Dic.* Also *poke, po'e.*

kuea *kik* Frame, as in bowling; space, as on a game board such as Monopoly. *Dic., ext. mng.* See *kapua'i kuea. Kuea maika.* Bowling frame. *Kuea huki pepa.* Chance space, in Monopoly.

kueka ha'uki *kik* Sweatshirt. *Lit.,* sports sweater. *Lole kueka ha'uki.* Warm-up suit.

Kue·kene *i'oa* Sweden; Swede; Swedish. *Eng.*

kue·kueni *heh* To vibrate. *Ke ho'okani 'ia ka mīkini pāleo a nui ka leo, hiki ke ho'opā i ke kuekueni o ka pahu leo me ka lima.* If you play the stereo loudly, you can feel the vibration of the speaker with your hand. *Dic.*

kuemi *heh* To bring back out, in basketball; to slow down, as in a fast break. *Kuemi iki akula 'o Mina ma ke po'o o ka pukakī i hiki i nā hoa kime ke ho'onohonoho iā lākou iho.* Mina brought out the ball a little outside the top of the key so that his teammates could position themselves. *Lit.,* step back. Also *kuemi iki.*

kuene moku·lele *kik* Flight attendant. *Lit.,* airplane steward.

Kuete *i'oa* Kuwait; Kuwaiti. *Eng.*

kui See entries below and *pulu kui.*

kū i ka hai *'a'* Freelance. *Hana 'o Keoki ma ke 'ano he kanaka pa'i ki'i kū i ka hai.* Keoki works as a freelance photographer. *Lit.,* ready to be hired.

kū i ka hewa *Ho'oholo i ke kū i ka hewa.* To convict, i.e. to find or prove to be guilty.

kū·ika·wā *Kumu kūikawā.* Extenuating circumstances. *Pū'ali koa kūikawā.* Militia.

kū i ke au *'a'* Trend. *Lit.,* existing in the era. See *mea kū i ke au.*

kū i ke ka'ina kā·nā·wai *'a'* Due process of law, i.e. the process by which the government must treat accused persons fairly according to rules established by law. *I ka mana'o o ka mea i ho'āhewa 'ia, 'a'ole i kū kōna hihia i ke ka'ina kānāwai.* The accused felt that his case was not given due process of law. *Lit.,* appropriate to the order (of) law.

kuiki kukui *kik* Light switch. *Mān.* Also *pana kukui.*

Kuiki·lana *i'oa* Switzerland; Swiss. *Dic.* Also *Kuikilani.*

Kuiki·lani *i'oa* Switzerland; Swiss. *Eng.* Also *Kuikilana. Waiūpa'a Kuikilani.* Swiss cheese.

kui·kina *kik* Narcissus. (Cantonese *suisin.*) *Kuikina haole.* Daffodil.

kui kolū *kik* Bolt, as in nuts and bolts. *Ni'ihau.* See *pihi wili.*

kui·kui *kik* Candlenut; light (var. of *kukui*). *Ni'ihau.*

kui lā·'au *kik* Wooden peg. *Dic.*

kui mō·pina *kik* Hypodermic needle. *Ni'ihau.*

kui nao *kik* Screw. *Dic.* See *kolūkalaiwa.*

kui pahu *kik* Thumbtack. *Dic.*

kui 'ū·mi'i pepa *kik* Staple, for paper. *Ni'ihau.* See *mea 'ūmi'i pepa, mea wehe 'ūmi'i.*

kū·olo·kū See *manu kūolokū.*

kū·ono *kik* First off the bench or six man, i.e. first alternate or substitute player, in basketball. *'O Kimo ke kūono; 'o ia ka mea e pani ana no Palani.* Kimo is the six man; he's the one taking Palani's place. *Sh. kūlana + 'eono.*

kū·hā *kik* Power forward or four man, in basketball. *'O Larry Johnson ke kūhā po'okela o ka NBA no kōna lō'ihi a māmā.* Larry Johnson is the best power forward in the NBA because he is so tall and quick. *Sh. kūlana + 'ehā.*

kū·haha'i *heh* To narrate orally, as in a speech. *Comb. kū + redup. of ha'i. Ha'i'ōlelo kūhaha'i.* Narrative speech.

kū hano ho'o·kolo·hua *kik* Ring stand, as for a test tube. *Lit.,* test tube stand. See *hano ho'okolohua.*

kū·helu *'a'* Official, as a language or representative. *Sh. kū i ka helu* (can be counted). *Cf. pōnolu. Ho'opi'i kūhelu.* Indictment; to indict. *Kūhelu 'ole.* Unofficial; non-standard, as in units of measurement.

kuhi See *mana'o kuhi.*

kuhia *kik* Referent, in math (O class). *Sh. kuhi + 'ia.*

kuhia *kik* Note, as in a book or research paper. *Dic., ext. mng. Kuhia o hope.* Endnote. *Kuhia o lalo.* Footnote.

kuhi·akau *kik* Hypothesis. *Comb. kuhi + a + kau.* See entry below.

kuhi·akau kū·papa *kik* Null, in math. *Lit.,* neutral hypothesis.

kū hiō *Mākala kū hiō o waho.* External abdominus oblique muscle. *Mākala kū hiō o loko.* Internal abdominus oblique muscle.

kuhi hewa o ka maka Optical illusion. *Lit.,* illusion of the eyes.

kuhi·kuhi *ham* To point, as a mouse arrow in a computer program. *Dic., ext. mng.* See entries below and *papa kuhikuhi. Manamana kuhikuhi.* Index finger. Also *manamana miki.*

kuhi·kuhi *ham* To show, demonstrate, as how a math problem is solved. *E kuhikuhi mai ʻoe i kāu polopolema.* Show how you did your problem. *Dic.*

kuhi·kuhi *ham* To direct, as a movie or video production. *Dic., ext. mng.* See *hoʻomālamalama, hoʻopuka, pāheona. Luna kuhikuhi.* Director. *Hope luna kuhikuhi.* Assistant director. *Poʻo kuhikuhi.* Executive director (preceded by *ke*).

kuhi·kuhi *kik/ham* Indicator; to indicate. *Dic., ext. mng. Ninahaidirina kuhikuhi.* Ninhydrin indicator.

kuhi·kuhi lā·ʻau *kik/ham* Prescription for medicinal drugs or medication; to prescribe, as a medication). *Dic. + lāʻau.* Cf. *kūʻai wale. Lāʻau kuhikuhi.* Prescription drug or medication.

kuhi·kuhina *kik* Reference; coordinate, in math or science; absolute location, in geography. *Dic., ext. mng.* Cf. *pilina henua. Nā kuhikuhina hōʻike honua.* Geographical coordinates. *Papa kuhikuhina.* Coordinate plane. *Paʻa helu kuhikuhina.* Ordered pair, in math.

kuhi lihi *kik* Page guide, as in a computer document or dictionary. *Lit.,* margin pointing.

kuhi lima *kik/ham* Hand gesture; to gesture with the hands; to use sign language. *ʻŌlelo kuhi lima.* Sign language. *ʻŌlelo kuhi lima ʻAmelika.* American Sign Language (ASL).

kuhi·makani *kik* Weather vane, wind vane. *Comb. kuhi + makani.*

kuhina *ʻAha kuhina.* Cabinet, a council that advises a president, sovereign, etc.

kuhi puke See *helu kuhi puke.*

kuhi·ʻī *kik/ham* Specifications, specs; to specify. *Sh. kuhikuhi + kikoʻī.*

kuhō *ham* Swish, rimless, i.e. to make a basket without touching the rim, in basketball. *Dic., ext. mng.* See *kī.*

kū·hou *ʻa* New, used only in special terminology. *Comb. kū + hou. Au Palaʻo Kūhou.* New Kingdom, in Egyptology.

kū·hō·hō See *awāwa kūhōhō.*

kū honua See *papa kū honua.*

kū·hō·ʻai·lona *ham* To stand for, as in a math problem. *Kūhōʻailona ke X no ka nui o nā ʻikamu i hōʻike ʻia.* X stands for the number of objects given. *Comb. kū + hōʻailona.*

kū·ho·ʻe *kik* Record, greatest achievement or performance to date. *E hoʻāʻo ana ʻo ia e mākia i ke kūhoʻe.* S/he's going to try to set the record. *Comb. kū + hoʻe (Tah.,* one). Cf. *moʻokūʻikena, moʻomōʻali.* See *mākia.*

kū·kā *heh* To confer. *Dic. Kūkā ma ka pūʻulu.* To conference, as part of the writing process. See *hōʻike manaʻo. ʻAha kūkā poʻo aupuni.* Summit, i.e. a conference of highest-level officials, as heads of government.

kū·kae·pele ʻoki·kene lua *kik* Sulfur dioxide. *Lit.,* sulfur double oxygen. Also *sulufura diokesaside.*

kū kau *ʻa* Seasonal. *Lit.,* exist (in the) season. Also *kū i ke kau.*

kū·kau·kaʻi *ʻa* Interdependence; interdependent. *Comb. kū + kaukaʻi.*

kū·kahi *kik* Point guard or one man, in basketball; guard, in football. *'O ke kūkahi ka mea holo kikī nui a hiki i kekahi po'o o ke kahua.* The point guard is the one who sprints all the way to the other end of the court. Sh. *kūlana + 'ekahi. Kūkahi hema.* Left guard. *Kūkahi 'ākau.* Right guard.

Kū·kahi·kahi *i'oa* Northern Equatorial Current, in oceanography. *Mān. (HA).*

kū·kahiko *'a'* Old, olden, used only in special terminology. Comb. *kū + kahiko. Au Pala'o Kūkahiko.* Old Kingdom, in Egyptology.

kū·kā ho'ēmi·emi *heh* Plea bargain, as in the negotiation of an agreement between a prosecutor and a defendant. *Ma o ke kūkā ho'ēmiemi 'ana, ua hā'awi 'ia ka mea i ho'āhewa 'ia he ho'okahi wale nō makahiki ma ka hale pa'ahao.* Through plea bargaining, the accused was given only one year in prison. *Lit.,* consult (to) bargain.

kū kāki *kik* Metered parking or any parking for which there is a charge. *Lit.,* parking (with a) charge. See *mīka kāki.*

kū·kala maka·'ala *kik/ham* Watch, as in a weather report. *Lit.,* proclaim vigilance. Cf. *kūkala pō'ino. Kūkala maka'ala makani pāhili.* Hurricane watch. *Kūkala maka'ala wai hālana.* Flood watch.

kū·kala pō·'ino *kik/ham* Warning, as in a weather report. *Lit.,* proclaim danger. Cf. *kūkala maka'ala. Kūkala pō'ino makani pāhili.* Hurricane warning. *Kūkala pō'ino wai hālana.* Flood warning.

kuka makani *kik* Windbreaker, a kind of jacket. *Lit.,* wind coat.

kū kā·nā·wai *'a'* Legal. *Dic. (kū i ke kānāwai).*

kū·ka'i leka *kik/ham* Written correspondence; to correspond by letter. *Dic. Papa kūka'i leka.* Correspondence course.

kū·ka'i·pā *kik* Interactive, as computer programs. Comb. *kūka'i + pā.*

kū·ka'i 'ae·like 'uni·ona *h a m* Collective bargaining. *'Oiai 'a'ole i hiki i ka 'uniona a me ka hui ke ho'opa'a i ka 'aelike, ua kauoha 'ia ia mau 'ao'ao e komo pū i ke kūka'i 'aelike 'uniona e ka luna ho'okolokolo i mea e hō'alo ai i ka 'olohani.* Since the union and the company could not settle the contract, both sides were ordered by the judge to enter into collective bargaining to avert a strike. *Lit.,* union contract exchange.

kū·kā·'oko'a *kik* Freedom, liberty. *'Ivanahō.* Also *kūnoa.* See entry below.

Kū·kā·'oko'a Kia·ho'o·mana'o *i'oa* Statue of Liberty. *Lit.,* freedom monument. Also *Kūkā'oko'a, ke kiaho'omana'o 'o Kūkā'oko'a.*

kuke See *lumi kuke. Kumu paina Kuke.* Cook pine. Also *paina Kuke.*

kū·kini ho'o·ili *kik* Relay race. *Lit.,* transfer race. Also *heihei ho'oili.* Cf. *holo ho'oili.* See *maile ho'oili.*

kū·kohu *kik* Model, usually miniature. Comb. *kū + kohu.* See *kāpili. Kūkohu moku.* Model boat.

kū kō·kua *Mākala kū kōkua.* Striated muscle.

kū·kolu *kik* Swing man, shooting forward or three man, in basketball. *E maka'ala 'oe i ke kūkolu; he loea 'o ia i ke kī 'ai kolu.* Make sure you keep an eye out for the swing man; he's really good at the triple shot. Sh. *kūlana + 'ekolu.*

kū·konu *'a'* Neutral, neutrality, i.e. not taking sides, as in a dispute. *Ke noho kūkonu nei wau ma kēia hihia; 'a'ole e 'onou ia'u i loko.* I am remaining neutral in this matter; don't get me involved. Comb. *kū + -konu.* Cf. *ho'okūkonu.*

kuku *kik* Rim of basket, in basketball. *Lewa li'ili'i akula 'o David Robinson ma ke kuku ma hope o kāna 'ūpo'i 'ana.* David Johnson hung onto the rim a little while after dunking the ball. *Dic., ext. mng.* Also *hao.* See *hīna'i, hupa.*

kukui *'Ōpu'u kukui.* Light bulb.

kukui hā·weo *kik* Fluorescent light. See *hāweo.*

kukui ho'o·kū *kik* Stoplight, traffic light.

kukui ho'o·mehana *kik* Heating lamp. *Lit.,* light (for) warming.

kukui kū *kik* Floor lamp. *Ni'ihau.* Also *kukui kū hale. Kukui kū pākaukau.* Table lamp

kukui lā·kene *kik* Hanging lantern, as Japanese type. Comb. *kukui* + Eng.

kukui·po'o *kik* Headlight. *Ni'ihau.* Also *kukuipo'o o mua.*

kukui 'oaka *kik* Flash, as for a camera. Also *'oaka. Dic.*

kukui 'owaka·waka *kik* Reflector. Also *'owakawaka.*

kū·kulu *Nā kūkulu 'ehā.* The four cardinal points, or four primary directions of the compass, in geography. *Nā kūkulu o waena.* Intermediate directions. *'Oi'enehana kūkulu.* Construction industry.

kū·kulu·ae'o *kik* Stilt, either the bird or the toy. *Dic.*

kū·kulu hale *ham* To develop land, as the work of a developer. *Ua kū'ai aku nei lākou i kēlā 'āina no ke kūkulu hale 'ana.* They bought that land in order to develop it. *Lit.,* build houses. Also *kūkulu hale ma luna o ka 'āina.*

kū·kulu hō·'oia *ham* Proof, in math. *Lit.,* establish verification.

kū·kulu hula·hula *ham* Choreographer; to choreograph. *Lit.,* arrange dances.

kū·kulu kahua *Mea kūkulu kahua.* Stagehand, grip. *Luna kūkulu kahua.* Stage manager, key grip, as for movie or video production.

kū·kulu mā·mala *ham* To phrase, as in written compositions. *'Ano hemahema ke kūkulu māmala 'ana i nā hopuna'ōlelo i loko o kēia paukū.* The phrasing of the sentences in this paragraph is rather awkward. *Lit.,* arrange (sentence) fragments. Cf. *puana māmala.* See *paukūkū.*

kū·kulu puolo *ham* Music arranger; to arrange music. *Lit.,* arrange music.

kukuna *kik* Spoke, as on a bicycle wheel; antenna, as of a lobster, insect, television, etc. *Dic.* See entries below. *Kukuna huila paikikala.* Bicycle wheel spoke.

kukuna *kik* Ray, as in geometry. *Dic., ext. mng.* Also *wāwae, 'ao'ao.*

kukuna·oka·lā *kik* Mangrove. *Dic., sp. var.*

kukuna kua·wehi *kik* Ultraviolet ray. *Dic., ext. mng.*

kukuna lewa lipo *kik* Cosmic ray. *Lit.,* outer-space ray.

kukuna pō·pa'i·pa'i *kik* Volleyball antenna. Also *kukuna. 'A'ena kukuna.* Antenna violation.

kukuna wana·'ā *kik* Laser beam.

kula *Leka kūloko kula.* Campus mail.

kū·launa *'a'* In harmony, in music. *Kūlauna ka hīmeni 'ana o lākou.* Their singing is in harmony. *E ho'olohe kākou i nā leo kūlauna.* Let's listen to the harmonizing parts. Comb. *kū + launa.* See *ho'okūlauna. Hīmeni kūlauna like.* To sing in harmony.

kula ho'o·wela wai *kik* Water heater. *Mān.* Also *pahu ho'owela wai.*

kula kaia·puni Hawai'i *kik* Hawaiian-medium school. See *kaiapuni.*

kula kama·li'i *kik* Preschool. *Lit.,* school (for) children.

kula lau·laha *kik* Plain, an expanse of flat land. *Lit.,* widespread plain. Also *'āina kula laulaha.* Cf. *nu'u laulaha.*

kū·lale *kik/ham* Stimulus; to stimulate. *Sh. kumu + ho'olalelale.* Cf. *ha'inole.*

kulali *kik* Curare, a poison for South American Indians' arrows; also a muscle relaxant in modern medicine. *Carib.*

kulalo *kik* Stalagmite. Sh. *kulu* + *lalo.* Cf. *kuluna.*

kula mau'u *kik* Meadow, grassy field. *Dic.*

kula·maka·loa *kik* Water filter for a fish tank, in aquaculture. *Lit.,* sedge water container.

kū·lana *kik* Status, rank, as position or social standing. *Dic., ext. mng.* Cf. *pae.* See *kūlana pale, moho. Kūlana olakino.* Health status. *Kūlana 'elua.* Runner-up, second place. *Ua puka wau i ke kūlana 'elua.* I took second place.

kū·lana·kau·hale *kik* Town or city, general term. *Dic.* Cf. *kaona, kiwikā.*

kū lana·kila *Ho'okele waiwai kū lanakila.* Free-market economy, i.e. the economy of a country wherein buying and selling can take place without government restrictions.

kū·lana pā·ho'o·nui *kik* Order of magnitude, in math. *Lit.,* exponent position.

kū·lana pale *kik* Defensive stance, as in basketball. *Mākaukau 'o Pa'a ma ke kūlana pale e kali ala i ka mea kūlele e holo mai.* Pa'a is set in the defensive stance waiting for the offender to come at him. *Lit.,* defense stance.

kula·nui kaia·ulu *kik* Community college. *Kulanui Kaiaulu o 'Ewa.* Leeward Community College.

kula'i *kik/ham* Tackle, i.e. the act of seizing and throwing down an opposing player with the ball, in football; to tackle (someone). *Dic., ext. mng.* Also *ho'ohina.* Cf. *kūlua.*

kula'i hā·pu'u *heh* To be sleeping or snoring, as a response when asked where someone is. *Aia 'o ia ke kula'i hāpu'u ala ma ka hale.* S/he's sleeping in the house. *Mān.* (MMLH).

kule *kik* Joule, a unit of energy. *Eng. Kule pāpiliona.* Gigajoule.

kule·ana *kik* Privilege or rights, as in a computer network. *Dic., ext. mng. Ke'ena Kuleana Hawai'i.* Office of Hawaiian Affairs (OHA).

kule·ana hā·nau *kik* Natural or inalienable rights, i.e. rights that people are born with and that a government should not attempt to deny. *'O ke kuleana o ke ola, ka noho kūkā'oko'a a me ka 'imi hau'oli, he mau kuleana hānau ia o kānaka.* The right to life, liberty, and the pursuit of happiness are natural rights of man. *Lit.,* birth rights.

kule·ana koho pā·loka *kik* Suffrage, i.e. the right to vote. *Lit.,* voting right.

kule·ana lau·'au'a *kik* Executive privilege, i.e. the right of the President to withhold information about his activities from the legislature or judiciary. *Ho'ā'o aku nei ka Pelekikena e ho'ohana aku i kōna kuleana lau'au'a ma kōna hihia ma ka 'aha ho'okolokolo.* The President tried to exercise his executive privilege in his court case. *Lit.,* right (to) withhold.

kule·hana *kik* Principle, as an accepted rule of action. Sh. *kuleana + hana.* Also *kahua hana.* Cf. *kulekele. Ke kulehana a 'Akimika.* Archimedes' principle, i.e. the buoyant force on an object submerged in a fluid is equal to the weight of the fluid displaced by that object, in science. *Ke kulehana a Penuli.* Bernoulli's principle. *Kulehana huinahā lō'ihi hapalua.* Half-rectangle principle. *Kulehana no ka helu 'ana.* Basic counting principle.

Kuleke *i'oa* Turkey; Turk; Turkish. *Dic.* Also *Tureke.*

kule·kele *kik* Policy. Sh. *kuleana + ho'okele.*

kule·kele kāohi *kik* Containment, as a government policy of preventing the expansion of a hostile power or ideology. *Lit.,* policy (to) repress.

kule·kele kū·loko *kik* Domestic policy, i.e. plans for dealing with national problems, in government.

kule·kele ʻāina ʻē *kik* Foreign policy, as a government function. *Kūkulu maila ka Pelekikena i kāna kulekele ʻāina ʻē ma ka launa ʻana me nā luna o nā ʻāina ʻē like ʻole.* The President established his foreign policy by associating with leaders of various foreign countries. *Lit.*, policy (for) foreign lands. Cf. *kōkua ʻāina ʻē.*

kū·lele *heh* Offense, as in sporting events; to play offense. *Dic., ext. mng.* Cf. *kūpale, pale.* See entries below.

kū·lele alo *kik* Man offense, i.e. offense for attacking face defense, in basketball. *Kū koke ihola ka ʻaoʻao kūlele ma ke kūlele alo.* The offense quickly set themselves up in the man offense. *Lit.*, face offense.

kū·lele kā·ʻei *kik* Zone offense, in basketball. *Ua kū nā mea kūlele ma waho o ke kī ma ke kūlele kāʻei.* The offense stood outside the key in zone offense.

kū·liu·kolu *heh* Triple-threat position, in basketball; to execute such a position. *ʻAʻohe kūliukolu ke ʻole ka paʻa o ke kinipōpō i ka lima.* In order to be in a triple-threat position, one must be in possession of the ball. *Sh. kū + liuliu + ʻekolu.*

kū·liu loko *kik* Low post, in basketball. *Sh. kūliukolu + loko.* Cf. *kūliu waho.*

kū·liu waho *kik* High post, in basketball. *Sh. kūliukolu + waho.* Cf. *kūliu loko.*

kū lima *kik/heh* Handstand; to do a handstand. Cf. *kū poʻo.* See *iwi kū lima.*

kū·lima *kik* Center or five man, in basketball. *He būtalo ʻo Shaq ma ke kūlana kūlima.* Shaq is the bull in the center position. *Sh. kūlana + ʻelima.* Cf. *huki pōpō.*

kulo *kik* Judo. *Niʻihau (Eng.).* See *paʻi kulo.*

kū·lohe·lohe *ʻa* Natural, lacking human intervention or contamination; raw, unprocessed, as raw materials. *Comb. kū- + lohelohe* (bare, uninterfered with). See *puni ao kūlohelohe, ʻakika ʻūpalu kūlohelohe. Ao kūlohelohe.* Nature. *Kaiameaola kūlohelohe.* Natural biological community. *Haku kūlohelohe.* Eolithic, in anthropology. *Ke au haku kūlohelohe.* Eolithic age, period. *Manehu kūlohelohe.* Natural force. *Makelia kūlohelohe.* Raw material. Also *memea kūlohelohe. Meaʻai kūlohelohe.* Natural food. *ʻŌnaehana Hoʻomalu ʻĀina Kūlohelohe.* Natural Areas Reserves System (NARS).

kū·loko *ʻa* Internal; closed, as a primary election. *Dic., ext. mng.* Cf. *kūākea, kūwaho, paʻaloko.* See entry below. *Kakena kūloko.* Internal drive, on a computer. *Kelepona kūloko.* Local call; to make such a call. *Leka kūloko.* Internal mail, as in an office or school. *Leka kūloko keʻena.* Office mail. *Leka kūloko kula.* Campus mail. *Memo kūloko.* Internal memo, as in tele-communication. *Wae moho kūloko.* Closed primary. *ʻIli kūloko.* Subcutus, in biology.

kū·loko *Haunaele kūloko.* Civil unrest. *Kānāwai kūloko.* Ordinance, i.e. a municipal regulation. *Kulekele kūloko.* Domestic policy, i.e. plans for dealing with national problems, in government.

kū·lua *kik* Twin, in math. *Dic., ext. mng. Helu kumu kūlua.* Twin primes.

kū·lua *kik* Shooting guard or two man, in basketball; tackle, either an offensive or defensive player, in football. *Sh. kūlana + ʻelua.* Cf. *kulaʻi. Kūlua hema.* Left tackle. *Kūlua ʻākau.* Right tackle.

kuluna *kik* Stalactite. *Sh. kulu + luna.* Cf. *kulalo.*

kuluna hau *kik* Icicle. *Lit.,* ice stalactite. *Dic.* Also *kulu hau pa'a.*

kū·mau *'a'* Standard, as in deviation, in math. *Dic., ext. mng.* Cf. *ma'amau.* See *papa hua'ōlelo kūmau. Haiahū kūmau.* Standard deviation. *Waihona kālā kūmau.* Endowment fund. Also *waihona ō.*

kū·maka *'a'* Visible. *Dic.* See *kūnalohia.*

kū·mī·kini *'a'* Mechanical, mechanics. *He mau 'āpana 'oni kō ka hāme'a kūmīkini.* Mechanical devices have moving parts in them. Comb. *kū + mīkini.*

kū·moe *kik* Headboard, of a bed. *Dic., ext. mng.* See *hao pela.*

kū·mole *kik* Reference, source, as a dictionary or other reference material. Sh. *kumu + mole.* Cf. *molekumu, puke noi'i.*

kumu *kik* Cause. *Dic.* See entries below and *hopena. Kānāwai kumu.* Common law.

kumu *kik* End of a sporting field or court. *Dic., ext. mng.* Also *po'o.* Cf. *iwi. Laina kumu.* End line. Also *laina po'o.*

kumu *Hua helu kumu.* Counting number, in math. *Kōkua helu kumu ho'ohui pālima.* Base-five counting piece. *Pepa maka'aha kumu ho'ohui pā'umi.* Base-ten grid paper.

kumu ala·ka'i *kik* Precedent, i.e. something done or said that may act as an example to justify it being done again. *Ma kēia hihia, ua ho'okumu 'ia he kumu alaka'i e nānā 'ia ana ma kēia hope aku.* This case sets a precedent that will be looked at from this time forward. *Lit.,* leading reason.

kumu i'a *kik* Large school of fish, such as *akule* or *aku. Mān.* Cf. *naho i'a.*

kumu·hana *kik* General subject or topic, as in literature. *Dic.*

Hopuna'ōlelo wehe kumuhana. Topic sentence, as of a paragraph. *Palapala 'āina kumuhana.* Thematic map. *Puke kumuhana.* Information book.

kumu honua *kik* Creation, origin of the world. *Dic. Mo'okalaleo kumu honua.* Creation literature, i.e. literature which describes the origin of the world.

kumu hō·'ai·'ē *kik* Credit, as at a bank or store. *'Ehia ka palena kumu hō'ai'ē ma kāu 'ea kāki?* What's the credit limit on your credit card? *Lit.,* credit base.

kumu ho'o·hau·mia *kik* Source pollution. *'O ke kumu kahi e ho'ohaumia 'ia nei ka 'āina, kapa 'ia ia 'ano haumia 'ana he kumu ho'ohaumia.* The source of pollution of the land is referred to as source pollution. *Lit.,* source causing pollution. *Kumu ho'ohaumia 'ike 'ia.* Point source pollution. *Kumu ho'ohaumia 'ike 'ole 'ia.* Non-point source pollution.

kumu ho'o·hā·like *kik* Example, model, as of behavior. *Ua lilo ke kumu kula i kumu ho'ohālike no kāna mau haumāna.* The schoolteacher became a model for his students. *Mān.* Cf. *la'ana.*

kumu ho'o·hā·like·like *kik* Control or control group, as in an experiment. *Lit.,* basis (for) comparison.

kumu ho'o·hui *kik* Base, in math. *Lit.,* base (for) joining. *Kumu ho'ohui pālima.* Base five. Also *kumu pālima. Kumu ho'ohui pālua.* Binary, i.e. a base-two system of numeration.

kumu ho'o·pi'i *kik* Complaint, i.e. a legal document that charges someone with having caused harm. *Dic.*

kumu·kolu *Mākala kumukolu.* Triceps, i.e. the muscle of the back of the upper arm.

kumu kū·ika·wā *kik* Extenuating circumstances. *Lit.,* special reason.

kumu·kū·ʻai *kik* Price, cost; quote, i.e. a stated price, as for merchandise. *Dic., ext. mng., sp. var.* Cf. *kumukūʻai koho.* See entries below. *Huli kumukūʻai.* Cost analysis.

kumu·kū·ʻai ana·kahi *kik* Unit price, in math. *Lit.,* price (per) unit of measurement.

kumu·kū·ʻai hale kū·ʻai *kik* Retail price. *Lit.,* store price. Cf. *kumukūʻai kālepa.*

kumu·kū·ʻai kā·lepa *kik* Wholesale price. *Lit.,* merchant price. Cf. *kumukūʻai hale kūʻai.*

kumu·kū·ʻai koho *kik* Estimated price, as for goods. Cf. *kāki koho.* See *koho.*

kumu·lā·ʻau ʻō·pio·pio *kik* Sapling. *Lit.,* young tree.

kumu·lilo *kik* Loss. *Dic.* Cf. *kumuloaʻa.*

kumu·loa·ʻa *kik* Profit. *Dic.* Cf. *kumulilo* and dictionary entries. See entry below.

kumu·loa·ʻa kā·ʻoko·ʻa *kik* Gross national product (GNP), i.e. the total monetary value of all goods and services produced in a country in a year. *Lit.,* complete profit.

kumu·loli *kik* Variable, as in a scientific experiment. *Lit.,* changing base. Cf. *hualau. Kumuloli kaukaʻi.* Dependent variable. *Kumuloli kūʻokoʻa.* Independent variable.

kumu loni·kū *kik* Prime meridian, in geography. *Lit.,* longitude base. Also *kumu lonitū.*

kumu·mana·ʻo *Papa kumumanaʻo.* Agenda, as for a meeting.

kumu·mea *kik* Element. *ʻO nā kumumea ʻehā o ke ao nei, ʻo ia nō ka honua, ka wai, ke ea, a me ke ahi.* The four basic elements of the earth are earth, water, air, and fire. Comb. *kumu + mea.* See *pūhui kumumea lua.*

kumu paina Kuke *kik* Cook pine. *Lit.,* Cook pine tree. Also *paina Kuke.*

kumu pā·hoʻo·nui *kik* Base, in exponential notation, in math. *Lit.,* exponent base. See entry below.

kumu pā·hoʻo·nui lua *kik* Square root, in math. *Lit.,* square base. See *kumu pāhoʻonui.*

kumu pā·lima See *kumu hoʻohui pālima.*

kumu·pa·ʻa *kik* Principal, i.e. money loaned, usually at a given interest rate and for a specified time. *Dic.* Also *kālā kumupaʻa.* See *uku paneʻe.*

kumu puʻu·naue *kik* Dividend, in math. *Dic., sp. var.*

kumu wai *ʻĀina kumu wai.* Watershed, i.e. an area from which water drains. *ʻĀina kumu wai kiwikā.* Municipal water shed.

kumu waina *kik* Grapevine, the plant. *Dic.*

kumu·wai·wai *kik* Resource, i.e. a source of supply. *Dic., sp. var. Kumuwaiwai kūlohelohe.* Natural resource. *Māhele Kumuwaiwai Kai.* Division of Aquatic Resources. *ʻOihana Kumuwaiwai ʻĀina.* Department of Land and Natural Resources (DLNR).

kumu welo *kik* Heredity. *Lit.,* basis (of) hereditary traits. See *welo.*

kumu·wili *kik* Drill. *Niʻihau.* See *makawili, wili.*

kumu ʻā·kō·lī See *kōkua hua mele.*

kumu·ʻi·ʻo *kik* Protein. Comb. *kumu + ʻiʻo.* Also *polokina.*

kumu ʻū·hā See *mākala ʻūhā.*

kūna ka·ʻa ʻō·hua *kik* Bus stop. *Lit.,* bus stopping place.

kū·nalo·hia *ʻa* Invisible. *Lit.,* (in a) state of disappearance. See *kūmaka.*

kū·nā·nahu *kik* Black, porous, light rock used to scrape the interior of gourds. *Niʻihau (KKK).*

Kunesi *iʻoa* Guernsey. *Eng. Ka mokupuni ʻo Kunesi.* Guernsey Island.

kuni See *peni kuni.*

kuni·kia *kik* Trademark. Comb. *kuni + kia.*

kuni·pona *kik* Abacus. (Cantonese *shunpon.*)

kū·noa *ʻa* Freedom; free, exempt from external restrictions. Sh. *kū i ka noa.* Cf. *kaʻawale,* not in use; *kūʻokoʻa,* independent; *manuahi,* no charge.

kunuko *kik* Junco, a kind of bird. *Eng.* Also *manu kunuko.*

kupa *kik* Citizen. *Hoʻomalu ʻia nā pono o nā kupa o ka ʻāina e ke kānāwai.* The rights of the citizens of the country are protected by law. *Dic.* Also *makaʻāinana. Kiule hoa kupa.* Jury of peers, as in court trials. *Kupa kaumokuʻāina pālua.* Dual citizen. Also *makaʻāinana kaumokuʻāina pālua.*

Kupa *iʻoa* Cuba; Cuban. *Dic.* Also *Kuba.*

kū·pale *ham* To defend, as your basket, in basketball. *Hoʻi hikiwawe akula ka ʻaoʻao kūpale e kūpale aku i ka hīnaʻi.* The defense quickly returned to defend their basket. *Dic.* Cf. *kaupale, pale.* See entry below.

kū·pale *Loio kūpale.* Defense attorney, attorney for the defendant. *Mea kūpale.* Defendant, in court. *ʻAoʻao kūpale.* Defense, i.e. the defendant's case or counsel in a lawsuit.

kū·papa *ʻa* Neutral, as neither base nor acid on a pH scale. *Māori. Kuhiakau kūpapa.* Null, in math.

kū·papa·kū *kik* Bedrock. *Dic.*

kupe·kio *kik* Edible oyster. Comb. *kupe + kio.* Cf. *pipi.*

Kupelo *iʻoa* Cyprus; Cypriot. *Dic.* Also *Kupero.*

Kupero *iʻoa* Cyprus; Cypriot. *Dic.* Also *Kupelo.*

kū·pī *heh* To reflect, as light, heat, or sound. *Ke kūpī nei ka mālamalama mai ke aniani mai.* Light is reflecting off the mirror. Sh. *kūpinaʻi.* See *hoʻokūpī, huina kūpī.*

kū·pili *ʻa* Logic; logical. *Lit.,* (in a) state of close association. See *hewa kūpili. Noʻonoʻo kūpili.* Logical thinking.

kū·pita *kik* Cubit, an ancient unit of measurement used in Bible times. *Dic.,* sp. var.

kū·pona *kik* Coupon. *Eng.*

kū·pono *ʻa* Reasonable. *Dic.,* ext. mng. See entry below. *Kumukūʻai kūpono.* Reasonable price.

kū·pono *ʻa* Perpendicular, in math. *Dic.* See *hoʻopiha kūpono. Kaha ʻoki hapalua kūpono.* Perpendicular bisector. *Nā kaha kūpono.* Perpendicular lines. *Kiʻe kūpono.* Altitude of a triangle. Cf. *kiʻekiʻe, kiʻekiʻena.*

kū poʻo *kik/heh* Headstand; to do a headstand. Cf. *kū lima.*

kupua See *kaʻao kupua.*

kupu·lau *kik* Spring. *Dic.* See *māuiili.*

kupu·riku *ʻa* Cupric. *Kupuriku karabonahate.* Cupric carbonate. *Kupuriku ʻokesaside.* Cupric oxide. *Kupuriku sulafahate.* Cupric sulfate. *Kupuriku sulafaside.* Cupric sulfide.

kū·waena *ʻa* Median; middle, used only in special terminology. *Lit.,* exist (in the) middle. See *laina kūwaena. Au Palaʻo Kūwaena.* Middle Kingdom, in Egyptology. *Helu kūwaena.* Median (number), in math. *ʻIli kūwaena.* Dermis, in biology.

kū·waho *ʻa* External. Comb. *kū + waho.* Cf. *kūloko, paʻaloko. Huina kūwaho.* Exterior angle, in math. *Kakena kūwaho.* External drive, on a computer. *Kelepona kūwaho.* Long-distance call; to make such a call. *ʻIli kūwaho.* Epidermis, in biology.

kū wā·wae See *iwi kū wāwae. Aʻa kino kū wāwae.* Tibial vein. *Aʻa puʻuwai kū wāwae.* Tibial artery.

kū·ʻai *Hoʻolaha kūʻai.* Advertisement, ad; commercial.

kū·ʻai·emi *kik/ham* Sale; to be or put on sale. Comb. *kūʻai + emi. Nā kīwī kūʻaiemi.* TVs on sale. *Kūʻaiemi ʻia nā kīwī.* The TVs are on sale.

kū·ʻai wale *ham* Over-the-counter. *Lāʻau kūʻai wale.* Over-the-counter drug or medication. Cf. *kuhikuhi lāʻau.*

kū·ʻau alelo *kik* Back of the tongue. *Lit.,* tongue stem. See *lau alelo, mole alelo, waena alelo, wēlau alelo.*

kū·ʻē *Hoʻopiʻi kūʻē.* To appeal, i.e. ask a higher court to review a decision made by a lower court.

kū·ʻē lula *ham* Exception to a rule. *Lit.,* contrary (to) rules.

kuʻe·maka See *pena kuʻemaka.*

kuʻe ʻamo *kik* Coccyx, i.e. the terminus of the spinal column; tailbone. Sh. *kuʻekuʻe + ʻamo.* Also *iwi kuʻe ʻamo.*

kū·ʻē·ʻē See *paʻa manehu kūʻēʻē.*

kuʻi *ham* To set, as an imu. *Niʻihau.* Cf. *huaʻi.* See entries below. *Kuʻi i ka imu.* To set an imu.

kuʻi *ham* Convergent, i.e. meeting in plate techtonics, in geology. *Dic., ext. mng.* Cf. *kākele, neʻe ʻoā. Palena kuʻi.* Convergent boundary.

kuʻia *kik* Error, as in a computer program. *Ua loaʻa kekahi kuʻia ma ke paʻi ʻana.* An error occurred while printing. *Dic. ext. mng.*

kuʻia *ʻa* Foul, in team sports such as basketball. *Ua kuʻia iā Keoni ʻo Kekoa, a kīpaku ʻia ʻo Keoni, no ka mea, ʻelima āna kuʻia.* Keoni fouled Kekoa, and Keoni was ejected because he had committed five fouls. *Dic., ext. mng.* Cf. *hoʻokuʻia.* See entries below.

kuʻia kime *ʻa* Team foul, in team sports such as basketball. *Na ʻŌlani ke kuʻia kime mua; ua paʻi hewa ʻo ia i ka lima o kōna hoa paio iā ia e kī ana.* ʻŌlani committed the first team foul; he accidentally hit his opponent's arm as he was shooting.

kuʻia kū·helu *ʻa* Technical foul, in team sports such as basketball. *Ua kū ʻia ka naʻau o ke kime i ke kuʻia kūhelu i kā lākou kaʻi.* The team felt bad about the technical foul that their coach had committed. *Lit.,* official foul.

kuʻia kū·lele *ʻa* Offensive foul, in team sports such as basketball. *Na ka mea kūlele ke kuʻia kūlele inā nāna e kulaʻi ʻino i kōna mea kūpale.* The offender commits the offensive foul if he was the one to knock down his defender. *Lit.,* offense foul.

kuʻia pili·kino *ʻa* Personal foul, in team sports such as basketball. *Ke hoʻāʻo nei ʻo Moe e akahele i kōna pāʻani ʻana, no ka mea, ʻehā āna kuʻia pilikino; hoʻokahi koe a e kīpaku ʻia ʻo ia.* Moe is trying to be careful while playing, since he already has four personal fouls; one more and he'll be ejected.

kuʻia ʻā·keʻa *ʻa* Blocking foul, in basketball. *Ua kuʻia ʻākeʻa iā Hāloa ʻo Nani Boy, ʻoiai ua neʻe mai ʻo Hāloa i mua pono o Nani Boy iā ia ala e kaha mai ana i ka hupa.* Hāloa committed a blocking foul against Nani Boy, since Hāloa moved directly in front of Nani Boy as he was driving towards the basket. *Lit.,* block-out foul.

kuʻi·hao *ham* To weld. *Niʻihau.*

kuʻi·kahi *kik* Consortium. *Ua komo nā ʻahahui pāʻoihana a me kekahi ʻoihana o ke aupuni i ke kuʻikahi no ka hoʻokō ʻana i ka papahana.* Commercial enterprises and a government agency entered into a consortium to implement the program. *Dic., ext. mng.* See entries below. *Hui kuʻikahi.* Alliance, i.e. a group of nations that have agreed to help or protect each other; to form such an alliance.

kuʻi·kahi *kik* League, in sports. *Dic.* See entries below and *hui.*

Kuʻi·kahi Pō·hili Au·puni *kik* National Baseball League.

Ku·i·kahi Pō·hili 'Ame·lika *kik*
American Baseball League.

Ku'i·kahi Pō·peku Au·puni *kik*
National Football League (NFL).

kū·'ike See *kālā kū'ike, waiwai kū'ike.*

kū·'ikena *kik* Fact. Comb. *kū +
'ikena. Puke noi'i kū'ikena.*
Encyclopedia.

ku'i·koli *ham* To compromise. Comb.
ku'i + koli.

ku'ina *kik* Connection, as in a
computer program. *Dic., ext. mng.* See
entries below and *ho'oku'i.*

ku'ina *kik* Front, as of weather. *Lit.,*
junction. *Ku'ina hu'ihu'i.* Cold front.
Ku'ina mehana. Warm front. *Ku'ina
pa'a.* Stationary front.

ku'ina una honua *kik* Plate
techtonics, in geology. See *kākele, ku'i,
ne'e 'oā, palena.*

ku'ina ko'o *kik* Plug-in, as in a
computer program. *Lit.,* support
connection.

ku'ina mea·'ai *kik* Food chain. *Lit.,*
food joining. Cf. *'upena mea'ai.*

ku'i nuke·liu *kik* Nuclear fusion.
Lit., joining (of) nuclei.

ku'i paipu *kik* Pipe fitting. *Ni'ihau.*

ku'i pā·na'i *ham* Counterpunch. Cf.
ho'ouka pāna'i.

ku'i·pē *ham* To cancel, i.e. the
compression of one wave at the same
time as the rarefaction of another wave,
in science. *Dic., ext. mng., sp. var.* See
ku'ipēhia.

ku'i·pē·hia *'a* To be cancelled (out),
in science or argumentation; cancellation.
Comb. *ku'ipē + -hia.* See *ku'ipē.*

ku'i pu'u·pu'u *ham* To spike with a
closed fist, in volleyball. *Ni'ihau.* Cf.
hānai pu'upu'u. See *hili, pa'i
pālahalaha.*

ku'i 'ā·mana *ham* To bump (the ball),
in volleyball. *Lit.,* Y-shaped strike.

ku'i 'ū·hā See *mākala 'ūhā.*

kū·'oko'a *Kumuloli kū'oko'a.*
Independent variable. *Mākala kū'oko'a.*
Smooth muscle.

kū·'ono *kik* Inside corner, nook. *Dic.*
Also *po'opo'o.* Cf. *kihi.* See entry below.

kū·'ono *kik* Cell, as in databases or
tables. *Ua piha nā kū'ono o ka pakuhi
maka'aha.* The cells of the spreadsheet
are full. *Dic., ext. mng.*

ku'u *heh* To land, as an airplane or
bird. *Ni'ihau.*

ku'u·loko *Lōku'u ku'uloko.*
Endocrine gland. Cf. *lōku'u ku'uwaho.*

ku'una *'a* Traditional. *He hana
ku'una ka hana lei 'ana.* Lei making is a
traditional activity. *Dic. A'o kahua 'ike
ku'una.* Traditional knowledge-based
learning. *Mo'okalaleo ku'una.*
Traditional literature. *'Ike ku'una.*
Traditional knowledge.

kū 'ū·niu *kik* Pivot, as a position in
basketball; pivot point. *Lit.,* pivot stand.
See *'ūniu.*

ku'u·pau *heh* To do with all one's
might or strength. *Dic./Ni'ihau.* Cf.
lawe pīlahi

ku'u·waho *Lōku'u ku'uwaho.*
Exocrine gland. Cf. *lōku'u ku'uloko.*

ku'u wela *ham* Exothermic, i.e. giving
off heat. Cf. *omo wela.*

Kuba *i'oa* Cuba; Cuban. *Dic.* Also
Kupa.

kh Abbreviation for *kī'aha* (cup).

khh Abbreviation for *kahahānai*
(radius).

kk Abbreviation for *kuaka* (quart).

Kk. Abbreviation for *Kauka* (Doctor), for
use as a title before a person's name.
Kk. Halenui (Kauka Halenui). Dr.
Halenui.

kkal Abbreviation for *kenikalame*
(centigram).

KKK Abbreviation for *kā'ei ku'ina
kopikala* (intertropical convergent zone;
ITCZ).

kkkal Abbreviation for *kekikalame* (decigram).

kkl Abbreviation for *kekilika* (deciliter).

kkm Abbreviation for *kekimika* (decimeter).

kkn Abbreviation for *kekona* (second).

kl Abbreviation for *kilo* (kilo), *kenilika* (centiliter).

Klk Abbreviation for *Kelekia* (Celsius).

klkal Abbreviation for *kilokalame* (kilogram).

kll Abbreviation for *kilolika* (kiloliter).

klm Abbreviation for *kilomika* (kilometer).

kln Abbreviation for *kālani* (gallon).

klt Abbreviation for *kilouate* (kilowatt).

Km Abbreviation for *komohana* (west).

knm Abbreviation for *kenimika* (centimeter).

kp Abbreviation for *kapuaʻi* (foot).

kp ph² Abbreviation for *kapuaʻi pāhoʻonui lua* (square foot).

L

l Abbreviation for *lika* (liter).

lā *kik* Day, date. *Dic.* No abbreviation. See *palena pau.* Format for date in Hawaiian: Day/month/year: *11 Iune 2002.* June 11, 2002. Abbreviations use Roman numerals for month to avoid confusion: *10/VI/02 6/10/02.*

lā *kik* Fin, as of a fish, general term. *Dic. Nā lā o ka iʻa.* The fins of a fish. *Nīʻau lā.* Ray, i.e. one of the bony spines supporting the membrane of a fish's fin.

lā *kik* La, the sixth note on the musical scale. *Dic.* See *pākōlī.*

laeʻoʻo *kik* Master's, as a degree at a university. *Ke kākau nei wau i kaʻu pepa no ka loaʻa ʻana o koʻu kēkelē laeoʻo.* I'm writing my thesis to get my Master's degree. *Dic., ext. mng., sp. var.* Also *MA* or *MS (pronounced* mūʻā, mūsā). Cf. *laepua, laeʻula.* See *muli*

puka. Kēkelē laeoʻo. Master's degree. Also *palapala laeoʻo.*

Lae·uli·uli *iʻoa* Cape Verde. *Lit.,* green cape. *Nā mokupuni ʻo Laeuliuli.* Cape Verde Islands.

lae·hano *ʻa* Honored. *Comb. lae + hano. Papa laehano.* Honor roll, as in elementary through high school.

lae·kahi *kik* Specialist. *Comb. lae + kahi.* Cf. *laeʻula* (dic.).

lae·pua *kik* Baccalaureate, bachelor's, as a degree at a university. *Loaʻa maila koʻu kēkelē laepua ma ke Kulanui o Hawaiʻi.* I got my bachelor's degree at the University of Hawaiʻi. *Lit.,* emerging wisdom. Also *BA* or *BS (pronounced* bēʻā, bēsā). Cf. *laeoʻo, laeʻula.* See *mua puka. Kēkelē laepua.* Bachelor's degree. Also *palapala laepua.*

lae·ʻula *kik* Doctorate, as a degree at a university. *Ke hana nei ʻo Kale no kōna kēkelē laeʻula ma ke kālaimeaola.* Kale is working on his doctorate degree in biology. *Dic., ext. mng.* Also *kauka.* Cf. *laeoʻo, laepua. Kēkelē laeʻula.* Doctorate degree. Also *palapala laeʻula.*

laiki *kik* Rice. *Dic.* Also *lāisi. Laiki keʻokeʻo.* White rice. Also *lāisi keʻokeʻo. Laiki mākuʻe.* Brown rice. Also *lāisi mākuʻe. Laiki mōchī.* Mochi rice. Also *lāisi mōchī. Pōpō laiki.* Rice ball, musubi. Also *pōpō lāisi, musubī.*

lai·kī *kik* Lychee, litchi. *Dic.*

laimi *kik* Lime. *Eng.*

laina *kik* Line, as on a basketball court. *Dic., ext. mng.* See entries below. *Laina iwi kī.* Side line of the key on a basketball court. *Laina kumu.* Base or end line. *Laina ʻaoʻao.* Side line.

laina o ke kō·kua hua mele *kik* Horizontal line on a musical staff. *Lit.,* line of the musical staff. Also *laina o ke kōkua.* Cf. *wā o ke kōkua hua mele.*

laina helu *kik* Number line, in math.

laina helu lā *kik* International date line. *Lit.,* line (for) counting days.

laina hī·naʻi *kik* End line, on a basketball court. *Nou wale akula ʻo Barkley i ke kinipōpō mai ka laina hīnaʻi a hiki i ka hoa kime ma kekahi poʻo o ke kahua.* Barkley whipped the ball from the base line to his teammate at the other end of the court. *Lit.,* basket line. Also *laina hupa, laina kumu, laina poʻo.*

laina hoʻo·uka *kik* Scrimmage line, in football. *Lit.,* attack line.

laina hupa *kik* End line, on a basketball court. *Hoʻomaka ka ʻaoʻao kūlele mai ka laina hupa a holo i kekahi ʻaoʻao.* The offense starts from the end line and goes all the way to the other end. *Lit.,* basket line. Also *laina hīnaʻi, laina kumu, laina poʻo.*

laina kā·lai·lai *kik* Transect, i.e. a sample area, as of vegetation, usually in the form of a long strip. *Lit.,* line (to) analyze.

laina kī noa *kik* Free throw line, in basketball. *Inā hoʻokuʻia ʻia ʻoe iā ʻoe e kaha ana i ka hīnaʻi ma loko o ka puka kī, e hele ʻoe i ka laina kī noa.* If you are fouled while driving to the basket within the key, you will go to the free throw line.

laina kū·lele *kik* Offensive line, in football. *Lit.,* offense line.

laina kū·pale *kik* Defensive line, in football. *Lit.,* defending line. Also *laina pale.*

laina kū·waena *kik* Half-court line, on a basketball court. *Ua kī ʻia ke kinipōpō mai ka laina kūwaena mai, a ʻuāʻuā aʻela ke anaina i ke komo ʻana i loko o ka hīnaʻi.* The ball was shot from the half-court line, and the crowd screamed when the ball went in the basket. *Lit.,* median line.

laina lahi·lahi *kik* Hairline, as in a computer program. *Lit.,* thin line.

laina laki·kū *kik* Parallel, i.e. an imaginary circle on the earth's surface parallel to the equator and designated in degrees of latitude. *Lit.,* latitude line. Also *laina latitū.*

laina lena *kik* Line of sight, sight line. Also *laina ʻike.*

laina manawa *kik* Time line.

laina pale *kik* Defensive line, in football. *Lit.,* defense line. Also *laina kūpale.*

laina pā·weo *kik* Skew line, in math. See *pāweo.*

laina ʻekolu mika *kik* Three-meter line, in volleyball. See *laina ʻumi kapuaʻi, ʻaʻena ʻekolu mika.*

laina ʻike *kik* Line of sight, sight line. *Lit.,* line (to) see. Also *laina lena.*

laina ʻike·pili *kik* Data stream, as in a computer program. *Lit.,* data line.

laina ʻumi kapu·aʻi *kik* Ten-foot line, in volleyball. Niʻihau. See *laina ʻekolu mika, ʻaʻena ʻumi kapuaʻi.*

lāisi *kik* Rice. Niʻihau. See *laiki.*

laoa See *lāʻau make laoa.*

Laosa *iʻoa* Laos; Laotian. *Eng.*

lau- A prefix meaning multi- or many. *Dic., ext. mng.* *Nā moku ahikao lauʻenekini.* Multiengined spaceships.

lau alelo *kik* Blade of the tongue. *Lit.,* tongue blade. See *kūʻau alelo, mole alelo, waena alelo, wēlau alelo.*

lau·alo *kik* Ventral, in biology. Comb. *lau + alo.* Cf. *lauhope, laukua, laumua.*

lau·ana *kik* Pattern, repeating series. Comb. *lau + ana.* See entry below. *Lauana helu.* Number pattern. *Lauana hoʻokahua.* Settlement pattern, in geography.

lau·ana wā *kik* Meter, in music. *Lit.,* time pattern.

lau·ele *heh* To daydream. *Dic., ext. mng.*

lau·ika *kik* Mode, as the number or numbers that occur most often in a set, in math. Comb. *lau + ika* (strong pattern).

lau hihi pā *kik* Ivy. *Lit.,* leaf (which) creeps (on) walls. Also *ʻaiwi.*

lau·hope *kik* Posterior, in biology.
Comb. *lau* + *hope.* Cf. *laualo, laukua,
laumua. Kualā lauhope.* Posterior dorsal
fin, of a fish.

lau huina·hā lō·ʻihi *kik* Rectangular
array, in math. *Lit.,* rectangle pattern.

lau kala·koa *kik* Croton. *Lit.,* varie-
gated leaves. Cf. *lau noʻe.*

lau kā·pala *kik* Print, as something
impressed or stamped with a print. *Lit.,*
printed design. See *kāpala.*

lau·ka·ʻi *ʻa* Coordinated, put in order.
Comb. *lau* + *kaʻi.* See *hoʻolaukaʻi.*

lau·ka·ʻina *kik* Sequence, in math.
Comb. *lau* + *kaʻina.*

lau·kua *ʻa* Irregular, as in shape;
amorphous, i.e. having no regular
crystalline form. *Dic., ext. mng.* Cf.
analahi. Kinona laukua. Irregular shape.
ʻAkano laukua. Amorphous substance.

lau·kua *kik* Dorsal, in biology. Comb.
lau + *kua.* Cf. *laualo, lauhope, laumua.
Kualā laukua.* Dorsal fin, of a fish.

lau·lā *ʻa* Wide. *Dic.* See entries below
and *kokoke, lōpū.* See also *pahuhopu
laulā. Paʻi laulā.* Wide shot, as of a
photograph or in movie or video
production (preceded by *ke*). *Paʻi a
laulā.* To take a wide shot. *Paʻi laulā
loa.* Extreme wide shot. *Paʻi a laulā loa.*
To take an extreme wide shot.

lau·lā *ʻa* Width or breadth, in math.
Dic. Abb. *ll.* Also *ana laulā, ākea.* Cf.
loa, lōʻihi, hohonu, kiʻekiʻe. See *laulā
loli.* Range, i.e. the difference between
the largest and smallest number or value.
Dic., ext. mng. Also *laulā loa.*

lau·lā *Koho pāloka laulā.* General
election, in politics.

lau·lau *kik* Brim, as of a floppy hat.
Mān. (MW). Cf. *kihikihi, pekekeu.*

lau·laha See *kula laulaha.*

lau·lā hawewe *kik* Amplitude, i.e. the
greatest distance the particles in a wave
rise or fall from their rest position, in
science. *Lit.,* vibration width. See
hoʻolaulā hawewe, ʻanini laulā hawewe.

lau·lahi *kik* Sheet, as of stamps.
Comb. *lau* + *lahi. Laulahi poʻoleka.*
Sheet of stamps.

lau·lā kala *kik* Tint, as of a television
screen. *Lit.,* breadth (of) color. Cf.
ʻauina kala.

lau·lā loli *kik* Variable width, as in a
computer program.

lau·like See *manaʻo laulike.*

lau liʻi *ʻAʻapehihi lau liʻi.*
Philodendron.

lau loa *ʻa* Lengthwise. *Dic.*

lau·mua *kik* Anterior, in biology.
Comb. *lau* + *mua.* Cf. *laualo, lauhope,
laukua. Kualā laumua.* Anterior dorsal
fin, of a fish.

launa *ʻa* Compatible, as of computer
programs. *Ua launa kēia lako
polokalamu hou me kāu kamepiula.*
This new software is compatible with
your computer. *Dic., ext. mng.* Cf.
launa ʻole. See entries below and *ʻaʻohe
launa. Hulu waihona launa.* Compatible
file format.

launa *ʻa* Corresponding, in math.
Huina launa. Corresponding angle, of a
triangle. *ʻAoʻao launa.* Corresponding
side, of a triangle.

lau nahele ʻō·iwi *kik* Natural
vegetation. *Lit.,* native plants.

launa kanaka *Aʻo launa kanaka.*
Socialization; to socialize, i.e. fit, teach, or
train (someone) for a social environment
or to associate sociably with others.

launa ʻole *ʻa* Incompatible, as of
computer programs. *He hulu waihona
launa ʻole kēia.* This is an incompatible
file format. *Lit.,* not compatible. Cf.
launa.

lau·nea *ʻa* Bare, as a tree without
leaves. *Dic.*

lau noʻe *kik* Coleus. *Lit.,* colored leaf.
Cf. *lau kalakoa.*

lau·pa·ʻa·hapa *ʻAilakele laupaʻahapa.*
Polyunsaturated fat.

lau po'o kuni *kik* Letterhead design. See *po'o kuni.*

lau·'ai *kik* Vegetable. *Maika'i ka lau'ai no ke olakino.* Vegetables are good for you. *Dic., ext. mng., sp. var.* See *'aila meakanu.*

lau·'au'a *Kuleana lau'au'a.* Executive privilege, i.e. the right of the President to withhold information about his activities from the legislature or judiciary.

lau·'ala *kik* Herb, as basil, thyme, etc. *'O ke kōko'olau, he lau'ala lapa'au ia i kī maika'i no ka lapa'au 'ana i kekahi mau 'ano ma'i.* Kōko'olau is a kind of herb with medical properties which makes a good tea for treating some kinds of sickness. Comb. *lau + 'ala.*

lau 'ī·nana *kik* Cotyledon. *Lit.,* leaf (from) stirring of life. *Lau 'īnana kahi.* Monocotyledon. *Lau 'īnana lua.* Dicotyledon.

lahi See *pūaina lahi.*

lahi·lahi *Laina lahilahi.* Hairline, as in a computer program.

laho·mā·pū *kik* Kiwi fruit. Comb. *laho + māpū.* Also *hua'ai kiwi.*

lā·hui *kik* Species, in biology. *Dic.* Also *lāhulu.* See entries below and *kālaipuolo lāhui, lāhulu.*

lā·hui *Paiha'akei lāhui.* Racism, i.e. adhering to a belief that one's own race is superior to another race. Also *paiha'akei 'ili. 'Āpana 'aha'ōlelo lāhui.* Congressional district, in government.

lā·hui emi *kik* Depleted species. Also *lāhulu emi.* Cf. *'ane halapohe.*

lā·hulu *kik* Species, in biology. Sh. *lāhui + hulu.* Also *lāhui. Lāhulu emi.* Depleted species. *Pili lāhulu.* Related species. *Kānāwai Lāhulu 'Ane Halapohe.* Endangered Species Act.

laka *kik/ham* Lock; to lock. *E laka 'oe i ka 'īpuka a pa'a.* Lock the door. *Dic.* See *pahu laka.*

lakau·ā *'a'* Domesticated, as a pet or for work. Sh. *laka + kauā.* Cf. *'āhiu, lōhiu.*

laka uai *kik* Sliding latch. *Lit.,* sliding lock.

laka helu *kik* Combination lock. *Lit.,* lock (with) numbers. Cf. *helu laka.*

laka ma'aka *kik* Caps lock, as on a computer or typewriter keyboard. *Pihi laka ma'aka.* Caps lock key (preceded by *ke*). Also *pihi laka.*

Laka·wia *i'oa* Latvia. *Eng.*

lāke See *manu lāke.*

lakeke *kik* Blouse. *Dic./Ni'ihau.* Also *palauki.* Cf. *lākeke.*

lā·keke *kik* Jacket. *Eng.* Cf. *lakeke.*

laki *Pili helu laki.* Lottery.

lā·kiō *kik* Ratio; rate, i.e. a ratio that compares different kinds of units, in math; quantity, amount, or degree of something measured per unit of something else, as of time. *Eng.* See entries below and *pakuhi lākiō. Ma ka lākiō he 60 mil/hl.* At the rate of 60 mph.

lā·kiō ana·puni *kik* Constant of proportionality, in math. *Lit.,* ratio (of) circumference.

lā·kiō like *kik* Proportion, proportional, in math; equal ratio. *Lit.,* same ratio.

lā·kiō pa'a·pū wai *kik* Specific gravity, relative gravity. *Lit.,* water density ratio.

lakika *kik* Radish. *Eng.*

laki·kū *kik* Latitude. *Dic.* Also *latitū.* Cf. *lonikū. Laina lakikū.* Parallel, i.e. an imaginary circle on the earth's surface parallel to the equator and designated in degrees of latitude. Also *laina latitū.*

lako hao *kik* Hardware, such as tools made of metal. *Lit.,* supply (of) metal tools. Cf. *lako pa'a. Hale kū'ai lako hao.* Hardware store.

lako hanu *kik* Breathing equipment, as for use in space exploration.

lako ho'o·nani *kik* Jewelry. Also *lako kāhiko.* Cf. *lako kula* (dic.).

lako hoʻo·puka *kik* Factors of production, in economics. *Lit.,* supplies (for) producing.

lako kā·hiko *kik* Jewelry. Also *lako hoʻonani.* Cf. *lako kula* (dic.).

lako·lako *kik* Accessories, peripherals, as for a computer. *Dic., ext. mng.*

lako paʻa *kik* Hardware, as for a computer. *Lit.,* solid gear. Cf. *lako polokalamu, lako hao.*

lako polo·kalamu *kik* Software, as for a computer. *Lit.,* program gear. Cf. *lako paʻa.*

lako ʻai·ʻē *kik/ʻa* Loan, i.e. money lent at interest; to have a loan. *Lit.,* provision (through) debt. Also *ʻaiʻē.* Cf. *hoʻolako ʻaiʻē, lawe ʻaiʻē.*

lakuna *kik* Raccoon. *Dic.*

lala *kik* Diagonal. *E kau i kēia mau kikohoʻe i like ka huinanui ma nā lala pākahi me ka -3.* Arrange these digits so that their total will be -3 on each diagonal. *Dic.* See *lala kūpono, kaha lala.*

lala *kik* Split end, in football. *Dic., new mng.* Cf. *muku.* See *ʻāwaʻa lala.*

lā·lā *kik* Member, as of an organization. *Dic. Nā lālā o ka papa.* Board members.

lā·lā *kik* Phrase, in grammar. *Dic., ext. mng.* Cf. *māmalaʻōlelo.*

lā·lahi·lewa *Ao lālahilewa.* Cirrus cloud. *Sh. lahilahi + lewa.*

lala kū·pono *kik* Hypotenuse. *Lit.,* perpendicular diagonal.

lā·lani *Haʻihelu lālani.* Linear equation. *Pālākiō lālani.* Linear scale, in geography. *Pepa anakuhi lālani.* Linear unit paper, in math.

lala·ʻē *ʻa* Eccentric. Comb. *lala + ʻē.* See *ʻūlala* (dic.).

lā·lelo *kik* Lateral, in linguistics. *Sh. lā + alelo.*

lali·noka *kik* Hieroglyph, hieroglyphics. *ʻAʻole i maopopo ʻia ka lalinoka a ka poʻe ʻAikupita a hiki i ka hoʻomaopopo ʻia ʻana ma ka hoʻohālike ʻana i ka lalinoka o ka pōhaku Roseta me kekahi mau ʻōlelo i kākau pū ʻia ma luna o ia pōhaku.* Egyptian hieroglyphics was not understood until it was figured out by comparing hieroglyphs found on the Rosetta stone with other languages which were also enscribed on that stone. (Assyrian *rahleenos.*)

lā·liʻi *ʻa* Detailed, intricate, as a design. *He lau lāliʻi maoli kēia lau kapa kuiki.* This is a very intricate quilt design. *Dic.*

lalo Sub-, under-. *Dic., ext. mng.* See entries below and *papa o lalo.*

lalo one *kik* Subsand.

lalo honua *kik* Underground. *Lit.,* beneath (the) land.

lalo kai *kik* Submarine, submerged, undersea. *Lit.,* beneath (the) sea. *Lua pele lalo kai.* Submerged volcano. *Papa ʻanuʻu lalo kai.* Underwater terrace.

lalo kopi·kala *kik* Subtropical.

lalo lepo *kik* Subsoil. Cf. *lepo uhi.*

lalo ʻala·paina *kik* Subalpine. *Lit.,* below alpine. See *ʻalapaina. Ululāʻau lalo ʻalapaina.* Subalpine forest.

lama *Ana lama hanu.* Breathalyzer. *Nui lama koko.* Blood alcohol level.

lā·meka *kik* Ceramic. *Eng. Kile lāmeka.* Ceramic tile.

lā·mia *kik* Lemur. *He pili lāhui ka lāmia me ke keko ma kekahi ʻano, akā, no ka nui kūpono o ka ʻokoʻa i ke keko, ua manaʻo ʻia he lāhui ʻokoʻa aʻe nō.* The lemur is a related species to the monkey, but because of some marked differences, it is considered a different species altogether. *Greek.*

lami·neka *ham* To laminate. *Eng.*

lā·nahu *kik* Coal. *Dic.* Cf. *nānahu. Kākinoea lānahu.* Coal gasification.

lana·kia *kik* Ranger. *Eng.* See *hale kiaʻi ululāʻau.*

lana·kila *Hele lanakila.* To go freely, i.e. have freedom to go wherever one pleases, "have the run of the place." *Hoʻokele waiwai kū lanakila.* Free-market economy, i.e. the economy of a country wherein buying and selling can take place without government restrictions. *Māhele lanakila.* Winner's bracket, as in a sports tournament.

lani·uma *kik* Geranium. *Dic.*

Lani·haʻi *iʻoa* Al Nair-Alpha Gruis, a star. *Mān. (HA).*

Lani·hou *iʻoa* Mira, a star. *Mān. (HA).*

Lani·holo·ʻokoʻa *iʻoa* Segin, a star. *Mān. (HA).*

lapa *ʻa* Wild or roughhousing, as an overactive or unruly child. *Dic.* Cf. *ʻāhiu.*

lapa *ʻa* Improper, in math. *Dic., ext. mng. Hakina lapa.* Improper fraction.

lāpa *kik* Raft. *Bounty. Lāpa laholio.* Rubber raft. *Lāpa lāʻau.* Wooden raft.

lapa ahi lā *kik* Solar flare. *Lit.,* flash (of) solar fire. Cf. *kiko lā, puapuaʻi lā, ʻale ahi lā.*

lā·paki *kik* Rabbit. *Dic.* Also *lāpiki, ʻiole lāpiki.* See entries below.

lā·paki huelo pulu·pulu *kik* Cottontail rabbit. Also *lāpiki huelo pulupulu, ʻiole lāpiki huelo pulupulu.*

lā·paki kini·kila *kik* Chinchilla rabbit. Comb. *lāpaki* + Eng. Also *lāpiki kinikila, ʻiole lāpiki kinikila.*

lapa koko *kik* Blood clot. *Dic.*

lapa niho *kik* Alveolar, in linguistics. *Lit.,* tooth ridge.

lapa puki *kik* Rubber boot. *Eng.* Also *laba puki, puki lapa.*

lapa·ʻau hoʻo·miki uila *kik* Shock therapy. *Hana ʻia ka lapaʻau hoʻomiki uila no ka lapaʻau ʻana i kekahi mau ʻano maʻi o ka lolo.* Shock treatment is used for some kinds of mental disorders. *Lit.,* treat (by) causing alertness (with) electricity.

Lapa·tewe *iʻoa* Laptev. *Eng. Ke kai ʻo Lapatewe.* Laptev Sea.

lā·piki *kik* Rabbit. Usu. *ʻiole lāpiki. Niʻihau.* Also *lāpaki.* See entries under *lāpaki.*

lapu *ʻa* Haunted. *Dic. Hale lapu.* Haunted house, not the Halloween variety. *Kiliki o lapu.* Trick or treat.

Lā·pule *kik* Sunday. *Dic.* Abb. *Lp.*

lawaiʻa *Hoʻomalu lawaiʻa a me ka hahai holoholona.* Fish and game management; to manage fish and game. *ʻAha Hoʻomalu Lawaiʻa o ka Pākīpika Komohana.* Western Pacific Fishery Management Council. *ʻOihana Lawaiʻa Kai Pekelala.* National Marine Fisheries Service.

lawe *ham* Minus. *Dic.* Cf. *hoʻolawe.*

lawe·hala *Keiki lawehala.* Juvenile delinquent. See entry below.

lawe·hala ʻō·pio·pio *kik* Juvenile delinquency. Cf. *keiki lawehala.*

lawe·kahiki *ham* To introduce, as plants and animals to a particular place; to borrow, as a word from another language. *Lit.,* bring (from) a foreign land. Cf. *malihini. Nā lāʻau a me nā holoholona i lawekahiki ʻia mai.* Introduced plants and animals. *He huaʻōlelo i lawekahiki ʻia.* A borrowed word.

lawe·lawe *kik* Service. *Dic.* See *Papa Lawelawe Hoʻolaha. Unu lawelawe.* Processor, as in computer hardware. *Lawelawe hana.* Function, as on a calculator. *Lawelawe kōkua.* Social services. *Lawelawe poʻokela.* High-quality service. *ʻOihana lawelawe.* Service industry.

lawe·lima *ham* Portable; laptop, as a computer. *Lit.,* (can be) taken (by) hand. *Kamepiula lawelima.* Laptop computer. Also *lolouila lawelima.*

lawe mā·lama *ham* To adopt, as a highway or other public area for environmental cleanup or maintenance. *Ma ka papahana lawe mālama alaloa na*

*ke aupuni, hiki ke lawe mālama kekahi
ʻahahui i kekahi māhele o ke alaloa, a
hōʻikeʻike ʻia ka inoa o ka hui nāna e
mālama.* In the highway adoption
program of the government, an
organization can adopt a section of
highway to take care of, and the name of
the organization that cares for that
section is displayed. *Lit.,* take (to) care for.
Cf. *lawe hānai* (dic.).

lawena *kik* Behavior, as the way people
or animals act. *Dic., ext. mng. Aʻo
kahua lawena.* Performance-based
learning, kinesthetic-based learning.
Lawena ʻike hānau. Instinctive behavior.
Lawena ʻapo. Learned behavior.

lawe pī·lahi *ham* To go for it; go for
broke; geevum. *Mān.* Cf. *kuʻupau.*

lawe ʻai·ʻē *ham* To borrow, take on
credit. *Dic.* Cf. *hoʻolako ʻaiʻē, lako ʻaiʻē,
ʻae.*

lā·ʻau *kik* Medicine, medicinal drug,
medication; wood. *Dic., ext. mng.* See
entries below and *papa pānela. Inu i ka
lāʻau.* To take (liquid) medicine. *ʻAi i
ka lāʻau.* To take medicine. *Lāʻau
kuhikuhi.* Prescription drug or medication. *Lāʻau kūʻai wale.* Over-the-counter
drug or medication.

lā·ʻau ana ki·ʻe·ki·ʻena *kik* Elevation
pole, as for surveying. *Lit.,* elevation
surveying rod. See *lāʻau ana ʻāina, lena
māka.*

lā·ʻau ana ʻāina *kik* Range pole,
surveying rod. Comb. dic. + *ʻāina.* See
lāʻau ana kiʻekiʻena, lena māka.

lā·ʻau ha·ʻi·nole *kik* Stimulant.
Lit., drug (for) stimulating.

lā·ʻau ho·ʻo·loha *kik* Depressant.
Lit., drug which causes depression.

lā·ʻau ho·ʻo·mā·lū *kik* Barbiturate.
*He lāʻau ka lāʻau hoʻomālū no ka hana
ʻana a mālie ke kino me ka hoʻomaka
hiamoe nō hoʻi.* Barbiturates are used to
calm the body and make one drowsy.

Comb. *lāʻau + hoʻo- + mālū* (Tokelau,
calm).

lā·ʻau ho·ʻo·ma·ʻe·ma·ʻe hale *kik*
Household product, i.e. any of a variety of
products used for cleaning floors, sinks,
etc. *Niʻihau.*

lā·ʻau ho·ʻo·mā··ʻe·ele *kik*
Anesthetic. *Lit.,* medicine (to)
anesthetize. See *hoʻomāʻeʻele.*

lā·ʻau kau·kahi *kik* Balance beam.
Lit., solitary rod. Cf. *lāʻau kaulua.*

lā·ʻau kau lole *kik* Hanger, when
made of wood. *Lit.,* wood (for) placing
clothes. See *uea kau lole, mea kau lole,
ʻea kau lole.*

lā·ʻau kau·lua *kik* Parallel bars. *Lit.,*
double rods. Cf. *lāʻau kaukahi. Lāʻau
kaulua kaulike.* Even parallel bars.
Lāʻau kaulua kaulike ʻole. Uneven
parallel bars.

lā·ʻau ko·ʻo·ko·ʻo *kik* Vaccine. *Lit.,*
support medicine.

lā·ʻau kuhi·kuhi *kik* Pointer, as used
in a classroom. *Dic.* See *lāʻau.*

lā·ʻau make *kik* Poison. *Dic.* See
entries below and *ʻalidirina, dielidirina.
Lāʻau make hanu.* Fumigant. *Lāʻau
make laoa.* Systemic insecticide. *Lāʻau
make pā ʻili.* Contact poison. *Lāʻau
make ʻai.* Stomach poison.

lā·ʻau make hai·pili·kia *kik*
Pesticide. *Lit.,* poison (for) pests. Also
lāʻau haipilikia.

lā·ʻau make nā·hele·hele *kik*
Herbicide. *Lit.,* poison (for) weeds.

lā·ʻau pulu·pulu *kik* Cotton swab,
Q-tip. *Lit.,* cotton stick.

lā·ʻau ʻai *kik* Chopstick. *Dic*

lā·ʻau ʻona *kik* Narcotic drug. *Lit.,*
intoxicating drug.

la·ʻa·lā·ʻau *kik* Bush, shrub. *Dic.
Wao laʻalāʻau.* Alpine shrubland.

la·ʻa·loa *ʻElelū laʻaloa.* German
cockroach (Blattella germanica).

la'ana *kik* Example; specimen. *E ha'i mai i la'ana o ka i'a ke'oke'o.* Give me an example of a white fish. Comb. *la'a* + *-na.* Cf. *kumu ho'ohālike, hāpana. La'ana hō'ole.* Counterexample.

lā·'ape *kik* Monstera. Comb. *lau* + *'ape.*

Labara·dora *i'oa* Labrador. *Eng. Ke kai 'o Labaradora.* Labrador Sea.

lati·tū See *lakikū.*

lā·toma *kik* Molecule. Sh. *lā-* (as in *lāhui, lālei*) + *'atoma. Kino lātoma.* Allotrope, i.e. a different molecular form of an element, in science.

lea·ka·a·'ike *kik* Protocol, in a computer system. Comb. *lea* (*Tongan,* language) + *ka'a'ike.*

lei *Iwi lei.* Clavicle, collarbone.

lei o Pele *kik* Ring of fire, in geology. *Lit.,* Pele's lei.

lei 'ā·'ī *kik* Necktie. *Dic.* Also *lei 'ā'ī kalawake, lei kalawake.* Cf. *hīpu'u pewa. Lei 'ā'ī pewa.* Bow tie.

leo *kik* Melody, tune. *Dic.* Also *'ea.* See entries below and *hō'ailona mele, pahu leo, pahu ho'onui leo.*

leo *kik* Voice, as in linguistics. *Dic.* See *palapala leo.*

leo ala·ka'i *kik* One who sings the melody of a song. *Ni'ihau.*

leo·paki kikī *kik* Cheetah. *Lit.,* swift leopard.

leo 'ekahi *kik* Soprano. *Lit.,* first voice. *'Ukulele leo 'ekahi.* Soprano 'ukulele.

leo 'ekolu *kik* Tenor. *Lit.,* third voice. *'Ukulele leo 'ekolu.* Tenor 'ukulele.

Leuni·ona *i'oa* Reunion. *Eng. Ka mokupuni 'o Leuniona.* Reunion Island.

lehe·lehe *kik* Labial, in linguistics. *Lit.,* lips. See *pena lehelehe, 'umi'umi lehelehe.*

lehi·lehia *'a* Coordinated, having physical dexterity. Redup. of *lehia,* deft.

lehu·lehu See *ho'omana akua lehulehu. Aupuni na ka lehulehu.* Democracy. *Aupuni kānāwai na ka lehulehu.* Direct democracy, i.e. a government in which laws are made directly by the citizens. *Pono o ka lehulehu.* Common good, i.e. the well-being of all members of society. *'Āina no ka lehulehu.* Public land.

leka *kik* Slat. *Ua ho'ololi 'ia nā leka o ka pukaaniani 'ōlepe i nehinei.* The jalousie slats were changed yesterday. *Mān.* (HHLH, MMLH). See *pepa leka.*

leka uila *kik* Electronic mail, E-mail, as in telecommunication. *Lit.,* electric letter.

leka kū·loko *kik* Internal mail, as in an office or school. *Leka kūloko ke'ena.* Office mail. *Leka kūloko kula.* Campus mail.

leka·pī *kik* Recipe. *Eng.*

leka wehe·wehe *kik* Cover letter. *Lit.,* letter (of) explanation.

leke·uma *kik* Legume. *Eng.*

lekesa *kik* Latex. *Eng.*

leki *kik* Tape. *Dic.* See entries below.

leki a·'a *kik* Strapping tape, filament tape. *Lit.,* rootlet tape.

lē·kiō *kik* Radio. *Dic.* Also *pahu ho'olele leo.*

leki uea *kik* Cloth duct tape, electrician's tape. *Lit.,* tape (for) wires.

leki nao *kik* Teflon tape, for use in plumbing. *Ni'ihau.*

leki pahu *kik* Masking tape, freezer tape. *Lit.,* tape (for) boxes.

leki pepa *kik* Paper tape, as for packages. *Lit.,* tape (made of) paper.

leki 'ea *kik* Transparent tape, Scotch tape. *Lit.,* plastic tape.

lele *heh* To log off, log out, as of a network or other computer system. *Dic., new mng.* See *kī lele.* Cf. *'e'e. E lele i.* "Goto," as in a computer program. *Helu lele.* To skip count, in math.

lele ai *Ma'i lele ai.* Sexually transmitted disease (STD).

lele haʻa·luna *heh* Vertical jump. *Lit.*, upward jump.

lele hoʻo·nanā *ham* Aggression, as a threat of attack by one country upon another. *Manaʻo ʻia he lele hoʻonanā ka holo ʻana o nā pūʻali koa o ʻIraka ma waho o ka palena i hoʻopaʻa ʻia e kō ka hui kuʻikahi.* The crossing over of Iraqi troops outside the borders set by the alliance was considered an act of aggression (not an attack). *Lit.*, rush out aggressively (as to provoke a fight). Cf. *lele kaua.*

lele kaua *ham* Aggression, as an attack by one country upon another. *Ua lele kaua ʻo Kihaapiʻilani me kōna ʻau moku i kō Maui hikina i mea e hoʻopau ai i ka noho aliʻi ʻana o Piʻilani.* In an act of agression, Kihaapiʻilani and his fleet attacked east Maui in order to topple the reign of Piʻilani. *Lit.*, rush out (to) make war. Cf. *lele hoʻonanā.*

lele kaula *heh* To jump rope. Cf. *kaula lele. Hōʻike lele kaula kanakolu kekona.* Thirty-second jump rope test.

lele·kē Palaunu *heh* Brownian motion, in chemistry. *Lit.*, Brown leaping here and there.

lele·kī·kē *heh* To volley, as a volleyball. *Lit.*, fly back and forth. Cf. *paʻi manamana, pohu.*

lele kiʻe·kiʻe *heh* High jump, in track.

lele koali *kik* Free swing, as a single rope hanging from a tree branch. *Dic.* Cf. *paiō.*

lele koʻo *heh* To pole vault. See *koʻo lele.*

lele lewa lipo kanaka *heh* Manned space flight. *Lit.*, human space flight.

lele loloa *heh* Standing long jump, in track. *Lit.*, long jump.

lele·neo *heh* To bounce, as a check. *Ua leleneo ka pila kīkoʻo no ka lawa ʻole o ke kālā ma ka waihona panakō.* The check bounced because there wasn't enough money in the account. Comb. *lele + neo.*

lele niniu *heh* Centrifugal, i.e. acting in a direction away from a center. *Lit.*, spinning flying. Cf. *ʻume niniu. Manehu lele niniu.* Centrifugal force.

lele paʻi *heh* Jump ball, in basketball. *Lilo ihola ke kinipōpō iā Waimea ma ka lele paʻi ʻana ma ka hoʻomaka ʻana o ka hoʻokūkū.* The ball went to Waimea on the jump ball at the start of the game. *Lit.*, jump (and) slap.

lele·pinao *heh* To use a trapeze. *Dic., ext. mng.* See *koali lelepinao.*

lele pine·pine *Helu lele pinepine.* Frequent-flyer number, as used in airline promotions.

lele ʻē *heh* Encroachment, in football. *Lit.*, premature jump. Cf. *mīʻoi. Lele ʻē na ke kūpale.* Defensive encroachment.

lele ʻole *Moho lele ʻole.* Flightless rail.

lele ʻō·pū *heh* To dive, in volleyball. *Lit.*, stomach jump. Also *luʻu, moe pālahalaha.*

lemi See *wai lemi.*

lena *Laina lena.* Line of sight, sight line. Also *laina ʻike.* See entry below.

lena māka *kik* Sighter, as for surveying. *Lit.*, sight (a) target. *Lima lena māka.* Sighter arm.

lene·kila *kik* Lentil. *Dic.*

Lepa·nona *iʻoa* Lebanon; Lebanese. *Dic.* Also *Lebanona.*

lepe *kik* Tab, as the tab on an audio cassette which can be removed to prevent erasing of what has been recorded, or an index tab on a notebook divider page. *Dic., ext. mng.* See entries below.

lepe unuhi *kik* Subtitle. *Lit.*, translation hem.

lepe kiʻi *kik/ham* Caption, as for a picture; to caption. *Lit.*, picture hem.

lepe pepei·ao *kik* Ear lobe. *Lit.*, ear wattles.

lepe puke *kik* Bookmark. *Lit.*, book attachment.

lepili *kik* Label, tag; to label. *Eng.*
Lepili māhuaola. Food label, as for
giving product information on a package
of food.

lepo *kik* Soil. *Dic.* See entries below.
Hōkeo kūmau hoʻāʻo lepo. Standard
soil-testing kit. *Lalo lepo.* Subsoil.
Lepo uhi. Topsoil. *Lepo makaili.*
Alluvial soil.

lepo kanu mea·kanu *kik* Potting
soil. *Lit.,* dirt (for) planting plants. Cf.
ʻelekanu.

lepo·piloki *kik* Leptospirosis. *Eng.*

lepo pohō *kik* Mud. *Niʻihau.* Also
ʻūkele.

**Lepupa·lika Hui Pū ʻia ʻo
Tana·zania** *iʻoa* United Republic of
Tanzania.

**Lepupa·lika Kemo·kalaka ʻo
Kono·kō** *iʻoa* Democratic Republic of
the Congo.

Lepupa·lika Komi·nika *iʻoa*
Dominican Republic. *Dic.* See
Kominika.

Lepupa·lika ʻApe·lika Waena *iʻoa*
Central African Republic.

Lepupa·lika ʻo Kili·paki Republic of
Kiribati.

lewa *kik* Space. *Dic.* See *lewapuni.*
Lewa lipo. Outer space. *Kukuna lewa
lipo.* Cosmic ray. *Palapala lewa lipo.*
Space map. *Paʻalole hele lewa.* Space
suit. *Pūʻali kaua lewa.* Air force.

lewa·lana *ʻa* Weightless, as when in
outer space. Comb. *lewa + lana.* Cf.
ʻumekaumaha ʻole.

lewa·lani·ha·ʻa *kik* Troposphere.
Comb. *lewa + lani + haʻa.*

lewa·puni *kik* Atmosphere, as around
planets. *Lit.,* surrounding atmosphere.
See *lewa.*

Leba·nona *iʻoa* Lebanon; Lebanese.
Dic. Also *Lepanona.*

Lesoto *iʻoa* Lesotho. *Eng.*

lī *kik* Mi, the third note on the musical
scale. *Dic.* See *pākōlī.*

lī·oho *kik* Algae, general term. Sh.
limu + oho.

liona *Kanaka kino liona.* Sphinx, a
mythological monster with the head of a
woman and the body of a lion.
Sapenika Liona. The huge Sphinx found
near the pyramids at Giza in Egypt.

liona kai *kik* Sea lion.

lio pai·pai *kik* Rocking horse.

lio pone *kik* Pony. Comb. *lio* + Eng.

lihi *kik* Margin, as on a printed page.
Dic., ext. mng. See *pili lihi. Lihi hema.*
Left margin. *Lihi ʻākau.* Right margin.
Lihi o luna. Top margin. *Lihi o lalo.*
Bottom margin. *Hoʻopaʻa i nā lihi.* To
set the margins.

lihi·lihi maka ku·ʻi *kik* False
eyelashes. *Niʻihau.* See *pena lihilihi
maka. Kau i ka lihilihi maka kuʻi.* To
put on false eyelashes. Also *komo i ka
lihilihi maka kuʻi.*

lika *kik* Liter. *Dic.* Abb. *l.*

lī·kaia *heh* To retire. *Eng.* Also
hoʻomaha loa, rītaia.

lī·kao *kik* Lotus. (Chinese *lingao.*)
Also *kalo Pākē.*

like *ʻa* Common, as in math terms;
equal or equality, as a mathematical
relation of being exactly the same. *Dic.,
ext. mng.* See *huinakolu like. Helu
hoʻonui like.* Common factor. *Helu
māhua like.* Common multiple. *Hoa
like.* Like term. *Lākiō like.* Equal ratio,
proportional. *Like ka papaha o nā mea
e loaʻa ana.* Equally likely outcomes.

like·like See *paʻa likelike.*

Likene·kaina *iʻoa* Liechtenstein.
Eng.

liko *kik* Newly opened leaf. *Dic.* Cf.
muʻo. See *piko.*

lī·lia ʻAiku·pika *kik* Agapanthus.
Lit., Egyptian lily. Also *līlia ʻAigupita.*

lī·lia ʻApe·lika *kik* Amaryllis. *Lit.,*
African lily.

liliu·ewe *heh* To evolve. Sh. *liliu* (*Tongan*, to adapt) + *ōewe*. Cf. *hoʻoliliuewe*. *Ka liliuewe ʻana.* Evolution.

liliu·welo *ʻa* To be biologically adapted to. *Ua liliuwelo ka ʻiʻiwi i ka ulu ʻōhiʻa.* The *ʻiʻiwi* is biologically adapted to the *ʻōhiʻa* forest. Comb. *liliu* (*Tongan*, to adapt) + *welo*. See *hoʻoliliuwelo*.

Liliʻu See *ʻukulele Liliʻu*.

lilo *ʻa* Turnover, in basketball. *Ua lilo ke kinipōpō iā Georgetown ʻumi manawa i ka hapa mua wale nō o ka hoʻokūkū.* The ball was turned over to Georgetown ten times in only the first half of the game. *Dic., ext. mng.* See entry below.

lilo ka ʻai iā Mea Point for Mea. *Niʻihau.*

lilo pā·keu *kik* Deficit, as an excess of expenditure over revenue. *He ulu a māhuahua mau ka lilo pākeu o ke aupuni.* The government deficit keeps growing. *Lit.,* excessive expenditure. Cf. *loaʻa pākeu*. See *hoʻolilo pākeu*.

lima See *iwi kū lima, iwi manamana lima, iwi pili lima.*

lima ā·ohi·ohi *kik* Resistance arm, i.e. the distance from the fulcrum to the resistance force in a lever.

lima·haka·haka *kik* Print, as in handwriting. *E kākau limahakahaka ʻoe i kēia mau huaʻōlelo.* Print these words. *Lit.,* space hand. Cf. *limahiō*. See *kākau pākahikahi*.

lima·hana *kik* Member of a work crew. *Dic., ext. mng. Nā limahana paʻi wikiō.* Video production crew.

lima·hiō *kik* Script, as in handwriting. *E kākau limahiō i kou inoa.* Write your name in script. *Lit.,* slant hand. Cf. *limahakahaka*. See *kākau maoli*.

lima·hilu *kik* Calligraphy. Comb. *lima* + *hilu*.

lima kau·lua *kik* Ambidextrous. *Lit.,* two-natured hands.

lima kia pihi *kik* Remote manipulator arm, space crane. *Lit.,* remote control crab claw. See *kia pihi*.

lima kuhi·kuhi *kik* Hand, as of an analog clock or watch. *Lima kuhikuhi minuke.* Minute hand. *Lima kuhikuhi hola.* Hour hand.

limu ko·a *kik* Coraline algae. *Lit.,* coral algae.

lina *kik* Green onion, having a white bulb with purple inside. *Mān. (RNM).* Cf. *ʻoʻa*.

lina hoʻo·komo *kik* A circle around a period, colon, or semicolon to show that it has been inserted, in proofreading. *Lit.,* ring (for) inserting. Cf. *kaha hoʻokomo*.

lina hoʻo·lana *kik* Swimming tube. *Lit.,* ring (for) floating. Cf. *pela hoʻolana*.

lina kui *kik* Ring, as in a ring binder. *Lit.,* ring to string (paper). *Puke lina kui.* Ring binder.

lina·lina *Palaoa linalina.* Unleavened pancake.

lina poe·poe *kik* Circular shape; circle, as in preschool programs; to sit in a circle. *E noho lina poepoe kākou.* Let's sit in a circle. *Lit.,* round ring.

lina poe·poe holo wā·wae *kik* Track, course for running events in track and field. *Lit.,* round track (for) running.

lina puhi hu·ʻa·hu·ʻa *kik* Bubble wand, for blowing bubbles. *Lit.,* ring (for) blowing bubbles.

lina ʻulī·keke *kik* Tambourine. *Lit.,* baby rattle ring.

lino·hau See *lumi linohau*.

linole·uma *kik* Linoleum, linoleum flooring. *Dic.* Also *moena ʻili*.

Lipe·lia *iʻoa* Liberia; Liberian. *Dic.* Also *Liberia*.

lī·pine *kik* Film, as for a movie or video; footage, as of video tape; recording tape. *Dic., ext. mng., sp. var.* Cf. *minuke līpine.* See entries below. *Līpine ma'ema'e.* Blank footage. *Līpine pa'i maka.* Raw footage.

lī·pine ana *kik* Tape measure, as a tailor's or for track events, etc. *Lit.,* measuring ribbon. Cf. *lula poho.*

lī·pine pō·ka'a *kik* Reel-to-reel tape. *Lit.,* reel tape. Cf. *pōka'a līpine.*

li'i Abbreviation for *li'ili'i* (small).

li'i·li'i *'a'* Little, small. *Dic.* See entry below. *Manamana li'ili'i.* Little finger. Also *manamana iki. Mea li'ili'i.* Detail. Also *mea li'ili'i kiko'ī, mea kiko'ī.*

li'i·li'i *'a'* Small, as drink size. *Dic.* Abb. *li'i.* See *lōpū, nui, nui keu. Koloaka li'ili'i.* Small soda.

Libe·ria *i'oa* Liberia; Liberian. *Eng.* Also *Lipelia.*

Libia *i'oa* Libya; Libyan. *Eng.*

liti·uma *kik* Lithium. *Eng.*

Litua·nia *i'oa* Lithuania. *Eng.*

lō Abbreviation for *lōpū* (medium), *lō'ihi* (length).

loa *'a'* Long. *Dic. Manamana loa.* Middle finger. Also *manamana waena.*

loa *'a'* Length, in math. *Dic.* No abbreviation. Also *ana loa.* See *lō'ihi.* Cf. *ākea, laulā, hohonu, ki'eki'e.*

loa Extra, i.e. beyond the usual size, extent, or degree. *Dic., ext. mng. Pākā loa.* Extra lean, as meat.

loa *Ao loa.* Stratus cloud.

loa'a pā·keu *kik* Surplus, as a quantity or amount over and above what is needed. *Ke loa'a i ke aupuni moku'āina ka loa'a pākeu, he ho'iho'i 'ia paha i nā kupa ma ka wā 'auhau.* When the state government has a surplus, it may be returned to the citizens at tax time. *Lit.,* excessive earnings. Cf. *lilo pākeu.*

loa'a pa'a mau *kik* Sustained yield, as in crop production. *Ma ka mahi 'ai 'ana, kanu hou 'ia ka meaulu i 'ohi 'ia i mea e mālama ai i ka loa'a pa'a mau.* In farming, crops are replanted after harvesting to ensure sustained yield. *Lit.,* constant harvest.

loea holo·holona lō·hiu *kik* Wildlife expert.

loi *ham* To look over critically; to scrutinize. *Dic. No'ono'o loi.* Critical thinking.

loio See entries below and *pepa loio.*

loio ho'o·pi'i *kik* Prosecutor, prosecuting attorney, plaintiff attorney. *Lit.,* lawyer (who) accuses in court. Cf. *loio kūpale.* See *mea ho'opi'i, 'ao'ao ho'opi'i.*

loio kū·pale *kik* Defense attorney, attorney for the defendant. Cf. *loio ho'opi'i.* See *mea kūpale, 'ao'ao kūpale.*

loi·hape *ham* To proofread. *Lit.,* scrutinize (for) inaccuracies.

loi·loi holo·mua hau·māna *ham* Student assessment. *Lit.,* scrutinize student progress.

loi·pā·lā·kiō *ham* To rate, as on a scale. *Lit.,* scrutinize (on a) scale.

loi·pela *kik/ham* Spell checker; to spell check, as of a computer document. *Lit.,* scrutinize spelling.

lou *kik* Hook, as for hanging things. *Dic.* See entries below. *Lou kau lole.* Clothes hook.

lou *kik* Bond. *Dic., ext. mng.* See *'ūlou. Lou 'ātoma.* Bond between atoms or ions as a result of gaining, losing or sharing electrons.

lou *ham* To save, in volleyball. *Ni'ihau.* Also *ho'iho'i.*

lou·lou *ham* To link, as in a computer program. *Dic., ext. mng.* See entry below. *Hua loulou.* Edition, as in a computer program. *Loulou waihona.* File link. *Loulou 'ikepili.* Data link.

lou·lou ki'i *ham* To subscribe, as in a computer program. *Lit.*, link pictures. Cf. *ho'omoe* (dic.).

lou·pili *kik* Velcro. Comb. *lou + pili. Mea ho'opa'a loupili.* Velcro fastener.

loha·loha *kik* Larva of damselfly and other dragonflies. *Dic.* Also *lohelohe.*

lohe·lohe *kik* Larva of damselfly and other dragonflies. *Dic.* Also *lohaloha.*

lohi *kik* Tendon. *Ni'ihau.* Also *uaua.*

lō·hiu *'a'* Naturally wild, as tiger, *'i'iwi, 'a'ali'i,* etc. Sh. *loko + 'āhiu.* See *'āhiu, lākauā, 'ōhuka. Holoholona lōhiu.* Wildlife. *Pōpoki lōhiu.* Wildcat. *Ho'omalu holoholona lōhiu.* State wildlife official. Also *luna ho'omalu holoholona lōhiu. 'Āina Ho'omalu Holoholona Lōhiu o Hawai'i.* Hawaiian Islands National Wildlife Refuge. *'Oihana I'a me ka Holoholona Lōhiu o 'Amelika.* US Fish and Wildlife Service.

loke lā·'au *kik* Wood rose.

lokeni *kik* Rotenone, a chemical compound. (Japn. *roten.*)

Loke 'Ai·lana *i'oa* Rhode Island; Rhode Islander. *Dic.* Also *Rode 'Ailana.*

lō·kino *kik* Organ, as of an animal. Sh. *loko + kino.* See entry below. *'Ōnaehana lōkino.* Organ system, in biology.

lō·kino hua·'ine *kik* Ovary. *Lit.*, ovum organ. See *hua'ine.*

loko *Aia i loko o ka papa.* To take a class. Also *komo i loko o ka papa, komo i ka papa.*

lō·kō *kik* Logo. *Eng.*

lō·ku'u *kik* Gland. Sh. *loko + ho'oku'u.* See entries below.

lō·ku'u hā·'ae *kik* Salivary gland. *Lit.*, saliva organ.

lō·ku'u ho'o·konu·konu pū·nao *kik* Thyroid gland. *Lit.*, gland (which) regulates metabolism.

lō·ku'u ku'u·loko *kik* Endocrine gland. Comb. *lōku'u + ku'u + loko.* Cf. *lōku'u ku'uwaho.* See *'ōnaehana hōmona.*

lō·ku'u ku'u·waho *kik* Exocrine gland. Comb. *lōku'u + ku'u + waho.* Cf. *lōku'u ku'uloko.*

lō·ku'u 'ana·pu'u *kik* Lymph gland, lymph node.

lola *kik* Cassette, as for music tapes or videos. *Ni'ihau.* See *mīkini lola. Lola wikiō.* Video cassette.

lola *kik* Roller; to roll. *Dic.* See entry below. *Kimalola.* Steamroller. *Lola pena.* Paint roller. *Pena lola.* To paint with a roller.

lola palaoa *kik* Rolling pin. *Lit.*, bread rolling pin.

lole See entries below and *hao kau lole, pepa lole pipi, 'āpā lole.*

lolea *'a'* Inside out. *Dic.* See *hulihia.*

lole ana kino·ea *kik* Gas fading control fabric, as in meteorology. *Lit.*, cloth (that) measures gas.

lole ana 'oki·kene kolu *kik* Ozone-sensitive fabric. *Lit.*, cloth (that) measures ozone.

lole o lalo *kik* Bottom, as clothing. Cf. *lole o luna; pale'ili o lalo* (dic.).

lole o luna *kik* Top, as clothing. Cf. *lole o lalo; pale'ili o luna* (dic.).

lole kueka ha'uki *kik* Warm-up suit, as for sports. *Lit.*, sweatshirt clothes. See *kueka ha'uki.*

lole·lole *ham* To thumb through, as a magazine. *Ni'ihau.* To scroll or scan, as in a computer program. *Lolelole i mua.* To scan forward. *Lolelole i hope.* To scan backward.

lole moe pō *kik* Pajamas, nightgown. *Dic.*

lole pipi See *mea lole pipi, pepa lole pipi.*

lole wā·wae kā·'awe *kik* Coveralls, overalls. *Ni'ihau.* Also *lole wāwae 'epane.*

lole wā·wae pala·ʻili *kik*
Underpants. *Niʻihau.* Also *palemaʻi.*
See *palemaʻi.*

lole wā·wae ʻepane *kik* Coveralls,
overalls. *Dic.* Also *lole wāwae kāʻawe.*

loli ulu·ō *kik* Impulse, i.e. the change
in momentum produced by a force, in
physics. *Lit.,* change (in) momentum.
See *uluō.*

loli honua *kik* Geologic change. *Lit.,*
earth change.

loli kemi·kala *kik* Chemical change.

lolo *kik* Brain. *Dic.* See entries below.

lolo·uila *kik* Computer. *Comb. lolo*
+ *uila.* Also *kamepiula, mīkini
hoʻonohonoho ʻikena. Lolouila
lawelima.* Laptop computer. Also
kamepiula lawelima.

lolo·kū *ʻŌnaehana lolokū.* Nervous
system.

lololo *Hoʻonaʻauao haumāna lololo.*
Gifted education, as a school program.

Loma *Helu Loma.* Roman numeral.

lona hulei *kik* Fulcrum. *Lit.,* seesaw
block.

loni·kū *kik* Longitude. *Dic.* Also
lonitū. Cf. *lakikū. Kumu lonikū.* Prime
Meridian. Also *kumu lonitū.*

loni·tū See *lonikū.*

lonoa *kik* Sense, as of taste, smell, etc.
(PPN *rongo* + *-a*). *Kahana lonoa.* Lateral
line, i.e. a linear series of sensory pores
and tubes along the side of a fish, in
biology. *Lonoa alelo.* Sense of taste.
Lonoa ihu. Sense of smell. *Lonoa
maka.* Sense of sight. *Lonoa pepeiao.*
Sense of hearing. *Lonoa ʻili.* Sense of
touch.

lopako *kik* Robot. *Eng.*

lopi niho *kik/ham* Dental floss; to
floss one's teeth. *E lopi ʻoe i nā niho ou
me kēia lopi niho.* Floss your teeth with
this dental floss. *Lit.,* thread (for) teeth.

lō·pū *ʻaʻ* Medium, as a drink size or of
a photograph or in movie or video
production. *Sh. roto* (Tah., *waena*) +
pū. Abb. lō. See *liʻiliʻi, nui, nui keu;
kokoke, laulā. Koloaka lōpū.* Medium
soda. *Paʻi lōpū.* Medium shot (preceded
by *ke*). *Paʻi a lōpū.* To take a medium
shot. *Wela lōpū.* Medium heat.

lō·ʻihi *ʻaʻ* Length, in math. *Dic. Abb.
lō.* Also *ana lōʻihi, loa.* Cf. *ākea, laulā,
hohonu, kiʻekiʻe.* See *hānai lōʻihi.*

lū See *pakuhi lū.*

lua *kik* Bathroom; toilet. *Dic.* See
lumi ʻauʻau, lumi hoʻopaupilikia.

lua hā See *papa lua hā.*

lua kī·lau·ea *kik* Caldera. *Lit.,*
kīlauea crater (named for the caldera on
Hawaiʻi).

lua like *kik* Duplicate, as in a computer
program. *Dic.*

lua pele *kik* Volcano. *Dic.* See
kuahene, pele. Lua pele kuahene. Shield
volcano. *Lua pele kuahene kuamua.*
Primary shield volcano. *Lua pele lalo
kai.* Submerged volcano. *Lua pele ʻā.*
Active volcano.

lua·po·ʻi *kik* Prey. *He luapoʻi ka ʻiole
na ka ʻio.* Mice are a prey of the hawk.
Sh. luaahi + *poʻi.* Cf. *poʻiiʻa.*

Luiki·ana *iʻoa* Louisiana; Louisianan,
Louisianian. *Dic.* Also *Luisiana.*

Luisi·ana *iʻoa* Louisiana; Louisianan,
Louisianian. *Dic.* Also *Luikiana.*

Lukema·puka *iʻoa* Luxembourg.
Eng.

Lū·kia *iʻoa* Russia; Russian. *Dic., sp.
var.* Also *Rūsia.*

lū·kī·mia *kik* Leukemia. *Eng.*

lū·kini pō·ʻae·ʻae *kik* Deodorant.
Lit., underarm perfume.

Luku·ʻāina *iʻoa* Komephoros, a star.
Mān. (HA).

lula *kik* Ruler, the measuring device.
Dic. See *lula poho. Lula lāʻau.* Wooden
ruler.

lula *Home lula.* Home rule, i.e. self-government or limited autonomy, as in a city or county.

lula hahaina *kik* Function rule, in math.

lula poho *kik* Tape measure, as used by carpenters. *Lit.*, ruler (in a) pouch. *Cf. līpine ana.*

luli·luli See *waiū luliluli.*

luli poʻo *Mākala luli poʻo.* Sternocleido-mastoid muscle, i.e. the muscles between the sternum and the base of the ear.

lulumi *ham* To press, in basketball. *Lulumi nui akula nā kūpale iā Pila i loko o nā kekona hope loa o ka hoʻokūkū.* The defense pressed hard on Pila in the last few seconds of the game. *Dic., ext. mng. Lulumi hapa.* Half-court press. *Lulumi ʻekolu hapahā.* Three-quarter-court press. *Lulumi piha.* Full-court press. *Pale lulumi.* Press defense.

lulu ʻala·neo *kik* Rain shadow. *Aia ka ʻaoʻao Kona ma ka ʻaoʻao lulu ʻalaneo o nā kuahiwi Koʻolau.* The leeward side is found on the rain shadow side of the windward mountains. *Lit.*, unclouded shelter.

lū·maua *ʻa* Fertilized, as an egg. Comb. *lū + mau + -a.* See *hoʻolūmaua.*

lumi hoʻāhu *kik* Storeroom. *Dic.* Cf. *waihona hoʻāhu.*

lumi hoʻo·kipa *kik* Living room. *Dic.*

lumi hoʻo·lulu *kik* Waiting room.

lumi hoʻo·pau·pili·kia *kik* Bathroom. *Lit.*, room (for) going to the bathroom. Also *lua, lumi ʻauʻau.*

lumi huna *kik* Attic. *Lit.*, ceiling room. See *lumi kaupaku.*

lumi kau·paku *kik* Attic. *Lit.*, room (under the) roof. Also *lumi kaupoku, lumi kaupuku, lumi huna.*

lumi kuke *kik* Kitchen. *Dic.*

lumi lino·hau *kik* Deluxe room, as in a hotel. *Lit.*, ornamented room. Cf. *lumi maʻamau.*

lumi maʻa·mau *kik* Standard room, as in a hotel. *Lit.*, ordinary room. Cf. *lumi linohau.*

lumi moe *kik* Bedroom. *Dic. Lumi moe haku.* Master bedroom. *Lumi moe malihini.* Guest room.

lumi ʻaina *kik* Dining room. *Dic.*

lumi ʻau·ʻau *kik* Bathroom. *Dic.* Also *lua, lumi hoʻopaupilikia.*

lumi ʻohana *kik* Family room.

luna *kik* One in charge of a particular activity, such as a coordinator, editor, manager, etc. *Dic., ext. mng.* See entries below and other entries under *hiʻohiʻona naʻiau, hoʻokuʻikuʻi, hoʻoponopono kani, hoʻopuka, huahana, kūkulu kahua, pāhaʻoweli, ʻenehana,* etc.

luna *kik* Dean, as in a college or university. *Dic., ext. mng.* See *luna kulanui. Luna koleke pāheona me ka ʻepekema.* Dean of the college of arts and sciences.

luna aʻo·ā·kumu *kik* Student teacher field service supervisor. *Lit.*, supervisor (of) student teachers. See *aʻoākumu.*

luna uila *kik* Gaffer, as for movie or video production. *Lit.*, electrical supervisor. *Hope luna uila.* Best boy, i.e. an assistant gaffer.

luna hō·ʻoia *kik* Auditor. *Dic.*

luna hoʻo·kele *kik* Director, i.e. one who serves as a leader in conducting any kind of business. *Lit.*, leader (who) conducts business. *Papa luna hoʻokele.* Administration, i.e. a team of executive branch officials appointed by the President, in government.

luna hoʻo·mā·lama·lama *kik* Lighting director, as for movie or video production. *Lit.*, supervisor (for) illuminating.

luna hoʻo·malu *kik* Moderator, as of a panel. *Dic., ext. mng.*

luna hoʻo·malu holo·holona lō·hiu *kik* State wildlife official. *Lit.,* officer (who) protects wildlife. Also *hoʻomalu holoholona lōhiu.*

luna kā·lai·ʻāina *Kīpaku luna kālaiʻāina.* Recall, i.e. the right or procedure by which an elected official may be removed from office. Also *kīpeku luna kālaiʻāina.*

luna kula·nui *kik* Provost, as of a college or university. *Lit.,* college supervisor. Cf. *pelekikena, poʻo kulanui.*

luna noho *kik* Incumbent, i.e. the holder of a political office. *ʻO ke kahua kālaiʻāina o ka luna noho, ʻo ia ke kūleʻa o kāna hana i kōna wā noho.* The platform of the incumbent is his success during his term. *Dic., ext. mng.*

luna pai·pai pila *kik* Floor leader, as a member of a legislative body. *Lit.,* leader (who) urges bills.

luna pā·heona *kik* Art director, as for movie or video production. *Lit.,* art supervisor.

luna·ʻike·hala *kik* Conscience. *Dic. Noho ka hewa i ka lunaʻikehala.* To have a guilty conscience.

lū·pahū *kik* "Pop-pop" fireworks that explode on impact. Comb. *lū + pahū.* See *ahihoʻoleʻaleʻa.*

lupe·kau *kik* Hang glider. *Lit.,* kite (for) riding.

lū·ʻau *Honu lūʻau.* Green sea turtle. Also *honu.*

lū·ʻau Haole *kik* Spinach. *Lit.,* foreign taro tops.

luʻu *heh* To dive, in volleyball. *Niʻi-hau.* Also *lele ʻōpū, moe pālahalaha.*

luʻu kini ea *heh* Scuba diving; to scuba dive. *Lit.,* dive (with a) scuba tank. See *kanaka luʻu kai, kini ea luʻu kai.*

luʻu lewa *heh* To sky dive. *Mea luʻu lewa.* Sky diver.

luʻu nalu poʻi *heh* Running under the jump rope. *Mān.* See *ʻoni a ka moku.*

ll Abbreviation for *laulā* (width).

Lp Abbreviation for *Lāpule* (Sunday).

M

m Abbreviation for *mika* (meter).

MA *kik* Master's, Master of Arts, as a degree at a university (*pronounced* mūʻā). *Eng.* See *laeoʻo, MS.*

māio *ʻa* Calm, cool-headed, even-tempered. *Mān.* See *kiʻi māio.*

mā·ioio mana·mana lima *kik* Groove on a finger as appears in a fingerprint. See *meheu manamana lima.*

Mai·ota *iʻoa* Mayotte. *Eng. Ka mokupuni ʻo Maiota.* Mayotte Island.

maika *kik/ham* Bowling. *Dic. Kuea maika.* Bowling frame. *Pine maika.* Bowling pin.

mai·keni *kik* Maytansine, a chemical compound once investigated for therapeutic uses but later found to be too toxic for human use. (Spanish *maiten.*)

māiki *ʻa* Microscopic; micro-. *Kiko nā hua he piohē māiki.* Eggs hatch into microscopic larvae. *Dic., ext. mng.* Cf. *mānui. ʻUmekaumaha māiki.* Micro-gravity. *Meaola māiki.* Microorganism.

māiki·kalame *kik* Microgram. Comb. *māiki + kalame.*

maiko·lona *kik* Micron (0.0001 cm). *Eng.*

Mai·kone·sia *iʻoa* Micronesia. *Eng. Nā Mokuʻāina Hoʻohui ʻia o Maikonesia.* Federated States of Micronesia.

maile hoʻo·ili *kik* Baton used in relay race. See *holo hoʻoili, kūkini hoʻoili, heihei hoʻoili.*

maile pana *kik* Bandmaster's baton. *Lit.,* wand (for) beating time. Cf. *ʻaukaʻi pāna, ʻaukaʻi wili.*

māina *kik* Minor, as a minor academic field of study. *Eng.* Cf. *mēkia.*

Maine *i'oa* Maine. *Dic.* Also *Meine.*

mai·'ao *kik* Hoof. *Dic.*

mai·'u'u *kik* Claw. *Dic.*

ma o In terms of, in math. *Dic., ext. mng. Ma o ke X.* In terms of X.

maoli See *kākau maoli.*

mao·meka *kik* Apparatus, device, mechanism, ordinarily including some mechanical part or parts. Sh. *ma o + mekanika.* See *hāme'a, mauha'a, mea hana.*

mao·popo *I mea e maopopo ai 'oe.* For your information. Also *i maopopo iā 'oe, he mea ho'omaopopo kēia.*

Maui *i'oa* Maui, the island. *Dic.* Cf. *Māui.*

Māui *i'oa* Māui, the demigod. *Dic.* Cf. *Maui.* See entries below.

māui·ili *kik* Equinox. Comb. *māui + ili.* Cf. *māuiki'iki'i. Ka māuiili o ka hā'ulelau.* Autumnal equinox. *Ka māuiili o ke kupulau.* Vernal equinox.

māui·ki'i·ki'i *kik* Solstice. Comb. *māui + ki'iki'i.* Cf. *māuiili. Ka māuiki'iki'i o ke kauwela.* Summer solstice. *Ka māuiki'iki'i o ka ho'oilo.* Winter solstice.

mau·ha'a *kik* Instrument, as a specialized tool for a particular occupation. *Tah.* See *hāme'a, maomeka, mea hana.*

mauna *kik* Mount. *Dic., ext. mng. Mauna 'Eweleka.* Mount Everest. *Mauna 'Olumepika.* Mount Olympus; Olympus Mons, a volcano on Mars.

mauna kai *kik* Seamount. *Mauna kai pālahalaha.* Guyot. *Ka pae mauna kai 'o 'Emepela.* Emperor Seamounts.

Mauna Kana Helena *i'oa* Mount Saint Helens. *Eng.* Also *Mauna Sana Helena.*

Mauna Pō·haku *i'oa* Utah; Utahan, Utahn. *Dic.* Also *'Ūtā.*

māunu *heh* To molt, as a snake its skin. *Dic.* Cf. *ho'omalule.*

mau·pa'a *'a'* To consist of, be composed of, be made up of. Comb. *mau + pa'a.* See *'ūmaupa'a.*

mau·'a'e *ham* To override, as in a computer program. *Dic., ext. mng.*

mau'u *kik* Grass, general term; lawn. *Dic.* Also *mahiki.* See entries below. *'Oki i ka mau'u.* To mow the lawn.

mau'u Kale·poni *kik* California grass. *He lā'au malihini ka mau'u Kaleponi e laha 'ino nei ma ka 'āina o nā mokupuni nui a pau o Hawai'i.* California grass is an introduced plant that is overrunning the land on all the major islands of Hawai'i.

mau'u pī·neki *kik* Nutgrass.

mau'u 'ohe *kik* Reed. *Lit.,* bamboo grass.

Mau·rita·nia *i'oa* Mauritania; Mauritanian. *Eng.*

Mau·riti·usa *i'oa* Mauritius. *Eng. Ka mokupuni 'o Mauritiusa.* Mauritius Island.

maha *Mākala maha.* Temporalis muscle, i.e. the muscle of the side of the head.

mahaka *kik* Outline, as a line marking the outer limits of an object or figure. *Ni'ihau* (from *māka*). Cf. *meheu. Anakuhi mahaka.* Stencil.

mahaka maka *kik* Eye liner. *Lit.,* eye tracing.

maha·kea *Mahi 'ai mahakea.* Shifting cultivation, in geography.

mahako·nia *kik* Mahogany, the wood. *Eng.*

mahalo pā·na'i *kik* Patronage, i.e. a political system in which party leaders do favors for loyal supporters. *Lit.,* reciprocal gratitude. *Mea mahalo pāna'i.* Patron.

maha·melo *kik* Marshmallow. *Eng.* Also *masamelo.*

mahana ʻaʻ Temperature, when weather considered warm. *ʻEhia ka mahana o kēia lā? Lit.*, warm. Also *mehana. Cf. anu, wela.* See *kēkelē, mehana.*

mā·hele *kik/ham* Division, piece, portion, department, category, part, land division; to divide, apportion. *Dic., sp. var. Cf. keʻena, ʻoihana.* See entries below.

mā·hele *kik* Branch, as of a government. *Dic., ext. mng., sp. var. Māhele mana hoʻokō.* Executive branch. *Māhele ʻaha hoʻokolokolo.* Judicial branch. *Māhele ʻahaʻōlelo.* Legislative branch.

mā·hele *kik* Bracket, as in a sports tournament. *Dic., ext. mng., sp. var. Māhele hāʻule.* Consolation bracket. *Māhele lanakila.* Winner's bracket.

mā·hele hana *Nā māhele hana.* Jobs, as for movie or video production. *Lit.*, work categories. *Papa māhele hana.* Call sheet, i.e. a list of jobs.

mā·hele hapa *kik* Fractional part. *Māhele hapalua.* One-half (part).

mā·hele haʻa·wina Hawaiʻi *kik* Hawaiian studies department, as at a university or community college. *Lit.*, Hawaiian lessons department.

Mā·hele Kumu·wai·wai Kai *kik* Division of Aquatic Resources.

mā·hele manawa *ham* To take turns. *Lit.*, apportion turns.

mā·hele pā *kik* Disk partitioning, in a computer hard drive. *Lit.*, disk division.

mā·hele ʻāina *kik* Geographic region; regional. *Cf. aupuni. ʻAhahui māhele ʻāina.* Regional organization.

mā·hie·lewa *kik* Mobile, as a piece of artwork which dangles and moves in the wind. *Comb. māhie + lewa.*

mahi iʻa *ham* Aquaculture. *He hiki ke lilo ka ʻoihana mahi iʻa i ʻoihana puka maoli o ke kālā ke hana laulā ʻia.* The aquaculture industry can become a very lucrative one if done widely. *Lit.*, cultivate marine animals or plants.

mahi ulu·lā·ʻau *ham* Agroforestry. *Lit.*, cultivate forests.

mahiki *kik* Grass, general term; lawn. *Niʻihau.* Also *mauʻu. ʻOki i ka mahiki.* To mow the lawn.

mahi·kua *kik* Defensive linebacker, in football. *Sh. mahimahi + kua.*

mahi māla *ham* To garden; gardening. *Lit.*, cultivate (a) garden. *Hale kūʻai mahi māla.* Garden store, gardening store. *Puke mahi māla.* Gardening book.

mahina *kik* Month. *Dic. Abb. mhn.* Also *māhina.*

mahi ʻai See entry below. *Koleke mahi ʻai.* College of agriculture. *ʻOihana Mahi ʻAi o ka Mokuʻāina.* State Department of Agriculture.

mahi ʻai maha·kea *ham* Shifting cultivation, in geography. *Lit.*, fallow-land cultivation.

mā·hoe *kik* Double, as when throwing dice. *Dic., ext. mng. Helu māhoe.* Double number, i.e. the same number used twice, in math.

mahola ʻaʻ Expanded or exploded, as a file in a computer program. *Ua mahola ka waihona ʻopihia.* The compressed file has been expanded. *Dic., ext. mng. Cf. māhuahua, ʻopi.* See *hoʻomahola. Waihona mahola.* Expanded file.

mahola·hune ʻaʻ Diffusion; to be diffused. *Ua maholahune ke kinoea i loko o ke ea, a ʻaʻohe pilikia i kēia manawa.* The gas has diffused into the air, and now there's no danger. *Comb. mahola + hune.*

māhu *Kokoleka me ka waiū māhu.* Chocolate with steamed milk.

mā·hua *kik* Multiple, in math. *Dic., ext. mng.* Also *helu māhua.*

mā·hua·ola *kik* Nutrient. *Lit.,*
increase life. *Lepili māhuaola.* Food
label, as for giving product information
on a package of food. *Māhuaola māiki.*
Micronutrient. *Māhuaola mānui.*
Macronutrient. *'Oulu māhuaola.*
Nutrient culture.

mā·hua·hua *'a'* Expanded, as of
computer memory. *Dic., ext. mng.* Cf.
keu, mahola. Waihona 'ike māhuahua.
Expanded memory.

māhu·ea *kik* Vapor. *Dic., ext. mng.*

māhu pele See *uila māhu pele.*

maka *Palaoa maka.* Flour. *Palaoa
maka huika piha.* Whole wheat flour.
See entries under *palaoa.*

māka *kik* Target. *Dic.*

mā·kā *kik* Obsidian. *Dic., ext. mng.*

maka·ani·ani kau·pale *kik* Safety
glasses, protective glasses or goggles.
Lit., glasses placed (to) protect.

maka·ani·ani kala *kik* Sunglasses.
Ni'ihau. Also *makaaniani lā.*

maka·ani·ani lā *kik* Sunglasses.
Also *makaaniani kala.*

maka·ani·ani lu'u kai *kik* Diving
goggles or mask. *Lit.,* glasses (for) diving
(in the) sea. Also *makaaniani lu'u.*

maka·ili *kik* Alluvial. *Loa'a ka lepo
makaili ma kahi e kahe ai nā kahawai.*
Alluvial soil is found in areas where
streams flow. *Dic., ext. mng. Lepo
makaili.* Alluvial soil.

Makao *i'oa* Macao. *Eng.*

mā·kau *kik* Skill. *Sh. mākaukau.* See
entries below.

mā·kau ola *kik* Practical life skill.

mā·kau ho'o·holo mana'o *kik*
Decision-making skill. *Lit.,* skill (to)
cause (to) decide.

mā·kau ho'o·ka'a·'ike *kik*
Communication skill.

mā·kau ho'o·lā·lā *kik* Planning
skill.

mā·kau ho'o·mohala mana'o *kik*
Productive-thinking skill. *Lit.,* skill (to)
develop thought.

mā·kau ho'o·pakele ola *kik* Life-
saving skill.

mā·kau hua·'ō·lelo *kik* Word skill.

mā·kau kino *kik* Physical education.
Lit., physical skill.

makau·nalo *kik* Fly, a fishhook with
feathers. *Lit.,* fly fishhook.

mā·kau nohona home *kik* Home
economics, as a course at school. *Lit.,*
skills (for) home life.

mā·kau no'o·no'o *kik* Thinking
skills. *Puke mākau no'ono'o.* Building
thinking skills book.

mā·kau pilina·'ō·lelo *kik*
Grammar or sentence-structure skill.

mā·kau wā·nana *kik* Prediction skill.

mā·kau 'ō·lelo *kik* Language arts.
Lit., language skill.

Mā·kahi *i'oa* Scheat, a star. *Mān.*
(HA).

maka·hiki *kik* Year. *Dic.* Abb. MH.
Makahiki holo kukuna lā. Light year.
See *māmā kukuna lā.*

maka·hi'o *ham* To explore. *E hele
kākou i ka makahi'o 'ana.* Let's go
exploring. Comb. *maka + hi'o* (*Tah.,*
look). *Huaka'i makahi'o.* Excursion,
field trip.

maka·kau *kik* Awareness. Comb.
maka + kau. Makakau 'ōlelo. Language
awareness.

maka·kema *kik* Macadamia. *Eng.*
Also *makeima, makekemia.*

maka·kina *kik* Magazine. *Eng.* Also
makasina.

maka·ki'i See *nananana makaki'i.*

maka·koho *kik* Priority. Comb.
maka + koho. See *ho'omakakoho.*
Ho'oka'ina makakoho. To prioritize, set
priorities

maka·kū *kik/heh* Creative imagination; to use one's imagination. *Dic.* Cf.
moeā. Kākau makakū. Creative writing.

maka·kui *kik* Fine point, fine line, as of a pen point. *Dic., ext. mng., sp. var. Peni makakui.* Fine-point pen.

Maka·kukeka *iʻoa* Massachusetts. *Dic.* Also *Masakuseta.*

maka·kumu *ʻa* Primitive. Comb. *maka + kumu.*

mā·kala *kik* Muscle. *Niʻihau (Eng.).* See entries below. *ʻŌnaehana mākala.* Muscular system, in biology.

Mā·kala *iʻoa* Marshall Islands; Marshallese. *Dic.* Also *Mākala ʻAilana, ka pae moku ʻo Mākala.*

mā·kala alo ʻū·hā See *mākala ʻūhā.*

maka·lau *kik* Tesselation, in math. Comb. *maka + lau.*

mā·kala uma iki *kik* Pectoralis minor muscle of the upper chest. *Lit.,* small chest muscle. *Cf. mākala uma nui.*

mā·kala uma nui *kik* Pectoralis major muscle of the upper chest. *Lit.,* large chest muscle. *Cf. mākala uma iki.*

maka·launa *ʻa* Compatible, as numbers, in math. *Dic., ext. mng. Helu makalauna.* Compatible number.

mā·kala hope alo ʻū·hā See *mākala ʻūhā.*

mā·kala kau·pē *kik* Deltoid muscle of the upper arm. *Lit.,* muscle (to) put a paddle forward.

mā·kala·kala *ʻa* Decoded, solved. *Dic., new mng.* See *hoʻomākalakala.*

mā·kala kaʻa·kepa ʻū·hā *kik* Sartorius muscle crossing the anterior portion of the upper leg. *Lit.,* diagonal thigh muscle.

mā·kala keʻa·haka *kik* Rectus abdominus muscle of the anterior torso. *Sh. mākala + keʻahakahaka.*

mā·kala kū hiō *kik* Abdominus oblique muscle. *Lit.,* oblique muscle. *Mākala kū hiō o loko.* Internal abdominus oblique muscle. *Mākala kū hiō o waho.* External abdominus oblique muscle.

mā·kala kū kō·kua *kik* Striated muscle. *Trad. (Anatomia).*

mā·kala kumu·kolu *kik* Triceps, i.e. the muscle of the back of the upper arm. *Lit.,* muscle (with) three sources.

mā·kala kumu ʻū·hā See *mākala ʻūhā.*

mā·kala kuʻi ʻū·hā See *mākala ʻūhā.*

mā·kala kū·ʻokoʻa *kik* Smooth muscle. *Trad. (Anatomia).*

mā·kala luli poʻo *kik* Sternocleido-mastoid muscle, i.e. the muscles between the sternum and the base of the ear. *Lit.,* head-shaking muscle.

mā·kala maha *kik* Temporalis muscle, i.e. the muscle of the side of the head. *Lit.,* temple muscle.

mā·kala nuku *kik* Orbicularis oris, i.e. the muscles surrounding the mouth and lips. *Lit.,* snout muscle.

mā·kala pelu mua *kik* Tibialis muscle, i.e. the muscle of the lower leg and foot region. *Lit.,* muscle (that) bends first.

mā·kala ʻamo *kik* Sphincter, i.e. an annular muscle surrounding and able to contract or close a bodily opening or channel. *Lit.,* anal muscle. See *puka ʻamo.*

mā·kala ʻō·pū *kik* Abdominal muscle. *Lit.,* abdomen muscle.

mā·kala ʻuala *kik* Biceps, i.e. the muscle of the front of the upper arm. *Lit.,* biceps muscle.

mā·kala ʻū·hā *kik* Any muscle of the quadriceps femoris group, the group of muscles that extend the leg. *Lit.,* thigh muscle. *Mākala alo ʻūhā.* Rectus femoris. *Mākala hope alo ʻūhā.* Vastus intermedius. *Mākala kumu ʻūhā.* Vastus medialis. *Mākala kuʻi ʻūhā.* Vastus lateralis.

mā·kala ʻulu *kik* Gastrocnemius or calf muscle of the anterior of the lower leg. *Dic.* Also *ʻoloʻolo wāwae.*

mā·kala ʻū·pā *kik* Masseter muscle, i.e. the muscle that closes the jaw. *Lit.,* muscle (that) opens and shuts (the mouth).

Mā·kala ʻAi·lana *iʻoa* Marshall Islands; Marshallese. *Dic.* Also *Mākala, ka pae moku ʻo Mākala.*

maka·like *kik* Daisy, marguerite. *Dic.*

maka·lina *kik* Margarine, oleomargarine. *Eng.*

maka·liʻi See *pākū makaliʻi, waiehu makaliʻi.*

maka·loni *kik* Macaroni. *Eng.*

māka mana·mana lima *kik* Fingerprint. *Niʻihau.* Also *kiʻi manamana lima, meheu manamana lima.* See *kāpala, māioio manamana lima. ʻOhi i ka māka manamana lima.* To collect fingerprints.

makana *kik* Cookie, i.e. a small tag file left on a computer hard drive by a server in order to gather information about the end-user. *Dic., ext. mng.* See *palapala makana.*

maka·neki·uma *kik* Magnesium. *Eng.*

makani *kik* Wind. *Dic.* See entries below and *pohu, kolonahe, aheahe, hoʻoholunape, ulūlu, ʻena makani.* See also *holona makani, huila makani, kuka makani.*

makani kaʻa·wili·wili *kik* Tornado. *Dic., sp. var.*

makani pā·hili *kik* Hurricane. *Dic. Kūkala makaʻala makani pāhili.* Hurricane watch. *Kūkala pōʻino makani pāhili.* Hurricane warning.

maka pū·alu *kik* Twill plaiting. *Mān. (MW).* Also *ʻoʻeno.*

maka puhi *kik* Herringbone weave. *Mān. (MW).* Also *iwipuhi.*

maka·wela *Kā makawela.* To slash and burn, a method of land cultivation.

Maka·wela *iʻoa* Miaplacidus, a star in the constellation Carina. *Mān. (HA).*

maka·wili *kik* Bit, as for a drill. *Niʻihau.* See *kumuwili, wili.*

maka·ʻāi·nana *kik* Citizen. *Dic.* Also *kupa.* See entry below. *Makaʻāinana kaumokuʻāina pālua.* Dual citizen. Also *kupa kaumokuʻāina pālua.*

maka·ʻāi·nana ʻā·pana *kik* Constituent, i.e. a voter in a district who is represented by an elected official. *Lit.,* citizen (of a) district.

maka·ʻaha *kik* Grid. *Dic., ext. mng., sp. var.* See *pakuhi makaʻaha. Pepa makaʻaha.* Graph paper. *Pepa makaʻaha kumu hoʻohui pāʻumi.* Base-ten grid paper.

maka·ʻaha *kik* Screen, as for windows. *Niʻihau.* Also *uea makika.* See *pani puka uea makika.*

maka·ʻala maʻaka *ham* Case sensitive, as in a computer program. *Lit.,* alert (for) capitals.

maka·ʻala ʻupena *Kanaka makaʻala ʻupena.* Referee, in volleyball. See *ʻuao.*

mā·kaʻi *Manu mākaʻi.* Cardinal. *Mān.* Also *manu ʻulaʻula.*

Mā·kaʻi *iʻoa* Enif, a star. *Mān. (HA).*

ma ka ʻikamu À la carte, as on a menu. Also *ʻoka pākahikahi.*

mā·kaʻi·kaʻi *heh* To browse, as through a computer program script or on the Internet. *Dic., ext. mng.* Cf. *kele.*

mā·kaʻi kiaʻi *kik* Security guard. *Lit.,* guard (who) watches. Also *kiaʻi, kiaʻi pō, mākaʻi kiaʻi pō.*

maka ʻole See *nananana maka ʻole.*

make See *lāʻau make. Pūnuku ea make.* Gas mask, as used during World War II.

makeima *kik* Macadamia. *Eng.* Also *makakema, makekemia.*

make·hana *ʻa* Useful. Cf. *makepono* (dic.).

make hopena *ʻa* To die a bad death, as in punishment for evil deeds. *Mān. (JPM).*

make·kana *kik* Mustang. *Eng.* Also *masetana.*

makeke·mia *kik* Macadamia. *Eng.* Also *makakema, makeima.*

make·lia *kik* Material, a general term but not relating to cloth. *Dic.* Also *memea. Makelia kūlohelohe.* Raw material.

make loa *'a'* Extinct. *Dic., ext. mng.* Also *halapohe, nalowale loa. 'Ane make loa.* Endangered.

make·make *kik* Preference. *Dic., ext. mng. Nā makemake.* Preferences, as in a computer program. *Heluna makemake.* Demand, i.e. a desired commodity within the consumer's ability to pay.

make·makika na'au *kik* Mental math. *Lit.,* mathematics (in the) mind. Also *helu na'au.*

make·naiko·kene *'a'* Chlorosis, i.e. a condition in plants as a result of deficient nitrogen. Comb. *make + naikokene.* Cf. *make wai, make 'ai* (dic.).

mā·kē·neki *kik* Magnet. *Dic.*

mā·kia *ham* To set, as a record. *Na wai i mākia i ke kūho'e o ka lele loloa i ka makahiki 1988?* Who is it that set the record for the standing long jump in 1988? *Dic., ext. mng.* Cf. *kūho'e.*

makili ka no'o·no'o To "see the light" after not understanding or after being in opposition to an idea. *Mān.*

Mā·koi *i'oa* The star in the center of the constellation Carina. *Mān. (HA).*

mā·kole *Manu wiliō mākole.* Red-eyed vireo.

mā·kō·pi'i *kik* Moss, general term. *Dic., ext. mng.* See *hulupō'ē'ē. Mākōpi'i 'elenahu.* Peat moss.

mā·kua·kua *heh/'a'* To age, as a person; aged. *Dic., ext. mng. Ka mākuakua 'ana.* Aging.

Makulu *i'oa* Saturn. *Dic.*

mā·ku'e *Palaoa māku'e.* Brown bread, a layman's term for any bread made with dark flour. See entries under *palaoa.*

Mal. Abbreviation for *Malaki* (March).

māla *Mahi māla.* To garden; gardening. See *mahi māla.*

māla·a'o *kik* Kindergarten. *Na ka'u kumu mālaa'o i a'o mai ia'u i ka heluhelu 'ana.* My kindergarten teacher taught me how to read. Comb. *māla + a'o.*

Malai·sia *i'oa* Malaysia; Malaysian. *Eng.*

Malaui *i'oa* Malawi; Malawian. *Eng.*

māla hō·'ike·'ike mea·kanu *kik* Botannical garden. *Lit.,* garden for displaying plants.

mala·keke *kik* Syrup. *Dic., ext. mng.* Also *hone.*

Malaki *i'oa* March. *Dic.* Abb. *Mal.*

mala·kona *kik* Marathon. *Eng.*

mā·lalai·oa *kik* Artisan, craftsman. *'O ke kanaka mālalaioa, he mākaukau loa i kekahi hana no'eau e hō'ike'ike 'ia ai, a i 'ole, e ho'ohana maoli 'ia ai ma ka noho 'ana.* An artisan is someone who is skilled at a particular trade or art to be displayed or for practical everyday use. *Dic., ext. mng.*

mā·lama *ham* To save, as in a computer program. *Dic., ext. mng.* See entry below. *Mālama ma ka inoa 'o.* To save as. *Ho'i i ka mālama.* To revert to previous save.

mā·lama *Lawe mālama.* To adopt, as a highway or other public area for environmental cleanup or maintenance. *'Aelike mālama kānāwai.* Compact, i.e. a written agreement to make and obey laws for the welfare of the group.

mā·lama·lama au·kahi *kik* Coherent light, i.e. light in which all the waves vibrate in a single plane with the crests and troughs all aligned. *Lit.,* flowing together light.

Mala·diwa *iʻoa* Maldives. *Eng.*

mala·ria *kik* Malaria. *Eng. Malaria manu.* Avian malaria.

Malata *iʻoa* Malta. *Eng. Ka mokupuni ʻo Malata.* Malta Island.

mala·tiona *kik* Malathion. *Eng.*

malele *heh* Radiation; to radiate. *Dic., ext. mng.* Cf. *pāhawewe. Malele hoʻoliliuwelo.* Adaptive radiation, in biology.

Māli *iʻoa* Mali; Malian. *Eng.*

mā·lī *kik* Mallee bird, of Australia. *Eng.* Also *manu mālī.*

mali·hini *ʻaʻ* Introduced, as plants and animals to a particular place. *Dic.* Cf. *lawekahiki.* See entry below and *lumi moe malihini.*

mali·hini noho loa *kik* Permanent resident, as an alien residing in one country over an extended period of time. *Lit.,* visitor (who) resides permanently.

mā·liko *kik* Transparency, as for an overhead projector. *Dic., ext. mng.*

Mali·neli *iʻoa* Marineris. *Eng. Ke awāwa ʻo Malineli.* Valles Marineris, a valley on Mars.

mā·lō *ʻaʻ* Tense, as articulation, in linguistics. *Dic., ext. mng.* Cf. *ʻalu. Woela mālō.* Tense vowel.

mā·lolo *ʻAu mālolo.* Butterfly stroke, in swimming; to swim the butterfly stroke. *Lit.,* swim (like) *mālolo* fish.

malū *Hālāwai malū.* Subconference, in telecommunications. *Pae malū.* Illegal alien; to arrive as an illegal alien. Cf. *pae kānāwai.*

mā·lua·wai *kik* Large pond, lake. *Niʻihau.*

malu·ō *kik* Conservation, i.e. careful use of natural resources to prevent depletion. Comb. *malu* + *ō* (thrive). See *hoʻomaluō. Helu wawe maluō.* Conservation hotline.

malu·hale *kik* Indoor. Comb. *malu* + *hale.* Cf. *kaupokulani. Haʻuki maluhale.* Indoor sport. *Mākeke maluhale.* Indoor market. *ʻAha mele maluhale.* Indoor concert.

malule *ʻaʻ* Floppy, as a computer disk. *Dic., ext. mng. Pā malule.* Floppy disk (preceded by *ke*). Cf. *pā paʻaloko.*

mā·mā *kik* Tempo, in music. *Dic., ext. mng.* See entries below.

mamao·alike *ʻaʻ* Equidistant, in math. Comb. *mamao* + *a* + *like.*

mā·mā holo *ʻaʻ* Speed, velocity. *Lit.,* going speed. See *piʻi ka māmā holo, hoʻopiʻi i ka māmā holo, emi ka māmā holo, hoʻēmi i ka māmā holo. ʻAwelike māmā holo.* Average speed.

mā·mā kani *kik* Speed of sound. Also *māmā holo o ke kani.* Cf. *māmā kukuna lā.* See *palena holo kani.*

mā·mā kukuna lā *kik* Speed of light. *Lit.,* speed (of) sun's ray. Also *māmā holo o ke kukuna lā.* Cf. *māmā kani.* See *makahiki holo kukuna lā.*

mā·mala·mala *kik* Sliver, splinter. Redup. of *māmala.*

mā·mala·ʻō·lelo *kik* Phrase, in literary or general use. *Dic.* Cf. *lālā.*

mā·mela *kik* Mammal. *Eng.* Also *holoholona ʻai waiū. Kānāwai Māmela Kai.* Marine Mammals Act. *Komikina Māmela Kai.* Marine Mammal Commission.

mā·mota *kik* Groundhog, marmot. *Eng.*

mana *kik* Version, as of a computer program, network, etc. *Dic., ext. mng.*

manā *ʻaʻ* Nasal, in linguistics. *Onomatopoeia.*

mana hoʻo·kō *Māhele mana hoʻokō.* Executive branch, of a government.

mana ho·o·kolo·kolo *kik* Appellate jurisdiction, i.e. a court's authority to hear an appeal of a decision made by another court. *Ke ho'okō nei ka 'Aha Ho'okolokolo Ki'eki'e i kōna mana ho'okolokolo ma ke kauoha 'ana e ho'okolokolo 'ia ka mea i ho'āhewa 'ia ma ka 'Aha Ho'okolokolo Ki'eki'e.* The Supreme Court is exercising it's appellate jurisdiction in ordering the accused be tried in the Supreme Court. *Lit.,* authority (to) try in court. See entry below.

mana ho·o·kolo·kolo maka mua *kik* Original jurisdiction, in law. *Lit.,* first appellate jurisdiction. See *mana ho'okolokolo.*

mana kau kā·nā·wai *kik* Legislative powers. *Trad.*

mana kahi *Ho'okele waiwai mana kahi.* Command economy, i.e. an economic system in which the government controls the factors of production and makes the basic economic decisions.

mana·kanika *kik* Manganese. *Eng.*

mana kā·'ili o ke au·puni *kik* Eminent domain, i.e. the right of the government to take, or to authorize taking of, the private property of a citizen for public use with just compensation being given to the citizen whose property has been taken. *Ma muli o ka mana kā'ili o ke aupuni, ua kā'ili 'ia kekahi hapa o ka 'āina o ka 'ohana Manu no ke kūkulu 'ana i alaloa.* Due to eminent domain, a portion of the Manu family's property was taken to build a highway. *Lit.,* seizing power of the government.

mana kē·nā kahi *Aupuni mana kēnā kahi.* Dictatorship.

mana·kia *kik* Manager. *Eng.* See *ho'opuka. Manakia 'enehana.* Production manager, as for a movie or video production.

mana·koho *'Elele manakoho.* Elector, as in the United States Electoral College.

mana·mana *kik* Finger. *Dic.* Also *manamana lima.* See entries below and *pa'i manamana.*

mana·mana iki *kik* Little finger. *Dic.* Also *manamana li'ili'i.*

mana·mana i'a *kik* Fish stick. *Lit.,* fish finger.

mana·mana komo *kik* Ring finger. *Ni'ihau.* Also *manamana pili.*

mana·mana kuhi·kuhi *kik* Index finger. *Ni'ihau.* Also *manamana miki.*

mana·mana lima See *manamana. Iwi manamana lima.* Phalanx (*plural* phalanges), i.e. the bones of the fingers.

mana·mana li·i·li·i *kik* Little finger. *Dic.* Also *manamana iki.*

mana·mana loa *kik* Middle finger. *Dic.* Also *manamana waena.*

mana·mana miki *kik* Index finger. *Dic.* Also *manamana kuhikuhi.*

mana·mana nui *kik* Thumb. *Dic.*

mana·mana pili *kik* Ring finger. *Dic.* Also *manamana komo.*

mana·mana waena *kik* Middle finger. *Ni'ihau.* Also *manamana loa.*

mana·mana wā·wae *Iwi manamana wāwae.* Phalanx (*plural* phalanges), i.e. the bones of the toes.

manawa *kik* Time. *Dic.* See entries below and *uaki. Helu manawa.* Time, as recorded duration; to time, as speed, duration, etc. *Laina manawa.* Time line. *Ma mua o ka manawa.* Early. Also *ma mua o ka hola. No ka manawa.* Pro tem, pro tempore. *Pelekikena no ka manawa.* President pro tem.

manawa *Ho'oka'awale i ka manawa.* To take the time, as to do something. Also *ho'olilo i ka manawa.*

manawa hili *kik* At bat, up (to bat), in baseball. *Lit.,* time (to) bat.

manawa ho·o·maha *kik* Time out, in team sports such as volleyball. *Ni'ihau.*

manawa ʻā·nō *kik* Real time, as in a computer program. *Hiki ke kolekole i ka manawa ʻānō ma ka Leokī.* You can chat in real time in Leokī. *Lit.,* present time.

mana ʻā·kule·ana *kik* Delegated powers, as of Congress. *Lit.,* power (to) delegate responsibility.

mana ʻā·like *kik* Concurrent power, as powers shared by federal and state governments. *Lit.,* identical power.

manaʻo *kik* Concept. *Dic., ext. mng. Au manaʻo.* Tone, as of a literary work. *Hoʻokaʻina manaʻo.* To sequence ideas, as in a composition. *Mākau hoʻoholo manaʻo.* Decision-making skill. *Mākau hoʻomohala manaʻo.* Productive-thinking skill. *Nīnau hoʻomohala manaʻo.* Open-ended question. *Puaʻi manaʻo.* To brainstorm.

manaʻo·ha·ʻi *kik* Theorem, in math. *Dic. Manaʻohaʻi o Paekakoleo.* Pythagorean theorum.

manaʻo kā·ko·ʻo *kik* Supporting idea, as in a composition.

manaʻo kuhi *kik/ham* Assumption; to assume. *Lit.,* assuming thought.

manaʻo lau·like *kik* Thesaurus entry. *Comb. manaʻo + lau + like. Puke manaʻo laulike.* Thesaurus. *Papa manaʻo laulike.* Thesaurus, as in a computer program.

manaʻo nui *kik* Main idea or thought, as of a paragraph or story. *Dic., ext. mng.*

manehu *kik* Force, power to affect physical relations or conditions. *Sh. mana + ehu.* See entry below and *paʻa manehu kūʻēʻē. Kāʻei manehu uila.* Electrical force field. *Manehu āohiohi.* Resistance force. *Manehu hoʻolana.* Buoyant force, i.e. the upward force of a fluid on an object in it. *Manehu kūlohelohe.* Natural force. *Manehu lā.* Solar power. *Manehu lele niniu.* Centrifugal force. *Manehu kaulike.* Balanced force. *Manehu ʻume niniu.* Centripetal force.

manehu ʻā·nai *kik* Friction, as when one thing rubs against another. *Lit.,* friction force. Also *ʻānai.*

maneki·neko *kik* Japanese lucky welcome cat. *Japn.*

mania *Pena paʻa mania.* Enamel.

mā·noa·noa *ʻa* Coarse, as sand. *Niʻihau/dic.* Cf. *ʻaeʻae.*

manono *ham* To percolate, as water passing through a porous substance. *Dic., ext. mng.*

māno·wai *ʻŌnaehana mānowai.* Cardiovascular system, circulatory system. Also *ʻōnaehana mānowai koko.*

mā·no·ʻa·no·ʻa *ʻa* Thick. *Dic.,* var. of *mānoanoa.*

manu *kik* Bird. *Dic.* See entries below.

mā·nui *ʻa* Macro-. *ʻO ka māhuaola mānui, he kumumea kemikala ia i pono e loaʻa nui i ka lāʻau no ka ulu maikaʻi ʻana o ka lāʻau.* A macronutrient is a chemical element that plants need in large amounts for the good growth of plants. *Sh. māiki + nui.* Cf. *māiki.*

manu hekili *kik* Thunderbird.

manu hū *kik* Hummingbird. *Lit.,* bird (that) hums.

manu kā·lā *kik* Sparrow. *Niʻihau.*

manu kelaka *kik* Thrasher, a bird related to the thrush. *Comb. manu + Eng.*

manu keluka *kik* Thrush. *Lit.,* thrush bird. *Manu keluka ululāʻau.* Wood thrush.

manu kika·kī *kik* Chickadee. *Comb. manu + Eng.*

manu kū·olo·kū *kik* Warbler. *Lit.,* warbling bird.

manu lāke *kik* Lark. *Comb. manu + Eng.*

manu mā·ka·ʻi *kik* Cardinal. *Mān.* Also *manu ʻulaʻula.*

manu mū·kī·kī *kik* Honeycreeper, general term. *Lit.,* bird (that) sucks.

manunu *kik/heh* Tremor, as of an earthquake; to tremor. *Dic.*

manu nū·hata *kik* Nuthatch, a kind of bird. *Comb. manu +* Eng.

manunu muli ō·laʻi *kik* Aftershock, i.e. a minor shock following an earthquake. *Ua nui ʻino nā manunu muli ōlaʻi he mau lā ma hope o ke ōlaʻi nui.* Many aftershocks were felt days after the big earthquake. *Lit.*, after-earthquake tremor.

manu pao lā·ʻau *kik* Woodpecker. *Lit.*, bird (that) pecks wood.

manu pala·miko *kik* Flamingo. *Comb. manu +* Eng. *Also palamiko.*

manu pale·kaiko *kik* Bird of paradise, the bird. *Cf. pua manu.*

manu peleita *kik* Mejiro. *Niʻihau.*

manu pī·uī·lā·ʻau *kik* Wood peewee, a kind of bird. *Comb. manu +* Eng. *+ lāʻau.*

manu pō·poki *kik* Catbird.

manu pupē *kik* Puffin. *Comb. manu +* Eng. *Also pupē.*

manu wili·ō *kik* Vireo, a kind of bird. *Comb. manu +* Eng. *Manu wiliō mākole.* Red-eyed vireo.

manu ʻini·kō *kik* Indigo bunting. *Lit.*, indigo bird.

manu ʻī·piki *kik* Ibis, a flightless bird in prehistoric Hawaiʻi. *Comb. manu +* Eng.

manu ʻoli·ō *kik* Oriole. *Comb. manu +* Eng.

manu ʻula·ʻula *kik* Cardinal. *Dic.* Also *manu mākaʻi.*

māpa *kik/ham* Mop; to mop. *Mān. Hulu māpa.* Mop head.

mā·pina *kik* Muffin. *Eng. Māpina pelene.* Bran muffin.

Mā·pono *iʻoa* Alpheratz, a star. *Mān.* (HA).

mā·pū·naka *kik* Primate, an order of animals including man, apes, and monkeys. *kik* Sh. *māpū + kanaka.*

mā·puna ʻō·lelo *kik* Expression, in grammar, i.e. a term of more than one word which has one meaning, e.g. *a laila. Dic.*

mā·wae See *awāwa māwae.*

maʻa *ʻa* To become adapted to. *Dic.* See *hoʻomaʻa.*

maʻa ana kawa·ū·ea kū·lua *kik* Sling psychrometer. *Lit.*, psychrometer sling. See *ana kawaūea.*

maʻaka *ʻa* Upper case, capital. (*Rarotongan,* big.) *Cf. naʻinaʻi.* See *hua maʻaka. Makaʻala maʻaka.* Case sensitive, as in a computer program.

mā·ʻalo·ʻalo See *uila au māʻaloʻalo.*

mā·ʻama·ola *kik* Bioluminescence. Sh. *māʻamaʻama + ola.*

maʻa·mau See *lumi maʻamau.*

mā·ʻele·nono *ʻa* Tilth, i.e. the nature of soil with porous texture and well-aggregated crumb structure. *Comb. mā- + ʻele* (sh. *kelekele,* PPN *lepo*) *+ nono.* See *pūhuna.*

maʻi See entries below and *hoʻomalu maʻi.*

maʻi hehena *kik* Maniacal delirium. *Lit.*, maniac illness.

maʻi huo·huoi *kik* Schizophrenia. *Comb. maʻi +* redup. of *huoi.* See *maʻi huki.*

maʻi huki *kik* Convulsion. *Dic. Maʻi huki huohuoi.* Schizophrenic convulsion.

maʻi kō·paʻa *kik* Diabetes. *Niʻihau.* Also *mimi kō.*

maʻi lele ai *kik* Sexually transmitted disease (STD). *He loaʻa i ka maʻi lele ai ma ka hana ai palekana ʻole.* You can get sexually transmitted diseases through unprotected sex. *Comb. maʻi lele + ai.* See *ai palekana.*

maʻi pale ʻea pau *kik* AIDS, i.e. acquired immune deficiency syndrome. *Lit.*, disease (of) finished resistance (against) infectious diseases. Also *pale ʻea pau.* See *mū hōlapu pale ʻea pau.*

ma'i 'a'ai 'ana·pu'u *kik* Lymphoma. *Lit.,* lymph cancer.

ma'ono *kik* Flavor. Comb. *ma-* + *'ono.* Cf. *mea hō'ono'ono.*

mā·'ō·'ā *'a'* To be in solution, a scientific term. Sh. *mea* + *'ō'ā.* See *mā'ō'āna, pēmā'ō'ā.*

mā·'ō·'āna *kik* Solution, i.e. a homogeneous mixture. Comb. *mā'ō'ā* + *-na.* Cf. *pūaina.* See *mā'ō'ā, pēmā'ō'ā. Mā'ō'āna kāmāhuaola.* Hydroponic solution. See *kāmāhuaola. Mā'ō'āna kemikala.* Chemical solution. *Mā'ō'āna 'ūhehe'e wai.* Aqueous solution. See *'ūhehe'e wai. 'Ūhōlo'a mā'ō'āna.* Buret, i.e. a precision-made piece of glassware used to measure and deliver accurate volumes of solutions.

ma'u·kele *Nahele ma'ukele.* Rain forest.

mā·'umi *kik* Denier, i.e. a unit of fineness for nylon, etc. Comb. *mā-* + *'umi.*

Mada·gaseka *i'oa* Madagascar; Madagascan. *Dic.*

maria *kik* Maria, a crater-free plain on the surface of the moon. *Eng.*

masa·keke *kik* Mustard. *Eng.*

Masa·kuseta *i'oa* Massachusetts. *Dic.* Also *Makakukeka.*

masa·melo *kik* Marshmallow. *Eng.* Also *mahamelo.*

mea ao 'ē *kik* Extraterrestrial, space alien. *Loa'a maoli anei nā mea ao 'ē ma nā ao 'ē a'e?* Are there actually space aliens on other worlds? *Lit.,* one (from a) different world.

mea ana *kik* Gauge, a measuring instrument. *Lit.,* thing (for) measuring.

mea·inu *kik* Drink, beverage. *Dic., sp. var.*

mea·ola *kik* Organism. *Lit.,* living thing. See *kōpū meaola. Kāohi meaola.* Biological control. *Kemika meaola.* Biochemistry. *Meaola māiki.* Microorganism.

mea·omōmo *kik* Drinking straw. *Lit.,* object (for) sucking.

mea omo 'elala *kik* Insect sucker, an instrument for drawing an insect into a tube by suction. *Lit.,* thing (that) sucks insects.

mea uholo uila *kik* Conductor, of electricity. *Lit.,* thing (through which) electricity runs. Cf. *awe uholo uila.*

mea·ulu *kik* Crop, i.e. a plant that is grown and harvested, usually for profit. *Dic., ext. mng.* Cf. *kanu.*

mea hana *kik* Tool, as a shovel, crowbar, etc. *Dic.* See *hāme'a, maomeka, mauha'a.*

mea hā·pai pila *kik* Sponsor, i.e. a legislator who presents and/or assumes responsibility for the passing of a bill. *Lit.,* one (who) raises (a) bill.

mea hehe'e *kik* Solute. *Lit.,* melted thing. See *'ūhehe'e.*

mea hehi wā·wae *kik* Pedal. *Lit.,* thing (to) pedal (by) foot.

mea hi'o·hia *kik* Find, as an archeological find. *Lit.,* discovered thing.

mea holo *kik* Running back, general term, in football. *Lit.,* one (who) runs.

mea holoi *kik* Eraser. *Dic.* Also *pale holoi, 'ileika.*

mea ho'o·hana *kik* End user, as of computer programs. *Lit.,* one (who) uses.

mea ho'o·hinu·hinu *kik* Polish, i.e. a substance used to give smoothness or shine. *Lit.,* matter (for) polishing.

mea ho'o·kani pila *kik* Musician, particularly one who plays Hawaiian music. *Lit.,* one (who) plays instruments. Cf. *mea puolo.*

mea ho'o·momona lepo *kik* Fertilizer. Comb. *mea* + dic. *Mea ho'omomona lepo kā'oko'a.* Complete fertilizer, i.e. fertilizer which contains the six necessary elements for plant growth.

mea hō·'ono·'ono *kik* Flavoring. *Lit.,* thing to make tasty. Cf. *ma'ono.*

mea hoʻo·pai·pai *kik* Lobbyist. *Lit.*, one (who) lobbies. See *hoʻopaipai*.

mea hoʻo·piʻi *kik* Plaintiff. *Dic.* Cf. *mea kūpale*. See *loio hoʻopiʻi, ʻaoʻao hoʻopiʻi*.

mea hoʻo·puka·puka kā·lā *kik* Investment. See *hoʻopukapuka*.

mea kau lole *kik* Hanger. *Lit.*, thing (for) placing clothes. Also *uea kau lole, lāʻau kau lole, ʻea kau lole*.

mea kā·lai·kanu *kik* Horticulturist. *Lit.*, horticulture person.

mea·kanu *kik* Plant. *Dic., sp. var.* See *pahu hoʻoulu meakanu. Meakanu pua.* Flowering plant. *ʻAila meakanu.* Vegetable oil.

mea kaʻa launa *kik* Contact, i.e. a person to whom certain information is communicated. *Lit.*, one in charge of associating.

mea kemu *kik* Consumer, i.e. a person who uses a commodity or service. *Lit.*, person (who) consumes. See *kemu*.

mea kiko·ʻī *kik* Detail. *Lit.*, specific thing. Also *mea liʻiliʻi, mea liʻiliʻi kikoʻī*.

mea·kino *kik* Matter, i.e. physical substance. Comb. *mea + kino*.

mea kō·kua helu *kik* Counter, as beans or bottle caps to help with a math problem. *Lit.*, thing (which) helps count.

mea kū i ke au *kik* Trend. *Lit.*, thing existing in the era. See *kū i ke au*.

mea kū·pale *kik* Defendant, in court proceedings. *Lit.*, one (who) defends. Cf. *mea hoʻopiʻi*. See *loio kūpale, ʻaoʻao kūpale*.

mea kū·ʻai *kik* Merchandise. *Lit.*, thing (to) buy.

mea liʻi·li·ʻi *kik* Detail. *ʻO ka mea wale nō i koe, ʻo ia ka hoʻoponopono ʻana i nā mea liʻiliʻi o ka huakaʻi ma mua o ka hele ʻana.* The only thing left to do is to take care of some details for the trip before leaving. *Lit.*, small thing. Also *mea kikoʻī, mea liʻiliʻi kikoʻī*.

mea lole pipi *kik* Butcher. *Dic.* Also *kanaka lole pipi*. See *pepa lole pipi*.

mea mahalo pā·na·ʻi See *mahalo pānaʻi*.

mea pā·ʻani See *pahu mea pāʻani, waihona mea pāʻani*.

mea puolo *kik* Musician, general term. *Lit.*, one (who does) music. Cf. *mea hoʻokani pila*.

mea puka *kik* Winner, as in the consolation bracket of a sports tournament. *ʻO mākou ka mea puka o ka māhele hāʻule.* We were the winners of the consolation bracket. *Lit.*, one (who) emerges (victorious).

mea wehe kini *kik* Can opener. *Dic.*

mea wehe ʻū·mi·ʻi *kik* Staple remover. *Niʻihau.* Cf. *kui ʻūmiʻi pepa, mea ʻūmiʻi pepa*.

mea·ʻai *kik* Food. *Dic., sp. var.* See entry below and *pūʻulu meaʻai, ʻailakele. Meaʻai waiū.* Dairy product. *Kuʻina meaʻai.* Food chain. *Pūnaewele meaʻai.* Food web.

mea·ʻai hiki·wawe *kik* Fast food. *ʻO ka mea maʻamau, nui ka ʻailakele o ka meaʻai hikiwawe.* Fast foods usually contain a lot of fat. *Lit.*, quickly done food. *Hale ʻaina meaʻai hikiwawe.* Fast-food restaurant.

mea ʻapo *kik* Receiver, in football. *Lit.*, one (who) catches. See *ʻapo*.

mea ʻene·hana *kik* Technician. *Lit.*, technology person. *Mea ʻenehana kani.* Sound technician, as for movie or video production. *Mea ʻenehana kiʻi.* Graphics technician.

mea·ʻono palauni *kik* Brownie, the dessert. Comb. *meaʻono + Eng.* Also *palauni*.

mea ʻū·mi·ʻi pepa *kik* Stapler, for paper. *Niʻihau.* See *kui ʻūmiʻi pepa, mea wehe ʻūmiʻi*.

Mei *iʻoa* May. *Dic.* No abbreviation.

Meine *iʻoa* Maine. *Eng.* Also *Maine*.

meiwi *kik* Traditional elements of Hawaiian poetry, story telling, oratory, and narration. *Sh. mele + iwi.*

meo·neki *kik* Mayonnaise. *Eng.* *Kāpiki meoneki.* Cole slaw.

mehana *ʻaʻ* Warm; temperature, when weather considered warm. *ʻEhia ka mehana o kēia lā?* What's the temperature today? *Dic.* Also *mahana. Cf. anu, wela.* See *kēkelē. Mehana ea.* Room temperature. Also *mehana lumi. Kuʻina mehana.* Warm front, as of weather.

me he Like, as if, as though. *Dic., sp. var.* Also *me he mea lā.*

meheu *ʻaʻ* Outlined, as on a computer or in typesetting. *Lit.,* trace. *Cf.* mahaka. See entries below and *hoʻomeheu.*

mē·heu·heu *kik* Custom, i.e. a learned cultural value or behavior. *Dic., ext. mng. Cf. moʻomeheu.*

meheu kalaima *kik* Evidence, as in the commission of a crime. *Lit.,* crime clue. See *kālaimeheu kalaima.*

meheu mana·mana lima *kik* Fingerprint. *Lit.,* finger trace. Also *māka manamana lima, kiʻi manamana lima.* See *kāpala, māioio manamana lima. ʻOhi i ka meheu manamana lima.* To collect fingerprints.

mekala *kik* Metal. *Dic.* Also *metala.* See entries below. *Mekala ʻōʻā.* Alloy. Also *metala ʻōʻā.*

mekala honua ʻā·kili·kai *kik* Alkaline earth metal, i.e. one of the family of elements in Group 2 of the periodic table. *Cf. mekala ʻākilikai.*

mekala ʻā·kili·kai *kik* Alkali metal, i.e. one of the family of elements in Group 1 of the periodic table. *Cf. mekala honua ʻākilikai.*

meka·lika *kik* Metric. *Eng. Anakahi mekalika.* Metric unit of measure. *ʻŌnaehana mekalika.* Metric system.

me ke kau i ka hano Cum laude, with distinction, with honors, as in academics. *Ua puka ʻo ia mai ke kulanui me ke kau i ka hano.* S/he graduated from college with honors. *Lit.,* with placing in honor. See entries below. Also *me ka hanohano, me ka hoʻomaikaʻi*

me ke kau i ka hano hoʻo·nani Magna cum laude, with high honors, as in academics. *ʻO ka mea e kiʻekiʻe kāna mau kaha ma ke kula a puka, he puka nō ʻo ia me ke kau i ka hano hoʻonani.* One whose grades are high in school until graduation will graduate with high honors. *Lit.,* with placing in honor (to) glorify. Also *me ka hoʻomaikaʻi nui.* See *me ke kau i ka hano, me ke kau i ka hano hāweo.*

me ke kau i ka hano hā·weo Summa cum laude, with highest honors, as in academics. *Keu loa ke akamai o Nani, a puka ʻo ia me ke kau i ka hano hāweo no ka maikaʻi loa o kāna hana ma ke kula.* Nani was brilliant enough that she graduated with highest honors since her school work was excellent. *Lit.,* with placing in glowing honor. See *me ke kau i ka hano, me ke kau i ka hano hoʻonani.*

mē·kene *kik* Methane. *Eng.* Also *mētene.*

meki *kik* Iron, the element. *Dic.*

mē·kia *kik* Major, as an academic field of specialization. *ʻO ka ʻōlelo Hawaiʻi kaʻu mēkia.* My major is Hawaiian language. *Eng. Cf. māina.*

Mekiko *iʻoa* Mexico; Mexican. *Dic.*

mela·lemu *kik* Sloth, the animal. *Sh. māmela + lemu. Melalemu pilikua.* Giant sloth.

mele *kik* Poem, poetry, general term (preceded by *ke*). *Dic.*

mele·hune *kik* Mushroom. *Niʻihau.* Also *kūkaelio. Melehune pōpōehu.* Puffball, a kind of mushroom.

mele·kulia *kik* Mercury, the metallic element, in chemistry. *Eng.*

Mele·lana *i'oa* Maryland; Marylander. *Dic.* Also *Merelana.*

mele·mele *Ke Kai Melemele.* Yellow Sea.

meleni *kik* Melon. *Tah.* Also *ipu.* See *ipu'ala.*

meli 'ele·ao *kik* Honeydew, i.e. a sweet juice secreted by aphids. *Lit.,* aphid honey.

melo·kiana *kik* Melodeon. *Dic.*

memea *kik* Material, a general term but not relating to cloth. Redup. of *mea.* Also *makelia. Memea kūlohelohe.* Raw material.

memo *kik* Memo, memorandum; a memo or note for conveying a message to someone; message. *Eng.* Cf. *kakaha. Kākau i memo.* To take a message; to write a memo. *Memo kūloko.* Internal memorandum, as in telecommunication.

mē·pala *kik* Maple. *Eng.*

me'e See *ka'ao me'e.*

Mere·lana *i'oa* Maryland; Marylander. *Dic.* Also *Melelana.*

meta·nola *kik* Methanol. *Eng.*

meto *kik* Methyl. *Eng.*

mī *kik* Ti, the seventh note on the musical scale. *Dic.* See *pākōlī.*

mī·ana *kik* Urinal. *Dic.* See *ipu mimi.*

mio *'a'* Streamlined, sleek. *Ni'ihau. Ka'a mio.* Sports car.

mio·mio *'a'* Precision, as high-quality print resolution on a computer printer. *Dic., ext. mng.* Cf. *kalakala. Kākiko miomio.* Precision bitmapping.

mio·'awi *kik* Mole, the animal. Comb. *miyo + ci'avi* (Ute).

mika *kik* Meter, the unit of measurement. *Dic.* Abb. *m.*

Mika See *kapuahi Mika.*

mīka *kik* Meter, an instrument that automatically measures and registers quantity. *Eng.* See *pahu mīka. Mīka kāki.* Parking meter. See *kū kāki.*

mī·kā *kik* Pressure. *Dic., ext. mng. Ana mīkā ea.* Barometer. *A'alonoa mīkā.* Pressure receptor. *Mīkā anakonu.* Isostasy, i.e. the equilibrium of the earth's crust, in geology. *Mīkā ea.* Air pressure, as in a tire. *Mīkā koko.* Blood pressure. *'Ōnaehana mīkā emi.* Low-pressure system, in meteorology. *'Ōnaehana mīkā pi'i.* High-pressure system.

mika·ō *kik* Utilities, as electricity, gas, etc. Comb. *mīka + ō.*

miki *ham* To take up with the fingers, as poi. *Dic. Manamana miki.* Index finger. Also *manamana kuhikuhi.*

miki *ham* To give an electric shock. *Ke 'oe ho'ō i kou manamana lima i loko o ka puka 'ōpu'u, e miki 'ia ana 'oe.* If you stick your finger in the light socket, you will get shocked. *Mān.* Also *omo.* Cf. *'ūmi'i.*

Miki·kana *i'oa* Michigan; Michigander, Michiganite. *Dic.*

Miki·kipi *i'oa* Mississippi; Mississippian. *Dic.* Also *Misisipi.*

miki·lima pō·hili *kik* Baseball glove, mitt.

mī·kini *kik* Appliance. *Dic., ext. mng.* See entries below. *Hale kū'ai mīkini.* Appliance store. *Mīkini home.* Home appliance. *Mīkini ke'ena.* Office appliance.

mī·kini ana ō·la'i *kik* Seismograph. *Dic.* Also *ana ōla'i.*

mī·kini helu *kik* Calculator. *Dic., ext. mng. Papakaumaka mīkini helu.* Calculator display screen.

mī·kini helu·helu pā *kik* Co-processor unit (CPU), as for a computer. *He holo lohi wale nō kēia MHP kahiko.* This old CPU runs so slow. *Lit.,* machine (for) reading disks. Abb. *MHP.*

mī·kini holoi pā *kik* Dishwasher. *Lit.,* machine (for) washing dishes. *Kopa mīkini holoi pā.* Dishwasher soap.

mī·kini hoʻāʻo *kik* Tester, as a battery tester, when the tester is a machine. *Lit.*, machine (for) testing. Cf. *hāmeʻa hoʻāʻo. Mīkini hoʻāʻo iho.* Battery tester, a machine.

mī·kini hoʻo·ili kiʻi *kik* Scanner, as for a computer program. *Lit.*, machine (to) transfer pictures.

mī·kini hoʻo·kani pā·leo *kik* Record player. Also *mīkini pāleo.*

mī·kini hoʻo·lele kiʻi·aka *kik* Slide projector. *Lit.*, machine (for) projecting slides. Also *mīkini kiʻiaka.* See *pākū hoʻolele kiʻi.*

mī·kini hoʻo·lele kiʻi·ʻoni·ʻoni *kik* Movie projector. *Lit.*, machine (for) projecting movies. Also *mīkini kiʻiʻoniʻoni.* See *pākū hoʻolele kiʻi.*

mī·kini hō·ʻolu ea *kik* Air conditioner. *Lit.*, machine (which) cools air. Also *hōʻolu ea.*

mī·kini hoʻo·moe hua *kik* Incubator, for eggs. *Lit.*, machine (for) hatching eggs.

mī·kini hoʻo·pau ʻume·kau·maha *kik* Antigravity machine. *Lit.*, machine (that) cancels gravity. See *ʻumekaumaha.*

mī·kini hoʻo·paʻa leo *kik* Tape recorder. *Lit.*, machine (for) recording voices. See *mīkini lola, mīkini pōkaʻa leo.*

mī·kini kā·kuhi *kik* Graphing calculator. *Lit.*, machine (for) graphing.

mī·kini kipi·kipi lepo *kik* Rotary tiller, rotary cultivator, Rototiller. *Lit.*, machine (that) digs dirt.

mī·kini lola *kik* Cassette recorder/player. *Lit.*, cassette machine. See *mīkini pōkaʻa leo. Mīkini hoʻokani lola.* Cassette player. *Mīkini hoʻopaʻa lola.* Cassette recorder.

mī·kini pana·kō *kik* Automated-teller machine (ATM). *Lit.*, bank machine.

mī·kini paʻi *kik* Printer, as for a computer. *Lit.*, machine (for) printing.

mī·kini pō·kaʻa leo *kik* Reel-to-reel tape recorder/player. *Lit.*, sound reel machine. See *mīkini lola. Mīkini hoʻokani pōkaʻa.* Reel-to-reel tape player. *Mīkini hoʻopaʻa pōkaʻa.* Reel-to-reel tape recorder.

mī·kini ʻohi kā·lā *kik* Cash register. *Lit.*, machine (for) collecting money. See *ʻohi kālā.*

Miko·uli *iʻoa* Missouri; Missourian. *Dic.* Also *Misouri.*

miko·kene *kik* Mitogen, i.e. any substance or agent that stimulates mitotic cell division. *Eng.*

miko·lolo·lehua *ham* To entertain, as in a speech. *Kawelo.* See dic. for other variations of *mikolololehua. Haʻiʻōlelo mikolololehua.* Expressive speech, a speech to entertain.

mil Abbreviation for *mile* (mile).

mile *kik* Mile. *Dic.* Abb. *mil. Mile o ka hola.* Miles per hour. Abb. *mil/hl.*

mili- Milli-, i.e. a prefix meaning one thousandth. *Eng.* Also *hapa kaukani.* See entries below.

mili·ona See *hapa miliona.*

mili·kalame *kik* Milligram. *Eng.* Abb. *mkal.*

mili·lika *kik* Milliliter. *Eng.* Abb. *ml.*

mili·mika *kik* Millimeter. *Eng.* Abb. *mm.*

Mima *iʻoa* Mimas, a moon very near to Saturn. *Eng.*

mimiki *Wahī mimiki.* Shrink-wrapping; to shrink-wrap.

mimi kō *kik* Diabetes. *Dic.* Also *maʻi kōpaʻa.*

min Abbreviation for *minuke* (minute).

Mine·koka *iʻoa* Minnesota; Minnesotan. *Dic.*

mine·lala *kik* Mineral. *Eng.* Also *minerala.*

minuke *kik* Minute, of time. *Dic.* Abb. *min.*

minuke lī·pine *kik* Footage, as the number of minutes of video tape shot. *Lit.,* footage minutes. Cf. *līpine.*

mī·'oi *heh* Offsides, in football. *Dic., ext. mng.* Cf. *lele 'ē.* See entry below. *Mī'oi na ke kūlele.* Offsides on the offense.

mī·'oi wale *heh* To fake or hit, in volleyball. *Ni'ihau.* Also *hana kolohe.*

Misi·sipi *i'oa* Mississippi; Mississippian. *Dic.* Also *Mikikipi.*

Miso·uri *i'oa* Missouri; Missourian. *Dic.* Also *Mikouli.*

moa *Pu'upu'u moa.* Chicken pox.

mō·akāka *'a'* Clear, plain, intelligible. *Ua wehewehe 'ia nā 'ōkuhi a mōakāka.* The instructions were explained clearly. *Dic., sp. var.*

moana *kik* Oceanic. *'O ka Polenekia, he po'e moana lākou.* Polynesians are an oceanic people. *Dic., ext. mng.* See entry below and *waena moana. Pāpa'a moana.* Ocean crust. *Pū'ali kaua moana.* Navy. Also *'au moku kaua, 'oihana moku. Kahua pū'ali kaua moana.* Navy base.

Moana Pā·kī·pika *i'oa* Pacific Ocean. *Dic.*

moe See entries below and *lumi moe.*

moe·ā *heh* To imagine oneself to be something or someone; imaginary. *Sh. moemoeā.* Cf. *ho'omoeā, makakū. Helu hapa moeā.* Complex number, in math. *Helu moeā.* Imaginary number. Cf. *helu maoli. Ho'ohele moeā.* To utilize guided imagery. *Laina moeā.* Imaginary line.

moe·apupa *heh* To pupate. *Comb. moe + a + pupa.* See *pupa.*

moe·kau *heh* Hibernation; to hibernate. *Comb. moe + kau.*

moe·kahi *'a'* Consecutive, in sequence. *Pā'ina aku nei wau ma laila 'ekolu ahiahi moekahi i kēlā pule aku nei.* I had dinner there three consecutive evenings last week. *Dic.*

moe·moeā *kik* Fantasy. *Dic.*

moena *kik* Rug, as for a living room or any large room. *Dic., ext. mng.* Also *hāli'i papahele.* See *pale papahele. Moena weleweka.* Carpet.

moena helu hapa haneli *kik* Hundredths square, in math. *Lit.,* mat (to) count hundredths. See *papa 'aukā helu, 'aukā helu hapa 'umi.*

moena kō·kua helu *kik* Counting mat, flat, or stripmat, in math. *Lit.,* mat (to) help count. Also *moena.* Cf. *pa'a'iliono kōkua helu, 'aukā kōkua helu.*

moena 'ili *kik* Linoleum, linoleum flooring. *Ni'ihau.* Also *linoleuma. Moena 'ili 'āpanapana.* Floor tile. Also *kile papahele, kile 'ili.*

moe pā·laha·laha *heh* To dive, in volleyball. *Ni'ihau.* Also *lele 'ōpū, lu'u.*

moe pē·pē *kik* Crib, as for babies. *Lit.,* baby bed.

moe·'alā *kik* Polychaete worm, a kind of worm found underneath stream rocks. *Comb. moe + 'alā.* Also *ko'e moe'alā.* Cf. *moeone (dic.).*

mohala *'a'* Blossoming, blooming, unfolded, as a flower; spread open. *Dic.*

mō·hihi'o *kik* Science fiction. *Sh. mō'ike + hihi'o. Ki'i'oni'oni mōhihi'o.* Science fiction movie.

moho *kik* Candidate, as in politics. *Nui maoli nō ka 'eu o ka paio kālai-mana'o o nā moho nui 'ehā i hō'ike'ike 'ia ma ke kelewikiona i ka pō nei.* The debate between the four main candidates that was broadcast on television last night was very lively. *Dic.* See entry below and *wae moho.*

moho *kik* Champion, champions. *'O mākou ka moho.* We're the champions. *Dic.* See *kūlana 'elua. Ho'okūkū moho.* Tournament, as for sports. Also *ho'okūkū.* See *ho'okūkū kio, ho'okūkū kahului.*

moho lele ʻole *kik* Flightless rail. *Lit.,* nonflying rail.

moka *kik* Waste, as of plants and animals. *Dic.*

mō·kema *kik* Modem. *Eng.*

mō·kio *ʻa* Rounded, in linguistics. *Dic., ext. mng. Woela mōkio.* Rounded vowel.

moko·huila·hā *kik* All-terrain vehicle (ATV). *Sh. mokokaikala + huila + ʻehā.*

moko·kai·kala holo lepo *kik* Dirt bike. *Lit.,* motorcycle (for) riding (on) dirt.

moku *ʻAu moku kaua.* Navy. Also *pūʻali kaua moana, ʻoihana moku.*

moku ahi·kao *kik* Spacecraft, spaceship, rocket ship. *Comb. moku + ahikao.* See *ahikao. Kelena moku ahikao.* Space capsule.

moku·hau·lana *kik* Iceberg. *Lit.,* island (of) floating ice.

moku·hali lewa lipo *kik* Space shuttle. *Sh. mokulele + halihali + lewa lipo.*

moku·honua *kik* Continent; continental. *Lit.,* earth island. Also *ʻāinapuniʻole. Hene mokuhonua.* Continental slope. *Holopapa mokuhonua.* Continental shelf. *Pāpaʻa mokuhonua.* Continental crust.

moku kau·lua *kik* Catamaran. *Lit.,* double boat.

moku kua·ʻau *kik* Atoll. *Lit.,* lagoon island.

moku·lele hali koa *kik* Military transport aircraft. *Lit.,* military carrying airplane.

moku·lele hele·kopa *kik* Helicopter. *Ua kuʻu ka mokulele helekopa ma luna o ke kahua kū kaʻa no ke kiʻi ʻana i ke kanaka i loaʻa i ka pōulia.* The helicopter landed on the parking lot to pick up the man who was having an emergency. *Niʻihau.* Also *helekopa.*

Moku·mana·mana *iʻoa* Necker, the island. *Trad.*

moku·moku See *palaoa mokumoku.*

mokuna *kik* A division of a legislative bill, larger than a section or article. *Dic., ext. mng.* See *kānāwai, kānāwai kūloko, kānāwai ʻahaʻōlelo, poʻo kānāwai.*

Moku·pā·papa *iʻoa* Kure, the island. *Lit.,* low, flat islet.

moku·peʻa holo mā·mā *kik* Clipper, a kind of ship. *Lit.,* sailing ship (that) travels fast.

moku·ʻāina *kik* State, as one of the United States. *Dic.* Cf. *aupuni, kaumokuʻāina, kauʻāina, māhele ʻāina, pekelala. Hōʻikeʻike mokuʻāina.* State fair. *Kānāwai hoʻolilo mokuʻāina.* Admission act, statehood act. *Nā Mokuʻāina Hoʻohui ʻia o Maikonesia.* Federated States of Micronesia. *Pāka mokuʻāina.* State park.

molai·bada·hate *kik* Molybdate. *ʻAmoniuma molaibadahate.* Ammonium molybdate.

molai·bede·numa *kik* Molybdenum. *Eng.*

mole alelo *kik* Root of the tongue. *Lit.,* tongue root. See *kūʻau alelo, lau alelo, waena alelo, wēlau alelo.*

mole·ana·honua *kik* Geometry. *Dic.* Also *anahonua.*

mō·lehu *Ala mōlehu.* Crepuscular, i.e. appearing or flying in the twilight. Cf. *ala ao, ala pō.*

mō·lehu·lehu *ʻa* Dusk, twilight. *Ua hoʻi wau i ka hale i ka mōlehulehu ʻana o ka lā.* I returned home at dusk. *Dic.* Also *hola mōlehulehu.*

mole·kumu *kik* Root, source, derivation, or origin, as the etymology of a word. *Comb. mole + kumu.* Cf. *kūmole.*

mō·lina *kik* Molding, as around windows or doors; frame or mount, as for pictures. *Dic. Mōlina pukaaniani.* Window frame. *Mōlina kiʻi.* Picture frame. *Mōlina kiʻiaka.* Slide mount.

mō·lina *kik* Frame, as in a computer program. *Dic., ext. mng. Mōlina kaʻakaʻa.* Open frame. *Mōlina paʻa.* Closed frame.

mō·lina *kik/ham* A single frame of a movie or video film; to frame, as to arrange the content of a photograph, movie, or video picture within certain borders. *Dic., ext. mng.*

Moloko *iʻoa* Morocco; Moroccan. *Dic.* Also *Moroko.*

Molo·dowa *iʻoa* Moldova. *Eng.*

Moluka *iʻoa* Molluca. *Eng. Ke kai ʻo Moluka.* Molluca Sea.

Mona·kana *iʻoa* Montana; Montanan. *Dic.* Also *Monekana.*

mona·kō *kik* Glucose. *Loaʻa nui ka monakō ma loko o kekahi mau ʻano huaʻai a me nā ʻaʻaʻa holoholona kekahi, a he hapa mai kōna momona i ke kōpaʻa maʻamau.* Glucose is usually found in some fruits and animal tissues and is about half as sweet as regular sugar. *Sh. momona + kō. Cf. huakō. Monakō koko.* Blood glucose.

Monako *iʻoa* Monaco. *Eng.*

mona·mona *kik* Dessert. *Sh./redup.* of *momona.*

mō·neka·kai *kik* Monkfish. *Comb. mōneka + kai.*

Mone·kana *iʻoa* Montana; Montanan. *Dic.* Also *Monakana.*

moni See *haka moni, paipu moni.*

mono·kesa·side *kik* Monoxide. *Eng. Karabona monokesaside.* Carbon monoxide.

Mono·kolia *iʻoa* Mongolia; Mongolian. *Dic.* Also *Monogolia.*

Mono·golia *iʻoa* Mongolia; Mongolian. *Dic.* Also *Monokolia.*

mō·pina *Kui mōpina.* Hypodermic needle.

mō·pine *kik* Morphine. *Eng.*

mō·ʻaui *kik/heh* Reaction; to react, as chemical compounds. *Sh. moʻo- + ʻaui. Cf. ʻūmōʻaui. Hōʻeleu mōʻaui.* Catalyst. Also *ʻūmōʻauiwawe.* Catalyst. *Mea mōʻaui.* Reactor. *Mōʻaui kemikala.* Chemical activity.

mō·ʻau·kala *kik* History. *Sh. moʻo + au + kala.*

moʻa hapa *ʻa* Medium rare, as meat. *Lit.,* partial cooked. Also *hapa moʻa.*

mō·ʻali·haku *kik* Fossil. *Sh. mōʻali + pōhaku.* Also *wīhaku.*

moʻa loa *ʻa* Well done, as meat. *Lit.,* very cooked.

mō·ʻī *Aupuni Mōʻī Hui Pū ʻia.* United Kingdom. *Aupuni Mōʻī ʻo Tonga.* Kingdom of Tonga.

moʻo·hana *kik* Reptile. *Sh. moʻo + ʻohana.*

moʻo·haʻa·wina *kik* A catalog listing of lessons; a sequence of lessons of a curriculum. *Lit.,* sequence (of) lessons. *Cf. ʻolokeʻa koina papa.*

moʻo·helu *kik* Budget, i.e. a listing of expenditures and receipts. *Trad.* Also *moʻohelu kālā. Hoʻopaʻa moʻohelu kālā.* To make a budget. *Mālama moʻohelu kālā.* Accounting.

moʻo·kāki *kik* Account, as in a computer program or any listing of charges. *Comb. moʻo + kāki.*

moʻo·kala·leo *kik* Literature, general term. *Comb. moʻo + kala + leo. Moʻokalaleo haʻi waha.* Oral literature. *Moʻokalaleo kumu honua.* Creation literature. *Moʻokalaleo kuʻuna.* Traditional literature. *Moʻokalaleo palapala.* Written literature. *Puke moʻomanaʻo moʻokalaleo.* Literature response log, as a student's journal for recording reactions to literature.

moʻo·kaʻao *kik* A traditional tale, especially one relating to a particular culture; folktale. *Dic., sp. var.* Also *kaʻao.* See *kaʻao.*

moʻo·kiʻina *kik* Routine. *Lit.,* sequence (of) movements.

mo‘o·kū·lana wai·wai *kik* Balance sheet, i.e. a listing of assets, liabilities, and owner's equity. Comb. *mo‘o* + *kūlana* + *waiwai.*

mo‘o·kū·‘au·hau *kik* Genealogy. *Dic., sp. var.* Mo‘olelo mo‘okū‘auhau. Genealogical story.

mo‘o·kū·‘ikena *kik* Record, i.e. a quantity of facts treated as a unit. *Lit.,* fact unit. Cf. *kūho‘e, mo‘omō‘ali.*

mo‘o·lako *kik* Inventory. Sh. *mo‘olelo* + *lako.*

mo‘o·lelo hana keaka *kik* Script, as for a play or movie. Usu. *mo‘olelo. Dic., ext. mng.* Cf. *mo‘olelo ki‘i‘oni‘oni. Mea kākau mo‘olelo.* Scriptwriter. *Luna kākau mo‘olelo.* Script supervisor.

mo‘o·lelo ha‘i waha *kik* Narration, as in movie or video production. *Lit.,* story (for) narrating verbally.

mo‘o·lelo kaha *kik* Storyboard, as in movie or video production. *Dic., ext. mng. Lima kaha mo‘olelo.* Storyboard artist. *Hua‘ōlelo kaha mo‘olelo.* Storyboard terms.

mo‘o·lelo ki‘i·‘oni·‘oni *kik* Screenplay. *Lit.,* movie story. See *kākau mo‘olelo ki‘i‘oni‘oni. Mea kākau mo‘olelo ki‘i‘oni‘oni.* Screenwriter. Also *mea kākau ki‘i‘oni‘oni.*

mo‘o·lio *kik* Sea horse. *Dic.*

mo‘o·mana‘o *Puke mo‘omana‘o.* Journal, diary. *Puke mo‘omana‘o mo‘okalaleo.* Literature response log, as a student's journal for recording reactions to literature.

mo‘o·meheu *kik* Culture; cultural. Comb. *mo‘o* + *meheu.* Cf. *mēheuheu.*

mo‘o·mō·‘ali *kik* Record, as a list of facts about achievements or tasks accomplished; résumé, vita, curriculum vitae. Comb. *mo‘o* + *mō‘ali.* Cf. *kūho‘e, mo‘okū‘ikena.*

mo‘ona *kik* Succession. Comb. *mo‘o* + *-na.*

mo‘o·pane *Palapala mo‘opane.* Deposition, i.e. testimony taken down in writing under oath to be used in court proceedings.

mo‘o pila kī·ko‘o *kik* Check register. *E ho‘opa‘a i kēia mau pila kīko‘o i loko o ka mo‘o pila kīko‘o.* Record these checks in the register. *Lit.,* succession of bank checks.

mo‘o pō·haku pele *kik* Lava lizard. *Lit.,* lava rock lizard.

mō·chī *kik* Mochi. *Japn. Laiki mōchī.* Mochi rice. Also *lāisi mōchī.*

Moroko *i‘oa* Morocco; Moroccan. *Eng.* Also *Moloko.*

Mozama·bika *i‘oa* Mozambique; Mozambican. *Eng.*

mū *kik* Checkers. *Dic. Mū Pākē.* Chinese checkers. *Mū kākela.* Chess.

mua See *‘ōlelo mua. Ma mua o ka manawa.* Early. Also *ma mua o ka hola.*

mua puka *kik* Undergraduate level, as of a student in a college or university. *Ho‘oikaika nui ka po‘e haumāna mua puka a loa‘a ka palapala laepua.* Undergraduate students strive hard to obtain a bachelor's degree. *Lit.,* before graduating. Cf. *muli puka. Haumāna mua puka.* Undergraduate student.

mū·he‘e *kik* Cuttlefish (local definition); squid (Haole definition). *Dic.* Cf. *he‘e. Mūhe‘e iwi.* Cuttlebone.

mū hōlapu *kik* Virus, as in a computer program. *Lit.,* spreading bug. See entry below.

mū hō·lapu pale ‘ea pau *kik* HIV, i.e. human immunodeficiency virus. *Lit.,* virus (for) finished resistance (against) infectious diseases. See *pale ‘ea pau.*

mū·hune *kik* Germ. Comb. *mū* + *hune. Huila mūhune.* Biofilter for a fish tank, in aquaculture. Also *hōkele mūhune* (slang). *Mūhune ‘ino.* Pathogen, a disease-producing agent. See *pale mūhune ‘ino.*

mū·kī·kī *Manu mūkīkī.* Honey-creeper, general term. *Lit.*, bird (that) sucks.

muku *kik* Starboard or right side of a single-hulled canoe when looking forward. *Dic., ext. mng.* Cf. *'ākea, ama.* See entry below.

muku *kik* Tight end, in football. *Dic., new mng.* Cf. *lala.* See *'āwa'a muku.*

muli *kik* Coda of a syllable, in linguistics. *Lit.*, last.

muli After-, post-. *Dic., ext. mng.* See entry below and *hō'ike muli a'o, kaumoku'āina muli panalā'au. Ha'uki muli kula.* After-school sports. *Ho'opa'i 'au'a muli kula.* After-school detention. *Manunu muli ōla'i.* Aftershock, i.e. a minor shock following an earthquake.

muli puka *kik* Graduate level, as of a student in a university who has already achieved an undergraduate degree. *Ma hope o ke kula muli puka, e hana nō paha wau no ke aupuni.* After graduate school I will probably work for the government. *Lit.*, after graduating. Cf. *mua puka. Haumāna muli puka.* Graduate student.

muli·wai *Kaha nuku muliwai.* Delta, of a river. *Nuku muliwai.* Estuary. *'Aumana muliwai.* River tributary.

munu·kō *kik* Mung. (Ilocano *monggo.*) *Pāpapa munukō.* Mung bean.

mū pao lau *kik* Leaf miner. *Lit.*, insect (that) bores leaves.

mu'o *kik* Bud of a leaf. *Dic.* Cf. *liko.*

musu·bī *kik* Rice ball, musubi. *Japn.* Also *pōpō laiki, pōpō lāisi.*

MH Abbreviation for *makahiki* (year). *Dic.*

mhn Abbreviation for *mahina* (month).

MHP Abbreviation for *mīkini heluhelu pā* (co-processor unit).

mkal Abbreviation for *milikalame* (milligram).

ml Abbreviation for *mililika* (milliliter).

mm Abbreviation for *milimika* (millimeter).

MS *kik* Master's, Master of Science, as a degree at a university (*pronounced mūsā*). *Eng.* See *laeo'o, MA.*

N

nāele *kik* Bog, with no trees and soft ground. *Dic.* See *ālialia, 'olokele.*

nae·lona *kik* Nylon. *Eng.*

naiko·kene *kik* Nitrogen; nitric. *Eng. Ko'ohune naikokene.* Azobacter, a type of bacteria containing nitrogen. *Naikokene diokesaside.* Nitrogen dioxide. Also *naikokene 'okikene lua. Pō'aiapuni naikokene.* Nitrogen cycle. *Pūhui naikokene ka'awale.* Free nitrogen compound. *'Akika naikokene.* Nitric acid. Also *'akika nikiriku.*

Nai·gera *i'oa* Niger; Nigerien. *Eng.*

Nai·geria *i'oa* Nigeria; Nigerian. *Eng.*

nao *Leki nao.* Teflon tape, for use in plumbing.

nau kuai *ham* To grind, as one's teeth. *E nau kuai ana 'o ia i kōna niho i ka pō nei.* He was grinding his teeth last night. *Comb. nau + kuai.*

naha i'a *kik* Small school of reef fish, such as *manini. Mān.* Also *naho i'a.* Cf. *kumu i'a.*

nahau *kik* Arrow, an indicator; arrowhead. (PPN *ngāsau.*) See *pua, ihe* (dic.). *Haku kā nahau.* Mesolithic, in anthropology. *Ke au haku kā nahau.* Mesolithic age, period. *Nahau 'iole.* Mouse arrow, pointer, or cursor, as in a computer program. Usu. *nahau.* Cf. *kaha'imo.* See *pihi nahau.*

nā·hā·hā *'a* Crumbled. *Dic., ext. mng.*

nahā wale *'a* Fragile, as glass. *Lit.*, easily broken. Cf. *haki wale, pāloli.*

nā·hele·hele *kik* Weed. *Dic.* Also *nā'ele'ele.* See *lā'au make nāhelehele.*

nā·hele·hesa *kik* Snakeweed. Sh. *nāhelehele + nāhesa.*

nahele maʻu·kele *kik* Rain forest. *Lit.,* rain-forest area forest.

nā·hesa pulu *kik* Bullsnake. Comb. *nāhesa +* Eng.

nahi *kik* Lichen, general term. Sh. *unahi.*

Nā·hiku *iʻoa* Big Dipper. *Dic.*

naho iʻa *kik* Small school of reef fish, such as *manini. Mān.* Also *naha iʻa.* Cf. *kumu iʻa.*

Nā Hui Nui ʻElima *kik* The Big Five, i.e. the five corporations that controlled most of the sugar industry in Hawaiʻi. *Lit.,* the five big corporations.

nakeke *ʻa* Crunchy, as fresh potato chips. *Niʻihau.* Also *nakekeke, kakani.* See *kamumu.*

nake·keke *ʻa* Crunchy, as an apple. Redup. of *nakeke.* Also *nakeke, kakani.* See *kamumu.*

nāki *kik* Tribe of people, outside of Hawaiʻi. *He hoʻokahi ka lāhui Māori o Aotearoa, akā, hoʻomāhelehele ʻia ka poʻe ma nā nāki like ʻole.* The Māori race of New Zealand are one race, but they are distinguished by various tribes. (Māori *ngāti.*) See *hapū, ʻalaea.*

nakili·naka *kik* Tundra. (Inuit *natirnaq.*)

Nā·kiʻi·kiʻi *iʻoa* Zuben Elschamali, a star. *Mān.* (HA).

nalala *kik* Dinosaur. (PPN *ngarara.*)

nalea *kik* Trick, as a dog's. Sh. *nanea + maʻalea.* Cf. *kēpuka, pāhaʻohuna.*

nalo·peʻe *ʻa* Camouflaged. Comb. *nalo + peʻe.* See *hoʻonalopeʻe.*

nalo·wale loa *ʻa* Extinct. Also *halapohe, make loa. ʻAne nalowale loa.* Endangered.

nalo wiʻu *kik* Midge fly. *Lit.,* fly (whose bite) smarts with pain.

nalo ʻui·ʻuiki *kik* Firefly. *Lit.,* glimmering fly.

nalu *kik* Wave, as surf near the land. *Dic.* Cf. *ʻale.* See *hokua, honua, kiʻekiʻena, kōā. Poʻina nalu.* Where a wave breaks; surf break (preceded by *ke*).

Nalu·kā·kala *iʻoa* Kingman Reef. *Lit.,* surf that arrives in combers.

Nami·bia *iʻoa* Namibia; Namibian. *Eng.*

nā·mua *kik* Preview. Sh. *nānā + mua.* See *nānaina. Nāmua paʻi.* Print preview, as in a computer program.

nā·naina *kik* View, as in a computer program; scene or scenery, as for a stage production. *Dic., ext. mng.* See *nāmua. Nānaina ululāʻau.* Forest scene.

nā·nahu *kik* Charcoal. *Dic.* Cf. *lānahu.*

nanana See *nananana.*

nana·nana *kik* Spider. *Dic.* Also *nanana.* See entries below and *kalanakula.*

nana·nana hese ʻele·ʻele *kik* Black widow, a spider. *Lit.,* black witch spider. Also *nanana hese ʻeleʻele.*

nana·nana maka·kiʻi *kik* Happy face spider. *Lit.,* mask spider. Also *nanana makakiʻi.*

nana·nana maka ʻole *kik* No-eyed big-eyed hunting spider, from Kauaʻi. *Lit.,* no-eyed spider. Also *nanana maka ʻole.*

nane *kik* Puzzle. *Dic. Nane ʻāpana.* Jigsaw puzzle. *Nane huahelu.* Number puzzle. *Nane huaʻōlelo.* Crossword puzzle.

nani·kupu·lau *kik* Spring beauty, a kind of flower. Comb. *nani + kupulau.*

napoe *kik* Grain. (*Filipino,* rice.)

Nawa·hō *iʻoa* Navaho, Navajo. *Mai kumupaʻa mai nei nō nā hana a me ka moʻomeheu o ka Lāhui Nawahō.* The traditions and culture of the Navajo Nation stem from very ancient times. *Eng.*

na‘au *Helu na‘au.* Mental math. Also *makemakika na‘au. Pō‘ai na‘au.* Affective domain, as relating to the learning process.

na‘au·kake ‘Ame·lika *kik* Hot dog. *Lit.,* American sausage.

nā·‘ana *kik* Review, checkpoint. *Sh. nānā + ‘ana.*

nā·‘ele·‘ele *kik* Weed. *Maui.* See *nāhelehele.*

na‘i·au *‘a‘* To have special effects, be enhanced. *Dic., ext. mng.* See *hi‘ohi‘ona na‘iau, ho‘ona‘iau.*

nā·‘ī·ā·‘umi *ham* To boycott, i.e. abstain from buying from or dealing with (a company) as a means of coercion. *Ke hō‘eu‘eu mai nei nā ‘ahahui he nui e nā‘īā‘umi i nā huahana o Palani no ka ho‘ā‘o ho‘opahū nukelea ma ka Pākīpika.* Many organizations are encouraging that French products be boycotted due to nuclear bomb testing in the Pacific. *Sh. nā‘ī‘ike + a + ‘umi.*

na‘i·na‘i *‘a‘* Lower case, small. *Tah.,* small. Cf. *ma‘aka.* See *hua na‘ina‘i.*

na‘o·koko *kik* Cholesterol. *Nui ‘ino nā mea‘ai ma‘amau o kēia wā me ka na‘okoko he nui o loko, a hiki ke pilikia ke kino i ke a‘aha‘apupū inā ‘a‘ole mālama pono ‘ia ke ‘ano o ka ‘ai ‘ana.* Many kinds of typical foods these days contain a lot of cholesterol and can result in arteriosclerosis if one's diet is not checked. (Māori *ngakototo.*)

Naseka *i‘oa* Nazca. *Eng. Ka Una Honua Naseka.* Nazca Plate.

nehe *heh* To rustle, as leaves or the sea. *Dic.*

Neke·lana *i‘oa* The Netherlands; Netherlander; Netherlandian. *Eng.*

nele *Kōkua nele.* Welfare, i.e. public financial assistance for needy persons.

nele wai *‘a‘* Anhydrous, i.e. without water. *Lit.,* lack water. Cf. *‘anahaidaraside.*

nemo·nemo *‘a‘* Bald, "balahead / bolohead," as a tire. *Ua ‘ai ‘ia ka nihoniho o ka taea a nemonemo.* The tread of the tire was worn bald. *Ni‘ihau.* See *nihoniho.*

nenelu *‘a‘* Marshy. *Dic., ext. mng.*

Nepala *i‘oa* Nepal; Nepalese. *Eng.*

Nepa·laka *i‘oa* Nebraska; Nebraskan. *Dic.* Also *Nebaraka.*

Nepe·kune *i‘oa* Neptune. *Eng.*

Newaka *i‘oa* Nevada; Nevadan. *Dic.* Also *Newada.*

Newada *i‘oa* Nevada; Nevadan. *Dic.* Also *Newaka.*

ne‘e *Ikehu ne‘e.* Kinetic energy.

ne‘e·kau *heh* Migration; to migrate; migratory. *Lit.,* move (with the) seasons.

ne‘ena *kik* Movement. *Dic.* See *holo lola, pu‘u ne‘ena hau. Ne‘ena pahu pa‘i wikiō.* Video camera movement.

ne‘e ‘oā *heh* Divergent, i.e. spreading, in plate techtonics, in geology. *Dic., ext. mng.* Cf. *kākele, ku‘i. Palena ne‘e ‘oā.* Divergent boundary.

Neba·raka *i‘oa* Nebraska; Nebraskan. *Dic.* Also *Nepalaka.*

nī·ane *kik* Neon. *Eng.*

nī·ele *‘a‘* Curious. *Dic.* Also *pena.*

nioe *kik* Tone, in linguistics, as relating to Chinese or Navaho languages. *Sh. pūpū kani oe.*

niu haku *kik* Sprouting coconut or one with eye emerging. *Dic.* Cf. *haku.*

niho *kik* Tooth. *Dic.* See entries below and *kauka ho‘opololei niho, wili niho, ‘ōhiki kauka niho. Nau kuai i ka niho.* To grind the teeth. *Puka niho.* Cavity in a tooth, caries. Cf. *haka waha.*

niho *kik* Dental, in linguistics. *Dic., ext. mng.*

niho *‘a‘* To have whitecaps. *Ua niho ke kai i nehinei.* The sea had whitecaps yesterday. *Mān. (Daisy Pai).* See *‘ale kuakea.*

Nī·hoa Nīhoa, the island. *Ni'ihau.* *'Ainohu Nīhoa.* Nīhoa finch (telespiza ultima).

niho kepa *kik* Boar's tusk. *Ni'ihau.*

niho·niho *kik* Tread, as on a tire. *Ni'ihau.* See *nemonemo.*

niho palaka *kik* Prong of electrical plug. *Lit.,* plug tooth. See *palaka, puka uila. Palaka niho lua.* Two-pronged plug. *Palaka niho kolu.* Three-pronged plug.

nikala *kik* Nickel, the metallic element. *Eng.* Cf. *hapa'umi.*

Nikala·kua *i'oa* Nicaragua; Nicaraguan. *Dic.* Also *Nikarakua.*

Nikara·kua *i'oa* Nicaragua; Nicaraguan. *Eng.* Also *Nikalakua.*

niki·riku Nitric. *Eng.* *'Akika nikiriku.* Nitric acid. Also *'akika naikokene.*

niko·roma *kik* Nichrome. *Eng.* *Uea nikoroma.* Nichrome wire.

niko·tina *kik* Nicotine. *Eng.*

nī·nau *kik* Issue, i.e. a matter in dispute between two or more parties. *Ua nui nā 'ano nīnau like 'ole e no'ono'o ai e pili ana i kēia kumuhana ko'iko'i.* There are all kinds of issues to consider concerning this urgent topic. *Trad.*

nī·nau·ele *ham* To interview. *Dic., ext. mng.* Cf. *ninaninau.*

nī·nau ho'o·mohala mana'o *kik* Open-ended question. *E nīnau wau iā 'oe i kekahi nīnau ho'omohala mana'o.* Let me ask you an open-ended question. *Lit.,* question (to) develop thoughts.

nī·nau koho·koho *kik* Multiple-choice question. *Lit.,* question (to) select (answers).

nī·nau pā·kā·kā *kik* Leading question. *Dic.*

nina·hai·dirina kuhi·kuhi *kik* Ninhydrin indicator.

nina·nina *kik* Scar. *Ni'ihau.* Also *'ālina* (preceded by *ke*).

nina·ninau *ham* To interrogate. *Dic.* Cf. *nīnauele. Palapala ninaninau.* Questionnaire.

niniu See *'ume niniu.*

niniki *kik* Membrane. Sh. *nikiniki.* See entry below.

niniki wahī iwi *kik* Periosteum, i.e. the tough membrane adhering tightly to a bone. *Lit.,* membrane (that) wraps around (a) bone.

nī·'au *kik* Nut, as on an 'ukulele or guitar. *Ni'ihau.* See *'ukulele. Nī'au li'ili'i.* Head nut. *Nī'au nui.* Bridge.

nī·'au·kani *kik* Jew's harp. *Dic., sp. var.*

nī·'au lā *kik* Ray, i.e. one of the bony spines supporting the membrane of a fish's fin. *Lit.,* fin midrib.

nitara·hate *kik* Nitrate. *Eng.*

nitara·hite *kik* Nitrite. *Eng.*

nō *kik* So, the fifth note on the musical scale. *Dic.* See *pākōlī.*

noa See *kī noa.*

noi *Palapala noi ho'ololi kānāwai.* Constitutional initiative, i.e. a process by which one can propose an amendment by gathering signatures on a petition.

nō·iki *kik* Alveolus, i.e. an air sac of the lungs, in anatomy. (Māori *ngōiti.*) *Pū'ali nōiki.* Alveolar duct.

noi'i *ham* Investigation; to investigate; to research. *Ke noi'i nei wau e pili ana i nā lā'au lapa'au like 'ole o nā kūpuna Hawai'i.* I am doing research on the medicinal practices of the Hawaiian people of old. *Dic. Kanaka noi'i.* Researcher. *Kanaka noi'i 'epekema.* Scientific researcher. *Puke noi'i.* Reference or resource book, as an encyclopedia. Cf. *kūmole. Puke noi'i kū'ikena.* Encyclopedia.

nou *ham* To throw overhand; baseball pass, in basketball; to throw such a pass. *Nou 'ia ke kinipōpō ma luna o ka po'ohiwi.* A baseball pass is thrown over the shoulder. *Dic., ext. mng.* Cf. *kiola.*

nō·hie *'a'* Simple, basic, uncomplicated. *PPN.* Cf. *nōhihi.*

nō·hihi *'a'* Complex. Comb. *nō-* (from *nōhie*) + *hihi.* Cf. *nōhie.*

noho *Ikehu noho.* Potential energy. *Luna noho.* Incumbent, i.e. the holder of a political office.

noho kū *kik* Stool without a back. *Lit.,* standing chair.

noho loa *Malihini noho loa.* Permanent resident, as an alien residing in one country over an extended period of time.

noho lua *kik* Toilet seat. Cf. *ipu lua.*

nohona home *Mākau nohona home.* Home economics, as a course at school.

noho paiki·kala *kik* Bicycle seat.

noho pi'i mauna *kik* Lift, as a ski lift. *Lit.,* chair (for) ascending mountains.

noho 'ā·mana *kik* Pack saddle. *Dic.*

nō·kahea *'a'* Drainage; to have good drainage. Comb. *nō* + *kahe* + *-a.*

no ka manawa *kik* Pro tem, pro tempore. *Trad. Pelekikena no ka manawa.* President pro tem.

Nole·wai *i'oa* Norway; Norwegian, Norse. *Dic. Ke kai 'o Nolewai.* Norwegian Sea.

nonia·kahi *'a'* Integrated, i.e. incorporated into a whole. *He noniakahi nā kula o waenakonu o nā kūlanakauhale nui me nā 'ano lāhui a me nā kūlana noho kū'ono'ono like 'ole mai 'ō a 'ō.* The schools in the inner cities are integrated with all types of races and economic backgrounds from all around. Comb. *noni* + *-a* + *kahi.* See *ho'ononiakahi.*

nono *'a'* Permeability, permeable. *Dic., ext. mng. Ālialia nono.* Anchialine pool.

Now. Abbreviation for *Nowemapa* (November).

nō·wela *kik* Novel, as a work of literature. *Eng. Nōwela pōkole.* Novelette.

Nowe·mapa *i'oa* November. *Dic.* Abb. *Now.*

no'o·no'o *Makili ka no'ono'o.* To "see the light" after not understanding or after being in opposition to an idea. *Pō'ai no'ono'o.* Cognitive domain, as relating to the learning process.

no'o·no'o kanaka *kik/ham* Common sense; to use common sense. *Trad. (Kekūhaupi'o).*

no'o·no'o kū·pili *ham* Logical thinking. See *kūpili.*

no'o·no'o loi *ham* Critical thinking. *Lit.,* thought (which) scrutinizes.

nui *'a'* Large, as drink or shirt size. *Dic.* See *li'ili'i, lōpū, nui keu. Koloaka nui.* Large soda. *Manamana nui.* Thumb.

nui *kik/'a'* Dimension, in math. *Dic.* Also *ana.*

nui a'e *'a'* Greater than, in math. Also *'oi aku ka nui.* Cf. *emi iho.*

Nū·ie·rese *i'oa* New Jersey; New Jerseyite. *Dic., sp. var.* Also *Nūkelese.*

Nū·ioka *i'oa* New York; New Yorker. *Dic., sp. var.*

nui keu *'a'* Extra large (XL), as shirt size. *Lit.,* extra big. *Nui keu pālua.* Double-extra large (XXL). *Nui keu pākolu.* Triple-extra large (XXXL).

nui lama koko *ham* Blood alcohol level. *Lit.,* amount (of) intoxicating drink (in) blood. Cf. *ana lama hanu.*

nui·pa'a *kik* Mass, bulk. *Lit.,* solid bulk. See entry below.

nui·pa'a 'ā·toma *kik* Atomic mass. *Anakahi nuipa'a 'ātoma.* Atomic mass unit. *'Awelike nuipa'a 'ātoma.* Average atomic mass.

Nū·hame·kia *i'oa* New Hampshire; New Hampshirite, New Hampshireman. *Dic., sp. var.* Also *Nūhamesia.*

Nū·hame·sia *i'oa* New Hampshire; New Hampshirite, New Hampshireman. *Dic., sp. var.* Also *Nūhamekia.*

nū·hata See *manu nūhata.*

Nū·hō·lani *i'oa* Australia; Australian. *Dic.* See *'Inionūhōlani.* *'Elelū Nūhōlani.* Australian cockroach (Periplaneta australasiae).

nuka·haku *kik* Boulder, generic term, particularly outside of Hawai'i. *'O ka nukahaku kū ka'awale nunui loa i loa'a ma luna o ka 'ili o ka honua, aia ma Nūhōlani.* The largest free standing boulder that can be found on the surface of the earth is located in Australia. *Comb. nuka + haku.* Cf. *pōhaku 'alā.*

Nū·kale·donia *i'oa* New Caledonia. *Eng.*

nuke·lea *kik* Nuclear. *Eng.* Cf. *nukeliu. Ikehu nukelea.* Nuclear energy.

Nū·kelese *i'oa* New Jersey; New Jerseyite. *Eng.* Also *Nūierese.*

nuke·liu *kik* Nucleus, as in an atom. *Eng.* Cf. *nukelea.*

nū·kihu *kik* Proboscis, as of a butterfly. *Sh. nuku + ihu.*

Nuki·lani *i'oa* New Zealand; New Zealander. *Dic., sp. var.* See *Aotearoa.*

Nū·kini *i'oa* New Guinea; New Guinean. *Dic., sp. var.* See *Pāpua Nūkini.*

nuku See entries below. *Mākala nuku.* Orbicularis oris, i.e. the muscles surrounding the mouth and lips.

nuku *ham/kik* Oral reprimand; to scold. *'O ka 'anu'u mua o ka ho'opa'i, 'o ia ka nuku.* The first level of punishment is an oral reprimand. *Dic., ext. mng.*

nuku *kik* Head or foot of trail; pass, in mountains; mouth, as of a river; nozzle. *Dic., ext. mng.* See *hānuku. Kaha nuku muliwai.* Delta, of a river. *Nuku muliwai.* Estuary. *Nuku 'ūpā makani.* Bellows nozzle.

nuku·kikiwi *kik* Jade plant. *Comb. nuku + kikiwi.*

nuku 'ekue *kik* King Kong finch (chloridops regiskongi). *Sh. nuku + pepe'ekue.* See *hona, 'ainohu Kauō, 'ainohu Nīhoa.*

nulu *kik* Noodle. *Eng. Nulu 'Īkālia.* Pasta.

Nū·mekiko *i'oa* New Mexico; New Mexican. *Dic., sp. var.*

nū·mō·nia *kik* Pneumonia. *Mān./dic., sp. var.*

nū·nū *ham* To hum, as a tune. *Ni'ihau.*

nupa pele·maka *kik* Magma chamber. *Lit.,* magma cave.

nu'u·o'a *kik* Highrise, as a building. *Lit.,* protruding blunt height. Cf. *ki'enao'a, nu'uha'a.*

nu'u·ha'a *kik* Lowrise, as a building. *Sh. nu'u + ha'aha'a.* Cf. *nu'uo'a.*

nu'u·kia *kik* Vision, as in the vision statement of an organization. *Comb. nu'u + kia.* See *ala nu'ukia. 'Ōlelo nu'ukia.* Vision statement.

nu'u lau·laha *kik* Plateau, high level land. *Lit.,* spread-out heights. Cf. *kula laulaha.*

P

P1 Abbreviation for *Po'akahi* (Monday).

P2 Abbreviation for *Po'alua* (Tuesday).

P3 Abbreviation for *Po'akolu* (Wednesday).

P4 Abbreviation for *Po'ahā* (Thursday).

P5 Abbreviation for *Po'alima* (Friday).

P6 Abbreviation for *Po'aono* (Saturday).

pā *kik* Disk (preceded by *ke*). *Dic., ext. mng. Pā kamepiula.* Computer disk. *Pā malule.* Floppy disk. *Pā ma'ema'e.* Blank disk. *Pā ho'omaka.* Startup disk. *Pā polokalamu.* Program disk. *Pā pa'aloko.* Hard disk. *Pā pa'aloko wehe.* Removable hard disk.

pā *kik* Do, the first note on the musical scale. *Dic.* See *pākōlī.*

pā *Huina pā.* Intercept, in math. *Huina pā X.* X-intercept.

pā *Mīkini holoi pā.* Dishwasher. *Kopa mīkini holoi pā.* Dishwasher soap.

pā ana *kik* Balancing tray for scales (preceded by *ke*). *Lit.*, measuring plate.

pā·ani·ani *kik* Yarn. *Dic., sp. var.* See *kā pāaniani*.

pae *kik* Stage, level of development; level of difficulty, as intermediate or advanced; rank, as in an orderly arrangement. *Niʻihau; dic., ext. mng.* Cf. *kūlana.* See entries below and *hoʻokaʻina pae.*

pae *kik* Chain, range, series of geographical features. *Dic., ext. mng.* See entries below.

pae *kik* Platform, as DOS, UNIX, Macintosh, etc., for a computer program. *Dic., ext. mng.* Pae *ʻōnaehana.* Operating system.

pae awāwa *kik* Series of valleys.

pae oʻo *kik* Varsity, as a league of sports at school. *Maikaʻi maoli nō kēia kau no ke kime pae oʻo.* The varsity team is having a great season. *Lit.*, mature level. Cf. *pae ʻōpio.*

pae holo·mua *kik* Advanced level.

pae hoʻo·maka *kik* Beginning or introductory level.

pā ehu lepo *kik* Dustpan (preceded by *ke*).

pae·humu *kik* Railing, ballustrade. *Dic.* Cf. *ʻūlili, hūlili.*

Pae·kako·leo *iʻoa* Pythagoras, Pythagorean. *Greek. Manaʻohaʻi o Paekakoleo.* Pythagorean theorum.

pae kā·nā·wai *heh* Legal alien; to arrive as a legal alien. *ʻO ka poʻe pae kānāwai, he mālama ʻia kō lākou mau pono ma lalo o ke kānāwai o ka ʻāina.* Legal aliens have rights that are protected under the laws of the land. *Lit.*, come ashore legally. Cf. *pae malū.*

pae kua·hiwi *kik* Mountain range.

pae lua pele *kik* Chain of craters.

pae mauna kai *kik* Chain of seamounts. *Ka pae mauna kai ʻo ʻEmepela.* Emperor Seamounts.

pae malū *heh* Illegal alien; to arrive as an illegal alien. *Hiki mai ka poʻe pae malū ma nā ʻano like ʻole: ma luna o ka ʻāina, ka moku, a me ka mokulele kekahi.* Illegal aliens arrive by different means: by land, on ship, and by air as well. *Lit.*, come ashore illegally. Cf. *pae kānāwai.*

pae moku *kik* Group of islands, archipelago. *Dic.* Also *pae ʻāina.* See *pae moku hoaka, pae ʻāina. Ka pae moku ʻo Kalolaina.* Caroline Isles. Also *ka pae moku ʻo Karolina. Ka pae moku ʻo Kenele.* Canary Isles. *Ka pae moku ʻo Mākala.* Marshall Islands. Also *Mākala, Mākala ʻAilana. Ka pae moku ʻo Fakalana.* Falkland Islands, Falklands.

pae moku hoaka *kik* Island arc. *ʻO nā pae moku ʻo Hawaiʻi a me ʻAleuta he mau laʻana o ia mea he pae moku hoaka.* The Hawaiian and Aleutian archipelagos are examples of island arcs. *Lit.*, arch archipelago.

pae·pae ala·pi·ʻi *kik* Staircase landing. *Lit.*, stairs platform.

pae·pae ani·ani kau·pane·ʻe *kik* Stage, as of a microscope. *Usu. paepae. Lit.*, platform (for) slides. See *aniani kaupaneʻe.*

pae·pae komo huila *kik* Axle, i.e. a shaft on which a wheel turns. *Dic.* Also *iho.*

pae·pae poho *kik* Chalk tray.

pae·pae puka *kik* Threshold, of a door. *Dic.*

pae·pae puka·ani·ani *kik* Window sill. *Dic.*

pae pū·ʻulu mea·ʻai See *pūʻulu meaʻai.*

pae waena *kik* Intermediate level.

pae ʻāina *kik* Group of islands, archipelago. *Dic.* Also *pae moku.* See *pae moku. Ka pae ʻāina ʻo ʻAleuta.* Aleutian Islands.

pae ʻakahi akahi *kik* Novice level.

pae ʻō·pio *kik* Junior varsity, as a league of sports at school. *Lit.,* young level. Cf. *pae oʻo.*

pai- *ham* A prefix meaning to laud, encourage; -ism, a suffix in English meaning devotion or adherence to something. *Dic., ext. mng.* See entries below.

pai *kik* Pi (π), in math. *Eng.* See *kī pai, pakuhi pai. Helu kohu pai.* Transcendental number.

pai·alewa *ham* Convectional, i.e. to circulate, as air or liquid, between a lower and higher stratum due to variations in density, heat; and gravity; convection; convective. *No ka paialewa, ʻike ʻia nā ao ʻōpua nui ma luna o ka mokupuni a me ka ua nui ma uka o nā pali.* Because of convection, large clouds form over the island and rain falls over the interior mountainous sections. *Comb. pai + a + lewa.*

pai·alou *ham* To make a pitch, as a sales pitch, or to "sell" an idea. *Comb. pai + a + lou.*

pai·ō *kik* Fixed swing, as with two or more ropes or chains. *Niʻihau.* Cf. *lele koali.*

paio kā·lai·manaʻo *ham* Debate; to debate. *Dic. Hui paio kālaimanaʻo.* Debate club.

pai·ola *ʻa* Nutritious. *Comb. pai + ola.* Cf. *ʻaiaola.*

pai·hā·nau *kik* Pro-life, i.e. opposed to abortion; right to life. *Comb. pai- + hānau.* Cf. *paikoho.* See *kaupalena hānau.*

pai·ha·kei lā·hui See *paihaʻakei ʻili.*

pai·ha·ʻa·kei ʻili *ham* Racism, i.e. adhering to a belief that one's own race is superior to another race. *Comb. pai- + haʻakei + ʻili.* Also *paihaʻakei lāhui.* Cf. *hoʻokae, hoʻokae ʻili* (dic.).

pai·hoʻāhu kā·loaʻa See *paikāloaʻa.*

pai·kā·loaʻa *ham* Capitalism. *Ua hoʻohiki maila ke aupuni o Kina e hoʻomau ʻia ana ka ʻōnaehana paikāloaʻa ma Honokaona ma hope o ka hoʻihoʻi ʻia ʻana o ia panalāʻau Beretānia o ka wā ma mua iā Kina.* The Chinese government has promised that it would maintain a capitalistic system in Hong Kong after the former British colony reverts back to China. *Comb. pai- + kāloaʻa.* Also *paihoʻāhu kāloaʻa.* See *ahu kāloaʻa.*

pāiki *kik* Suitcase, purse. *Dic.* Also *pāisi.*

pāiki hā·ʻawe *kik* Backpack, knapsack. *Lit.,* backpack bag. Also *pāisi hāʻawe, ʻawe.*

paiki·kala *kik* Bicycle. *Dic.* Cf. *kalaikikala. Kaea paikikala.* Bicycle tire. Also *taea paikikala. Kaulahao paikikala.* Bicycle chain. *Kalaiwa paikikala.* Bicycle handlebars. Also *ʻau paikikala* (preceded by *ke*). *Kua hao paikikala.* Bicycle crossbar. *Noho paikikala.* Bicycle seat. *Paikikala holo kuahiwi.* Mountain bike.

pāiki lola *kik* Tape case, cassette holder. Cf. *poho lola.*

pai·koho *kik* Pro-choice, i.e. advocating legalized abortion. *Comb. pai- + koho.* Cf. *paihānau.* See *kaupalena hānau.*

pai·kū ka·ʻa·wale *kik* Isolationism. *Lit.,* adhering to (the principle of) standing separate.

paila *heh* To boil. *Dic. Kēkelē paila.* Boiling point. See *kēkelē.*

pai·laha *kik* Credit, as the name of a person who has contributed to a performance. *Comb. hāpai + hoʻolaha.*

pai·leki *kik* Pyrex. *Eng. Hano hoʻokolohua paileki.* Pyrex test tube.

pai·lola *kik* Wintergreen. *Eng.* (scientific name *pyrola*).

pai·mana au·puni *ham* Communism. *Lit.,* adhering to government power.

pai·mana ka‘a·wale *kik* Federalism, i.e. the principle of division of power between the state and national governments. *Lit.*, adhering to separate power.

paina *kik* Pint. *Dic.* Abb. *pin.*

paina *kik* Pine, conifer, or any tree which resembles a pine. Also *paina lau kukuna, paina tidara* (Bib.). See entries below.

paina Kuke *kik* Cook pine. Also *kumu paina Kuke.*

paina luhe *kik* Ironwood. *Lit.*, drooping pine. Also *paina.*

paina Puki·kī *kik* Portuguese cypress. Also *paina tireza* (Bib.).

paina·‘ā·pala *kik* Pineapple. *Mān.* Also *hala kahiki.* *‘Ea paina‘āpala.* Polyethylene.

pai·pai *Luna paipai pila.* Floor leader, as a member of a legislative body.

pai pika *kik* Pizza. *Eng.* Also *pika.*

paipu See entries below. *Kala paipu.* Pipe wrench. *Kanaka ho‘omoe paipu.* Plumber. *Ku‘i paipu.* Pipe fitting. *Wai paipu.* Tap water. *Tuko paipu ‘ea.* Plastic pipe cement. Also *tuko paipu.*

paipu ahi *kik* Exhaust pipe, as on a car. *Ni‘ihau.* Cf. *kini paipu ahi.*

paipu omo wai *kik* Drain. *Ni‘ihau.*

paipu hanu *kik* Windpipe, trachea, in anatomy. *Lit.*, pipe (for) breathing. Also *paipu hanu o lalo.* Cf. *paipu moni.* See entry below and *kani‘ā‘ī. Paipu hanu o luna.* Larynx. *Pani paipu hanu.* Epiglottis (preceded by *ke*).

paipu hanu *kik* Snorkel. *Lit.*, pipe (for) breathing. *‘Au‘au paipu hanu.* To snorkel.

paipu kinai ahi *kik* Fire hydrant. *Lit.*, pipe (for) extinguishing fire. Also *piula wai*

paipu ko‘o *kik* Pipe used to hold up clear plastic sheeting over an aquaculture tank. *Lit.*, support pipe.

paipu lawe ‘ino *kik* Sewer, the pipe. *Dic. Pani paipu lawe ‘ino.* Manhole cover, as for a sewer (preceded by *ke*).

paipu·li‘i *kik* Pipette. Comb. *paipu + li‘i. Paipuli‘i ‘umelauoho.* Capillary pipette.

paipu moni *kik* Esophagus. *Lit.*, pipe (for) swallowing. Cf. *paipu hanu.*

paiwa *kik* Drama; dramatic. Tongan *faiva* (entertainment). *Hana keaka paiwa.* Dramatic play.

pai·roga·lola *kik* Pyrogallol. *Eng.*

pao See *ōpuhe pao lā‘au, kila pao, manu pao lā‘au, mū pao lau.*

pao·meki *kik* Hollow tile. Sh. *pao + kimeki.*

paona *kik* Pound, a unit of weight. *Dic.* Abb. *pon.*

pau *A pau.* All, entirely. *Ka pau ‘ana.* Closing, as of a composition or story. See *ho‘omaka, kino.*

pāua *kik* Abalone. *Māori.*

pā uila *kik/‘a* Electrolysis; to be affected by electrolysis. *Lit.*, touched (by) electricity. See *ho‘opā uila.*

pauka *Waiū pauka.* Powdered milk. Also *waiū ehu.*

pauka hele·helena *kik* Face powder. *Ni‘ihau. Hana i ka pauka helehelena.* To put on face powder. Also *kau i ka pauka helehelena.*

pauka koka *kik* Baking soda. *Lit.*, soda powder. See *hū.*

pauka maka *kik* Eye shadow. *Ni‘ihau. Hana i ka pauka maka.* To put on eye shadow.

pauka niho *kik* Toothpaste. *Mān.* See *pani, poho pauka niho.*

pauka ‘ī·nika *kik* Toner, as for a computer printer. *Lit.*, ink powder.

pau·kū *kik* Paragraph. *Dic.* See entries below and *paukūkū.*

pau·kū *kik* Term, in math. *Dic., ext. mng.* See *hoa like, hua pa‘a. Ho‘onui paukū pākahi.* To multiply through.

pau·kū iwi kua·mo·ʻo *kik* Vertebra, i.e. a segment of the backbone. *Lit.,* section (of the) spine. Cf. *iwi kuamoʻo.*

pau·kū kā·lele *kik* Accent unit or measure, in linguistics. *Lit.,* stress section.

pau·kū kino *kik* Thorax. *Lit.,* body section. Also *paukū.*

pau·kū·kū *ham* To paragraph, as in written compositions. Redup. of *paukū.* See *kūkulu māmala.*

pau·kū ʻolo·kaʻa *kik* Cylinder, the shape. *Dic.* See *hano.*

pāuma *kik/ham* Pump; to pump, as air or water. *Dic.* See *peni pāuma. Pāuma ea.* Air pump, as for tires. Also *pāuma paikikala. Pihi pāuma ea.* Air valve, as on a tire (preceded by *ke*).

pāuma lua *kik* Plunger, as for cleaning clogged drains. *Niʻihau.*

pāumu *kik* Farm. *Māori.*

pau ʻole *ʻa* Infinity, in math. *Dic., ext. mng.*

pā·hai *kik* Plaque, i.e. a commemorative tablet. Sh. *papa + ʻahai.* Cf. *kiahai.*

pā hali·hali *kik* Tray (preceded by *ke*). *Dic.*

Pahama *iʻoa* Bahamas; Bahamian. *Dic.* Also *Bahama.*

pā·hana *kik* Project, as for a class. Sh. *papahana.*

pā·haneli Hecto-, a prefix meaning hundred (h). *Dic., ext. mng.* Abb. *ph.*

pā·hawewe *heh* Radiation; to radiate, as in the form of waves. Comb. *pā + hawewe.* Cf. *malele. Pāhawewe ikehu.* Radioactivity. *Pāhawewe lā.* Solar radiation. *Pāhawewe nukelea.* Nuclear radiation. *Pāhawewe ʻātoma.* Atomic radiation.

pā·ha·ʻo·huna *kik/ham* Magic trick, illusion, sleight of hand; to perform a magic trick. *Ua pāhaʻohuna ʻo ia i ke ale pahi kaua.* He performed the sword-swallowing trick. *Lit.,* secretly mysterious. Cf. *hoʻokalakupua.* See *kēpuka.*

pā·ha·ʻo·weli *kik/ham* Stunt, a feat which requires unusual daring or skill, as in movie or video production; to do or perform a stunt. *E pāhaʻoweli au i ka ulia kaʻa ma ka wikiō.* I'll perform the car-accident stunt in the video. Sh. *pāhaʻohuna + weliweli. Kanaka pāhaʻoweli.* Stuntperson. *Luna pāhaʻoweli.* Stunt coordinator.

pā·heona *kik* Art, artwork; fine arts. *Nui koʻu hoihoi i ka pāheona Pākē.* I'm very interested in Chinese art. Comb. *pā + heona.* See *heona. Luna pāheona.* Art director, as for movie or video production.

pā·heu *kik* Allergy. *Ua loaʻa wau i ka pāheu i kekahi mau ʻano pua.* I am allergic to some kinds of flowers. Comb. *pā + heu* (*Niʻihau*, dust). *Hopena pāheu.* Allergic reaction.

pā·helene *kik* Discus. *Lit.,* Greek disk. *Kīloi pāhelene.* To throw a discus.

pahemo *ʻa* Off-line, i.e. describing the state of an electronic device not ready to receive data, or not connected to a computer or computer network. *Ke ʻā maila kaʻu kamepiula, akā, ʻaʻole pahemo, no ka mea, ʻaʻole i hoʻokuʻi ʻia me ka pūnaewele.* My computer is on, but it is not on-line because it is not connected to the network. *Dic., ext. mng.* Cf. *paʻeʻe.* See *hoʻopahemo.*

paheʻe wai *heh* Water slide; to go on a water slide (Slip 'n' Slide). *Moena paheʻe wai.* Water-slide mat.

pahi *Haku kā pahi.* Paleolithic, in anthropology. *Ke au haku kā pahi.* Paleolithic age, period.

pā·hia How many to each, to a group? *Pāhia nā ʻōhiʻa a kekahi?* How many ʻōhiʻa for each one? *E pāhia ia na kekahi keiki?* How many was it for each child? *Dic.*

pā·hia·hia *kik* Performing art. Sh. *papahana + redup. of hia.*

pahiki *kik* Probability, in math. Sh.
paha + hiki. Cf. *papaha. Pahiki li'ili'i.*
Low probability. *Pahiki nui.* High
probability. *Pahiki ho'okolohua.* Experimental probability. *Pahiki make-*
makika. Mathematical probability.

pā·hili hau *kik* Blizzard. *Lit.,* strong,
snowy wind. Also *makani pāhili hau.*
See *makani pāhili.*

pā·hina *kik* Topping, as for ice cream.
Sh. *pāpahi + -na.*

pā·hi'a See *'oki pāhi'a.*

pā·hi'u *kik* Dart, as for a dart game.
Sh. *pāhi'uhi'u.*

pā·ho'o·nui *kik* Exponent, in math;
power, i.e. a product in which each factor
is the same. Comb. *pā- + ho'onui.* See
entry below and *kapua'i pāho'onui lua,*
kumu pāho'onui lua. Kūlana
pāho'onui. Order of magnitude.
Pāho'onui lua. Square. *Ka pāho'onui*
lua o ka helu. The square of the number.
Pāho'onui kolu. Cubed, as in exponential
counting.

pā·ho'o·nui lua *kik* Quadratic.
Comb. *pāho'onui + lua.* See *pāho'onui.*
Hahaina pāho'onui lua. Quadratic
function. *Ha'ihelu pāho'onui lua.*
Quadratic equation.

pahu *kik* Case. *Dic.* Cf. *'ope.* See
pū'olo, 'eke'eke. Pahu koloaka. Case of
soda. *Pahu pia.* Case of beer.

pahu *kik* Base or plate, as on a baseball
diamond. *Mān. Pahu eo.* Home plate.
Pahu 'ekahi. First base. *Pahu 'elua.*
Second base. *Pahu 'ekolu.* Third base.

pahu *kik* Court, as for volleyball.
Ni'ihau. Also *kahua pōpa'ipa'i.*

pahu *ham* To push. *Dic.* Also *pohu.*

pahu a'o *kik* Dialog box, in a computer
program. *Ua 'ō'ili 'emo 'ole mai nei*
kekahi pahu a'o. A dialog box suddenly
appeared. *Lit.,* teaching box.

pahu·honua·ea *kik* Terrarium. *Lit.,*
aerated box (of) earth. Cf. *pahumea-*
olaea, pahuwaiea.

pahu·hope *kik* Finish point, as in a
race. Comb. *pahu + hope.* Cf. *pahukū.*
Laina pahuhope. Finish line.

pahu·hopu *kik* Goal. *Dic., sp. var.*
Also *pahuhopu laulā. Pahuhopu hāiki.*
Objective.

pahu ho'o·ulu mea·kanu *kik*
Planter, as for growing plants. *Lit.,* box
(for) growing plants.

pahu ho'o·kele *kik* Controller, as in
Nintendo games. *Lit.,* box (to) steer.

pahu ho'o·lele leo *kik* Radio.
Ni'ihau. Also *lēkiō.*

pahu ho'o·nui leo *kik* Amplifier.
Lit., box (for) increasing sound. Cf. *pahu*
leo.

pahu ho'o·wela wai *kik* Water
heater. *Lit.,* tank (for) heating water.
Also *kula ho'owela wai.*

pahu kā·hea *kik* Walkie-talkie.
Ni'ihau.

pahu kā·leka kuhi puke *kik* Card
catalog, as in a library. Sh. *pahu +*
kāleka helu kuhi puke. See *kāleka helu*
kuhi puke.

pahu kī·kā See *'ukulele pahu kīkā.*

pahu·kū *kik* Starting point, as in a
race. Comb. *pahu + kū.* Cf. *pahuhope.*
Laina pahukū. Starting line.

pahu laka *kik* Locker. Comb. *pahu +*
Eng. Also *waihona pāiki.*

pahu leo *kik* Speaker, as for a stereo.
Lit., sound box. Cf. *pahu ho'onui leo.*

pahu·mea·ola·ea *kik* Vivarium.
Lit., aerated box (of) living things. Cf.
pahuhonuaea, pahuwaiea.

pahu mea pā·'ani *kik* Toy chest, toy
box. Also *waihona mea pā'ani.*

pahu mīka *kik* Meter box.

pā·hune *kik* Platelet (preceded by *ke*).
Lit., tiny disk.

pahū·pahū *kik* Firecracker (preceded
by *ke*). *Dic.* See *ahiho'ole'ale'a. Kālī*
pahūpahū. String of firecrackers.

pahu papa·kau·maka *kik* Monitor, as for a computer or in movie or video production. *Lit.,* screen box. See *papakaumaka. Pahu papakaumaka kamepiula.* Computer monitor. *Pahu papakaumaka kīwī.* TV monitor.

pahu pa·a·hau *kik* Freezer. See *pa'ahau.*

pahu pa'i wiki·ō *kik* Camcorder, video camera. *Lit.,* video camera. See *pa'i. Ne'ena pahu pa'i wikiō.* Video camera movement.

pahu pepa *kik* Cardboard box. *Lit.,* paper box. Cf. *pepa pahu.*

pahu pono ha'a·wina *kik* Schoolbox. *Lit.,* box (for) lesson supplies.

pahu·wai·ea *kik* Aquarium. *Lit.,* aerated box (of) water. Cf. *hale hō'ike'ike i'a* (dic.), *pahuhonuaea, pahumeaolaea.*

pahu wai·ū *kik* Milk carton.

pahu wai·hona pepa *kik* File cabinet. *Lit.,* container (for) paper files. Also *pahu waihona, waihona pepa.*

pahu wai·hona wai·wai *kik* Treasure chest. *Lit.,* chest (for) storing valuables.

pahu wā·wahie kū·waho *kik* External fuel tank, as on a spaceship.

pā·hu'a *kik* Open dirt area in pasture, clearing in range land. *Dic.*

pahu 'ai holo *kik* End zone, on a football field. *Lit.,* touchdown box.

pahu 'uiki uila *kik* Fuse box.

pahu 'ume *kik* Bureau, dresser. *Dic.* See *'ume.*

pakā *ham* To dunk (the ball), in basketball. *Ua ka'a ke eo o ka ho'okūkū pakā iā Spud Web.* Spud Web took the slam dunk contest. *Onomatopoeia.* Also *'ūpo'i.* Cf. *pākī.*

pāka See entries below. *'Oihana o nā Pāka a me nā Hana Ho'onanea.* Department of Parks and Recreation.

pā·kā *'a'* Lean, as meat. *Dic. Pākā loa.* Extra lean.

pā·kā *ham* To skin, as a pig or sheep. *Ni'ihau. Pākā hapahā.* To quarter, as an animal.

pāka au·puni *kik* National park. *Pāka Aupuni 'o Iosemite.* Yosemite National Park. *Pāka Aupuni 'o Haunene'e.* Glacier National Park. *Pāka Aupuni 'o Kīlauea.* Hawai'i Volcanoes National Park. *'Oihana Pāka Aupuni.* National Park Service.

pā·kau *kik* Podium. Also *pākau ha'i'ōlelo. Dic., ext. mng.*

pā·kau·kau See *puna pākaukau.*

pā·kau·kau moe *kik* Bedside table, nightstand. *Lit.,* bed table.

pā·kau·kau wai *kik* Water table, as used in preschools. Cf. *papa wai.*

pā·kau·kani Kilo-, a prefix meaning thousand (k). *Dic., ext. mng.* Abb. *pk.* See *'ai pākaukani. Ikehu'ā pākaukani.* Kilocalorie.

pā·kahi *Ho'onui paukū pākahi.* To multiply through, in math. *Pepa pākahi.* One-dollar bill.

pā·kahi·kahi See *kākau pākahikahi, 'oka pākahikahi.*

pā·kā·kā *Heluhelu pākākā.* To skim read. *Ka heluhelu pākākā 'ana.* Skim reading.

pāka kāni·wala *kik* Amusement park. *Lit.,* carnival park.

paka·lī *kik* Parsley. *Eng.*

pā kapu·ahi *kik* Burner, as on a stove. *Lit.,* stove plate. Cf. *kapuahi papakau.*

pā kawa·ū·ea *kik* Relative humidity. Sh. *pākēneka kawaūea.*

pā·ka'a·pohe *kik* Rosette. Comb. *pāka'a + pohe.*

pā·ka'a·wili *kik* Spiralateral, in math. *Dic., ext. mng. Kaha pāka'awili.* To draw a spiralateral.

pake *kik* Putty. *Dic. Pahi pake.* Putty knife.

Pā·kē *i'oa* Chinese. *Dic.* See *kalo Pākē, 'ōpae Pākē. 'Āina Pākē.* China. Also *Kina.*

pā·keu *Hoʻolilo pākeu.* Deficit spending. *Lilo pākeu.* Deficit, as an excess of expenditure over revenue. *Loaʻa pākeu.* Surplus, as a quantity or amount over and above what is needed.

pā·keke *liʻiliʻi kik* Pail. *Lit.,* small bucket.

pakeki *kik* Spaghetti. *Eng.*

pā·kela *koko piʻi kik* Hypertension, i.e. abnormally high arterial blood pressure. *Hiki ke pilikia i ka pākela koko piʻi ke nui loa ka ʻaloʻahia.* Extremely high stress can lead to hypertension. *Lit.,* excessive high blood pressure.

pā·kela *ʻai lā·ʻau ʻaʻ* To overdose on drugs. *Lit.,* take drugs to excess.

pake·leke *Pea pakeleke.* Pear, usually Bartlett. See *pea.*

pā·kē·neka *kik* Percent, percentage; rate. *Dic., sp. var; ext. mng.* See entries below. *Pākēneka uku paneʻe.* Rate of interest. *Pākēneka ʻauhau.* Tax rate.

pā·kē·neka o ka papa·ʻai *kik* Percent Daily Value, formerly known as percentage of US Recommended Daily Allowances (USRDA). *Lit.,* percent of diet.

pā·kē·neka hoʻo·piʻi *kik* Markup, as in the price of an article. *Lit.,* percentage (of) raising.

pakē pī·neki *kik* Peanut brittle.

pā·kī *ham* To slam dunk, in basketball. *Dic., ext. mng.* See entry below and *kī.*

pā·kī *ham* To spike (the ball), in volleyball. *Dic., ext. mng.* Also *hili.* See *hili, ʻai hele wale. Mea pākī.* Hitter. Also *pākī. Pākī ʻepa.* An off-speed shot, i.e. to make a fake spike.

pāki·huila *kik* Flatbed trailer. *Lit.,* barge (with) wheels. Cf. *kaleila.*

pakika *heh* To skid, as a car; to slip, as on a wet sidewalk. *Dic.*

pā·kili·ona Tera-, a prefix meaning trillion (T). Comb. *pā- + kiliona.* Abb. *pkl.*

pā·kimo·kimo *ham* To dribble, as a basketball. Comb. *pā- + kimokimo.* Also *pāloiloi, paʻipaʻi. Pākimokimo pālua.* To double dribble.

Pakipi *iʻoa* Poughkeepsie. *Eng.*

Pā·kī·pika *Moana Pākīpika.* Pacific Ocean. *ʻAha Hoʻomalu Lawaiʻa o ka Pākīpika Komohana.* Western Pacific Fishery Management Council.

pakiʻi *ʻaʻ* Flat, as a tire. *Niʻihau.* Cf. *ʻananuʻu.*

Paki·tana *iʻoa* Pakistan; Pakistani. *Eng.*

pā·kō *kik* Operand, as a digit in a computer mathematical operation. Comb. *pā + kō.* Cf. *haʻi hoʻokō.*

pā·kō·lea *ham* To provide physical therapy. *Ma hope o koʻu ulia kaʻa, ua pono wau e hele pinepine i ka pākōlea ʻia ma ke kikowaena pākōlea.* After my car accident, I had to go often for physical therapy at the physical therapy center. *Dic., ext. mng. Mea pākōlea.* Physical therapist. Also *kanaka pākōlea.*

pā·kō·lī *kik* Musical scale: *pā, kō, lī, hā, nō, lā, mī, pā. Dic.* Also *alapiʻi mele.*

pā·kolu *Pepeiao pākolu.* Tricuspid valve, of the heart.

pā kopa *kik* Soap dish (preceded by *ke*).

paku *ham* To block (a shot), in basketball. *Dic., ext. mng.* See entries below. *Paku ʻino.* To roof. *Ua paku ʻino ʻia kā ia nei e ia ala.* He was roofed by that guy.

paku *ham* To block (the ball), in volleyball. *Dic., ext. mng.* Also *pālulu.* See *ʻai hele wale. Mea paku.* Blocker. Also *paku.*

paku *ʻaʻ* Physical, as a scientific term relating to physical matter. *Sh. pōhaku.* Cf. *kālaiaopaku. Nā ʻanopili paku.* Physical properties.

pakuhi *kik* Chart, graph, plot. Sh. *papa* + *kuhikuhi*. See entries below. *Piko pakuhi*. Origin of a graph. Also *piko*.

pakuhi hoʻo·loli *kik* Conversion chart. *Lit.*, chart (for) changing. *Pakuhi hoʻololi mekalika*. Metric conversion chart.

pakuhi huina ʻike·pili *kik* Cross-tab graph, in math. *Lit.*, data juncture graph.

pakuhi kaʻina *kik* Flow chart. See *kākuhi kaʻina*.

pakuhi kiko·kiko *kik* Scattergram, in math. *Lit.*, graph (of) points. Cf. *pakuhi lū*.

pakuhi kiʻi *kik* Pictogram, pictograph, as in a computer program. *Lit.*, picture chart.

pakuhi lā·kiō *kik* Line graph. *Lit.*, ratio chart.

pakuhi lū *kik* Scattergraph, in math. Cf. *pakuhi kikokiko*.

pakuhi maka·ʻaha *kik* Spreadsheet, as in a computer program. *Lit.*, grid chart. *Polokalamu pakuhi makaʻaha*. Spread-sheet program.

pakuhi pai *kik* Pie chart, as for showing statistics.

pakuhi pahu me ka ʻumi·ʻumi *kik* Box and whiskers graph, in math.

pakuhi papa *kik* Table, as of statistics, etc. *Lit.*, list chart.

pakuhi paʻa ʻau·kā *kik* Double bar graph, in math. *Lit.*, pair (of) bars graph. Cf. *pakuhi ʻaukā*.

pakuhi pō·ʻai *kik* Circle graph, in math.

pakuhi ʻau·kā *kik* Bar graph. Cf. *pakuhi paʻa ʻaukā*. *Pakuhi ʻaukā alapine*. Histogram, i.e. a bar graph showing frequencies, in math.

pakuhi ʻau me ka lau *kik* Stem and leaf plot, in math.

pā·kū hoʻo·lele kiʻi *kik* Screen for projecting slides or movies. *Lit.*, screen (for) projecting pictures.

pakū·kaʻā *kik* Kingfisher. (Ute *pagūcaʻā*.)

pā·kule·kele *kik* Bureaucracy; bureaucratic. *No ka nui pupū o ka holo o ka pākulekele, ʻaʻohe puka o kaʻu noi i nā luna*. Because of bureaucratic stalling, my request to the administration was not approved. Comb. *pā-* + *kulekele*. *Kanaka pākulekele*. Bureaucrat.

pā·kū maka·liʻi *kik* Marquisette, a kind of curtain. *Lit.*, small-meshed curtain.

pā·kū makika *kik* Mosquito netting. *Dic.*

pakū·pakū See *palaoa pakūpakū*.

pā·kuʻi *ham* To graft. *Dic.* See entries below and *papa huaʻōlelo pākuʻi*. *Hoʻoulu pākuʻi*. To grow by grafting. *Pīlali pākuʻi*. Grafting wax.

pā·kuʻi *ham* To annex, in math, as in annexing a zero to show both decimal parts as a hundreth: $6.10 - 3.25 = $. *Dic., ext. mng.*

pā·kuʻi hoʻo·loli *kik/ham* Amendment, i.e. an addition or change to a bill, constitution, etc.; to amend. *Nui nā pākuʻi hoʻololi i pākuʻi ʻia i ke kumukānāwai o ka Mokuʻāina*. There have been many amendments added to the State constitution. *Lit.*, addendum (to) amend.

pā·kuʻina *kik* Affix, in grammar; appendix, as in a book. Comb. *pākuʻi* + *-na*. *Pākuʻina kau hope*. Suffix. *Pākuʻina kau mua*. Prefix. *Pākuʻina kau loko*. Infix.

palaea *kik* Pliers. *Niʻihau*. Also *palaea huki*.

palai hoʻo·luʻu *ham* To deep-fry. *Ma ka palai hoʻoluʻu ʻana, hoʻowela nui ʻia ka ʻaila ma loko o ka ipu hao, a hoʻoluʻu maoli ʻia ka meaʻai i ke kuke ʻana*. In deep-frying, the oil is made very hot in a pot, and the food is actually dipped into it to cook. *Lit.*, fry (by) immersing.

palaina hele·helena *kik* Foundation, for makeup. *Lit.*, smooth (the) face.

palaina puna An exclamation used by the winner in a card game to the loser meaning "you got wiped out!" *Man.* Also *pāpaʻa piele.*

palaoa *kik* Bread *Dic.* See entries below. *Hunahuna palaoa.* Bread crumbs.

palaoa huika *kik* Wheat bread. Cf. *palaoa huika piha.* See *palaoa mākuʻe.*

palaoa huika piha *kik* Whole wheat bread. Cf. *palaoa huika.* See *palaoa mākuʻe.*

palaoa keko *kik* Dumplings. *Man.* Also *palaoa mokumoku, palaoa pakūpakū.*

palaoa keʻo·keʻo *kik* White bread.

palaoa kī·poʻo·poʻo *kik* Waffle. *Lit.*, pitted bread.

palaoa lina·lina *kik* Unleavened pancake. *Dic.*

palaoa lū·lū *kik* Hawaiian-style mush, made of flour and water. *Dic.*

palaoa maka *kik* Flour. *Dic. Palaoa maka huika piha.* Whole wheat flour.

palaoa mā·kuʻe *kik* Brown bread, a layman's term for any bread made with dark flour. See *palaoa hapa huika, palaoa huika.*

palaoa moku·moku *kik* Dumplings. *Dic.* Also *palaoa pakūpakū, palaoa keko.*

palaoa pakū·pakū *kik* Dumplings. *Man.* Also *palaoa keko, palaoa mokumoku.*

palaoa pikeke *kik* Biscuit. Comb. *palaoa* + Eng. Also *pikeke.*

palaoa pū·haʻu·haʻu *kik* Popover. *Lit.*, puffed-out bread.

palaua·lea *kik* Slang. Sh. *pālau* + *walea.*

palauki *kik* Blouse. *Dic.* Also *lakeke.*

pā·lau·moa *kik* Drumstick, as of a chicken. Comb. *pālau* + *moa.* See *ʻūhā moa.*

palauni *kik* Brownie, i.e. the dessert. Usu. *meaʻono palauni. Eng.*

Palaunu *iʻoa* Brown, Brownian. *Eng. Lelekē Palaunu.* Brownian motion, i.e. the random motion of colloidal particles due to their bombardment by molecules of the solvent, in chemistry.

pā·laha·laha See *moe pālahalaha, paʻi pālahalaha.*

pala·hē *ʻa* Mushy, as rice cooked with too much water. *Niʻihau.*

pala·hē·hē *ʻa* Infection; infected. *Dic., ext. mng.*

pala·hō *Pale palahō.* Antiseptic.

pala·holo *kik* Gel. *Dic., new mng.* Cf. *ʻūnina. Palaholo lauoho.* Hair gel, Dep. *Palaholo silaka g.* Silica gel g, i.e. a powder used as the sorbent layer in thin-layer chromatography (pronounced *palaholo silaka gā*).

palaka *kik* Shirt, with short or long sleeves. *Man.* See entries below. *Palaka aloha.* Aloha shirt.

palaka *kik* Plug. *Niʻihau (Eng.).* See *niho palaka, puka uila. Palaka uila.* Electrical plug. *Palaka niho lua.* Two-pronged plug. *Palaka niho kolu.* Three-pronged plug.

palaka *kik* Block, i.e. the child's toy. *Dic., ext. mng.* See *pōlaka.*

palaka kepa *kik* Snap cube. *Lit.*, snap block.

palaka kimeki *kik* Pier block, in construction. *Lit.*, cement block. Cf. *paomeki. Palaka kimeki pale mū.* Termite block.

palaka·lī *kik* Broccoli. *Eng.*

pā·lā·kiō *kik* Scale, in math. Comb. *pā* + *lākiō.* See entries below. *Kiʻi pālākiō.* Scale drawing. *Pane pālākiō.* Rating response. *Papa pālākiō.* Conversion scale.

pā·lā·kiō ikehu ōlaʻi *kik* Richter scale. *Lit.*, earthquake power scale.

pā·lā·kiō lā·lani *kik* Linear scale, in geography. *Lit.*, line scale.

Pala·kila *iʻoa* Brazil; Brazilian. *Dic.* Also *Barazila.*

palaki·niuma *kik* Platinum. *Eng.*

palaki ʻau·ʻau *kik* Brush for bathing.

palaku *kik* Palate, in linguistics. *Eng. Palaku iwi.* Hard palate. *Palaku kīleo.* Soft palate.

Pala·kuae *iʻoa* Paraguay; Paraguayan. *Dic.* Also *Paraguae.*

palala See *pānini palala.*

palami *kik* Brumby, a wild Australian horse. *Eng.*

pala·miko *kik* Flamingo. *Eng.* Also *manu palamiko.*

Palana·heika *kik* Fahrenheit. *Dic.* Abb. *Ph.* See *kēkelē.*

Palani *iʻoa* France; French. *Dic.* Also *Farani. Polenekia Palani.* French Polynesia.

pala·pala *kik/ham* Document, as in a computer program; to transcribe; written. *Dic., ext. mng.* Cf. *haʻi waha, palapala leo.* See entries below. *Hōʻike palapala.* Written report. *Moʻokalaleo palapala.* Written literature.

pala·pala hiʻona ʻāina *kik* Topographic map. See *hiʻona ʻāina.*

pala·pala holo ʻāina ʻē *kik* Passport. *Lit.,* document (for) traveling abroad.

pala·pala hopu *kik* Arrest warrant, warrant for arrest, i.e. a document issued by a magistrate authorizing an officer to make an arrest. *He palapala hopu nō kā mākou e hopu ai iā ʻoe.* We have a warrant for your arrest. *Dic.*

Pala·pala Hō·ʻike Hopena Kaia·puni *kik* Environmental Impact Statement. *Lit.,* document showing environmental consequences.

pala·pala hoʻo·hiki *kik* Guarantee, an assurance of quality or length of use with promise of reimbursement. *Lit.,* promising document. Cf. *palapala hoʻokō.*

pala·pala hoʻo·kō *kik* Warranty, a written guarantee of integrity of a product with promise to repair or replace. *Lit.,* confirming document. Cf. *palapala hoʻohiki.*

pala·pala hoʻo·kō *kik* Certificate of achievement. *Lit.,* accomplishing certificate.

pala·pala hoʻo·kumu *kik* Charter, a document defining the organization of a city, colony, or corporate body. *Ma ka hālāwai o kēlā makahiki aku nei i ʻāpono ʻia ai ka palapala hoʻokumu o ka ʻahahui ʻo Nā Pua a Hāloa, a mai ia manawa mai, ua ulu a he mau kaukani ka nui o nā lālā.* At last year's meeting the charter for the association called Nā Pua a Hāloa was approved, and since that time membership has grown into the thousands. *Dic.*

pala·pala kā·inoa *kik* Registration form.

pala·pala kā·ʻei mea·kanu *kik* Vegetation zonation sheet.

pala·pala leo *kik* Transcription. *Lit.,* voice document. See *palapala.*

pala·pala lewa lipo *kik* Space map. *Lit.,* outer-space document.

pala·pala makana *kik* Gift certificate.

pala·pala moʻo·pane *kik* Deposition, i.e. testimony taken down in writing under oath to be used in court proceedings. Comb. *palapala + moʻo- + pane.*

pala·pala nina·ninau *kik* Questionnaire. *Dic.*

pala·pala noi hoʻo·loli kā·nā·wai *kik* Constitutional initiative, i.e. a process by which one can propose an amendment by gathering signatures on a petition. *Lit.,* document asking (to) change (the) law.

pala·pala pono kanaka *kik* Bill of rights. Sh. *palapala o nā pono pilikino o ke kanaka* (dic.).

pala·pala ʻāina ua *kik* Rainfall map.

pala·pala ʻāina kahua *kik* Site map.

pala·pala ʻāina kumu·hana *kik* Thematic map. *Lit.*, topic map.

pala·pala ʻoi·hana aʻo *kik* Professional diploma for teaching. *Lit.*, diploma (for) teaching career.

pala·pala ʻoka *kik* Order form. *Lit.*, document for ordering. See *palapala ʻoka kūʻai*.

pala·pala ʻoka kū·ʻai *kik* Purchase order, PO. *Lit.*, order form (for) buying.

pala·pola *kik* Parabola, parabolic. *Eng. Uma palapola*. Parabolic curve.

pala·ʻai *kik* Pumpkin. *Dic.* See *ipu*.

pala·ʻai hele·uī *kik* Jack-o'-lantern. *Lit.*, Halloween pumpkin. Also *pū heleuī*.

pala·ʻili *kik* T-shirt; any pullover-style shirt. *Niʻihau.* Cf. *paleʻili*.

pala·ʻili kā·ʻawe *kik* Tank top. *Lit.*, T-shirt (with) strap. Also *paleʻili kāʻawe*. Cf. *palaʻili, paleʻili*.

pala·ʻo *kik* Walrus. *Dic.* Also *ʻelepani o ke kai*.

Pala·ʻo *iʻoa* Pharaoh. *Dic.* See *Au Palaʻo Kūhou, Au Palaʻo Kūkahiko, Au Palaʻo Kūwaena*.

pala·sema *kik* Plasma. *Eng.* Also *wai koko*.

pala·sika *kik* Plastid, i.e. tiny structures inside plant cells that contain pigment as well as chlorophyll. *Eng.*

pale *ham* To cover or shield, as one's mouth. *Ke kunu ʻoe, e pale i kou waha me ka lima.* When you cough, cover your mouth with your hand. *Dic.* See entries below and *pūʻali pale kapa kai*.

pale *kik* Inning. *Dic., ext. mng. Pale pōhili.* Baseball inning.

pale *ham* To defend, in sports; defense. *E ka hoa, nāu e pale ka mea lōʻihi, a naʻu e pale kēia mea poupou.* Eh, you defend the tall guy, and I'll watch this short, stubby one. Cf. *kaupale, kūpale; kūlele.* See *pale alo, pale kāʻei, pale lulumi*.

pā·lē *kik* Ballet. *Eng.* Also *hulahula pālē, bālē*.

pale ahi *ham* Flame retardant. *Ninini nui ʻia ka lāʻau pale ahi ma luna o ke ahi hōlapu o ka nahele i mea e hoʻēmi ai i ka laha ʻana.* Large amounts of flame retardent chemicals were dumped onto the raging forest fire to slow its spread. *Lit.*, protect (against) fire. See *awe pale ahi*.

pale alo *ham* Man-to-man defense, as in basketball; to execute such a play. *Ke pale alo kākou, iā ʻoe ʻo Noʻeau.* When we do a man-to-man defense, you take Noʻeau. *Lit.*, face defense.

pā·leo *kik* Record, record album, as for a record player. Comb. *pā + leo.* Also *pāʻōlelo. Mīkini hoʻokani pāleo.* Record player. Also *mīkini pāleo. Wahī pāleo.* Record album cover.

pā·leo·leo *kik/ham* Rap music; to rap. *Dic., ext. mng.*

pale uluna *kik* Pillowcase. *Dic.*

pale·upoʻo *kik* Helmet. Comb. *pale + u (Tah., head) + poʻo.*

pale holoi *kik* Eraser. *Niʻihau.* Also *mea holoi, ʻileika.*

pale hoʻo·ka·a·wale *kik* Buffer. *Lit.*, shield (for) separating.

pale·kaiko *Manu palekaiko.* Bird of paradise, the bird.

pale kaua *kik* Shield, as for battle. *Dic.* Cf. *kuahene.*

pale·kana *Ai palekana.* Safe sex; to practice safe sex. *Ai palekana ʻole.* Unprotected sex; to practice unprotected sex. See *maʻi lele ai.*

pale kā·nā·wai *ham* To break laws, act as an outlaw. Cf. *haʻihaʻi kānāwai, ʻae kānāwai. Mea pale kānāwai.* Outlaw.

pale kā·ʻei *ham* Zone defense, as in basketball; to execute such a play. *Mai hahai wale iā ia; e hoʻi kākou i ka pale kāʻei.* Don't just follow him all over; let's go back to a zone defense.

palē·kele *kik* Flubber or Gak, a game. Sh. *palēkō* + *'ūkele.*

pale kili·lau *kik* Shower curtain. Cf. *pale pukaaniani.* See *kililau.*

palē·kō *kik* Play-Doh. *Eng.*

pale·kona kā·lu'u *kik* Peregrine falcon. *Lit.*, falcon (that) sweeps and swerves.

pale kuene *kik* Apron. *Ni'ihau.* Also *'epane.*

pale kukui *kik* Lampshade. *Trad.*

pale lā See *'aila pale lā.*

palela *kik* Barrel, a unit of measurement. *Dic.* Abb. *pll.*

pā·lele *kik* Flying saucer. Comb. *pā* + *lele.*

pale lepo *kik* Mud guard. *Pale lepo paikikala.* Bicycle mud guard.

pale lulumi *ham* Press defense, as in basketball; to execute such a play. *I loko o nā minuke hope 'elima, e pale lulumi nui kākou.* In the last five minutes of the game, let's concentrate on the press defense. *Lit.*, defense (by) crowding uncomfortably.

pale·ma'i *kik* Underpants. *Dic.* Also *lole wāwae pala'ili.* Sanitary pad. *Ni'ihau.*

palemo See *kīloi palemo.*

pale mū·hune 'ino *kik* Antibiotic. *Lit.*, ward off pathogens.

palena *kik* Boundary. *Dic.* See entries below. *Palena kākele.* Transform boundary, in plate techtonics, in geology. *Palena ku'i.* Convergent boundary. *Palena ne'e 'oā.* Divergent boundary.

palena *kik* Terms of a fraction, in math. *Dic. Palena ha'aha'a loa.* Lowest terms.

palena iki *kik* Minimum. *Lit.*, small limit. Cf. *palena nui. Ka palena iki o ke kaumaha.* The minimum weight.

palena ulu *kik* Grow limit, as in a computer program.

palena ū wai *kik* Field capacity, for holding water. *Lit.*, water-soaked limit.

palena holo kani *kik* Sound barrier. *Lit.*, limit (of) flowing sound. Cf. *māmā kani.*

palena nui *kik* Maximum. *Lit.*, large limit. Cf. *palena iki. Ka palena nui o ke kaumaha.* The maximum weight.

palena pau *kik* Deadline. *Lit.*, final limit. See *kaupalena. Hola palena pau.* Deadline, the hour. *Lā palena pau.* Deadline, the day.

palena papaha *kik* Potential. *Lit.*, limit (of) possibility.

palena pi'i *kik* Amplitude, as of a pendulum. *Lit.*, limit (to) ascend.

palena 'ā·luna o ka hewa *kik* Greatest possible error, in math. *Lit.*, loosening boundary of error. Abb. *P'ĀH.*

pale pala·hō *ham* Antiseptic. *Ho'ohana 'ia ka lā'au pale palahō no ka ho'oma'ema'e 'ana i ka lumi ho'opau pilikia a ma'ema'e loa.* Antiseptics are used to clean the bathroom so that it is thoroughly clean. *Lit.*, protect (against) rot.

pale papa·hele *kik* Small rug, as in a bathroom or beside a bed. *Lit.*, floor protection. Also *pale wāwae.* See *hāli'i papahele, moena, moena weleweka.*

pale peleki *kik* Brake pad.

pale puka·ani·ani *kik* Window curtain. *Dic.* Cf. *pale kililau, pale pukaaniani 'ōlepelepe.*

pale puka·ani·ani 'ō·lepe·lepe *kik* Venetian blinds. *Lit.*, Venetian blinds window curtain.

pale 'ea See entry below. *'Ōnaehana pale 'ea.* Immune system, as in mammals.

pale 'ea pau *kik* AIDS, i.e. acquired immune deficiency syndrome. *Lit.*, finished resistance (against) infectious diseases. Also *ma'i pale 'ea pau.* See *mū hōlapu pale 'ea pau.*

pale·'eke *kik* Liner for a fish tank, in aquaculture. Comb. *pale* + *'eke.* See *pe'a.*

pale·‘ili *kik* T-shirt. *Dic., ext. mng.* Also *pala‘ili.*

pale·‘ili kā·‘awe *kik* Tank top. *Lit.,* T-shirt (with) strap. Also *pala‘ili kā‘awe.* Cf. *pala‘ili, pale‘ili.*

pali See *pili pali.*

pā·like *kik* Reciprocal, in math. Sh. *pāna‘i + like.*

pā·lima *Kōkua helu kumu ho‘ohui pālima.* Base-five counting piece, in math. *Kumu ho‘ohui pālima.* Base five, in math. Also *kumu pālima. Pepa pālima.* Five-dollar bill.

pā·loi·loi *ham* To dribble, as a basketball. Sh. *pā* + redup. of *kīloi.* Also *pākimokimo, pa‘ipa‘i. Pāloiloi pālua.* To double dribble.

pā·loka *Anamana‘o pāloka.* To canvass, i.e. go door to door handing out political information and asking people which candidate they support. *Koho pāloka wae moho.* Primary election. Also *wae moho. Koho pāloka laulā.* General election. *Kuleana koho pāloka.* Suffrage, i.e. the right to vote.

pā·loke *kik* Parrot. *Eng.* Also *manu pāloke.*

pā·loke·‘i‘i *kik* Parakeet. *Lit.,* under-sized parrot.

pā·loli *‘a* Fragile, susceptible to change. *Ua kū ke kaiaola i ka pāloli.* The ecosystem was fragile. Comb. *pā + loli.* Cf. *haki wale, nahā wale.*

pā·lolo *kik* Clay, as for ceramics; clay dirt. *Dic., ext. mng.* Cf. *kalē.*

pā·lomi *ham* Chiropractic; to practice chiropractic. Comb. *pā- + lomi. Kauka pālomi.* Chiropractor.

pā·lua See *kupa kaumoku‘āina pālua. Pepeiao pālua.* Bicuspid valve, of the heart.

palu·hē See *pepa paluhē.*

pā·lule *kik* Shirt, with short or long sleeves. *Dic.* Also *palaka.*

pā·lulu *ham* To block (the ball), in volleyball. *Ni‘ihau.* Also *paku.* See

paku, ‘ai hele wale. Hala ka pālulu. To pass through the block.

pāma *Pā‘ā pāma.* Raffia, the fiber of the raffia palm of Madagascar.

pāma hihi *kik* Rattan. *Lit.,* creeping palm.

pā·make *‘a* Fatal. *Make aku nei ‘elua keiki ma ka ulia ka‘a pāmake ma ke alaloa o Pāhoa i ka pō nei.* Two boys were killed in a fatal car crash on the Pāhoa highway last night. *Dic.*

pā·malae *kik* Courtyard. Comb. *pā + malae* (Māori *marae*).

pā·ma‘i *‘a* To be susceptible or vulnerable to disease. *Ua kū ke keiki i ka pāma‘i.* The child was susceptible to disease. *Dic.* Cf. *pā wale.*

pame·sana *kik* Parmesan. *Eng. Waiūpa‘a pamesana.* Parmesan cheese.

pā·mia *‘a* Used, second-hand. Comb. *pā + -mia. Ka‘a pāmia.* Used car.

pā·mili·ona Mega-, a prefix meaning million (M). Comb. *pā- + miliona.* Abb. *pm.* See *‘ai pāmiliona.*

pana *kik* Beat, as in music or linguistics; pulse. *Dic. Helu pana pu‘uwai.* Heart rate, pulse rate. *Pu‘uwai pana ‘ewa‘ewa.* Cardiac arrythmia.

pā·nai·nai *‘a* Shallow, as a dish. *Dic.*

pana ho‘o·lei *ham* To flip, as a coin. Comb. *pana + ho‘olei.* See *hi‘u, po‘o.*

pana·kiō *kik* Banjo. *Eng.*

pana·kiō·lele *kik* Banjolele. *Eng.*

pana·kō hale *kik* Piggy bank. *Lit.,* house bank. See *mīkini panakō.*

pana kukui *kik* Light switch. *Dic., ext. mng.* Also *kuiki kukui.*

pana·lā·‘au *kik* Colony, as a territory ruled by a more powerful nation. *He panalā‘au ke kūlanakauhale ‘o Makao no Pokukala, aia ma kahi kokoke i Honokaona.* The city of Macao is a colony of Portugal located near Hong Kong. *Dic.* See *kaumoku‘āina muli panalā‘au.*

Pana·mā *i'oa* Panama; Panamanian.
Dic.

pā·nā·nā *kik* Compass, as for navigation (preceded by *ke*). *Dic.* Cf. *'ūpā kāpō'ai.* See *kikowaena pānānā.* *Pānānā pa'a lima.* Pocket compass.

pana·pana *ham* To pick, as an 'ukulele or guitar. *Mān.* Also *hiku.*

pā·na'i *Uku pāna'i.* Compensation, as to make amends for loss or damage; payment for services. *Mahalo pāna'i.* Patronage, i.e. a political system in which party leaders do favors for loyal supporters. *Mea mahalo pāna'i.* Patron.

pane ho'o·pi'i *'Aha pane ho'opi'i.* Arraignment, i.e. a court hearing in which a defendant is formally charged with a crime and enters a plea of guilty or not guilty. See *ho'opi'i kū'ē.*

pane koho·koho *kik* Multiple-choice. *Lit.*, multiple-choice reply. Also *kohokoho.*

pā·nela *kik* Panel. *Eng.* Cf. *papa pānela.*

pane pā·lā·kiō *kik* Rating response, in math. *Lit.*, scale response.

pani *kik* Cap, as for a toothpaste tube; lid, as for a jar (preceded by *ke*). *Dic., ext. mng.* Cf. *po'i peni.* See *kekimala, paipu lawe 'ino.*

pani *ham* To close, as in a computer program. *Dic., ext. mng.* See *wehe.*

pani *ham* Substitute, as in sports; also to substitute (preceded by *ke*). *Auē! Ua 'unu ke ku'eku'e wāwae o Lopaka; 'o wai ana lā kōna pani?* Shucks! Lopaka's ankle is sprained; who's going to substitute for him? *Dic.* Also *pani hakahaka.*

pani haka·haka *kik* Stand-in, as for an actor in movie or video production (preceded by *ke*). *Dic., ext. mng.* Also *pani.*

pā·niho·niho *kik* Cog. *Ni'ihau.* *Pānihoniho o ke kaulahao paikikala.* Bicycle chain cog.

Pani·kipe *i'oa* Principe. *Ka mokupuni 'o Saotome me Panikipe.* Sao Tome and Principe Island.

pā·niki pepa *kik* Hole punch, for paper. *Dic.*

pā·nini *kik* Prickly pear cactus; cactus, general term. *Dic., ext. mng.* Also *pānini maoli, pāpipi.* See entries below.

pā·niniu *kik* Spinner, as in board games (preceded by *ke*). Comb. *pā + niniu.*

pā·nini kioia *kik* Cholla, a kind of cactus. Comb. *pānini* + Spanish.

pā·nini palala *kik* Barrell cactus. Comb. *pānini* + Eng.

pā·nini 'okana *kik* Organ pipe cactus. Comb. *pānini* + Eng.

pā·nini 'oko·tio *kik* Ocotillo, a kind of cactus. Comb. *pānini* + Spanish.

pani paipu hanu *kik* Epiglottis, in anatomy (preceded by *ke*). *Lit.*, windpipe stopper. See *paipu hanu.*

pani po'o *kik* Capping, as the last stage of volcano formation (preceded by *ke*). *Dic., ext. mng.* Cf. *panepo'o (dic.).*

pani puka *kik* Door, as opposed to doorway (preceded by *ke*). *Ua kau 'o ia i ka wehi Kalikimaka ma ke pani puka.* She placed the Christmas ornament on the door. *Dic.* See *pani puka uea makika.*

pani puka uea makika *kik* Screen door (preceded by *ke*). Also *pani puka maka'aha.* See *uea makika, maka'aha.*

pani wai 'ula *kik* Tampon (preceded by *ke*). *Lit.*, menstrual flow stopper.

pani 'ene·kini *kik* Hood, as of a car or truck (preceded by *ke*). *Lit.*, engine cover.

panoa *kik* Desert. *Dic.*

panoko *kik* Metathesis, i.e. transposition of letters, syllables, or sounds in a word: e.g., *hā'uke'uke/hāku'eku'e.* *Rapanui.*

panua *kik* Styrofoam. *Ni'ihau.* Also *'ūpīhu'a.*

papa *kik* List. *Mān.* See entries below and *kī papa. Papa helu wahi.* Mailing list. *Papa kauoha kamepiula.* List of computer commands.

papa *Aia i loko o ka papa.* To take a class. Also *komo i loko o ka papa, komo i ka papa.*

papa *kik* Board, lumber. *Dic. Papa lua hā.* Two-by-four board or lumber. *Papa hā hā.* Four-by-four board or lumber.

papa *kik* Two-dimensional, in math. *Dic., ext. mng.* Cf. *paʻa. Kinona papa.* Two-dimensional figure.

papa *kik* Layer, as of skin or tissue beneath the skin. *Dic.*

Papa See *Hoʻohokuikalani.*

papā See *huina papā.*

papaina *kik* Papain, an enzyme found in papayas and used as a meat tenderizer. *Eng.*

papa o lalo *kik* Substrate, as in a stream. *Lit.,* bottom stratum.

papaha *kik* Chance, possibility of an indicated outcome, in math. Redup. of *paha.* Cf. *pahiki. Like ka papaha o nā mea e loaʻa ana.* Equally likely outcomes. *Palena papaha.* Potential.

papa hana *kik* Plan. *Dic.* Cf. *papa hoʻolālā.*

papa·hana *kik* Project, as in a curriculum program. *Dic., sp. var.* Cf. *pāhana. Papahana ʻŌhiʻa.* ʻŌhiʻa Project.

Papa Hana Hoʻo·pakele Sila *kik* Seal Recovery Program. *Lit.,* program (to) protect seals.

papa hapa·malu *kik* Understory layer of vegetation, as low trees and shrubs. *Lit.,* partially shaded layer. See *papa kū honua, papa kaupoku, papa ʻoiʻoi.*

papa haʻa·wina *kik* Curriculum. *Lit.,* list (of) lessons. See entries below.

papa haʻa·wina koina *kik* Required curriculum or coursework. *Lit.,* required curriculum. Cf. *papa haʻawina koho.* See *papa koina.*

papa haʻa·wina koho *kik* Elective curriculum or coursework. *Lit.,* curriculum (of) choice. Cf. *papa haʻawina koina.* See *papa koho.*

papa·hele *kik* Story, floor, as in a building. *Dic.* See *hāliʻi papahele, kīloi papahele, pale papahele.*

papa helu·haʻa Lower-division course. *Lit.,* lower-division class.

papa helu·kiʻe Upper-division course. *Lit.,* upper-division class.

papa helu·ʻai *kik* Scoreboard, as for sports. *He papakaumaka nunui kō ka papa heluʻai o ka hale haʻuki hou o ke Kulanui o Hawaiʻi.* The scoreboard at UH's new special events arena has a huge monitor.

papa hī·naʻi *kik* Backboard, in basketball. *Nāhāhā a okaoka ka papa hīnaʻi ma muli o ka pākī nui a Shaq.* The backboard completely shattered on Shaq's massive slam dunk. *Lit.,* basket board. Also *papa hupa, papa.* See *hīnaʻi, hupa.*

pā·paho *kik* Media, as radio, TV, etc. (Māori *pāpāho.*)

papa·honua *kik* Ground zero, as in field mapping. Comb. *papa + honua.*

papa hō·ʻike·ʻike *kik* Bulletin board; gallery, as in a computer program. *Lit.,* board (for) displaying.

papa hoʻo·holo *kik* Control panel, on a computer. *Lit.,* board to cause to run.

papa hoʻo·laha *kik* Sign, as political or business, etc. *Niʻihau.* Also *hōʻailona.*

papa hoʻo·lā·lā *kik* Plan, particularly one which involves thought and decision-making. Sh. *papa hana + hoʻolālā.* Cf. *papa hana.* See *hikiāpoko, hikiālōpū, hikiāloa.*

pā·pahu *kik* Cartridge, as for a computer printer. Comb. *pā + pahu. Pāpahu kinona hua.* Font cartridge. *E hoʻokomo i ka pāpahu kinona hua ma loko o ka mīkini paʻi, a paʻi hou.* Insert the font cartridge into the printer and print again.

papa hua·'ōlelo *kik* Dictionary, as in a computer program. *Lit.,* list (of) words. Cf. *papa wehewehe 'ōlelo. Papa hua'ōlelo kūmau.* Main dictionary. *Papa hua'ōlelo pāku'i.* User dictionary.

papa huila *kik* Skateboard. *Lit.,* wheel board. *He'ena papa huila.* Skateboard ramp.

papa hulei *kik* Seesaw, teetertotter. *Dic.* See *hulehulei.*

papa hupa *kik* Backboard, in basketball. *Lit.,* basket board. Also *papa hīna'i, papa.* See *hīna'i, hupa.*

pā·paka *kik* Crustacean. PPN *pāpaka* (crab). *Pāpaka 'āina.* Land crustacean.

papa kaia·puni Hawai'i *kik* Hawaiian-medium class. See *kaiapuni.*

papa·kau *kik* Counter, as in a kitchen. *Mān. Kapuahi papakau.* Hot plate.

papa·kau·maka *kik* Screen, as on a TV or computer monitor. *Lit.,* flat surface (for) fixing eyes (upon). See *pahu papakaumaka. Papakaumaka kamepiula.* Computer monitor screen. *Papakaumaka kīwī.* TV screen. *Papakaumaka mīkini helu.* Calculator display screen.

papa kau·poku *kik* Canopy layer of vegetation between *papa hapamalu* and *papa 'oi'oi. Lit.,* ceiling layer. See *papa kū honua, papa hapamalu, papa 'oi'oi.*

papa kā·nā·wai *kik* Code, i.e. a systematic collection of existing laws. *Lit.,* list (of) laws. *Papa kānāwai wai o ka moku'āina.* State water code.

pā·pā kā·nā·wai *ham* To outlaw, i.e. make something illegal. *Lit.,* prohibit (by) law.

papa kēmu *kik* Game board. See *kēmu.*

papa ke'o·ke'o *kik* White board, dry erase board. Also *papa peni kuni.*

papa kī *kik* Head, as of an 'ukulele or guitar. *Ni'ihau.* See *'ukulele.*

papa koina *kik* Required course or class, as in school. *Lit.,* required class. Cf. *papa koho.* See *papa ha'awina koina.*

papa koho *kik* Elective course or class, as in school. *Lit.,* class (of) choice. Cf. *papa koina.* See *papa ha'awina koho.*

papa koho *kik* Menu bar, on a computer screen. *Lit.,* selection list. Cf. *papa kuhikuhi, papa 'ō'ili.*

papa·kū *kik* Riverbed; streambed. *Dic.* Also *papakū muliwai; papakū kahawai, kahena wai.*

papa·kū *'a'* Vertical. *Dic., ext. mng.* Cf. *ho'opapakū, papamoe. Ulu papakū.* To grow vertically.

papa·kui ana·honua *kik* Geoboard, in math. *Lit.,* geometry nail board.

papa kuhi·kuhi *kik* Table of contents. *Dic. Papa kuhikuhi kiko'ī.* Index. See entry below.

papa kuhi·kuhi *kik* Menu, as in a computer program. *Dic., ext. mng.* Cf. *papa koho, papa 'ō'ili. Papa kuhikuhi kahua pa'a.* Main menu.

papa kuhi·kuhina *kik* Coordinate plane, in math.

papa kuhi wai·hona *kik* Directory, of computer files. *Lit.,* list pointing out files.

papa kū honua *kik* Ground layer of vegetation. *Lit.,* layer reaching earth. See *papa hapamalu, papa kaupoku, papa 'oi'oi.*

papa kumu·mana'o *kik* Agenda, as for a meeting. *Ho'omakakoho 'ia ka mo'ohelu he makakoho ko'iko'i ma ka papa kumumana'o o ka hālāwai.* The budget was made an important priority at the meeting. *Lit.,* list (of) topics.

papa lae·hano *kik* Honor roll, as in elementary through high school. *Lit.,* honored list.

pā palai *kik* Frying pan (preceded by *ke*). *Dic. 'Au pā palai.* Frying pan handle (preceded by *ke*).

papa·lala *'a'* Diagonally. Comb. *papa + lala.* Cf. *papakū, papamoe.* See *lala.*

Papa Lawe·lawe Hoʻo·laha *kik* Bulletin Board Service (BBS), on computer programs. *Ua hoʻolaha ʻia ka ʻaha hālāwai o kēia pule aʻe ma ke PLH.* Next week's conference was posted on the BBS. *Lit.,* billboard service. *Abb. PLH.*

pā·pale *kik* Cap, hat. *Dic. Pāpale kapuhau.* Ski cap, stocking cap. *Pāpale kililau.* Shower cap. *Pāpale kone.* Dunce cap, clown hat. *Pāpale ʻau.* Swim cap.

pā·pale·kimo *kik* Condom, for men. *Comb. pāpale + kimo.*

papa lua hā *kik* Two-by-four board or lumber. *Dic.*

papa luna hoʻo·kele *kik* Administration, i.e. a team of executive branch officials appointed by the President, in government. *Ua manaʻo mai ka papa luna hoʻokele e uku manawaleʻa aku i nā poʻe limahana no ka maikaʻi loa o kā lākou hana i kēia makahiki.* The administration thought to reward the employees for their excellent work done this year. *Lit.,* board (of) directors. See *luna hoʻokele.*

papa mā·hele hana *kik* Call sheet, as a list of jobs for movie or video production. *Lit.,* list (of) job categories.

papa manaʻo lau·like *kik* Thesaurus, as in a computer program. *Lit.,* list (of words with) similar meanings. See *manaʻo laulike, puke manaʻo laulike.*

papa mea·kanu *kik* Vegetation layer. *Lit.,* plant layer. See *papa hapamalu, papa kaupoku, papa ʻoiʻoi.*

papa·moe *ʻa* Horizontal. *Dic., ext. mng.* Cf. *papakū.* See *hawewe papamoe. Ulu papamoe.* To grow horizontally.

papana *kik* Rhythm, in music. *Redup. of pana.* Cf. *aupana.*

pā·papa *kik* Bean. *Dic., sp. var.* See *ula pāpapa. Pāpapa haʻa.* Bush bean.

Pāpapa hihi. String bean. *Pāpapa kele.* Jelly bean. *Pāpapa koiū.* Soybean, soya bean. *Pāpapa laima.* Lima bean. *Pāpapa loloa.* Long bean, a common Filipino dish. *Pāpapa munukō.* Mung bean. *Pāpapa poepoe.* Pea. *Pāpapa ʻūhinihone.* Honey locust bean.

papa pā·lā·kiō *kik* Conversion scale. *Lit.,* scale list.

papa pā·nela *kik* Paneling. *Comb. papa + Eng. Papa pānela lāʻau.* Wood paneling.

papa pena *kik* Palette, as in a computer program. *Lit.,* paint board.

papa peni kuni *kik* Dry erase board, white board. *Lit.,* felt pen board. Also *papa keʻokeʻo.*

papa peʻa *kik* Board for windsurfing. *Lit.,* sail board. *Holo papa peʻa.* To windsurf.

papa pihi *kik* Keyboard, as on a computer or typewriter. *Papa pihi kamepiula.* Computer keyboard. *Papa pihi keu.* Enhanced keyboard, expanded keyboard.

papa wai *kik* Water table, in geology. *Lit.,* water stratum. Cf. *papa wai kau luna, pākaukau wai.*

papa·wai *kik* Plywood for building boats. *Niʻihau.* Cf. *papa ʻililahi.*

papa wai kau luna *kik* Water lens, in geology. *Lit.,* water layer placed on top. Cf. *papa wai.*

papa wehe·wehe ʻō·lelo *kik* Glossary. *Lit.,* list (to) explain words. Cf. *papa huaʻōlelo.*

papaʻa *kik* Archive, backup, as in a computer program. *Dic., ext. mng.* See *hoʻopapaʻa. Kope papaʻa.* Backup copy. *Waihona papaʻa.* Backup file.

pā·paʻa *kik* Crust, in geology. *Dic., ext. mng. Pāpaʻa honua.* Earth's crust. *Pāpaʻa moana.* Ocean crust. *Pāpaʻa mokuhonua.* Continental crust.

papa·ʻai *kik* Diet, i.e. the food that is eaten. *Lit.*, list (of) food. See *hoʻēmi kino, paiola, ʻaiaola. Pākēneka o ka papaʻai.* Percent Daily Value, formerly known as percentage of US Recommended Daily Allowances (USRDA).

papa ʻau·kā helu *kik* Ten-strip board, in math. *Lit.*, strip board (to) count. See *moena helu hapa haneli, ʻaukā helu hapa ʻumi.*

papa ʻā·lua·lua *kik* Multiplication tables. Cf. *ʻalualua* (dic.).

papa ʻanuʻu lalo kai *kik* Underwater terrace. *Lit.*, undersea terrace layer.

pā·pa·ʻa piele An exclamation used by the winner in a card game to the loser meaning "you got wiped out!" *Mān.* Also *palaina puna.*

Papa·ʻā·poho *iʻoa* Lisianski, the island. *Lit.*, flat (with a) depression.

papaʻi See *kīloi papaʻi, kī papaʻi.*

pā·pa·ʻi *heh* To execute a defensive slide, in basketball. *Ke hiki mai ke kūkahi ma ʻaneʻi, e pāpaʻi ʻoe me ia.* When the point guard comes here, slide over to him. *Lit.*, crab.

papa ʻili·lahi *kik* Plywood. *Lit.*, board (with) thin layers. Cf. *papawai.*

papa ʻoi·ʻoi *kik* Emergent layer of vegetation, as trees sticking out at top. *Lit.*, layer above. See *papa kū honua, papa hapamalu, papa kaupoku.*

pā·pā·ʻō·lelo *kik* Dialogue, as in a play, movie, or video production. *Dic., ext. mng.*

papa ʻō·ʻili *kik* Pop-up menu, as in a computer program. *Lit.*, appearing list.

papa ʻū·mi·ʻi *kik* Clipboard, as in a computer program. *Hōʻike papa ʻūmiʻi.* To show clipboard.

pā·peka *kik* Puppet. Usu. *pāpeta. Eng.* Also *kiʻi lima. Pāpeka kaula.* Marionette. Also *pāpeta kaula.*

pā peleki *kik* Brake disk (preceded by *ke*).

papi *kik* California poppy. *Eng. Pua papi.* Poppy flower.

pā piki *kik* Petri dish (preceded by *ke*). Comb. *pā* + *Eng.*

pā·pili·ona Giga-, a prefix meaning billion (G). Comb. *pā-* + *piliona.* Abb. *pp.* See *ʻai pāpiliona. Kule pāpiliona.* Gigajoule.

pā·pipi *kik* Prickly pear cactus. *Dic.* Also *pānini, pānini maoli.*

Pā·pua Nū·kini *iʻoa* Papua New Guinea; Papua New Guinean. Comb. *Eng.* + *dic., sp. var.*

pā puni *Hoʻokūkū pā puni.* Round robin, as in sports.

pā wai *kik* Water dish (preceded by *ke*).

pā wale *ʻa* Susceptible, vulnerable. *He pā wale nā manu ʻōiwi o Hawaiʻi i nā maʻi a me nā poʻiiʻa malihini.* Native birds are susceptible to introduced diseases and predators. Comb. *pā* + *wale.* Cf. *pāmaʻi.*

pā·weo *heh* To skew, as a deviation from a straight line, in math. *Dic., ext. mng. Laina pāweo.* Skew line.

pā wili *kik* Dial (preceded by *ke*). *Lit.*, circular object (for) twisting. See *wili.*

paʻa *kik* Geometric solid. *Dic.* See entries below and *kuʻina paʻa, pena paʻa mania. Hua paʻa.* Constant term, in math. Cf. *hoa like, paukū.*

paʻa *ʻa* Three-dimensional, in math. *Dic., ext. mng.* Cf. *papa. Kinona paʻa.* Three-dimensional figure. *Kohu paʻa.* Three-dimensional or 3D, as a picture or movie. *Kiʻiʻoniʻoni kohu paʻa.* 3D movie.

paʻa *ʻa* Closed, as a frame in a computer program. *Dic., ext. mng.* Cf. *kaʻakaʻa. Mōlina paʻa.* Closed frame.

paʻa·alewa *heh* Flexed-arm hang. *Lit.*, hanging fixed.

paʻa ea *ʻa* Airtight. *Lit.*, hold air. *He hōkelo paʻa ea.* An airtight container.

paʻa·hau *ʻa* Frozen. *Paʻahau ka wai i ke kēkelē ʻole o ke Kelekia.* Water freezes at zero degrees Celsius. Sh. *paʻa i ka hau.* Cf. *hoʻopaʻahau.* See *kēkelē. Au paʻahau.* Ice age. *Pahu paʻahau.* Freezer. *ʻAila ʻaʻalo paʻahau.* Antifreeze.

paʻa·hapa *ʻAilakele paʻahapa.* Unsaturated fat.

paʻa helu *kik* Number pair. *Paʻa helu kuhikuhina.* Coordinates; ordered pair, i.e. two numbers used to give the location of a point on a graph, in math.

paʻa·kai ʻepe·soma *kik* Epsom salt. Comb. *paʻakai* + Eng.

paʻa·kū·kū *ʻa* Coagulated, as blood. *Dic., ext. mng.*

paʻa like·like *kik* Suit, as in a deck of playing cards. *Niʻihau.*

paʻa lima *ʻa* Held in the hand, hand-held. *Dic. Aniani paʻa lima.* Hand mirror. *Pānānā paʻa lima.* Pocket compass.

paʻa·loko *ʻa* Built-in. *He mōkema paʻaloko kō kēia kamepiula.* This computer has a built-in modem. Comb. *paʻa* + *loko.* Cf. *kūloko.* See *kakena paʻaloko, pā paʻaloko. Waihona ʻike paʻaloko.* Built-in memory, in a computer.

paʻa·lole hele lewa *kik* Space suit. *Lit.,* suit (for) walking (in) space.

pā·ʻā·lua *kik* Code. Sh. *pāpālua* + *ʻalualua.* See *hoʻopāʻālua, poʻo pāʻālua. Hoʻokala pāʻālua.* To unencrypt, as a code or computer data. *Pāʻālua kaʻina hana.* Key code, as for the order to press keys on a calculator to find an answer.

paʻa mau *ʻa* Sustained. *Dic., ext. mng. Loaʻa paʻa mau.* Sustained yield, as in crop production.

paʻa·mau *kik* Default, as in a computer program. *Ua hoʻopaʻa ʻia ke kinona hua paʻamau ma ka Times.* The default font is set at Times. Comb. *paʻa* + *mau.*

paʻa·mā·hua·ola *kik* Nutrient salts, i.e. the deposits that remain after a liquid has been removed. Sh. *paʻakai* + *māhuaola.*

paʻa manehu kū·ʻē·ʻē *kik* Action-reaction pair, i.e. two forces having equal strength but opposite directions, in science. *Lit.,* opposing force pair.

pā·ʻani iwi *ham* To play dominoes. *Lit.,* play bones. See *iwi pāʻani.*

pā·ʻā pāma *kik* Raffia, the fiber of the raffia palm of Madagascar. *Lit.,* palm fiber.

paʻa·paʻa·ʻina *ʻa* Crisp or brittle, as dry *hala* leaves. *Dic.*

paʻa·poe·poe *kik* Sphere, in math. Comb. *paʻa* + *poepoe.*

paʻa pō·haku *ʻa* Lithified. *He pōhaku ke kumuone i paʻa pōhaku maila i ke au o nā makahiki he nui loa.* Sandstone is a rock which has gone through lithification over a period of many years. *Lit.,* solidified (into) rock.

paʻa·pū *kik* Density, as of a computer disk. *Dic., ext. mng.* See entry below. *Paʻapū emi.* Low density. *Paʻapū ʻoi.* High density. *Paʻapū pūʻuo kanaka.* Population density, for humans only.

paʻapū *Lākiō paʻapū wai.* Specific gravity, relative gravity. *ʻAilakele paʻapū.* Saturated fat.

paʻa·pū·hia *ʻa* Concentrated. Comb. *paʻapū* + *-hia.* Cf. *kaiaka.* See *hoʻopaʻa-pūhia. Wai paʻakai paʻapūhia.* Brine, a concentrated solution of salt or ocean water. Also *wai paʻakai.* See *wai kai.*

paʻa·puna *kik* Calcareous. Comb. *paʻa* + *puna. Pōhaku paʻapuna.* Calcareous rock, calcium carbonate.

paʻa·ʻili See entries below.

paʻa·ʻili iwa·kā·lua *kik* Icosahedron, a space figure with twenty faces, in math. Comb. *paʻaʻili* + *iwakālua.*

pa'a·'ili·ono *kik* Hexahedron, a space figure with six faces, in math; cube, cubic. *Dic., ext mng.* See *pa'a'iliono analahi, pa'a'iliono kōkua helu.* '*Īā pa'a'iliono.* Cubic yard.

pa'a·'ili·ono ana·lahi *kik* Cube, in math. Comb. *pa'a'iliono + analahi.* Also *pa'a'iliono.* See *pa'a'iliono.*

pa'a·'ili·ono kō·kua helu *kik* Counting cube, in math. *Lit.,* cube (to) help count. Also *pa'a'iliono.* Cf. *moena kōkua helu, 'aukā kōkua helu.*

pa'a·'ili·hā *kik* Tetrahedron, a space figure with four faces, in math. Comb. *pa'a'ili + hā.*

pa'a·'ili lehu·lehu *kik* Polyhedron, a space figure with many faces, in math. Comb. *pa'a'ili + lehulehu.* Also *pa'a'ili.*

pa'a·'ili·walu *kik* Octahedron, a space figure with eight faces, in math. Comb. *pa'a'ili + walu.*

pa'a·'ili 'umi·kū·mā·lua *kik* Dodecahedron, a space figure with twelve faces, in math. Comb. *pa'a'ili + 'umikūmālua.*

pa'a 'ohe·nā·nā *kik* Binoculars. *Lit.,* pair (of) telescopes.

pa'a·'olo·laha *kik* Ovoid. Comb. *pa'a + 'ololaha.*

pā·'eke *kik* Corral. *Dic.*

pa'ewa *kik* Bias, i.e. systematic error in gathering data, in math. Sh. *pā'ewa·'ewa.* See *kīloi pa'ewa.*

pā·'ewa·'ewa *kik/'a* Bias; biased. *He ho'ā'o ka po'e ha'ilono e ha'i aku i ka nū hou me ka pā'ewa'ewa 'ole i 'ole e mana'o 'ia ua 'ume 'ia ka mea ha'ilono e kekahi 'ao'ao.* Journalists attempt to report the news without bias so as not to appear that they are influenced by one side or another. *Dic.*

pa'e'e *'a* On-line, i.e. describing the state of an electronic device ready to receive data, connected to a computer network, or accessible by means of a computer or computer network. *Ke*

pa'e'e hou mai nei nā kamepiula ma hope o ka ho'ā hou 'ia 'ana o ka pūnaewele e ka luna pūnaewele. The computers are coming on-line again after the network supervisor restarted the network. Comb. *pa- + 'e'e.* Cf. *pahemo.* See *ho'opa'e'e.*

pa'i *kik* Portuguese man-of-war (*Physalia*). *Ni'ihau.* Also *pa'imalau.* See *pa'ipe'a, pa'ipihi.*

pa'i *ham* To print, as on a computer (preceded by *ke*). *Dic.* See entries below. *Mīkini pa'i.* Printer.

pa'i *kik* Shot, as of a photograph or in movie or video production (preceded by *ke*). *Dic., ext. mng.* See *kokoke, laulā, lōpū, pa'i ki'i.* *Nā 'ano pa'i.* Types of shots. *Pa'i laulā.* Wide shot. *Pa'i laulā loa.* Extreme wide shot. *Pa'i lōpū.* Medium shot. *Pa'i kokoke.* Close-up. *Pa'i kokoke loa.* Extreme close-up.

pa'i *ham* To take, shoot, or snap, as a photograph (preceded by *ke*). *Dic.* Cf. *'āpona.* See entries below and *pahu pa'i wikiō.* *Mea pa'i ki'i.* Photographer, cameraperson. *Pa'i ki'i'oni'oni.* To shoot a movie film. *Pa'i wikiō.* To shoot a video.

pa'i ulele *ham* Service, in volleyball; to serve (the ball). *Lit.,* hit (to) get into action. Cf. *hānai, hānai pu'upu'u.* *Ka'a pa'i ulele.* Side out. *'A'ena pa'i ulele.* Service violation.

pa'i haka·haka *ham* To type. *Ni'ihau.* Also *kikokiko.*

pa'i kā·hela *ham* To pan, as with a movie or video camera (preceded by *ke*). *Lit.,* take (a picture) sweeping backward and forward

pa'i ki'i *ham* To photograph or take a picture, either still or motion (preceded by *ke*). *Dic.* See *ki'i pa'i, pa'i.*

pa'i kulo *ham* To make a sidewinder serve, in volleyball. *Ni'ihau.*

pā 'ili See *lā'au make pā 'ili.*

pa'i lihi *ham* To dink, i.e. to mishit or clip (the ball), in volleyball. *Lit.,* slight hit. Also *ho'okulu.* See *'ai hele wale.*

pa'i lua *'A'ena pa'i lua.* Double-hit violation, in volleyball.

pa'i·malau *kik* Portuguese man-of-war (*Physalia*). *Dic.* Also *pa'i.* See *pa'ipe'a, pa'ipihi.*

pa'i mana·mana *ham* To volley, i.e. keep the ball in play, in volleyball. *Lit.,* hit (with) fingers. Also *pohu.* Cf. *lelekīkē.*

pa'ina *kik* Click, as the sound produced when clicking a computer mouse. *He kuli nui ka pa'ina o kēia 'iole.* This mouse has a loud click to it. *Dic.* See *kaomi, kōmi.*

pa'i·palaoa *kik* Dough. *Lit.,* mix flour.

pa'i pā·laha·laha *ham* To spike with open hand, in volleyball. *Ni'ihau.* See *hili, ku'i pu'upu'u.*

pa'i·pa'i *ham* To dilute or mix, as a drink. *Dic.* Cf. *ho'okaiaka. Ua pa'ipa'i 'ia ka lama i ka wai.* The alcoholic beverage was diluted with water.

pa'i·pa'i *ham* To dribble, as a basketball. *Ni'ihau.* Also *pākimokimo, pāloiloi.* Cf. *pekupeku.*

pa'i·pa'i pā·lua *ham* To double dribble, in basketball. Also *pākimokimo pālua, pāloiloi pālua.*

pa'i·pe'a *kik* By-the-wind-sailor, a kind of jellyfish. Comb. *pa'i + pe'a.* See *pa'i, pa'ipihi.*

pa'i·pihi *kik* Blue-button, a kind of jellyfish. Comb. *pa'i + pihi.* See *pa'i, pa'ipe'a.*

pā·'oi·hana *kik* Business, i.e. a person or company engaged in business; commercial, i.e. relating to commerce or business. *Nui nā pā'oihana o ke kaona 'o Honolulu, 'o ka hale 'aina 'oe, 'o ka panakō 'oe, a pēlā aku.* There are many businesses in the city of Honolulu: restaurants, banks, etc. Comb. *pā + 'oihana.* Cf. *kaona, 'oihana. Pā'oihana*

ho'oulu meakanu. Commercial growers. *Pā'oihana ka'alilo.* A business or company which has a monopoly. *'Āpana pā'oihana kauwaena.* Central business district.

pā·'ō·lelo *kik* Record, as for a record player. *Ni'ihau.* Also *pāleo.*

pā 'oma *kik* Baking pan (preceded by *ke*).

pa'u See *kalina pa'u.*

pā·'umi Deka-, a prefix meaning ten (da). *Dic., ext. mng.* Abb. *p'm. Pepa maka'aha kumu ho'ohui pā'umi.* Base-ten grid paper. *Pepa pā'umi.* Ten-dollar bill.

pa'ū·pa'ū *kik* Tapa, bark cloth. *Dic.*

pa'u·popo *'a* Organic, i.e. relating to the branch of chemistry concerning the carbon compounds of living things. Comb. *pa'u + popo.*

pā CD See *CD.*

Para·guae *i'oa* Paraguay; Paraguayan. *Dic.* Also *Palakuae.*

pā sē·dē See *C D.*

pē- A prefix used for certain scientific terms with the meaning able to, -able, -ability, -ibility, etc. NOTE: pē- + *'a'ano;* pē- + *hamani/hehele* + -hia. Var. of *pae.* See *pēhāpopopo, pēmā'ō'ā, pēne'e, pē'āhia, pē'ano, pē'umelauoho,* etc.

pea *kik* Avocado. *Dic.* Also *pea Hawai'i. Pea pakeleke.* Pear, usually Bartlett.

pea Kina *kik* Panda. *Lit.,* China bear.

pea ki'i *kik* Teddy bear. Also *pea pā'ani.* Cf. *pēpē ki'i.*

pea pā·'ani *kik* Teddy bear. *Lit.,* bear (for) playing. Also *pea ki'i.* Cf. *pēpē ki'i.*

peawa *kik* Beaver. *Eng. Peawa kuahiwi.* Mountain beaver.

pea 'Ā·lika *kik* Polar bear. *Lit.,* Arctic bear.

pē·hā·popopo *'a* Biodegradable. *'O nā huahana kūpono no ke kaiapuni, he pēhāpopopo ke 'ano o ka pū'olo e wahī 'ia ai.* Products which are environmentally sound are packaged with biodegradable packaging. *Comb. pē-* + *hāpopopo.*

pē·heu *kik* Mumps. *Niʻihau.*

peka *kik* Peck, a unit of measurment. *Eng.*

peke *kik* Child's scooter. *Inv.* Also *kaʻa peke.* See *pueo peke.*

peke·keu *kik* Brim, of a hat. *Mān.* *(MW).* Also *kihikihi.* Cf. *laulau.*

peke·lala *ʻa* Federal. *Dic.* Cf. *aupuni. ʻAhahui pekelala.* Federal organization.

pēki *heh* To back up. *E pēki ʻoe i hope!* Back up! *Mān.*

pēki *heh* To escape, as in a computer program. *Mān., ext. mng. Pihi pēki.* Escape key (preceded by *ke*). *E kōmi i ke pihi pēki a hiki loa i ka papa kuhikuhi kahua paʻa.* Press the escape key all the way back to the main menu.

peki·kulali *kik* Lousewort. *Latin,* pedicularis.

pekona *kik* Bacon. *Eng.*

peku·nia *kik* Petunia. *Dic.*

peku·peku *ham* To dribble, as with kicks, in soccer. *Dic., ext. mng.* Cf. *paʻipaʻi.*

pela *kik* Mattress. *Dic.* Bed. *Niʻihau.* Also *pela moe. Hao pela.* Bedframe. *Pela hoʻolana.* Air mattress.

pēla *kik* Bail, i.e. money a defendant gives a court as a promise to return for trial. *E hoʻopaʻa ana ka luna hoʻokolo-kolo i ka pēla he ʻumi kaukani kālā no ka hopohopo e mahuka ka mea i hoʻāhewa ʻia i kahi ʻāina ʻē.* Bail has been set by the judge at ten thousand dollars for fear the accused may flee the country. *Dic., sp. var.*

pelaha *kik* Poster. *Sh. pepa* + *hoʻo-laha. Pena pelaha.* Tempera paint.

pela hewa *Kaha pela hewa.* A circle around a misspelled word with the letters *ph* (*pela hewa*) written above the word, in proofreading.

pela·hū *kik* Pinwheel, the toy. *Sh. pelamakani* + *hū.*

pela·makani *kik* Electric fan. *Niʻi-hau.*

pela·mika *kik* Pyramid shape. *Dic. Pelamika ikehu.* Energy pyramid. *Puʻu pelamika.* Pyramid, as in Egypt.

pele *kik* Volcano, volcanic; alarm bell, as on a clock or fire alarm. *Dic.* See *oeoe, uila māhu pele, lua pele, ʻūhini nēnē pele. Moʻo pōhaku pele.* Lava lizard. *Piko pele.* Hot spot, in geology. *Puʻu pele.* Volcanic cone.

peleita See *manu peleita.*

peleka *kik* Felt, a type of fabric. *Eng.*

Pele·kāne *iʻoa* Britain, England; British, English person; English (of England). *Mān./dic., sp. var.* Cf. *Pelekānia.* See *ʻEnelani.*

Pele·kā·nia *iʻoa* Britain, British; English. *Mān./dic., sp. var.* Cf. *Pelekāne. ʻŌlelo Pelekānia.* English (language).

peleki *kik* Brake. *Dic. Peleki pā.* Disk brake. *Pā peleki.* Brake disk (preceded by *ke*). *Pale peleki.* Brake pad.

Pele·kiuma *iʻoa* Belgium; Belgian. *Dic.* Also *Belegiuma.*

pele·kikena *kik* President, as of a college or university. *Dic.* Cf. *luna kulanui, poʻo kulanui.*

pele·leu *ʻa* Obtuse. *Dic. Huina peleleu.* Obtuse angle. *Huinakolu peleleu.* Obtuse triangle.

pele·leu *kik* Extension, as of a computer file. *Dic., ext. mng. Peleleu waihona.* File extension.

pele·maka *kik* Magma. *Lit.,* raw lava. *Nupa pelemaka.* Magma chamber. *Pōhaku pelemaka.* Igneous rock, i.e. rock formed by the solidification of molten magma.

pelena peʻa *kik* Pretzel. *Lit.,* crossed cracker.

pelene *kik* Bran. *Eng. Māpina pelene.* Bran muffin.

pelu *kik* Hem, as of a dress. *Dic.* See *kaʻa kaupaku pelu. Pelu ʻupena.* Hem of a net.

Pelū *iʻoa* Peru; Peruvian. *Dic.* Also *Perū.*

pelu mua *Mākala pelu mua.* Tibialis muscle, i.e. the muscle of the lower leg and foot region.

pelu ʻō·pū *kik/ham* Situp; to do sit-ups. *Lit.,* bend stomach.

pē·mā·ʻō·ʻā *ʻa* Solubility; soluble. Comb. *pē-* + *māʻōʻā.* Cf. *māʻōʻā, māʻōʻāna. Pēmāʻōʻā wae ʻano.* Selective solubility.

pena *ʻa* Curious, *nīele. Maui.* See entries below and *papa pena.*

pena *kik* Paint, i.e. the area within the key below the free throw line on a basketball court. *Kīhele wale hoʻi hā ʻo Kaunu ma ʻō, ma ʻaneʻi ma ka pena.* Kaunu was all over the paint. *Dic., ext. mng.*

pena holoi *kik* Primer for PVC pipe cement. *Niʻihau.* See *tuko paipu ʻea.*

pena kī·kina *kik/ham* Spray paint; to spray paint.

pena kua·papa wai *kik* Water-base paint. Cf. *pena wai.*

pena kuʻe·maka *kik* Eyebrow pencil. *Niʻihau. Hana i ka pena kuʻemaka.* To "put on" or "do" one's eyebrows.

pena lehe·lehe *kik/ham* Lipstick. *Lit.,* lip paint. Also *pena waha.*

pena lihi·lihi maka *kik* Mascara. *Niʻihau. Hana i ka pena lihilihi maka.* To put on mascara.

pena lola *ham* To paint with a roller. Cf. *lola pena.*

pena maka *kik/ham* Makeup; to put on makeup. *Lit.,* paint (the) face. *Mea pena maka.* Makeup artist, as for a play, movie, or video production.

pena paʻa mania *kik* Enamel. *Lit.,* paint (that) hardens smooth.

pena pelaha *kik* Tempera paint. *Lit.,* poster paint.

pena wai *kik* Watercolor. *Lit.,* water paint. Cf. *pena kuapapa wai.*

pena waha *kik/ham* Lipstick. *Niʻihau.* Also *pena lehelehe.* Cf. *peni pena waha. Hana i ka pena waha.* To put on lipstick.

pena·tomino *kik* Pentomino, in math. *Eng.*

pene *kik* Cage. (*Eng.* pen.) Cf. *hale mālama ʻīlio. Pene halihali.* Kennel or crate for transporting animals. *Pene ʻīlio.* Kennel, as a shelter for a dog.

Pene·kele·winia *iʻoa* Pennsylvania; Pennsylvanian. *Dic.* Also *Peneselevinia.*

pene·kui *kik* Benzoin, a resin used in perfume and cosmetics. (Old Catalan *benjui.*)

pē·ne·e *kik* Mobility, in geography. Comb. *pē-* + *neʻe.*

pene ʻio·ʻio *kik* Brooder. *Lit.,* cheeping pen.

Pene·sele·vinia *iʻoa* Pennsylvania; Pennsylvanian. *Dic.* Also *Penekelewinia.*

peni *kik* Pen. *Dic.* Also *peni ʻīnika.* See *peni kuni, poʻi peni.*

peni·aliʻi *kik* Pennyroyal, a kind of flower. Comb. *Eng.* + *aliʻi.*

peni·kala kala *kik* Colored pencil.

peni kuni *kik* Marsh pen, felt pen. Sh. *peni kuni pahu,* pen (for) etching (on) boxes. *Niʻihau. Papa peni kuni.* Dry erase board, white board. Also *papa keʻokeʻo.*

peni pāuma *kik* Fountain pen. *Lit.,* pen (that) pumps.

peni pena lehe·lehe *kik* Lipliner. *Lit.,* pen (for) painting lips. Also *peni pena waha.* Cf. *pena waha.*

peni pena waha *kik* Lipliner. *Niʻihau.* Also *peni pena lehelehe.* Cf. *pena waha.*

peni ʻī·nika *kik* Pen. *Niʻihau.* Also *peni.*

Penuli *i'oa* Bernoulli. *Eng. Ke kulehana a Penuli.* Bernoulli's principle, in science.

Pep. Abbreviation for *Pepeluali* (February).

pepa ana·kuhi lā·lani *kik* Linear unit paper, in math. *Lit.,* template paper (with) rows.

pepa ana 'akika *kik* Litmus paper, for measuring pH. *Lit.,* paper (for) measuring acid.

pepa·ā·nue *kik* Construction paper. *Sh. pepa + ānuenue.*

pepa hō·'aui·kala *kik* Chromatographic paper. *Lit.,* chromatography paper. See *hō'auikala.*

pepa kā·lā *kik* Bill, i.e. a piece of paper money. *Lit.,* money paper. See *pepa pākahi, 'ōkeni.*

pepa kiko ana·like *kik* Isometric dot paper, in math.

pepa kini *kik* Aluminum foil, tin foil. *Lit.,* tin paper.

pepa leka *kik* Letter-size paper (8-1/2 X 11). *Lit.,* letter paper. See pepa loio, *pepa 11" X 17".*

pepa loio *kik* Legal-size paper (8-1/2 x 14). *Lit.,* lawyer paper. See *pepa leka, pepa 11" X 17".*

pepa lole pipi *kik* Butcher paper. *Sh. pepa + mea lole pipi.* See *mea lole pipi.*

pepa·loni *kik* Pepperoni. *Eng.*

pepa maka·'aha *kik* Grid paper, in math. *Pepa maka'aha kumu ho'ohui pā'umi.* Base-ten grid paper.

pepa mā·noa·noa *kik* Posterboard. *Lit.,* thick paper.

pepa paia *kik* Wallpaper.

pepa pahu *kik* Cardboard, corrugated paper. *Lit.,* box paper. Cf. *pahu pepa.*

pepa pā·kahi *kik* One-dollar bill. *Sh. pepa kālā + pākahi.* See entries below.

pepa pā·lima *kik* Five-dollar bill. *Sh. pepa kālā + pālima.*

pepa palu·hē *kik* Papier mâché. *Lit.,* paper reduced to pulp.

pepa papa 'oka *kik* Oaktag, a strong cardboard used for posters; also called tagboard. *Lit.,* oak board paper.

pepa pā·'umi *kik* Ten-dollar bill. *Sh. pepa kālā + pā'umi.*

pepa pī·lali *kik* Wax paper. Also *pepa 'aila.*

pepa 'aila *kik* Wax paper. *Ni'ihau.* Also *pepa pīlali.*

pepa 11" X 17" *kik* Tabloid paper (pronounced *pepa 'umikūmākahi 'īniha i ka 'umikūmāhiku 'īniha*). See *pepa leka, pepa loio.*

pepei·ao *kik* Valve of the heart. *Dic. Pepeiao 'a'apu.* Semilunar valve. *Pepeiao pālua.* Bicuspid valve. *Pepeiao pākolu.* Tricuspid valve.

pepei·ao *'Uala kahiki pepeiao.* Scalloped potatoes. Also *'uala pepeiao.*

pepeke *kik* Grammatical sentence or clause. Redup. of *feke* (PPN *he'e*). See entries below.

pepeke haku *kik* Main clause, in grammar. *Lit.,* master *pepeke.*

pepeke 'ō·hua *kik* Dependent clause, in grammar. *Lit.,* dependent *pepeke.*

pē·pē ki'i *kik* Doll, a child's plaything. *Ni'ihau.* Cf. *pea ki'i.*

pepelu *kik* Brochure, flyer, pamphlet. *Sh. pepa + pelu.*

Pepe·luali *i'oa* February. *Dic.* Abb. *Pep.*

pepewa *'a'* Webbed, as a duck's feet. Redup of *pewa.*

pepe'e·kua *kik* Amphibian. Māori, *pepeketua* (frog).

pepili *kik* Sticker. *Sh. pepa + pipili.*

pe'a *kik* Cover for a fish tank, in aquaculture. *Dic., ext. mng.* See *papa pe'a, pale'eke, pelena pe'a. 'Ōmaka kau pe'a.* Universal fitting, for putting pipes together.

pē·'ā·hia *'a'* Flammable, flammability; also inflammable, inflammability. Comb. *pē- + 'ā + -hia.*

pe'ahi lima *kik* Hand, as opposed to arm. *Dic.*

pē·'ano *kik* Mode, as in a computer program. Comb. *pē-* + *'ano.*

pē·'ume·lau·oho *'a'* Capillarity. Comb. *pē-* + dic., sp. var. Cf. *ohowele.*

pero·kesa·side *kik* Peroxide. *Eng.* See *haikokene lua 'okikene lua.*

Perū *i'oa* Peru; Peruvian. *Eng.* Also *Pelū.*

pia·'ai *kik* Starch, i.e. a white, tasteless, solid carbohydrate found in plants. *He mea'ai nui ka pia'ai ma ka papa'ai o kānaka.* Starch is a staple in the diet of humans. *Lit.,* edible starch.

piele *kik* Scab. *Ni'ihau.* See *pāpa'a piele.*

pio·hē *kik* Larva. *Sh. 'ōpiopio* + *hē* (caterpillar).

pio·pio *kik* Young chick; sound used to call chickens by imitating a young chick. *Dic.*

pī·uī·lā·'au See *manu pīuīlā'au.*

piula wai *kik* Fire hydrant. *Dic.* Also *paipu kinai ahi.*

piha See *helu piha, waiū piha.*

pihana·haka *kik* Volume. Comb. *pihana* + *haka.* Cf. *pihana'ū.* Abb. *phk. Kinona pihanahaka.* Space figure, in math.

pihana·'ū *kik* Capacity. Comb. *pihana* + *-'ū.* Cf. *pihanahaka.*

piha·piha *kik* Gills, of a fish. *Dic.*

Pihe·manu *i'oa* Midway island. *Lit.,* loud din (of) birds.

pihi *kik/ham* Button; to button (preceded by *ke*). *Dic.* Also *pihi lole.* See entries below.

pihi *kik* Key, as on a typewriter or computer keyboard (preceded by *ke*). *Dic., ext. mng.* See entries below. *Inoa o ke pihi.* Name of key. *Papa pihi.* Keyboard.

pihi *kik* Switch, as on a radio, TV set, etc. (preceded by *ke*). *Dic., ext. mng.*

pihi hō·'ai·lona *kik* Badge (preceded by *ke*). *Lit.,* symbol button. *Pihi māka'i.* Police badge.

pihi ho'o·holo *kik* Control key, as on a computer keyboard (preceded by *ke*). See *ho'oholo.*

pihi ho'o·kō·ā *kik* Space bar, on a typewriter or computer keyboard, variant term (preceded by *ke*). *Ni'ihau.* Also *pihi ka'ahua.*

pihi ho'o·mana'o *kik* Memory key, as on a calculator keyboard (preceded by *ke*).

pihi ho'o·nui lohe *kik* Hearing aid (preceded by *ke*). *Lit.,* button (to) increase hearing.

pihi ho'o·piha *kik* Washer, as used in plumbing. *Lit.,* button (for) filling. Also *ho'opiha, pihipihi.*

pihi ho'o·polo·lei *kik* Adjuster, as on triple-beam balance scales. *E ho'oponopono i ke pihi ho'opololei a kaulike ke kaupaona.* Fix the adjuster so that the scales are balanced. *Lit.,* button (for) straightening.

pihi kā·ho'i *kik* Return key, as on a typewriter or computer keyboard (preceded by *ke*). See *kāho'i.*

pihi kake *kik* Shift key, as on a typewriter or computer keyboard (preceded by *ke*). *Lit.,* key (for) slipping back and forth. See *kake.*

pihi kā·wā·holo *kik* Tab key, as on a typewriter or computer keyboard (preceded by *ke*). See *kāwāholo.*

pihi ka'a·hua *kik* Space bar, on a typewriter or computer keyboard (preceded by *ke*). See *ka'ahua.*

pihi laka ma'aka *kik* Caps lock key, on a typewriter or computer keyboard (preceded by *ke*). *Ua pa'a ke pihi laka ma'aka.* The caps lock key is stuck. Also *pihi laka.*

pihi lohe *kik* Earphone (preceded by *ke*). *Lit.,* hearing button. See *apo lohe.*

pihi nahau *kik* Arrow key, as on a computer keyboard (preceded by *ke*). *Pihi nahau holo ʻākau (hema, i luna, i lalo).* Arrow key for moving right (left, up, down).

pihi pāuma ea *kik* Air valve, as on a tire (preceded by *ke*). *Niʻihau.* See *pāuma.*

pihi·pihi *kik* Washer, as used in plumbing (preceded by *ke*). *Dic.* Also *pihi hoʻopiha, hoʻopiha.*

pihi pī·naʻi *kik* Turbo button, as in Nintendo games (preceded by *ke*). *Lit.,* repeat button. See *kaʻakepa.*

pihi·poho *kik* Locket (preceded by *ke*). Comb. *pihi* + *poho.*

pihi wiki *kik* Hot key, as on a computer keyboard (preceded by *ke*). *Lit.,* fast key. *Nā pihi wiki.* Hot keys.

pihi wili *kik* Nut, as in nuts and bolts (preceded by *ke*). *Lit.,* screw nut. Also *pihi.* See *kui kolū. Pihi wili ono.* Hex nut. *Pihi wili ʻēheu.* Wing nut.

pihi ʻū·miʻi *kik* Snap, fastener (preceded by *ke*). *Dic., ext. mng.* Also *ʻūmiʻi.*

pika *kik* Pizza. *Eng.* Also *pai pika.*

pika pua *kik* Flower vase. *Dic.*

pī·kaʻo *ʻa* Dehydrated. *Hoʻāhu nui ʻia ka meaʻai pīkaʻo i lako ai i ka wā pōpilikia.* Dehydrated food is stored up in order to be well supplied during times of disaster. *Dic.* See *hoʻopīkaʻo.*

pike *kik* Beet. *Eng.*

pikeke *kik* Biscuit. *Eng.* Also *palaoa pikeke.*

piki See *pā piki.*

piko *kik* Node, where a leaf is connected to the stem. *Dic.* See entries below.

piko *kik* Endpoint, in math. *Dic., ext. mng.*

piko·lō *kik* Piccolo. *Eng.*

pī·kō·nia *kik* Begonia. *Dic., sp. var.*

piko pakuhi *kik* Origin of a graph. *Lit.,* graph center. Also *piko.*

piko pele *kik* Hot spot, in geology. *Lit.,* volcanic center.

piko ʻume·kau·maha *kik* Center of gravity. See *ʻumekaumaha.*

pila *kik* Bill, a draft of a law presented to a legislature. *Dic. Luna paipai pila.* Floor leader, as a member of a legislative body. *Mea hāpai pila.* Sponsor, i.e. a legislator who presents and/or assumes responsibility for the passing of a bill.

pila *kik* Any musical instrument, but especially string instruments. *Dic., ext. mng.* See entries below.

pila hāpa *kik* Autoharp. *Dic.* Also *hāpa paʻa lima.*

pī·lahi *Lawe pīlahi.* To go for it; go for broke; geevum. Cf. *kuʻupau.*

pila kī·koʻo *kik* Bank Check. *Dic.* See entries below.

pila kī·koʻo hua·kaʻi *kik* Traveler's check. *Lit.,* travel check.

pila kī·koʻo pana·kō *kik* Bank draft, cashier's check, certified check. *Lit.,* bank check.

pila kū nui *kik* Bass viol, string bass. *Lit.,* large standing fiddle. Also *pila nui.*

pī·lali *kik* Wax. *Dic.* Also *uepa. Pepa pīlali.* Wax paper. Also *pepa ʻaila. Pīlali pākuʻi.* Grafting wax. See *pākuʻi. Tuko pīlali.* Silicone, used as an adhesive.

pila nui See *pila kū nui.*

pila puhi·puhi *kik* Harmonica. *Dic., sp. var.*

pila ʻoka kā·lā *kik* Money order. *Lit.,* bill (to) order money.

pila ʻū·poho *kik* Bagpipe. *Lit.,* bagpipe fiddle. Also *ʻūpoho.*

pī·leka·leka *kik/ʻa* Adhesion; adhesive. *Dic., ext. mng.* Cf. *pūʻuoʻuo.*

pili *ʻAoʻao pili.* Adjacent leg or side of a right triangle. See *manamana pili, ʻaoʻao.*

pili·olana *kik* Biography; biographical. Comb. *pili + ola + ana.* Cf. *hikapili-olana. Nōwela piliolana.* Biographical novel.

pili·ona See *hapa piliona.*

pili helu laki *kik* Lottery. *Lit.,* lucky number betting.

pili ho·o·kahi pala·pala *'a'* Document specific, as in a computer program. *He pilikia pili ho'okahi palapala nō ia.* That problem is definitely document specific. *Lit.,* relative (to) one document.

pili·kanaka *kik* Social studies. *Lit.,* concerning man.

pili·kino *'a'* Custom, custom-made, i.e. made to individual specifications. *Penei ka hana a ka'u papa pihi pilikino.* This is how my custom-made keyboard works. *Dic., ext. mng. Ho'onoho-nohona pilikino.* Custom format.

pili lihi *'a'* Contiguous. *Lit.,* edges touching.

pili lima See *iwi pili lima.*

pilina henua *kik* Relative location, in geography. Comb. *pilina + fenua* (Tah., earth). Cf. *kuhikuhina.*

pilina moe *kik* Bedsprings. *Dic.*

pilina·'ō·lelo *kik* Grammar. Comb. *pilina + 'ōlelo. Ha'awina pilina'ōlelo.* Grammar lesson, a lesson related to sentence structure. *Mākau pilina'ōlelo.* Grammar or sentence-structure skill.

pili·pā *'a'* Parallel. *Dic., ext. mng.* See *ala pilipā. Nā kaha pilipā.* Parallel lines.

pili pali *kik* Orographic, i.e. dealing with mountains. *Lit.,* associated with cliffs. *Ua pili pali.* Orographic rainfall.

Pilipino *i'oa* Filipino. *Dic.* Also *Pinopino. Ke Kai Pilipino.* Philippine Sea. *'Āina Pilipino.* Philippines.

pili·wai *'a'* Flush, as in carpentry. *Ni'ihau.* Cf. *'unu'unu.*

pili wā·wae See *iwi pili wāwae.*

pili·'āina *Kelepona pili'āina.* Interisland call; to make such a call.

pimeka *kik* Allspice. (Latin *pimenta dioica.*)

pin Abbreviation for *paina* (pint).

pī·naki *kik* Var. of *pīneki* (peanut). *Mān.*

pī·nalo·nalo *kik* Thrips, a kind of insect. Comb. *pī- + nalonalo.*

pina·pinao *kik* Damselfly (Megalagrion spp). Redup. of *pinao.*

pī·na'i *heh* To repeat, as the action of a computer key when held down. *Dic., ext. mng.* See *kekimala. Māmā pīna'i.* Repeat rate. *Pihi pīna'i.* Turbo button, as in Nintendo games (preceded by *ke*).

pī·na'i·apuni *heh* Loop, as in a computer program. Comb. *pīna'i + a + puni.*

pine *kik/ham* Clip; to clip together. *Ni'ihau. Pine pepa.* Paper clip.

pine hale·pe'a *kik* Tent stake. *Ni'i-hau.*

pine kai·apa *kik* Safety pin. *Dic.*

pī·neki *kik* Peanut, groundnut. *Dic., sp. var.* Any edible nut. *Ni'ihau.* Also *pīnaki, pineki. Mau'u pīneki.* Nutgrass.

pī·neki·paka *kik* Peanut butter. *Eng.*

pine lau·oho *kik* Hairclip, barrette. *Ni'ihau.*

pine maika *kik* Bowling pin.

pine·pine *Helu lele pinepine.* Frequent-flyer number, as used in airline promotions.

pine 'elala *ham* Insect mounting; to mount insects. *Lit.,* pin insects.

pini·aka *kik* Piñata. *Spanish.* Also *piniata.*

Pino·pino *i'oa* Filipino. *Ni'ihau.* Also *Pilipino. 'Āina Pinopino.* Philippines.

pīpa *kik* Beep, as a sound effect on a computer. *Eng.*

pipi *kik* Pearl oyster. *Dic.* Cf. *kupekio. Pepa lole pipi.* Butcher paper. *'Aleku'u kau pipi.* Cattle egret.

pipi Kele·mā·nia *kik* Fresh corned beef, as opposed to canned. *Lit.,* German beef. Cf. *pipi kini.*

pipi kini *kik* Canned corned beef. *Lit.,* can beef. Cf. *pipi Kelemānia.* See *kini pipi.*

pipi·nola *kik* An edible variety of squash. *Dic.*

pipi ʻĀ·lika *kik* Musk-ox. *Lit.,* Arctic ox.

pī·ʻai *kik* Berry. *Dic.* See entries below.

pī·ʻai ho·ʻo·ilo *kik* Winterberry. Comb. *pīʻai + hoʻoilo.*

pī·ʻai kī *kik* Teaberry. Comb. *pīʻai +* Eng.

pī·ʻai poku *kik* Pokeweed. Comb. *pīʻai +* Eng.

pī·ʻai ʻele·peli *kik* Elderberry. Comb. *pīʻai +* Eng.

pī·ʻā·pā *kik* Alphabet. *Dic.* *Hoʻokaʻina pīʻāpā.* To alphabetize, put in alphabetical order.

pī·ʻa·ʻaka *ʻa* Shrivelled, as grass or leaves. *Niʻihau.*

pi·ʻi *ʻŌnaehana mīkā piʻi.* High-pressure system, in meteorology. Cf. *ʻōnaehana mīkā emi.*

pi·ʻi ka mā·mā holo *heh* To accelerate. *Lit.,* the running speed advances. Cf. *hoʻopiʻi i ka māmā holo, piʻi māmā holo.* See also *emi ka māmā holo, hoʻēmi i ka māmā holo.*

pi·ʻi ki·ʻe·ki·ʻe loa *kik* Greatest increase, in math. *Lit.,* ascend (to the) highest. Cf. *emi haʻahaʻa loa.*

pi·ʻi·komo·ā·ea *kik* Evapotranspiration. Sh. *piʻikū + omoāea.* See *piʻikū.*

pi·ʻi·kū *kik* Transpiration; to transpire. *Dic.* See *piʻikomoāea.*

pi·ʻi mā·mā holo *kik* Acceleration. *He aha ka ʻokoʻa ma waena o ka māmā me ka piʻi māmā holo?* What's the difference between speed and acceleration? *Lit.,* increase (of) progress. Cf. *piʻi ka māmā holo, emi māmā holo.*

pi·ʻi·pi·ʻi See *wai piʻipiʻi.*

pi·ʻo *kik* Arc, in math. *Dic.* See *kaula hōʻike piʻo, kī piʻo, kīloi piʻo.*

pī·ʻoe *kik* Barnacle, general term. *Dic.* See entries below.

pī·ʻoe ʻō·hā kai *kik* Gooseneck barnacle. Comb. *pīʻoe + ʻōhā + kai.*

pī·ʻoe ʻō·ku·ʻe·ku·ʻe *kik* Acorn barnacle. *Lit.,* knuckles barnacle.

pi·ʻū Abbreviation for *pihanaʻū* (capacity).

pō·aka *kik* Crystal. Sh. *pōhaku + ʻoaka.*

poe lā *kik* Solar system. *Judd.*

poe·lele *kik* Satellite. *Lit.,* flying buoy. Also *ukali.* Cf. *hōkū ukali.*

poe·lele ho·ʻo·kolo·hua wā loa *kik* Long Duration Exposure Facility (LDEF), a kind of experimentation satellite placed in orbit by a space shuttle. *Lit.,* long-time experiment satellite.

Poepe *iʻoa* Phoebe, the most distant moon of Saturn. *Eng.*

poe·poe *kik* Sphere, globe. *Dic.* See *poepoe hapa. Poepoe Honua.* Globe of Earth.

poe·poe hapa *kik* Hemisphere. *Lit.,* half sphere. See *poepoe. Poepoe hapa hema.* Southern hemisphere. *Poepoe hapa hikina.* Eastern hemisphere. *Poepoe hapa komohana.* Western hemisphere. *Poepoe hapa ʻākau.* Northern hemisphere.

Poila *iʻoa* Boyle. *Eng. Ke kānāwai a Poila.* Boyle's law, i.e. decreasing the volume of a gas will increase the pressure the gas exerts if the temperature remains constant, in science.

pō·ulia *kik* Emergency. Sh. *pōʻino + ulia. Keʻena mālama pōulia.* Emergency facility, emergency room.

pou moe *kik* Bedpost.

pou·namu *kik* Jade, jadeite. *Māori.*

pou ʻau·makua ʻIli·kini *kik* Totem pole. *Lit.,* pole (of) Indian personal gods.

pohā *kik* Stop, in linguistics. *Dic., ext. mng.*

pō·hā·one *kik* Sandstone. Comb. *pōhā* + *one*.

pō·hā·hā *kik* Volcanic ejecta. *Ua lele ka pōhāhā ma loko o ke kai.* The volcanic ejecta flew into the sea. *Dic. Puʻu pōhāhā.* Spatter cone.

pō·hahī *kik* Affricate, in linguistics. *Onomatopoeia.*

pō·haku See entries below. *Paʻa pōhaku.* Lithified. *Pōhaku paʻapuna.* Calcareous rock, calcium carbonate.

pō·haku hoʻo·paʻa wai *kik* Caprock, in geology. *Lit.,* rock (which) plugs water.

pō·haku·kū·kahi *kik* Monolith. Comb. *pōhaku* + *kū* + *kahi.*

pō·haku makua *kik* Parent rock, i.e. rocks in upper surface of the earth which break down to form rocks, sand, dirt, etc.

pō·haku pele *Moʻo pōhaku pele.* Lava lizard.

pō·haku pele·maka *kik* Igneous rock, i.e. rock formed by the solidification of molten magma. *Lit.,* magma rock.

pō·haku puka ea *kik* Air stone, i.e. the porous rock in an aquarium that creates tiny bubbles at the surface of the water to facilitate the exchange of gases. *Lit.,* stone (from which) air emerges.

pō·haku ʻalā *kik* Boulder, in Hawaiʻi, referring to poi pounder-size stones and larger. *Lit., ʻalā* stone. Cf. *nukahaku.*

pō·heo *kik* Slang term for top of the key on a basketball court. Usu. *uma kī. Dic., ext. mng.* See entries below.

pō·heo *kik* Knob, handle (knob-style only). Also *pōheoheo. Dic.* Cf. *kākai, ʻau.*

pō·heo·heo puka *kik* Doorknob. *Niʻihau.* Also *pōheo puka.*

pō·heo puka *kik* Doorknob. Also *pōheoheo puka. Niʻihau.*

pō·heo ʻume *kik* Drawer knob. Cf. *ʻau ʻume.*

pō·hili *kik* Baseball, the sport. Sh. *kinipōpō* + *hili. Kaimana pōhili.*

Baseball diamond, infield. *Kahua pōhili.* Baseball field. *Kinipōpō pōhili.* Baseball, the ball. *Mikilima pōhili.* Baseball glove, mitt. *Pale pōhili.* Baseball inning. *Kuʻikahi Pōhili Aupuni.* National Baseball League. *Kuʻikahi Pōhili ʻAmelika.* American Baseball League.

pō·hī·na·ʻi *kik* Basketball, the sport. Sh. *kinipōpō* + *hinaʻi. Kinipōpō pōhīnaʻi.* Basketball, the ball.

poho *kik* Chalk (preceded by *ke*). *Dic. Poho kala.* Colored chalk. *Ehu poho.* Chalk dust. *Paepae poho.* Chalk tray.

pohō *ʻaʻ* Vain attempt, "missed out." *ʻAha koi pohō ʻuʻuku.* Small-claims court, small-debts court.

pohō *kik* Pond mud. *Dic. Lepo pohō.* Mud. Cf. *ʻūkele.*

poho·alo *ʻaʻ* Forehand, i.e. with palms facing forward. Comb. *poho* + *alo.* Cf. *pohokua.* See *hukialewa, kīpehi.*

poho·kua *ʻaʻ* Backhand, i.e. with palms facing back. Comb. *poho* + *kua.* Cf. *pohoalo.* See *hukialewa, kīpehi.*

poho·kuiki·lani *kik* Music box. *Lit.,* Switzerland container.

poho lā·ʻau pō·ulia *kik* First aid kit. *Lit.,* emergency medical pouch. Also *kini lapaʻau.*

pohole *ʻaʻ* Easy to peel, as small corms of cooked taro. *Mān.*

poho lola *kik* Cassette case, usually made of plastic. *Lit.,* container (for) cassettes. Cf. *pāiki lola.*

poho·luna *ham* To carry or palm (the ball), in basketball. *Ua puhi ka ʻuao i ka ʻūlili iā Ūlei no kāna poholuna ʻana i ke kinipōpō.* The official blew the whistle on Ūlei for palming the ball. *Lit.,* (with) palm (facing) up.

poho mea·kanu *kik* Flower pot. *Dic.*

poho pauka niho *kik* Toothpaste tube. *Niʻihau.* See *pauka niho, pani.*

poho pā·ku'i *kik* Additional sheet feeder, as for a computer printer. *Lit.,* additional receptacle. Cf. *poho pepa.*

poho palaki niho *kik* Toothbrush container, usually made of plastic.

poho pepa *kik* Sheet feeder, paper tray or cassette, as for a computer printer. *Lit.,* paper container. Cf. *poho pāku'i.* See *pāku'ina, 'āpo'o poho pepa.*

pohu *'a* Calm, as the wind; smoke rises vertically, and direction of wind is shown by smoke drift rather than wind vanes, in meteorology. *Dic., ext. mng.* See *makani.*

pohu *ham* To push. *Ni'ihau.* Also *pahu.*

pohu *ham* To volley, i.e. keep the ball in play, in volleyball. *Ni'ihau.* Also *pa'i manamana.* Cf. *lelekīkē.*

pohu·pani *ham* Displacement; to displace. Comb. *pohu* (push) + *pani. Pohupani ea.* Air displacement. *Pohupani wai.* Water displacement.

poka·ka'a *Hāme'a pokaka'a.* Block and tackle, an arrangement of pulleys and rope or cable used to lift or haul.

pokala *kik* Potash, i.e. potassium carbonate or potassium insoluble compounds. *Sh. potasiuma + kalapona.*

poka mai'a *kik* Banana poka.

pō·ka'a lī·pine *kik* Reel for recording tape. Cf. *līpine pōka'a.* See *mīkini pōka'a leo.*

poke *ham* To remove, as an *'opihi* from its shell. *Dic.* Also *kua'i, po'e.*

poke *kik* Period, i.e. each set of three numerals, in math. *Dic., ext. mng.*

poke kaola *kik* Dowel. *Lit.,* bar section.

poki·poki *kik* Sow bug. *Dic.* See entry below.

poki·poki ā·lia *kik* Brine shrimp, genus artemia. *Lit.,* brackish *pokipoki.*

poko *kik* Cutworm. *Dic.* Also *'enuhe hele pō.*

pō·kole *Hānai pōkole.* To make a short set, in volleyball.

Poko·liko *i'oa* Puerto Rico; Puerto Rican. *Dic.*

poku See *pī'ai poku.*

Poku·kala *i'oa* Portugal. *Dic.* Also *Potugala.*

polai- Poly-, a prefix for chemical terms. *Eng.* See entry below.

polai·posa·pahate *kik* Polyphosphate. *Eng.*

pō·laka *kik* City block. *Trad.* Cf. *palaka.*

pola·lau·ahi *kik* Vog. *Dic., ext. mng.*

Pō·lani *i'oa* Poland; Pole; Polish. *Dic.*

Pola·pola *'Ōpae Polapola.* Tahitian prawn.

Pole·nekia Palani *i'oa* French Polynesia.

pole·wao *kik* Tadpole, polliwog. *Mān. (HKM).*

poli·ō *kik* Polio. *Eng.*

pō·liu *kik* Mystery, as a story or movie. *Dic., ext. mng. Nōwela pōliu.* Mystery novel.

poli wā·wae *Iwi poli wāwae.* Metatarsus, i.e. one of the five bones of the foot immediately proximal to the phalanges.

poloka *kik* Frog. *Dic. Poloka kau lā'au.* Tree frog. *Poloka kau lā'au 'alani.* Orange tree frog. *Poloka mimino.* Wrinkled frog. *Poloka pulu.* Bullfrog.

polo·kalamu *kik* Program, as on TV. *Eng. Po'o inoa polokalamu.* Program title, as for a TV program (preceded by *ke*).

polo·kalamu *kik* Program, as for a computer; application, as in a computer program. *Eng.* See *pakuhi maka'aha. Haku polokalamu.* To write a program, as for a computer. *Pā polokalamu.* Program disk (preceded by *ke*). *Polokalamu hōkeo 'ikepili.* Database program. *Polokalamu kikokiko palapala.* Word processor.

polo·kalamu lewa lipo *kik* Space program.

polo·kina *kik* Protein. *Eng.* Also *kumuʻiʻo.*

polo·lei *kik* Precision, as in math. *Dic., ext. mng.* See *kaʻe pololei.*

polo·lei aʻe *ʻa* Across, as in a crossword puzzle.

polo·lia *kik* Jellyfish. *Dic.*

Polo·lika *iʻoa* Florida; Floridan, Floridian. *Dic.* Also *Folorida.*

polo·mine *kik* Bromine. *Eng. Kinoea polomine.* Bromine gas.

polo·polema *kik* Problem, as in math. *Eng.*

pō·mai·kaʻi *Ūlialia pōmaikaʻi.* Serendipity, i.e. making a fortunate discovery by accident.

poma·lina *kik* Formalin. *Eng.*

pomelo *kik* Pomelo. *Eng.* See *iāpona.* *ʻĀlani pomelo.* Grapefruit.

pon Abbreviation for *paona* (pound).

pona *kik* Bond, a certificate bought from a government or corporation which agrees to pay back the cost of the bond plus interest after a set period of time. *Dic.*

pona *kik* Atrium, of the mammalian heart. *Lit.,* heart socket. Also *pona puʻuwai.* See entries below and *keʻena.*

pona hema *kik* Left atrium, of the mammalian heart. Also *pona puʻuwai hema.*

pō·nalo *kik* Pomace fly, family Drosophilidae. *Dic., ext. mng. Pōnalo huaʻai.* Fruit fly.

pona puʻu·wai *kik* Atrium, of the mammalian heart. *Lit.,* heart socket. Also *pona.* See *keʻena. Pona puʻuwai hema.* Left atrium. *Pona puʻuwai ʻākau.* Right atrium.

pona ʻā·kau *kik* Right atrium, of the mammalian heart. Also *pona puʻuwai ʻākau.*

ponī *kik* Skunk. (Ute *poniyi.*)

poni·ʻala *kik* Lavender, both the flower and plant. *Lit.,* fragrant purple.

pono *kik* Equipment. *Dic.* See entries below. *Pono hana wikiō.* Video equipment.

pono o ka lehu·lehu *kik* Common good, i.e. the well-being of all members of society. *Lit.,* well-being of the public.

pono haʻa·wina *kik* School supplies. *Lit.,* lesson supplies. *Pahu pono haʻawina.* School box.

pono kau·like *kik* Justice, i.e. the quality of being impartial or fair. *Lit.,* just equity.

pono kahua *kik* Props, as for a play, movie or video production. *Lit.,* stage accessories. See *kahua. Nā pono kahua e pono ai.* Props needed. *Luna pono kahua.* Prop master.

pono kanaka *Palapala pono kanaka.* Bill of rights.

pono keu *kik* Fringe benefit, i.e. any employee benefit other than salary, such as medical insurance, etc. *Lit.,* extra benefit.

pono koho *ʻa* Random. *Lit.,* select any old way. *Hāpana pono koho.* Random sample.

pono lako *kik* Facility, i.e. something that is built, installed, or established to serve a particular purpose. *Ua kūpono loa nā pono lako o kēia kulanui.* The facilities at this university are entirely adequate. *A pehea nā pono lako ma ka*

pō·nolu *ʻa* Informal. *Dic., ext. mng.* Cf. *kūhelu.*

hale hoʻoikaika kino? And how are the facilities at the fitness center? *Lit.,* well-equipped resources.

ponu *kik* Beetle. (PPN *fonu.*)

ponu·momi *kik* Ladybug. *Lit.,* jeweled beetle.

ponu ʻili *kik* Dermestid, larder beetle. *Lit.,* skin beetle.

pō·paʻi·paʻi *kik* Volleyball, the sport. Sh. *kinipōpō + paʻipaʻi. Hoʻokūkū*

pōpaʻipaʻi. Volleyball tournament.
Kahua pōpaʻipaʻi. Volleyball court.
Kinipōpō pōpaʻipaʻi. Volleyball, the ball.
Kukuna pōpaʻipaʻi. Volleyball antenna.
ʻUpena pōpaʻipaʻi. Volleyball net.

pō·peku *kik* Football, the sport. *Sh.*
kinipōpō + peku. Kinipōpō pōpeku.
Football, the ball.

pō·pene *kik* Propane. *Eng.*

pō·pō ani·ani *kik* Glass ball, i.e. a
Japanese fishing float.

pō·pō·ehu *Melehune pōpōehu.*
Puffball, a kind of mushroom. *Lit.,*
pollen ball mushroom.

Popoka *iʻoa* Phobos, a moon of Mars.
Eng.

pō·poki See *manu pōpoki.*

pō·pō kī·lepa·lepa *kik* Pompom.
Dic., ext. mng. Also *kīlepalepa.*

pō·poki lō·hiu *kik* Wildcat. *Lit.,*
naturally wild cat.

pō·pō laiki *kik* Rice ball, musubi.
Also *musubī, pōpō lāisi.*

pō·pō pale mū *kik* Mothball. *Lit.,* ball
(to) ward off moths.

pō·pō wehi lā·ʻau Kaliki·maka
kik Christmas ball, the tree ornament.

pō·wā·wae *kik* Soccer. *Sh. kinipōpō*
+ wāwae. Kinipōpō pōwāwae. Soccer
ball.

Pō·ʻā *iʻoa* Algol, a star. *Mān. (HA).*

pō·ʻai *kik* Circle, i.e. the geometric
shape. *Dic.* Cf. *lina poepoe.* See entries
below and *pakuhi pōʻai.*

pō·ʻai *kik* Domain, as a sphere or field
of activity or influence. *Dic., ext. mng.*
See *pōʻai naʻau, pōʻai noʻonoʻo, pōʻai*
ʻonina kino.

pō·ʻai *heh* To orbit. *Ala pōʻai.* Orbit.
Dic.

pō·ʻai·apili *kik* Context. *Comb.*
pōʻai + a + pili.

pō·ʻai·apuni *kik* Cycle. *Comb. pōʻai*
+ a + puni. See entry below and
hoʻopōʻaiapuni. Pōʻaiapuni ola. Life
cycle.

pō·ʻai·apuni kā·loa·ʻa *kik* Business
cycle, i.e. a repeated series of economic
growth and recession. *Ma ke au o ka*
pōʻaiapuni kāloaʻa o kēia manawa, ke
puka mai nei ke kūlana hoʻokele wai-
wai mai kōna wā nāwaliwali. According
to the current business cycle, the
economy is coming out of its weak
period.

pō·ʻai hapa·lua *kik* Semicircle. *Dic.*

pō·ʻai lō·ʻihi *kik* Oval. *Dic.* Also
ʻololaha. Pōʻai lōʻihi analahi. Ellipse.

pō·ʻai na·ʻau *kik* Affective domain, as
relating to the learning process. *Lit.,*
heart domain. Cf. *pōʻai noʻonoʻo, pōʻai*
ʻonina kino.

pō·ʻai no·ʻo·no·ʻo *kik* Cognitive
domain, as relating to the learning
process. *Lit.,* thinking domain. Cf. *pōʻai*
naʻau, pōʻai ʻonina kino.

pō·ʻai waena *kik* Center circle, on a
basketball court.

pō·ʻai waena honua *kik* Equator.
Dic. Also *Kapikoowākea.* Cf. *pōʻai*
waena lani.

pō·ʻai waena lani *kik* Celestial
equator. *Sh. pōʻai waena honua + lani.*
Cf. *pōʻai waena honua.*

pō·ʻai·wai·akai *ʻa* Amphidromous,
i.e. migrating from fresh to salt water, or
from salt to fresh water, at some stage of
the life cycle other than the breeding
period. *He pōʻaiwaiakai ka noho ʻana o*
ka ʻoʻopu nākea, no ka mea, hānau ʻia ia
iʻa ma uka o ke kahawai ma ke ʻano he
piohē, a huki ʻia i kai, a ulu he pua, a
laila, hoʻi hou i uka o ke kahawai, a ulu
he makua. The life of the ʻoʻopu nākea
fish is amphidromous since it is born
upland in the stream as larvae and taken
out to sea where it grows into its
post-larvae stage of development, then
returns upstream where it becomes an
adult. *Comb. pōʻai + wai + a + kai.*

pō·ʻai ʻonina kino *kik* Psychomotor domain, as relating to the learning process. *Lit.*, domain (of) body movement. Cf. *pōʻai naʻau, pōʻai noʻonoʻo.*

Poʻa·ono *kik* Saturday. *Dic., sp. var.* Abb. *P6.*

Poʻa·hā *kik* Thursday. *Dic., sp. var.* Abb. *P4.*

Poʻa·kahi *kik* Monday. *Dic., sp.var.* Abb. *P1.*

Poʻa·kolu *kik* Wednesday. *Dic., sp. var.* Abb. *P3.*

Poʻa·lima *kik* Friday. *Dic., sp. var.* Abb. *P5.*

Poʻa·lua *kik* Tuesday. *Dic., sp. var.* Abb. *P2.*

poʻe *ham* To remove, as an *ʻopihi* from its shell. Var. of *poke.* Also *kuaʻi.*

poʻi·iʻa *kik/ham* Predator; to prey; predatory. *He poʻiiʻa ka ʻio i ka ʻiole.* A hawk is a predator of mice. Comb. *poʻi + iʻa.* Cf. *luapoʻi.*

poʻina nalu *kik* Where a wave breaks; surf break (preceded by *ka*). *Dic.*

poʻi peni *kik* Pen cap (preceded by *ke*). *Niʻihau.* Cf. *pani.*

poʻo *kik* Heads, as in coin toss (preceded by *ke*). *Dic., ext. mng.* Also *ʻaoʻao poʻo.* See entries below and *hiʻu, pana hoʻolei.* See also *hui poʻo, pani poʻo. Iwi poʻo.* Skull. *Mākala luli poʻo.* Sternocleido-mastoid muscle, i.e. the muscles between the sternum and the base of the ear.

poʻo *kik* End of a sporting field or court (preceded by *ke*). *Dic., ext. mng.* Also *kumu.* Cf. *iwi. Laina poʻo.* End line.

poʻo *kik* Base of leaf, as *hala* (preceded by *ke*). *Dic.* Cf. *hiʻu.*

poʻo au·puni *ʻAha kūkā poʻo aupuni.* Summit, i.e. a conference of highest-level officials, as heads of government.

poʻo inoa *kik* Title, as of a book or story, or at the beginning of a movie or video production (preceded by *ke*). *Lit.*, title heading. Also *inoa. Poʻo inoa polokalamu.* Program title, as for a TV program.

poʻo·hana *kik* Terminal, i.e. a computer device which is connected to a network system. Sh. *poʻopoʻo + hana.*

poʻo hou *kik* Paragraph symbol (¶), in proofreading (preceded by *ke*). *Dic.*

poʻo kā·nā·wai *kik* Title, i.e. the heading which names a legislative act or statute (preceded by *ke*). Sh. *poʻoʻōlelo + kānāwai.* See *kānāwai, kānāwai kūloko, kānāwai ʻahaʻōlelo, mokuna.*

poʻo kili·lau *kik* Shower head (preceded by *ke*). See *kililau.*

poʻo kula·nui *kik* Chancellor, as of a college or university (preceded by *ke*). *Lit.*, college director. Cf. *luna kulanui, pelekikena.*

poʻo kuni *kik* Letterhead (preceded by *ke*). *E ʻoluʻolu e pane mai ma ka pepa poʻo kuni.* Please reply on letterhead paper. *Lit.*, stamped heading. *Lau poʻo kuni.* Letterhead design.

poʻo·mana·ʻo *kik* Heading or subheading, as in a story. *Dic.*

poʻo pā·ʻa·lua *kik* Header information, file prefix, as codes at the beginning of each computer file (preceded by *ke*). *Lit.*, code heading.

poʻo·poʻo *kik* Inside corner. *Niʻihau.* Also *kūʻono.* Cf. *kihi.*

poʻo·poʻo *kik* Station, as for a computer network. *Dic., ext. mng. Poʻopoʻo pūnaewele.* Network station.

poroto·zoa *kik* Protozoa. *Eng.*

posa·pahate *kik* Phosphate. *Eng.*

poso·porusa *kik* Phosphorus. *Eng.*

potasi·uma *kik* Potassium. *Eng. Potasiuma kaianaside.* Potassium cyanide. *Potasiuma ʻiodiside.* Potassium iodide.

Potu·gala *iʻoa* Portugal. *Dic.* Also *Pokukala.*

pū *kik* Horn, a musical instrument. *Dic.* Also *pū hoʻokani.* See *pū keleawe, pū koa, pū pihi, pū puhi uai, pū puhi Palani, pū ʻoʻohe.*

pū Abb. for *pūkele* (bushel).

pua *kik* Post-larvae. *Dic., ext. mng.*

pū·ai *ʻa* To be suspended, as particles which are mixed but not dissolved in a fluid, solid, or gas. *Sh. pūailewa.* See *pūaina.*

pū·aina *kik* Suspension, i.e. a mixture in which the particles are mixed but not dissolved in a fluid, solid, or gas. *Comb. pūai + -na. Cf. māʻōʻā.* See *pūai, pūaina lahi.*

pū·aina lahi *kik* Colloid, i.e. a chemical mixture with particle size between that of solutions and suspensions. *Lit.,* delicate suspension. See *māʻōʻāna, pūaina.*

pua·hō·lani *kik* Tulip. *Lit.,* Dutch flower.

pua huika *kik* Straw. *Lit.,* wheat flower.

pua kalaunu See *pulelehua pua kalaunu.*

pua Kaliki·maka *kik* Poinsettia. *Lit.,* Christmas flower.

Pua·ka·i·lima *iʻoa* Baker Island, near the Phoenix Islands in the Pacific Ocean. *Trad.*

pua kaʻū·mana *kik* Azalea. *Lit.,* Kaʻūmana flower, so named because many azalea grow there.

pua kepela *kik* Zebrina, a kind of flower. *Lit.,* zebra flower. Also *kepela.*

pua·lā·paki *kik* Snapdragon. *Lit.,* rabbit flower.

pua·leo *heh* Timbre, in music. *Lit.,* voice emergence.

puale kai *kik* Sea vent. *Comb. puare* (*Māori,* open) + *kai.*

pua·lono *kik* Accent, in speech. *Sh. puana + hoʻolono. Pualono ʻē.* Foreign accent.

pū·alu See *maka pūalu.*

pua manu *kik* Bird of paradise, the flower. *Lit.,* bird flower. *Cf. manu palekaiko.*

puana *kik* Pronunciation. *Dic.*

puana hua·leo *kik* Allophone, in linguistics. *Lit.,* pronunciation (of) phoneme. See *hualeo.*

puana·leo *ham* Phone, in linguistics. *Lit.,* pronounce sound.

puana mā·mala *ham* To phrase, as in speaking or reading orally. *No ka puana māmala maikaʻi ma ka ʻōlelo Hawaiʻi, pono e maha ka leo ma hope wale nō o kekahi poke.* For good phrasing in Hawaiian, one must pause only after a *poke. Lit.,* (sentence) fragment pronunciation. *Cf. kūkulu māmala.*

puana·ʻī *kik/ham* Quotation; to quote (someone or something). *Comb. puana + ʻī.* See *kaha puanaʻī.*

pua·palani *kik* Iris, fleur-de-lis. *Lit.,* French flower.

pua pepa *kik* Bougainvillea. *Niʻihau.* Also *pukanawila.*

pua·pua·ʻi lā *kik* Solar prominences, i.e. puffs of gas which gently drift above the surface of the sun. *Lit.,* solar boiling. *Cf. kiko lā, lapa ahi lā, ʻale ahi lā.*

pua wī·kō·lia *kik* Rhododendron. *Lit.,* Victoria flower, named for the Victoria Gardens in Canada.

pua woela *kik* Vowel quality, in linguistics. *Lit.,* speak vowel. See *hoʻēmi woela* and entries under *woela.*

pua·ʻi manaʻo *heh* To brainstorm. *Lit.,* utter ideas.

pua·ʻi·wai *kik* Drinking fountain. *Dic. Cf. pūnāpuaʻi.*

pua ʻō·ʻili hau *kik* Crocus. *Lit.,* flower (that) appears (in) snow.

pueo kiwi hulu *kik* Great horned owl. *Lit.*, owl (with) feather horns.

pueo peke *kik* Elf owl.

puolo *kik* Music. Comb. *pū + olo*; also Māori *puoro*. See *mea hoʻokani pila*. *Kūkulu puolo.* Music arranger; to arrange music. *Mea puolo.* Musician, general term.

pū·hā·hā *heh* To spout, as a whale. *Dic., ext. mng.*

Pū·hā·honu *iʻoa* Gardner Pinnacles. *Lit.*, surfacing of turtle for air.

pū·ha·ʻu·ha·ʻu See *palaoa pūhaʻu-haʻu*.

pū hele·uī *kik* Jack-oʻ-lantern. Also *palaʻai heleuī. Lit.* Halloween pumpkin.

puhi *ham* To fire, as clay or ceramics. *Dic., ext. mng.* See *maka puhi*.

puhi a piha *ham* To inflate, fill with air. *Niʻihau.* Also *hoʻopūhalalū.* See *ʻananuʻu*.

puhi·paka *Hōkū puhipaka.* Comet.

puhi wā·wahie See *uila puhi wāwahie*.

pū·hō·mona *kik* Steroid. *Hiki ke ʻike ʻia he mau hopena ʻano ʻē o ke kino ke hoʻohana ʻia ka pūhōmona me ka naʻaupō.* Some strange physical effects can result from taking steroids ignorantly. *Sh. pūhui + hōmona.*

pū hoʻo·kani *kik* Horn, i.e. a musical instrument. *Lit.*, horn (to) play. Also *pū.* See *pū*.

pū·hui *kik* Compound, as in chemistry. Comb. *pū + hui.* See *kumumea, meakino, ʻakano. Pūhui kumumea lua.* Binary compound. *Pūhui naikokene kaʻawale.* Free nitrogen compound. *ʻAkika pūhui kalapona.* Carboxylic acid.

pū·hulu·hulu *ʻElepani pūhuluhulu.* Woolly mammoth. *Sila pūhuluhulu.* Fur seal.

pū·huna *kik* Crumb, i.e. clumps of mineral particles mixed into soil. *Sh. pū + pahunga* (*Māori*, crumb). See *māʻelenono*.

puk Abbreviation for *puna kī* (teaspoon).

puka *Mua puka.* Undergraduate level, as of a student in a college or university. *Haumāna mua puka.* Undergraduate student. *Muli puka.* Graduate level, as of a student in a university who has already achieved an undergraduate degree. *Haumāna muli puka.* Graduate student. *Mea puka.* Winner, as in the consolation bracket of a sports tournament.

puka·ani·ani　　ho·ʻo·pono·pono *kik* Edit screen, in a computer program. *Lit.*, edit window.

puka·ani·ani　kolamu　ʻike·pili *kik* List editor screen, in a computer program. *Lit.*, data column window.

puka·ani·ani　ʻō·lepe *kik* Jalousie. *Lit.*, blinds-style window. Also *puka-aniani ʻōlepelepe*.

puka ea *kik* Air vent. See *pōhaku puka ea*.

puka uai *kik* Sliding door. Also *ʻīpuka uai*.

puka uahi *kik* Chimney. *Dic.*

puka uila *kik* Electrical outlet. See *palaka*.

pū·kaha *kik* Defensive end, in football. Comb. *pū- + kaha. Pūkaha hema.* Left defensive end. *Pūkaha ʻākau.* Right defensive end.

puka·hanu *kik* Stoma. Comb. *puka + hanu.*

puka kahiko *kik* Anus, i.e. the posterior opening of the alimentary canal. *Dic.* Also *puka ʻamo*.

puka kani *kik* Sound hole, as on an ʻukulele or guitar.

puka·kī *kik* Key or keyhole, on a basketball court. *Ua komo ke kī ʻana a ʻĀlapa mai ka uma mai o ka pukakī.* ʻĀlapa made the shot from the top of the key. *Lit.*, key hole. See *uma kī*.

puka kikī hou *kik* Sweat duct. *Lit.*, hole (through which) sweat flows.

pū kako·pone *kik* Saxophone. *Comb. pū* + Eng. Also *kakopone*.

puka lā *heh* To come out daily, as a newspaper. *Comb. puka* + *lā*.

puka ma kekahi ʻaoʻao (o) Through. *Ua kī ʻia kōna lima a puka aku ma kekahi ʻaoʻao.* He was shot through the hand. *Lit.*, emerge on another side (of).

pukana·wila *kik* Bougainvillea. *Dic.* Also *pua pepa*.

puka·neʻe *heh* To emigrate. *Comb. puka* + *neʻe*. Cf. *komoneʻe*.

puka niho *kik* Cavity in a tooth, caries. *Dic.* Cf. *haka waha*.

puka·pakī *kik* Pore. *Dic.*

puka pihi *kik* Buttonhole. *Dic.*

puka·puka See *kapuahi pukapuka*.

puka ʻamo *kik* Anus, i.e. the posterior opening of the alimentary canal. *Mān.* Also *puka kahiko*. See *mākala ʻamo*.

pū·kaʻina *kik* Series. *Comb. pū* + *kaʻina*. See *ala pūkaʻina, ʻalakaine, ʻalakane, ʻalakene. Pūkaʻina hū pele.* Series of volcanic eruptions. *Pūkaʻina polokalamu kīwī.* TV series.

puke ala·kaʻi *kik* Teacher's guide, manual. *Lit.*, guiding book.

puke aʻo ana·lula *kik* Pattern book, as for teaching grammatical patterns in reading. *Lit.*, book (for) teaching patterns.

puke aʻo hou *kik* Reteaching book.

puke haʻa·wina *kik* Textbook. *Lit.*, lesson book.

puke helu·helu *kik* Reader, storybook. *Lit.*, book (for) reading.

puke hoʻo·haliʻa maka·hiki *kik* Yearbook, annual. *Lit.*, book (to) evoke year's reminiscence.

puke hoʻo·make·ʻaka *kik* Humorous book, in literature. *Lit.*, amusing book.

puke hoʻo·maʻa·maʻa haʻa·wina *kik* Workbook, practice book. *Usu. puke hoʻomaʻamaʻa. Lit.*, book (for) practicing lessons.

puke hoʻo·nui ʻike *kik* Enrichment book, challenge book. *Lit.*, book (for) increasing knowledge.

puke huna·huna *kik* Scrapbook, as in a computer program.

puke kā·koʻo *kik* Supplementary text or book; any book which supplements a primary text. *Lit.*, supporting book.

puke kiʻi kū *kik* Pop-up book, as for children's stories. *Lit.*, book (with) standing pictures.

puke kumu·hana *kik* Information book. *Ua hele wau i ka hale waihona puke no ke kāinoa ʻana i kekahi mau puke kumuhana e pili ana i ke kai.* I went to the library to check out some information books about the sea. *Lit.*, book (on a) topic.

pū·kele *kik* Bushel, a unit of measurement. *Dic. Abb. pū.*

pū kele·awe *kik* Any brass instrument. *Lit.*, brass horn.

puke lina kui *kik* Ring binder. *Lit.*, ring book. Cf. *kālana kākau*.

puke mā·kau noʻo·noʻo *kik* Building thinking skills book. *Lit.*, book (for) thinking skills.

puke manaʻo lau·like *kik* Thesaurus. *Lit.*, book (of words with) similar meanings. See *manaʻo laulike, papa manaʻo laulike*.

puke moʻo·manaʻo *kik* Journal, diary. *Lit.*, book (of) series of thoughts.

puke moʻo·manaʻo moʻo·kala·leo *kik* Literature response log, as a student's journal for recording reactions to literature. *Lit.*, literature journal.

puke noiʻi *kik* Reference or resource book, as an encyclopedia. *Lit.,* book (for) research. Cf. *kūmole.* See *puke noiʻi kūʻikena.*

puke noiʻi kū·ʻikena *kik* Encyclopedia. *Lit.,* fact reference book.

puke pane koho·koho *kik* Multiple-choice book.

puke ʻale·manaka *kik* Almanac. *Lit.,* almanac book. Cf. *ʻalemanaka puke.*

puke ʻō·lepe *kik* Flap book, as for children's stories. *Lit.,* hinged book.

pū koa *kik* Bugle. *Lit.,* soldier horn. See *pū pihi.*

pū·kolo *kik* Team of draft animals. *Dic.*

pū·kowi *kik* Birch. *Czech.*

pula·pula *kik* Cutting, as of a plant. *Dic.*

pule *kik* Week. *Dic.* Abb. *pl.*

pule·lehua Kameha·meha *kik* Kamehameha butterfly.

pule·lehua pua kalaunu *kik* Monarch butterfly. *Lit.,* crown flower butterfly.

pū·lima *kik/ham* Signature; to sign one's name. *Dic., ext. mng.* See *hua inoa. Pūlima hua.* To initial. *Iwi pūlima.* Any one of the eight carpal bones of the wrist.

pulu *Poloka pulu.* Bullfrog.

puluka *kik* Flute. *Dic.* Also *ʻohekani puluka.*

Pulu·kalia *iʻoa* Bulgaria; Bulgarian. *Dic.* Also *Bulugaria.*

pulu kui *kik* Pin cushion. *Dic.*

pulu·pulu *kik* Cotton. *Dic. Lāʻau pulupulu.* Cotton swab, Q-tip. *Pulupulu uea.* Steel wool, wire gauze.

puna *kik* Cast, as for a broken arm. *Dic., ext. mng.* Also *kimeki iwi.* See *palaina puna.*

pū·nae·wele *kik* Network. Comb./ sh. *pūnāwelewele* + *nae.* See entries below. *ʻŌnaehana pūnaewele.* Network system.

pū·nae·wele mea·ʻai *kik* Food web. *Lit.,* food network. Cf. *kuʻina meaʻai.*

Pū·nae·wele Puni Honua *kik* World Wide Web (www), as on the Internet. *Lit.,* network around (the) world.

pū·nao *kik* Metabolism. (Māori *pūngao.*) *Lōkuʻu hoʻokonukonu pūnao.* Thyroid gland.

puna·helu *kik* Mold. *Dic., ext. mng.*

puna kī *kik* Teaspoon, a unit of measurement (preceded by *ke*). Abb. *puk.*

puna kī·ʻo·ʻe *kik* Ladle (preceded by *ke*). *Lit.,* ladle spoon. Also *puna ukuhi.*

pū·nana *kik* Nest. *Dic.* See *hoʻopūnana.*

puna pā·kau·kau *kik* Tablespoon, a unit of measurement (preceded by *ke*). Abb. *pup.*

puna Pā·lisa *kik* Plaster of Paris. *Lit.,* Paris plaster.

pū·nā·pua·ʻi *kik* Fountain, as for decoration. Sh. *pūnāwai* + *puaʻi.* Cf. *puaʻiwai.*

pū·nā·wai ʻau·ʻau *kik* Swimming pool. *Lit.,* spring (for) swimming.

puni *kik* Lap, complete circuit, revolution. *Ua ʻau ʻo ia ʻekolu puni o ka pūnāwai ʻauʻau.* He swam three laps in the pool. *Ua puni ʻekolu manawa iā ia.* He did three laps. *Trad.* Round, as in boxing. *Dic., ext. mng.* Hand, as a single round in a game of cards. *Dic., ext. mng.*

puni *Hoʻokūkū pā puni.* Round-robin, as in sports. *Puni o ka minuke (p/min).* Revolutions per minute (rpm).

puni ao kū·lohe·lohe *kik* Naturalist. *Lit.,* fond (of) nature. Also *kanaka puni ao kūlohelohe.*

pū·niu See *ʻukulele pūniu.*

puni uila *kik* Electric circuit. *‘Ū‘oki puni uila.* Circuit breaker, i.e. a device which automatically interrupts electric current before wires in a circuit get too hot.

puni honua *Pūnaewele Puni Honua.* World Wide Web (www), as on the Internet.

pū·nuku ea make *kik* Gas mask, as used during World War II. *Ua komo ka po‘e kinai ahi i kō lākou pūnuku ea make ma mua o ke komo ‘ana i loko o ka hale e ‘ā ana i ke ahi me ka puapua nui o ka uahi.* The firemen put on their gas masks before entering the burning house with all the smoke that was spewing out of it. *Trad.*

pup Abbreviation for *puna pākaukau* (tablespoon).

pupa *kik* Pupa; pupal. *Eng.* See *moeapupa.*

pupē *kik* Puffin. *Eng.* Also *manu pupē.*

pū pihi *kik* Trumpet. *Lit.,* horn (with) buttons. See *pū koa. Pū pihi poko.* Cornet.

pupū *‘a* To be hung, as a network system in a computer program. *Ke pupū maila ka ‘ōnaehana pūnaewele.* The network system is hung. *Dic., ext. mng.*

pū puhi uai *kik* Trombone. *Lit.,* sliding horn.

pū puhi Palani *kik* French horn.

pū·‘ali ho‘o·uka kaua *kik* Marine corps. *Lit.,* army (for) attacking.

pū·‘ali kaua lewa *kik* Air force. *Lit.,* sky-war army.

pū·‘ali kaua moana *kik* Navy. *Lit.,* ocean-war army. Also *‘au moku kaua, ‘oihana moku. Kahua pū‘ali kaua moana.* Navy base.

pū·‘ali kia‘i mō·‘ī *kik* King's guard. *Lit.,* soldiers (for) guarding kings.

pū·‘ali koa *kik* Army; military service. *Mān. Kahua pū‘ali koa.* Military base.

pū·‘ali koa kū·ika·wā *kik* Militia. *Trad.*

pū·‘ali nō·iki *kik* Alveolar duct, in anatomy. *Lit.,* alveolus isthmus.

pū·‘ali pale kapa kai *kik* Coast guard. *Lit.,* coast guard army.

pū·‘olo *kik* Bag; twelve-pack, as of drinks. *Ni‘ihau.* Cf. *‘ope.* See entries below and *pahu, ‘eke, ‘eke‘eke. Pū‘olo koloaka.* Twelve-pack of soda. *Pū‘olo pia.* Twelve-pack of beer.

pū·‘olo koho·koho *kik* Guessing bag.

pū·‘olo pepa *kik* Paper bag. Cf. *‘eke ‘ea.*

pū·‘o‘a uahi *kik* Smokestack, as for a factory. *Lit.,* smoke tower.

pū ‘o‘ohe *kik* Any woodwind instrument. Comb. *pū* + redup. of *‘ohe.*

pu‘u *kik* Throat. *Dic.* See entries below.

pu‘u *kik* Cone, a geological feature. *Dic. Pu‘u ahupapa.* Composite cone. *Pu‘u hakuhune.* Tuff cone. *Pu‘u kuahene.* Shield cone. *Pu‘u lehu.* Ash cone. *Pu‘u ‘ākeke.* Cinder cone.

pū·‘uo *kik* Population, as in biology. Sh. *pū‘ulu* + *‘uo. Ili pū‘uo.* Population distribution, in geography. Also *ili pū‘uo kanaka. Pa‘apū pū‘uo kanaka.* Population density, for humans only.

pū·‘uo·‘uo *kik/‘a* Cohesion; cohesive. Comb. *pū* + *‘uo‘uo.* Cf. *pīlekaleka.*

pu‘u ha‘a·pupū *kik* Speed bump, as on a road or in a parking lot. *Lit.,* bump (for) holding back.

pu‘u·kani *kik* Singer. *Dic.*

pū·‘ulu *kik* Group. *Dic.* See *ho‘opū‘ulu, kūkā ma ka pū‘ulu. Pū‘ulu mea‘ai.* Food group, i.e. one of the six food groups, in nutrition. *Pae pū‘ulu mea‘ai.* The food groups, i.e. the collective union of all six food groups (calcium/milk, vegetable, fruit, starch, meat, and fat).

pu'u·naue *ham* Division; to divide, in math. *Dic.* See entries below. *Kaha pu'unaue.* Division sign. *Kumu pu'unaue.* Dividend.

pu'u·naue koena 'ole *ham* Divisible, in math. *Lit.,* division without remainder.

pu'u·naue lua *ham* Composite, in math. *Lit.,* double division. *Helu pu'unaue lua.* Composite number.

pu'u ne'ena hau *kik* Moraine. *Lit.,* hill (caused by) movement (of) ice.

pu'u pele *kik* Volcanic cone, in geology.

pu'u pō·hā·hā *kik* Spatter cone, in geology. *Lit.,* ejecta cone.

pu'u·pu'u *kik* Nodule, as on a leguminous plant. *Dic., ext. mng.* See entries below.

pu'u·pu'u *Hānai pu'upu'u.* To serve underhand, in volleyball. *Ku'i pu'upu'u.* To spike with closed fist.

pu'u·pu'u moa *kik* Chicken pox. *Ni'ihau.*

pu'u·wai See *ho'oikaika pu'uwai, ko'e pu'uwai. Pona pu'uwai.* Atrium, of the mammalian heart. Also *pona. Pona pu'uwai hema.* Left atrium. Also *pona hema. Pona pu'uwai 'ākau.* Right atrium. Also *pona 'ākau. 'Ōpū pu'uwai.* Ventricle, of the mammalian heart. Also *'ōpū. 'Ōpū pu'uwai hema.* Left ventricle. Also *'ōpū hema. 'Ōpū pu'uwai 'ākau.* Right ventricle. Also *'ōpū 'ākau.*

pu'u·wai pana 'ewa·'ewa *kik* Cardiac arrythmia. *Lit.,* heart (with) irregular beat.

Puruma *i'oa* Burma; Burmese. *Eng.* Also *Buruma.*

pū·tē *heh* To scowl. *Ua pūtē maila 'o Pāpā ia'u i ko'u ho'i lohi 'ana mai i ka hale.* Daddy scowled at me when I came home late. *Ni'ihau.* Cf. *ho'oku'emaka.*

ph Abbreviation for *pāhaneli* (hecto-).

Ph Abbreviation for *Palanaheika* (Fahrenheit).

phk Abbreviation for *pihanahaka* (volume).

pk Abbreviation for *pākaukani* (kilo-).

PK Abbreviation for *'ai pākaukani* (kilobyte).

pkl Abbreviation for *pākiliona* (tera-).

pl Abbreviation for *pule* (week).

PLH Abbreviation for *Papa Lawelawe Ho'olaha* (Bulletin Board Service).

pll Abbreviation for *palela* (barrel).

pm Abbreviation for *pāmiliona* (mega-).

p.m. Post meridium, p.m. (pronounced *pīmū*). *Eng.* See *a.m.*

PM Abbreviation for *'ai pāmiliona* (megabyte).

p/min Abbreviation for *puni o ka minuke* (revolutions per minute).

pp Abbreviation for *pāpiliona* (giga-).

PP Abbreviation for *'ai pāpiliona* (gigabyte).

P'ĀH Abbreviation for *palena 'āluna o ka hewa* (greatest possible error).

p'm Abbreviation for *pā'umi* (deka-).

W

wā *kik* Fret, as on an 'ukulele, guitar, etc. *Dic.* See *'ukulele.*

wā *kik* Interval, i.e. the number of units between spaces on a graph's scale, in math. *Dic., ext. mng.*

wae·le'a *ham* To distinguish. Comb. *wae* + *le'a* (clearly, thoroughly).

wae moho *ham* Primary, primary election, i.e. a preliminary election to nominate candidates for office. *Ma ka wae moho, e koho kekahi 'ao'ao kālai'āina i ka mea a lākou e kāko'o ai i ka holo moho 'ana no kekahi kūlana ko'iko'i o ke aupuni.* In the primary, a political party chooses the person they will support in running for election for an important government position. *Sh. koho wae moho* (dic.). Also *koho*

pāloka wae moho. *Wae moho kūākea.*
Open primary. *Wae moho kūloko.*
Closed primary.

waena *Manamana waena.* Middle
finger. *Ni'ihau.* Also *manamana loa.*

waena alelo *kik* Central portion of the
tongue. *Lit.,* tongue center. See *kū'au
alelo, lau alelo, mole alelo, wēlau alelo.*

waena honua *Ke Kai Waena Honua.*
Mediterranean Sea. *Pō'ai waena honua.*
Equator. Also *Kapikoowākea.*

waena moana Asea, at sea; midocean.
Aia nā moku a pau ōna i waena moana.
All his ships are at sea. *Trad. Kualapa
waena moana.* Midocean ridge.

wae·waele *ham* To thin, as plants
when gardening. Comb. *wae + waele.*

wae·'ano *ham* To classify, categorize.
Lit., sort (by) types.

wae 'ano See *pēmā'ō'ā wae 'ano.*

wai *kik* Water. *Dic.* See entries below
and *ana kaumaha wai, pena kuapapa
wai, pena wai. Nele wai.* Anhydrous, i.e.
without water. Cf. *'anahaidaraside.*
Papa kānāwai wai o ka moku'āina. State
water code. *'Āina kumu wai.* Watershed, i.e. an area from which water
drains.

wai·apuni *kik* Hydrosphere. Comb.
wai + a + puni.

wai·ehu *kik* File, the tool. *Dic.* Cf.
apuapu. Waiehu makali'i. Fine-cut file.

waio·leka niho·'ī·lio *kik* Dog's
tooth violet, a kind of flower. Comb. Eng.
+ *niho + 'īlio.*

wai·olina *kik* Violin, fiddle. *Dic.*

Waio·mina *i'oa* Wyoming;
Wyomingite. *Dic.*

wai·ū *kik* Milk. *Dic.* See entries below
and *pahu waiū, 'ōmole omo waiū.*
Kokoleka me ka waiū hu'ahu'a.
Chocolate with frothed milk. *Kokoleka
me ka waiū māhu.* Chocolate with
steamed milk.

wai ua *kik* Rain water.

wai·ū ehu *kik* Powdered milk.
Ni'ihau. Also *waiū pauka.*

wai·ū·haku·haku *kik* Cottage
cheese. *Dic.*

wai·ū he'e *kik* Skim milk. See *he'e.*

wai·ū luli·luli *kik* Milk shake. *Dic.*

wai·ū pauka *kik* Powdered milk.
Also *waiū ehu.*

wai·ū·pa'a *kik* Cheese. *Dic.*
Waiūpa'a keka. Cheddar cheese.
Waiūpa'a Kuikilani. Swiss cheese.

wai·ū piha *kik* Whole milk. *Lit.,*
complete milk.

wai·ū·tepe *kik* Yogurt. Comb. *waiū
+ tepe* (*Māori,* congealed).

wai hā·lana *kik* Flood. *Dic. Kāohi
wai hālana.* Flood control. *Kūkala
maka'ala wai hālana.* Flood watch.
Kūkala pō'ino wai hālana. Flood
warning.

wai hā·lo'a·lo'a *kik* Rapids, as in a
river. *Lit.,* turbulent water.

waiho *ham* To file, as files in a file
cabinet. *Dic., ext. mng.* Also *ho'okomo.*
See entries below.

waiho *ham* To leave as is, no change, as
in a computer program. *Dic., ext. mng.*
Kaha waiho. A series of dots written
under a word or words which have been
lined out to show that no change should
be made from the original, in proofreading; stet.

waiho *kik* Spread, as data on a graph, in
math. *Dic., ext. mng. Ka waiho o ka
'ikepili.* Data spread.

waiho inoa See *hāpai inoa.*

wai·hona *kik* File, as in a computer
program. *Dic., ext. mng.* Cf. *wahī.* See
entries below and *papa kuhi waihona,
po'o pā'ālua. Hulu waihona.* File format.
Loulou waihona. File link. *Peleleu
waihona.* File extension. *Waihona
mahola.* Expanded file. *Waihona
papa'a.* Backup file.

wai·hona *kik* Account, as in a bank. *Dic., ext. mng. Waihona kālā.* Bank account. *Waihona hoʻāhu kālā.* Savings account. *Waihona hoʻolilo.* Expense account. *Waihona kīkoʻo.* Checking account. *Waihona kāki.* Charge account, credit account.

wai·hona ō *kik* Endowment fund. *Lit.,* fund (which) endures. Also *waihona kālā kūmau.*

wai·hona hoʻāhu *kik* Storage cabinet. Cf. *lumi hoʻāhu.*

wai·hona kā·lā kū·mau *kik* Endowment fund. Sh. *waihona* + *puʻu kālā kūmau.* Also *waihona ō.*

wai·hona lā·ʻau lapa·ʻau *kik* Medicine cabinet. *Lit.,* cabinet (for) medicine.

wai·hona mea pā·ʻani *kik* Toy chest, toy box. *Lit.,* receptacle (for) toys. Also *pahu mea pāʻani.*

wai·hona pāiki *kik* Locker. *Lit.,* satchel cabinet. Also *pahu laka.*

wai·hona pepa *kik* File cabinet. *Lit.,* receptacle (for) paper. Also *pahu waihona, pahu waihona pepa.*

wai·hona wai·wai See *pahu waihona waiwai.*

wai·hona ʻike *kik* Memory, as in a computer program. *ʻEhia ka nui o ka waihona ʻike kaʻawale o kēia kamepiula?* How much available memory is there on this computer? *Lit.,* knowledge repository. *Waihona ʻike paʻaloko.* Built-in memory. *Waihona ʻike keu.* Extended memory. *Waihona ʻike māhuahua.* Expanded memory.

wai honua *kik* Groundwater. *Lit.,* earth water.

wai·hoʻo·lu·ʻu hui kea *kik* Additive color, i.e. one of the primary colors (red, blue, green) which, when added together, produce white light. *Lit.,* color (which) combines white.

wai kai *kik* Salty water. *Dic.* See *wai paʻakai paʻapūhia. Hoʻomānalo wai kai.* To desalinate/desalinize salty water.

wai kahe See *uila wai kahe.*

wai kō·ī *kik* Cataract, i.e. steep rapids in a large river. *Lit.,* water flowing with force. ·

wai koko *kik* Plasma. *Lit.,* blood fluid. Also *palasema.*

wai kō·ʻie·ʻie *kik* Run, as in a stream. *Lit.,* rushing water.

wai·lele *Kiʻo wai wailele.* Plunge pool, i.e. the pool at the base of a waterfall.

wai·lelele *kik* Cascade. Redup. of *wailele.*

wai lemi *kik* Lemonade. *Dic.*

wai·nola *kik* Vinyl. *Eng.*

wai paipu *kik* Tap water. *Lit.,* pipe water. *Wai wela paipu.* Hot tap water.

wai paʻa·kai paʻa·pū·hia *kik* Brine, i.e. a concentrated solution of salt or ocean water. *Lit.,* concentrated salt water. Also *wai paʻakai.* See *hoʻomānalo wai kai.*

wai·pele·kī *kik* Geyser. Comb. *wai* + *pele* + *kī.*

wai piʻi·piʻi *kik* Mineral or sparkling water. *Dic., ext. mng.*

wai pua *kik* Nectar, i.e. sweet liquid secreted by the nectaries of a plant. *Lit.,* flower liquid.

wai·wai *kik* Value. *Ua like ka waiwai o kēia ʻōkeni me ka ʻelima kēneka.* The value of this coin is five cents. *Dic. Waiwai kūʻai.* Market value. See entries below and *hokona, hoʻomohala waiwai, kālaihoʻokele waiwai. Waiwai kūʻike.* Face value. *Waiwai wānana.* Expected value. *Waiwai ʻiʻo.* Absolute value. *Waiwai ʻaiaola.* Nutritive value.

wai·wai *Hoʻokele waiwai.* Economy. *Moʻokūlana waiwai.* Balance sheet, i.e. a listing of assets, liabilities, and owner's equity.

wai·wai helu *kik* Numerical value, in math. *Lit.,* number value.

wai·wai kū lana·kila *Hoʻokele waiwai kū lanakila.* Free-market economy, i.e. the economy of a country wherein buying and selling can take place without government restrictions.

wai·wai mana kahi *Hoʻokele waiwai mana kahi.* Command economy, i.e. an economic system in which the government controls the factors of production and makes the basic economic decisions.

wai wili·au *kik* Side pool, as in a stream. *Lit.,* pool (that) moves in eddies.

wai ʻili honua *kik* Surface water. *Lit.,* earth-surface water. Also *wai ʻili.*

wai ʻula *Pani wai ʻula.* Tampon (preceded by *ke*).

wai ʻume·lau·oho *kik* Capillary water.

wā o ke kō·kua hua mele *kik* Space between horizontal lines on a musical staff. *Lit.,* space of the musical staff. Also *wā o ke kōkua.* Cf. *laina o ke kōkua hua mele.*

wao kua·hiwi *kik* Montane area. *Lit.,* mountain region. See *wao kumu kuahiwi. Wao kuahiwi haʻahaʻa.* Lower montane area. *Wao kuahiwi kiʻekiʻe.* Upper montane area.

wao kumu kua·hiwi *kik* Vegetation area at the base of a mountain. *Lit.,* region (at) base (of) mountain. See *wao kuahiwi.*

wao laʻa·lā·ʻau *kik* Alpine shrubland. *Lit.,* shrub region.

waha wali *kik* Smooth talk, smooth talker; to talk smooth; glib. *Ma muli o ka maikaʻi loa o kō kēlā kanaka kūʻai kaʻa me ka waha wali, nui ka poʻe kūʻai kaʻa maiā ia mai.* Because that car salesman is such a smooth talker, many people buy cars from him. *Niʻihau.*

wahi *kik* Region, a specific area, in math. *Dic., ext. mng.*

wahī *kik* Folder, as in a computer program. *Pono e hana kope ʻia kēlā waihona ma ka wahī ʻōnaehana.* That file needs to be copied to the system folder. *Dic., ext. mng.* Cf. *waihona.* See entries below. *Wahī o waho.* External folder.

wā·hia *ʻa* Decomposed, i.e. broken down into component parts, as through chemical reaction. *Dic., ext. mng.* Cf. *hāpopopo.*

wahī iwi *Niniki wahī iwi.* Periosteum, i.e. the tough membrane adhering tightly to a bone.

wahi hoʻo·malu *kik* Shelter. *Dic.*

wahī mimiki *kik/ham* Shrink-wrapping; to shrink-wrap. *Lit.,* wrapping (that) shrinks.

wahine *Hoʻokae wahine.* Misogyny, hatred of women. See *hoʻokae.*

wahi noho *kik* Residence. *Dic.* Also *hale noho.*

wahī pā·leo *kik* Record album cover. *Lit.,* record album wrapper.

wahī ʻano·ʻano *kik* Seed pod. *Lit.,* seed case.

wahī ʻea *kik* Any plastic film for wrapping food, as Saran Wrap. *Lit.,* plastic wrapper.

wahī·ʻeha *kik* Band aid. *Dic., ext. mng.*

waho loa *Hōkūhele o waho loa.* Outer planet.

wā hoʻo·hana *kik* Session, i.e. a period of time spent in an application of a computer program. *Lit.,* using time.

wā hoʻo·malu *kik* Probation, in law. *ʻO ka ʻōlelo hoʻopaʻi nōna, he ʻeono māhina ma ka wā hoʻomalu.* His sentence was six months probation. *Lit.,* time (of) probation. *Luna wā hoʻomalu.* Probation officer.

Wā·kea See *Hoʻohokuikalani.*

wā·kiuma *kik/ham* Vacuum; to vacuum. *Dic.*

Wakine·kona *i'oa* Washington; Washingtonian. *Dic.*

wale 'ili *kik* Cambium, i.e. the slippery layer under the bark of a plant which is the growing area of the stem. *Lit.*, bark slime.

wali *Waha wali.* Smooth talk, smooth talker; to talk smooth; glib.

walu *ham* To scratch with claws, as a cat. *Dic.* Cf. *wa'u.*

wā·nana *kik/ham* Prediction; to predict, as in a scientific experiment. *Dic., ext. mng.* See *waiwai wānana. Mākau wānana.* Prediction skill.

wana·'ā *kik* Laser. Comb. *wana + 'ā. Kukuna wana'ā.* Laser beam.

waniki *kik* Lacquer. *Dic., ext. mng.*

wani·lina *kik* Vanilin, a crystalline solid used chiefly as a flavoring agent and in perfumery. *Eng.*

wā pā·'ani *kik* Recess, as during school. *Lit.*, time (for) playing.

wā·wae *kik* Leg. *Dic.* See entry below and *a'a kino kū wāwae, a'a pu'uwai kū wāwae, iwi kū wāwae, iwi manamana wāwae, iwi pili wāwae, iwi poli wāwae. Wāwae noho.* Chair leg. *Wāwae pākaukau.* Table leg.

wā·wae *kik* Ray, as in geometry. *Legendre.* Also *'ao'ao.*

wā·wae·'ala·lā *kik* Crow's feet, a kind of plant. Comb. *wāwae + 'alalā.*

wā·wae·'ami *kik* Arthropod. *Lit.*, jointed legs.

wā·wahi *ham* To break, change, as a twenty-dollar bill. *Dic.* See entry below.

wā·wahi *ham* To break apart, i.e. breaking a number into addends or factors, in math. *Dic., ext. mng.*

wā·wahie *kik* Fuel. *Trad.* (redup. of *wahie*). See *uila puhi wāwahie. Wāwahie mō'alihaku.* Fossil fuel. Also *wāwahie wīhaku.*

wawe *Helu wawe.* Hotline. *Helu wawe maluō.* Conservation hotline.

wa'a kai·aka *kik* Kayak. Comb. *wa'a* + Eng.

wa'a 'Ili·kini *kik* Canoe without *'iako. Lit.*, Indian canoe.

wa'u *ham* To scratch, as an itch. *Dic.* Also *wa'uwa'u.* Cf. *walu.*

wā 'ukē *kik* Period of a pendulum. *Lit.*, time (of) pendulum swing.

wehe *ham* To open, remove. *Dic.* See entry below. *Mea wehe kini.* Can opener. *Mea wehe 'ūmi'i.* Staple remover.

wehe *ham* To open, as a file in a computer program. *Dic., ext. mng.* See *pani. Wehe i ke kī wai.* To turn on the water. *Ni'ihau.*

wehena papa·hana *kik* Opening ceremonies. *Lit.*, program opening.

wehe·wehe See *papa wehewehe 'ōlelo. Leka wehewehe.* Cover letter.

wehi *kik* Ornament. *Dic. Wehi lā'au Kalikimaka.* Christmas tree ornament. *Pōpō wehi lā'au Kalikimaka.* Christmas ball, the tree ornament.

weke·lia *kik* Wedelia, a ground cover. *Eng.*

wela 'a' Temperature, when weather considered hot. *'Ehia ka wela o kēia lā?* What's the temperature today? *Lit.*, hot. Cf. *anu, mahana, mehana.* See *kēkelē, wela lōpū.*

wē·lau *kik* Pole. *Dic. Wēlau 'ākau.* North pole. *Wēlau hema.* South pole.

wē·lau alelo *kik* Tip of the tongue. *Lit.*, tongue tip. See *kū'au alelo, lau alelo, mole alelo, waena alelo.*

wela lōpū 'a' Medium heat.

wele *kik* Rarefaction, i.e. the least dense concentration of wave particles in a compressional wave. Sh. *wāele.* Cf. *ulu.* See *hawewe papamoe.*

wele·lau *kik* Tip of a leaf, as hala. *Man.* Also *hi'u.* Cf. *po'o.*

Wele·moneka *i'oa* Vermont; Vermonter. *Dic.* Also *Veremona, Veremoneta.*

weli *kik* Scion. *Dic.*

welo *kik* Hereditary trait. *Dic., ext. mng.* Cf. *ōewe.* See *kumu welo.*

welo·welo *Hōkū welowelo.* Shooting star.

welu ʻeha *kik* Gauze. *Lit.,* injury rag. Also *welu wahīʻeha* (Niʻihau), *ʻaʻamoʻo* (dic.).

welu ʻili *kik* Chamois, chamois cloth. *Lit.,* leather rag.

wena·kawa *kik* Vena cava, i.e. any of the large veins by which the blood is returned to the right atrium of the heart. *Latin.* Also *aʻa kino wenakawa. Wenakawa o luna.* Superior vena cava. *Wenakawa o lalo.* Inferior vena cava.

Wene See *kiʻikuhi Wene.*

Wene·zuela *iʻoa* Venezuela. *Eng.*

Wenuke *iʻoa* Venus, the name. *Eng.* Also *Wenuse.*

Wedele *iʻoa* Weddell. *Eng. Ke kai ʻo Wedele.* Weddell Sea.

Wieka·nama *iʻoa* Vietnam; Vietnamese. *Eng.*

wī·haku *kik* Fossil. *Sh. iwi + pōhaku.* Also *mōʻalihaku.*

wika·mina *kik* Vitamin. *Eng.* Also *witamina.*

wiki See *pihi wiki.*

wiki·ō *kik* Video. *Eng. Lola wikiō.* Video cassette. *Pahu paʻi wikiō.* Camcorder, video camera.

wiki·ola *kik* Vitriol. *Eng.* Also *witiola.*

Wī·kini *kik* Viking. *Eng.*

wī·kō·lia *Pua wīkōlia.* Rhododendron.

Wikone·kina *iʻoa* Wisconsin; Wisconsinite. *Dic.* Also *Wikonesina.*

Wikone·sina *iʻoa* Wisconsin; Wisconsinite. *Dic.* Also *Wikonekina.*

wili *ham* To dial, as a telephone; to drill; to twirl, as a baton. *Dic.; dic., ext. mng.* See *kumuwili, makawili, pā wili, pihi wili, wili i hope, wili i mua, ʻaukaʻi wili.*

wili *ham* To turn, as a figure, in math. *Dic., ext. mng. Kikowaena wili.* Turn center. *Kinona like wili hapahā.* Quarter-turn image. *ʻĀlikelike wili.* Rotational symmetry. See *ʻālikelike.*

wili·au *kik* Eddy. *Dic. Wai wiliau.* Side pool, as in a stream. *Wiliau hōkū.* Galaxy.

wili·aho *kik* Reel, as for fishing. *Mān.* (comb. *wili + aho*). *Wiliaho hāmama.* Open reel. *Wiliaho hekau maunu.* Bait-casting reel.

wili i hope *ham* To rewind, as a film or audio tape. *Lit.,* wind back. See *wili i mua.*

wili i mua *ham* To fast forward, as a film or audio tape. *Lit.,* wind forward. See *wili i hope.*

wili·ō See *manu wiliō.*

wili hoʻo·mā·lō *kik* Banding tool, as for putting metal bands on boxes, water tanks, etc. *Lit.,* drill (for) stretching. See *kalapu hao.*

Wili·kinia *iʻoa* Virginia; Virginian. *Dic. Wilikinia Komohana.* West Virginia; West Virginian.

wili niho *ham* Dentist's drill. *Lit.,* tooth drill. See *ʻōhiki kauka niho.*

wili·pā *kik* Disc jockey. *Lit.,* "spin" records. Also *wilipāleo.*

wili·paipu *kik* Plumber. *Lit.,* turn pipe. Also *kanaka hoʻomoe paipu.* Cf. *wilikī* (dic.).

wili ʻaila *kik* Oil rig, for drilling oil on either land or sea. *Lit.,* oil drill.

wili·ʻō·kaʻi *kik* Chrysalis. *Dic.*

wini·kili·kini *kik* Vincristine, an alkaloid derived from the periwinkle. *Eng.*

wiʻu *ʻa* Pungent, sharp, as the smell of ammonia or vinegar. *Dic., new mng. Nalo wiʻu.* Midge fly.

wisa *kik* Visa, i.e. an endorsement made on a passport by proper authorities denoting it has been examined and that the bearer may proceed. *Eng.*

wita·mina *kik* Vitamin. *Eng.* Also *wikamina*.

witi·ola *kik* Vitriol. *Eng.* Also *wikiola*.

woela *kik* Vowel, in linguistics. *Eng.* See entries below and *ho'ēmi woela, pua woela*.

woela emi *kik* Reduced vowel, in linguistics.

woela ha'a·ha'a *kik* Low vowel, in linguistics.

woela kau·hope *kik* Back vowel, in linguistics. Comb. *woela + kau + hope*.

woela kau·mua *kik* Front vowel, in linguistics. Comb. *woela + kau + mua*.

woela kau·waena *kik* Central vowel, in linguistics. Comb. *woela + kau + waena*.

woela ki'e·ki'e *kik* High vowel, in linguistics.

woela mā·lō *kik* Tense vowel, in linguistics. *Lit.*, taut vowel.

woela mō·kio *kik* Rounded vowel, in linguistics. *Lit.*, pucker vowel.

woela 'alu *kik* Lax vowel, in linguistics. *Lit.*, slackened vowel.

'

'ā *'a'* Active, as a volcano. *Dic., ext. mng. Lua pele 'ā.* Active volcano.

'ae *ham* To lend, not to borrow. *E 'olu'olu e 'ae mai i kāu peni.* Please lend me your pen; may I borrow your pen? *Mān.*

'ae omo·waho *kik* Solvent front, i.e. the leading edge of a moving solvent as in a developing chromatogram. *Lit.*, adsorbing edge; cf. *'ae kai* (dic.).

'Ae·keana *i'oa* Aegean. *Eng. Ke kai 'o 'Aekeana.* Aegean Sea.

'āeko po'o hina *kik* Bald eagle. *Lit.*, white-haired eagle. Also *'āeto po'o hina*.

'ae·like See entries below. *Ho'oku'u 'aelike.* To cede, as land or territory. *Kūka'i 'aelike 'uniona.* Collective bargaining.

'ae·like ho'ōki *kik* Cloture, i.e. a method of ending debate and causing an immediate vote to be taken. *Ke hāpai maila ka luna ho'omalu o ka 'aha kenekoa e komo i ka 'aelike ho'ōki i hiki ke ho'opau i ka paio kālaimana'o a ho'oholo i ka pila.* The senate leader is proposing that the session enter into cloture so that the debate can end and the bill be decided. *Lit.*, agreement (to) terminate (debate).

'ae·like mā·lama kā·nā·wai *kik* Compact, i.e. a written agreement to make and obey laws for the welfare of the group. *Lit.*, agreement (to) maintain laws.

'ae··ae *'a'* Fine, as sand. *Ni'ihau/dic.* Cf. *mānoanoa*.

'āeto See *'āeko po'o hina*.

'ai *kik* Point, as in a game or sporting event. *Dic.* See entries below and *helu'ai, kāpuka 'ai, lā'au make 'ai, lilo ka 'ai iā Mea*.

'ai *kik* Byte, in computer terminology. *Dic., ext. mng.* See *huna, 'ai pākaukani, 'ai pāmiliona, 'ai pāpiliona*.

'ai *kik* Credit, as for a school course. *Dic., ext. mng. 'Ai koina.* Core credit. *'Ai koho.* Elective credit.

'ai *ham* To take, as medicine or a pill. *Dic., ext. mng.* Cf. *inu. 'Ai i ka huaale.* To take a pill. *'Ai i ka lā'au.* To take medicine.

'aia·ola *heh* To eat nutritious food. Comb. *'ai + a + ola.* Cf. *paiola. Kūlana 'aiaola.* Nutrition.

'Aio·ā *i'oa* Iowa; Iowan. *Eng.* Also *'Ioa*.

'ai hā·'awi wale *kik* Ace, in volleyball. *Ni'ihau.* Also *'eki*.

'ai hele wale *kik* Point from block, dink, or spike, in volleyball. *Ni'ihau.*

'ai hemo *ham* To remove food from one's mouth and then eat it again, as gum. *Mān. (MMLH).*

'ai hī·na'i *kik* Basket, a score in basketball. *Lit.,* basket score. See *'ai kolu.*

'ai holo *kik* Touchdown, in football. *Lit.,* run score. Cf. *'ai hopu, 'ai manuahi, 'ai peku.*

'ai hopu *kik* Touchback, in football. *Lit.,* catch score. Cf. *'ai holo, 'ai manuahi, 'ai peku.*

'ai·hue *ham* To steal, in basketball. *'Aihue akula 'o Kevin Johnson i ke kinipōpō, a holo akula no ka 'ai.* Kevin Johnson stole the ball and went in for the goal. *Dic.*

'ai·kalima *kik* Ice cream. *Dic. Kone 'aikalima.* Ice cream cone. *'Aikalima 'au.* Popsicle. Cf. *kanakē 'au.*

'ai keu *kik* Extra credit, bonus. *Lit.,* extra point. Also *ho'opi'i kaha. Nīnau 'ai keu.* Extra-credit question, bonus question. Also *nīnau ho'opi'i kaha.*

'Ai·kiopa *i'oa* Ethiopia; Ethiopian. *Dic.*

'ai kolu *kik* A successful three-point shot, in basketball. *Ua komo ka 'ai kolu a ke kī miomio 'ana a Pi'ikea.* Pi'ikea's expertly shot three-pointer went in. *Lit.,* three points. See *'ai hīna'i. Kī 'ai kolu.* Three-point shot; to attempt such a shot.

'Aiku·pika *i'oa* Egypt; Egyptian. *Dic.* Also *'Aikupita, 'Aigupita.*

'aila·hola *kik* Gasohol. *Sh. 'aila + 'alekohola.*

'aila ho'o·hinu·hinu *kik* Wax, as for polishing a car. *Lit.,* oil (for) polishing.

'aila kā *kik* Petroleum. *Lit.,* tar oil. Also *'aila tā.*

'aila·kele *kik* Fat. Comb. *'aila + kele.* See entries below and *ha'akupu 'ailakele, 'a'a'a hunaola 'ailakele. Mea'ai 'ailakele iki.* Low-fat food. Also *mea'ai li'ili'i o ka 'ailakele. Mea'ai 'ailakele nui.* High-fat food. Also *mea'ai nui o ka 'ailakele.*

'aila·kele lau·pa'a·hapa *kik* Polyunsaturated fat. Comb. *'ailakele + lau + pa'a + hapa.* Cf. *'ailakele pa'ahapa, 'ailakele pa'apū.*

'aila·kele pa'a·hapa *kik* Unsaturated fat. Comb. *'ailakele + pa'a + hapa.* Cf. *'ailakele laupa'ahapa, 'ailakele pa'apū.*

'aila·kele pa'a·pū *kik* Saturated fat. *Lit.,* dense fat. Cf. *'ailakele laupa'ahapa, 'ailakele pa'ahapa.*

'aila mea·kanu *kik* Vegetable oil. *Lit.,* plant oil. See *lau'ai.*

'Ai·lana Kanaka *i'oa* Isle of Man.

'aila pale lā *kik* Sunscreen, the lotion. *Lit.,* ointment (to) protect (against) sun. Cf. *'aila 'ōlala.*

'aila 'a'alo pa'a·hau *kik* Antifreeze. *Lit.,* oil (to) resist freezing.

'aila 'ō·lala *kik* Suntan lotion. *Lit.,* ointment (for) basking (in the sun). Cf. *'aila pale lā.*

'Ai·liki *i'oa* Irish. *Dic.* See *'Ilelani.*

'ai manu·ahi *kik* Point after touchdown, in football. *Lit.,* free point. See *'ai holo, 'ai hopu, 'ai peku. 'Ai manuahi holo.* Point after by passing or running. *'Ai manuahi peku.* Point after by kicking.

'aina See *lumi 'aina.*

'āina *kik* Country. *Dic.* See entries below. *Aloha 'āina.* Nationalism, patriotism. *'Āina 'oi'enehana.* Developed or First World Country. *'Āina hō'oi'enehana.* Developing or Third World Country.

'āina Hoʻohana ʻāina. Land use, in geography. Komikina Hoʻohana ʻĀina o ka Mokuʻāina. State Land Use Commission. ʻOihana Kumuwaiwai ʻĀina. Department of Land and Natural Resources (DLNR). ʻŌnaehana Hoʻomalu ʻĀina Kūlohelohe. Natural Areas Reserves System (NARS).

'ai·nao·nao kik Anteater. Comb. ʻai + naonao.

'āina hoʻo·malu kik Reserve, i.e. a reservation or tract of land set apart. Lit., land (to) protect. ʻĀina hoʻomalu ao kūlohelohe. Nature reserve. ʻĀina hoʻomalu ululāʻau. Forest reserve.

'Āina Hoʻo·malu Holo·holona Lō·hiu o Hawaiʻi kik Hawaiian Islands National Wildlife Refuge.

'āina kula lau·laha kik Plain, an expanse of flat land. Lit., widespread-plain land. Also kula laulaha. Cf. nuʻu laulaha.

'āina kumu wai kik Watershed, i.e. an area from which water drains. Lit., water source land. ʻĀina kumu wai kiwikā. Municipal watershed.

'āina loli·loli kik Transition area, i.e. an area where natural topography changes from one land feature to another. Lit., changing land.

'āina mauʻu kik Grassland.

'āina muli pana·lā·ʻau kik Post-colonial country. Lit., after-colony land. Also kaumokuʻāina muli panalāʻau.

'āina no ka lehu·lehu kik Public land. Kaʻa nā ʻāina no ka lehulehu ma lalo o ka hoʻomalu ʻia ʻana o ke aupuni o ka Mokuʻāina. Public lands fall under the administration of the State government. Lit., land for the public. Cf. ʻalokio.

'Āina Pā·kē iʻoa China. Dic. Also Kina. See Pākē.

'Āina Pili·pino iʻoa Philippines. Dic. Also ʻĀina Pinopino.

'Āina Pino·pino iʻoa Philippines. Niʻihau. Also ʻĀina Pilipino.

'āina·puni·ʻole kik Continent. Dic. Also mokuhonua. See mokuhonua.

'āina ʻē Kelepona ʻāina ʻē. International call; to make such a call. Kōkua ʻāina ʻē. Foreign aid, as a government policy. Kulekele ʻāina ʻē. Foreign policy, as a government function.

'Āina·ʻō·ma·ʻo·ma·ʻo Ke kai ʻo ʻĀinaʻōmaʻomaʻo. Greenland Sea.

'ai·nohu Kau·ō kik Laysan finch (telespiza cantanc). Comb. ʻai + nohu + Kauō. See hona, nuku ʻekue, ʻainohu Nīhoa.

'ai·nohu Nī·hoa kik Nīhoa finch (telespiza ultima). Comb. ʻai + nohu + Nīhoa. See hona, nuku ʻekue, ʻainohu Kauō.

'ai pā·kau·kani kik Kilobyte (K), in computer terminology. Lit., thousandfold byte. Abb. PK. See ʻai.

'ai pā·mili·ona kik Megabyte (Meg), in computer terminology. Lit., millionfold byte. Abb. PM. See ʻai.

'ai pā·pili·ona kik Gigabyte, in computer terminology. Lit., billionfold byte. Abb. PP. See ʻai.

'ai peku kik Field goal, in football. Lit., kick score. Cf. ʻai holo, ʻai hopu, ʻai manuahi.

'ai puni kik Home run. Lit., lap score.

'aiwi kik Ivy. Eng. Also lau hihi pā.

'ai·ʻē kik Loan, i.e. money lent at interest; to have a loan. Dic., ext. mng. Also lako ʻaiʻē. Cf. hoʻolako ʻaiʻē, lawe ʻaiʻē.

'Aigu·pita iʻoa Egypt; Egyptian. Dic., sp. var. Also ʻAikupika, ʻAikupita.

'ao Abbreviation for ʻaoʻao (page).

'ao·ʻao kik Leg or side, of a triangle. Dic., ext. mng. See entries below and kukuna, ʻaoʻao huli alo, ʻaoʻao launa, ʻaoʻao pili.

'ao·ʻao See kīloi ʻaoʻao. ʻAu ʻaoʻao. Side stroke, in swimming; to swim the side stroke.

'Ao·'ao *i'oa* Almak, a star. *Mān.* *(HA).*

'ao·'ao inoa See *'ao'ao ho'ākāka.*

'ao·'ao hapa nui *kik* Majority party, in politics. Cf. *'ao'ao hapa 'u'uku, 'ao'ao kālai'āina.*

'ao·'ao hapa 'u'uku *kik* Minority party, in politics. Cf. *'ao'ao hapa nui, 'ao'ao kālai'āina.*

'ao·'ao ho'ā·kāka *kik* Cover page. *Ua loa'a ka inoa a me ka helu wahi o ka mea kākau ma ka 'ao'ao ho'ākāka.* The author's name and address are found on the cover page. *Lit.,* explanation page. Also *'ao'ao inoa.*

'ao·'ao ho'o·pi'i *kik* Prosecution, i.e. the prosecuting party in a court case. *Lit.,* side (to) bring a complaint. Cf. *'ao'ao kūpale.* See *loio ho'opi'i, mea ho'opi'i.*

'ao·'ao huli alo *kik* Opposite leg or side, of a right triangle. *Lit.,* side (which) faces (the right angle). See *'ao'ao pili.*

'ao·'ao kau *kik* Base, as of a triangle, in math. *Lit.,* placing side. Abb. *'ak.*

'ao·'ao kā·lai·'āina *kik* Political party. See *'ao'ao hapa nui, 'ao'ao hapa 'u'uku.*

'ao·'ao kū·pale *kik* Defense, in sports. *Lit.,* defending side. See entry below. Also *'ao'ao pale.*

'ao·'ao kū·pale *kik* Defense, i.e. the defendant's case or counsel in a lawsuit. *Lit.,* side (which) defends. Cf. *'ao'ao ho'opi'i.* See *loio kūpale, mea ho'opi'i.*

'ao·'ao launa *kik* Corresponding side, of a triangle. *Lit.,* associating side. See *'ao'ao huli alo, 'ao'ao pili.*

'ao·'ao like 'ole *kik* Scalene, in math. *Lit.,* dissimilar sides. *Huinakolu 'ao'ao like 'ole.* Scalene triangle.

'ao·'ao pale *kik* Defense, in sports. *Lit.,* defense side. Also *'ao'ao kūpale.*

'ao·'ao pili *kik* Adjacent leg or side, of a right triangle. *Lit.,* adjoining side. See *'ao'ao huli alo.*

'ao·'ao 'elua *Aupuni 'ao'ao 'elua.* Two-party system of government.

'au *kik* Handle, as of a bureau drawer, faucet, frying pan, toilet, etc. (preceded by *ke*); neck, as of an 'ukulele, guitar, etc. *Dic.; Ni'ihau.* Cf. *kākai, pōheo.* See *'au ho'oku'u wai o ka lua, 'au kī wai, 'au paikikala, 'au pā palai, 'au 'ume.* See also *'ukulele.*

'au·ae See *'umi'umi 'auae.*

'au·a'a *kik* Rhizome. *Lit.,* root stem.

'au·ina *kik* Band, gradient, as of colors. *Dic., ext. mng. 'Auina kala.* Color band, color gradient.

'au umauma *heh* Breast stroke; to swim the breast stroke. *Dic.*

'au·hau *kik* Tax. *Dic. Mea uku 'auhau.* Taxpayer. *Pākēneka 'auhau.* Tax rate. *'Auhau komo pū.* Tax included. *'Auhau kumukū'ai.* Sales tax.

'au·hō·kū *kik* Delphinium. Comb. *'au + hōkū.* Also *pua 'auhōkū.*

'au ho'o·ku'u wai o ka lua *kik* Toilet handle (preceded by *ke*). Also *'au ho'oku'u.*

'au·hua *kik* Corm, scientific usage. Comb. *'au + hua.* See *hua.*

'Auk. Abbreviation for *'Aukake* (August).

'auka *'a'* Out, in baseball. *Ua 'auka wau iā ia.* He put me out. *Dic.* Cf. *hala akula i waho.* See *hō'auka.*

'au·kā See entries below. *Pakuhi 'aukā.* Bar graph. *Pakuhi pa'a 'aukā.* Double bar graph. *Papa 'aukā helu.* Ten-strip board, in math.

'au·kā helu hapa 'umi *kik* Tenth strip, in math. *Lit.,* strip (to) count tenths. See *moena helu hapa haneli, papa 'aukā helu.*

'au·kā holo·mua *kik* Fill bar, in a computer program. *Lit.,* bar (showing) progress.

'Au·kake *i'oa* August. *Dic.* Abb. *'Auk.*

'au·kā kō·kua helu *kik* Counting rod or strip, in math. *Lit.*, bar (to) help count. Also *'aukā*. Cf. *moena kōkua helu, pa'a'iliono kōkua helu*.

'au·ka'i *kik* Baton. Comb. *'au + ka'i*. See entries below.

'au·ka'i pāna *kik* Signal baton, as used by a marching bandleader. *Lit.*, baton (for directing) bands.

'au·ka'i wili *kik* Baton for twirling. See *wili*.

'Au·keku·lia *i'oa* Austria; Austrian. *Dic.* Also *'Auseturia*.

'au kī wai *kik* Faucet handle (preceded by *ke*). See *kī wai*.

'au kolo *heh* Free style, crawl, in swimming; to swim using this syle. *Dic.*

'au kua *heh* Back stroke, in swimming; to swim the back stroke. *Lit.*, swim (on the) back.

'au·lahi *kik* Strip, as in a stripmat counting system, in math (preceded by *ke*). Sh. *'au + lahilahi*.

'au·la'o *kik* Twig, small stick (preceded by *ke*). Sh. *'au + la'ola'o*.

'au·lili'i *'a'* Precision; precise. Redup. of *'auli'i*.

'au mā·lolo *heh* Butterfly stroke, in swimming; to swim the butterfly stroke. *Lit.*, swim (like) a *mālolo* fish.

'au·mana *kik* Tributary. *He 'aumana 'o Misouri no Misisipi.* The Missouri is a tributary of the Mississippi. Comb. *'au + mana*. *'Aumana kahawai.* Stream tributary. *'Aumana muliwai.* River tributary.

'Au·mani *i'oa* Alnitak, a star. *Mān.* (HA).

'au moku kaua *kik* Navy. *Trad.* Also *pū'ali kaua moana, 'oihana moku*.

'au·neki *kik* Ounce. *Dic.* Abb. *'an*. *'Auneki wai.* Fluid ounce. Abb. *'an w*.

'au pai·kikala *kik* Handlebars, on a bicycle (preceded by *ke*). Ni'ihau. Also *kalaiwa paikikala*.

'au pā palai *kik* Frying pan handle (preceded by *ke*).

'au·waha *kik* Geologic trench, as Aleutian Trench. *Dic., ext. mng. Ka 'auwaha 'o 'Aleuta.* Aleutian Trench.

'au·a *Ho'opa'i 'au'a.* Detention, as punishment at school. *Ho'opa'i 'au'a i ka wā kula.* In-school detention. *Ho'opa'i 'au'a muli kula.* After-school detention.

'au 'ao·'ao *heh* Side stroke, in swimming; to swim the side stroke. *Lit.*, swim (on the) side.

'au·'au kili·lau *heh* To take a shower, bathe by showering. See *kililau, lumi 'au'au*.

'au·'auna manu *kik* Birdbath. *Lit.*, bird bathing place.

'au·'au paipu hanu *heh* To snorkel. See *paipu hanu*.

'au 'ī·lio *heh* Dog paddle, in swimming; to dog paddle. *Lit.*, swim (like a) dog.

'au 'ume *kik* Drawer handle (preceded by *ke*). Cf. *pōheo 'ume*.

'Au·setu·ria *i'oa* Austria; Austrian. *Dic., sp. var.* Also *'Aukekulia*.

'aha *kik* Council. *Dic., ext. mng.* See entries below. *'Aha kalana.* County council.

'Aha Au·puni Hui Pū 'ia *kik* United Nations (UN). *Lit.*, conference of unified nations.

'aha ho'o·kolo·kolo *Māhele 'aha ho'okolokolo.* Judicial branch, of a government.

'aha ho'o·ku'i·kahi *kik* Convention, i.e. an assembly of people who meet for a common purpose, in politics. *Lit.*, convention (for) unifying.

'aha ho'o·lohe *kik* Hearing, i.e. a time for presenting official testimony or argument. *E mālama 'ia ana kekahi 'aha ho'olohe e pili ana i nā kuleana wai o ka 'ao'ao Ko'olau o O'ahu i Kāne'ohe i kēia ahiahi.* A hearing will be held regarding water rights on the windward side of O'ahu in Kāne'ohe this evening. *Lit.*, gathering (for) listening. Also *hālāwai ho'olohe*.

'Aha Ho'o·malu Lawai'a o ka Pā·kī·pika Komo·hana *kik* Western Pacific Fishery Management Council.

'aha ho'o·nā 'āina *kik* Land court. *Lit.*, court (for) settling land claims.

'Aha·hui Maka·'ala Holo·holona *kik* Humane Society. *Lit.*, society (which) attends to animals.

'aha·huina *kik* Corporation, i.e. a business that is separate from the people who own it and acts legally as a single entity. Comb. *'ahahui + -na*.

'aha koi pohō 'u·uku *kik* Small-claims court, small-debts court. *Ua ho'opi'i 'ia ka wahine i ka 'aha koi pohō 'u'uku e ho'onā ai i ka hihia o nā kini 'ōpala i hō'ino 'ia.* The woman was taken to small-claims court to settle the case of the damaged trash cans. *Lit.*, court (to) sue for small claims or damages.

'aha kuhina *kik* Cabinet, a council that advises a president, sovereign, etc. *Ua ho'okohu 'ia 'o Keoki Kahaele i ka 'aha kuhina no ka nui o kōna kāko'o a kōkua i ka Pelekikena i kōna holo moho 'ana.* Keoki Kahaele was appointed to the cabinet for his great support and help to the President in his campaign efforts. *Dic.*

'aha kū·kā *kik* Conference. *Dic.* Cf. *hui.* See entry below.

'aha kū·kā po'o au·puni *kik* Summit, i.e. a conference of highest-level officials, as heads of government. *'O ke po'omana'o kūkā nui ma ka 'aha kūkā po'o aupuni, 'o ia ka ho'okele waiwai 'ana.* The main topic of discussion at the summit was the economy. *Lit.*, conference (of) government heads.

'aha pane ho'o·pi'i *kik* Arraignment, i.e. a court hearing in which a defendant is formally charged with a crime and enters a plea of guilty or not guilty. *Ho'opi'i pa'alula 'ia ke kanaka ma ka 'aha pane ho'opi'i, a pane akula 'o ia 'a'ohe ōna kū i ka hewa.* The man was formally charged in the arraignment wherein he entered a plea of not guilty. *Lit.*, court (for) answering accusation. See *ho'opi'i kū'ē.*

'aha·'aina *kik* Banquet. *Dic.* *'Aha'aina ho'okipa.* Welcome banquet. *'Aha'aina panina.* Closing banquet.

'ā·ha'i *kik* Halfback, in football. *Dic., new mng.*

'aha·'ō·lelo *Kānāwai 'aha'ōlelo.* Statute, i.e. a law enacted by the legislative branch of a government. *Māhele 'aha'ōlelo.* Legislative branch, of a government. *'Āpana 'aha'ōlelo lāhui.* Congressional district.

'ā·hia *kik* Powdery tinder. *Dic.* Cf. *pulupulu* (dic.).

'ā·hiu *'a* Wild, general term; shy. *Dic.* Cf. *lapa.* See *lōhiu, lakauā.*

'ā·hina·hina 'ō·ma'o·ma'o *kik* Maui greensword. *Lit.*, green silversword.

'ā·holo *kik* Avalanche, landslide. *Dic., sp. var.* *'Āholo hau.* Snow avalanche.

'ahu honua *kik* Earth's mantle.

'ā·huli *kik/heh* Mutation; to mutate. *He 'āhuli ia o ke ōewe.* It's a mutation in the gene. Var. of *kāhuli.*

'ak Abbreviation for *'ao'ao kau* (base).

'Āk Abbreviation for *'ākau* (north).

'ā·kau *kik* North. *Dic.* Abb. *'Āk.* See *wēlau 'ākau. Ke Kai 'Ākau.* North Sea. *Kō'ai 'ākau.* Clockwise. *Poepoe hapa 'ākau.* Northern hemisphere.

'aka·kiu *kik* Cashew. (Tupi *acajú.*)

'Akana·kā *i'oa* Arkansas; Arkansan. *Dic., sp. var.* Also *'Akanasā.*

'**Akana·sā** *i'oa* Arkansas; Arkansan. *Dic., sp. var.* Also '*Akanakā.*

'**akano** *kik* Substance. PPN *kakano* (body). See *kumumea, meakino, pūhui.* '*Akano laukua.* Amorphous substance.

'**aka·'akai** See *ilo 'aka'akai, lina, 'o'a.*

'**ā·ka'a·ka'a** '*a*' To be peeling, as skin from sunburn. *Dic.*

'**ā·kea** *kik* Starboard hull of a double-hulled canoe or right side of a ship when looking forward. *Dic., ext. mng.* Cf. *ama, muku.*

'**ā·keka** *kik* Acetate, a salt/ester of ascetic acid. *Eng.* '*Ākeka 'eto.* Ethyl acetate.

'**ā·keke** *kik* Cinder. *Dic.* See *one 'ā.* *Pu'u 'ākeke.* Cinder cone.

'**ake·kona** *kik* Acetone. *Eng.*

'**Ake·lanika** *i'oa* Atlantic. *Dic.* Also '*Atelanika.*

'**Ake·pai·kana** *i'oa* Azerbaijan. *Eng.*

'**ā·ke'a** *ham* To block out or screen, in basketball. *Ua ne'e akula 'o Kalama i mua o Mānai no ka 'āke'a 'ana i kā ia ala 'āpō 'ana mai.* Kalama moved in front of Mānai to block out his attempt to rebound. Comb. '*ā- + ke'a.* See entries below.

'**ā·ke'a ne'e** *ham* Illegal screen, in basketball. '*A'ole hiki ke 'āke'a ne'e i ke kūpale me ka holo pū 'ana.* Screening while moving along with the defender is not allowed. *Lit.,* moving screen. See *ku'ia 'āke'a.*

'**ā·ke'a 'ū·niu** *ham* Pick and roll, in basketball; to make such a play. *Pa'akikī ke kaupale 'ana i ke ka'ane'e 'āke'a 'ūniu.* Defending the pick and roll play is tough. *Lit.,* pivot screen.

'**Ā·kia** *i'oa* Asia; Asian, Asiatic. *Dic.* Also '*Āsia.*

'**akiu** *ham* To probe. *Dic.* '*Akiu lewa lipo.* Space probe.

'**akika** *kik* Acid. *Dic. Pepa ana 'akika.* Litmus paper, for measuring pH. '*Akika haidorokoloriku.* Hydrochloric acid. '*Akika kalapona.* Carbonic acid. '*Akika naikokene.* Nitric acid. Also '*akika nikiriku.* '*Akika pūhui kalapona.* Carboxylic acid. '*Akika 'ūpalu kūlohelohe.* Naturally occurring weak acid. '*Akika forimiku.* Formic acid. '*Akika sulufuriku.* Sulfuric acid. '*Akika tanika.* Tannic acid. '*Anahaidaraside 'akika.* Acidic anhydride.

'**ā·kili·kai** *kik* Alkali; alkaline. Comb. '*ā- + kili + kai.* *Mekala 'ākilikai.* Alkali metal, i.e. one of the family of elements in Group 1 of the periodic table. *Mekala honua 'ākilikai.* Alkaline earth metal, i.e. one of the family of elements in Group 2 of the periodic table.

'**Akili·kika** *i'oa* Adriatic. *Eng. Ke kai 'o 'Akilikika.* Adriatic Sea.

'**ā·kili·lehu** *kik* Lye. Sh. '*ākilikai + lehu.*

'**Aki·mika** *i'oa* Archimedes. *Eng. Ke kulehana a 'Akimika.* Archimedes' principle, i.e. the buoyant force on an object submerged in a fluid is equal to the weight of the fluid displaced by that object, in science.

'**akino·ika** *kik* Actinoid, i.e. one of the fourteen elements that follow actinium on the periodic table. *Eng.*

'**ā·kō·lī** See *kōkua hua mele.*

'**akomi** '*a*' Automatic. *Eng. Hānai 'akomi.* To auto feed, continuous feed, as paper into a computer printer.

'**ā·kope** *kik* Caffeine. Comb. '*ā- + kope.*

'**ako·pie** See *uinihapa 'akopie.*

'**ā kua·lua** '*a*' Secondary activity, of a volcano. Comb. '*ā + kualua.*

'**aku·iki** *kik* Chipmonk. (Ute '*akwii-si.*) Also *kiulela 'akuiki.*

'**ā·kule·ana** *Mana 'ākuleana.* Delegated powers, as of Congress.

'ā·kuli·kuli kula *kik* Portulaca.
Dic.

'alā *Iwi 'alā.* Cortical bone. *Pōhaku
'alā.* Boulder, in Hawai'i, referring to poi
pounder-size stones and larger. Cf.
nukahaku.

'alaea *kik* Tribe, i.e. people in a district
who have intermarried, specifically
referring to Hawai'i. *Dic.* Cf. *hapū,
nāki.*

'Ā·laka *i'oa* Alaska; Alaskan. *Dic.*
Also *'Alaseka.*

'ala·kaine *kik* Alkyne. *Eng.* Cf.
'alakane, 'alakene. Pūka'ina 'alakaine.
Alkyne series, i.e. the group of
unsaturated hydrocarbons with one triple
bond.

'ala·kaloida *kik* Alkaloid. *Eng.*

'ala·kane *kik* Alkane. *Eng.* Cf.
'alakaine, 'alakene. Pūka'ina 'alakane.
Alkane series, i.e. saturated hydrocarbons
where all the carbon atoms are joined by
single covalent bonds.

'ala·keka *kik* Alligator. *Eng.*

'ala·kene *kik* Alkene. *Eng.* Cf.
'alakaine, 'alakane. Pūka'ina 'alakene.
Alkene series, i.e. the group of
unsaturated hydrocarbons with one
double bond.

'Alala *i'oa* Aral. *Eng. Ke kai 'o 'Alala.*
Aral Sea.

'ala·meka *kik* Nutmeg. *Sh. hua'ala* +
Eng.

'ala·neo *Lulu 'alaneo.* Rain shadow.

'ā·lani *Poloka kau lā'au 'ālani.* Orange
tree frog.

'ala·nine *kik* Alanine, an amino acid.
Eng.

'ā·lani pomelo *kik* Grapefruit. *Lit.,*
pomelo orange. See *iāpona, pomelo.*

'ā·lapa *kik/'a'* Athlete; athletic. *Dic.
Ha'awina kālā 'ālapa.* Athletic scholarship.

'ala·paina *'a'* Alpine, i.e. relating to
the biogeographic zone above timberline.

Eng. See *lalo 'alapaina, wao la'alā'au.
Panoa 'alapaina.* Alpine desert.

'ā·lapa·kona- *Prefix (Haw.); suffix
(Eng.)* -athalon. *Comb. 'ālapa + kona.*
See entries below.

'ā·lapa·kona·kolu *kik* Triathalon.
Comb. 'ālapakona- + *kolu.*

'ā·lapa·kona·lima *kik* Pentathalon.
Comb. 'ālapakona- + *lima.*

'ā·lapa·kona·'umi *kik* Decathalon.
Comb. 'ālapakona- + *'umi.*

'Ala·pama *i'oa* Alabama; Alabaman,
Alabamian. *Dic.* Also *'Alabama.*

'Ala·pia *i'oa* Arabia, Arabian. *Dic.*
Also *'Arabia. Aupuni 'Emira 'Alapia
Hui Pū 'ia.* United Arab Emirates. *Ke
kai 'o 'Alapia.* Arabian Sea. *Saudi
'Alapia.* Saudi Arabia; Saudi. Also
Saudi 'Arabia.

'Ala·bama *i'oa* Alabama; Alabaman,
Alabamian. *Dic., sp. var.* Also
'Alapama.

'Ala·bania *i'oa* Albania; Albanian.
Eng. Also *'Alepania.*

'Ala·seka *i'oa* Alaska; Alaskan. *Dic.,
sp. var.* Also *'Ālaka.*

'ale *kik* Wave, as a swell in the open
ocean. *Dic.* Cf. *nalu.* See *hokua,
honua, ki'eki'ena, kōā.*

'ale ahi lā *kik* Solar granule, i.e.
gigantic waves of gas which roll across
the surface of the sun. *Lit.,* wave (of)
solar fire. Cf. *kiko lā, lapa ahi lā,
puapua'i lā.*

'Ale·uta *i'oa* Aleut; Aleutian. *Eng.
Ka pae 'āina 'o 'Aleuta.* Aleutian Islands.
Ka 'auwaha 'o 'Aleuta. Aleutian Trench.

'ale·kea *kik* Heron, general term.
Dic. See *'aleku'u.*

'Ale·kelia *i'oa* Algeria; Algerian.
Dic. Also *'Alegeria.*

'Ale·kina *i'oa* Argentina; Argentine,
Argentinean. *Eng.*

'ale·kohola *kik* Alcohol. *Dic.*

'ale kua·kea *kik* Whitecap. *Dic.* See
niho.

'ale·ku·u *kik* Egret, general term. *Papapū ka 'āina mahi kō i ka 'aleku'u kau pipi ma hope o ka puhi 'ana i ke kō.* The cane field is covered with cattle egrets after the cane is burned. *Sh.* *'alekea + 'auku'u.* See *'alekea.* *'Aleku'u kau pipi.* Cattle egret.

'ale·manaka *kik* Calendar. *Dic.* *'Alemanaka puke.* Date book, appointment book. Cf. *puke 'alemanaka.*

'ā·lepa *kik* Alpha. *Dic., sp. var.* *Huna 'ālepa.* Alpha particle, i.e. a positively charged particle made up of two protons and two neutrons.

'Ale·pania *i'oa* Albania; Albanian. *Dic.* Also *'Alabania.*

'ale·'ale See *hawewe 'ale'ale.*

'Ale·geria *i'oa* Algeria; Algerian. *Dic., sp. var.* Also *'Alekelia.*

'ali *ham* To dig (the ball), in volleyball. *Dic., ext. mng.* See *'ali 'ūlau. Mea 'ali.* Digger. Also *'ali. 'Ali 'ūlau.* Pancake dig.

'ali·upa *ham* Alley-oop, a basketball play. *E kakali wale ana 'o Loa i ke kīloi 'ia mai i hiki ai iā ia ke 'aliupa.* Loa was just waiting to be passed the ball so that he could make the alley-oop play. *Eng.*

'alihi See *'alihikūlele.*

'alihi·kū·lele *kik* Quarterback, in football. *Sh. 'alihikaua + kūlele.* Also *'alihi.*

'Ā·lika *i'oa* Arctic. *Dic.*

'ā·like *'a* Identical, matching. *Dic.* *Nā hapa 'ālike.* Identical parts. *Mana 'ālike.* Concurrent power, as powers shared by federal and state governments.

'ā·like·like *kik/'a* Symmetry; symmetric, symmetrical, in math. Redup. of *'ālike. Kaha 'ālikelike.* Line of symmetry, a line on which a figure can be folded so the two parts fit exactly, in math. *Kinona 'ālikelike.* Symmetric figure. *'Ālikelike aka.* Reflection symmetry. *'Ālikelike kau.* Translation symmetry. *'Ālikelike wili.* Rotational symmetry.

'ali·koka *kik* Artichoke. *Eng.*

'Ali·kona *i'oa* Arizona; Arizonan, Arizonian. *Dic.* Also *'Arizona.*

'ā·lina *kik* Scar (preceded by *ke*). *Dic.* Also *ninanina.*

'ali·dirina *kik* Aldrin, a kind of insecticide. *Eng.* Cf. *dielidirina.* See *lā'au make.*

'alo ho'o·pi'i 'elua *ham* Double jeopardy, i.e. to be tried in court twice for the same offense. *Lit.,* endure two court cases.

'alo·kio *kik* Private land. *Dic., ext. mng.* Also *'alodio.* Cf. *'āina no ka lehulehu.*

'alo·peke 'Ā·lika *kik* Arctic fox. Also *'alopeka 'Ālika.*

'alo'a·hia *kik* Emotional stress. *Mān.* (MMLH).

'alo·dio *kik* Private land. *Dic., ext. mng., sp. var.* Also *'alokio.* Cf. *'āina no ka lehulehu.*

'alu *'a* Lax, as articulation, in linguistics. *Dic., ext. mng.* Cf. *mālō.* *Woela 'alu.* Lax vowel.

'ā·lua·lua *Papa 'ālualua.* Multiplication tables. *Comb. papa + dic.* See *'ālualua* (dic.).

'alumi·numa *kik* Aluminum. *Eng.*

'ā·luna See *palena 'āluna o ka hewa.*

'alu·'alu *kik* Bark, of a plant; skin. *Ni'ihau.* Also *'ili.*

'ama·kila *kik* Armadillo. *Eng.*

'ā·mana *Ku'i 'āmana.* To bump (the ball), in volleyball.

'ā·mana koho *kik* Dichotomous key. *Lit.,* Y-shaped branch (for) choosing.

'ā·mana·pu'u *kik* Bronchus, bronchiole; bronchial. *Comb. 'āmana + pu'u. 'Āmanapu'u kuamua.* Primary bronchus. *'Āmanapu'u kualua.* Secondary bronchus, lobar bronchus. *'Āmanapu'u kuakolu.* Tertiary bronchus, segmental bronchus. *'Āmanapu'u kuahope.* Terminal bronchiole.

ʻā·ma·ʻa·mau *heh* In rapid succession. *Dic.*

ʻAma·sona *iʻoa* Amazon. *Eng. Ka muliwai ʻo ʻAmasona.* Amazon river.

ʻAme·lika *iʻoa* America; American. *Dic.* See entries below.

ʻAme·lika Hema *iʻoa* South America; South American. *Dic.*

ʻAme·lika Hui Pū ʻia *iʻoa* United States of America; American. *Dic., sp. var.*

ʻAme·lika Waena *iʻoa* Central America, Latin America; Central American, Latin American. *Dic.*

ʻAme·lika ʻĀ·kau *iʻoa* North America; North American. *Dic.*

ʻĀ·mē·nia *iʻoa* Armenia. *Eng.*

ʻami *kik* Hinge. *Dic. ʻAmi puka.* Door hinge. Also *ʻami ʻīpuka.*

ʻamino *kik* Amino. *Eng. ʻAkika ʻamino.* Amino acid.

ʻamo See *iwi kuʻe ʻamo. Mākala ʻamo.* Sphincter, i.e. an annular muscle surrounding and able to contract or close a bodily opening or channel. *Puka ʻamo.* Anus, i.e. the posterior opening of the alimentary canal. Also *puka kahiko.*

ʻamo·nia *kik* Ammonia. *Eng.*

ʻamoni·uma *kik* Ammonium. *Eng. ʻAmoniuma molaibadahate.* Ammonium molybdate.

ʻā·mui *kik* Assembly, i.e. a gathering of people for a specific purpose. *Tah.*

ʻan Abbreviation for *ʻauneki* (ounce).

ʻana *Iwi ʻana.* Cancellous bone.

ʻā·nai *ham* To rub, as one's eyes. *Niʻihau.* Cf. *ʻanaʻanai.* See entry below.

ʻā·nai *Haku ʻānai.* Neolithic, in anthropology. *Ke au haku ʻānai.* Neolithic age, period.

ʻana·hai·dara·side *kik* Anhydride, i.e. a compound formed from another by the removal of water. *Eng.* Cf. *nele wai. ʻAnahaidaraside kuapapa.* Basic

anhydride, a metallic oxide that forms a base when added to water. *ʻAnahaidaraside ʻakika.* Acidic anhydride.

ʻAna·heu·heu *iʻoa* Corona Borealis, a constellation. *Tah.*

ʻana·kio·pua *kik* Angiosperm. *Comb. angio* (Gr.) + *pua.*

ʻAna·kola *iʻoa* Andorra. *Eng.*

ʻAna·kolo·meka *iʻoa* Andromeda. *Eng. Ka wiliau hōkū ʻo ʻAnakolomeka.* Andromeda galaxy.

ʻAna·muli *iʻoa* Alderamin, a star. (Tah. *ʻAnamuri.*)

ʻana·naka *kik* Jackfruit. (Ilocano *ananka.*)

ʻana·nuʻu *ʻa* Deflated, as a balloon. *Dic., ext. mng.* Also *puhalu* (dic.), *emi* (Niʻihau). Cf. *pakiʻi.* See *hoʻopūhalalū.*

ʻana·puʻu *kik* Lymph. *Mān. Lōkuʻu ʻanapuʻu.* Lymph gland, lymph node. *Maʻi ʻaʻai ʻanapuʻu.* Lymphoma.

ʻana·ʻanai *ham* To rub repeatedly, as one's eyes. *Niʻihau.* Cf. *ʻānai.*

ʻAna·damana *iʻoa* Andaman. *Eng. Ke kai ʻo ʻAnadamana.* Andaman Sea.

ʻAna·gola *iʻoa* Angola; Angolan. *Eng.*

-ʻāne *Huaʻāne.* Spermatozoon, sperm, in biology. Cf. *huaʻine.*

ʻāne *ʻa* Positive, as of electrical charge or north pole of a magnet. *Inv.* See *hohoki, ʻine, ʻūholo uila ʻāne. Huna ʻāne.* Proton.

ʻane hala·pohe *ʻa* Endangered. *Lit.,* almost extinct. Also *ʻane make loa, ʻane nalowale loa. Kānāwai Lāhulu ʻAne Halapohe.* Endangered Species Act.

ʻane make loa *ʻa* Endangered. *Lit.,* almost extinct. Also *ʻane halapohe, ʻane nalowale loa.*

ʻane nalo·wale loa *ʻa* Endangered. *Lit.,* almost extinct. Also *ʻane halapohe, ʻane make loa.*

ʻAne·ā·lika *iʻoa* Antarctica; Antarctic. *Dic., sp. var.*

'anini *kik* Eaves (preceded by *ke*). *Dic., ext. mng.*

'anini lau·lā hawewe *kik* Amplitude modulation. *Lit.,* amplitude variation. Also *AM* (pronounced *'āmū*). Cf. *FM.*

'ano like *'a'* Similar, in math. *Lit.,* somewhat alike. *Kinona 'ano like.* Similar figure.

'ano·pili *kik* Property, i.e. distinctive attribute, as of a number, in math (preceded by *ke*). *Dic., sp. var.* See entries below.

'ano·pili o ka 'ē·ko'a *kik* Opposites property, in math (preceded by *ke*). *Lit.,* property of the opposite.

'ano·pili helu *kik* Number property, in math (preceded by *ke*).

'ano·pili ho'i hope See *'anopili ka'ina ho'i hope.*

'ano·pili ho'o·ili *kik* Distributive property, in math (preceded by *ke*). *Lit.,* transferring property. Cf. *'anopili ka'ina ho'i hope.*

'ano·pili ho'o·like *kik* Associative property, in math (preceded by *ke*). *Lit.,* equalizing property.

'ano·pili ho'o·pū·'ulu *kik* Grouping property, in math (preceded by *ke*).

'ano·pili kau·like *kik* Equality property, in math (preceded by *ke*).

'ano·pili ka'ina ho'i hope *kik* Commutative property, in math (preceded by *ke*). *Lit.,* property (with) order reversed. Also *'anopili ho'i hope.* Cf. *'anopili ho'oili.*

'ano·pili kemi·kala *kik* Chemical property (preceded by *ke*).

'ano·pili 'ekahi *kik* One property, in multiplication (preceded by *ke*).

'ano·pili 'ole *kik* Zero property (preceded by *ke*). *'Anopili 'ole o ka ho'onui.* Zero property of multiplication.

'ano·'ano *kik* Seed. *Dic. Wahī 'ano'ano.* Seed pod.

'anu'u *kik* Stair, step. *Dic.* See entry below. *Papa 'anu'u lalo kai.* Underwater terrace.

'anu'u hana *kik* Step, as in problem solving. *Dic., ext. mng.* Also *'anu'u.*

'an w Abbreviation for *'auneki wai* (fluid ounce).

'Ap. Abbreviation for *'Apelila* (April).

'ā·pahu·pahu *ham* To repel, as like charges in a magnet. Comb. *'ā-* + *pahupahu.* See entry below.

'ā·pahu·pahu *'a'* Faded, as material which has been left in the sun. *Ni'ihau.*

'ā·pā lole *kik* Bolt of material. *Dic.* See *'iālole.*

'ā·pana *Maka'āinana 'āpana.* Constituent, i.e. a voter in a district who is represented by an elected official.

'ā·pana hana *kik* Errand. *Trad.* Also *hana.*

'ā·pana hapa·hā *kik* Quadrant. *Lit.,* quarter piece. Cf. *'āpana noi'i.*

'ā·pana kaha *kik* Line segment, in math.

'ā·pana·kahi *kik* Increment, i.e. one of a series of additions in groups or quantity. Comb. *'āpana* + *kahi.*

'ā·pana noi'i *kik* Quadrat, i.e. a rectangular plot used for ecological or population studies. *Lit.,* research section. Cf. *'āpana hapahā.*

'ā·pana·pana *Moena 'ili 'āpanapana.* Floor tile. Also *kile 'ili, kile papahele.*

'ā·pana pā·'oi·hana kau·waena *kik* Central business district. Cf. *kaona.*

'ā·pana 'aha·'ō·lelo lā·hui *kik* Congressional district, in government. *Ua ho'i aku nei ke Kenekoa i kōna 'āpana 'aha'ōlelo lāhui pono'ī e hō'ike ai no nā kānāwai i puka.* The Senator returned to his congressional district to report about the laws that had passed.

'ā·papapa *kik* Reef. *Ni'ihau. Ula 'āpapapa.* Slipper lobster. Also *ula pāpapa.* See *'ōmā.*

'ā·pa·a·kuma *'a* Endemic. *Dic., ext. mng.* Cf. *'ōiwi. Meakanu 'āpa'akuma.* Endemic plant.

'Ape·kani·kana *i'oa* Afghanistan; Afghan, Afghani. *Dic.* Also *'Afekanisana.*

'Ape·lika *i'oa* Africa; African. *Dic.* Also *'Aferika. Lepupalika 'Apelika Waena.* Central African Republic. *Lilia 'Apelika.* Amaryllis. *'Apelika Hema.* South Africa; South African.

'Ape·lila *i'oa* April. *Dic.* Abb. *'Ap.*

'ā·pika·pika *Halo 'āpikapika.* Suction cup fin, as beneath the stomach of an *'o'opu.*

'apo *ham* To catch, as a ball; to receive or reception, in football. *Ua 'apo kōna hoa kime i ke kinipōpō, a holo akula i ke kī pai.* His teammate caught the ball and went in for a layup. *Dic., ext. mng.* See *lawena, 'apo lilo.*

'ā·pō *ham* To rebound, in basketball. *He 45 'ai a me 8 'āpō a Karl Malone.* Karl Malone has 45 points and 8 rebounds. Var. of *'apo.*

'ā·poho 'āina *kik* Geologic depression, as Death Valley. Comb. *'āpoho* (dic., ext. mng.) + *'āina.*

'ā·pohu *kik* Fullback, in football. Comb. *'ā-* + *pohu* (var. of *pahu*).

'apo kani kā·kau *kik* Phonics. *Lit.,* catch written sounds.

'apo kele·pona *kik* Telephone receiver. *Lit.,* telephone grasp.

'apo lilo *ham* To intercept (the ball), in football. *Lit.,* take-possession catch.

'apo·mana'o *heh* Comprehension; to comprehend. *Lit.,* grasp meaning. *Nīnau 'apomana'o.* Comprehension question.

'ā·pona *kik* A take, i.e. a successful shot in movie or video production. *He 'āpona!* It's a take! *Dic., ext. mng.* See *pa'i.*

'ā·pono *ham* To ratify, as a legislative bill or a treaty. *Ua 'āpono 'ia ka pila ma ka 'Aha'ōlelo Lāhui.* The bill was ratified in Congress. *Dic., ext. mng. Ka 'āpono 'ana.* Ratification.

'ā·pō·pō *kik* Tomorrow. *Dic., sp. var.*

'ā·po'e *kik* Camp, i.e. a gathering of people to learn or practice certain skills. Sh. *'āpo'epo'e.* See *ho'omoana. 'Āpo'e kamepiula.* Computer camp. *'Āpo'e pōhīna'i.* Basketball camp.

'ā·po'o poho pepa *kik* Paper tray slot, as for a computer printer. *Lit.,* paper-tray hole (*Tah.*). See *poho pepa, poho pāku'i.*

'ā·pu'u See *'āpu'upu'u.*

'ā·pu'u·pu'u *Ka'a holo 'āpu'upu'u.* Any off-road vehicle, e.g. ATV, dirt bike, 4x4, etc. Also *ka'a 'āpu'u.*

'awa·hia *'a* Toxic. *Dic., ext. mng.*

'awa·keke *kik* Gingerbread. Sh. *'awapuhi* + *malakeke.*

'ā·wa'a *kik* Safety, in football. *Dic., new mng.* See *lala, muku. 'Āwa'a lala.* Weak safety. *'Āwa'a muku.* Strong safety.

'awe *kik* Backpack, knapsack. *Dic.* Also *pāiki hā'awe, pāisi hā'awe.*

'awe·hā *kik* Hemoglobin. Comb. *'awe* + *hā;* Māori *kawehā.*

'awe·like *kik* Average; mean, in math. *Eng. 'Awelike o ka ua.* Average rainfall. *'Awelike māmā holo.* Average speed. *'Awelike nuipa'a 'ātoma.* Average atomic mass.

'awe·'awe *kik* Tentacle. *Dic.*

'ā·we·a·we·a *'a* Trace, small amount. *Dic. Kumumea 'āwe'awe'a.* Trace element.

'a·ai *Ma'i 'a'ai 'anapu'u.* Lymphoma.

'a·aia·ani·lā *'a* Weathered; weathering. *Lit.,* eroded by weather.

'a·aia·nalu *'a* Eroded or cut by waves, as a cliff. *Lit.,* eroded by surf. *Pali 'a'aianalu.* Wave-cut cliff.

'a·aia·wā *heh/'a'* Erosion; to erode; eroded. *Lit.*, eroded (by) time.

'a·ahu *kik* Clothing. *Dic. Nā 'a'ahu hana keaka.* Wardrobe, as stage costumes for a play, movie or video production. *Usu. nā 'a'ahu.*

'a·a kā·nā·wai *ham* Civil disobedience, i.e. breaking a law because it goes against personal morals. *Ua kaulana 'o Martin Luther King no kōna a'o 'ana i ka 'a'a kānāwai 'ana me ka hakakā 'ole.* Martin Luther King was famous for his teaching of non-violent civil disobedience. *Lit.*, defy law.

'a·alo *ham* To resist, as water on corrosive things. *Dic., ext. mng. Uaki 'a'alo wai.* Water-resistant watch. Also *uāki 'a'alo wai. 'Aila 'a'alo pa'ahau.* Antifreeze. *'A'alo pili.* Teflon. *'A'alo wai.* Waterproof, water-resistant.

'a·a·nahoa *kik* Adventure, as a story or movie. *Comb. 'a'a + nahoa.*

'a·ape·hihi *kik* Pothos. *Redup. of 'ape + hihi. 'A'apehihi lau li'i.* Philodendron.

'ā·'apo *kik* Flanker, in football. *Comb. 'ā- + 'apo.*

'a·apu *Pepeiao 'a'apu.* Semilunar valve, of the heart.

'a·a·a huna·ola *kik* Tissue, as structural material of a plant or animal. *Lit.*, cell tissue. *'A'a'a hunaola 'ailakele.* Adipose tissue, i.e. animal tissue in which fat is stored. See *ha'akupu 'ailakele, 'ailakele.*

'a·ehi *heh* To cross, as a street. *Comb. 'A'e + -hi* (transitive ending). See *'a'ehina.*

'a·e·hina *kik* Crosswalk. *Comb. 'a'ehi + -na.* See *'a'ehi. Kukui 'a'ehina.* Crosswalk light.

'a·e kā·nā·wai *ham* To break the law. *Dic.* Also *ha'iha'i kānāwai. Cf. pale kānāwai.*

'a·ena *kik* Violation, as in basketball. *'O ke kake iki akula nō ia o Niu, a ho'ōho maila ka 'uao i ka 'a'ena 'ekolu kekona.* Niu just shifted a little, and the official called him on the three-second violation. *Comb. 'a'e + -na.* See entry below. *'A'ena laina kūwaena.* Backcourt violation. *'A'ena 'ekolu kekona.* Three-second violation. *'A'ena 'umi kekona.* Ten-second violation.

'a·ena *kik* Violation, as in volleyball. *Comb. 'a'e + -na. 'A'ena hāpai.* Carrying violation. *'A'ena kukuna.* Antenna violation. *'A'ena pa'i ulele.* Service violation. *'A'ena pa'i lua.* Double-hit violation. *'A'ena 'ekolu mika.* Three-meter line violation. See *laina 'ekolu mika. 'A'ena 'umi kapua'i.* Ten-foot line violation. See *laina 'umi kapua'i. 'A'ena 'upena.* Net violation.

'a·e palena *ham* To go out of bounds, in sports. *Lit.*, trespass (a) boundary.

'ā·'ī *kik* Collar. *Mān.* Also *'ā'ī lole, 'ā'ī kala, kala. A'a kino 'ā'ī.* Jugular vein. *A'a pu'uwai 'ā'ī.* Carotid artery. *Ho'omālō 'ā'ī.* Neck stretches, i.e. a warm-up exercise for sports such as volleyball; also to do this exercise.

'ā·'iwa *kik* Defensive corner back, in football. *Comb. 'ā- + 'iwa.*

'a·ohe launa *'a'* Inappropriate. *Ni'ihau.*

'a·ole i pau "Stay tuned," "to be continued," as during a TV program. *Lit.*, not finished.

'Afe·kani·sana *i'oa* Afghanistan; Afghan, Afghani. *Eng.* Also *'Apekanikana.*

'Afe·rika *i'oa* Africa; African. *Dic., sp. var.* Also *'Apelika. 'Aferika Hema.* South Africa; South African.

'Ara·bia *i'oa* Arabia, Arabian. *Eng.* Also *'Alapia. Saudi 'Arabia.* Saudi Arabia; Saudi. Also *Saudi 'Alapia.*

'ara·gona *kik* Argon, an element. *Eng.*

ʻAri·zona *iʻoa* Arizona; Arizonan, Arizonian. *Dic., sp. var.* Also *ʻAlikona.*

ʻasete·line *kik* Acetylene. *Eng.*

ʻĀ·sia *iʻoa* Asia; Asian, Asiatic. *Dic., sp. var.* Also *ʻĀkia.*

ʻAte·lanika *iʻoa* Atlantic. *Dic., sp. var.* Also *ʻAkelanika.*

ʻā·toma *kik* Atom, atomic. *Eng. Lou ʻātoma.* Bond between atoms or ions as a result of gaining, losing, or sharing electrons.

ʻea *kik* Melody, tune. *Eng.* (air). Also *leo.* See entries below and *mū hōlapu pale ʻea pau, ʻōnaehana pale ʻea, ʻukulele ʻea honu.*

ʻea *kik* Plastic. *Niʻihau. Kanaka ʻea.* Mannequin. *ʻEke ʻea.* Plastic bag (preceded by *ke*). Cf. *pūʻolo pepa. Tuko paipu ʻea.* Plastic pipe cement. Also *tuko paipu.*

ʻea kau lole *kik* Hanger, when made of plastic. *Lit.,* plastic (for) placing clothes. See *uea kau lole, lāʻau kau lole, mea kau lole.*

ʻea kāki *kik* Charge card. *Lit.,* plastic (for) charging. Also *kāleka kāki.*

ʻea paina·ā·pala *kik* Polyethylene. *Lit.,* pineapple plastic (from the plastic used when planting pineapples). See *hāliʻi ʻea.*

ʻea ʻeke·ʻeke *kik* Six-pack ring, i.e. the plastic ring which holds the cans together. *Lit.,* six-pack plastic. *ʻEa ʻekeʻeke koloaka.* Six-pack soda ring. *ʻEa ʻekeʻeke pia.* Six-pack beer ring.

ʻeono ʻī·niha *kik* Six inches, i.e. a warm-up exercise for sports such as volleyball.

ʻEu·lā·sia *iʻoa* Eurasia; Eurasian. *Eng. Ka Una Honua ʻEulāsia.* Eurasian Plate.

ʻEu·lopa *iʻoa* Europe. *Dic.* See entry below. *ʻEulopa Hikina.* Eastern Europe; Eastern European. *ʻEulopa Komohana.* Western Europe; Western European.

ʻEu·lopa *iʻoa* Europa, a moon of Jupiter. *Eng.*

ʻē·heu See *pihi wili ʻēheu.*

ʻehia How, what, as in asking about any kind of measurement. *ʻEhia ka lōʻihi o kēlā pākaukau?* How long is that table? *Niʻihau.* Also *he aha.*

ʻē·kā *kik* Agar, a gelatin-like product of certain seaweeds used as a thickening agent. *Eng.*

ʻē·kakaʻa *heh* To separate easily, as a nut from its shell. *Ke pūlehu kūpono ʻoe i ka hua kukui, a i ke ʻano o kou kīkē ʻana i ka iwi, e ʻēkakaʻa wale mai nō ka ʻiʻo mai ka iwi mai.* If you broil the kukui nut well, as you break open the shell, the meat will separate easily from the shell. *Mān.* (LKK).

ʻeke *kik* Bag (preceded by *ke*). See entries below and *pūʻolo.*

ʻeke ukana *kik* Basket, as on a bicycle (preceded by *ke*). *Niʻihau.* See *ʻie.*

ʻeke hia·moe *kik* Sleeping bag (preceded by *ke*). Also *ʻeke moe.*

ʻeke keni·keni *kik* Coin purse (preceded by *ke*). *Lit.,* bag (for) loose change.

ʻeke mimi *kik* Bladder (preceded by *ke*). *Mān.*

ʻeke moe *kik* Sleeping bag (preceded by *ke*). Also *ʻeke hiamoe.*

ʻeke pela *kik* Mattress cover (preceded by *ke*). *Lit.,* mattress bag.

ʻeke ʻea *kik* Plastic bag (preceded by *ke*). Cf. *pūʻolo pepa.*

ʻeke·ʻeke *kik* Six-pack, as of drinks. *Niʻihau.* Cf. *ʻope.* See *pahu, pūʻolo, ʻea ʻekeʻeke. ʻEkeʻeke koloaka.* Six-pack of soda. *ʻEkeʻeke pia.* Six-pack of beer.

ʻeki *kik* Ace, in volleyball. *Dic., ext. mng.* Also *ʻai hāʻawi wale.*

ʻekolu mika See *laina ʻekolu mika, ʻaʻena ʻekolu mika.*

ʻē·kona *kik* Acorn. *Eng.* Also *hua kumu ʻoka.*

'ē·ko'a 'a' Opposite. Sh. 'ē + 'oko'a.
'Ēko'a me. To be the opposite of. Ua
'ēko'a ka 'ele'ele me ke ke'oke'o. Black is
the opposite of white.

'Ekua·kola i'oa Ecuador; Ecuadoran,
Ecuadorean, Ecuadorian. Dic. Also
'Ekuadora.

'Ekua·kolia Kini 'Ekuakolia.
Equatorial Guinea.

'Ekua·dora i'oa Ecuador; Ecuadoran,
Ecuadorean, Ecuadorian. Dic. Also
'Ekuakola.

'ekue Nuku 'ekue. King Kong finch
(chloridops regiskongi). See hona,
'ainohu Kauō, 'ainohu Nīhoa.

'ē·lau kik Crown, as on a pineapple.
Dic., ext. mng. 'Ēlau hala kahiki. Pineapple crown. Also 'ēlau paina'āpala.

'elala kik Insect, bug. (Wallis Futuna
ngarara.) Pine 'elala. Insect mounting; to
mount insects. 'Ōmole mālama 'elala.
Insect holding jar. 'Ōmole pepehi 'elala.
Insect killing jar. 'Upena 'elala. Insect
net. 'Upena 'elala ho'olewalewa. Insect
fixed net. 'Upena 'elala kā'e'e. Insect
sweep net. 'Upena 'elala 'eke. Insect bag
net.

'Ela Sala·vadora i'oa El Salvador;
Salvadoran, Salvadorian. Eng.

'ele Ke Kai 'Ele. Black Sea.

'ele·ao kik Aphid, a kind of insect.
Dic. Meli 'eleao. Honeydew, i.e. a sweet
juice secreted by aphids.

'ele·hune kik Silt. Sh. kelekele (PPN
lepo) + hune.

'ē·leka kik Moose. Dic. (elk).

'ele·kanu kik Planting medium. Sh.
kelekele (PPN lepo) + kanu. Cf. lepo
kanu meakanu.

'elele mana·koho kik Elector, as in
the United States Electoral College. Lit.,
voter delegate.

'ele·lū kī·kē·kē kik American
cockroach (Periplaneta americana). Dic.

'ele·lū la'a·loa kik German
cockroach (Blattella germanica). Comb.
'elelū + dic.

'ele·lū Nū·hō·lani kik Australian
cockroach (Periplaneta australasiae).

'ele·makua kik Loam. Sh. kelekele
(PPN lepo) + onematua (Māori, loam).

'ele·muku Ko'e 'elemuku. Nematode.

'ele·nahu kik Peat. Sh. kelekele (PPN
lepo) + nanahu.

'ele·pani o ke kai kik Walrus. Lit.,
elephant of the sea. Also pala'o.

'ele·pani pū·hulu·hulu kik
Woolly mammoth. Lit., hairy elephant.

'ele·peli Pī'ai 'elepeli. Elderberry.

'ele·popo kik Humus. Sh. kelekele
(PPN lepo) + popopo.

'Eli·kilea i'oa Eritrea. Eng.

'elima Nā Hui Nui 'Elima. The Big
Five, i.e. the five corporations that
controlled most of the sugar industry in
Hawai'i.

'elua Kūlana 'elua. Runner-up, second
place.

'elua hale kik Bicameral, as a
legislature. 'Elua hale o ka 'aha'ōlelo.
The legislature is bicameral. Lit., two
houses. Cf. aupuni 'ao'ao 'elua.

'elua 'ao·'ao like Isosceles. Lit., two
equal sides. Huinakolu 'elua 'ao'ao like.
Isosceles triangle.

'eme·pela Aupuni 'emepela. Empire.
Ka pae mauna kai 'o 'Emepela. Emperor
Seamounts.

'emila kik Emir. Dic. Also 'emira.
Aupuni 'emila. Emirate. Also aupuni
'emira. 'Emira 'Alapia Hui Pū 'ia. United
Arab Emirates.

'emira See 'emila.

'ena makani kik Gale, stormy wind;
whole trees in motion and inconvenience felt in walking against the wind, in
meteorology. Dic., ext. mng. See
makani.

'ene·hana *kik* Technology. Sh. *'enekini* + *mea hana.* Cf. *'oi'enehana. Mea 'enehana.* Technician. *Luna 'enehana.* Production engineer, as for movie or video production. *Hope luna 'enehana.* Assistant production engineer. *Manakia 'enehana.* Production manager. *Mea 'enehana kani.* Sound technician. *Mea 'enehana ki'i.* Graphics technician.

'Ene·kela·kuke *i'oa* Enceladus, a small moon of Saturn. *Eng.*

'ene·kini *Pani 'enekini.* Hood, as of a car or truck.

'ene·kinia *kik* Engineer. *Dic. 'Ene-kinia mīkini.* Mechanical engineer.

'ene·kini kī·kaha *kik* Maneuvering engine, as for a spacecraft.

'Ene·lani *i'oa* England, English person; English (of England). *Dic.* Also *Pelekāne.* Cf. *Pelekānia.*

'enuhe hamu·i'a *kik* Carnivorous caterpillar (Eupithecia spp).

'enuhe hele pō *kik* Cutworm. *Lit.,* caterpillar (that) goes (at) night. Also *poko.*

'epa *ham* To fake out, in basketball. *'Epa aku nei 'o ia ma ka 'ākau, ka hema; kaha ihola 'o ia ma waena o nā kūpale 'elua.* He faked to the right, the left; he made the drive right through the two defenders. *Lit.,* deceive. See *pākī 'epa.*

'epaki *kik* Phase. *Mān.* (HKM)/Eng. *'Epaki mahina.* Phase of the moon (Western concept).

'epane *kik* Apron. *Dic.* Also *pale kuene.*

'epe·kema *kik* Science. (Greek *epetema.*) Also *akeakamai. Kauhelu 'epekema.* Scientific notation. *Kanaka noi'i 'epekema.* Scientific researcher.

'epe·soma *kik* Epsom. *Eng. Pa'akai 'epesoma.* Epsom salt.

'Ewa *Kulanui Kaiaulu o 'Ewa.* Leeward Community College.

'ewa·'ewa *Pu'uwai pana 'ewa'ewa.* Cardiac arrythmia.

'Ewe·leka *i'oa* Everest. *Eng. Mauna 'Eweleka.* Mount Everest.

'e'e *heh* To log on, log in, as of a network or other computer system. *Dic., new mng.* Cf. *lele.*

'e'ele *'a'* Concave, i.e. hollowed or rounded inward, as the inside of a bowl. Sh./redup. of *ka'ele.* Cf. *'e'emu. Aniani 'e'ele.* Concave mirror. *Aniani kaulona 'e'ele.* Concave lens.

'e'emu *'a'* Convex, i.e. curved or rounded, as the exterior of a sphere or circle. Sh./redup. of *lemu.* Cf. *'e'ele. Aniani 'e'emu.* Convex mirror. *Aniani kaulona 'e'emu.* Convex lens.

'e'epa pau·'aka *kik* Goblin. *Lit.,* grotesque person with miraculous powers.

'Ese·tonia *i'oa* Estonia. *Eng.*

'eto *kik* Ethyl. *Eng. 'Ākeka 'eto.* Ethyl acetate.

'I Abbreviation for *'ili* (area).

'ī·ā *kik* Yard, a unit of measurement. *Eng.* No abbreviation. *'Īā pa'a'iliono.* Cublic yard.

'ī·ā·lole *kik* Material, cloth. *Mān.* (MMLH, HHLH). See *'āpā lole.*

'ie *kik* Basket (preceded by *ke*). *Dic.* See *'eke ukana.*

'Ioa *i'oa* Iowa; Iowan. *Dic., sp. var.* Also *'Aioā.*

'io·kine *kik* Iodine. *Eng.* See *hō'iokine.*

'iole *kik* Mouse, as for a computer. *Dic., ext. mng.* See *nahau 'iole.*

'iole *kik* Mouse, rat. *Dic.* See entries below. *'Iole kaupoku.* Roof rat. *'Iole kia.* Deer mouse. *'Iole wāwae kea.* White-footed mouse.

'iole kawia *kik* Guinea pig. Comb. *'iole* + *cavia* (Latin).

'iole kepila *kik* Gerbil. Comb. *'iole* + Eng. Also *'iole kebira.*

'iole lā·piki *kik* Rabbit. *Ni'ihau.* Also *lāpiki, lāpaki.* See entries under *lāpaki.*

'iona *kik* Ion.

'io·'io *Pene* 'io'io. Brooder.

'iodi·side *kik* Iodide. *Eng.*
Potasiuma 'iodiside. Potassium iodide.

'Ika·hō *i'oa* Idaho; Idahoan. *Dic.*

'Ī·kā·lia *i'oa* Italy; Italian. *Dic., sp. var.* Also *'Ītālia.*

'ikamu *kik* Entry, item, object. *E koho i kekahi o nā 'ikamu i hō'ike 'ia.* Choose one of the given objects. *Dic., ext. mng. Ma ka 'ikamu.* À la carte, as on a menu. Also *'oka pākahikahi.*

'ike *kik* Information. *Dic., ext. mng.* See entries below and *po'o pā'ālua.*

'ike *Laina* 'ike. Line of sight, sight line. Also *laina lena.*

'ike hā·nau See *lawena.*

'ike ku'una *kik* Traditional knowledge. *A'o kahua 'ike ku'una.* Traditional knowledge-based learning.

'ike·pili *kik* Data. *Lit.,* associated information. See entry below and *ili, kāhuakomo, kāhuapuka, kākuhi, waiho. Hōkeo* 'ikepili. Data bank, database. *Ho'okuene* 'ikepili. To browse, as in a database program having the capability to rearrange data. *Laina* 'ikepili. Data stream, as in a computer program. *Pakuhi huina* 'ikepili. Cross-tab graph, in math. *Pukaaniani kolamu* 'ikepili. List editor screen, in a computer program.

'ike·pili helu *kik* Statistics, i.e. numerical facts or data, in math. *Lit.,* number data.

'ī·koi honua *kik* Earth's core. *Dic., ext. mng.*

'ī·komo *kik* Filling, as for a sandwich. Comb. *'ī-* (Tah.) + *komo.* Cf. *'īpiha.*

'iku·ana *kik* Iguana. *Eng.*

'Ilaka *i'oa* Iraq; Iraqi. *Dic.* Also *'Iraka.*

'Ilana *i'oa* Iran; Iranian. *Dic.* Also *'Irana.*

'ileika *kik* Eraser. *Eng.* Also *mea holoi, pale holoi.*

'Ile·lani *i'oa* Ireland; Irish. *Dic.* Also *'Irelani.* See *'Ailiki.*

'ili *kik* Skin. *Dic.* Also *'alu'alu.* See entries below and *moena* 'ili. *Welu* 'ili. Chamois, chamois cloth. *'Ili kūloko.* Subcutus, in biology. *'Ili kūwaena.* Dermis. *'Ili kūwaho.* Epidermis. *'Ōnaehana* 'ili. Integumentary system, in biology.

'ili *kik* Bark, of a plant. *Dic.* Also *'alu'alu. Wale* 'ili. Cambium, i.e. the slippery layer under the bark of a plant which is the growing area of the stem. *'Ili iho.* Inner bark. *'Ili o waho.* Outer bark.

'ili *Paiha'akei* 'ili. Racism, i.e. adhering to a belief that one's own race is superior to another race. Also *paiha'akei lāhui.*

'ili alo *kik* Surface area, in math. Comb. *'ili + alo.* Also *'ili.*

'ī·lio *'Au* 'ilio. Dog paddle, in swimming; to dog paddle. *Lit.,* swim (like a) dog.

'ī·lio kē·lia *kik* Terrier. (Latin *terrarius.*) Also *kēlia.*

'Ili·oki *i'oa* Pluto, the planet. *Inv.*

'ili ho'o·lohe pu'u·wai *kik* Stethoscope. *Lit.,* tube (for) listening (to the) heart. Also *kiupe ho'olohe.*

'ili·kai *kik* Sea level. *Dic., ext. mng.* Cf. *'iliwai.*

'ili kalapu wā·wae *kik* Jess, a leg strap for falcons. *Lit.,* leg strap.

'Ili·kini See *wa'a 'Ilikini, 'Īnia.*

'ili kuapo *Apo* 'ili kuapo. Belt loop, as on a pair of pants.

'ili lau·lā *kik* Area, a quantitative measurement. *'Ehia ka 'ili laulā o kēia huinakolu?* What is the area of this triangle? *Lit.,* surface width and breadth. Also *'ili.* Abb. *'I.*

'ili·lahi *Papa* 'ililahi. Plywood. Cf. *papawai.*

'Ili·noe *i'oa* Illinois; Illinoisan. *Dic.*

'ili·wai *kik* Carpenter's level. *Dic.* Cf. *'ilikai.*

'ili·wehi *kik* Veneer. Comb. *'ili* + *wehi*.

'ili·'ili *kik* Cobble. *Dic., ext. mng.*

'ī·maka *kik* Lookout, scenic viewpoint. *Dic.*

'imi hā·'ina *ham* To solve a problem, look for a solution. *E 'imi 'oe i ka hā'ina o ka polopolema helu 'ekolu.* Solve problem three. Cf. *ho'oponopono pilikia, huli hā'ina.*

'īn Abbreviation for *'īniha* (inch).

'ī·nana See *lau 'īnana.*

'inā·'inā *'a* Hypothetical. Redup./var. of *inā.*

-'ine *Hua'ine.* Ovum, in biology. Cf. *hua'āne.*

'ine *'a* Negative, as of an electrical charge or south pole of a magnet. *Inv.* See *hohoki, 'āne, 'ūholo uila 'ine. Huna 'ine.* Electron.

'Ī·nia *i'oa* India; Indian, i.e. referring to India and its peoples. *Dic.* Cf. *'Iniana.*

'Ini·ana *Moana 'Iniana.* Indian Ocean. *Dic.* Cf. *'Īnia.*

'Ī·nio- Indo-. Sh. *'Īnia* + *o.* See entry below.

'Ī·nio·nū·hō·lani *i'oa* Indo-Australian. Comb. *'Īnio-* + *Nūhōlani. Ka Una Honua 'Īnionūhōlani.* Indo-Australian Plate.

'ī·niha *kik* Inch. *Dic.* Abb. *'īn.*

'Ini·kiana *i'oa* Indiana; Indianian. *Dic.* Also *'Inidiana.*

'inik·ō See *manu 'inikō.*

'ini·kua *kik* Insurance. *Dic. Uku 'inikua.* Insurance premium. *'Inikua olakino.* Medical insurance. *Helu 'inikua olakino.* Medical coverage number.

'Ini·diana *i'oa* Indiana; Indianian. *Dic., sp. var.* Also *'Inikiana.*

'Ini·done·sia *i'oa* Indonesia; Indonesian. *Eng.*

'Inu·ika *kik* Eskimo person, language, or culture. *Usu. 'Inuita. Inuit.*

'Inu·ita See *'Inuika.*

'ī·pale *kik* Insulation. Comb. *'ī-* + *pale.* See *hō'īpale.*

'ī·piha *kik* Filling, as of a tooth. Comb. *'ī-* (Tah.) + *piha.* Cf. *'īkomo.*

'ī·piki *Manu 'īpiki.* Ibis, a flightless bird in prehistoric Hawai'i.

'ī·puka *kik* Alias or gateway, as in a computer program. *Dic., ext. mng.*

'ī·puka uai *kik* Sliding door. Also *puka uai.*

'ī·puka pakele pahū *kik* Explosive escape hatch, as in a spaceship. *Lit.,* explosive escape door.

'Iwa·keli'i *i'oa* Cassiopeia, a constellation. *Mān. (HA).*

'iwa·'iwa *kik* Maidenhair fern. *Dic.*

'i'o See *helu 'i'o, helu 'i'o 'ole, helu piha, waiwai 'i'o, 'i'o 'ole.*

'i'o wili·wili *kik* Meat meal. *Lit.,* ground meat. Cf. *iwi wiliwili.*

'i'o 'ole *Kaha 'i'o 'ole.* Negative sign, in math (-). Cf. *kaha ho'olawe.*

'Iraka *i'oa* Iraq; Iraqi. *Dic., sp. var.* Also *'Ilaka.*

'Irana *i'oa* Iran; Iranian. *Dic., sp. var.* Also *'Ilana.*

'Ire·lani *i'oa* Ireland; Irish. *Dic., sp. var.* Also *'Ilelani.* See *'Ailiki*

'Ise·ra'ela *i'oa* Israel; Israeli. *Dic., sp. var.*

'ita *kik* Ether. *Eng.*

'Ī·tā·lia *i'oa* Italy; Italian. *Dic., sp. var.* Also *'Īkālia.*

'o2 Abbreviation for *'oki hapalua* (bisect).

'oā *kik/heh* Crack or split, as in a sidewalk; to crack or split. *Dic.* Cf. *kōā.* See *ne'e 'oā.*

'oi *'a* Acute, in math. *Dic. Huina 'oi.* Acute angle. *Huinakolu 'oi.* Acute triangle.

'oi aku ka nui Greater than, in math. Also *nui a'e.* See *'oi aku ke emi.*

'oi aku ke emi Less than, in math. Also *emi iho.* See *'oi aku ka nui.*

'oi·hana *kik* Business, career, occupation; professional, professionally. *Dic.* Cf. *kāloaʻa, pāʻoihana.* See entries below and *kākoʻo ʻoihana olakino. Mea hulahula ʻoihana.* Professional dancer. *Paʻi ʻoihana ʻia.* Professionally printed. *ʻOihana pōhili.* Baseball career.

'oi·hana *kik* Department, office. *Dic., ext. mng.* Also *keʻena.* Cf. *māhele.* See entries below.

'Oi·hana Iʻa me ka Holo·holona Lō·hiu o ʻAme·lika *kik* US Fish and Wildlife Service. *Lit.,* fish and wildlife department of America.

'Oi·hana o nā Pāka a me nā Hana Hoʻo·nanea *kik* Department of Parks and Recreation. *Dic.*

'oi·hana haʻi·lono *kik* Journalism. *Lit.,* occupation (to) tell the news.

'Oi·hana Hoʻo·lā·lā a me ka Hoʻo·mohala Wai·wai o ka Moku·ʻāina ʻo Hawaiʻi *kik* Hawaiʻi State Department of Planning and Economic Development. *Lit.,* planning and economic development department of the state of Hawaiʻi.

'Oi·hana Kā·lā o ka Moku·ʻāina ʻo Hawaiʻi *kik* Hawaiʻi State Department of Finance. *Lit.,* money department of the State of Hawaiʻi.

'oi·hana kā·pili *kik* Manufacturing industry. Sh. *ʻoihana + hana kāpili.* Also *ʻoiʻenehana kāpili.*

'Oi·hana Kumu·wai·wai ʻĀina *kik* Department of Land and Natural Resources (DLNR). *Lit.,* land resources department.

'Oi·hana Lawaiʻa Kai Peke·lala *kik* National Marine Fisheries Service. *Lit.,* federal sea-fishing bureau.

'oi·hana lawe·lawe *kik* Service industry.

'Oi·hana Mahi ʻAi o ka Moku·ʻāina *kik* State Department of Agriculture. *Lit.,* agricultural department of the state.

'oi·hana moku *kik* Navy. *Dic.* Also *pūʻali kaua moana, ʻau moku kaua.*

'Oi·hana Pāka Au·puni *kik* National Park Service. *Lit.,* national park department.

'oi·hana ani·lā *kik* Weather service.

'ō·iho·iho *ʻa* Waxy, as in texture. Comb. *ʻō- + ihoiho.*

'ō·iwi *ʻa* Indigenous, native. *Dic., ext. mng.* Cf. *ʻāpaʻakuma. Lau nahele ʻōiwi.* Natural vegetation. *Manu ʻōiwi.* Native bird. *Meakanu ʻōiwi.* Indigenous plant.

'oi·'ene·hana *kik* Industry, especially that with a highly technological structure of production or service; industrialized; developed, as a First World Country. *He ʻāina ʻoiʻenehana ʻo Kelemānia; ʻo ka hana kaʻa kekahi o nā ʻoiʻenehana o laila.* Germany is an industrialized country; car manufacturing is one of its businesses. Sh. *hōʻoi + ʻenehana.* Cf. *hōʻoiʻenehana.* See entries below and *ʻenehana. ʻĀina ʻoiʻenehana.* Developed country; First World Country.

'oi·'ene·hana kā·pili *kik* Manufacturing industry. Sh. *ʻoiʻenehana + hana kāpili.* Also *ʻoihana kāpili.*

'oi·'ene·hana kū·kulu *kik* Construction industry. *Inā emi ka nui o nā pāhana kūkulu, a laila, ʻike ʻia ka ʻalu nui ma ka ʻoiʻenehana kūkulu.* If there are not many construction projects going on, the construction industry falls into a real slump.

'oi·'oi See *papa ʻoiʻoi.*

'ō·ula·ula *kik* Plankton. Redup. of *koura (Eastern Polynesian,* shrimp).

'oulu *kik* Culture, as bacteria grown in a prepared nutrient. *Dic., ext. mng. ʻOulu one.* Sand culture. *ʻOulu māhuaola.* Nutrient culture.

'Ohaio *iʻoa* Ohio; Ohioan. *Dic.*

'ō·hā kai *Pīʻoe ʻōhā kai.* Gooseneck barnacle. See *pīʻoe.*

'ohana kā·lai·mea·ola *kik* Biological family. *Lit.,* biology family.

'ohana 'ā·lani *kik* Citrus. *Lit.,* orange family.

'ohana sila *kik* Pinniped, i.e. any of the suborder of aquatic mammals including the seal and walrus. *Lit.,* seal family.

'ō·ha'i *kik* Ore. *Tah.* *'ōfa'i* (stone).

'ō hā·'ule hua *kik* Ovipositor. *Lit.,* piercing instrument (for) laying eggs.

'ohe See entries below and *mau'u 'ohe*.

'ohe ho'o·nui 'ike *kik* Microscope. *Lit.,* tube (for) enlarging sight. See *aniani kaupane'e, paepae aniani kaupane'e*.

'ohe·kani puluka *kik* Flute. Comb. *dic. (sp. var.)* + *dic.* Also *puluka*.

'ohe kī·wī *kik* Cathode-ray tube (CRT). *Lit.,* TV tube. See *'ūholo uila 'ine*.

'ohe·nā·nā *kik* Telescope. *Dic., sp. var. Pa'a 'ohenānā*. Binoculars.

'ohi *ham* To collect, as fingerprints at the scene of a crime. *Dic. 'Ohi i ka meheu manamana lima (māka manamana lima, ki'i manamana lima)*. To collect fingerprints. Cf. *kāpala*. See entries below and *hano 'ohi*.

'ohi hiki *ham* COD, cash on delivery. *Lit.,* collect (on) arrival.

'ohi kā·lā *Mīkini 'ohi kālā*. Cash register. *Lit.,* machine (for) collecting money. *Mea 'ohi kālā*. Cashier. Also *kanaka 'ohi kālā, wahine 'ohi kālā*.

'ō·hiki kauka niho *kik* Dentist's pick, probe. See *wili niho*.

'ohina *kik* Fact family, as in math. *Lit.,* gathering selection.

'ō ho'o·kani *kik* Tuning fork (preceded by *ke*). *Lit.,* musical fork. Also *hao ho'okani*.

'ō·hua *kik* Extra, i.e. one hired for crowd scenes in movie or video production. *Dic., ext. mng.* See *pepeke 'ōhua*.

'ō·hui *kik* Batch, as of cookies or recruits. Comb. *'ō-* + *hui*.

'ō·huka *'a'* Feral but formerly domesticated, as feral goats. Comb. *'ō-* + *mahuka*. See *'āhiu*.

'Ok. Abbreviation for *'Okakopa* (October).

'oka See *palapala 'oka, palapala 'oka kū'ai, pepa papa 'oka, pila 'oka kālā, 'oka pākahikahi*.

'Oka·kopa *i'oa* October. *Dic.* Abb. *'Ok.*

'ō·kala *kik* Sea anemone. *Dic.* Also *'ōkole*.

'Okala·homa *i'oa* Oklahoma; Oklahoman. *Dic.*

'oka·mila *kik* Oatmeal. *Eng. Ulahi 'okamila*. Oatmeal flake.

'okana See *pānini 'okana*.

'oka pā·kahi·kahi *ham* À la carte, as on a menu. *Ni'ihau*. Also *ma ka 'ikamu*.

'oka·tene *kik* Octane. *Eng.*

'ō·keni *kik* Coin. *Dic., ext. mng.* See *pepa kālā*.

'okesa·ili·hate *Kalipuna 'okesailihate*. Calcium oxilate.

'okesa·side *kik* Oxide. *Eng. Kupuriku 'okesaside*. Cupric oxide. *Feriku 'okesaside*. Ferric oxide. *Ferousa 'okesaside*. Ferrous oxide. *Ferosoferiku 'okesaside*. Ferrosoferric oxide.

'oki *ham* To cut, mow. *Dic.* See entries below. *'Oki i ka mau'u*. To mow the lawn. Also *'oki i ka mahiki*.

'oki *ham* To stop or break, as an electric circuit. *Dic., ext. mng.* See *ho'oku'i*.

'oki *ham* To record, as on a cassette. *Ni'ihau*. Also *ho'opa'a*.

'okia *'a'* Cutaway. *Dic., ext. mng. 'Ukulele 'okia*. Cutaway 'ukulele.

'oki hapa·lua *ham* To bisect, in math. *Lit.,* cut in half. Abb. *'o2*. See *kaha 'oki hapalua*.

'oki·kaha *ham* To slice off. Comb. *'oki* + *kaha*.

'oki·kene *kik* Oxygen. *Dic.*

'oki·kene kolu *kik* Ozone. *Lit.*, triple oxygen. See *lole ana 'okikene kolu.*

'oki pā·hi'a *ham* To cut diagonally. *Dic.* Also *'oki ma ka pāhi'a.*

'oki pō·kole *kik/heh* Shortcut; to take a shortcut. *Calque from Eng. idiom.*

'ō·kole *kik* Sea anemone. *Dic.* Also *'ōkala.*

'oko'a *Ho'omaha 'oko'a.* Whole rest, in music. *Hua mele 'oko'a.* Whole note, in music.

'Oko·soka *i'oa* Okhostk. *Eng. Ke kai 'o 'Okosoka.* Sea of Okhostk.

'oko·tio See *pānini 'okotio.*

'ō·kuene *kik* Layout, as of a computer keyboard. *Comb.* '*ō- + kuene.* Cf. *ka'akuene.* *'Ōkuene papa pihi.* Keyboard layout.

'ō·kuhi *kik* Directions. *Sh. 'ōlelo + kuhikuhi.* *Kōmi 'ōkuhi.* Script, i.e. a set of computer codes programmed to run consecutively in a computer system. *Haku kōmi 'ōkuhi.* To write a (computer) script; scripting.

'ō·ku'e·ku'e *Pī'oe 'ōku'eku'e.* Acorn barnacle. See *pī'oe.*

'ō·lala See *'aila 'ōlala.*

'ō·lali *kik* Glide, in linguistics. *Dic., ext. mng.*

'ō·lapa *heh* Lift-off, as of a rocket or missile; to blast off. *Dic., ext. mng.* Cf. *ho'ōlapa.* See *helu 'ōlapa.*

'ō·lapa haole *kik* Aspen. *Lit.,* foreign *'ōlapa.*

'ōlē *kik* Horn, as on a car or bicycle. *Mān.* Also *'ōlea.*

'ō·lea *kik* Horn, as on a car or bicycle. *Ni'ihau.* Also *'ōlē. Mān.*

'ole Kele·wine Absolute zero, i.e. a hypothetical temperature characterized by complete absence of heat; 0 degrees K (Kelvin). *Lit.,* zero Kelvin.

'Ole·kona *i'oa* Oregon; Oregonian. *Dic.* Also *'Oregona.*

'ō·lelo *kik* Language; statement. *Dic.* See entries below. *A'o kahua 'ōlelo.* Language-based learning. *Makakau 'ōlelo.* Language awareness. *'Ōlelo ala nu'ukia.* Mission statement. *'Ōlelo nu'ukia.* Vision statement.

'ō·lelo ha'i mua *kik* Foreword, preface, as in a book. *Dic.* Also *'ōlelo mua.* Cf. *'ōlelo ho'ākāka.*

'ō·lelo ho'ā·kāka *kik* Introduction, as in a book. *Lit.,* word (of) explanation. Cf. *'ōlelo ha'i mua, 'ōlelo mua.*

'ō·lelo hō·'ike *kik* Oral report. Also *hō'ike ha'i waha.*

'ō·lelo ho'o·hani *kik* Hint. *Comb. 'ōlelo + ho'ohani.* See *ho'ohani.*

'ō·lelo ho'ōho *ham* Exclamatory statement; to make such a statement. *Dic., ext. mng.*

'ō·lelo·kona *kik* Talkathon. *Comb. 'ōlelo + Eng.*

'ō·lelo kuhi lima *kik* Sign language. *Lit.,* hand-gesture language. See *kuhi lima.*

'ō·lelo mua *kik* Preamble. *Trad.* Foreword, preface, as in a book. *Dic.* Also *'ōlelo ha'i mua.* Cf. *'ōlelo ho'ākāka.*

'ō·lepe *kik* Impatiens. *Dic.* See *pukaaniani 'ōlepe, puke 'ōlepe.*

'ō·lepe·lepe See *pale pukaaniani 'ōlepelepe, pukaaniani 'ōlepe.*

'ō·lewa *'a* Flexible, as a policy. *Penei ke kulekele, akā na'e, he 'ōlewa nō i ka wā kūpono.* This is the policy, but it can be flexible when appropriate. *Dic., ext. mng.*

'oli·ō See *manu 'oliō.*

'oli·liko *kik* Ostracod, a tiny crustacean having a shrimplike body enclosed in a hinged bivalve shell. *Lit.,* shimmering.

'olili·'ula *kik* Aurora borealis, northern lights. *Lit.,* ghostly shimmering.

'olo *kik* Bob, as of a pendulum. *Dic., ext. mng.*

'olo·ka'a See *paukū 'oloka'a.*

'olo·kele *kik* Swamp. *Dic.* See *ālia-lia, nāele.*

'olo·ke'a *kik* Outline, as a summary using letters and numbers in headings to indicate topics and subtopics. NOTE: Only vowels with subscript numbers used as letters in outlining: A, E, I, O, U, A_1, E_1, I_1, O_1, U_1, A_2, E_2.... Pronounced: *'ā (ma'aka) kahi, 'ā (ma'aka) lua.... Dic., new mng.* See entry below and *hō'oloke'a. 'Oloke'a palapala.* Document outline, as in a computer program.

'olo·ke'a koina papa *kik* Syllabus, as for a college course. *Lit.,* outline (of) class requirements. Cf. *mo'oha'awina.*

'olo·laha *kik* Oval. *Ni'ihau.* Also *pō'ai lō'ihi. 'Ololaha analahi.* Ellipse.

'olume·pika *kik* Olympics; olympic. *Eng. Nā Pā'ani 'Olumepika Ho'oilo.* Winter Olympic Games.

'Olume·pika *i'oa* Olympus. *Eng. Mauna 'Olumepika.* Mount Olympus; Olympus Mons, a volcano on Mars.

'oma *Pā 'oma.* Baking pan (preceded by *ke*).

'ō·mā *kik* Maine lobster. (French *homard.*)

'ō·maka hua kanu *kik* Bulb tip. *Lit.,* bulb budding. See *hua kanu.*

'ō·maka kau pe'a *kik* Universal fitting, for putting pipes together. *Ni'ihau.* Cf. *'ōmaka T.*

'ō maka kolu *kik* Trident (preceded by *ke*). *Lit.,* three-pointed spear.

'ō·maka T *kik* T-fitting, for putting pipes together. *Ni'ihau.* Cf. *'ōmaka kau pe'a.*

'oma kō·'ala *kik* Broiler oven. *Lit.,* oven (for) broiling.

'Omana *i'oa* Oman; Omani. *Eng.*

'oma·wawe *kik* Microwave oven. *Lit.,* fast oven.

'ō·ma'o·haku *kik* Olivine. Comb. *'ōma'o + haku.*

'ome *kik* Ohm, a unit of resistance in electricity. *Eng.* Cf. *anakahi uila. Ana 'ome.* Ohmmeter.

'omo·hau *kik* Icecap. *Lit.,* ice cover.

'ō·mole iho uila *kik* Battery jar, i.e. a large cylindrical container of heavy glass with an open top as used in laboratories. *Lit.,* electric battery jar.

'ō·mole omo wai·ū *kik* Baby bottle. *Lit.,* bottle (for) sucking milk. Also *'ōmole waiū.*

'ō·mole ho'o·kulu *kik* Dropping bottle, i.e. a bottle used much like an eyedropper. *Lit.,* bottle (used to) cause drops.

'ō·mole kā·lani *kik* Gallon jar, gallon jug.

'ō·mole·li'i *kik* Vial. *Lit.,* small bottle.

'ō·mole mā·lama 'elala *kik* Insect holding jar. *Lit.,* jar (for) keeping insects. Cf. *'ōmole pepehi 'elala.*

'ō·mole pepehi 'elala *kik* Insect killing jar. *Lit.,* jar (for) killing insects. Cf. *'ōmole mālama 'elala.*

'ō·mole 'apo huna·huna *kik* Dustfall jar, as for scientific experiments. *Lit.,* jar (for) catching particles.

'ō·mo'o noho *kik* Bleachers. *Lit.,* ridge (of) seats.

'ōnae·ao *kik* Universe, as a scientific term only. Sh. *'ōnaehana + ao.*

'ō·nae·hana *kik* System. Comb. *'ō- + nae + hana.* See entries below.

'ō·nae·hana ola·kino kaia·ulu *kik* Community-based health system. *Lit.,* community health system.

'ō·nae·hana hanu *kik* Respiratory system. *Lit.,* respiration system.

'ō·nae·hana hō·mona *kik* Endocrine system, in biology. *Lit.,* hormone system.

'ō·nae·hana ho'o·hehe'e mea·'ai *kik* Digestive system.

'ō·nae·hana ho'o·hua *kik* Reproductive system, in biology.

ʻō·nae·hana hoʻo·kau·apono *kik* Balancing mechanism, in biology. *Lit.,* system (for) compensating.

ʻŌ·nae·hana Hoʻo·malu ʻĀina Kū·lohe·ohe *kik* Natural Areas Reserves System (NARS). *Lit.,* system (for) protecting natural land. Cf. *ʻāina hoʻomalu ao kūlohelohe.*

ʻō·nae·hana hoʻo·nā ʻāina *kik* Land registration system. *Lit.,* system (for) settling land claims.

ʻō·nae·hana kauka no ka lapa·ʻau like ʻana *kik* Coordinated physician referral system. *Lit.,* doctors' system for treating medicinally together.

ʻō·nae·hana keki·mala *kik* Decimal system, in math. See *kekimala.*

ʻō·nae·hana lō·kino *kik* Organ system, in biology.

ʻō·nae·hana lolo·kū *kik* Nervous system.

ʻō·nae·hana mā·kala *kik* Muscular system, in biology. *Lit.,* muscle system.

ʻō·nae·hana māno·wai *kik* Cardio-vascular system, circulatory system. Also *ʻōnaehana mānowai koko.*

ʻō·nae·hana mī·kā emi *kik* Low-pressure system, in meteorology. *Pā ka ʻōnaehana mīkā emi ma ke komohana ʻākau o Hawaiʻi.* Low pressure systems develop northwest of Hawaiʻi. *Lit.,* waning pressure system. Cf. *ʻōnaehana mīkā piʻi.*

ʻō·nae·hana mī·kā piʻi *kik* High-pressure system, in meteorology. *Lit.,* ascending pressure system. Cf. *ʻōnaehana mīkā emi.*

ʻō·nae·hana pale ʻea *kik* Immune system, as in mammals. *Lit.,* system (to) ward off infectious diseases.

ʻō·nae·hana pū·nae·wele *kik* Network system, as in a computer system.

ʻō·nae·hana ʻili *kik* Integumentary system, in biology. *Lit.,* skin system.

ʻoneki *kik* Desktop, in a computer program. *Dic., ext. mng.* See entries below.

ʻoneki hana *kik* Payload bay, i.e. the part of a spacecraft where scientific instruments and passengers are carried. *Lit.,* work deck.

ʻoneki pai·laka *kik* Flight deck, as on a spaceship. *Lit.,* pilot deck.

ʻoni a ka moku "Rock the boat," a jump rope game of jumping and bouncing a ball at the same time. *Mān.* See *luʻu nalu poʻi.*

ʻoni·lele *kik* Aerobics. *Lit.,* jumping movements. See *hoʻoikaika puʻuwai.*

ʻonina *kik* Move, as in a sports play; movement, as of body parts. *ʻIke aku nei ʻoe i kēlā ʻonina? Hō ka maʻe!* Did you see that move? Wow, that was sweet! *Comb. ʻoni + -na. Pōʻai ʻonina kino.* Psycho-motor domain, as relating to the learning process.

ʻoni·pā *ʻa* Thigmotactic. *Lit.,* move (when) touched.

ʻono *A ʻalonoa ʻono.* Taste receptor.

ʻŌ·nohi ʻUla Kū·ā·hewa *iʻoa* Giant Red Spot, a huge gaseous feature on Jupiter. *Lit.,* vast red eyeball.

ʻō·pā *kik* Rowboat, skiff. Niʻihau var. of *waʻapā.*

ʻō·pae Pā·kē *kik* Crayfish. *Mān.*

ʻō·pae Pola·pola *kik* Tahitian prawn. *Lit.,* Tahitian shrimp.

ʻō·pao *kik* Cellar. *Comb. ʻō- + pao* (somewhat cavernous).

ʻō·paka *kik* Prism. *Dic. ʻŌpaka huinahā lōʻihi.* Rectangular prism.

ʻopa·kuma *kik* Opossum. *Eng. ʻOpakuma ʻAmelika ʻĀkau.* North American opossum.

ʻō·paʻa *kik* Set, in math; also as of golf clubs or silverware. *Comb. ʻō- + paʻa.* Cf. *huikaina.* See entry below.

ʻō·paʻa hopena *kik* Sample space, i.e. the set of all possible outcomes of an experiment, in math. *Lit.,* outcome set.

'ō·pa'u *kik* Carbon, not in chemistry. Comb. *'ō-* + *pa'u*. Cf. *kalapona*. *Pepa 'ōpa'u*. Carbon paper.

'ope *kik* Pack, for items other than drinks, as gum, baseball cards, or cigarettes. *Dic., ext. mng.* See *pahu, pū'olo, 'eke'eke*. *'Ope hā*. Four-pack. *'Ope ono*. Six-pack.

'opi *kik* Crease, as on a pair of pants. *Dic.* Also *haki*. See entry below.

'opi *ham* To compress or collapse, as a file in a computer program. *E 'opi i ka waihona i hiki ke loa'a ma ke pā malule*. Compress the file so that it can be put onto the floppy disk. *E 'opi i ka papa kuhikuhi a i ke kū'ono 'ākau o lalo*. Collapse the menu to the lower right-hand corner. *Dic., ext. mng.* Cf. *ho'omahola*. See *'opihia*.

'ō·pio *Pae 'ōpio*. Junior varsity, as a league of sports at school.

'ō·pio·pio *Lawehala 'ōpiopio*. Juvenile delinquency.

'opi·hia *'a'* Compressed or collapsed, as a file in a computer program. *Pehea 'oe e wehe ai i ka waihona 'opihia?* How do you open a compressed file? Comb. *'opi* + *-hia*. See *'opi, ho'omahola*. *Waihona 'opihia*. Compressed file, collapsed file.

'ō·piki·piki *kik/'a'* Anxiety. *Nui ka 'ōpikipiki o ku'u mana'o i ka no'ono'o i ka holo 'ana i luna o ke kai a mamao loa*. My mind was filled with anxiety when thinking about the long trip over the sea. *Dic.*

'ō·pili *heh* To close up tight, as a flower bud. *Dic.*

'ō·pū *kik* Body, as of an 'ukulele, guitar, etc. *Ni'ihau*. See *'ukulele*. *Mākala 'ōpū*. Abdominal muscle.

'ō·pū *kik* Ventricle, of the mammalian heart. *Trad.* Also *'ōpū pu'uwai*. See entries below.

'ō·pua *Ao 'ōpua*. Cumulus cloud. Comb. *ao* + *dic*.

'ō·pū hema *kik* Left ventricle, of the mammalian heart. Also *'ōpū pu'uwai hema*.

'ō·pū pu'u·wai *kik* Ventricle, of the mammalian heart. *Trad.* Also *'ōpū*. See *ke'ena*. *'Ōpū pu'uwai hema*. Left ventricle. *'Ōpū pu'uwai 'ākau*. Right ventricle.

'ō·pū 'ā·kau *kik* Right ventricle, of the mammalian heart. Also *'ōpū pu'uwai 'ākau*.

'ō·pu'u *kik* Bulb. *Ni'ihau*. See *'ōpu'uahi*. *Ana kawaūea 'ōpu'u pulu a malo'o*. Wet-and-dry-bulb hygrometer. *'Ōpu'u kukui*. Light bulb.

'ō·pu'u *kik* Geometric cone. *Dic.*

'ō·pu'u·ahi *kik* Spark plug. *Ni'ihau*.

'ō·pu'u·hame *kik* Clove, the spice. Comb. *'ōpu'u* + *hame*.

'owaka·waka *kik* Reflector. *Dic., ext. mng.* Also *kukui 'owakawaka*.

'ō·wī *ham* To peer, i.e. look narrowly or searchingly at something. *Ni'ihau*. Also *ki'ei*.

'ō·wili *kik* Roll, as of film. *Ni'ihau*. *'Ōwili ki'i*. Roll of film. *'Ōwili ki'iaka*. Filmstrip.

'o'a *kik* Green onion with a purple bulb becoming white close to the tip. *Mān. (RNM).* Cf. *lina*.

'ō·'ā *'a'* Mixed, combined, in math and science. *Dic., ext. mng. Helu 'ō'ā*. Mixed number. *Kekimala 'ō'ā*. Mixed decimal. *Mekala 'ō'ā*. Alloy. Also *metala 'ō'ā*. *'Ō'ā kemikala 'ia*. Chemically combined.

'ō·'aki *kik* Geometrid moth. *Ua maopopo 'ia ka po'ii'a 'ana o ka piohē a ka 'ō'aki i ka luapo'i ola*. Larvae of the geometrid moth has been known to catch active prey. *Sh. 'ōka'i* + *'aki* / metathesis of *'ōka'i*.

'o'e *ham* To skim, as oil from the top of stew. *Mān.* Also *kī'o'e*.

'ō 'eli *kik* Spading fork (preceded by *ke*). *Lit.,* fork (for) digging.

'o'eno *kik* Twill plaiting. *Dic.* Also *maka pūalu.*

'ō·'ili See *papa 'ō'ili.*

'o'opu Pā·kē *kik* Catfish. *Mān.*

'ō·'ū *ham* To abort, as in a computer program. *Ua 'ō'ū 'ia ka ho'one'e waihona 'ana.* The file transfer was aborted. *Dic., ext. mng.*

'ora·gano·poso·pahate *kik* Organophosphate. *Eng.*

'Ore·gona *i'oa* Oregon; Oregonian. *Eng.* Also *'Olekona.*

'ota *kik* Otter. *Eng.*

'ū- A prefix indicating the instrument or cause of a particular action. *Dic., ext. mng.* See *'ūomo, 'ūhehe'e, 'ūhili, 'ūholo uila, 'ūhōlo'a,* etc.

'uao *kik/ham* Referee, umpire; to referee. *Dic.* Also *'uao ha'uki.* See entry below and *kanaka maka'ala 'upena.*

'uao *ham* To arbitrate. *Ma kekahi mau 'ano hihia o kekahi hui me nā po'e limahana, na kekahi luna ho'okolokolo e 'uao.* In some disputes between a company and the employees, a judge will arbitrate. *Dic. Ka 'uao 'ana.* Arbitration.

'uala *Mākala 'uala.* Biceps, i.e. the muscle of the front of the upper arm.

'uala kahiki See entries below. *Kipi uala kahiki.* Potato chip.

'uala kahiki koli·koli *kik* Hash-brown potatoes. *Lit.,* whittled potato. Also *'uala kolikoli.*

'uala kahiki pepei·ao *kik* Scalloped potatoes. *Lit.,* potatoes (like) scallops. Also *'uala pepeiao.*

'uala koli·koli See *'uala kahiki kolikoli.*

'uala pepei·ao See *'uala kahiki pepeiao.*

'uiki uila *kik* Fuse. *Lit.,* electric fuse. *Pahu 'uiki uila.* Fuse box.

'uiki 'ā *kik* Filament, as in a light bulb. *Lit.,* wick (for) lighting. *Kukui 'uiki 'ā.* Incandescent light.

'ui·'uiki See *nalo 'ui'uiki.*

'ū·omo *kik* Sorbent, an absorbent material such as used in chromatography. Comb. *'ū- + omo.* See *omo.*

'ū·omo ikehu lā *kik* Solar panel. *Lit.,* instrument (for) sucking solar energy.

'ū·hā See *mākala ka'akepa 'ūhā, mākala 'ūhā.*

'ū·hā moa *kik* Chicken thigh. See *pālaumoa.*

'uhane *A'o kahua 'uhane.* Spiritually-based learning.

'ū·hehe'e *kik* Solvent. Comb. *'ū- + hehe'e.* See *mea hehe'e. 'Ūhehe'e wai.* Aqueous, i.e. having water as a solvent, in science. *Mā'ō'āna 'ūhehe'e wai.* Aqueous solution.

'ū·hili *kik* Bat, club, racket. Comb. *'ū- + hili. 'Ūhili kolepa.* Golf club.

'ū·hini *kik* Grasshopper. *Dic.*

'ū·hini·hone *Pāpapa 'ūhinihone.* Honey locust bean.

'ū·hini nēnē *kik* Cricket. *Lit.,* chirping cricket. *'Ūhini nēnē kahakai.* Beach cricket. *'Ūhini nēnē pele.* Lava cricket.

'ū·hini·pule *kik* Praying mantis. *Lit.,* praying grasshopper.

'ū·holo uila *kik* Electrode. *Lit.,* instrument (for) conducting electricity. *'Ūholo uila 'āne.* Anode, i.e. the positive electrode in an electrical circuit. *'Ūholo uila 'ine.* Cathode, i.e. the negative electrode in an electric circuit.

'ū·hō·lo'a *kik* Dispenser, i.e. a dispensing container of any kind. Comb. *'ū- + hōlo'a.* See entries below and *hōlo'a. 'Ūhōlo'a kāwele pepa.* Paper towel dispenser. *'Ūhōlo'a kopa.* Soap dispenser.

'ū·hō·lo'a kaka·lina *kik* Carburetor, as in an internal-combustion engine. *Lit.,* gasoline dispenser.

'ū·hō·lo'a mā·'ō·'āna *kik* Buret, i.e. a precision-made piece of glassware used to measure and deliver accurate volumes of solutions, in science. *Lit.,* solution dispenser.

'ū·hū *kik* Enzyme. Comb. *'ū- + hū.*

'ū·kaomi hano kui *kik* Syringe plunger. Comb. *'ū- + kaomi + hano kui.* Also *'ūkaomi, 'ūkōmi, 'ūkōmi hano kui.* Cf. *pāuma.*

'ū·kake uila *kik* Commutator, i.e. a switch on a motor running on direct current that causes the current to reverse every half turn. *Lit.,* instrument (for) slipping electricity back and forth.

'ukē *heh* To swing, as a pendulum. *Dic.* See *ule'o.* *Wā 'ukē.* Period of a pendulum.

'ū·kele *kik* Mud. *Dic.* Also *lepo pohō.*

'Uke·lena *i'oa* Ukraine. *Eng.*

'ū·kōmi See *'ūkaomi hano kui.*

'uku·lele *kik* 'Ukulele. *Dic.* See entries below. For parts, see *kaula, nī'au, nī'au li'ili'i, nī'au nui, papa kī, wā, 'au, 'ōpū.*

'uku·lele Ohta-san *kik* Ohta-san 'ukulele.

'uku·lele hā·'oi *kik* Baritone 'ukulele. See *hā'oi.*

'uku·lele leo 'ekahi *kik* Soprano 'ukulele. See *leo 'ekahi.*

'uku·lele leo 'ekolu *kik* Tenor 'ukulele. See *leo 'ekolu.*

'uku·lele Lili'u *kik* Lili'u 'ukulele.

'uku·lele pahu kī·kā *kik* Cigar-box 'ukulele.

'uku·lele pū·niu *kik* Coconut shell 'ukulele.

'uku·lele 'ea honu *kik* Turtle shell 'ukulele.

'uku·lele 'elua puka *kik* Double-hole 'ukulele. *Lit.,* 'ukulele (with) two holes.

'uku·lele 'ewalu kaula *kik* Eight-string 'ukulele.

'uku·lele 'okia *kik* Cutaway 'ukulele. See *'okia.*

'uku wai *kik* Daphnia. *Lit.,* water flea.

'ula *Ke Kai 'Ula.* Red Sea.

'ū·lau *kik* Spatula, pancake turner. Comb. *'ū- + lau* (flat instrument). See *ali 'ūlau.* *'Ūlau kahi.* Rubber spatula.

'ula·kai·ano *kik* Anthocyanin, i.e. a kind of pigment producing blue to red coloring in flowers and plants. Comb. *'ula + kyanos* (*Greek,* blue).

'ulā·li'i *kik* Measles. *Dic.*

'ula mā·ku'e 'a' Magenta. *Dic., ext. mng.*

'ula·'ula *Manu 'ula'ula.* Cardinal. Also *manu māka'i.*

'ulea *kik* Urea. *Eng.*

'ulī·keke *kik* Baby rattle. Sh. *'ulī'ulī + nakeke.* *Lina 'ulīkeke.* Tambourine.

'ū·lili *kik* Whistle, as a referee's. *Dic.*

'ū·lili *kik* Railing support, balluster. *Dic.* Also *hūlili.* Cf. *paehumu.*

'ū·lou *kik* Bonding instrument. Comb. *'ū- + lou.*

'ulu *Mākala 'ulu.* Gastrocnemius or calf muscle of the anterior of the lower leg.

'ū·lū *ham* To pack, as a suitcase. *Wilcox:* u-lu.

'Ulu·kuae *i'oa* Uruguay; Uruguayan. *Eng.* Also *'Uruguae.*

'ū·mau·pa'a *kik* Component, constituent. Comb. *'ū- + maupa'a.*

'ume *kik* Drawer. *Dic., ext. mng.* See *pahu 'ume.*

'ume *kik* Fermata, i.e. the symbol placed over a note, chord, or rest indicating the extension of duration longer than the indicated time value, in music. *Dic.*

'ume·kau·maha *kik* Gravity. *Dic.* *Mīkini ho'opau 'umekaumaha.* Anti-gravity machine. *Piko 'umekaumaha.* Center of gravity. *'Umekaumaha māiki.* Microgravity. *'Umekaumaha 'ole.* Zero gravity.

'ume·lau·oho *kik* Capillary. Comb. 'ume + lauoho. *Paipuli'i 'umelauoho.* Capillary pipette. *Wai 'umelauoho.* Capillary water.

'ume mā·kē·neki *kik* Magnetism. *Lit.,* magnet attraction.

'ume niniu *ham* Centripetal, i.e. acting in a direction toward a center. *Lit.,* spinning attraction. Cf. *lele niniu. Manehu 'ume niniu.* Centripetal force.

'umi See entries below and *hapa 'umi.*

'umi *ham* To pressure, in basketball. *'Umi nui 'ia 'o Karl Malone e 'ekolu mea kūpale i nā minuke hope loa o ka ho'okūkū.* Karl Malone usually gets pressured by three defenders in the last few minutes of the game. *Dic., ext. mng.*

'umi·ā·pau *kik* Damping-off, i.e. a diseased condition of seedlings or cuttings caused by fungi and characterized by wilting or rotting. Comb. *'umi + ā + pau.*

'umi kapu·a'i See *laina 'umi kapua'i, 'a'ena 'umi kapua'i.*

'ū·mi'i *ham* To give a severe electric shock. *'O ka noho 'ūmi'i kekahi 'ano o ka ho'opa'i kū i ka make.* The electric chair is one form of capital punishment. *Mān.* Cf. *miki, omo.* See entries below.

'ū·mi'i *ham* To staple. *Ni'ihau.* See *kui 'ūmi'i pepa, mea 'ūmi'i pepa, mea wehe 'ūmi'i, papa 'ūmi'i, pihi 'ūmi'i.*

'ū·mi'i *ham* Clamp. *Dic. 'Ūmi'i hano ho'okolohua.* Test tube clamp. *'Ūmi'i ho'opa'a.* Utility clamp. Cf. *'ūpā ho'opa'a. 'Ūmi'i pani.* Pinch clamp.

'ū·mi'i kaula *kik* Capo, as used on a fretted instrument to raise the pitch of all strings. *Lit.,* string clamp.

'ū·mi'i·lau *kik* Planthopper (Oliarus tamehameha). Comb. *'ūmi'i + lau.* Cf. *'ūmi'ikō* (dic.).

'ū·mi'i lau·oho *ham* Bobby pin. *Ni'ihau.*

'ū·mi'i·nalo *kik* Venus flytrap. Comb. *'ūmi'i + nalo.*

'ū·mi'i 'ili·kuapo *ham* Belt buckle. Also *'ūmi'i.*

'umi·'umi See *pakuhi pahu me ka 'umi'umi.*

'umi·'umi lehe·lehe *kik* Moustache. *Lit.,* lip beard. Cf. *'umi'umi 'auae.*

'umi·'umi 'au·ae *kik* Beard, excluding the moustache. Usu. *'umi'umi. Lit.,* chin beard. Cf. *'umi'umi lehelehe.*

'ū·mō·'aui *kik* Reactant, reagent. Comb. *'ū- + mō'aui.* See *mō'aui.*

'ū·mō·'aui·wawe *kik* Catalyst, i.e. a substance which increases the rate of a chemical reaction without being permanently changed itself. Comb. *'ūmō'aui + wawe.* Also *hō'eleu mō'aui.*

'uni·ona *kik* Union. *Dic., sp. var. Kūka'i 'aelike 'uniona.* Collective bargaining.

'ū·niu *heh* To pivot. Sh. *'ū- + 'ōniu.* See *kū 'ūniu.*

'ū·nina *kik* Gelatin. Var. of *'ūlina,* ext. mng. Cf. *palaholo.*

'unu *'a'* Sprained. *Mān.*

'unu·'unu *ham* To overlap, as shingles on a roof. *Dic., ext. mng.* Cf. *piliwai.*

'ū·pā *Mākala 'ūpā.* Masseter muscle, i.e. the muscle that closes the jaw.

'ū·pā ho·'o·pa'a *kik* Forceps. *Lit.,* tongs (that) hold fast. Cf. *'ūmi'i ho'opa'a.*

'ū·pā kā·pō·'ai *kik* Compass, an instrument for describing circles or transferring measurements, in math. Comb. *'ūpā + -kāpō'ai.* Cf. *pānānā.*

'ū·palu *'a'* Mild, as a solution. *E ho'omākaukau i kekahi mā'ō'āna kopa 'ūpalu.* Prepare a mild solution of soap. *Dic.* See *'akika 'ūpalu kūlohelohe.*

'upena *kik* Net, as of a basket on a basketball court or a volleyball net. *He 'upena wale iho nō.* Nothing but net. *Dic., ext. mng. Ua 'upena ke kinopōpō.* Net ball, in volleyball. *Ni'ihau.* Also

ua 'upena. *Kanaka maka'ala 'upena.*
Referee, in volleyball. See *'uao.* *'A'ena
'upena.* Net violation. *'Upena
pōpa'ipa'i.* Volleyball net.

'upena 'elala *kik* Insect net. See
entries below.

'upena 'elala ho'o·lewa·lewa *kik*
Insect fixed net, as hung in a wind corridor to catch insects. *Lit.,* hung insect net.

'upena 'elala kā·'e'e *kik* Insect sweep
net. *Lit., kā'e'e*-style net (for) insects.

'upena 'elala 'eke *kik* Insect bag net,
as for collecting insects from a small
bush. *Lit.,* bag insect net.

'ū·pī·hu'a *kik* Styrofoam. *Lit.,* foam
sponge. Also *panua.*

'ū·piki *ham* Trap, in basketball; to
make such a play. *Dic., ext. mng.*

'ū·piki lima *kik* Handcuffs. *Dic.*

'ū·pī·lā·'au *kik* Cork, the material or
the tree. *Lit.,* wooden sponge.

'ū·pī·'ū *'a* Spongy, as leaves of the
pānini. Comb. *'ūpī* + *'ū-.*

'ū·poho *kik* Bagpipe. *Dic.* Also *pila
'ūpoho.*

'ū·po'i *ham* To dunk (the ball), in
basketball. *Dic., ext. mng.* Also *pakā.* Cf.
pākī.

'ū·'oki puni uila *kik* Circuit breaker,
i.e. a device which automatically
interrupts electric current before wires in
a circuit get too hot. *Lit.,* instrument
(which) breaks electric circuit.

'u'uku *Kāko'o hapa 'u'uku.*
Affirmative action. *'Ao'ao hapa 'u'uku.*
Minority party, in politics. *'Aha koi
pohō 'u'uku.* Small-claims court,
small-debts court.

'Ugana *i'oa* Uganda; Ugandan. *Eng.*

'Uru·guae *i'oa* Uruguay; Uruguayan.
Eng. Also *'Ulukuae.*

'Use·peki·kana *i'oa* Uzbekistan.
Eng.

'Ū·tā *i'oa* Utah; Utahan, Utahn. *Dic.,
sp. var.* Also *Mauna Pōhaku.*

B

Bahama *i'oa* Bahamas; Bahamian.
Dic. Also *Pahama.*

Baha·raina *i'oa* Bahrain. *Eng.*

Bala·tika *i'oa* Baltic. *Eng. Ke kai 'o
Balatika.* Baltic Sea.

bā·lē *kik* Ballet. *Eng.* Also *pālē,
hulahula pālē.*

Bale·neta *i'oa* Barents. *Eng. Ke kai
'o Baleneta.* Barents Sea.

Banada *i'oa* Banda. *Eng. Ke kai 'o
Banada.* Banda Sea.

Bana·gala·desa *i'oa* Bangladesh.
Eng.

Bara·zila *i'oa* Brazil; Brazilian. *Dic.*
Also *Palakila.*

bari·uma *kik* Barium. *Eng.*

Bela·rusa *i'oa* Belarus. *Eng.*

Bele·giuma *i'oa* Belgium; Belgian.
Dic. Also *Pelekiuma.*

Belize *i'oa* Belize; Belizean. *Eng.*

bene·zene *kik* Benzene. *Eng.*

Berina *i'oa* Bering. *Eng. Ke kai 'o
Berina.* Bering Sea.

beta *kik* Beta. *Eng. Huna beta.* Beta
particle, in chemistry.

bisula·fahate *kik* Bisulfate. *Eng.
Sodiuma bisulafahate.* Sodium bisulfate.

Boli·via *i'oa* Bolivia; Bolivian. *Eng.*

Bose·nia *i'oa* Bosnia. *Eng. Bosenia
me Hesegowina.* Bosnia and
Herzogovina.

Botu·ana *i'oa* Botswana. *Eng.*

Bulu·garia *i'oa* Bulgaria; Bulgarian.
Dic. Also *Pulukalia.*

Bura·kina Faso *i'oa* Burkina Faso.
Eng.

Buruma *i'oa* Burma; Burmese. *Eng.*
Also *Puruma.*

Buruni *i'oa* Burundi. *Eng.*

Butana *i'oa* Bhutan; Bhutanese. *Eng.*

butane *kik* Butane. *Eng.*

C

CD *kik* CD, compact disk (pronounced *sēdē*). *Eng.* Also *sēdē; pā CD, pā sēdē* (preceded by *ke*).

D

Dakota Hema *i'oa* South Dakota; South Dakotan. *Eng.* Also *Kakoka Hema.*

Dakota 'Ā·kau *i'oa* North Dakota; North Dakotan. *Eng.* Also *Kakoka 'Ākau.*

Dek. Abbreviation for *Dekemapa* (December). See *Kekemapa.*

Deke·mapa *i'oa* Var. of *Kekemapa* (December). *Abb. Dek.*

Dela·uea *i'oa* Delaware; Delawarean. *Dic., sp. var.* Also *Kelauea.*

Dene·maka *i'oa* Denmark; Dane; Danish. *Dic.* Also *Kenemaka.*

diazi·nona *kik* Diazinon. *Eng.*

dieli·dirina *kik* Dieldrin, a kind of insecticide. *Eng.* Cf. *'alidirina.* See *lā'au make.*

dio·kesa·side *kik* Dioxide. *Eng. Sulufura diokesaside.* Sulfur dioxide. *Naikokene diokesaside.* Nitrogen dioxide.

Dibuti *i'oa* Djibouti. *Eng.*

disuli·faside *kik* Disulfide. *Eng. Karabona disulifaside.* Carbon disulfide.

F

Faka·lana *Ka pae moku 'o Fakalana.* Falkland Islands, Falklands.

Falo *i'oa* Faroe. *Eng. Ka pae 'āina 'o Falo.* Faroe Islands.

Farani *i'oa* France; French. *Dic.* Also *Palani.* See *Palani.*

Faso *Burakina Faso.* Burkina Faso.

fea *kik* Fair. *Eng.* Also *hō'ike'ike.*

feriku 'okesa·side *kik* Ferric oxide.

fero·usa Ferrous. *Eng.* See entries below.

fero·usa kara·bona·hate *kik* Ferrous carbonate. *Eng.*

fero·usa 'okesa·side *kik* Ferrous oxide. *Eng.*

fero·usa sula·fahate *kik* Ferrous sulfate. *Eng.*

fero·usa sula·faside *kik* Ferrous sulfide. *Eng.*

fero·sofe·riku 'okesa·side *kik* Ferrosoferric oxide. *Eng.*

Fini·lana *i'oa* Finland; Finn; Finnish. *Dic.* Also *Finilani.*

Fini·lani *i'oa* Finland; Finn; Finnish. *Eng.* Also *Finilana.*

Folo·rida *i'oa* Florida; Floridan, Floridian. *Dic.* Also *Pololika.*

fori·miku Formic. *Eng. 'Akika forimiku.* Formic acid.

FM *kik* FM, frequency modulation (pronounced *fāmū*). *Eng.* Cf. *AM.*

G

galai·sine *kik* Glycine. *Eng.*

Gāna *i'oa* Ghana; Ghanaian, Ghanian. *Eng.*

Gabona *i'oa* Gabon; Gabonese. *Eng.* Also *Kapona.*

Guama *i'oa* Guam; Guamanian. *Eng.*

R

Rea *i'oa* Rhea, the second largest moon of Saturn. *Eng.*

rese·pine *kik* Reserpine, an alkaloid used as a tranquilizer. *Eng.*

rī·taia *heh* To retire. *Eng.* Also *līkaia, ho'omaha loa.*

Romā·nia *i'oa* Romania; Romanian. *Eng.*

Rode 'Ai·lana *i'oa* Rhode Island; Rhode Islander. *Dic.* Also *Loke 'Ailana.*

Rua·nada *i'oa* Rwanda; Rwandan. *Eng.*

Rū·sia *i'oa* Russia; Russian. *Dic., sp. var.* Also *Lūkia.*

S

Sao·tome me Pani·kipe *i'oa* Sao Tome and Principe. *Eng. Ka mokupuni 'o Saotome me Panikipe.* Sao Tome and Principe Island.

Saudi 'Ala·pia *i'oa* Saudi Arabia; Saudi. *Comb. Eng.* + *'Alapia.* Also *Saudi 'Arabia.*

Saudi 'Ara·bia *i'oa* Saudi Arabia; Saudi. *Eng.* Also *Saudi 'Alapia.*

Sahara Komo·hana *i'oa* Western Sahara; Western Saharan. *Comb. Eng.* + *komohana.*

sala·mena *kik* Salamander. *Eng.* Also *kalamena.*

Sana Helena *Mauna Sana Helena.* Mount Saint Helens. Also *Mauna Kana Helena.*

Sape·nika Liona *i'oa* The huge Sphinx found near the pyramids at Giza in Egypt. *'Akahi nō a pau ka ho'oponopono 'ia 'ana o Sapenika Liona ma 'Aikupita.* The work of renovation on the Sphinx in Egypt has just been completed. *Lit.,* lion sphinx *(Eng.).* Cf. *kanaka kino liona.*

sawana *kik* Savanna, i.e. a tropical or subtropical grassland containing scattered trees. *Eng.*

sasa·palasa *kik* Sassafras. *Eng.*

satano·usa kolori·side *kik* Stannous chloride. *Eng.*

Sekele *i'oa* Seychelles. *Eng. Ka pae moku 'o Sekele.* Seychelles Islands.

Seko·tia *i'oa* Scotland; Scot, Scots, Scottish. *Dic.* Also *Kekokia.*

Selepe *i'oa* Celebes. *Eng. Ke kai 'o Selepe.* Celebes Sea.

semi·nā *kik* Seminar. *Eng.*

Sene·kala *i'oa* Senegal. *Eng.*

Sepa·nia *i'oa* Spain. *Dic.* Also *Kepania.*

sē·dē See *CD.*

Siela·leone *i'oa* Sierra Leone. *Eng.*

sila *kik* Seal. *Mān. Papa Hana Ho'opakele Sila.* Seal Recovery Program. *Sila Hawai'i.* Hawaiian monk seal. *Sila pūhuluhulu.* Fur seal. *'Ohana sila.* Pinniped, i.e. any of the suborder of aquatic mammals including the seal and walrus.

silaka *kik* Silica. *Eng. Palaholo silaka g.* Silica gel g, a powder used as the sorbent layer in thin-layer chromatography (pronounced *palaholo silaka gā*).

sili·kone *kik* Silicon. *Eng.*

Sili·lanaka *i'oa* Sri Lanka. *Eng.*

Sina·poa *i'oa* Singapore. *Eng.*

sī·wila *Kānāwai sīwila.* Civil law. Also *kānāwai kīwila.*

Sibe·ria *i'oa* Siberia, Siberian. *Eng. Ke kai 'o Siberia Hikina.* East Siberian Sea.

-side Suffix in chemical compounds and terms: -ide.

siri·ala *kik* Cereal. *Eng.* Also *kiliala.*

solono·kiuma *kik* Strontium. *Eng.*

Solo·wakia *i'oa* Slovakia. *Eng.*

Solo·wenia *i'oa* Slovenia. *Eng.*

Soma·lia *i'oa* Somalia; Somalian. *Eng.*

sodi·uma *kik* Sodium. *Eng. Sodiuma kitarahate.* Sodium citrate. *Sodiuma bisulafahate.* Sodium bisulfate.

Suazi·lana *i'oa* Swaziland. *Eng.*

sū·kini *kik* Zucchini. *Eng.*

sula·fahate *kik* Sulfate. *Eng. Kupuriku sulafahate.* Cupric sulfate.

sula·faside *kik* Sulfide. *Eng. Kupuriku sulafaside.* Cupric sulfide. *Ferousa sulafaside.* Ferrous sulfide.

Suli·name *i'oa* Surinam. *Eng.*

Sulu *i'oa* Sulu. *Eng. Ke kai 'o Sulu.* Sulu Sea.

sulu·fura dio·kesa·side *kik* Sulfur dioxide. *Eng.* Also *kūkaepele 'okikene lua.*

sulu·furiku Sulfuric. *Eng. 'Akika sulufuriku.* Sulfuric acid.

supero·posa·pahate *kik* Superphos-phate. *Eng.*

Sudana *i'oa* Sudan; Sudanese. *Eng.*

Suria *i'oa* Syria; Syrian. *Trad.*

T

T *'Ōmaka T.* T-fitting, for putting pipes together.

tā *kik* Tar. *Dic.* Also *kā.*

taea *kik* Tire. *Eng.* Also *kaea.* *Taea paikikala.* Bicycle tire.

Tai·uana *i'oa* Taiwan; Taiwanese. *Eng.*

taika *kik* Taiga. *Eng.*

Tai·lani *i'oa* Thailand. *Eng.*

Takisi·tana *i'oa* Tajikistan. *Eng.*

tala·pia *kik* Tilapia. *Eng.*

Tana·zania *i'oa* Tanzania; Tanzanian. *Eng. Lepupalika Hui Pū 'ia 'o Tanazania.* United Republic of Tanzania.

tanika *'a'* Tannic. *Eng. 'Akika tanika.* Tannic acid.

Tekasa *i'oa* Texas; Texan. *Eng.* Also *Kekeka, Teseta.*

Tene·sī *i'oa* Tennessee; Tennessean. *Dic., sp. var.* Also *Kenekī*

Teseta *i'oa* Texas; Texan. *Dic.* Also *Kekeka, Tekasa.*

Tetisa *i'oa* Tethys, a moon of Saturn. *Eng.*

Tieka *i'oa* Czech. *Eng.* See *Tieka-solowakia. Ka Lepupalika 'o Tieka.* Czech Republic.

Tieka·solo·wakia *i'oa* Czechoslovakia; Czech, but only when referring to the former country of Czechoslovakia. *Eng.* See *Tieka.*

Tō·kō *i'oa* Togo. *Eng.*

Tonga *Aupuni Mō'ī 'o Tonga.* Kingdom of Tonga.

tō·fū *kik* Tofu, bean curd. *Japn.*

tō·tia *kik* Tortilla. *Spanish.*

tū·kana *kik* Toucan. *Eng.*

Tuke·meni·kana *i'oa* Turkmenistan. *Eng.*

tuko *kik* Glue. *Ni'ihau* (Eng. *Duco*). See entries below. *Tuko ke'oke'o.* Paste. *Tuko laholio.* Rubber cement.

tuko paipu 'ea *kik* Plastic pipe cement. *Lit.,* plastic pipe glue. Also *tuko paipu.* See *pena holoi.*

tuko pī·lali *kik* Silicone, used as an adhesive. *Lit.,* sticky glue.

tuna *kik* Tuna. *Eng. Kini tuna.* Can of tuna.

Tuni·sia *i'oa* Tunisia; Tunisian. *Eng.*

Tureke *i'oa* Turkey; Turk; Turkish. *Dic.* Also *Kuleke.*

V

Vere·mona *i'oa* Vermont; Vermonter. *Eng.* Also *Welemoneka, Veremoneta.*

Vere·moneta *i'oa* Vermont; Vermonter. *Dic.* Also *Welemoneka, Veremona.*

Z

Zā·ire *i'oa* Zaire; Zairian. *Eng.*

Zami·bia *i'oa* Zambia; Zambian. *Eng.*

Zima·babue *i'oa* Zimbabwe; Zimbabwean. *Eng.*

Māhele ʻŌlelo Pelekānia
English-Hawaiian

A

abacus Kunipona.

abalone Pāua.

abbreviation Hua hōʻailona. See *initial*.

abdominal aorta Ewe o lalo. See *aorta*.

abdominal muscle Mākala ʻōpū.

abdominus See entry below and *rectus abdominus*.

abdominus oblique muscle *Internal ~.* Mākala kū hiō o loko. *External ~.* Mākala kū hiō o waho.

-able *See Hawaiian entry* pē-.

abort *To ~, as in a computer program.* ʻŌʻū.

abortion See *pro-choice, pro-life*.

absolute location *In geography.* Kuhikuhina. See *relative location*.

absolute value *In math.* Waiwai ʻiʻo. See *value*.

absolute zero *A hypothetical temperature characterized by complete absence of heat; also zero degrees K (Kelvin).* ʻOle Kelewine.

absorb Omo. See *adsorb, sorbent*.

AC *Alternating current.* Au māʻaloʻalo. *~ electricity.* Uila au māʻaloʻalo. See *DC*.

academics *Also academic.* Kālaiʻike.

accelerate Hoʻopiʻi i ka māmā holo; piʻi ka māmā holo. See *acceleration, decelerate*.

acceleration Piʻi māmā holo. See *accelerate, deceleration*.

accent *Or stress, in linguistics.* Kālele. *~ unit or measure.* Paukū kālele. *In speech.* Pualono. *Foreign ~.* Pualono ʻē.

access *To ~, as in a computer program.* Komo (i loko o).

accessories *Or peripherals, as for a computer.* Lakolako.

accident Ulia. *Car ~.* Ulia kaʻa.

account *As in a bank.* Waihona kālā. *Charge or credit ~.* Waihona kāki. *Checking ~.* Waihona kīkoʻo. *Expense ~.* Waihona hoʻolilo. *Savings ~.* Waihona hoʻāhu kālā. *As in a computer program or any listing of charges.* Moʻokāki.

accounting Mālama moʻohelu kālā. See *budget*.

accumulate *To lay away, store away.* Hoʻāhu.

ace *In volleyball.* ʻAi hāʻawi wale, ʻeki.

acetate *A salt/ester of ascetic acid.* ʻĀkeka. *Ethyl ~.* ʻĀkeka ʻeto.

acetone ʻAkekona.

acetylene ʻAseteline.

Achernar *A star.* Hinalua.

achievement *Certificate of ~.* Palapala hoʻokō. See *record*.

acid ʻAkika. *~ indicator.* Ana ʻakika. See *litmus paper. Amino ~.* ʻAkika ʻamino. *Carbonic ~.* ʻAkika kalapona. *Carboxylic ~.* ʻAkika pūhui kalapona. *Formic ~.* ʻAkika forimiku. *Hydrochloric ~.* ʻAkika haidorokoloriku. *Naturally occurring weak ~.* ʻAkika ʻūpalu kūlohelohe. *Nitric ~.* ʻAkika naikokene, ʻakika nikiriku. *Sulfuric ~.* ʻAkika sulufuriku. *Tannic ~.* ʻAkika tanika.

acidic anhydride ʻAnahaidaraside ʻakika. See *anhydride*.

acorn Hua kumu ʻoka, ʻēkona.

acorn barnacle Pīʻoe ʻōkuʻekuʻe.

acoustics *The science of ~.* Kālaikani.

acquired immune deficiency syndrome *AIDS.* Maʻi pale ʻea pau, pale ʻea pau. See *HIV*.

across *As in a crossword puzzle.* Pololei aʻe. See *down. Pages ~, as in a computer program.* ʻEhia ʻaoʻao haʻaʻe?

acrylic Hūkaʻa ʻea.

act *As a law, decree, or edict, in government.* Kānāwai. *See Hawaiian entries under* kānāwai. *Admission* ~, *statehood* ~. Kānāwai hoʻolilo mokuʻāina. *Endangered Species* ~. Kānāwai Lāhulu ʻAne Halapohe.

act *To* ~, *as in a play, movie, or video production.* Hana keaka. *See actor, act out.*

act cocky *To strut about looking for a fight.* Hoʻonanā.

actinoid *One of the fourteen elements that follow actinium on the periodic table.* ʻAkinoika.

action *Affirmative* ~. Kākoʻo hapa ʻuʻuku.

action movie Kiʻiʻoniʻoni ehuehu.

action-reaction pair *Two forces having equal strength but opposite directions, in science.* Paʻa manehu kūʻēʻē.

active *As a volcano.* ʻĀ. *See activity.* ~ *volcano.* Lua pele ʻā.

activity *Chemical* ~. Mōʻaui kemikala. *Secondary* ~, *of a volcano.* ʻĀ kualua. *See active.*

actor Mea hana keaka. *See extra, role.*

act out *To* ~, *as a math problem.* Hana keaka.

acute *In math.* ʻOi. ~ *angle.* Huina ʻoi. ~ *triangle.* Huinakolu ʻoi.

ad *Also advertisment, commercial.* Hoʻolaha kūʻai.

adapt *To* ~, *as a written document by shortening or lengthening, or by changing the form or style.* Hakuloli. *See modernize.*

adapt Hoʻomaʻa. *See adaptive radiation. To become* ~*ed to.* Maʻa. *To* ~ *biologically.* Hoʻoliliuwelo. *See adaptive radiation. To be biologically* ~*ed to.* Liliuwelo.

adaptive radiation *In biology.* Malele hoʻoliliuwelo. *See adapt.*

add *In math.* Hoʻohui. *See addition, plus sign.*

addend *In math.* Helu hoʻohui.

addiction *Also addicted.* Hei.

addition *In math.* Hōʻuluʻulu. *See add, plus sign.*

additive color *One of the primary colors (red, blue, green) which, when added together, produce white light.* Waihoʻoluʻu hui kea.

adhesion *Also adhesive.* Pīlekaleka. *See cohesion.*

adhesive *See silicone.*

adipogenesis *The formation of fat or fatty tissue in a body; also adipogenetic.* Haʻakupu ʻailakele. *See adipose tissue.*

adipose tissue *Animal tissue in which fat is stored.* ʻAʻa hunaola ʻailakele. *See adipogenesis.*

adjacent *See side of a triangle.*

adjuster *As on triple-beam balance scales.* Pihi hoʻopololei.

administration *A team of executive branch officials appointed by the President, in government.* Papa luna hoʻokele. *See director.*

administrator *As a controller for a computer network.* Kahu. *Network* ~. Kahu pūnaewele.

admission act *Also statehood act.* Kānāwai hoʻolilo mokuʻāina.

adobe ʻAkopie. ~ *block.* Uinihapa ʻakopie.

adopt *As a highway or other public area for environmental cleanup or maintenance.* Lawe mālama.

Adriatic ʻAkilikika. ~ *Sea.* Ke kai ʻo ʻAkilikika.

adsorb Omowaho. *See absorb, solvent front.*

advanced level Pae holomua.

advantage Keu pono.

adventure *As a story or movie.* ʻAʻanahoa.

advertisement *Also ad, commercial.* Hoʻolaha kūʻai.

Aegean 'Aekeana. ~ *Sea.* Ke kai 'o 'Aekeana.

Aeneolithic *In anthropology.* Haku keleawe'ula. ~ *age, period.* Ke au haku keleawe'ula.

aerate Hō'eaea. See *aerobic. Aerated.* Eaea.

aerobic *Living, active, or occurring only in the presence of oxygen.* Eaea. See entry below and *anaerobic decomposition.* ~ *decomposition or putrefaction.* Ka ho'ohāpopopo eaea 'ana.

aerobic Ho'oikaika pu'uwai. See *aerobics.* ~ *activity.* Hana ho'oikaika pu'uwai. ~ *point.* 'Ai ho'oikaika pu'uwai.

aerobics 'Onilele. See *aerobic.*

aerophone *A musical instrument whose sound is produced by air passing through it.* Oloea. See *Hawaiian entries beginning with olo-.*

aerosol can Kini kīkī.

affective domain *As relating to the learning process.* Pō'ai na'au. See *domain.*

affinity *To have an ~ for something.* Hia'ume.

affirmative action Kāko'o hapa 'u'uku.

affix *In grammar.* Pāku'ina. See *prefix, infix, suffix.*

affricate *In linguistics.* Pōhahī.

Afghanistan *Also Afghan, Afghani.* 'Apekanikana, 'Afekanisana.

Africa *Also African.* 'Apelika, 'Aferika. *Central African Republic.* Lepupalika 'Apelika Waena. *South* ~. 'Apelika Hema, 'Aferika Hema.

after- Muli. See entries below and *post-.* ~*school sports.* Ha'uki muli kula.

after-school detention *As punishment at school.* Ho'opa'i 'au'a muli kula. See *in-school detention.*

aftershock *A minor shock following an earthquake.* Manunu muli ōla'i.

agapanthus Līlia 'Aikupika, līlia 'Aigupita.

agar *A gelatin-like product of certain seaweeds used as a thickening agent.* 'Ēkā.

age *Also epoch, era, period, as in athropology.* Au. See *Eolithic, Paleolithic, Mesolithic, Neolithic, Aeneolithic. Ice* ~. Au pa'ahau.

age *To* ~, *as a person; aged.* Mākuakua. *Aging.* Ka mākuakua 'ana.

agenda *As for a meeting.* Papa kumumana'o.

aggregate *To bind together.* Ho'opili pū.

aggression *As an attack by one country upon another.* Lele kaua. *As a threat of attack by one country upon another.* Lele ho'onanā.

agriculture *College of* ~. Koleke mahi 'ai. *State Department of* ~. 'Oihana Mahi 'Ai o ka Moku'āina.

agroforestry Mahi ululā'au.

agronomy Kālailepomahi.

aid *Foreign* ~, *as a government policy.* Kōkua 'āina 'ē. *Hearing* ~. Pihi ho'onui lohe (*preceded by* ke).

AIDS *Acquired immune deficiency syndrome.* Ma'i pale 'ea pau, pale 'ea pau. See *HIV.*

air ball *Also missed shot, in basketball; to make such a shot.* Kī halahī, kī halahū.

air conditioner Mīkini hō'olu ea, hō'olu ea.

aircraft *Military transport* ~. Mokulele hali koa.

air displacement Pohupani ea.

air force Pū'ali kaua lewa.

airmail *Also to send by airmail.* Halilele. ~ *letter.* Leka halilele. ~ *stamp.* Po'oleka halilele (*preceded by* ke).

air mass *As in weather.* Ahu ea.

air mattress Pela ho'olana.

air pollution Haumia ea.

air pressure *As in a tire.* Mīkā ea.

air resistance Āohiohi ea. See *resistance.*

air stone *The porous rock in an aquarium that creates tiny bubbles at the surface of the water to facilitate the exchange of gases.* Pōhaku puka ea.

airtight Pa'a ea. *An ~ container.* He hōkelo pa'a ea.

air valve *As on a tire.* Pihi pāumu ea (*preceded by* ke).

air vent Puka ea.

aisle *As in a supermarket.* Ala, alakaha.

ajar *Also unlocked, open for business.* Hemo. See *open wide.*

Alabama *Also Alabaman, Alabamian.* 'Alapama, 'Alabama.

à la carte *As on a menu.* Ma ka 'ikamu, 'oka pākahikahi.

alanine *An amino acid.* 'Alanine.

alarm *~ bell, as on a clock or fire alarm.* Oeoe, pele. *~ clock.* Uaki ho'āla, uāki ho'āla. *Smoke ~.* Oeoe uahi.

Alaska *Also Alaskan.* 'Ālaka, 'Alaseka.

Albania *Also Albanian.* 'Alepania, 'Alabania.

album *Record ~.* Pāleo. *Record ~ cover.* Wahī pāleo.

alcohol 'Alekohola. *Blood ~ level.* Nui lama koko. See *breathalyzer.*

Alderamin *A star.* 'Anamuli.

aldrin *A kind of insecticide.* 'Alidirina. See *dieldrin, poison.*

Aleut See *Aleutian.*

Aleutian *Also Aleut.* 'Aleuta. *~ Islands.* Ka pae 'āina 'o 'Aleuta. *~ Trench.* Ka 'auwaha 'o 'Aleuta.

alfalfa sprout Kawowo 'alapapa.

algae *General term.* Līoho. *Coraline ~.* Limu ko'a.

algebra Hō'ailona helu. *Algebraic expression.* Ha'i hō'ailona helu.

Algeria *Also Algerian.* 'Alekelia, 'Alegeria.

Algol *A star.* Pō'ā.

alias *Also gateway, in a computer program.* 'Īpuka.

alien See *permanent resident. Illegal ~; to arrive as an illegal ~.* Pae malū. *Legal ~; to arrive as a legal ~.* Pae kānāwai. *Space ~, extraterrestrial.* Mea ao 'ē.

align *To ~, as type in a computer program.* Ho'olālani.

alkali *Also alkaline.* 'Ākilikai. See *entries below.*

alkali metal *One of the family of elements in Group 1 of the periodic table.* Mekala 'ākilikai. See *alkaline earth metal.*

alkaline earth metal *One of the family of elements in Group 2 of the periodic table.* Mekala honua 'ākilikai. See *alkali metal.*

alkaloid 'Alakaloida.

alkane 'Alakane. See *alkene, alkyne. ~ series, i.e. saturated hydrocarbons where all the carbon atoms are joined by single covalent bonds.* Pūka'ina 'alakane.

alkene 'Alakene. See *alkane, alkyne. ~ series, i.e. the group of unsaturated hydrocarbons with one double bond.* Pūka'ina 'alakene.

alkyne 'Alakaine. See *alkane, alkene. ~ series, i.e. the group of unsaturated hydrocarbons with one triple bond.* Pūka'ina 'alakaine.

all *Entirely.* A pau.

allergic reaction Hopena pāheu. See *allergy.*

allergy Pāheu. See *allergic reaction.*

alley *Also alleyway.* Ala hānuku.

alley-oop *A basketball play.* 'Aliupa.

alliance *A group of nations that have agreed to help or protect each other; to form such an ~.* Hui ku'ikahi. See *consortium.*

allied health professional Kāko'o 'oihana olakino.

alligator 'Alakeka.

allophone *In linguistics.* Puana hualeo. See *phoneme.*

allotrope *A different molecular form of an element, in science.* Kino lātoma.

alloy Mekala 'ō'ā, metala 'ō'ā.

allspice Pimeka.

all-terrain vehicle *ATV.* Mokohuilahā. See *off-road vehicle.*

alluvial soil Lepo makaili.

Almak *A star.* 'Ao'ao.

almanac Puke 'alemanaka. See *appointment book.*

Al Nair-Alpha Gruis *A star.* Laniha'i.

Alnilam *A star.* Kauano.

Alnitak *A star.* 'Aumani.

aloha ball *In volleyball.* Kinipōpō aloha.

aloha shirt Palaka aloha.

alphabet Pī'āpā. See *alphabetize.*

alphabetical order Ka'ina pī'āpā. See *alphabetize.*

alphabetize *To put in alphabetical order.* Ho'oka'ina pī'āpā.

alpha particle *A positively charged particle made up of two protons and two neutrons.* Huna 'ālepa. See *beta particle.*

Alphekka *A star in the constellation Corona Borealis.* Keaopō.

Alpheratz *A star.* Māpono.

alpine *Relating to the biogeographic zone above timberline.* 'Alapaina. See *subalpine.* ~ *desert.* Panoa 'alapaina. ~ *shrubland.* Wao la'alā'au.

Alpha Tuscanae *A star.* Kapo'e.

alternate *To ~, as in a computer program.* Hō'alo. ~ *key.* Pihi hō'alo (*preceded by* ke).

alternate player *First ~ or substitute, also called first off the bench or six man, in basketball.* Kūono.

alternating current *AC.* A u mā'alo'alo. See *direct current.* ~ *electricity.* Uila au mā'alo'alo.

alternative education *As a school program.* Ho'ona'auao ka'a'oko'a.

altimeter Ana ki'eki'ena. See *altitude.*

altitude Ki'eki'ena. See *elevation, height. Of a triangle.* Ki'e kūpono.

aluminum 'Aluminuma. ~ *foil.* Pepa kini.

alveolar *In linguistics.* Lapa niho.

alveolus *An air sac of the lungs, in anatomy.* Nōiki. *Alveolar duct.* Pū'ali nōiki.

a.m. *Ante meridium.* A.m. (*pronounced* 'āmū). See *p.m.*

AM *Amplitude modulation.* AM (*pronounced* 'āmū), 'anini laulā hawewe. See *FM.*

amaryllis Līlia 'Apelika.

Amazon 'Amasona. ~ *river.* Ka muliwai 'o 'Amasona.

ambassador Kanikela nui. See *consul.*

ambidextrous Lima kaulua.

amend See *amendment.*

amendment *An addition or change to a bill, constitution, etc.; also to amend* Pāku'i ho'ololi.

America *Also American.* 'Amelika. *See entries below. Central ~ or Latin ~.* 'Amelika Waena. *North ~.* 'Amelika 'Ākau. *South ~.* 'Amelika Hema. *United States of ~.* 'Amelika Hui Pū 'ia.

American Baseball League Ku'ikahi Pōhili 'Amelika.

American cockroach *Periplaneta americana.* 'Elelū kīkēkē.

American Football Conference *AFC.* Hui Pōpeku 'Amelika.

American Sāmoa *Also American Sāmoan.* Kāmoa 'Amelika, Ha'amoa 'Amelika.

amino 'Amino. ~ *acid.* 'Akika 'amino.

ammeter *An instrument used to measure the amount of electric current in a circuit.* Ana au uila.

ammonia 'Amonia.

ammonium 'Amoniuma. ~
molybdate. 'Amoniuma molaibadahate.

amorphous *Having no regular
crystalline form.* Laukua. ~ *substance.*
'Akano laukua.

amount Helu, heluna.

amphibian Pepeʻekua.

amphidromous *Migrating from fresh
to salt water, or from salt to fresh water,
at some stage of the life cycle other than
the breeding period.* Pōʻaiwaiakai.

amplifier Pahu hoʻonui leo. See
speaker.

amplify *To increase the amplitude of a
wave.* Hoʻolaulā hawewe. See
amplitude.

amplitude *The amount of energy in a
sound wave.* Ikaika hawewe kani. See
entry below and *sound wavelength.*

amplitude *The greatest distance the
particles in a wave rise or fall from their
rest position, in science.* Laulā hawewe.
~ *modulation.* 'Anini laulā hawewe. See
entry above and *AM. As of a pendulum.* Palena piʻi.

amusement park Pāka kāniwala.

anaerobic decomposition *Also
anaerobic putrefaction.* Ka hoʻohāpopo
eaea ʻole ʻana. See *aerobic.*

anagram Huaneʻe.

analog ~ *watch or clock, i.e. having
hands.* Uaki lima kuhikuhi, uāki lima
kuhikuhi. See *digital.*

analysis *Cost* ~. Huli kumukūʻai.

analyze Kālailai.

anchialine pool Ālialia nono.

and *Also when, until, to, etc.* A.

Andaman 'Anadamana. ~ *Sea.* Ke kai
ʻo 'Anadamana

Andorra 'Anakola.

Andromeda 'Anakolomeka. ~ *galaxy.*
Ka wiliau hōkū ʻo 'Anakolomeka.

anemometer Ana māmā makani.

anemone *Sea* ~. 'Ōkala, ʻōkole.

aneroid barometer Ana mīkā ea
kuhikuhi.

anesthetic Lāʻau hoʻomāʻeʻele.

anesthetize Hoʻomāʻeʻele.

angiosperm 'Anakiopua.

angle *In math.* Huina. *See entries
below. Acute* ~. Huina ʻoi. *Central* ~,
*an angle that has its vertex at the center
of a circle.* Huina kikowaena.
Complementary ~s, *two angles whose
measures have a sum of 90°.* Nā huina
hoʻopiha kūpono. *Corresponding* ~.
Huina launa. *Exterior* ~. Huina kūwaho.
Obtuse ~. Huina peleleu. *Right* ~. Huina
kūpono. *Straight* ~, *an angle that has a
measure of 180°.* Huina kaha.
Supplementary ~s, *two angles whose
measures have a sum of 180°.* Nā huina
hoʻopiha kaha.

angle of incidence *The angle made
between a wave striking a barrier and
the normal to the surface.* Huina papā.
See *angle of reflection.*

angle of reflection *The angle
between a reflected wave and the
normal to the barrier from which it is
reflected.* Huina kūpī. See *angle of
incidence.*

angle spike *In volleyball.* Hili ʻaoʻao.
See *spike.*

Angola *Also Angolan.* 'Anagola.

anhydride *A compound formed from
another by the removal of water.*
'Anahaidaraside. See *anhydrous.*
Acidic ~. 'Anahaidaraside ʻakika. *Basic*
~, *a metallic oxide that forms a base
when added to water.* 'Anahaidaraside
kuapapa.

anhydrous *Without water.* Nele wai.
See *anhydride.*

animal Holoholona. *Fish or any
marine* ~. Iʻa, iʻa kai. See *fish.*
Vertebrate ~. Holoholona iwi kuamoʻo.
Invertebrate ~. Holoholona iwi kuamoʻo
ʻole.

animated *Also violent.* Ehuehu. See *action movie.*

Ankaa *A star.* Kapela.

annex *To ~, in math, as in ~ing a zero to show both decimal parts as a hundredth.* Pākuʻi.

anniversary card Kāleka piha makahiki. See *birthday card.*

annual *Yearbook.* Puke hoʻohaliʻa makahiki.

anode *The positive electrode in an electrical circuit.* ʻŪholo uila ʻāne. See *cathode, electrode.*

answer *A solution to a problem.* Hāʻina.

Antarctica *Also Antarctic.* ʻAneʻālika.

anteater ʻAinaonao.

ante meridium *A.m.* A.m. *(pronounced* ʻāmū). See *post meridium.*

antenna *As of a lobster, insect, television, etc.* Kukuna. *Volleyball ~.* Kukuna pōpaʻipaʻi. *~ violation.* ʻAʻena kukuna.

Antennariv Commersonil *A kind of fish.* Hahili poloka.

anterior *In biology.* Laumua. See *dorsal, posterior, ventral. ~ dorsal fin, of a fish.* Kualā laumua.

anthocyanin *A kind of pigment producing blue to red coloring in flowers and plants.* ʻUlakaiano.

anthropology Hulikanaka. See *age.*

antibiotic Pale mūhune ʻino. See *pathogen.*

antifreeze ʻAila ʻaʻalo paʻahau.

antigravity machine Mīkini hoʻopau ʻumekaumaha. See *gravity.*

antiseptic Pale palahō.

antonym Huaʻōlelo manaʻo ʻēkoʻa. See *homonym, synonym.*

anus *The posterior opening of the alimentary canal.* Puka kahiko, puka ʻamo. See *sphincter.*

anxiety ʻŌpikipiki.

aorta Ewe o luna. *Abdominal ~.* Ewe o lalo.

aphid *A kind of insect.* ʻEleao. See *honeydew.*

apocope *In linguistics.* Hua hope hāʻule.

apostrophe Koma luna.

apparatus *Device or mechanism, ordinarily including some mechanical part or parts.* Maomeka. See *device, instrument, tool.*

appeal *To ask a higher court to review a decision made by a lower court.* Hoʻopiʻi kūʻē. See *appellate jurisdiction.*

appearance *General ~ or impression.* Hiʻona. See *feature.*

appellate jurisdiction *A court's authority to hear an appeal of a decision made by another court.* Mana hoʻokolokolo. See *appeal.*

appendix *As in a book.* Pākuʻina.

appliance Mīkini. *Home ~.* Mīkini home. *Office ~.* Mīkini keʻena. *~ store.* Hale kūʻai mīkini home.

application *As in a computer program; also program, as for a computer.* Polokalamu.

appointment book *Also date book.* ʻAlemanaka puke. See *almanac.*

apportion *Also division, piece, portion, department, category, part, land division; to divide.* Māhele.

apprentice See *intern.*

approach *Or strategy, as in solving a math problem.* Kaʻakālai.

approximate *Also approximation.* Kokekau.

April ʻApelila. *Abb.* ʻAp.

apron Pale kuene, ʻepane.

aquaculture Mahi iʻa. See *biofilter, pipe.*

aquarium Pahuwaiea. See *hale hōʻikeʻike iʻa* (dic.).

Aquatic Resources *Division of ~.* Māhele Kumuwaiwai Kai.

aqueous *Having water as a solvent, in science.* ʻŪheheʻe wai. ~ *solution.* Māʻōʻāna ʻūheheʻe wai.

Arab *See Arabia. United ~ Emirates.* Aupuni ʻEmira ʻAlapia Hui Pū ʻia.

Arabia *Also Arab, Arabian.* ʻAlapia, ʻArabia. ~ *Sea.* Ke kai ʻo ʻAlapia. *Saudi ~, Saudi.* Saudi ʻAlapia, Saudi ʻArabia.

Arabian Sea Ke kai ʻo ʻAlapia.

Aral ʻAlala. ~ *Sea.* Ke kai ʻo ʻAlala.

arbitrate ʻUao. *Arbitration.* Ka ʻuao ʻana.

arborial Kau lāʻau. *See orange tree frog, treehouse.*

arc *In math.* Piʻo. *See chord. Island ~.* Pae moku hoaka. *Three-point ~, in basketball.* Hoaka kīkolu.

arch *As the Arch of Triumph in Paris.* Hoaka kū.

archaeology Hulikoehana. *Archaeological site.* Kahua hulikoehana. *Archaeologist.* Kanaka hulikoehana, mea hulikoehana.

Archimedes ʻAkimika. ~' *principle, i.e. the buoyant force on an object submerged in a fluid is equal to the weight of the fluid displaced by that object, in science.* Ke kulehana a ʻAkimika.

archipelago Pae moku, pae ʻāina. *See Hawaiian entries.*

archive *Or backup, as in a computer program.* Papaʻa. *See backup.*

Arctic ʻĀlika. ~ *fox.* ʻAlopeka ʻĀlika, ʻalopeke ʻĀlika. ~ *ground squirrel.* Kiulela ʻĀlika.

area *In math.* ʻIli. *Abb.* ʻI. *Quantitative measurement.* ʻIli laulā, ʻili. *Surface ~.* ʻIli alo.

area *Transition ~, an ~ where natural topography changes from one land feature to another.* ʻĀina loliloli.

Argentina *Also Argentine, Argentinean.* ʻAlekina.

argon *An element.* ʻAragona.

Arizona *Also Arizonan, Arizonian.* ʻAlikona, ʻArizona.

Arkansas *Also Arkansan.* ʻAkanakā, ʻAkanasā.

arm *Resistance ~, i.e. the distance from the fulcrum to the resistance force in a lever.* Lima āohiohi.

armadillo ʻAmakila.

Armenia ʻĀmēnia.

army *Also military service.* Pūʻali koa.

arraignment *A court hearing in which a defendant is formally charged with a crime and enters a plea of guilty or not guilty.* ʻAha pane hoʻopiʻi.

arrange music *Also music arranger.* Kūkulu puolo.

array *Rectangular ~, in math.* Lau huinahā lōʻihi.

arrest warrant *A document issued by a magistrate authorizing an officer to make an arrest.* Palapala hopu.

arrow *An indicator.* Nahau. ~ *key, as on a computer keyboard.* Pihi nahau (*preceded by* ke). ~ *key for moving right (left, up, down).* Pihi nahau holo ʻākau (hema, i luna, i lalo). *Mouse ~, pointer, or cursor, as in a computer program.* Nahau ʻiole, nahau.

arrowhead Nahau.

arrythmia *Cardiac ~.* Puʻuwai pana ʻewaʻewa.

art *Also artwork.* Pāheona. *See artistic, fine arts.* ~ *director, as for movie or video production.* Luna pāheona. *Performing ~.* Pāhiahia.

artemia *Brine shrimp.* Pokipoki ālia.

arteriolosclerosis *In medicine.* Aʻahaʻapupū. *See arteriosclerosis.*

arteriosclerosis *Also atherosclerosis or hardening of the arteries, in medicine.* Aʻalāʻau. *See arteriolosclerosis.*

artery Aʻa koko puʻuwai, aʻa puʻuwai. *See Hawaiian entries under aʻa puʻuwai and arteriosclerosis, vein.*

arthropod Wāwaeʻami.

artichoke ʻAlikoka.

artifact Koehana. *See archaeology.*

artificial reef Umukoʻa.

artisan *Also craftsman.* Mālalaioa.

artist *Storyboard ~, as in movie or video production.* Lima kaha moʻolelo. See *storyboard*.

artistic *Esthetically appealing or having ~ talent.* Heona. See *art. To make ~, decorate ~ally.* Hoʻoheona.

arts and sciences *College of ~.* Koleke pāheona me ka ʻepekema. See *dean*.

asbestos Awe pale ahi.

asea *At sea.* I waena moana. See *midocean*.

ash cone *In geology.* Puʻu lehu.

Asia *Also Asian, Asiatic.* ʻĀkia, ʻĀsia.

as if *Also as though, like.* Me he.

aspen ʻŌlapa haole.

asphalt Unukā. See *pave. ~ compound, a brown or black tar-like substance, a variety of distilled tar (bitumen) found in a natural state or obtained by evaporating petroleum; pitch.* Kēpau kā.

assemble *As when splicing film or video segments together for movie or video production.* Hoʻokuʻikuʻi. *~ editor.* Luna hoʻokuʻikuʻi.

assembly *A gathering of people for a specific purpose.* ʻĀmui.

assessment *Student ~.* Loiloi holomua haumāna.

assign *To ~ a value or power, as in math problems.* Hoʻāmana.

assimilate Hoʻokemua. *Assimilated.* Kemua. See *assimilation*.

assimilation *In linguistics.* Kīlikelike.

assist *To feed or ~, as in basketball and most team sports except baseball.* Hānai.

associative *In math.* Hoʻolike. *~ property.* ʻAnopili hoʻolike (*preceded by* ke).

assume *Also assumption.* Manaʻo kuhi.

asteroid Hōkūnaʻi. *~ belt.* Kāʻei hōkūnaʻi.

as though *Also as if, like.* Me he.

astronaut Kelalani.

at bat *Also up (to bat), in baseball.* Manawa hili.

-ate *Suffix in chemical compounds and terms.* -hate.

-athalon *Suffix (Eng.); prefix (Haw).* ʻĀlapakona-. See *decathalon, penta- thalon, triathalon, -thon*.

atherosclerosis *Also arteriosclerosis or hardening of the arteries, in medi- cine.* Aʻalāʻau. See *arteriolosclerosis*.

athlete ʻĀlapa. See *athletic*.

athletic *Also athlete.* ʻĀlapa. *~ scholarship.* Haʻawina kālā ʻālapa. *~ club, fitness center.* Hale hoʻoikaika kino. See *gymnasium*.

Atlantic ʻAkelanika, ʻAtelanika.

ATM *Automated-teller machine.* Mīkini panakō.

atmosphere *Around planets.* Lewapuni. See *space*.

atoll Moku kuaʻau.

atom ʻĀtoma. See *atomic*.

atomic *Also atom.* ʻĀtoma. See entries below and *bond, nucleus, particle. ~ radiation.* Pāhawewe ʻatoma.

atomic mass Nuipaʻa ʻatoma. *~ unit.* Anakahi nuipaʻa ʻatoma. *Average ~.* ʻAwelike nuipaʻa ʻatoma.

atomic number Heluna huna ʻāne.

atrium *Of the mammalian heart.* Pona puʻuwai, pona. See *chamber. Left ~.* Pona puʻuwai hema, pona hema. *Right ~.* Pona puʻuwai ʻākau, pona ʻākau.

attack *Raid; also to attack or raid.* Hoʻouka. *Counter~; also to counter~.* Hoʻouka pānaʻi.

attempt See *vain attempt*.

attendant *Flight ~.* Kuene mokulele.

attic Lumi huna; lumi kaupaku, lumi kaupoku, lumi kaupuku.

attorney Loio. See *defense attorney, prosecuting attorney*.

attribute *Style, as italic or bold in printing or a computer program.* Kaila hua. *See code style, font, property.*

ATV *All-terrain vehicle.* Mokohuilahā. *See off-road vehicle.*

auditor Luna hōʻoia.

August ʻAukake. *Abb.* ʻAuk.

aurora borealis *Also northern lights.* ʻOliliʻula.

Australia *Also Australian.* Nūhōlani. *See entry below and Indo-Australian.*

Australian cockroach *Periplaneta australasiae.* ʻElelū Nūhōlani.

Austria *Also Austrian.* ʻAukekulia, ʻAuseturia.

auto- *Or self- (prefix).* Hika-. *See entries below.*

autobiographical Hikapiliolana. *See biographical. Autobiography.* Moʻolelo hikapiliolana, hikapiliolana.

auto feed *To ~, as paper into a computer printer.* Hānai ʻakomi.

autoharp Hāpa paʻa lima, pila hāpa.

automated-teller machine *ATM.* Mīkini panakō.

automatic ʻAkomi. *See auto feed.*

autopsy *Also necropsy.* Kālaikupapaʻu.

autumn *Fall.* Hāʻulelau. *~al equinox.* Ka māuiili o ka hāʻulelau. *See equinox.*

avalanche *Also landslide.* ʻĀholo. *Snow ~.* ʻĀholo hau.

average ʻAwelike. *~ atomic mass.* ʻAwelike nuipaʻa ʻātoma. *~ rainfall.* ʻAwelike o ka ua. *~ speed.* ʻAwelike māmā holo.

avian malaria Malaria manu.

Avior *A star.* Kīnaʻu.

avocado Pea Hawaiʻi, pea. *See pear.*

awareness Makakau. *Language ~.* Makakau ʻōlelo.

axe Koʻi, koʻi lipi.

axis *In math.* Iho. *Coordinate axes, i.e. two intersecting perpendicular number lines used for graphing ordered number pairs.* Iho kuhikuhina.

axle *A shaft on which a wheel turns.* Iho, paepae komo huila.

azalea Pua kaʻūmana.

Azerbaijan ʻAkepaikana.

azobacter *A type of bacteria containing nitrogen.* Koʻohune naikokene.

B

baby bottle ʻŌmole omo waiū, ʻōmole waiū.

baby carriage Kaʻapēpē. *See crib.*

baby rattle ʻUlīkeke. *See tambourine.*

baccalaureate *See bachelor's.*

bachelor's *As a degree at a university; baccalaureate.* Laepua, BA (*pronounced* bēʻā), BS (*pronounced* bēsā). *See undergraduate, graduate, Master's, doctorate. ~ degree.* Kēkelē laepua, palapala laepua.

back *Of seat.* Kua noho. *Of tongue.* Kūʻau alelo. *See tongue. ~ vowel.* Woela kauhope. *See vowel.*

back *Defensive corner ~, in football.* ʻĀʻiwa. *Running ~, general term.* Mea holo.

backboard *In basketball.* Papa hīnaʻi, papa hupa, papa.

backbone *Spine.* Iwi kuamoʻo. *See vertebra.*

backcourt violation *In basketball.* ʻAʻena laina kūwaena. *See violation.*

back-door pass *In basketball; to throw such a pass.* Kīloi palemo.

background *As in a photo, movie, or video scene, or on a computer screen.* Kāʻei kua. *See foreground.*

backpack *Knapsack.* Pāiki hāʻawe, pāisi hāʻawe, ʻawe.

back set *To make a ~, in volleyball.* Hānai i hope, hānai kīkala.

backslash *In printing (\).* Kaha hiō iho. *See slash.*

backspace *To ~, as on an IBM computer.* Holoi i hope. *See delete.*

back stroke *Also to swim the ~.* 'Au kua. See *stroke.*

back up Pēki (i hope).

backup *Archive, as in a computer program.* Papa'a. *~ copy.* Kope papa'a. *~ file.* Waihona papa'a. *To ~, as a file.* Ho'opapa'a.

backward *With palms facing ~.* Pohokua. See *chin-up, forward, hit.*

bacon Pekona.

bacteria Ko'ohune. See *azobacter.* *Mesophilic ~.* Ko'ohune ola mehana. *Thermophilic ~.* Ko'ohune ola wela.

baculum *A slender bone reinforcing the penis in many mammals.* Iwi ule.

badge *General term.* Pihi hō'ailona (*preceded by* ke). *Police ~.* Pihi māka'i.

badminton Kenika manu.

bag Pū'olo; 'eke (*preceded by* ke). See *insect bag net. Guessing ~.* Pū'olo kohokoho. *Paper ~.* Pū'olo pepa. *Plastic ~.* 'Eke 'ea. *Sleeping ~.* 'Eke moe, 'eke hiamoe.

bagpipe Pila 'ūpoho, 'ūpoho.

Bahamas *Also Bahamian.* Pahama, Bahama.

Bahrain Baharaina.

bail *Money a defendant gives a court as a promise to return for trial.* Pēla.

bait-casting reel *As for fishing.* Wiliaho hekau maunu. See *reel.*

Baker Island *Near the Phoenix Islands in the Pacific Ocean.* Puaka'ilima.

baking pan Pā 'oma (*preceded by* ke).

baking powder Hū. See *baking soda.*

baking soda Pauka koka. See *baking powder.*

balance *To ~ something.* Ho'okaualewa. See *entries below and scales.*

balance beam Lā'au kaukahi. See *parallel bars.*

balanced *As equal distribution of weight.* Kaualewa. *Also evenly ~, in science; fair, just, equitable.* Kaulike. *~ chemical equation.* Ha'ihelu kemikala kaulike. *~ force.* Manehu kaulike.

balances *Checks and ~, as in government.* Ho'oku'ia.

balance sheet *A listing of assets, liabilities, and owner's equity.* Mo'okūlana waiwai.

balancing mechanism *In biology.* 'Ōnaehana ho'okauapono.

bald *"Balahead/bolohead," as a tire.* Nemonemo. See *tread.*

bald eagle 'Āeko po'o hina, 'āeto po'o hina.

ball Kinipōpō. See *air ball, glass ball; baseball, basketball, football, volleyball, etc. Aloha ~, in volleyball.* Kinipōpō aloha. *Christmas ~, the tree ornament.* Pōpō wehi lā'au Kalikimaka.

ballet Hulahula pālē, pālē, bālē.

balluster *Railing support.* 'Ūlili, hūlili. See *ballustrade.*

ballustrade *Railing.* Paehumu. See *balluster.*

balsa Haulāpa.

Baltic Balatika. *~ Sea.* Ke kai 'o Balatika.

banana poka Poka mai'a.

band *Or gradient, as of colors.* 'Auina. *Color ~.* 'Auina kala. *Metal ~ or strap, as for banding around metal boxes, water tanks, etc.* Kalapu hao. See *banding tool.*

Banda Banada. *~ Sea.* Ke kai 'o Banada.

band aid Wahī'eha.

banding tool *As for putting metal bands on boxes, water tanks, etc.* Wili ho'omālō. See *band.*

bandmaster's baton Maile pana.

Bangladesh Banagaladesa.

banjo Panakiō.

banjolele Panakiōlele.

bank Panakō. See *ATM, account, check. ~ check.* Pila kīko'o. *~ draft.* Pila kīko'o panakō. *Piggy ~.* Panakō hale.

banked curve *Also banked turn.* Uakeʻe hiō.

bank shot *In basketball; to make such a shot.* Kī papa.

banquet ʻAhaʻaina. *Welcome* ~. ʻAhaʻaina hoʻokipa. *Closing* ~. ʻAhaʻaina panina.

bar *See* bars. ~ *graph.* Pakuhi ʻaukā. *See* histogram. *Double* ~ *graph.* Pakuhi paʻa ʻaukā. *Fill* ~, *in a computer program.* ʻAukā holomua. *Menu* ~, *on a computer screen.* Papa koho. *Space* ~, *on a typewriter or computer keyboard.* Pihi hoʻokōā, pihi kaʻahua *(preceded by* ke).

barbiturate Lāʻau hoʻomālū.

bare *As a tree without leaves.* Launea.

Barents Baleneta. ~ *Sea.* Ke kai ʻo Baleneta.

bargain *Plea* ~, *as in the negotiation of an agreement between a prosecutor and a defendant.* Kūkā hoʻēmiemi.

bargaining *Collective* ~. Kūkaʻi ʻaelike ʻuniona.

baritone Hāʻoi. ~ ʻukulele. ʻUkulele hāʻoi.

barium Bariuma.

bark *Of a plant.* ʻIli, ʻaluʻalu. *Inner* ~. ʻIli iho. *Outer* ~. ʻIli o waho.

bark cloth *Tapa.* Paʻūpaʻū.

barnacle *General term.* Pīʻoe. *Acorn* ~. Pīʻoe ʻokuʻekuʻe. *Gooseneck* ~. Pīʻoe ʻōhā kai.

barometer Ana mīkā ea. *Aneroid* ~. Ana mīkā ea kuhikuhi.

barrel *A unit of measurement.* Palela. *Abb.* pll.

barrel cactus Pānini palala.

barrette *Hairclip.* Pine lauoho.

barrier *Sound* ~. Palena holo kani.

bars *Parallel* ~. Lāʻau kaulua. *Even parallel* ~. Lāʻau kaulua kaulike. *Uneven parallel* ~. Lāʻau kaulua kaulike ʻole. *See* balance beam. *Monkey* ~, *as playground equipment.* Haokeko. *See* jungle gym.

barter Hailawe. ~ *system.* Ka hailawe ʻana.

-base Kuapapa. *Water-base paint.* Pena kuapapa wai.

base Kahua. *See entries below.* *Military* ~. Kahua pūʻali koa. *Navy* ~. Kahua pūʻali kaua moana. *Of a leaf, as* hala. Poʻo *(preceded by* ke).

base *As on a baseball diamond.* Pahu. *See* home plate. *First* ~. Pahu ʻekahi. *Second* ~. Pahu ʻelua. *Third* ~. Pahu ʻekolu.

base *In math.* Kumu hoʻohui. *See* base five, binary. *In exponential notation.* Kumu pāhoʻonui. *As of a triangle.* ʻAoʻao kau. *Abb.* ʻak.

baseball *The sport.* Pōhili. *The ball.* Kinipōpō pōhili. ~ *glove or mitt.* Mikilima pōhili. ~ *field.* Kahua pōhili. ~ *diamond, infield.* Kaimana pōhili. ~ *inning.* Pale pōhili. *American* ~ *League.* Kuʻikahi Pōhili ʻAmelika. *National* ~ *League.* Kuʻikahi Pōhili Aupuni.

baseball pass *In basketball; to throw such a pass.* Nou.

base five *In math.* Kumu hoʻohui pālima, kumu pālima. ~ *counting piece.* Kōkua helu kumu hoʻohui pālima.

base line *End line, as on a basketball court.* Laina kumu. *See* line, *as on a basketball court.*

base-ten grid paper *In math.* Pepa makaʻaha kumu hoʻohui pāʻumi.

basic *Simple, uncomplicated.* Nōhie. *See entries below and* complex.

basic anhydride *A metallic oxide that forms a base when added to water.* ʻAnahaidaraside kuapapa. *See* anhydride.

basic counting principle *In math.* Kulehana no ka helu ʻana.

basket ʻIe *(preceded by* ke). *As on a bicycle.* ʻEke ukana *(preceded by* ke).

basket *In basketball.* Hīnaʻi, hupa. See *backboard, rim, shoot, three-point shot.* *A score.* ʻAi hīnaʻi. *To make or sink a* ~. Hoʻokomo i ke kinipōpō. *Made a* ~. Komohia.

basketball *The sport.* Pōhīnaʻi. *The ball.* Kinipōpō pōhīnaʻi. ~ *net.* Hīnaʻi. ~ *court.* Kahua pōhīnaʻi, kahua. ~ *camp.* ʻĀpoʻe pōhīnaʻi.

bass clef *In music.* Hōʻailona mele leo kāne, leo kāne. See *treble clef.*

bass viol *Also string bass.* Pila kū nui, pila nui.

bat *Also club, racket.* ʻŪhili. *At* ~, *up (to* ~*), in baseball.* Manawa hili.

batch *As of cookies or recruits.* ʻŌhui.

bathe See *shower.*

bathroom Lua, lumi hoʻopaupilikia, lumi ʻauʻau. ~ *scales.* Anapaona home, *usu.* anapaona.

bathtub Kapu ʻauʻau.

baton Maile, ʻaukaʻi. *Bandmaster's* ~. Maile pana. ~ *used in a relay race.* Maile hoʻoili. ~ *for twirling.* ʻAukaʻi wili. *Signal* ~, *as used by a marching band-leader.* ʻAukaʻi pāna.

batter *As when making pancakes.* Kale palaoa.

battery Iho, pakalē. See *entries below.* *Button-shape* ~. Iho pihi. *For flashlight, radio, etc.* Iho poke. *Six-volt* ~. Iho ʻeono. *Twelve-volt* ~. Iho ʻumikūmālua.

battery jar *A large cylindrical container of heavy glass with an open top as used in laboratories.* ʻŌmole iho uila.

battery tester *A machine.* Mīkini hoʻāʻo iho. *Not a machine.* Hāmeʻa hoʻāʻo iho.

bay *Payload* ~, *the part of a spacecraft where scientific instruments and passengers are carried.* ʻOneki hana.

BBS *Bulletin Board Service, on computer programs.* PLH (Papa Lawelawe Hoʻolaha).

B-complex vitamin Kauwikamina B.

beach cricket ʻŪhini nēnē kahakai.

bead Olopī.

beaker Hano kānuku.

beam *Balance* ~. Lāʻau kaukahi. See *parallel bars. Laser* ~. Kukuna wanaʻā. ~ *of a boat.* Kua uma.

beam reach (port) *Beam reach on the port side, i.e. sailing at a 90° angle from the direction of the wind, with the port side windward.* Kele ama kāmoe. See *beam reach (starboard), broad reach (port, starboard), close hauled (port, starboard), downwind.*

beam reach (starboard) *Beam reach on the starboard side, i.e. sailing at a 90° angle from the direction of the wind, with the starboard side windward.* Kele ʻākea kāmoe. See *beam reach (port), broad reach (port, starboard), close hauled (port, starboard), downwind.*

bean Pāpapa. See entries below and *pea. Bush* ~. Pāpapa haʻa. *Honey locust* ~. Pāpapa ʻūhinihone. *Jelly* ~. Pāpapa kele. *Lima* ~. Pāpapa laima. *Long* ~. Pāpapa loloa. *Mung* ~. Pāpapa munukō. *Soya* ~. Pāpapa koiū. *String* ~. Pāpapa hihi.

bean curd *Also tofu.* Tōfū.

bean sprout Kawowo pāpapa.

bear Pea. *Polar* ~. Pea ʻĀlika. *Teddy* ~. Pea kiʻi, pea pāʻani. See *panda.*

beard *Excluding the moustache.* ʻUmiʻumi ʻauae, *usu.* ʻumiʻumi. See *moustache.*

beat *As in music or linguistics.* Pana.

beaver Peawa. *Mountain* ~. Peawa kuahiwi.

bed See entries below and *mattress, riverbed, streambed.*

bedframe Hao pela. See *headboard.*

bedpan *Also urinal.* Ipu mimi. See *toilet bowl, urinal.*

bedpost Pou moe.

bedrock Kūpapakū.

bedroom Lumi moe. *Master ~.* Lumi moe haku. *Guest room.* Lumi moe malihini.

bedsheet Hāliʻi moe, hāliʻi pela.

bedside table *Also nightstand.* Pākaukau moe.

bedspread Uhimoe.

bedsprings Pilina moe.

beef See *corned beef.*

beep *As a sound effect on a computer.* Pīpa.

beer *Six-pack of ~.* ʻEkeʻeke pia. *Twelve-pack of ~.* Pūʻolo pia. *Case of ~.* Pahu pia.

beet Pike.

beetle Ponu. *Larder ~, dermestid.* Ponu ʻili.

beforehand *Early, as registration for a conference.* Hiki mua. See *early, late.*

begin *To start, as a computer program.* Hoʻomaka. See *quit.*

beginning level *Also introductory level.* Pae hoʻomaka.

begonia Pīkōnia.

behavior *As the way people or animals act.* Lawena. *Instinctive ~.* Lawena ʻike hānau. *Learned ~.* Lawena ʻapo.

behavioral science Kālailawena.

behind-the-back pass *In basketball; to throw such a pass.* Kīloi kua.

Belarus Belarusa.

Belgium *Also Belgian.* Pelekiuma, Belegiuma.

Belize *Also Belizean.* Belize.

bell Pele. *Alarm ~, as on a clock or fire alarm.* Oeoe, pele.

Bellatrix *A star.* Kaluakoke.

bellows nozzle Nuku ʻūpā makani.

belt *Asteroid ~.* Kāʻei hōkūnaʻi.

belt buckle ʻŪmiʻi ʻilikuapo, ʻūmiʻi.

belt loop *As on a pair of pants.* Apo ʻili kuapo.

bench See *first off the bench.*

benchmark *In math.* Kaha ana.

benefit *Fringe ~, as any employee ~ other than salary, such as medical insurance, etc.* Pono keu.

benzene Benezene.

benzoin *A resin used in perfume and cosmetics.* Penekui.

Bering Berina. *~ Sea.* Ke kai ʻo Berina.

Bernoulli's principle *In science.* Ke kulehana a Penuli.

berry Pīʻai. See *Hawaiian entries under* pīʻai.

best boy *An assistant gaffer.* Hope luna uila. See *gaffer.*

beta particle *A negatively charged electron moving at high speed.* Huna beta. See *alpha particle.*

beverage *Drink.* Meainu.

Bhutan *Also Bhutanese.* Butana.

bias *Also biased.* Pāʻewaʻewa. *Systematic error in gathering data, in math.* Paʻewa.

bicameral *As a legislature.* ʻElua hale.

biceps *The muscle of the front of the upper arm.* Mākala ʻuala.

bicuspid valve *Of the heart.* Pepeiao pālua. See *valve.*

bicycle Paikikala. See *basket, bike.* *~ chain.* Kaulahao paikikala. *~ chain cog.* Pānihoniho o ke kaulahao paikikala. *~ crossbar.* Kua hao paikikala. *~ handlebars.* Kalaiwa paikikala, ʻau paikikala (*preceded by* ke). *~ mud guard.* Pale lepo paikikala. *~ seat.* Noho paikikala. *~ tire.* Kaea paikikala, taea paikikala.

Big Dipper Nāhiku.

Big Five *The ~, the five corporations that controlled most of the sugar industry in Hawaiʻi.* Nā Hui Nui ʻElima.

bike *Dirt ~.* Mokokaikala holo lepo. *Mountain ~.* Paikikala holo kuahiwi. See *bicycle.*

bill *A piece of paper money.* Pepa kālā. See *coin.* *One-dollar ~.* Pepa pākahi. *Five-dollar ~.* Pepa pālima. *Ten-dollar ~.* Pepa pāʻumi.

bill *A draft of a law presented to a legislature.* Pila. *Division of a legislative ~, larger than a section or article.* Mokuna. *See Hawaiian entries under* kānāwai *and* title.

billion *See* giga-, nano-.

bill of rights Palapala pono kanaka.

binary *A base-two system of numeration, in math.* Kumu hoʻohui pālua. *~ compound.* Pūhui kumumea lua.

binary compound Pūhui kumumea lua.

binder *Ring ~.* Puke lina kui. *See* notebook, ring.

bingo *Name of Hawaiian language version.* Keola.

binoculars Paʻa ʻohenānā.

biochemistry Kemika meaola.

biodegradable Pēhāpopopo.

biofilter *For a fish tank, in aquaculture.* Huila mūhune, hōkele mūhune *(slang).*

biographical *Also biography.* Piliolana. *See* autobiographical. *~ novel.* Nōwela piliolana.

biological *See entries below. ~ community.* Kaiameaola. *Natural ~ community.* Kaiameaola kūlohelohe. *~ control.* Kāohi meaola. *~ family.* ʻOhana kālaimeaola. *To be ~ly adapted to.* Liliuwelo.

biologist Kanaka kālaimeaola, mea kālaimeaola.

biology Kālaimeaola. *See* biological, cell, microbiology.

bioluminescence Māʻamaola.

biomass Kōpū meaola.

biome Kaiawao.

birch Pūkowi.

bird *See Hawaiian entries under* manu.

birdbath ʻAuʻauna manu. *See* feeder.

bird of paradise *The bird.* Manu palekaiko. *The flower.* Pua manu.

birthday card Kāleka lā hānau, kāleka piha makahiki. *See* anniversary card.

biscuit Palaoa pikeke, pikeke.

bisect *To ~, in math.* ʻOki hapalua. *Abb.* ʻo2. *See* bisector.

bisector *In math.* Kaha ʻoki hapalua. *See* bisect. *Perpendicular ~.* Kaha ʻoki hapalua kūpono.

Bissau *See* Guinea-Bissau.

bisulfate Bisulafahate. *Sodium ~.* Sodiuma bisulafahate.

bit *A computer unit of information.* Huna. *See* byte. *As for a drill.* Makawili. *See* drill.

bitmap *To ~, a style of printing a graphic image as on a computer printer.* Kākiko. *A ~ped graphic image.* Kiʻi kiko. *Precision ~ping.* Kākiko miomio.

Black Sea Ke Kai ʻEle.

black widow *A kind of spider.* Nananana hese ʻeleʻele, nanana hese ʻeleʻele.

bladder ʻEke mimi *(preceded by* ke).

blade *Of tongue.* Lau alelo. *See* tongue.

blanket Kapa, kapa moe. *See* quilt, shawl. *Electric ~.* Kapa uila. *Heavy or woolen ~.* Kapa huluhulu, huluhulu.

blank footage *As of video tape.* Līpine maʻemaʻe. *See* footage.

blast off *To ~, as a rocket.* ʻŌlapa. *To cause to ~.* Hoʻōlapa.

Blattella germanica *German cockroach.* ʻElelū laʻaloa.

bleachers ʻŌmoʻo noho.

blind pass *Also no-look pass, in basketball; to throw such a pass.* Kīloi hoʻopalai.

blinds *Venetian ~.* Pale pukaaniani ʻōlepelepe.

blizzard Pāhili hau, makani pāhili hau.

block *A child's toy.* Palaka. *Adobe ~.* Uinihapa ʻakopie. *City ~.* Pōlaka. *Pier ~, in construction.* Palaka kimeki. *Termite ~.* Palaka kimeki pale mū.

block *To ~ or highlight text, as in a computer program.* Kahiāuli. *See shade.*

block *To ~ (a shot), in basketball.* Paku. *See roof. To ~ out or screen.* 'Āke'a. *To ~ (the ball), in volleyball.* Paku, pālulu. *To pass through the ~.* Hala ka pālulu. *~er.* Mea paku, paku. *Point from ~.* 'Ai hele wale.

block and tackle *An arrangement of pulleys and rope or cable used to lift or haul.* Hāme'a pokaka'a.

blocking foul *In basketball.* Ku'ia 'āke'a. *See foul.*

blood Koko. *See entries below. ~ cell.* Hunaola koko. *~ glucose.* Monakō koko. *~ pressure.* Mīkā koko. *~stream.* Kahena koko. *~ type.* Hulu koko. *White ~ cell.* Hunaola koko ke'oke'o. *Red ~ cell.* Hunaola koko 'ula'ula. *Cold-~ed.* Koko hu'ihu'i. *Warm-~ed.* Koko mehana.

blood alcohol level Nui lama koko. *See breathalyzer.*

blood clot Lapa koko. *See coagulated.*

blooming *Also blossoming, unfolded, as a flower; spread open.* Mohala.

blossoming *See blooming.*

blouse Lakeke, palauki. *See jacket.*

blow *As the wind. See wind. To ~ one's nose.* Hūkē, ho'okē.

blue-button *A kind of jellyfish.* Pa'ipihi. *See by-the-wind-sailor, Portuguese man-of-war.*

bluefish I'auli.

blue jay Manu kēuli, kēuli.

blueprint Ki'i kūkulu, ki'i kūkulu hale. *To draft or draw ~s; also draftsman or drafter.* Kaha ki'i kūkulu.

blush *Also rouge, as makeup.* Hehelo pāpālina.

boar's tusk Niho kepa.

board Papa. *See BBS, member, sten-strip board, white board, windsurf. Four-by-four ~.* Papa hā hā.

Two-by-four ~. Papa lua hā. *Bulletin ~.* Papa hō'ike'ike. *~ game, as checkers.* Kēmu. *Game ~.* Papa kēmu.

bob *As of a pendulum.* 'Olo.

bobby pin 'Ūmi'i lauoho.

body *As of a composition or text.* Kino. *See opening, closing. As of an 'ukulele, guitar, etc.* 'Ōpū. *See 'ukulele.*

bog *With no trees and soft ground.* Nāele. *See marsh, swamp.*

boil Paila. *~ing point.* Kēkelē paila. *See freezing point, melting point.*

bold *See boldface.*

boldface *On a computer or in typesetting; also bold.* Kā'ele. *To bold, i.e. set in ~ type.* Ho'okā'ele.

Bolivia *Also Bolivian.* Bolivia.

bolt *As in nuts and ~s.* Kui kolū. *See nut. Of material.* 'Āpā lole.

bomb *Missile ~.* Kao lele pahū.

bond Lou. *Between atoms or ions as a result of gaining, losing, or sharing electrons.* Lou 'ātoma. *~ing instrument.* 'Ūlou. *A certificate bought from a government or corporation which agrees to pay back the cost of the bond plus interest after a set period of time.* Pona.

bone *See Hawaiian entries beginning with* iwi.

bonemeal Iwi wiliwili. *See meat meal.*

bonus *Extra credit, as a class assignment or question on a quiz.* Ho'opi'i kaha, 'ai keu. *~ question.* Nīnau ho'opi'i kaha, nīnau 'ai keu.

book *See Hawaiian entries beginning with* puke. *Humorous ~.* Puke ho'omake'aka. *Information ~.* Puke kumuhana. *Pattern ~.* Puke a'o analula.

bookmark Lepe puke.

bookshelf Haka kau puke.

boom *To operate a ~, as for movie or video production.* Kīko'o ipuleo. *~ operator.* Mea kīko'o ipuleo.

booster *Solid rocket ~.* Kao wāwahie kinopaʻa, kao wāwahie paʻa.

boot *Rubber ~.* Lapa puki, laba puki, puki lapa. *Ski ~.* Kāmaʻa puki heʻe hau.

booth *As at a carnival, etc.* Kāmala.

borealis *See aurora borealis, Corona Borealis.*

borer *A kind of insect.* Huhupao.

borrow *To ~, take on credit.* Lawe ʻaiʻē. See *lend, loan. To ~ or check out something by signing for it, as a book.* Kāinoa. *To ~, as a word from another language; also to introduce, as plants and animals to a particular place.* Lawekahiki. See *introduce. A ~ed word.* He huaʻōlelo i lawekahiki ʻia.

Bosnia Bosenia. *~ and Herzogovina.* Bosenia me Hesegowina.

botannical garden Māla hōʻikeʻike meakanu.

botany Kālailau nahele.

Botswana Botuana.

bottle *Baby ~.* ʻŌmole omo waiū, ʻōmole waiū. *Dropping ~, a bottle used much like an eyedropper.* ʻŌmole hoʻokulu.

bottom *Clothing.* Lole o lalo. See *top.*

bottom margin Lihi o lalo. See *margin.*

bougainvillea Pua pepa, pukanawila.

boulder *Generic term, particularly outside of Hawaiʻi.* Nukahaku. *In Hawaiʻi, referring to poi pounder-size stones and larger.* Pōhaku ʻalā.

bounce *To ~, as a check.* Leleneo.

bounce pass *In basketball; to throw such a pass.* Kīloi papahele.

boundary *Convergent ~ in plate techtonics, in geology.* Palena kuʻi. *Divergent ~.* Palena neʻe ʻoā. *Transform ~.* Palena kākele.

bounds *To go out of ~, in sports.* ʻAʻe palena.

bow *As ribbon or string.* Hīpuʻu pewa. See *knot. ~ tie.* Lei ʻāʻī pewa.

bow *Of a boat.* Ihu.

bowl *Toilet ~.* Ipu hoʻopaupilikia. See *chamber pot, urinal.*

bowling Maika. *~ frame.* Kuea maika. *~ pin.* Pine maika.

box *Cardboard ~.* Pahu pepa. *Fuse ~.* Pahu ʻuiki uila. *Meter ~.* Pahu mika. *Toy ~.* Pahu mea pāʻani, waihona mea pāʻani.

box *Dialog ~, in a computer program.* Pahu aʻo.

box and whiskers graph *In math.* Pakuhi pahu me ka ʻumiʻumi.

boxcar *As of a train.* Kaʻapahu.

boxing round Puni.

box turtle Honu pahu.

boycott *To abstain from buying from or dealing with (a company) as a means of coercion.* Nāʻīāʻumi.

Boyle Poila. *~'s law, i.e. decreasing the volume of a gas will increase the pressure the gas exerts if the temperature remains constant.* Ke kānāwai a Poila.

brace *As for body parts.* Kāliki. *Wrist ~.* Kāliki pūlima.

bracket *In punctuation.* Kahaapo kihikihi. See entry below and *parenthesis. Open ~.* Kahaapo kihikihi wehe. *Close ~.* Kahaapo kihikihi pani.

bracket *As in a sports tournament.* Māhele. *Consolation ~.* Māhele hāʻule. *Winner's ~.* Māhele lanakila.

brain Lolo. See *computer.*

brainstorm Puaʻi manaʻo.

brake Peleki. *~ cable, as on a bicycle.* Uea peleki. *~ disk.* Pā peleki (*preceded by* ke). *Disk ~.* Peleki pā. *~ pad.* Pale peleki.

bran Pelene. *~ muffin.* Māpina pelene.

branch *As of a government.* Māhele. *Executive ~.* Māhele mana hoʻokō. *Judicial ~.* Māhele ʻaha hoʻokolokolo. *Legislative ~.* Māhele ʻahaʻōlelo.

brand new Hou loa.

brass Keleawe. ~ *instrument.* Pū keleawe.

Brazil *Also Brazilian.* Palakila, Barazila.

bread Palaoa. *See Hawaiian entries under* palaoa. ~ *crumbs.* Hunahuna palaoa. *Brown* ~, *a layman's term for any bread made with dark flower.* Palaoa māku'e. *Wheat* ~. Palaoa huika. *Whole wheat* ~. Palaoa huika piha. *White* ~. Palaoa ke'oke'o.

breadth *Also width, in math.* Ākea, ana ākea, laulā (*abb.* ll), ana laulā. *See height, length.*

break *To* ~ *the law.* Ha'iha'i kānāwai, 'a'e kānāwai. *See* outlaw.

break *To* ~ *apart, in math, i.e.* ~*ing a number into addends or factors; also to* ~ *or change, as a twenty-dollar bill.* Wāwahi.

break *To* ~ *or stop, as an electric circuit.* 'Oki. *See* open. *Circuit breaker, a device which automatically interrupts electric current before wires in a circuit get too hot.* 'Ū'oki puni uila.

break *Page* ~, *as in a computer program.* Ho'oka'awale 'ao'ao.

break *Fast* ~, *in basketball; also to make a fast* ~. Ulele kikī. *See* lead pass.

breast *Chicken* ~. Umauma moa.

breast stroke *Also to swim the* ~. 'Au umauma.

breathalyzer Ana lama hanu. *See blood alcohol level.*

breathing equipment *As for use in space exploration.* Lako hanu.

breed *Also to impregnate.* Ho'opi'i. *To* ~ *animals or propagate plants.* Ha'akipu. *See* crossbreed.

breeze *Gentle* ~; *dust raised and small branches move, in meteorology.* Aheahe. *See* wind. *Leaves in constant motion.* Kolonahe.

breezeway *As an open area between buildings.* Holona makani.

bridge *As on an 'ukulele or guitar.* Nī'au nui. *See* 'ukulele.

brim *Of a hat.* Kihikihi, pekekeu. *Of a floppy hat.* Laulau.

brine *A concentrated solution of salt or ocean water.* Wai pa'akai pa'apūhia, wai pa'akai.

brine shrimp *Artemia.* Pokipoki ālia.

bring back out *To* ~, *in basketball; also to slow down, as in a fast break.* Kuemi, kuemi iki.

Britain *Also British.* Pelekāne, Pelekānia. *See* England, English.

British *See* Britain.

brittle *As dry* hala *leaves.* Pa'apa'a'ina. *See* peanut brittle.

broad reach (port) *Broad reach on the port side, i.e. sailing downwind at an angle between 90° and directly downwind, with the port side windward.* Kele ama ka'akepa. *See broad reach (starboard), beam reach (port, starboard), close hauled (port, starboard), downwind.*

broad reach (starboard) *Broad reach on the starboard side, i.e. sailing downwind at an angle between 90° and directly downwind, with the starboard side windward.* Kele 'ākea ka'akepa. *See broad reach (port), beam reach (port, starboard), close hauled (port, starboard), downwind.*

broccoli Palakalī.

brochure *Also flyer, pamphlet.* Pepelu.

broiler oven 'Oma kō'ala.

broke *Go for* ~; *also go for it, geevum.* Lawe pīlahi. *See do with all one's might or strength.*

bromine Polomine. ~ *gas.* Kinoea polomine.

bronchial *Also bronchiole, bronchus.* 'Āmanapu'u. *See entries below.*

bronchiole *Also bronchial, bronchus.* 'Āmanapu'u. *Terminal* ~. 'Āmanapu'u kuahope.

bronchus *Also bronchiole, bronchial.* 'Āmanapu'u. *Primary ~.* 'Āmanapu'u kuamua. *Secondary or lobar ~.* 'Āmanapu'u kualua. *Tertiary or segmental ~.* 'Āmanapu'u kuakolu.

bronze Keleawekini. *The ~ (cap.) age, period.* Ke au keleawekini. *See Hawaiian entry* au.

brooder Pene 'io'io.

broom closet Ke'ena pūlumi.

Brown *Also Brownian.* Palaunu. *See entries below. ~ian motion, in chemistry.* Lelekē Palaunu.

brown bread *A layman's term for any bread made with dark flour.* Palaoa māku'e. *See Hawaiian entries under* palaoa.

brownie *The dessert.* Mea'ono palauni, palauni.

brown rice Laiki māku'e, lāisi māku'e.

browse *As in a database program having the capability to rearrange data.* Ho'okuene 'ikepili. *See surf. As through a computer program script or on the Internet.* Māka'ika'i.

browser *An animal that eats twigs and leaves.* Hamulau lā'au. *See grazer.*

brumby *A wild Australian horse.* Palami.

brush *A contact that supplies electric current to a commutator.* Awe uholo uila. *See commutator, conductor. For bathing.* Palaki 'au'au. *Paint ~.* Hulu pena.

bubble chamber *In chemistry.* Hōkelo hu'a.

bubble wand *For blowing bubbles.* Lina puhi hu'ahu'a.

buckle *Belt ~.* 'Ūmi'i 'ilikuapo, 'ūmi'i.

bud *Of a leaf.* Mu'o. *See leaf.*

budget *A listing of expenditures and receipts.* Mo'ohelu kālā, mo'ohelu. *See accounting. To make a ~.* Ho'opa'a mo'ohelu kālā.

buffer Pale ho'oka'awale.

bug *See insect, sow bug.*

buggy *Dune ~.* Ka'a holo one.

bugle Pū koa. *See cornet, trumpet.*

build *To put together, as a model.* Kāpili. *See manufacture. To ~ a model airplane.* Kāpili kūkohu mokulele.

build *To ~, in math.* Ho'omāhele. *See undo. To ~ a shield (volcano).* Ho'āhua kuahene.

built-in Pa'aloko. *See hard disk, hard drive. ~ memory, in a computer.* Waihona 'ike pa'aloko.

bulb 'Ōpu'u. *Light ~.* 'Ōpu'u kukui. *As of a lily or tulip.* Hua kanu. *~ tip.* 'Ōmaka hua kanu. *Wet-and-dry-~ hygrometer.* Ana kawaūea 'ōpu'u pulu a malo'o.

Bulgaria *Also Bulgarian.* Pulukalia, Bulugaria.

bulk *Mass.* Nuipa'a.

bulletin board Papa hō'ike'ike.

Bulletin Board Service *On computer programs (BBS).* Papa Lawelawe Ho'olaha. *Abb.* PLH.

bullfrog Poloka pulu.

bullsnake Nāhesa pulu.

bump *Speed ~, as on a road or in a parking lot.* Pu'u ha'apupū. *To bang into; to crash, as cars.* Ho'oku'i. *To ~ (the ball), in volleyball.* Ku'i 'āmana.

Bunsen burner Kapuahi ula kahi. *See burner.*

bunting *Indigo ~.* Manu 'inikō.

buoyant force *The upward force of a fluid on an object in it.* Manehu ho'olana.

bureau *Dresser.* Pahu 'ume.

bureaucracy *Also bureaucratic.* Pākulekele. *Bureaucrat.* Kanaka pākulekele.

buret *A precision-made piece of glassware used to measure and deliver accurate volumes of solutions, in science.* 'Ūhōlo'a mā'ō'āna.

Burkina Faso Burakina Faso.

Burma *Also Burmese.* Puruma, Buruma.

burn *Slash and ~, a method of land cultivation.* Kā makawela.

burner *As on a stove.* Pā kapuahi. See *hot plate.* *Bunsen* ~. Kapuahi ula kahi. *Fisher* ~. Kapuahi pukapuka. *Meeker* ~. Kapuahi Mika.

Burundi Buruni.

bush *Shrub.* La'alā'au. See *shrubland, twig.*

bush bean Pāpapa ha'a.

bushel *A unit of measurement.* Pūkele. *Abb.* pū.

business *Career or occupation.* 'Oihana. *Purchase and sale of goods and services.* Kāloa'a. *A person or company engaged in* ~. Pā'oihana. ~ *cycle, a repeated series of economic growth and recession.* Pō'aiapuni kāloa'a. *Central* ~ *district.* 'Āpana pā'oihana kauwaena. See *downtown.*

bus stop Kūna ka'a 'ōhua.

butane Butane.

butcher Mea lole pipi, kanaka lole pipi. ~ *paper.* Pepa lole pipi.

butter *Peanut* ~. Pīnekipaka.

butterfly *Kamehameha* ~. Pulelehua Kamehameha. *Monarch* ~. Pulelehua pua kalaunu. ~ *stroke; also to swim the* ~ *stroke.* 'Au malolo. See *stroke.*

button *Also to* ~. Pihi, pihi lole *(preceded by* ke*).* *Turbo* ~, *as in Nintendo games.* Pihi pīna'i. See *warp zone.*

buttonhole Puka pihi.

byte *In computer terminology.* 'Ai. See *bit, kilobyte, megabyte, gigabyte.*

by-the-wind-sailor *A kind of jellyfish.* Pa'ipe'a. See *blue-button, Portuguese man-of-war.*

C

cabbage *Skunk* ~. Kāpiki ponī.

cabinet *A council that advises a president, sovereign, etc.* 'Aha kuhina.

cabinet *File* ~. Pahu waihona pepa, pahu waihona, waihona pepa. *Medicine* ~. Waihona lā'au lapa'au. *Storage* ~. Waihona ho'āhu.

cable Kaula uea. *Also* uea. *Brake* ~, *as on a bicycle.* Uea peleki.

cache *As in a computer program.* Ahu ho'okoe. *To* ~, *as a computer function.* Ho'okoe. *To* ~ *disks.* Ho'okoe pā.

cactus *General term; also prickly pear* ~. Pānini. See *barrel cactus, cholla, ocotillo, organ pipe cactus, prickly pear cactus.*

café au lait *Hot coffee served with an equal amount of hot or scalded milk.* Kope ke'oke'o.

caffeine 'Ākope.

cage Pene. See *kennel.*

caladium Kalo kalakoa.

calcareous Pa'apuna. ~ *rock, calcium carbonate.* Pōhaku pa'apuna.

calcite Ōpuna.

calcium Kalipuna. ~ *carbonate, calcareous rock.* Pōhaku pa'apuna. ~ *oxilate.* Kalipuna 'okesailihate.

calculate Huli a loa'a, huli, ho'omaulia.

calculator Mīkini helu. ~ *display screen.* Papakaumaka mīkini helu. *Graphing* ~. Mīkini kākuhi.

caldera Lua kīlauea.

Caledonia See *New Caledonia.*

calendar 'Alemanaka.

calf *Gastrocnemius muscle of the anterior of the lower leg.* Mākala 'ulu, 'olo'olo wāwae.

calibrate *Also calibration.* Kauanakahi.

California *Also Californian.* Kaleponi. ~ *grass.* Mau'u Kaleponi.

call *As a* ~ *made on a telephone.* See *Hawaiian entries under* kelepona.

calligraphy Limahilu.

Callisto *A moon of Jupiter.* Kalito.

call number *As for a library book.* Helu kuhi puke. See *card catalog, catalog card.*

call sheet *A list of jobs for movie or video production.* Papa māhele hana. See *jobs.*

calm *As the wind; smoke rises vertically, and direction of wind shown by smoke drift rather than wind vanes, in meteorology.* Pohu. See *wind. Also cool-headed, even-tempered.* Māio.

calorie Ikehu'ā.

calorimeter *An instrument used to measure changes in thermal energy.* Ana ikehu kā'oko'a.

cambium *The slippery layer under the bark of a plant which is the growing area of the stem.* Wale 'ili.

Cambodia *Also Cambodian.* Kamabodia.

camcorder *Video camera.* Pahu pa'i wikiō.

Cameroon *Also Cameroun, Cameroonian, Camerounian.* Kameruna.

camouflaged Nalope'e. *To camouflage.* Ho'onalope'e.

camp *Gathering of people to learn or practice certain skills.* 'Āpo'e. See *camper, campground. Computer ~.* 'Āpo'e kamepiula. *Basketball ~.* 'Āpo'e pōhīna'i. *To ~.* Ho'omoana.

camper *Camping vehicle.* Ka'a ho'omoana.

campground Kahua ho'omoana.

campus mail Leka kūloko kula. See *internal mail, office mail.*

can *Aerosol ~.* Kini kīkī. *~ of corned beef.* Kini pipi. *~ of tuna.* Kini tuna. *~ opener.* Mea wehe kini. *Watering ~.* Kini ho'opulu meakanu.

Canada *Also Canadian.* Kanakā.

Canary Isles Pae Moku Kenele.

cancel *To ~, as a computer function.* Ho'ōki. See *put away, undo.*

cancel *To ~, i.e. the compression of one wave at the same time as the rarefaction of another wave, in science.* Ku'ipē. *To be ~led (out), in science or argumentation; ~lation.* Ku'ipēhia.

cancellous bone Iwi 'ana. See *cortical bone.*

candidate *As in politics.* Moho. See *election.*

candlenut Kukui, kuikui.

candy *~ cane.* Kanakē ko'oko'o. *Caramel ~.* Kanakē kalamela. See *lollipop.*

canned fish Kini i'a.

cannibal *Among animals, insects, etc.* Hamuhika. See *cannibal (dic.). ~ snail.* Homeka hamuhika.

canoe *Without 'iako.* Wa'a 'Ilikini. *The portion of a ~ between forward and aft outrigger booms.* Ukuwai. See *port, starboard.*

canopy *~ layer of vegetation between understory and emergent layers.* Papa kaupoku. See *vegetation layer.*

cantaloupe Ipu'ala. See *melon.*

canteen Kini huewai.

canvass *To go door to door handing out political information and asking people which candidate they support.* Anamana'o pāloka.

canyon Awāwa kūhōhō. See *passageway. Grand ~.* Ke awāwa kūhōhō nui 'o Haka'ama, Haka'ama.

cap *Dunce ~.* Pāpale kone. *Shower ~.* Pāpale kililau. *Ski ~, stocking ~.* Pāpale kapuhau. *Swim ~.* Pāpale 'au.

cap *As for a toothpaste tube; lid, as for a jar.* Pani (*preceded by* ke). See *manhole cover. Pen ~.* Po'i peni (*preceded by* ke).

capacity Pihana'ū. *Abb.* pi'ū. See *volume. Field ~, for holding water.* Palena ū wai.

Cape Verde Laeuliuli. *~ Islands.* Nā mokupuni 'o Laeuliuli.

capillary 'Umelauoho. *Capillarity.* Pē'umelauoho. *~ pipette.* Paipuli'i 'umelauoho. *~ water.* Wai 'umelauoho. *One of the minute blood vessels between the arteries and the veins.* Oho.

capital *Upper case.* Ma'aka. See *capitalize, letter. ~ letter.* Hua ma'aka.

capital *Anything produced in an economy that is accumulated or used to produce other goods and services.* Ahu kāloaʻa. See *capitalism.*

capitalism Paikāloaʻa, paihoʻāhu kāloaʻa.

capitalize *To ~ (a letter of the alphabet).* Hoʻomaʻaka. See *lower case. Three lines drawn under a letter to indicate that the letter is to be ~d, in proofreading.* Kaha hoʻomaʻaka. *A line drawn diagonally through a capital letter to indicate the letter is not to be ~d.* Kaha hoʻonaʻinaʻi.

capo *As used on a fretted instrument to raise the pitch of all strings.* ʻŪmiʻi kaula.

capping *As the last stage of volcano formation.* Pani poʻo *(preceded by* ke).

cappuccino *Espresso coffee and steamed milk.* Kapukino.

caprock *In geology.* Pōhaku hoʻopaʻa wai.

caps *Key ~, on a computer program.* Hōʻike hua pihi. *~ lock, as on a computer or typewriter keyboard.* Laka maʻaka. *~ lock key.* Pihi laka maʻaka, pihi laka *(preceded by* ke).

capsule *Space ~.* Kelena moku ahikao.

caption *Also to ~.* Lepe kiʻi. See *subtitle.*

caramel Kalamela. *~ candy.* Kanakē kalamela.

carbohydrate Kōpia.

carbon *Not in chemistry.* ʻŌpaʻu. See *entries below. ~ paper.* Pepa ʻōpaʻu.

carbon Karabona, kalapona. See *entries below.*

carbonate Karabonahate. See *calcareous. Calcium ~, calcareous rock.* Pōhaku paʻapuna. *Cupric ~.* Kupuriku karabonahate. *Ferrous ~.* Ferousa karabonahate.

carbon dating *Also radiocarbon date.* Helu makahiki kalapona.

carbon dioxide Karabona diokesaside, kalapona ʻokikene lua. *Oxygen-~ cycle.* Pōʻaiapuni ʻokikene kalapona ʻokikene lua.

carbon disulfide Karabona disulifaside.

carbonic acid ʻAkika kalapona.

carbon monoxide Karabona monokesaside.

carboxylic acid ʻAkika pūhui kalapona.

carburetor *As in an internal-combustion engine.* ʻŪhōloʻa kakalina.

card Kāleka. See entries below and postcard. *Birthday ~.* Kāleka lā hānau. *Birthday or anniversary ~.* Kāleka piha makahiki. *Graduation ~.* Kāleka puka kula, kāleka hemo kula. *Greeting ~.* Kāleka aloha.

card *Charge ~.* Kāleka kāki, ʻea kāki. *Fitness ~, as for sports or physical education.* Kāleka olakino. *Flash ~.* Kāleka aʻo. *Index ~.* Kāleka pahu.

cardboard *Corrugated paper.* Pepa pahu. *~ box.* Pahu pepa.

card catalog *As in a library.* Pahu kāleka kuhi puke. See *call number, catalog card.*

card game See *wiped out.*

cardiac arrythmia Puʻuwai pana ʻewaʻewa.

cardinal *The bird.* Manu mākaʻi, manu ʻulaʻula.

cardinal number Helu heluna. See *ordinal number.*

cardinal points *The four ~, or four primary directions of the compass, in geography.* Nā kūkulu ʻehā.

cardiovascular system *Also circulatory system.* ʻŌnaehana mānowai, ʻōnaehana mānowai koko.

career *Occupation.* ʻOihana. See *business. Baseball ~.* ʻOihana pōhili.

caret *An editing mark (^) used to show where something is to be inserted, in proofreading.* Kaha hoʻokomo. See *pound sign.*

Caribbean Kalepiana, Karebiana.

caries *Cavity in a tooth.* Puka niho. See *oral cavity.*

Carina *The star in the center of the constellation* ~. Mākoi. *Another star in this constellation.* Makawela.

carnival See *amusement park.*

carnivore *Also carnivorous.* Hamui'a.

carnivorous caterpillar *Eupithecia spp.* 'Enuhe hamui'a.

Carolina *Also Carolinian.* Kalolaina. See *Caroline Isles. North* ~. Kalolaina 'Ākau. *South* ~. Kalolaina Hema.

Caroline Isles Ka pae moku 'o Kalolaina, ka pae moku 'o Karolaina.

carotid artery A'a pu'uwai 'ā'ī.

carpal bone *Any one of the eight* ~s *of the wrist.* Iwi pūlima.

carpenter's level 'Iliwai.

carpet Moena weleweka. See *rug.*

carriage *Baby* ~. Ka'apēpē.

carrier *As of a radio-wave signal.* Hāpaina.

carry *To palm or* ~ *(the ball), in basketball.* Poholuna.

carrying violation *In volleyball.* 'A'ena hāpai. See *lift.*

cart *Shopping* ~. Ka'a mākeke. *Push*~. Ka'a pahu.

cartilage Iwi kamumu.

carton *Milk* ~. Pahu waiū.

cartoon Kātuna, kākuna, kākuni. See *comic book.*

cartridge *As for a computer printer.* Pāpahu. *Font* ~. Pāpahu kinona hua.

cascade Wailelele.

case *Cassette* ~, *usually made of plastic.* Poho lola. *Tape* ~, *cassette holder.* Pāiki lola.

case Pahu. See *pack, six-pack, twelve-pack. Of beer.* Pahu pia. *Of soda.* Pahu koloaka.

case sensitive *As in a computer program.* Maka'ala ma'aka.

cash Kālā kū'ike. *Petty* ~. Kālā kini.

cashbox Kini kālā.

cashew 'Akakiu.

cashier Mea 'ohi kālā, kanaka 'ohi kālā, wahine 'ohi kālā. See *cash register.*

cashier's check Pila kīko'o panakō.

cash on delivery *COD.* 'Ohi hiki.

cash register Mīkini 'ohi kālā. See *cashier.*

Caspian Kasepiana. ~ *Sea.* Ke kai 'o Kasepiana.

cassette *As for music tapes.* Lola. See *entry below.* ~ *recorder/player.* Mīkini lola. ~ *player.* Mīkini ho'okani lola. ~ *recorder.* Mīkini ho'opa'a lola. See *recorder.* ~ *case, usually made of plastic.* Poho lola. ~ *holder or tape case.* Pāiki lola. *Video* ~. Lola wikiō.

cassette *Paper* ~, *as for a computer printer.* Poho pepa.

Cassiopeia *A constellation.* 'Iwakeli'i.

cast *As for a broken arm.* Kimeki iwi, puna.

cat *Japanese lucky welcome* ~. Manekineko.

catalog card *As in a library.* Kāleka helu kuhi puke. See *call number, card catalog.*

catalyst *A substance which increases the rate of a chemical reaction without being permanently changed itself.* 'Ūmō'auiwawe, hō'eleu mō'aui.

catamaran Moku kaulua.

cataract *Steep rapids in a large river.* Wai kōī.

catbird Manu pōpoki.

catch *To* ~, *as a ball.* 'Apo. See *receive.*

categorize *Also to classify.* Wae'ano.

category *Also division, piece, portion, department, part, land division; to divide, apportion.* Māhele.

caterpillar *Carnivorous* ~ *(Eupithecia spp).* 'Enuhe hamui'a.

catfish 'O'opu Pākē.

cathode *The negative electrode in an electrical circuit.* 'Ūholo uila 'ine. See *anode, electrode.* ~-*ray tube (CRT).* 'Ohe kīwī.

Catskills *A mountain range.* Katakila.

cattail Huelopōpoki.

cattle egret 'Aleku'u kau pipi.

caucus *A meeting of political party leaders to determine policy, choose candidates, etc.* Haiamui.

cauliflower Kalipalaoa.

cause Kumu. See *effect. A prefix indicating the instrument or ~ of a particular action.* 'ū-.

cavity *In a tooth, caries.* Puka niho. *Inner ear ~, cochlea.* Haka mo'oni. *Nasal ~, in linguistics.* Haka ihu. *Oral ~.* Haka waha.

CD *Also compact disc.* CD (*pronounced* sēdē), sēdē; pā CD, pā sēdē (*preceded by* ke).

cede *As land or territory.* Ho'oku'u 'aelike.

ceiling Kilina, huna.

Celebes Selepe. *~ Sea.* Ke kai 'o Selepe.

celestial equator Pō'ai waena lani.

cell *As in databases or tables.* Kū'ono.

cell *Biological ~.* Hunaola. See *blood, tissue. One ~, one-celled; single ~, single-celled.* Hunaola kahi.

cellar 'Ōpao.

cellulose Kelulose.

Celsius Kelekia. *Abb.* Klk.

cement *Plastic pipe ~.* Tuko paipu 'ea, tuko paipu. See *primer. Rubber ~.* Tuko laholio. See *glue, paste.*

census *A periodic official enumeration of a population and its characteristics.* Helu kanaka.

cent Kēneka. *~ sign.* Kaha kēneka.

center *Of a circle.* Kikowaena. See entries below and *learning center, shopping center. Of tongue.* Waena alelo. *Turn ~, in math.* Kikowaena wili.

center *To ~, as type on a printed page.* Kauwaena. *To ~ justify.* Ho'okauwaena.

center *Also five man, in basketball.* Kūlima. *In football.* Huki pōpō. See *hike.*

center circle *On basketball court.* Pō'ai waena.

center feed *To ~, as paper into a printer or copy machine.* Hānai waena.

center of gravity Piko 'umekaumaha. See *gravity.*

centi- *A prefix meaning one hundredth (c).* Hapa haneli. *Abb.* hhn. *Also* keni-. *See entries below and* deci-, *milli-, micro-, nano-, pico-.*

centigram Kenikalame. *Abb.* kkal.

centiliter Kenilika. *Abb.* kl.

centimeter Kenimika. *Abb.* knm.

Central African Republic Lepupalika 'Apelika Waena.

Central America *Also Central American, Latin America, Latin American.* 'Amelika Waena.

central angle *An angle that has its vertex at the center of a circle, in math.* Huina kikowaena.

central business district 'Āpana pā'oihana kauwaena. See *downtown.*

central vowel *In linguistics.* Woela kauwaena. See *vowel.*

centrifugal *Acting in a direction away from a center.* Lele niniu. See *centripetal. ~ force.* Manehu lele niniu.

centripetal *Acting in a direction toward a center.* 'Ume niniu. See *centrifugal. ~ force.* Manehu 'ume niniu.

ceramic Lāmeka. *~ tile.* Kile lāmeka.

cereal Kiliala, siriala.

ceremonies *Opening ~.* Wehena papahana. See *closing banquet.*

certificate *Of achievement.* Palapala ho'okō. *Gift ~.* Palapala makana.

certified check Pila kīko'o panakō.

Chad *Also Chadian.* Kada.

chain Kaulahao; ku'ina; pae. See *food net, range, series. Bicycle ~.* Kaulahao paikikala. *~ of craters.* Pae lua pele. *~ of seamounts.* Pae mauna kai. *Food ~.* Ku'ina mea'ai.

chair leg Wāwae noho.

chalk Poho (*preceded by* ke). *~ dust.* Ehu poho. *~ tray.* Paepae poho. *Colored ~.* Poho kala.

challenge *~ or enrichment book.* Puke ho'onui 'ike.

chamber *A generalized term for any of the ~s of the heart.* Ke'ena. See entry below and *atrium, ventricle.*

chamber *Bubble ~, in chemistry.* Hōkelo hu'a. *Cloud ~, a scientific device which detects nuclear particles through the formation of cloud tracks.* Hōkelo ao. *Magma ~.* Nupa pelemaka.

chamois *Also chamois cloth.* Welu 'ili.

champion *Also champions.* Moho. See *championship.*

championship *In sports.* Ho'okūkū kahului. See *scrimmage, tournament.*

chance *Possibility of an indicated outcome, in math.* Papaha. See *outcome, probability. ~ space, as on a game board such as Monopoly.* Kuea huki pepa.

chancellor *As of a college or university.* Po'o kulanui. See *president, provost.*

change *As from a purchase.* Koena. *Loose ~.* Kālā helele'i, kenikeni. *To ~ or break, as a twenty-dollar bill.* Wāwahi.

change *To ~ or replace, as in a search-and-replace feature in a computer program.* Kuapo. *To find and ~, search and replace.* Huli a kuapo. *To not make any ~, leave as is, as in a computer program.* Waiho.

change *Chemical ~.* Loli kemikala. *Geologic ~.* Loli honua. *To ~ something into a different form or product.* Ho'olilo.

channel *Also station, as on radio or television.* Kānela.

character *As in a story, play, movie, etc.* Hāme'e.

character *As of type in a computer program.* Hua pa'i, hua.

character operator Mea ulele hua. See *set type.*

charcoal Nānahu. See *coal.*

charge Kāki. See entry below and *account, cost, price. ~ card.* Kāleka kāki, 'ea kāki. *~ or credit account, as in a bank.* Waihona kāki.

charge *Electric ~.* Ikehu uila. *Neutral ~.* Ikehu uila hohoki, ikehu hohoki. See *positive, negative. To ~, as a battery.* Ho'oikehu.

Charles Kale. *~' law, in science, i.e. the volume of a gas increases as its temperature increases if the pressure remains constant.* Ke kānāwai a Kale.

Charon *A moon of Pluto.* Kālona.

chart *Also graph, plot.* Pakuhi. See *Hawaiian entries under* pakuhi *and* graph, plot. *Conversion ~.* Pakuhi ho'ololi. *Metric conversion ~.* Pakuhi ho'ololi mekalika. *Flow ~.* Pakuhi ka'ina. *To ~, make a ~ or graph.* Kākuhi. *To make a flow ~.* Kākuhi ka'ina.

charter *A document defining the organization of a city, colony, or corporate body.* Palapala ho'okumu.

cheat Kikiki.

check *~ mark.* Kahamakau. *To verify or give proof, as for a math problem.* Hō'oia. *Spell-~er; to spell ~.* Loipela.

check *Bank ~.* Pila kīko'o. See *money order. Cashier's or certified ~; also bank draft.* Pila kīko'o panakō. *Traveler's ~.* Pila kīko'o huaka'i.

checkers Mū. See *chess. Chinese ~.* Mū Pākē.

check in *To ~ or register, as at a conference or hotel.* Kāinoa komo, kāinoa. See *check out, registration.*

checking account *As in a bank.* Waihona kīkoʻo. See *account.*

check out *To ~, as of a hotel.* Kāinoa puka. See *check in, registration. To ~ or borrow something by signing for it.* Kāinoa.

checkpoint *Also review.* Nāʻana.

check register Moʻo pila kīkoʻo.

checks and balances *As in government.* Hoʻokuʻia.

cheddar Keka. *~ cheese.* Waiūpaʻa keka.

cheese Waiūpaʻa. *Cheddar ~.* Waiūpaʻa keka. *Cottage ~.* Waiūhakuhaku. *Parmesan ~.* Waiūpaʻa pamesana. *Process(ed) ~.* Waiūpaʻa i haʻaliu ʻia. *Swiss ~.* Waiūpaʻa Kuikilani.

cheetah Leopaki kikī.

chemical Kemikala. See *coefficient. ~ activity.* Mōʻaui kemikala. *~ change.* Loli kemikala. *~ energy.* Ikehu kemikala. *~ equation.* Haʻihelu kemikala. *Balanced ~ equation.* Haʻihelu kemikala kaulike. *~ formula.* Haʻilula kemikala. *~ property.* ʻAnopili kemikala (*preceded by* ke). *~ solution.* Māʻōʻāna kemikala. *~ly combined.* ʻŌʻā kemikala ʻia. *To treat ~ly, as sewage.* Kāemikala.

chemistry Kemika.

cherry Keli.

chess Mū kākela. See *checkers.*

chest *Toy ~.* Pahu mea pāʻani, waihona mea pāʻani. *Treasure ~.* Pahu waihona waiwai.

chest pass *In basketball; to throw such a pass.* Kīloi umauma.

chick *Young ~; also sound to call chickens by imitating a young ~.* Piopio.

chickadee Manu kikakī.

chicken *Drumstick.* Pālaumoa. *~ breast.* Umauma moa. *~ thigh.* ʻŪhā moa.

chicken pox Puʻupuʻu moa.

Chile *Also Chilean.* Kile, Kili.

chili Kili.

chimney Puka uahi.

China Kina, ʻĀina Pākē. See *Chinese. East ~ Sea.* Ke kai ʻo Kina Hikina. *South ~ Sea.* Ke kai ʻo Kina Hema.

chinchilla rabbit Lāpaki kinikila, lāpiki kinikila, ʻiole lāpiki kinikila.

Chinese Pākē. See *China.*

Chinese checkers Mū Pākē.

chin-up Hukialewa, hukialewa pohokua. See *pull-up.*

chip *As used in checkers, counting, pocker, etc.* Hiu. *As in computer hardware.* Unu. See *processor. As a potato chip.* Kipi. *Potato ~.* Kipi ʻuala kahiki. *Taro ~.* Kipi kalo.

chipmonk ʻAkuiki, kiulela ʻakuiki.

chiropractic *Also to practice ~.* Pālomi. *Chiropractor.* Kauka pālomi.

chisel Kila, kila pao.

chi-squared distribution *In math.* Haʻihelu hoʻoili.

chloride Koloriside. *Cobalt ~.* Kobalata koloriside. *Stannous ~.* Satanousa koloriside.

chloridops *~ kona, grosbeak finch.* Hona. *~ regiskongi, King Kong finch.* Nuku ʻekue.

chlorine Kolorine.

chlorodane Kolorodane.

chlorofluorocarbon Kolorofolorokalapona.

chloroform Kolopoma.

chlorophyll Kolopila. See *plastid.*

chloroplast Kolopalake.

chlorosis *A condition in plants as a result of deficient nitrogen.* Makenaikokene.

chocolate *Also hot chocolate.* Kokoleka. *~ with whipped cream.* Kokoleka me ke kalima huipa. *~ with steamed milk.* Kokoleka me ka waiū māhu. *~ with frothed milk.* Kokoleka me ka waiū huʻahuʻa.

choice *As in a computer program.* Koho. See *pro-choice.*

cholesterol Naʻokoko.

cholla *A kind of cactus.* Pānini kioia.

choose *To ~, as in a computer program.* Koho.

chopstick Lāʻau ʻai.

chord *Of an arc, in math.* Kaula hōʻike piʻo.

chordophone *A musical instrument whose sound is produced by plucking, strumming, striking, or bowing strings.* Olokaula. *See Hawaiian entries beginning with* olo-.

choreographer *Also to choreograph.* Kūkulu hulahula.

Christmas ball *The tree ornament.* Pōpō wehi lāʻau Kalikimaka. *See ornament.*

chromatography Hōʻauikala. *See silica gel g. Paper ~.* Hōʻauikala pepa. *Thin-layer ~.* Hōʻauikala papa lahilahi. *Chromatograph.* Kiʻi hōʻauikala. *Chromatographic paper.* Pepa hōʻauikala.

chromosome Awe ōewe.

chrysalis Wiliʻōkaʻi.

cigar-box ʻukulele ʻUkulele pahu kīkā.

ciguatera *Poisoning caused by eating fish with accumulated toxic substance in its flesh.* Kaʻelo.

cilium *Also cilia.* Huluheu.

cinder ʻĀkeke. *~ cone.* Puʻu ʻākeke. *Volcanic ~.* One ʻā.

cinnamon Kinamona.

circle *Circular shape; as in preschool programs; to sit in a ~.* Lina poepoe. *The geometric shape.* Pōʻai. *~ graph.* Pakuhi pōʻai. *Center of a ~.* Kikowaena. *Radius of a ~.* Kahahānai. *Concentric ~s.* Nā pōʻai kikowaena kahi. *Semi~.* Pōʻai hapalua. *Center ~, on a basketball court.* Pōʻai waena. *To ~, i.e. draw a ~ around something.* Kahalina. *A ~ around a period, colon, or semicolon to show that it has been inserted, in proofreading.* Lina hoʻokomo.

circuit *Complete ~, lap.* Puni. *Electric ~.* Puni uila. *~ breaker, a device which automatically interrupts electric current before wires in a circuit get too hot.* ʻŪʻoki puni uila.

circulate *To ~, as blood.* Holo puni.

circulatory system *Also cardiovascular system.* ʻŌnaehana mānowai, ʻōnaehana mānowai koko.

circumference Anapuni.

circumstances *Extenuating ~.* Kumu kūikawā.

circus Keleku.

cirrus cloud Ao lālahilewa. *See cloud.*

citizen Kupa, makaʻāinana. *Dual ~.* Kupa kaumokuʻāina pālua, makaʻāinana kaumokuʻāina pālua.

citrate Kitarahate. *Sodium ~.* Sodiuma kitarahate.

citrus ʻOhana ʻālani.

city *General term; town.* Kūlanakauhale. *See municipality. ~ block.* Pōlaka. *Downtown.* Kaona. *Urban area.* Kiwikā.

civil disobedience *Breaking a law because it goes against personal morals.* ʻAʻa kānāwai.

civil law Kānāwai kīwila, kānāwai sīwila.

civil unrest Haunaele kūloko.

claim *~ for damages, as to an insurance company.* Koi pohō. *To make a ~ for damages.* Hoʻopiʻi i ke koi pohō. *To settle, as a ~.* Hoʻonā. *See land court, land registration system.*

clamp ʻŪmiʻi. *See forceps. Pinch ~.* ʻŪmiʻi pani. *Test tube ~.* ʻŪmiʻi hano hoʻokolohua. *Utility ~.* ʻŪmiʻi hoʻopaʻa.

clan *Also subtribe.* Hapū. *See tribe.*

clarify *To explain.* Hoʻākāka.

ClarisWorks *A nickname for the computer program.* Kaleiwahana.

class *To take a ~.* Aia i loko o ka papa, komo i loko o ka papa. *See Hawaiian entries* aia, komo *and course.*

classify *Also to categorize.* Wae'ano.

clause *Or grammatical sentence.*
Pepeke. *Dependent* ~. Pepeke 'ōhua.
Main ~. Pepeke haku.

clavicle *Collarbone.* Iwi lei.

claw Mai'u'u.

clay *Modeling* ~. Kalē. See *Play-Doh*.
As for ceramics; ~ *dirt.* Pālolo.

cleaner wrasse *Labroides Phthirophegus, a kind of fish.* Hīnālea nā'uke.

clear *Plain, intelligible.* Mōakāka. *To
~, as data in a computer program.* Holoi.

clearing *In pasture or range land.*
Pāhu'a.

clef *In music.* Hō'ailona mele. *Bass* ~.
Hō'ailona mele leo kāne, leo kāne.
Treble ~. Hō'ailona mele leo wahine, leo
wahine.

click *As the sound produced when
~ing a computer mouse.* Pa'ina. *To
press or depress, as in a computer
program.* Kōmi, kaomi.

cliff *Wave-cut* ~. Pali 'a'aianalu. See
weathered. Small ~s. Kīpāpali.

climate Aniau. See *climatology,
microclimate, weather.*

climatology Kālaianiau.
Climatologist. Kanaka kālaianiau, mea
kālaianiau.

climax community *In biology.*
Kaiaulu 'āha'i.

clip *Also to* ~ *together.* Pine. See *dink.
Paper* ~. Pine pepa.

clipboard *As in a computer program.*
Papa 'ūmi'i. *To show* ~. Hō'ike papa
'ūmi'i.

clipper *A kind of ship.* Mokupe'a holo
māmā.

clock *Also watch.* Uaki, uāki. *Alarm*
~. Uaki ho'āla, uāki ho'āla. *Analog* ~.
Uaki lima kuhikuhi, uāki lima
kuhikuhi. *Digital* ~. Uaki kikoho'e, uāki
kikoho'e.

clockwise Kō'ai 'ākau. See *counterclockwise.*

close *Near.* Kokoke. See entries below
and *close-up.*

close *To* ~, *as in a computer program.*
Pani. See *closed, bracket, parenthesis.
To* ~ *up tight, as a flower bud.* 'Ōpili.

closed *As a frame in a computer
program.* Pa'a. See *open.* ~ *frame.*
Mōlina pa'a. *As a primary election.*
Kūloko. ~ *primary.* Wae moho kūloko.

close hauled (port) *Close hauled on
the port side, i.e. sailing into the wind at
the closest angle possible, generally 67°,
with the port side windward.* Kele ama
kūnihi. See *beam reach (port,
starboard), broad reach (port, starboard),
close hauled (starboard), downwind.*

close hauled (starboard) *Close
hauled on the starboard side, i.e. sailing
into the wind at the closest angle
possible, generally 67°, with the
starboard side windward.* Kele 'ākea
kūnihi. See *beam reach (port,
starboard), broad reach (port, starboard),
close hauled (port), downwind.*

closet *Broom* ~. Ke'ena pūlumi.

close-up *As of a photograph or in
movie or video production.* Pa'i kokoke
(*preceded by* ke). See *medium shot,
wide shot. To take a* ~. Pa'i a kokoke.
Extreme ~. Pa'i kokoke loa. *To take an
extreme* ~. Pa'i a kokoke loa.

closing *As of a composition or story.* Ka
pau 'ana. See *opening, body.*

closing banquet 'Aha'aina panina.

clot *Blood* ~. Lapa koko.

cloth *Material.* 'Īālole. See *bolt.*

cloth duct tape *Electrician's tape.* Leki
uea.

clothes ~ *hook.* Lou kau lole. ~ *rack,
as on wheels in a clothing store.* Hao kau
lole, haka lole.

clothesline Kaula kaula'i lole.

clothing 'A'ahu. See *wardrobe.*

cloture *A method of ending debate
and causing an immediate vote to be
taken, as in a legislature.* 'Aelike ho'ōki.

cloud Ao. *Cirrus ~.* Ao lālahilewa. *Cumulus ~.* Ao 'ōpua. *Stratus ~.* Ao loa.

cloud chamber *A scientific device which detects nuclear particles through the formation of cloud tracks.* Hōkelo ao.

clove *The spice.* 'Ōpu'uhame.

clown Kalaona. *~ hat.* Pāpale kone.

club *Also bat, racket.* 'Ūhili. *Golf ~.* 'Ūhili kolepa.

clue *Also to give a ~ about.* Ahuoi.

cluster *A prefix which indicates a ~ing together.* Kaia-. *See Hawaiian entries under* kaia-.

cluster *To find addends or factors that are nearly alike, in math.* Ho'okokoke.

coach *Also to ~ or train (someone) for sports, etc.* Ka'i. *~ for sports or physical education.* Ka'i 'ālapa. *Drama ~.* Ka'i hana keaka. *Sports trainer.* Ka'i ha'uki. *Vocal ~.* Ka'i pu'ukani.

coagulated *As blood.* Pa'akūkū.

coal Lānahu. *See* charcoal. *~ gasification, i.e. the process in which steam and hot coal produce hydrocarbons.* Kākinoea lānahu.

coarse *As sand.* Mānoanoa. *See* fine.

coast *Ivory ~; Ivorian.* Kapa Kai Palaoa.

coast guard Pū'ali pale kapa kai.

cobalt Kobalata, kopalaka. *~ chloride.* Kobalata koloriside.

cobble 'Ili'ili.

cocaine Kōkeina.

coccyx *The terminus of the spinal column; tailbone.* Iwi ku'e 'amo, ku'e 'amo.

cochlea *Inner ear cavity.* Haka mo'oni.

cockroach *American ~ (Periplaneta americana).* 'Elelū kīkēkē. *Australian ~ (Periplaneta australasiae).* 'Elelū Nūhōlani. *German ~ (Blattella germanica).* 'Elelū la'aloa.

cocky *To act ~, strut about looking for a fight.* Ho'onanā.

coconut *Sponge-like material in a sprouting ~.* Haku. *Sprouting ~ or one with eye emerging.* Niu haku.

coconut shell 'ukulele 'Ukulele pūniu.

Cocos Kokosa. *~ Plate.* Ka Una Honua Kokosa.

COD *Cash on delivery.* 'Ohi hiki.

coda *Of a syllable, in linguistics.* Muli.

code Pā'ālua. *See entry below and* color code, encode, unencrypt, library, script. *~ style, as in a computer program.* Haka pā'ālua. *Key ~, as for the order to press keys on a calculator to find an answer.* Pā'ālua ka'ina hana.

code *A systematic collection of existing laws.* Papa kānāwai. *State water ~.* Papa kānāwai wai o ka moku'āina.

coefficient *A number placed in front of a chemical symbol or formula in order to balance the chemical equation.* Helu ho'onui kemikala. *In math.* Ka'ilau. *~ of X.* Ka'ilau o ke X. *Combinatorial ~.* Ha'i huihuina. *Permutatorial ~.* Ha'i kake ka'ina.

coffee *See* café au lait, cappuccino, espresso.

cog Pānihoniho. *Bicycle chain ~.* Pānihoniho o ke kaulahao paikikala.

cognitive domain *As relating to the learning process.* Pō'ai no'ono'o. *See* domain.

coherent light *Light in which all the waves vibrate in a single plane with the crests and troughs all aligned.* Mālamalama aukahi.

cohesion *Also cohesive.* Pū'uo'uo. *See* adhesion.

coin 'Ōkeni. *See* bill, heads, tails. *~ purse.* 'Eke kenikeni (*preceded by* ke).

coincidence Ūlialia. *See* serendipity.

cold-blooded *As an animal.* Koko hu'ihu'i. *See* warm-blooded.

cold front *As of weather.* Ku'ina hu'ihu'i. *See* front.

cold war *Intense rivalry between nations but without miliary combat.* Kaua ko'eko'e.

cole slaw Kāpiki meoneki.

coleus Lau no'e. See *croton.*

collapse See *compress.*

collar 'Ā'ī, 'ā'ī lole, 'ā'ī kala, kala.

collarbone *Clavicle.* Iwi lei.

collate Kakeka'i.

collect Hō'ili'ili. See *collection. As fingerprints.* 'Ohi. See *fingerprint. To ~ fingerprints.* 'Ohi i ka meheu manamana lima (māka manamana lima, ki'i manamana lima).

collect call *Also to make such a call.* Kelepona kāki hiki. See *Hawaiian entries under* kelepona.

collection Hō'ili'ilina. *Stamp ~.* Hō'ili'ilina po'oleka.

collection tube *A test tube used to collect gas generated in an experiment.* Hano 'ohi.

collective bargaining Kūka'i 'aelike 'uniona.

college *As a division or department within a university.* Koleke. *~ of agriculture.* Koleke mahi 'ai. *~ of arts and sciences.* Koleke pāheona me ka 'epekema. *Community ~.* Kulanui kaiaulu. *Leeward Community ~.* Kulanui Kaiaulu o 'Ewa.

colloid *A chemical mixture with particle size between that of solutions and suspensions.* Pūaina lahi. See *solution, suspension.*

Colombia *Also Colombian.* Kolomepia, Kolomebia.

colon *In punctuation.* Kolona. See *semicolon.*

colonial See *postcolonial.*

colonize *To ~, as a land by either people, animals, or plants.* Ho'opanalā'au. *To ~, particularly from the perspective of a people who have*

been *~d by a dominant culture or political entity.* Ho'okolonaio. *Colonized.* Kolonaio.

colony *As a territory ruled by a more powerful nation.* Panalā'au.

color *Additive ~, one of the primary colors (red, blue, green) which, when added together, produce white light.* Waiho'olu'u hui kea. *See entries below.*

Colorado *Also Coloradan.* Kololako, Kolorado. See *Grand Canyon. ~ River.* Ka muliwai 'o Kololako, ka muliwai 'o Haka'ama.

color code *Also to ~ something.* Kalakuhi.

colored pencil Penikala kala.

color gradient *Also color band.* 'Auina kala.

coloring *Food ~.* Kala mea'ai.

column Kolamu. *To place in ~s.* Ho'okolamu.

combination *Also mixture.* Huihuina. *As for a lock.* Helu laka. *~ lock.* Laka helu.

combinatorial coefficient *In math.* Ha'i huihuina. See *coefficient.*

combined *Also mixed.* 'Ō'ā. *Chemically ~.* 'Ō'ā kemikala 'ia.

comet Hōkū puhipaka. See *shooting star. Halley's ~.* Ka hōkū puhipaka 'o Hēli.

comic book Puke kātuna.

comma Kiko koma, kiko ho'omaha.

command economy *An economic system in which the government controls the factors of production and makes the basic economic decisions.* Ho'okele waiwai mana kahi. See *free-market economy.*

commercial *Also ad, advertisement.* Ho'olaha kū'ai. *Relating to business or commerce.* Pā'oihana. *~ growers.* Pā'oihana ho'oulu meakanu.

commission Komikina. *State Land Use Commission.* Komikina Hoʻohana ʻĀina o ka Mokuʻāina. *Water ~.* Komikina wai. *A fee paid to an agent for transacting business or performing a service.* Uku ʻēkena, uku ʻākena.

commodity *Anything bought or sold.* Huakūʻai.

common *As in math terms.* Like. *~ factor.* Helu hoʻonui like. *Greatest ~ factor.* Helu hoʻonui like kiʻekiʻe loa. *~ multiple.* Helu māhua like. *Least ~ multiple.* Māhua haʻahaʻa loa. *Least ~ denominator.* Kinopiha haʻahaʻa loa.

common good *The well-being of all members of society.* Pono o ka lehulehu.

common law Kānāwai kumu.

common sense *Also to use ~.* Noʻonoʻo kanaka.

communicate Hoʻokaʻaʻike. See *communication.*

communication Kaʻaʻike. See *telecommunication.* *~ skill.* Mākau hoʻokaʻaʻike. *Oral ~.* Kaʻaʻike haʻi waha, kaʻaʻike waha. *Two-way ~, inter~.* Kaʻaʻike pānaʻi.

communism Paimana aupuni.

community Kaiaulu. *~-based health system.* ʻŌnaehana olakino kaiaulu. *Biological ~, as in science.* Kaiameaola. *Natural biological ~.* Kaiameaola kūlohelohe. *Climax ~, as in biology.* Kaiaulu ʻāhaʻi.

community college Kulanui kaiaulu. *Leeward ~.* Kulanui Kaiaulu o ʻEwa.

commutative property *In math.* ʻAnopili kaʻina hoʻi hope, ʻanopili hoʻi hope (*preceded by* ke).

commutator *A switch on a motor running on direct current that causes the current to reverse every half turn.* ʻŪkake uila. See *brush.*

Comoros Komorosa.

compact *A written agreement to make and obey laws for the welfare of the group.* ʻAelike mālama kānāwai.

compact disc See *CD.*

compare Hoʻokūkū.

compass *An instrument for describing circles or transferring measurements, in math.* ʻŪpā kāpōʻai. See *directions.* *As for navigation.* Pānānā (*preceded by* ke). *Pocket ~.* Pānānā paʻa lima (*preceded by* ke).

compatible *As of computer programs.* Launa. See *incompatible.* *~ file format.* Hulu waihona launa. *As numbers in math.* Makalauna. *~ number.* Helu makalauna.

compensate *Also to counterbalance.* Hoʻokauapono. See *compensation.*

compensation *Something that constitutes an equivalent.* Kauapono. See *compensate.* *To make amends for loss or damage; payment for services.* Uku pānaʻi.

complaint *A legal document that charges someone with having caused harm.* Kumu hoʻopiʻi.

complement *To ~, as angles, in math.* Hoʻopiha kūpono. See *complementary angles, supplement.*

complementary angles *Two angles whose measures have a sum of 90°, in math.* Nā huina hoʻopiha kūpono. See *supplementary angles.*

complete *To ~, as a geometric figure, in math.* Kaha kinona.

complete *Also to open, as an electric circuit.* Hoʻokuʻi. See *break.*

complete fertilizer *Fertilizer which contains the six necessary elements for plant growth.* Mea hoʻomomona lepo kāʻokoʻa.

complex Nōhihi. See *simple.* *A prefix referring to vitamins.* Kau-. *B-~ vitamin.* Kauwikamina B.

complex number *In math.* Helu hapa moeā. See *imaginary number, real number.*

component *Also constituent.* ʻŪmaupaʻa.

composed *To be ~ of, consist of, be made up of.* Maupaʻa.

composer *Also to compose songs or chants.* Haku mele.

composite Huihuina. *~ sample.* Hāpana huihuina. *As volcanic cone.* Ahupapa. *~ cone.* Puʻu ahupapa. *In math.* Puʻunaue lua. *~ number.* Helu puʻunaue lua.

compost *Also to ~.* Kīpulu. See *fertilize. To make ~.* Hana kīpulu.

compound *As in chemistry.* Pūhui. See *element, matter, substance. Binary ~.* Pūhui kumumea lua. *Free nitrogen ~.* Pūhui naikokene kaʻawale. *~ machine.* Kaumīkini.

comprehend See *comprehension.*

comprehension *Also to comprehend.* ʻApomanaʻo. *~ question.* Nīnau ʻapomanaʻo.

compress *To ~ or collapse, as a file in a computer program.* ʻOpi. See *expand. ~ed or collapsed.* ʻOpihia. *~ed file.* Waihona ʻopihia.

compression *The most dense concentration of wave particles in a ~al wave.* Ulu. See *compressional wave, rarefaction.*

compressional wave *A wave in which matter vibrates in the same direction as the wave moves.* Hawewe papamoe. See *compression, transverse wave.*

compromise Kuʻikoli.

computer Kamepiula, lolouila, mīkini hoʻonohonoho ʻikena. *~ camp.* ʻĀpoʻe kamepiula. *~ keyboard.* Papa pihi kamepiula. *~ monitor.* Pahu papakaumaka kamepiula. See *screen. Laptop ~.* Kamepiula lawelima, lolouila lawelima. *To write a ~ program.* Haku polokalamu.

concave *Hollowed or rounded inward, as the inside of a bowl.* ʻEʻele. See *convex. ~ lens.* Aniani kaulona ʻeʻele. *~ mirror.* Aniani ʻeʻele.

concentrate *To make less dilute.* Hoʻopaʻapūhia. See *dilute. Concentrated.* Paʻapūhia.

concentric Kikowaena kahi. *~ circles.* Nā pōʻai kikowaena kahi.

concept Manaʻo.

concert *Indoor ~.* ʻAha mele maluhale. *Outdoor ~.* ʻAha mele kaupokulani.

conclusion Hopena. *To draw a ~.* Hoʻoholo i hopena.

concurrent power *As powers shared by federal and state governments.* Mana ʻālike.

condensation *Also to condense, as gas to liquid.* Kōkaha.

condense *To ~, as text in a computer document.* Hoʻohāiki. See *condensation, extend.*

conditioner *Air ~.* Mīkini hōʻolu ʻea, hōʻolu ʻea.

condom *For men.* Pāpalekimo.

conduct *To ~ a drive, as for cans or clean-up.* Alu. See *drive.*

conductor *Of electricity.* Mea uholo uila.

cone *Geometric ~.* ʻŌpuʻu. *Ice cream ~.* Kone ʻaikalima. *~ used as a traffic marker.* Kone alanui.

cone *A geological feature.* Puʻu. *Ash ~.* Puʻu lehu. *Cinder ~.* Puʻu ʻākeke. *Composite ~.* Puʻu ahupapa. *Shield ~.* Puʻu kuahene. *Spatter ~.* Puʻu pōhāhā. *Tuff ~.* Puʻu hakuhune. *Volcanic ~.* Puʻu pele.

confer Kūkā. See *conference.*

conference *To ~, as part of the writing process.* Kūkā ma ka pūʻulu. See entry below and *prewrite.*

conference ʻAha kūkā. *In sports.* Hui. See *league. American Football ~ (AFC).* Hui Pōpeku ʻAmelika. *National Football ~ (NFC).* Hui Pōpeku Aupuni.

Congo *Also Congolese.* Konokō. *Democratic Republic of the ~.* Lepupalika Kemokalaka ʻo Konokō.

congressional district *In government.* 'Āpana 'aha'ōlelo lāhui.

congruent *In math.* Komolike. ~ *figure.* Kinona komolike. ~ *triangle.* Huinakolu komolike.

conifer *Pine or any tree which resembles a pine.* Paina, paina lau kukuna, paina tidara. *See cypress, ironwood.*

connect *To ~, as in a computer program.* Ho'oku'i. *See connection, disconnect. As dots, etc.* Ho'ohui.

Connecticut Konekikuka, Konetikuta.

connection *As in a computer program.* Ku'ina. *See connect.*

conscience Luna'ikehala. *To have a guilty ~.* Noho ka hewa i ka luna'ikehala.

consecutive *In sequence.* Moekahi.

conservation *Careful use of natural resources to prevent depletion.* Maluō. *See conserve.* ~ *hotline.* Helu wawe maluō.

conserve *To use or manage wisely, as natural resources.* Ho'omaluō. *See conservation.*

consist *To ~ of, be composed of, be made up of.* Maupa'a.

consolation bracket *As in a sports tournament.* Māhele hā'ule. *See bracket.*

consonant Koneka.

consortium Ku'ikahi. *See alliance.*

constant *In math.* Helu ho'ohana. ~ *term.* Hua pa'a. *See like term, term.*

constant *Solar ~.* Kā'ei kau lā.

constant of proportionality *In math.* Lākiō anapuni.

constellation Huihui hōkū.

constituent *Also component.* 'Ūmaupa'a. *See entry below.*

constituent *A voter in a district who is represented by an elected official.* Maka'āinana 'āpana.

constitutional initiative *A process by which one can propose an amend-ment by gathering signatures on a petition.* Palapala noi ho'ololi kānāwai.

construct *In geometry, to ~, as in making a surveying figure with the use of only a compass and a straightedge; construction.* Kāpi'okaha.

construction industry 'Oi'enehana kūkulu.

construction paper Pepaānue.

consul Kanikela. *See ambassador.*

consume *To use a commodity or service.* Kemu. *See consumer.*

consumer *A person who uses a commodity or service.* Mea kemu. *See consume.*

contact *A person to whom certain information is communicated.* Mea ka'a launa.

contact poison Lā'au make pā 'ili.

container *General term.* Hōkelo. *An airtight ~.* He hōkelo pa'a ea. *Toothbrush ~, usually made of plastic.* Poho palaki niho.

containment *A government policy of preventing the expansion of a hostile power or ideology.* Kulekele kāohi.

contents *Table of ~.* Papa kuhikuhi. *See index.*

context Pō'aiapili.

contiguous Pili lihi.

continental *Also continent.* Mokuhonua, 'āinapuni'ole. ~ *crust.* Pāpa'a mokuhonua. ~ *shelf.* Holopapa mokuhonua. ~ *slope.* Hene mokuhonua.

continued *"To be ~," "stay tuned," as during a TV program.* 'A'ole i pau.

continuous feed *See auto feed.*

contour *As the elevations of a particular place.* Hi'ona 'āina.

contract labor Kepa.

control Kāohi. *See entries below. Biological ~.* Kāohi meaola. *Flood ~.* Kāohi wai hālana.

control *Also ~ group, as in an experiment.* Kumu ho'ohālikelike.

control *As in a computer program.* Ho'oholo. *General ~s.* Ho'oholo laulā. *~ key.* Pihi ho'oholo (*preceded by* ke). *~ panel.* Papa ho'oholo.

controller *As an administrator for a computer network.* Kahu. *Network ~.* Kahu pūnaewele. *As in Nintendo games.* Pahu ho'okele.

controls *Light ~, as for stage productions.* Une kukui.

convectional *To circulate, as air or liquid, between a lower and higher stratum due to variations in density, heat, and gravity; also convection, convective.* Paialewa.

convention *An assembly of people who meet for a common purpose, in politics.* 'Aha ho'oku'ikahi.

convergent *Meeting in plate techtonics, in geology.* Ku'i. *See divergent, intertropical convergent zone, transform. ~ boundary.* Palena ku'i.

conversion chart Pakuhi ho'ololi. *Metric ~.* Pakuhi ho'ololi mekalika.

conversion scale Papa pālākiō.

convertible *A car with a top that can be lowered or removed.* Ka'a kaupaku pelu, ka'a kaupoku pelu, ka'a kaupuku pelu.

convex *Curved or rounded, as the exterior of a sphere or circle.* 'E'emu. *See concave. ~ lens.* Aniani kaulona 'e'emu. *~ mirror.* Aniani 'e'emu.

convict *To find or prove to be guilty.* Ho'oholo i ke kū i ka hewa.

convulsion Ma'i huki. *Schizophrenic ~.* Ma'i huki huohuoi. *See schizophrenia.*

cookie *A small tag file left on a computer hard drive by a server in order to gather information about the end-user.* Makana.

Cook pine Kumu paina Kuke, paina Kuke.

cool-headed *Also even-tempered, calm.* Māio.

coordinate *To put in order.* Ho'olauka'i. *See entries below. Coordinated.* Lauka'i. *~d physician referral system.* 'Ōnaehana kauka no ka lapa'au like 'ana.

coordinate *Also reference, in math.* Kuhikuhina. *~s; ordered pair, i.e. two numbers used to give location of a point on a graph.* Pa'a helu kuhikuhina. *~ axes, i.e. two intersecting perpendicular number lines used for graphing ordered number pairs.* Iho kuhikuhina. *~ plane.* Papa kuhikuhina. *Geographical ~s.* Nā kuhikuhina hō'ike honua.

coordinated *Having physical dexterity.* Lehilehia.

coordinator *See Hawaiian entries under luna.*

copper Keleawe'ula. *See Aeneolithic.*

co-processor unit *As for a computer (CPU).* Mīkini heluhelu pā. *Abb. MHP.*

copy *As of a document.* Kope. *Original or master ~.* Kope kumu. *To make a ~.* Hana kope. *Backup ~.* Kope papa'a. *See backup.*

coraline algae Limu ko'a.

cord *A unit for measuring firewood.* Koka.

core *Earth's ~.* 'Īkoi honua. *See crust, mantle.*

core credit *As for a school course.* 'Ai koina. *See required.*

cork *The material or the tree.* 'Ūpīlā'au.

corm *As of taro.* Hua. *Scientific usage.* 'Auhua.

corned beef *Fresh ~, as opposed to canned.* Pipi Kelemānia. *Canned ~.* Kini pipi, pipi kini. *Can of ~.* Kini pipi.

corner *Particularly an outside ~.* Kihi. *Inside ~.* Kū'ono, po'opo'o.

corner back *Defensive ~, in football.* 'Ā'iwa.

cornet Pū pihi poko. See *bugle, trumpet.*

corn smut Kalina paʻu kūlina.

Corona Borealis *A constellation.* ʻAnaheuheu.

corporation *A business that is separate from the people who own it and acts legally as a single entity.* ʻAhahuina.

corps *Marine ~.* Pūʻali hoʻouka kaua.

corral Pāʻeke.

correspondence *Written ~; also to correspond by letter.* Kūkaʻi leka. *~ course.* Papa kūkaʻi leka.

corresponding *In math.* Launa. *~ angle, of a triangle.* Huina launa. *~ side.* ʻAoʻao launa.

corridor *Flight ~.* Ala lele mokulele.

corrugated paper *Cardboard.* Pepa pahu.

cortical bone Iwi ʻalā. See *cancellous bone.*

cortisone *A hormone used in the treatment of arthritis.* Kokikone. See *hydrocortisone.*

cosmic ray Kukuna lewa lipo.

cosmos *A kind of flower.* Komosa.

cost *Price.* Kumukūʻai. *~ analysis.* Huli kumukūʻai. *Estimated ~ or charge, as for services.* Kāki koho.

Costa Rica *Also Costa Rican.* Koka Rika.

cottage cheese Waiūhakuhaku.

cotton Pulupulu. *~ swab, Q-tip.* Lāʻau pulupulu.

cottontail rabbit Lāpaki huelo pulupulu, lāpiki huelo pulupulu, ʻiole lāpiki huelo pulupulu.

cotyledon Lau ʻīnana. *Mono~.* Lau ʻīnana kahi. *Di~.* Lau ʻīnana lua.

council ʻAha. *County ~.* ʻAha kalana.

count *To skip ~, in math.* Helu lele.

countdown *Also to count down, as in launching a rocket.* Helu ʻōlapa.

counter *As in a kitchen.* Papakau. *As beans or bottle caps to help with a math problem.* Mea kōkua helu.

counterattack Hoʻouka pānaʻi.

counterbalance See *compensation.*

counterclockwise Kōʻai hema. See *clockwise.*

Countercurrent *Equatorial ~, in oceanography.* Hiapo. See *current.*

counterexample Laʻana hōʻole.

counterpunch Kuʻi pānaʻi.

counting cube *In math.* Paʻaʻiliono kōkua helu, paʻaʻiliono. See *counting mat, counting rod.*

counting mat *Also counting flat, counting stripmat, in math.* Moena kōkua helu, moena. See *counting cube, counting rod.*

counting number *In math.* Hua helu kumu.

counting on *A strategy used in mental math.* Helu kūana. See *unit of counting.*

counting piece *Base-five ~, in math.* Kōkua helu kumu hoʻohui pālima.

counting principle *Basic ~, in math.* Kulehana no ka helu ʻana.

counting rod *Also counting strip, in math.* ʻAukā kōkua helu, ʻaukā. See *counting cube, counting mat.*

counting strip See *counting rod.*

country *Developed or First World ~.* ʻĀina ʻoiʻenehana. *Developing or Third World ~.* ʻĀina hōʻoiʻenehana. *Nation-state.* Kaumokuʻāina. *Postcolonial ~.* Kaumokuʻāina muli panalāʻau, ʻāina muli panalāʻau.

county Kalana. *~ council.* ʻAha kalana. *~ fair.* Hōʻikeʻike kalana. See *fair.* *~ Planning Department.* Keʻena Hoʻolālā o ke Kalana.

coupon Kūpona.

course *Elective ~.* Papa koho. *Required ~.* Papa koina. *Lower-division ~.* Papa heluhaʻa. *Upper-division ~.* Papa helukiʻe.

course *Slalom ~.* Ala heihei kīke'eke'e.

coursework See *curriculum.*

court *As for basketball.* Kahua. See entry below and *field. Basketball ~.* Kahua pōhīna'i, kahua. *Volleyball ~.* Kahua pōpa'ipa'i, pahu.

court *Land ~.* 'Aha ho'onā 'āina. See *land registration system, settle, small-claims court.*

courtyard Pāmalae.

cover *To ~ or shield, as one's mouth.* Pale. *~ page.* 'Ao'ao ho'ākāka. *Ground ~.* Kapauli. *Manhole ~, as for a sewer.* Pani paipu lawe 'ino (*preceded by* ke). See *cap. Mattress ~.* 'Eke pela (*preceded by* ke). *For a fish tank, in aquaculture.* Pe'a. See *fish tank liner, record album.*

coverage *Medical ~ number.* Helu 'inikua olakino.

coveralls *Overalls.* Lole wāwae kā'awe, lole wāwae 'epane.

cover letter Leka wehewehe.

CPU *Co-processor unit, as for a computer.* MHP (mīkini heluhelu pā).

crack *As space between fence boards.* Kōā. *As in a sidewalk; also to ~.* 'Oā.

craftsman *Also artisan.* Mālalaioa.

crane *Space ~, remote manipulator arm.* Lima kia pihi.

crash *To ~, as cars; to bump or bang into.* Ho'oku'i.

crater *Chain of ~s.* Pae lua pele. See *volcano.*

cravat Kalawake. See *necktie.*

crawl *Free style in swimming; also to swim using this style.* 'Au kolo. See *stroke.*

crayfish 'Ōpae Pākē.

crayon Kala, peni kala.

cream *Whipped ~.* Kalima huipa. See *chocolate.*

crease *As on a pair of pants.* Haki, 'opi.

creation *Also origin of the world.* Kumu honua. *~ literature.* Mo'okalaleo kumu honua.

creative writing Kākau makakū.

credit *As for a school course.* 'Ai. *Core ~.* 'Ai koina. *Elective ~.* 'Ai koho.

credit *As at a bank or store.* Kumu hō'ai'ē. *As the name of a person who has contributed to a performance.* Pailaha.

credit account *Also charge account, as in a bank.* Waihona kāki. See *bank account.*

crepuscular *Appearing or flying in the twilight.* Ala mōlehu. See *diurnal, nocturnal*

crest *Of a wave.* Hokua, hokua o ka nalu, hokua o ka 'ale. See *trough, wave.*

Crete *Also Cretan.* Keleke, Kerete.

crew *Member of a work ~.* Limahana. *Video production ~.* Nā limahana pa'i wikiō.

crib *As for babies.* Moe pēpē.

cricket 'Ūhini nēnē. *Beach ~.* 'Ūhini nēnē kahakai. *Lava ~.* 'Ūhini nēnē pele.

crime See *criminalistics, criminology.*

criminalistics *The scientific study of physical evidence in the commission of crimes.* Kālaimeheu kalaima. See *criminology. Criminalist.* Kanaka kālaimeheu kalaima, mea kālaimeheu kalaima.

criminal law *The law of crimes and their punishments.* Kānāwai kalaima.

criminology *The study of crime and criminals.* Kālaikalaima. See *criminalistics. Criminologist.* Kanaka kālaikalaima, mea kālaikalaima.

crisp *Or brittle, as dry* hala *leaves.* Pa'apa'a'ina.

critical thinking No'ono'o loi.

Croatia Koloatia.

crocus Pua 'ō'ili hau.

crop *Or planting, i.e. the number of plantings of a particular plant.* Kanu. *A plant that is grown and harvested, usually for profit.* Meaulu.

cross *To ~, as a street.* 'A'ehi. See entries below and *crosswalk.*

crossbar *On a bicycle.* Kua hao paikikala.

crossbreed Hoʻopiʻi kaʻakepa. See *breed, cross-pollinate.*

cross-country ski Heʻe hau peʻa ʻāina.

cross out Kahapeʻa.

cross-pollinate Hoʻēhu pua kaʻakepa. See *crossbreed, pollinate.*

cross product *In math.* Hualoaʻa kaupeʻa.

cross section Hiʻona kaha.

cross-tab graph *In math.* Pakuhi huina ʻikepili.

crosswalk ʻAʻehina. See *cross.* ~ *light.* Kukui ʻaʻehina.

crossword puzzle Nane huaʻōlelo.

croton Lau kalakoa. See *coleus.*

crow's feet *A kind of plant.* Wāwaeʻalalā.

crown *As on a pineapple.* ʻĒlau. *Pineapple* ~. ʻĒlau hala kahiki, ʻēlau painaʻāpala.

CRT *Cathode-ray tube.* ʻOhe kīwī. See *cathode.*

crumb *Bread* ~*s.* Hunahuna palaoa. *Clumps of mineral particles mixed into soil.* Pūhuna. See *tilth.*

crumbled Nāhāhā.

crunchy *General term, but especially for loli, ʻopihi, etc.* Kamumu. *As fresh potato chips.* Kakani, nakeke. *As an apple.* Nakekeke.

crust *In geology.* Pāpaʻa. See *core, mantle. Continental* ~. Pāpaʻa mokuhonua. *Earth's* ~. Pāpaʻa honua. *Ocean* ~. Pāpaʻa moana.

crustacean See *ostracod.* Pāpaka. *Land* ~. Pāpaka ʻāina.

crystal Pōaka.

Cuba *Also Cuban.* Kupa, Kuba.

cubby hole Kapi.

cube *In math.* Paʻaʻiliono analahi, paʻaʻiliono. See *cubic, hexahedron. Counting* ~. Paʻaʻiliono kōkua helu, paʻaʻiliono. *Snap* ~. Palaka kepa.

cubed *As in exponential counting, in math.* Pāhoʻonui kolu. See *square.*

cubic Paʻaʻiliono. See *cube.* ~ *yard.* ʻĪā paʻaʻiliono.

cubit *An ancient unit of measurement used in Bible times.* Kūpita.

cue *As in the game of pool.* Kiu. *Pool* ~. Kiu pahupahu.

cultivation *Shifting* ~, *in geography.* Mahi ʻai mahakea.

cultivator *Also to cultivate.* Kīkoʻu. See *rotary tiller. Hand* ~. Kīkoʻu paʻa lima.

culture *Also cultural.* Moʻomeheu. See entry below and *custom.*

culture *As bacteria grown in a prepared nutrient.* ʻOulu. *Nutrient* ~. ʻOulu māhuaola. *Sand* ~. ʻOulu one.

cum laude *Also with distinction, with honors, as in academics.* Me ke kau i ka hano, me ka hanohano, me ka hoʻomaikaʻi. See *magna cum laude, summa cum laude.*

cumulus cloud Ao ʻōpua. See *cloud.*

cup *As for measurement.* Kīʻaha. *Abb.* kh. *Measuring* ~. Kīʻaha ana.

cupric Kupuriku. ~ *carbonate.* Kupuriku karabonahate. ~ *oxide.* Kupuriku ʻokesaside. ~ *sulfate.* Kupuriku sulafahate. ~ *sulfide.* Kupuriku sulafaside.

curare *A poison for South American Indians' arrows; also a muscle relaxant in modern medicine.* Kulali.

curd *Bean* ~, *tofu.* Tōfū.

cure *To prepare by chemical or physical processing for keeping or use.* Hoʻohāoʻo. *Cured.* Hāoʻo.

curious Nīele, pena.

currency *Money.* Kālā.

current Au. *Dic. Electric* ~. Au uila. *Alternating* ~ *(AC) electricity.* Uila au māʻaloʻalo. *Direct* ~ *(DC) electricity.* Uila aukahi. *Drift* ~, *in oceanography.* Au 'ae'a. *Equatorial ~.* Au kā'ei pō'ai waena honua. *Northern Equatorial ~.* Kūkahikahi. *Southern Equatorial ~.* Kalekale. *Stream ~.* Au kikī.

curriculum *Also coursework.* Papa ha'awina. *Elective ~.* Papa ha'awina koho. *Required ~.* Papa ha'awina koina. *A catalog listing or sequence of lessons of a ~.* Mo'oha'awina.

curriculum vitae *Also résumé, vita.* Mo'omō'ali.

cursor *Also I-bar or insertion point in a computer program.* Kaha'imo. *Also mouse arrow or pointer.* Nahau 'iole, nahau.

curtain *Shower ~.* Pale kililau. *Window ~.* Pale pukaaniani.

curve *Or turn, as in a road or on a trail.* Uake'e. *Banked ~.* Uake'e hiō. *Geometric ~, or as on a graph.* Uma. *Parabolic ~.* Uma palapola.

curve-fitting *In math.* Ho'okūkū hahaina.

cushion *Pin ~.* Pulu kui.

custom *A learned cultural value or behavior.* Mēheuheu. See entry below and *culture.*

custom *~ format, as for a computer program.* Ho'onohonohona pilikino. *Or ~-made, i.e. made to individual specifications.* Pilikino.

cut *A command to stop the filming of a movie or video scene.* Ua oki (*pronounced* uoki)!

cut *To ~ diagonally.* 'Oki pāhi'a, 'oki ma ka pāhi'a.

cutaway 'ukulele 'Ukulele 'okia.

cutting *As of a plant.* Pulapula.

cuttlebone Mūhe'e iwi.

cuttlefish *As per local definition; squid, as per Haole definition.* Mūhe'e.

cutworm Poko, 'enuhe hele pō.

cyanide Kaianaside. *Potassium ~.* Potasiuma kaianaside.

cycle Pō'aiapuni. See *oxygen, recycle.* *Business ~, a repeated series of economic growth and recession.* Pō'aiapuni kāloa'a. *Life ~.* Pō'aiapuni ola.

cylinder *The shape.* Paukū 'oloka'a. *The container.* Hano. *Graduated ~.* Hano ana. See *test tube.*

cypress *Portuguese ~.* Paina Pukikī, paina tireza.

Cyprus *Also Cypriot.* Kupelo, Kupero.

Czech Tieka. See *Czechoslovakia. ~ Republic.* Ka Lepupalika 'o Tieka.

Czechoslovakia *Also Czech, but only when referring to the former country of ~.* Tiekasolowakia. See *Czech.*

D

daffodil Kuikina haole. See *narcissus.*

daikon Kaikona.

daily *To come out ~, as a newspaper.* Puka lā. See *Percent Daily Value.*

dairy product Mea'ai waiū.

daisy *Marguerite.* Makalike.

Dakota Kakoka, Dakota. *North ~.* Kakoka 'Ākau, Dakota 'Ākau. *South ~.* Kakoka Hema, Dakota Hema.

damages See *claim for damages.*

damp *~ or moist with fog or dew, wet from cold.* Kawaū.

damping-off *A diseased condition of seedlings or cuttings caused by fungi and characterized by wilting or rotting.* 'Umiāpau.

damselfly *Megalagrion spp.* Pinapinao. *Larva of ~ and other dragonflies.* Lohaloha, lohelohe.

dance-a-thon Hulahulakona.

Dane See *Denmark.*

Danish See *Denmark.*

daphnia 'Uku wai.

dart *As for a dart game.* Pāhi'u.

dash *In punctuation.* Kaha maha. See *hyphen.*

dash *Also to sprint.* Holo kikī.

data 'Ikepili. See *database. To distribute ~, as on a graph, in math.* Kākuhi,
kākuhi i ka 'ikepili. *~ distribution.* Ka ili
o ka 'ikepili. *~ spread.* Ka waiho o ka
'ikepili. *To input ~, as into a computer.*
Kāhuakomo 'ikepili. *To output ~.*
Kāhuapuka 'ikepili. *~ link.* Loulou
'ikepili. See *file link. ~ stream.* Laina
'ikepili.

data bank See *database.*

database *As in a computer program;
also data bank, i.e. an organized
collection of information, in math.*
Hōkeo 'ikepili. See *data. ~ program.*
Polokalamu hōkeo 'ikepili.

date Lā. *Format for ~ in Hawaiian:
June 10, 1998.* 10 Iune 1998. 6/10/98.
10/VI/98.

date book *Also appointment book.*
'Alemanaka puke. See *almanac.*

date line *International ~.* Laina helu lā.

dating *Carbon ~, radiocarbon date.* Helu
makahiki kalapona.

day Lā. *No abbreviation.* See *date.*

daydream Lauele.

DC *Direct current.* Aukahi. See *AC. ~
electricity.* Uila aukahi.

deadfall *A kind of animal trap.*
Hāʻuleāpaʻa.

deadline Palena pau. *~ hour.* Hola
palena pau. *~ day.* Lā palena pau. *To
set a ~.* Kaupalena.

deal *To ~, as cards; to distribute or pass
out, as papers in a class; to dole out.*
Kākaʻahi. See *shuffle.*

dean *As in a college or university.*
Luna. See *provost. ~ of the college of
arts and sciences.* Luna koleke pāheona
me ka ʻepekema.

debate Paio kālaimanaʻo. *~ club.* Hui
paio kālaimanaʻo.

deca- *A prefix meaning ten (da).*
Pāʻumi. *Abb.* pʻm. *Also* keka-. See
entries below and *hecto-, kilo-, mega-,
giga-, tera-.*

decade Kekeke.

decagon *A ten-sided polygon.* Huina
ʻumi.

decagram Kekakalame. *Abb.* kekal.

decaliter Kekalika. *Abb.* kel.

decameter Kekamika. *Abb.* kek.

decathalon ʻĀlapakonaʻumi. See
triathalon, pentathalon.

decelerate Hoʻēmi i ka māmā holo, emi
ka māmā holo. See *accelerate,
deceleration. Decelerated.* Emi ka māmā
holo.

deceleration Emi māmā holo. See
acceleration, decelerate.

December Kekemapa. *Abb.* Kek. *Also*
Dekemapa. *Abb.* Dek.

deci- *A prefix meaning one tenth (d).*
Hapa ʻumi *Abb.* hʻm. *Also* keki-. See
entries below and *centi-, milli-, micro-,
nano-, pico-.*

decibel Ikakani.

decigram Kekikalame. *Abb.* kkkal.

deciliter Kekilika. *Abb.* kkl.

decimal Kekimala. *~ place.* Kūana
kekimala. *~ point.* Kiko kekimala. *~
system.* ʻŌnaehana kekimala. *Mixed ~.*
Kekimala ʻōʻā. *Repeating ~.* Kekimala
pīnaʻi. *Terminating ~.* Kekimala pani.

decimeter Kekimika. *Abb.* kkm.

decision-making skill Mākau
hoʻoholo manaʻo.

deck *Flight ~, as on a spaceship.* ʻOneki
pailaka.

decode Hoʻomākalakala. *Decoded.*
Mākalakala.

decomposed *Also putrefied.*
Hāpopopo. See *decomposition. To
decompose or putrefy something.*
Hoʻohāpopopo. *Broken down into
component parts, as through chemical
reaction.* Wāhia.

decomposition *Aerobic ~ or
putrefaction.* Ka hoʻohāpopopo eaea ʻana.
Anaerobic ~ or putrefaction. Ka
hoʻohāpopopo eaea ʻole ʻana. See
decomposed.

decorate *To make artistic.* Hoʻoheona. *To ~ sets, as for a movie or video production.* Hoʻoponopono kahua. *Set decorator.* Mea hoʻoponopono kahua.

decrease *Greatest ~, in math.* Emi haʻahaʻa loa. *See increase.*

deep-fry Palai hoʻoluʻu.

deer *~ mouse.* ʻIole kia. *Roe ~.* Kia lō.

default *As in a computer program.* Paʻamau.

defend *To ~, in sports.* Pale. *See defense. As your basket in basketball.* Kūpale. *To ~ against, as an opponent.* Kaupale.

defendant *In court proceedings.* Mea kūpale. *See defense, defense attorney.*

defense *In sports.* Pale; ʻaoʻao pale, ʻaoʻao kūpale. *See entries below and defend, offense. Man-to-man ~, as in basketball.* Pale alo. *Press ~.* Pale lulumi. *Zone ~.* Pale kāʻei.

defense *The defendant's case or counsel in a lawsuit.* ʻAoʻao kūpale. *See defense attorney, prosecution.*

defense attorney *Also attorney for the defendant.* Loio kūpale. *See defendant, prosecuting attorney.*

defensive corner back *In football.* ʻĀʻiwa.

defensive encroachment *In football.* Lele ʻē na ke kūpale.

defensive end *In football.* Pūkaha. *Left ~.* Pūkaha hema. *Right ~.* Pūkaha ʻākau.

defensive line *In football.* Laina kūpale, laina pale.

defensive linebacker *In football.* Mahikua.

defensive middle guard *Also nose guard, nose tackle, in football.* Haunaku.

defensive slide *To execute a ~, in basketball.* Pāpaʻi.

defensive stance *As in basketball.* Kūlana pale.

deficit *An excess of expenditure over revenue.* Lilo pākeu. *See surplus. ~ spending.* Hoʻolilo pākeu.

deflated *As a balloon.* ʻAnanuʻu, emi, puhalu. *See flat.*

deforestation *Also to deforest.* Hoʻoneo ʻāina ululāʻau.

degree Kēkelē. *See boiling point, freezing point, melting point, temperature. ~ Celsius.* Kēkelē Kelekia. *~ Fahrenheit.* Kēkelē Palanaheika. *See also bachelor's, Master's, doctorate.*

dehydrate *To ~ something.* Hoʻopīkaʻo. *dehydrated.* Pīkaʻo.

Deimos *A moon of Mars.* Keimoka.

deka- *See deca-.*

Delaware *Also Delawarean.* Kelauea, Delauea.

delay *As in a computer program.* Kaʻukaʻu.

delegated powers *As of Congress.* Mana ʻākuleana.

delete *To ~, as in a computer program.* Holoi. *To ~ with ~ key on a Macintosh computer.* Holoi i hope. *See backspace. A line used to indicate that something is to be ~d, in proofreading.* Kaha kāpae. *To strike through or line out, also used to indicate that the letters or words lined out are to be ~d and replaced by those written above.* Kahawaena.

deliberately *To foul ~, in team sports such as basketball.* Hoʻokuʻia. *See foul.*

delinquency *Juvenile ~.* Lawehala ʻōpiopio. *See delinquent.*

delinquent *Juvenile ~.* Keiki lawehala. *See delinquency.*

delirium *Maniacal ~.* Maʻi hehena.

delivery *See COD.*

delphinium ʻAuhōkū, pua ʻauhōkū.

delta *Of a river.* Kaha nuku muliwai.

deltoid *A muscle of the upper arm.* Mākala kaupē.

deluxe Linohau. *See standard. ~ room, as in a hotel.* Lumi linohau.

demand *A desired commodity within the consumer's ability to pay.* Heluna makemake. *Supply and ~.* Hoʻolako me ka heluna makemake.

democracy Aupuni na ka lehulehu. *Direct ~, a government in which laws are made directly by the citizens.* Aupuni kānāwai na ka lehulehu.

Democratic Republic of the Congo Lepupalika Kemokalaka ʻo Konokō.

demonstrate *To show, as how a math problem is solved.* Kuhikuhi.

denier *A unit of fineness for nylon, etc.* Māʻumi.

Denmark *Also Dane, Danish.* Kenemaka, Denemaka.

denomination *Monetary ~.* Kūana kālā.

denominator *In math.* Kinopiha. *See numerator. Least common ~.* Kinopiha haʻahaʻa loa.

density *As of a computer disk.* Paʻapū. *High ~.* Paʻapū ʻoi. *Low ~.* Paʻapū emi.

density *Population ~, for humans only.* Paʻapū pūʻuo kanaka.

dental *In linguistics.* Niho.

dental floss *Also to floss (one's teeth).* Lopi niho.

dentist *See drill, orthodontist, pick.*

deodorant Lūkini pōʻaeʻae.

Dep *Hair gel.* Palaholo lauoho.

department *Also division, piece, portion, category, part, land division; to divide, apportion.* Māhele. *Also office.* Keʻena, ʻoihana. *See entries below. County Planning ~.* Keʻena Hoʻolālā o ke Kalana. *Hawaiʻi State ~ of Finance.* ʻOihana Kālā o ka Mokuʻāina ʻo Hawaiʻi. *Hawaiʻi State ~ of Planning and Economic Development.* ʻOihana Hoʻolālā a me ka Hoʻomohala Waiwai o ka Mokuʻāina ʻo Hawaiʻi. *State ~ of Agriculture.* ʻOihana Mahi ʻAi o ka Mokuʻāina.

Department of Land and Natural Resources *DLNR.* ʻOihana Kumuwaiwai ʻĀina.

Department of Parks and Recreation ʻOihana o nā Pāka a me nā Hana Hoʻonanea.

dependent clause *In grammar.* Pepeke ʻōhua.

dependent variable Kumuloli kaukaʻi. *See independent variable.*

depleted *As a species.* Emi. *See endangered. ~ species.* Lāhui emi, lāhulu emi.

deposit *As money placed into a bank account.* Kālā hoʻokomo.

deposition *Testimony taken down in writing under oath to be used in court proceedings.* Palapala moʻopane.

depress *To click or press, as in a computer program.* Kōmi, kaomi.

depressant Lāʻau hoʻoloha. *See stimulant.*

depression *Geologic ~, as Death Valley.* ʻĀpoho ʻāina.

depth *Or height, in math.* Hohonu. *See length, width. To measure ~, as in the ocean.* Hoʻopapā hohonu.

derivation *Root, source, or origin, as the etymology of a word.* Molekumu.

dermestid *Larder beetle.* Ponu ʻili.

dermis *In biology.* ʻIli kūwaena. *See epidermis.*

desalinate *Also to desalinize salty water.* Hoʻomānalo wai kai.

desalinize *Also to desalinate salty water.* Hoʻomānalo wai kai.

desert Panoa. *Alpine ~.* Panoa ʻalapaina.

desertification *The processes by which an area becomes a desert, in geography.* Hoʻopanoa.

design *Letterhead ~.* Lau poʻo kuni. *To make drawings or plans.* Hakulau. *To ~ sets, as for movie or video production.* Hakulau kahua. *Set ~er.* Mea hakulau kahua.

desktop *In a computer program.* 'Oneki.

dessert Monamona.

detail Mea kiko'ī, mea li'ili'i, mea li'ili'i kiko'ī. See *detailed.*

detailed *As a design.* Lāli'i. See *detail.*

detention *As punishment at school.* Ho'opa'i 'au'a. See *suspension.* *After-school* ~. Ho'opa'i 'au'a muli kula. *In-school* ~. Ho'opa'i 'au'a i ka wā kula.

develop *To ~ land, as the work of a developer.* Kūkulu hale, kūkulu hale ma luna o ka 'āina. *See entries below.*

developed *As a First World Country.* 'Oi'enehana. See *developing.* ~ *country.* 'Āina 'oi'enehana.

developing *As a Third World Country.* Hō'oi'enehana. See *developed.* ~ *country.* 'Āina hō'oi'enehana.

development *Economic* ~. Ho'omohala waiwai. *Hawai'i State Department of Planning and Economic* ~. 'Oihana Ho'olālā a me ka Ho'omohala Waiwai o ka Moku'āina 'o Hawai'i. *Housing* ~, *subdivision.* Kaiahale.

deviation *In math.* Haiahū. See *normal. Standard* ~. Haiahū kūmau.

device *Something made or used for a particular purpose; doohickey, gadget, gizmo, thingamajig.* Hāme'a. See *instrument, tool. Input* ~, *as on a computer.* Hāme'a huakomo. *Output* ~. Hāme'a huapuka. *Ordinarily including some mechanical part or parts.* Maomeka.

diabetes Ma'i kōpa'a, mimi kō.

diachronic *In linguistics.* Kōāwā. See *synchronic.* ~ *rule.* Lula kōāwā.

diagonal *In math.* Lala. See *horizontal, vertical. A segment other than a side connecting two vertices of a polygon.* Kaha lala. ~*ly.* Papalala. *To cut* ~*ly.* 'Oki pāhi'a, 'oki ma ka pāhi'a.

diagram *Schematic drawing.* Ki'ikuhi. *Tree* ~, *in math.* Ki'i kuhi pahiki. *Venn* ~, *a ~ using overlapping circles to show relationship of data.* Ki'ikuhi Wene.

dial Pā wili (*preceded by* ke). ~ *tone.* Kani 'ā. *To* ~, *as a telephone.* Wili.

dialog box *In a computer program.* Pahu a'o. See *dialogue.*

dialogue *As in a play, movie, or video production.* Pāpā'ōlelo.

diameter *In math.* Anawaena. *Abb.* anw.

diamond *Baseball* ~, *infield.* Kaimana pōhili. See *baseball field.*

diaphragm Houpo.

diary *Also journal.* Puke mo'omana'o.

diazinon Diazinona.

dichotomous key 'Āmana koho.

dicotyledon Lau 'īnana lua. See *cotyledon.*

dictatorship Aupuni mana kēnā kahi.

dictionary *As in a computer program.* Papa hua'ōlelo. See *glossary. Main* ~. Papa hua'ōlelo kūmau. *User* ~. Papa hua'ōlelo pāku'i.

die *To ~ a bad death, as in punishment for evil deeds.* Make hopena.

dieldrin *A kind of insecticide.* Dielidirina. See *aldrin, poison.*

diet *The food that is eaten.* Papa'ai. *To reduce.* Ho'ēmi kino.

difference *Remainder, in math.* Koena. *Abb.* K.

difficulty *Also problem, as in the plot of a story.* Hihia. See *resolution.*

diffusion *Also to be diffused.* Maholahune.

dig *To ~ (the ball), in volleyball.* 'Ali. See *pancake dig. Digger.* Mea 'ali, 'ali.

digest *To ~ food.* Ho'ohehe'e mea'ai, ho'owali 'ai, ho'onapele.

digestive system 'Ōnaehana ho'ohehe'e mea'ai.

digit *In math.* Kikoho'e. *Front end ~.* Kikoho'e hapa mua.

digital *~ clock or watch.* Uaki kikoho'e, uāki kikoho'e. See *analog.*

dike *Geological formation.* Huku 'ou pele.

dilute Ho'okaiaka. *Diluted.* Kaiaka. *To ~ or mix, as a drink.* Pa'ipa'i.

dime *Also loose change.* Kenikeni.

dimension *In math.* Ana, nui.

dimensional See *two-dimensional, three-dimensional.*

dining room Lumi 'aina.

dink *To mishit or clip (the ball), in volleyball.* Ho'okulu, pa'i lihi. *Point from ~.* 'Ai hele wale.

dinosaur Nalala.

Dione *A moon of Saturn.* Kione.

dioxide Diokesaside. *Nitrogen ~.* Naikokene diokesaside, naikokene 'okikene lua. *Sulfur ~.* Sulufura diokesaside.

diphthong Huēwoela.

diploma *Professional ~ for teaching.* Palapala 'oihana a'o.

Dipper *Big ~.* Nāhiku.

Diptha *A star.* Kapanui.

direct *To ~, as a movie or video production.* Kuhikuhi. See *director.*

direct current *DC.* Aukahi. See *alternating current.* *~ electricity.* Uila aukahi.

direct democracy *A government in which laws are made directly by the citizens.* Aupuni kānāwai na ka lehulehu. See *democracy.*

direction Huli. *The four primary ~s, or four cardinal points of the compass, in geography.* Nā kūkulu 'ehā. *Intermediate ~s.* Nā kūkulu o waena.

directions 'Ōkuhi. *To follow ~.* Hahai 'ōkuhi.

director *One who serves as a leader in conducting any kind of business.* Luna ho'okele. See *administration.* *As for movie or video production.* Luna kuhikuhi. *Assistant ~.* Hope luna kuhikuhi. *Executive ~.* Po'o kuhikuhi. *Art ~.* Luna pāheona. *Lighting ~.* Luna ho'omālamalama.

directory *Of computer files.* Papa kuhi waihona.

directrix *As a line from which a curve can be made by taking all equidistant points of a conic section.* Kaha kau. *As a line which divides a parabola into two equal areas, in math.* Kaha anaalike.

dirt bike Mokokaikala holo lepo. See *all-terrain vehicle, off-road vehicle.*

disc jockey Wilipā, wilipāleo.

disconnect *To ~, as in a computer program.* Ho'ohemo. See *connect.*

discount *Also to ~, as a price for merchandise.* Ho'ēmi.

discover Kaunānā. *~ed.* Hi'ohia.

discrepancy Kāwā.

discriminate See *discrimination.*

discrimination *Also prejudice; to discriminate or be prejudiced against.* Ho'okae. See *racism.*

discus Pāhelene. *To throw a ~.* Kīloi pāhelene.

disease *To be susceptible or vulnerable to ~.* Pāma'i.

dish Pā *(preceded by ke).* *~ rack.* Haka kaula'i pā. *Petri ~.* Pā piki. *Soap ~.* Pā kopa. *Water ~.* Pā wai.

dishwasher Mīkini holoi pā. *~ soap.* Kopa mīkini holoi pā.

disk Pā *(preceded by ke).* See *disk drive.* *Computer ~.* Pā kamepiula. *Blank ~.* Pā ma'ema'e. *Floppy ~.* Pā malule. *Program ~.* Pā polokalamu. *Startup ~.* Pā ho'omaka. *Hard ~.* Pā pa'aloko. *Removable hard ~.* Pā pa'aloko wehe. *~ partitioning.* Māhele pā. *~ space.* Hakahaka pā. *To cache ~s.* Ho'okoe pā.

disk brake Peleki pā. See *brake disk.*

disk drive *As on a computer.* Kakena. See *disk. Hard drive.* Kakena pa'aloko. *Internal drive.* Kakena kūloko. *External drive.* Kakena kūwaho.

disobedience *Civil ~, i.e. breaking a law because it goes against personal morals.* 'A'a kānāwai.

dispense *To provide in measured quantities.* Hōlo'a. See *dispenser.*

dispenser *A dispensing container of any kind.* 'Ūhōlo'a. See *dispense. Paper towel ~.* 'Ūhōlo'a kāwele pepa. *Soap ~.* 'Ūhōlo'a kopa. *Water ~, as in a bird cage.* Kāhāinu. See *feeder.*

displacement *Also to displace.* Pohupani. *Air ~.* Pohupani ea. *Water ~.* Pohupani wai.

display *As on a computer screen.* Hō'ike.

display screen *As on a calculator.* Papakaumaka. *Calculator ~.* Papakaumaka mīkini helu.

dissimilation *In linguistics.* Kī'ōko'ako'a.

dissolve *To ~ something.* Ho'ohehe'e.

distinction *With ~, also with honors, cum laude, as in academics.* Me ke kau i ka hano, me ka hanohano, me ka ho'omaika'i. *With high ~, magna cum laude.* Me ke kau i ka hano ho'onani, me ka ho'omaika'i nui. *With highest ~, summa cum laude.* Me ke kau i ka hano hāweo.

distinguish Waele'a.

distribute *To ~, as in delivering or making publications available to the public.* Ho'omalele. See *distribution. To ~ or pass out, as papers in a class.* Kāka'ahi. *To ~ data, as on a graph, in math.* Kākuhi, kākuhi i ka 'ikepili.

distribution *Also to distribute, distributive, in math.* Ho'oili. See *distribute, distributive. Chi-squared ~.* Ha'ihelu ho'oili. *Also to be distributed, as data on a graph.* Ili. *Data ~.* Ka ili o ka 'ikepili. *Normal ~, in math and science.* Ili haiakonu. *Population ~.* Ili pū'uo, ili pū'uo kanaka. *Rain ~.* Ka ili o ka ua.

distributive See *distribution. ~ law.* Kānāwai ho'oili. *~ property.* 'Anopili ho'oili (*preceded by* ke).

district *Central business ~.* 'Āpana pā'oihana kauwaena. See *downtown. Congressional ~, in government.* 'Āpana 'aha'ōlelo lāhui.

dither *To approximate the appearance of a graphic image from another computer operating system.* Ho'okohu a like.

diurnal *Active during the daytime.* Ala ao. See *crepuscular, nocturnal.*

dive *To ~, in volleyball.* Lele 'ōpū, lu'u, moe pālahalaha. *To sky ~.* Lu'u lewa. *Sky ~r.* Mea lu'u lewa. *Diving goggles or mask.* Makaaniani lu'u kai, makaaniani lu'u. See *scuba.*

divergent *Spreading, in plate techtonics, in geology.* Ne'e 'oā. See *convergent, transform. ~ boundary.* Palena ne'e 'oā.

divide See *division.*

dividend *In math.* Kumu pu'unaue.

divisible *In math.* Pu'unaue koena 'ole.

division *Also to divide, in math.* Pu'unaue. See *composite. ~ sign.* Kaha pu'unaue.

division *Also piece, portion, department, category, part, land division; to divide, apportion.* Māhele. See *lower division, upper division. Of a legislative bill, larger than a section or article.* Mokuna. *See Hawaiian entries under kānāwai and title.*

Division of Aquatic Resources Māhele Kumuwaiwai Kai.

divisor *In math.* Helu komo.

Djibouti Dibuti.

DLNR *Department of Land and Natural Resources.* 'Oihana Kumuwaiwai 'Āina.

do *To ~ with all one's might or strength.* Ku'upau. See *geevum.*

do *The first note on the musical scale.* Pā. See *Hawaiian entry* pākōlī.

Doctor *For use as a title before a person's name.* Kauka. *Abb.* Kk.

doctorate *As a degree at a university.* Lae'ula, kauka. See *bachelor's, Master's, undergraduate, graduate.* *~ degree.* Kēkelē lae'ula, palapala lae'ula.

document *As in a computer program.* Palapala. See *draft, subsummary. Text of a ~.* Kikokikona. *~ outline.* 'Oloke'a palapala. *~ specific.* Pili ho'okahi palapala. *~ summary.* Hō'ulu'ulu palapala.

dodecahedron *A space figure with twelve faces, in math.* Pa'a'ili 'umikūmālua.

dog's tooth violet *A kind of flower.* Waioleka niho'īlio.

doghouse Hale 'īlio.

dog paddle *Also to ~, in swimming.* 'Au 'īlio. See *stroke.*

dole out See *deal.*

doll *A child's plaything.* Pēpē ki'i.

dollar Kālā. See *bill, half dollar, quarter.* *~ sign.* Kaha kālā. *Silver ~.* Kālā ke'oke'o.

domain *As on the Internet.* Kā'ei kapu. *As a sphere or field of activity or influence.* Pō'ai. *Affective ~, as relating to the learning process.* Pō'ai na'au. *Cognitive ~.* Pō'ai no'ono'o. *Psychomotor ~.* Pō'ai 'onina kino. *Eminent ~, the right of the government to take, or to authorize taking of, the private property of a citizen for public use with just compensation being given to the citizen whose property has been taken.* Mana kā'ili o ke aupuni.

domesticated *As a pet or for work.* Lakauā. See *feral.*

domestic policy *Plans for dealing with national problems, in government.* Kulekele kūloko. See *foreign policy.*

Domincan Kominika. *~ Republic.* Lepupalika Kominika.

domino Iwi pā'ani. *To play ~es.* Pā'ani iwi.

don't you forget it *Also I told you so, you dummy, you should know; used only at the end of a sentence or phrase.* Ā. See *Hawaiian entry.*

doohickey *Device, gadget, gizmo, thingamajig.* Hāme'a. See *apparatus, instrument, tool.*

door *As opposed to doorway.* Pani puka (*preceded by* ke). See *molding.* *~frame.* Kikihi. *~ hinge.* 'Ami puka, 'ami 'īpuka. *~ threshold.* Paepae puka. *Screen ~.* Pani puka uea makika, pani puka maka'aha. *Sliding ~.* Puka uai, 'īpuka uai.

doorknob Pōheo puka, pōheoheo puka.

doorstop Ko'o puka, ko'o 'īpuka.

dormant Ka'oko.

dormitory Hale moe, hale noho haumāna.

dorsal *In biology.* Laukua. See *anterior, posterior, ventral.* *~ fin, of a fish, nonscientific term.* Kualā. *~ fin, scientific term.* Kualā laukua. *Anterior ~ fin.* Kualā laumua. *Posterior ~ fin.* Kualā lauhope.

dot *On a grid.* Kiko huina. See *entry below and intersection, isometric dot paper.*

dots *A series of ~ written under a word or words which have been lined out to show that no change should be made from the original, in proofreading; stet.* Kaha waiho.

dotted half note *In music.* Hua mele hapalua kiko.

dotted quarter note *In music.* Hua mele hapahā kiko.

double *In math.* Kaulua. *See entries below. As when throwing dice.* Māhoe. *~ number.* Helu māhoe.

double bar graph *In math.* Pakuhi pa'a 'aukā. See *bar graph.*

double dribble *In basketball.* Pākimokimo pālua, pāloiloi pālua, pa'ipa'i pālua.

double extra large *XXL, as a shirt size.* Nui keu pālua. See *large.*

double hit *To lift or make a ~, in volleyball.* Hāpai. See *carrying violation.* *~ violation.* 'A'ena pa'i lua.

double-hole 'ukulele 'Ukulele 'elua puka.

double jeopardy *To be tried in court twice for the same offense.* 'Alo ho'opi'i 'elua.

double space See *spacing.*

dough Pa'ipalaoa.

dowel Poke kaola.

down *Pages ~, as in a computer program.* 'Ehia 'ao'ao ha'alalo? See *across.*

download *To ~, as in a computer program.* Ho'oili. See *install, load.*

downtown Kaona. See *central business district, city.*

downward Ha'alalo. See *round off.*

downwind *To sail directly ~.* Kele ka'alalo. See *beam reach, broad reach, close hauled.*

draft *A preliminary version; also to prepare a ~.* Kāmua. *See entries below. First ~.* Kāmua 'ekahi. *Second ~.* Kāmua 'elua.

draft *To draw blueprints.* Kaha ki'i kūkulu. See *draftsman. To draw up documents.* Kāpalapala. *A person who ~s documents.* Kanaka kāpalapala.

draft *Bank ~.* Pila kīko'o panakō.

draft animals *A team of ~.* Pūkolo.

drafter See *draftsman.*

draftsman *One who draws blueprints.* Kaha ki'i kūkulu. See *draft.*

drag *To ~, as in a computer program.* Alakō, ki'i a alakō. *To ~ onto.* Alakō ma luna o, alakō a kau ma luna o.

dragon *As in fairy tales.* Kalekona, kelekona. See *skeleton.*

dragonfly See *damselfly.*

drain Paipu omo wai.

drainage *Also to have good drainage.* Nōkahea.

drama *Also dramatic.* Paiwa. *~ coach.* Ka'i hana keaka. *~tic play.* Hana keaka paiwa.

draw *To ~ a conclusion.* Ho'oholo i hopena. *To ~ or withdraw money from the bank.* Kīko'o.

drawer 'Ume. See *bureau.* *~ handle.* 'Au 'ume *(preceded by* ke*).* *~ knob.* Pōheo 'ume.

drawing *Scale ~, in math.* Ki'i pālākiō.

dresser *Bureau.* Pahu 'ume.

dribble *To ~, as a basketball.* Pākimokimo, pāloiloi, pa'ipa'i. *Double ~.* Pākimokimo pālua, pāloiloi pālua, pa'ipa'i pālua. *To ~, as with kicks in soccer.* Pekupeku.

dried See *freeze dried.*

drift current *In oceanography.* Au 'ae'a.

drill Kumuwili, wili. See *bit. Dentist's ~.* Wili niho. *To ~.* Wili.

drink *Beverage.* Meainu.

drinking fountain Pua'iwai.

drive *Disk ~, as on a computer.* Kakena. *Hard ~.* Kakena pa'aloko. *Internal ~.* Kakena kūloko. *External ~.* Kakena kūwaho.

drive *To ~, in basketball.* Kaha.

drive *As for cans; to conduct a ~.* Alu. *Newspaper ~.* Alu hō'ili'ili nūpepa. *School clean-up ~.* Alu ho'oma'ema'e pā kula.

drive-through *As at a restaurant or bank.* Holona ka'a.

driveway Alakalaiwa.

dropper Omo ho'okulu.

dropping bottle *A bottle used much like an eyedropper.* 'Ōmole ho'okulu.

Drosophilidae *Pomace fly, family ~.* Pōnalo.

drug *Medicinal ~, medication.* Lā'au. *Prescription ~.* Lā'au kuhikuhi. *Prescription for ~s or medication.* Kuhikuhi lā'au. *Over-the-counter ~.* Lā'au kū'ai wale. *Narcotic ~.* Lā'au 'ona. *To overdose on ~s.* Pākela 'ai lā'au.

drumstick *As of a chicken.* Pālaumoa.

dry erase board *Also white board.* Papa ke'oke'o, papa peni kuni.

dual citizen Kupa kaumoku'āina pālua, maka'āinana kaumoku'āina pālua.

duct *Alveolar ~, in anatomy.* Pū'ali nōiki. *Sweat ~.* Puka kikī hou.

due process *Also ~ of law.* Kū i ke ka'ina kānāwai.

dull *Not shiny.* Hāpa'upa'u.

dumb See *ignorance.*

dummy See *you dummy.*

dump Ho'ohanini. *~ truck.* Kalaka ho'ohanini. *To ~, in volleyball.* Hō'anu'u.

dumplings Palaoa mokumoku, palaoa pakūpakū, palaoa keko.

dunce cap Pāpale kone.

dune buggy Ka'a holo one.

dunk *To ~ (the ball), in basketball.* Pakā, 'ūpo'i. *To slam ~.* Pākī.

duplicate *As in a computer program.* Lua like.

duration *In music.* Kō hua mele.

dusk *Twilight.* Mōlehulehu, hola mōlehulehu.

dust Ehu lepo, ehu. *Chalk ~.* Ehu poho. *To brush or apply lightly a thin coat, such as sulphur to a plant.* Kāehuehu. *To ~ with a cloth.* Kāwele. *To ~ with a dry cloth.* Kāwele malo'o. *To ~ with a damp cloth.* Kāwele ma'ū. *To ~ with a duster.* Kāhilihili. See *duster.*

duster Mea kāhilihili. See *dust.*

dustfall jar *As for scientific experiments.* 'Ōmole 'apo hunahuna.

dustpan Pā ehu lepo (*preceded by* ke).

E

eagle *Bald ~.* 'Āeko po'o hina, 'āeto po'o hina.

ear *~ lobe.* Lepe pepeiao. *Inner ~ cavity, cochlea.* Haka mo'oni.

early Ma mua o ka manawa, ma mua o ka hola. *Beforehand, pre-.* Hiki mua. *~ registration.* Kāinoa hiki mua.

earphone Pihi lohe (*preceded by* ke). See *headphone.*

Earth *The planet.* Honua (*cap.*). See *core, crust, globe, mantle.*

earth metal *Alkaline ~, one of the family of elements in Group 2 of the periodic table.* Mekala honua 'ākilikai. See *alkali metal.*

earthquake Ōla'i. See *aftershock.* *Epicenter.* Kiko ōla'i.

earthworm Ko'e honua.

easel Kū pena ki'i.

east Hikina. *Abb.* Hk. *See entries below.*

East China Sea Ke kai 'o Kina Hikina.

Eastern Europe *Also Eastern European.* 'Eulopa Hikina.

eastern hemisphere Poepoe hapa hikina. See *hemisphere.*

East Siberian Sea Ke kai 'o Siberia Hikina.

eaves 'Anini (*preceded by* ke).

eccentric Lala'ē.

ecology Kālaikaiaola. See *ecosystem.*

economic development Ho'omohala waiwai. *Hawai'i State Department of Planning and ~.* 'Oihana Ho'olālā a me ka Ho'omohala Waiwai o ka Moku'āina 'o Hawai'i.

economics Kālaiho'okele waiwai. See *economy.* *Home ~.* Mākau nohona home.

economy Hoʻokele waiwai. See *economic development, economics. Command ~.* Hoʻokele waiwai mana kahi. *Free-market ~.* Hoʻokele waiwai kū lanakila.

ecosystem Kaiaola. See *ecology.*

Ecuador *Also Ecuadoran, Ecuadorean, Ecuadorian.* ʻEkuakola, ʻEkuadora.

eddy Wiliau. See *galaxy.*

edge *As of a three-dimensional geometric figure.* Kaʻe. See *straightedge.*

edge feed *To ~, as paper into a printer or copy machine.* Hānai kaʻe.

edit *To ~, as on a computer.* Hoʻololi. *See entries below. ~ screen, in a computer program.* Pukaaniani hoʻoponopono. *List editor or screen.* Pukaaniani kolamu ʻikepili.

edit *To ~, as movies or movie productions.* Hoʻoponopono kiʻiʻoniʻoni. See *editing facility, editor. To ~, as videos or video productions.* Hoʻoponopono wikiō. *To ~ sound, as for a movie or video production.* Hoʻoponopono kani.

editing facility *For movies.* Hale hoʻoponopono kiʻiʻoniʻoni. *For videos.* Hale hoʻoponopono wikiō.

edition *As in a computer program.* Hua loulou.

editor *Also coordinator, manager, etc., as in producing a movie or video.* Luna. *Assemble ~.* Luna hoʻokuʻikuʻi. *Sound ~.* Luna hoʻoponopono kani.

education *Alternative ~, as a school program.* Hoʻonaʻauao kaʻaʻokoʻa. *Gifted ~.* Hoʻonaʻauao haumāna lololo. *~ support staff.* Kākoʻo hoʻonaʻauao.

effect Hopena See *cause.*

effects Hiʻohiʻona. See *sound. Printer ~, as on a computer printer.* Hiʻohiʻona paʻi. *Special ~.* Hiʻohiʻona naʻiau. *To add special ~.* Hoʻonaʻiau (i ka hiʻohiʻona). *To have special ~.* Naʻiau.

egg *White or yolk.* Kauō. *~ white.* Kauō keʻokeʻo. *~ yolk.* Kauō melemele.

egret *General term.* ʻAlekuʻu. See *heron. Cattle ~.* ʻAlekuʻu kau pipi.

Egypt *Also Egyptian.* ʻAikupika, ʻAikupita, ʻAigupita.

eighth note *In music.* Hua mele hapawalu.

eighth rest *In music.* Hoʻomaha hapawalu.

eight-string ʻukulele ʻUkulele ʻewalu kaula.

EIS *Environmental Impact Statement.* Palapala Hōʻike Hopena Kaiapuni.

eject *To ~, as a disk from a computer or a video cassette from a VCR.* Kīpeku.

ejecta *Volcanic ~.* Pōhāhā. See *spatter cone.*

elapsed Kaʻahope. *~ time.* Hola kaʻahope.

elderberry Pīʻai ʻelepeli.

election *Primary ~.* Koho pāloka wae moho, wae moho. *Closed primary ~.* Wae moho kūloko. *Open primary ~.* Wae moho kūākea. *General ~.* Koho pāloka laulā.

elective Koho. See *required. ~ class, course, as in school.* Papa koho. *~ credit.* ʻAi koho. *~ coursework, curriculum.* Papa haʻawina koho.

elector *As in the United States Electoral College.* ʻElele manakoho.

electric *~ blanket.* Kapa uila. *~ circuit.* Puni uila. *~ current.* Au uila. *~ charge.* Ikehu uila. *Neutral charge.* Ikehu uila hohoki, ikehu uila. See items below and *brush, charge, conductor, fan.*

electrical *~ force field.* Kāʻei manehu uila. See *force. ~ outlet.* Puka uila. See *plug.*

electrician Kanaka hana uila.

electrician's tape *Cloth duct tape.* Leki uea.

electricity Uila. *Geothermal ~.* Uila māhu pele. *Hydro~.* Uila wai kahe. *Wind-generated ~.* Uila huila makani. See *thermoelectricity.*

electric shock *To give an ~.* Omo, miki. *To give a severe ~.* 'Ūmi'i.

electrode 'Ūholo uila. See *anode, cathode.*

electrolysis *Also to be affected by ~.* Pā uila. *To utilize the process of ~.* Ho'opā uila.

electron Huna 'ine. See *neutron, proton.*

electronic mail See *E-mail.*

elegant *Fancy.* Ho'ohiluhilu.

element Kumumea. *Traditional ~s of Hawaiian poetry, story telling, oratory, and narration.* Meiwi.

element *Trace ~.* Kumumea 'āwe'awe'a.

elevated train *As the Japan monorail.* Ka'aahi kau lewa.

elevation Ki'eki'ena. *~ pole, as for surveying.* Lā'au ana ki'eki'ena. See *range pole, sighter.*

elf owl Pueo peke.

ellipse Pō'ai lō'ihi analahi, 'ololaha analahi. See *oval.*

ellipsis *In punctuation.* Kiko kolu.

El Salvador *Also Salvadoran, Salvadorian.* 'Ela Salavadora.

E-mail *Electronic mail, as in telecommunication.* Leka uila.

emergency Pōulia. *~ room or facility.* Ke'ena mālama pōulia.

emergent *~ layer of vegetation, as trees sticking out at top.* Papa 'oi'oi. See *vegetation layer.*

emigrate Pukane'e. See *immigrate.*

eminent domain *The right of the government to take, or to authorize taking of, the private property of a citizen for public use with just compensation being given to the citizen whose property has been taken.* Mana kā'ili o ke aupuni.

emir 'Emila, 'emira. See *emirate.*

emirate Aupuni 'emila, aupuni 'emira. See *emir. United Arab ~s.* Aupuni 'Emira 'Alapia Hui Pū 'ia.

emotional stress 'Alo'ahia.

Emperor Seamounts Ka pae mauna kai 'o 'Emepela.

empire Aupuni 'emepela.

empty *As a bowl.* Hakahaka, ka'ele.

empty trash *To ~, as in a computer program.* Kīloi.

emulation *As in a computer printer.* Hoa māhu'i.

enamel Pena pa'a mania.

Enceladus *A small moon of Saturn.* 'Enekelakuke.

encode *To encrypt, as computer data.* Ho'opā'ālua. See *code, unencrypt.*

encourage *A prefix meaning to ~, laud; -ism, a suffix in English meaning devotion or adherence to something.* Pai-. *See Hawaiian entries beginning with* pai-.

encroachment *In football.* Lele 'ē. See *offsides. Defensive ~.* Lele 'ē na ke kūpale.

encrypt See *encode.*

encyclopedia Puke noi'i kū'ikena.

end *Of a sporting field or court.* Po'o (*preceded by* ke), kumu. See *line, side.* *~ line or base line, as on a basketball court.* Laina hīna'i, laina hupa, laina kumu, laina po'o. *~ zone, on a football field.* Pahu 'ai holo.

end *Defensive ~, in football.* Pūkaha. See *safety. Left defensive ~.* Pūkaha hema. *Right defensive ~.* Pūkaha 'ākau. *Split ~.* Lala. *Tight ~.* Muku.

endangered 'Ane halapohe, 'ane make loa, 'ane nalowale loa. See entry below and *extinct.*

Endangered Species Act Kānāwai Lāhulu 'Ane Halapohe.

endemic 'Āpa'akuma. *~ plant.* Meakanu 'āpa'akuma.

endnote *As in a book or research paper.* Kuhia o hope. See *note, footnote.*

endocrine gland Lōkuʻu kuʻuloko. See entry below and *exocrine gland.*

endocrine system *In biology.* ʻŌnaehana hōmona.

endoskeleton Iwi kūloko. See *exoskeleton.*

endothermic Omo wela. See *exothermic.*

endowment fund Waihona ō, waihona kālā kūmau.

endpoint *In math.* Piko.

end user *As of computer programs.* Mea hoʻohana.

energy Ikehu. *~ pyramid.* Pelamika ikehu. *Chemical ~.* Ikehu kemikala. *Kinetic ~.* Ikehu neʻe. *Nuclear ~.* Ikehu nukelea. *Potential ~.* Ikehu noho. *Solar ~ wave.* Hawewe ikehu lā. *Thermal ~, i.e. the total ~ of all the particles in an object.* Ikehu kāʻokoʻa. See *calorimeter.*

engine *Maneuvering ~, as for a spacecraft.* ʻEnekini kīkaha.

engineer ʻEnekinia. *Mechanical ~.* ʻEnekinia mīkini. *Production ~, as for movie or video production.* Luna ʻenehana. *Assistant production ~.* Hope luna ʻenehana. *To ~ genetically.* Hoʻoliliuewe. *Genetic ~ing.* Ka hoʻoliliuewe ʻana.

England *Also Britain, British, English (of England), English person.* Pelekāne, ʻEnelani. See *British, English.*

English *Also British, Britain.* Pelekānia. See *British, England. Of England.* Pelekāne, ʻEnelani. *~ language.* ʻŌlelo Pelekānia.

enhanced *To be ~, have special effects.* Naʻiau. See *effects.*

enhanced *Or expanded, as a computer keyboard.* Keu. *~ keyboard.* Papa pihi keu.

Enif *A star.* Mākaʻi.

enrich *To improve the nutritive value of something.* Hoʻopaiola. *~ed.* Hoʻopaiola ʻia. *To increase knowledge.* Hoʻonui ʻike. *~ment book, challenge book.* Puke hoʻonui ʻike.

enter *To ~ or input, as typing data into a computer database or calculator.* Kāhuakomo. *To send or ~ data into a computer database or calculator after it has been typed.* Hoʻouna. *To use the ~ or return key on a computer or typewriter keyboard in order to return the cursor or carriage to the left margin on a new line; ~ or return, as the key just above the shift key on a computer keyboard.* Kāhoʻi.

entertain *To ~, as in a speech.* Mikolololehua. See *speech. A speech to ~, expressive speech.* Haʻiʻōlelo mikolololehua.

entirely *All.* A pau.

entry *Also item, object.* ʻIkamu. See *thesaurus entry.*

environment Kaiapuni. See *medium. Learning ~.* Kaiapuni aʻo. *Total healing ~.* Kaiapuni hoʻōla piha.

Environmental Impact Statement *EIS.* Palapala Hōʻike Hopena Kaiapuni.

enzyme ʻŪhū. See *papain.*

Eolithic *In anthropology.* Haku kūlohelohe. *~ age, period.* Ke au haku kūlohelohe.

epenthetic sound *In linguistics.* Hua komo.

epicenter Kiko ōlaʻi.

epidermis *In biology.* ʻIli kūwaho. See *dermis.*

epiglottis Pani paipu hanu (*preceded by* ke). See *larynx, trachea.*

epoch *Also age, era, period, as in athropology.* Au. See *Eolithic, Paleolithic, Mesolithic, Neolithic, Aeneolithic.*

Epsom ʻEpesoma. *~ salt.* Paʻakai ʻepesoma.

equal *Or equality, as a mathematical relation of being exactly the same.* Like. ~ *sign.* Kaha like. ~ *ratio.* Lākiō like. ~*ly likely outcomes.* Like ka papaha o nā mea e loaʻa ana.

equality See *equal.* ~ *property, in math.* ʻAnopili kaulike (*preceded by* ke).

equation *In math and science.* Haʻihelu. See *problem. Chemical* ~. Haʻihelu kemikala. *Balanced chemical* ~. Haʻihelu kemikala kaulike. *Linear* ~. Haʻihelu lālani. *Quadratic* ~. Haʻihelu pāhoʻonui lua. See *quadratic function.*

equator Kapikoowākea, pōʻai waena honua. See *entries below. Celestial* ~. Pōʻai waena lani.

Equatorial Countercurrent *In oceanography.* Hiapo. See *entry below* and *current.*

equatorial current *In oceanography.* Au kāʻei pōʻai waena honua. See *current, Equatorial Countercurrent.*

Equatorial Guinea Kini ʻEkuakolia.

equidistant *In math.* Mamaoalike.

equilateral triangle Huinakolu like.

equilibrium Anakonu. See *isostasy.*

equinox Māuiili. See *solstice. Autumnal* ~. Ka māuiili o ka hāʻulelau. *Vernal* ~. Ka māuiili o ke kupulau.

equipment Lako, pono. See *props. Breathing* ~, *as for use in space exploration.* Lako hanu. *Video* ~. Pono hana wikiō.

equitable *Fair, just, balanced.* Kaulike.

equivalent expression *In math.* Haʻi heluna like.

equivalent fraction *In math.* Hakina heluna like.

era *Also age, epoch, period, as in athropology.* Au. See *Eolithic, Paleolithic, Mesolithic, Neolithic, Aeneolithic.*

erase See *white board.*

eraser Mea holoi, pale holoi, ʻileika.

Eritrea ʻElikilea.

erode *Also eroded, erosion.* ʻAʻaiawā. See *weathered.* ~*d smooth.* Koea a mania. ~*d or cut by waves, as a cliff.* ʻAʻaianalu. *Wave-cut cliff.* Pali ʻaʻaianalu.

errand Hana, ʻāpana hana.

error *As in a computer program.* Kuʻia. See entry below and *trial and error.*

error *Greatest possible* ~, *in math.* Palena ʻāluna o ka hewa. *Abb.* PʻĀH. *Overflow* ~, *as on a calculator display.* Hū. *Logic* ~, *as a message on a calculator display that shows an operation is not logical.* Hewa kūpili.

eruption *Series of volcanic* ~*s.* Pūkaʻina hū pele.

escape *To* ~, *as in a computer program.* Pēki. ~ *key.* Pihi pēki (*preceded by* ke).

escape hatch *Explosive* ~, *as in a spaceship.* ʻĪpuka pakele pahū.

Eskimo ~ *person, language, or culture.* ʻInuika, *usu.* ʻInuita.

esophagus Paipu moni. See *trachea.*

espresso *Strong black coffee prepared by forcing steam under pressure through ground dark-roast coffee beans.* Kopeika. See *cappuccino.*

estimate *Also estimated, estimation.* Koho. ~*d price, as for goods.* Kumukūʻai koho. ~*d cost or charge, as for services.* Kāki koho. *To over*~. Kohoʻoi. *To under*~. Kohoemi.

estimation See *estimate. Front end* ~. Koho hapa mua.

Estonia ʻEsetonia.

estuary Nuku muliwai.

etch Kaha koe. *Etching.* Kiʻi kaha koe.

ether ʻIta.

Ethiopia *Also Ethiopian.* ʻAikiopa.

ethnomusicology Kālaipuolo lāhui. See *musicology.*

ethyl ʻEto. ~ *acetate.* ʻĀkeka ʻeto.

etymology *Root, source, derivation, or origin of a word.* Molekumu.

Eupithecia spp *Carnivorous caterpillar.* 'Enuhe hamui'a.

Eurasia *Also Eurasian.* 'Eulāsia. ~*n Plate.* Ka Una Honua 'Eulāsia.

Europa *A moon of Jupiter.* 'Eulopa.

Europe 'Eulopa. *Eastern* ~. 'Eulopa Hikina *Western* ~. 'Eulopa Komohana.

evacuate *To* ~, *as a building.* Ha'alele. *To* ~, *as people from a building.* Ho'oha'alele.

evaluate *To find the number that an algebraic expression names, in math.* Huli.

evaporate Omoāea.

evapotranspiration Pi'ikomoāea.

even *See parallel bars.*

even number Helu kaulike.

event *As in math; also as a happening in a story.* Hanana.

even-tempered *Also calm, cool.* Māio.

Everest 'Eweleka. *Mount* ~. Mauna 'Eweleka.

evidence *As in the commission of a crime.* Meheu kalaima.

evolution Ka liliuewe 'ana. *See evolve, genetic engineering.*

evolve Liliuewe. *See evolution, genetic engineering.*

example La'ana. *Model, as of behavior.* Kumu ho'ohālike.

exception ~ *to a rule.* Kū'ē lula.

exchange *As of gases in the body.* Kuapo.

exclaim Ho'ōho. *See exclamatory statement.*

exclamation point Kiko pū'iwa.

exclamatory statement *Also to make an* ~. 'Ōlelo ho'ōho.

excursion *Field trip.* Huaka'i makahi'o, huaka'i. *See explore.*

executive branch *As of a government.* Māhele mana ho'okō. *See branch.*

executive privilege *The right of the President to withhold information about his activities from the legislature or judiciary.* Kuleana lau'au'a.

exhaust pipe *As on a car.* Paipu ahi. *See muffler.*

exocrine gland Lōku'u ku'uwaho. *See endocrine gland.*

exoskeleton Iwi kūwaho. *See endoskeleton.*

exothermic Ku'u wela. *See endothermic.*

expand *To* ~ *or explode, as a file in a computer program.* Ho'omahola. *See compress, expanded.*

expanded *Also exploded, as a file in a computer program.* Mahola. *See expand, extended.* ~ *file.* Waihona mahola. *As of computer memory.* Māhuahua. ~ *memory.* Waihona 'ike māhuahua. *Also enhanced, as a computer keyboard.* Keu. ~ *keyboard.* Papa pihi keu.

expanded ~ *form, in math; also to expand.* Unuhi kūana. ~ *numeral.* Helu unuhi kūana.

expected value *In math.* Waiwai wānana. *See value.*

expel *As from a school or institution.* Kīpaku, kīpeku.

expense account Waihona ho'olilo. *See account.*

experiment *Also to* ~, *as in a laboratory.* Ho'okolohua. *To* ~ *on.* Ho'okolohua no. *To* ~ *with.* Ho'okolohua me. ~*al probability.* Pahiki ho'okolohua.

expert *Wildlife* ~. Loea holoholona lōhiu.

explain *To clarify.* Ho'ākāka.

explode *See expand, expanded.*

explore Makahi'o. *See excursion.*

explosive escape hatch *As in a spaceship.* 'Īpuka pakele pahū.

exponent *Also power, i.e. a product in which each factor is the same, in math.* Pāhoʻonui. *See square. ~ial notation.* Kauhelu pāhoʻonui.

export Kāpuka. *See import.*

expression *In math.* Haʻi. *Algebraic ~.* Haʻi hōʻailona helu. *Equivalent ~.* Haʻi heluna like.

expression *In grammar, a term of more than one word which has one meaning.* Māpuna ʻōlelo.

expressive speech *Also speech to entertain.* Haʻiʻōlelo mikololohua. *See speech.*

extemporaneous writing *Also to freewrite, as writing about anything one chooses.* Kākau ulu wale.

extend *To ~, as text in computer word processing.* Hoʻākea. *See entry below and condense. As a math problem which can be ~ed into other similar problems or situations.* Hoʻomahola.

extended *As of computer memory.* Keu. *See expanded. ~ memory.* Waihona ʻike keu.

extension *As of a computer file.* Peleleu. *File ~.* Peleleu waihona.

extenuating circumstances Kumu kūikawā.

exterior angle *In math.* Huina kūwaho.

external Kūwaho. *See internal. ~ drive, as on a computer.* Kakena kūwaho. *~ folder, in a computer program.* Wahī o waho.

external abdominus oblique muscle Mākala kū hiō o waho.

external fuel tank *As on a spaceship.* Pahu wāwahie kūwaho.

extinct Halapohe, make loa, nalowale loa. *See endangered.*

extinguisher *Fire ~.* Kini hoʻopio ahi, kini kinai ahi.

extra *Beyond the usual size, extent, or degree.* Keu, loa. *See large. ~ large, XL, as shirt size.* Nui keu. *~ lean, as meat.* Pākā loa.

extra *One hired for crowd scenes in movie or video production.* ʻŌhua.

extra credit *As a class assignment or question on a quiz.* Hoʻopiʻi kaha, ʻai keu. *~ question.* Nīnau hoʻopiʻi kaha, nīnau ʻai keu.

extract Kāwina. *Vanilla ~.* Kāwina wanila. *To ~.* Kāwī.

extraterrestrial *Also space alien.* Mea ao ʻē.

eyebrow pencil Pena kuʻemaka. *To "put on" or "do" one's eyebrows.* Hana i ka pena kuʻemaka.

eyedropper Omo hoʻokulu.

eyelashes *False ~.* Lihilihi maka kuʻi. *To put on false ~.* Kau i ka lihilihi maka kuʻi, komo i ka lihilihi maka kuʻi.

eye liner Mahaka maka.

eye shadow Pauka maka. *To put on ~.* Hana i ka pauka maka.

F

fa *The fourth note on the musical scale.* Hā. *See Hawaiian entry* pākōlī.

fabric *Gas fading control ~, as in meteorology.* Lole ana kinoea. *Ozone-sensitive ~.* Lole ana ʻokikene kolu.

face *As one side of a space figure, in math.* Alo. *~ value.* Waiwai kūʻike. *See value.*

face powder Pauka helehelena. *To put on ~.* Hana i ka pauka helehelena, kau i ka pauka helehelena.

facility *Something that is built, installed, or established to serve a particular purpose.* Pono lako.

fact Kūʻikena.

factor *In math.* Helu hoʻonui. *See entries below. Common ~.* Helu hoʻonui like. *Greatest common ~.* Helu hoʻonui like kiʻekiʻe loa. *~ tree.* Papa helu hoʻonui kumu.

factorial *In math.* Hoʻonui pāʻanuʻu.

factorization *Prime ~.* Huli helu hoʻonui kumu.

factors of production *In economics.* Lako hoʻopuka.

faded *As material which has been left in the sun.* ʻĀpahupahu.

Fahrenheit Palanaheika. *Abb.* Ph. *Degrees ~.* Kēkelē Palanaheika.

fair Hōʻikeʻike, fea. *Science ~.* Hōʻikeʻike ʻepekema. *County ~.* Hōʻikeʻike kalana. *State ~.* Hōʻikeʻike mokuʻāina.

fair *Just, equitable, balanced.* Kaulike. *~ game, as one in which each player has the same chance of winning.* Pāʻani kaulike. *See justice.*

fake *To ~ or hit, in volleyball.* Hana kolohe, mīʻoi wale. *To make a ~ spike, an off-speed shot.* Pākī ʻepa. *To ~ out, in basketball.* ʻEpa.

falcon *Peregrine ~.* Palekona kāluʻu. *See jess.*

Falkland Islands *Also Falklands.* Ka pae moku ʻo Fakalana.

fall *Autumn.* Hāʻulelau.

false eyelashes Lihilihi maka kuʻi. *To put on false ~.* Kau i ka lihilihi maka kuʻi, komo i ka lihilihi maka kuʻi.

family *Of facts, as in math.* ʻOhina. *Biological ~.* ʻOhana kālaimeaola.

family planning *Also planned parenthood, population control.* Kaupalena hānau. *See pro-choice, pro-life.*

family room Lumi ʻohana.

fan *Electric ~.* Pelamakani.

fancy *Elegant.* Hoʻohiluhilu.

fantasy Moemoeā.

farm Pāumu.

Faroe Falo. *~ Islands.* Ka pae ʻāina ʻo Falo.

Faso *Burkina ~.* Burakina Faso.

fast break *In basketball; also to make a ~.* Ulele kikī. *See lead pass, slow down.*

fastener *Snap.* Pihi ʻūmiʻi (*preceded by ke*), ʻūmiʻi. *See Velcro.*

fast food Meaʻai hikiwawe. *Fast-food restaurant.* Hale ʻaina meaʻai hikiwawe.

fast forward *To ~, as a film or audio tape.* Wili i mua. *See rewind.*

fat ʻAilakele. *Low-~ food.* Meaʻai ʻailakele iki, meaʻai liʻiliʻi o ka ʻailakele. *High-~ food.* Meaʻai ʻailakele nui, meaʻai nui o ka ʻailakele. *Saturated ~.* ʻAilakele paʻapū. *Unsaturated ~.* ʻAilakele paʻahapa. *Polyunsaturated ~.* ʻAilakele laupaʻahapa.

fatal Pāmake.

faucet Kī wai. *~ handle.* ʻAu kī wai (*preceded by ke*).

fault *Geologic ~, as San Andreas Fault.* Hakinaheʻe.

favor *Party ~.* Alelomoʻo.

fax *Also to ~.* Kelepaʻi. *~ machine.* Mīkini kelepaʻi.

feature *General appearance, impression.* Hiʻona. *Land ~, as mountains, valleys, etc.* Hiʻona ʻāina. *See landscape. Water ~ or form.* Hiʻona wai. *Man-made topographical ~.* Hiʻona na ke kanaka.

February Pepeluali. *Abb.* Pep.

federal Pekelala. *See national. ~ organization.* ʻAhahui pekelala.

federalism *The principle of division of power between the state and national governments.* Paimana kaʻawale.

Federated States of Micronesia Nā Mokuʻāina Hoʻohui ʻia o Maikonesia.

feed *To ~ or assist, as in basketball and most team sports except baseball.* Hānai.

feed *To ~, as paper into a printer or copy machine.* Hānai. *To center ~.* Hānai waena. *To edge ~.* Hānai kaʻe. *To auto ~.* Hānai ʻakomi.

feeder *As for birds.* Kāhānai. See
water dispenser. Sheet ~, as for a
computer printer. Poho pepa.
Additional sheet ~. Poho pāku'i.

feign *To ~ ignorance.* Ho'ohūpō,
ho'opalō.

felt *A type of fabric.* Peleka.

felt pen Peni kuni.

femoral artery A'a pu'uwai hilo. *See*
Hawaiian entries under a'a pu'uwai.

femoral vein A'a kino hilo. *See*
Hawaiian entries under a'a kino.

femoris See *quadriceps femoris*.

femur *The long bone of the thigh.* Iwi
hilo.

feral *Formerly domesticated.* 'Ōhuka.
See *domesticated, wild*.

fermata *The symbol placed over a*
note, chord, or rest indicating the
extension of duration longer than the
indicated time value, in music. 'Ume.

fern *Maidenhair ~.* 'Iwa'iwa.

ferric oxide Feriku 'okesaside.

ferrosoferric oxide Ferosoferiku
'okesaside.

ferrous Ferousa. *~ carbonate.* Ferousa
karabonahate. *~ oxide.* Ferousa
'okesaside. *~ sulfate.* Ferousa sulafahate.
~ sulfide. Ferousa sulafaside.

fertilize *To ~, as an egg.* Ho'olūmaua.
Fertilized. Lūmaua. *See entry below.*

fertilizer Mea ho'omomona lepo. See
compost. Complete ~, i.e. ~ which
contains the six necessary elements for
plant growth. Mea ho'omomona lepo
kā'oko'a. *To fertilize.* Ho'omomona.

few *Also sparse, seldom, rarely.*
Kāka'ikahi.

fiber *As referring to diet.* Hā'a'a 'ai.

fiberglass Aniani awe. See *plexiglass*.

fibula *The outer and thinner bone of*
the lower leg. Iwi pili wāwae. See
radius, tibia.

fiction *Also fictitious.* Hakupuni. See
nonfiction. ~ book. Puke hakupuni.
Historical ~. Hakupuni mō'aukala.
Realistic ~. Hakupuni kohu 'oia'i'o.
Science ~. Mōhihi'o.

fiddle *Also violin.* Waiolina.

field *As in a database.* Kahua. See
entries below and *subfield*.

field *As for football.* Kahua. See
baseball, court, meadow. Football ~.
Kahua pōpeku, kahua.

field capacity *For holding water.*
Palena ū wai.

field goal *In football.* 'Ai peku.

field map *To ~ a site.* Kaha palapala
'āina.

field service supervisor *Student*
teacher ~. Luna a'oākumu. See *student*
teacher.

field station *As used when mapping*
a certain area. Kikowaena pānānā.

field trip *Excursion.* Huaka'i makahi'o,
huaka'i. See *explore*.

fight *To act cocky, strut about looking*
for a ~. Ho'onanā.

figure *Number (the character),*
numeral. Huahelu. *Geometric ~.*
Kinona. *Congruent ~.* Kinona
komoloko. *Plane ~.* Kinona papa.
Similar ~. Kinona 'ano like. *Solid ~.*
Kinona pa'a. *Space ~.* Kinona
pihanahaka. *Symmetric ~.* Kinona
'ālikelike. *As illustration in a textbook.*
v̇:'.

filament *As in a light bulb.* 'Uiki 'ā. *~*
tape, strapping tape. Leki a'a.

file *The tool.* Waiehu. *Fine-cut ~.*
Waiehu makali'i.

file *~ cabinet.* Pahu waihona pepa, pahu
waihona, waihona pepa. *To ~, as ~s in a*
~ cabinet. Ho'okomo, waiho.

file *As in a computer program.*
Waihona. See entries below and
backup, directory, folder. Backup ~.
Waihona papa'a. *Compressed ~.*
Waihona 'opihia. *Expanded ~.* Waihona
mahola.

file extension *As in a computer program.* Peleleu waihona.

file format *As in a computer program.* Hulu waihona. *Compatible ~.* Hulu waihona launa. *Incompatible ~.* Hulu waihona launa ʻole.

file link *As in a computer program.* Loulou waihona. *See data link.*

file prefix *Also header information, as codes at the beginning of each computer file.* Poʻo pāʻalua (*preceded by* ke).

filibuster *To make a long speech in order to prevent action on a legislative bill.* Hoʻopulelehua.

Filipino Pilipino, Pinopino. *See Philippines.*

fill bar *In a computer program.* ʻAukā holomua.

filling *As for a sandwich.* ʻĪkomo. *As of a tooth.* ʻĪpiha.

film *As for a movie or video.* Līpine. *See shoot. ~ movement, as in a movie or video camera.* Holo lola. *Roll of ~.* ʻŌwili kiʻi.

filmstrip ʻŌwili kiʻiaka.

filter *Water ~ for a fish tank, in aquaculture.* Kulamakaloa. *See fish tank.*

fin *As of a fish, general term.* Lā. *See dorsal fin, ray. The ~s of a fish.* Nā lā o ka iʻa. *Suction cup ~, as beneath the stomach of an ʻoʻopu.* Halo ʻāpikapika.

final *Terminal, as last in time, order, or importance.* Kuahope. *See primary, secondary, tertiary.*

finals *As in sporting events.* Hoʻokūkū moho.

finance *Hawaiʻi State Department of ~.* ʻOihana Kālā o ka Mokuʻāina ʻo Hawaiʻi.

finch *General term.* Ōpuhe. *Woodpecker ~.* Ōpuhe pao lāʻau. *Grosbeak ~.* Hona. *King Kong ~.* Nuku ʻekue. *Laysan ~.* ʻAinohu Kauō. *Nīhoa ~.* ʻAinohu Nīhoa.

find *As an archeological ~.* Mea hiʻohia.

find *To calculate, in math.* Huli a loaʻa, huli. *See calculate.*

find *To search for, as in a computer program.* Huli. *To ~ and change, search and replace.* Huli a kuapo.

fine *As sand.* ʻAeʻae. *See coarse.*

fine arts Pāheona.

fine-cut file Waiehu makaliʻi.

fine point *Also fine line, as of a pen point.* Makakui. *~ pen.* Peni makakui.

finger Manamana lima, manamana. *See phalanx. Thumb.* Manamana nui. *Index ~.* Manamana miki, manamana kuhikuhi. *Middle ~.* Manamana loa, manamana waena. *Ring ~.* Manamana pili, manamana komo. *Little ~.* Manamana iki, manamana liʻiliʻi.

fingerprint Meheu manamana lima, māka manamana lima, kiʻi manamana lima. *Groove on finger.* Māioio manamana lima. *To collect ~s.* ʻOhi i ka meheu manamana lima (māka manamana lima, kiʻi manamana lima). *To take the ~s of (someone).* Kāpala, kāpala i ka meheu manamana lima (māka manamana lima, kiʻi manamana lima).

fingertips *See jab.*

finish *~ point, as in a race.* Pahuhope. *See starting. ~ line.* Laina pahuhope.

Finland *Also Finn, Finnish.* Finilana, Finilani.

Finn *Also Finland, Finnish.* Finilana, Finilani.

fire *To ~, as clay or ceramics.* Puhi. *See ring of fire.*

firecracker Pahūpahū (*preceded by* ke). *See fireworks. String of ~s.* Kālī pahūpahū.

fire extinguisher Kini hoʻopio ahi, kini kinai ahi.

firefly Nalo ʻuiʻuiki.

fire hydrant Paipu kinai ahi, piula wai.

fireplace Kapuahi hoʻopumehana.

fireworks Ahihoʻoleʻaleʻa. *See firecracker, pop-pops, Roman candle.*

first aid kit Kini lapaʻau, poho lāʻau
pōulia.

first base *In baseball.* Pahu ʻekahi. See
base.

first draft Kāmua ʻekahi. See *draft.*

first off the bench *Also six man, i.e.
first alternate or substitute player, in
basketball.* Kūono.

first pass *Also to receive a serve, in
volleyball.* Kiʻi.

First World Country ʻĀina
ʻoiʻenehana. See *developed, Third
World Country.*

fish *Also any marine animal.* Iʻa. See
entries below and *aquaculture. Canned
~.* Kini iʻa. *~ cake, kamaboko.*
Kamapoko. *~ flake.* Ulahi iʻa. *~ food
flake.* Ulahi meaʻai iʻa. *Guppy.* Iʻa kapi.
Molly. Iʻa moli. *Mosquito ~, medaka.* Iʻa
makika. *Large school of ~ such as akule
or aku.* Kumu iʻa. *Small school of reef
~ such as* manini. Naho iʻa, naha iʻa.

fish and game management *Also
to manage fish and game.* Hoʻomalu
lawaiʻa a me ka hahai holoholona.

Fish and Wildlife Service *US ~.*
ʻOihana Iʻa me ka Holoholona Lōhiu o
ʻAmelika.

Fisher burner Kapuahi pukapuka. See
burner.

fishery *National Marine ~ies Service.*
ʻOihana Lawaiʻa Kai Pekelala. *Western
Pacific ~ Management Council.* ʻAha
Hoʻomalu Lawaiʻa o ka Pākīpika
Komohana.

fishing float See *glass ball.*

fish poisoning See *ciguatera.*

fish stick Manamana iʻa.

fish tank *Cover, in aquaculture.* Peʻa.
~ liner. Paleʻeke. See *water filter.*

fitness card *As for sports or physical
education.* Kāleka olakino.

fitness center *Athletic club.* Hale
hoʻoikaika kino. See *gymnasium.*

fitting *Pipe ~.* Kuʻi paipu. *T-fitting.*
ʻŌmaka T. *Universal ~.* ʻŌmaka kau
peʻa.

five *Base ~, in math.* Kumu hoʻohui
pālima, kumu pālima. *Base-~ counting
piece.* Kōkua helu kumu hoʻohui
pālima. *~-dollar bill.* Pepa pālima.

five man *Also center, in basketball.*
Kūlima.

fixed net See *insect fixed net.*

fixed swing *As with two or more
ropes or chains.* Paiō. See *free swing.*

flagrant *To commit a ~ foul, in team
sports such as basketball.* Hoʻokuʻia
kīpaku. See *foul.*

flake Ulahi. *Fish ~.* Ulahi iʻa. *Fish
food ~.* Ulahi meaʻai iʻa. *Oatmeal ~.*
Ulahi ʻokamila. *Snowflake.* Ulahi hau.

flame retardant Pale ahi.

flamingo Manu palamiko, palamiko.

flammable *Also flammability,
inflammable, inflammability.* Pēʻāhia.

flanker *In football.* ʻĀʻapo.

flap book *As for children's stories.*
Puke ʻōlepe.

flare *Solar ~.* Lapa ahi lā. See *solar,
sunspot.*

flash *As for a camera.* Kukui ʻoaka,
ʻoaka.

flash card Kāleka aʻo.

flat *As a tire.* Pakiʻi. See *counting mat,
deflated.*

flatbed trailer Pākihuila.

flatworm Koʻe pālahalaha.

flavor Maʻono. *To ~ or make tasty.*
Hōʻonoʻono. *~ing.* Mea hōʻonoʻono.

fleur-de-lis *Also iris.* Puapalani.

flexed-arm hang Paʻaalewa.

flexible *As a policy.* ʻŌlewa.

flight *~ attendant.* Kuene mokulele.
~ corridor. Ala lele mokulele. *~ deck,
as on a spaceship.* ʻOneki pailaka.
Manned space ~. Lele lewa lipo kanaka.

flightless rail Moho lele ʻole.

flip *To turn a figure to its reverse side, in math.* Hoʻohuli. *See* slide. *To ~, as a coin.* Pana hoʻolei. *See* heads, tails.

flood Wai hālana. *~ control.* Kāohi wai hālana. *~ warning, as in a weather report.* Kūkala pōʻino wai hālana. *~ watch.* Kūkala makaʻala wai hālana.

floor *Story, as in a building.* Papahele. *~ lamp.* Kukui kū, kukui kū hale. *~ tile.* Kile papahele, kile ʻili, moena ʻili ʻāpanapana. *See* linoleum.

floor leader *As a member of a legislative body.* Luna paipai pila.

floppy *As a computer disk.* Malule. *~ disk.* Pā malule (*preceded by* ke).

Florida *Also Floridan, Floridian.* Pololika, Folorida.

floss *Dental ~; also to ~ (one's teeth).* Lopi niho.

flour Palaoa maka. *See Hawaiian entries under* palaoa. *Whole wheat ~.* Palaoa maka huika piha.

flow chart Pakuhi kaʻina. *To make a ~.* Kākuhi kaʻina.

flower *~ pot.* Poho meakanu. *~ vase.* Pika pua. *~ing plant.* Meakanu pua.

Flubber *Also Gak, a game.* Palēkele.

fluctuate *To ~, as the tide.* Hanuʻu.

fluid ounce ʻAuneki wai. *Abb.* ʻan w.

fluke Koʻelau. *Liver ~.* Koʻelau ake.

fluorescent *As colors.* Hālino. *~ pink.* ʻĀkala hālino. *As light; also phosphorescent.* Hāweo. *~ light.* Kukui hāweo.

flush *To ~ a toilet.* Hoʻokuʻu i ka wai o ka lua, hoʻoholo i ka wai.

flush *As in carpentry.* Piliwai. *See overlap.*

flute ʻOhekani puluka, puluka.

fly *Fishhook with feathers.* Makaunalo. *Fruit ~.* Pōnalo huaʻai. *Midge ~.* Nalo wiʻu. *Pomace ~.* Pōnalo.

flyer *Also brochure, pamphlet.* Pepelu. *See frequent-flyer number.*

flying saucer Pālele.

flytrap *Venus ~.* ʻŪmiʻinalo.

FM *Frequency modulation.* FM (*pronounced* fāmū). *See AM.*

focus point Kiko kau.

foil *Aluminum ~.* Pepa kini.

folder *As in a computer program.* Wahī. *See* file. *External ~.* Wahī o waho.

folktale *A traditional tale, especially one relating to a particular culture.* Kaʻao, moʻokaʻao. *See Hawaiian entries under* kaʻao.

Fomalhaut *A star.* Ahiwela.

font *Typeface, as in printing or a computer program.* Kinona hua. *See style. ~ cartridge.* Pāpahu kinona hua.

food Meaʻai. *See entries below and nutritious, remove, serving. ~ coloring.* Kala meaʻai. *~ chain.* Kuʻina meaʻai. *~ web.* Pūnaewele meaʻai. *Health ~.* Meaʻai hāʻehuola. *High-fat ~.* Meaʻai nui o ka ʻailakele. *Low-fat ~.* Meaʻai liʻiliʻi o ka ʻailakele.

food group *As one of the six ~s.* Pūʻulu meaʻai. *The ~s, i.e. the collective union of all six ~s (calcium/milk, vegetable, fruit, starch, meat, and fat).* Pae pūʻulu meaʻai.

food label *As for giving product information on a package of food.* Lepili māhuaola.

foot *The unit of measurement.* Kapuaʻi. *Abb.* kp. *See square foot. ~ or head of a trail.* Nuku. *See pass.*

footage *As of a video tape.* Līpine. *Blank ~.* Līpine maʻemaʻe. *Raw ~.* Līpine paʻi maka. *As the number of minutes of video tape shot.* Minuke līpine.

football *The sport.* Pōpeku. *The ball.* Kinipōpō pōpeku. *~ field.* Kahua pōpeku, kahua. *American ~ Conference (AFC).* Hui Pōpeku ʻAmelika. *National ~ Conference (NFC).* Hui Pōpeku Aupuni. *National ~ League (NFL).* Kuʻikahi Pōpeku Aupuni.

footer *As in computer documents.* Kau lalo. See *header.*

footnote *As in a book or research paper.* Kuhia o lalo. See *endnote, note.*

foraminiferans *Paper shell.* Unahione.

force *Power to affect physical relations or conditions.* Manehu. *Balanced ~.* Manehu kaulike. *Buoyant ~, i.e. the upward force of a fluid on an object in it.* Manehu ho'olana. *Centrifugal ~.* Manehu lele niniu. *Centripetal ~.* Manehu 'ume niniu. *Electrical ~ field.* Kā'ei manehu uila. *Natural ~.* Manehu kūlohelohe. *Resistance ~.* Manehu āohiohi.

forceps 'Ūpā ho'opa'a. See *utility clamp.*

foreground *As in a photo, movie, or video scene.* Kā'ei alo. See *background.*

foreign accent Pualona 'ē.

foreign aid *As a government policy.* Kōkua 'āina 'ē.

foreign policy *As a government function.* Kulekele 'āina 'ē. See *domestic policy.*

forest Ululā'au, nahele. See *ranger watchtower. ~ reserve.* 'Āina ho'omalu ululā'au. *Rain ~.* Nahele ma'ukele. *Subalpine ~.* Ululā'au lalo 'alapaina. *Temperate ~.* Nahele kemepale.

foreword *Also preface, as in a book.* 'Ōlelo ha'i mua, 'ōlelo mua. See *introduction.*

forget it *Don't you ~; also I told you so, you dummy, you should know; used only at the end of a sentence or phrase.* Ā. See *Hawaiian entry.*

fork *Spading ~.* 'Ō 'eli *(preceded by* ke). *Tuning ~.* Hao ho'okani, 'ō ho'okani *(preceded by* ke).

form *Order ~.* Palapala 'oka. *Registration ~.* Palapala kāinoa.

form *Standard ~, as for numbers.* Kino huahelu. *Expanded ~.* Unuhi kūana.

formalin Pomalina.

format *As of a computer file.* Hulu. See *compatible, disk. File ~.* Hulu waihona. *To ~.* Ho'onohonoho. *As of a document in a computer program.* Ho'onohonohona. *Custom ~.* Ho'onohonohona pilikino. *To ~ or initialize, as a computer disk.* Ho'āla.

formic Forimiku. *~ acid.* 'Akika forimiku.

formula *In math and science.* Ha'ilula. *Chemical ~.* Ha'ilula kemikala.

forward *With palms facing ~.* Pohoalo. See *backward, hit, pull-up, fast forward. Power ~ or four man, in basketball.* Kūhā. *Shooting ~, swing man, or three man.* Kūkolu.

for your information I mea e maopopo ai 'oe, i maopopo iā 'oe, he mea ho'omaopopo kēia.

fossil Mō'alihaku, wīhaku. *~ fuel.* Wāwahie mō'alihaku, wāwahie wīhaku.

foul *In team sports such as basketball.* Ku'ia. *Blocking ~, in basketball.* Ku'ia 'āke'a. *Offensive ~.* Ku'ia kūlele. *Personal ~.* Ku'ia pilikino. *Team ~.* Ku'ia kime. *Technical ~.* Ku'ia kūhelu. *To deliberately ~.* Ho'oku'ia. *To commit an intentional ~.* Ho'oku'ia ahuwale. *To commit a flagrant ~.* Ho'oku'ia kīpaku.

foundation *For makeup.* Palaina helehelena.

fountain *Drinking ~.* Pua'iwai. *For decoration.* Pūnāpua'i.

fountain pen Peni pāuma.

four-by-four Hā hā. *~ board or lumber.* Papa hā hā.

four man *Also power forward, in basketball.* Kūhā.

four-pack See *pack.*

fox *Arctic ~.* 'Alopeka 'Ālika, 'alopeke 'Ālika.

fraction *In math.* Hakina. *Equivalent ~.* Hakina heluna like. *Improper ~.* Hakina lapa. *Terms of a ~.* Palena. See *terms.*

fractional part Māhele hapa. *One-half (part).* Māhele hapalua.

fragile *Easily broken.* Haki wale. *As glass.* Nahā wale. *Susceptible to change.* Pāloli.

frame *As in bowling.* Kuea. See entries below and *molding. Bowling ~.* Kuea maika. *Bed~.* Hao pela. *Door~.* Kikihi. *Picture ~.* Mōlina kiʻi. *Window ~.* Mōlina pukaaniani.

frame *As in a computer program.* Mōlina. *Open ~.* Mōlina kaʻakaʻa. *Closed ~.* Mōlina paʻa.

frame *A single ~ of a movie or video film; also to ~ or arrange the content of a photograph, movie, or video picture within certain borders.* Mōlina.

France *Also French.* Palani, Farani.

free *Exempt from external restrictions.* Kūnoa. *Independent.* Kūʻokoʻa. *No charge.* Manuahi. *Not in use.* Kaʻawale. See entries below and *toll free.*

freedom *Also liberty.* Kūnoa, kūkāʻokoʻa. See *free.*

freelance Kū i ka hai.

freely *To go ~, i.e. have freedom to go wherever one pleases, to "have the run of the place."* Hele lanakila.

free-market economy *The economy of a country wherein buying and selling can take place without government restrictions.* Hoʻokele waiwai kū lanakila. See *command economy.*

free nitrogen compound Pūhui naikokene kaʻawale.

free style *Crawl, in swimming; also to swim using this style.* ʻAu kolo. See *stroke.*

free swing *As a single rope hanging from a tree branch.* Lele koali. See *fixed swing.*

free throw *In basketball; to make such a shot.* Kī noa. *Single ~.* Kī noa pākahi. *One-and-one ~.* Kī noa kī hou. *Two-shot ~.* Kī noa pālua. *~ line.* Laina kī noa.

freewrite *To write about anything one chooses; also extemporaneous writing.* Kākau ulu wale.

freeze *To ~ something.* Hoʻopaʻahau. *See entries below. Frozen.* Paʻahau. *To ~ dry something.* Hoʻokaʻohau. *~ dried.* Kaʻohau. *Freezer.* Pahu paʻahau.

freezer tape *Masking ~.* Leki pahu.

freezing point Kēkelē paʻahau. See *boiling point, melting point.*

French Frigate Shoals Kānemilohaʻi.

French Guiana Kiana Palani.

French horn Pū puhi Palani.

French Polynesia Polenekia Palani.

frequency *In math.* Alapine.

frequency modulation *FM.* FM (*pronounced* fāmū). See *AM.*

frequent-flyer number *As used in airline promotions.* Helu lele pinepine.

fresh-water marsh Ālialia wai maoli.

fret *As on an ʻukulele, guitar, etc.* Wā. See *ʻukulele.*

fricative *In linguistics.* Hahī.

friction *As when one thing rubs against another.* Manehu ʻānai.

Friday Poʻalima. *Abb.* P5.

friendly See *user friendly.*

frieze Kāʻei kiʻi kālai.

fringe benefit *Any employee benefit other than salary, such as medical insurance, etc.* Pono keu.

frog Poloka. *Tree ~.* Poloka kau lāʻau. *Orange tree ~.* Poloka kau lāʻau ʻalani. *Wrinkled ~.* Poloka mimino.

front *As of weather.* Kuʻina. See *solvent front. Cold ~.* Kuʻina huʻihuʻi. *Warm ~.* Kuʻina mehana. *Stationary ~.* Kuʻina paʻa.

front-end *In math.* Hapa mua. *~ digit.* Kikohoʻe hapa mua. *~ estimation.* Koho hapa mua.

front vowel *In linguistics.* Woela kaumua. See *vowel.*

frothed milk *(Hot) chocolate with ~.* Kokoleka me ka waiū huʻahuʻa.

frown Hoʻokuʻemaka. See *scowl*.

frozen yogurt Hauwaiūtepe. See *freeze*.

fructose Huakō. See *glucose*.

fruit fly Pōnalo huaʻai.

fry See *deep-fry*.

frying pan Pā palai (*preceded by* ke). ~ *handle*. ʻAu pā palai (*preceded by* ke).

fudge Kokoleka pāhoehoe.

fuel Wāwahie. *External* ~ *tank, as on a spaceship*. Pahu wāwahie kūwaho. *Fossil* ~. Wāwahie mōʻalihaku, wāwahie wīhaku.

fulcrum Lona hulei.

fullback *In football*. ʻĀpohu.

full-court press *In basketball*. Lulumi piha. See *press*.

full justified *As type in printing*. Kaulihi like. See *justify*.

fume Ea puka, ea.

fumigant Lāʻau make hanu. See *poison*.

function *As on a calculator or a computer keyboard*. Hana. ~ *key*. Pihi hana (*preceded by* ke). *As on a calculator*. Lawelawe hana. *In math*. Hahaina. ~ *rule*. Lula hahaina. *Linear* ~. Hahaina lālani. *Quadratic* ~. Hahaina pāhoʻonui lua. See *quadratic equation*.

fund See *endowment fund*.

fungus *General term*. Kalina.

funnel Kānuku.

funny *Witty*. Hoʻomakeʻaka.

fur seal Sila pūhuluhulu.

fuse ʻUiki uila. ~ *box*. Pahu ʻuiki uila.

fusion *Nuclear* ~. Kuʻi nukeliu.

G

Gabon *Also Gabonese*. Kapona, Gabona.

gadget *Device, doohickey, gizmo, thingamajig*. Hāmeʻa. See *apparatus, instrument, tool*.

gaffer *As for movie or video production*. Luna uila. See *best boy*.

Gak *Also Flubber, a game*. Palēkele.

galaxy Wiliau hōkū. *Andromeda* ~. Ka wiliau hōkū ʻo ʻAnakolomeka.

gale Kelawini, makani kelawini. See *wind. Stormy wind; whole trees in motion and inconvenience felt in walking against the wind, in meteorology*. ʻEna makani.

Galileo *Also Galilean*. Kalileo. *Galilean moons*. Nā mahina ʻo Kalileo.

gallery *As in a computer program*. Papa hōʻikeʻike.

gallon Kālani. *Abb*. kln. *Half* ~. Hapalua kālani. ~ *jar or jug*. ʻŌmole kālani.

Gambia Kamapia.

game *Board* ~, *as checkers*. Kēmu. ~ *board*. Papa kēmu. *Fair* ~, *as one in which each player has the same chance of winning*. Pāʻani kaulike. *Fish and* ~ *management; also to manage fish and* ~. Hoʻomalu lawaiʻa a me ka hahai holoholona.

Ganymede *A moon of Jupiter*. Kanimeki.

garden *To* ~; *also* ~*ing*. Mahi māla. *Botannical* ~. Māla hōʻikeʻike meakanu. ~*ing book*. Puke mahi māla. ~ *rake*. Hao kope. ~ *store*, ~*ing store*. Hale kūʻai mahi māla. ~ *trowel*. Kopalā lima.

Gardner Pinnacles Pūhāhonu.

gas *Also gaseous, as opposed to solid or liquid*. Kinoea. *As in the digestive system*. Hūea. See entries below and *Charles' law. Bromine* ~. Kinoea polomine. ~ *generator, a device used for producing gases in a chemistry lab*. Hāmeʻa hana kinoea. ~ *mask, as used during World War II*. Pūnuku ea make.

gas fading control fabric *As in meteorology*. Lole ana kinoea.

gasification *Also to gasify, i.e. convert into gas*. Kākinoea. *Coal* ~, *i.e. the process in which steam and hot coal produce hydrocarbons*. Kākinoea lānahu.

gasify See *gasification*.

gasohol 'Ailahola.

gastrocnemius *Calf muscle of the anterior of the lower leg.* Mākala 'ulu, 'olo'olo wāwae.

gateway *Also alias, as in a computer program.* 'Īpuka.

gauge *A measuring instrument.* Mea ana.

gauze Welu 'eha, welu wahī'eha, 'a'amo'o. *Wire ~, steel wool.* Pulupulu uea.

gear *As in machinery.* Kia.

geevum *Also go for broke, go for it.* Lawe pīlahi. See *do with all one's might or strength.*

gel Palaholo. *Hair ~, Dep.* Palaholo lauoho. *Silica ~ g.* Palaholo silaka g (*pronounced* palaholo silaka gā).

gelatin 'Ūnina.

gene *Also genetic.* Ōewe. See *genetics, genetic engineering.* Kūkulu ōewe.

genealogy Mo'okū'auhau. *Genealogical story.* Mo'olelo mo'okū'auhau.

general controls *As in a computer program.* Ho'oholo laulā.

general election *In politics.* Koho pāloka laulā. See *primary election.*

generalize Ho'olaulā.

generator See *gas generator.*

genetic engineering Ka ho'oliliuewe 'ana.

genetics Kālaiōewe. See *gene.*

gentle breeze *Dust raised and small branches move, in meteorology.* Aheahe. See *wind. Leaves in constant motion.* Kolonahe.

geoboard *In math.* Papakui anahonua.

geographical coordinates Nā kuhikuhina hō'ike honua. See *geography.*

geography Hō'ike honua. See *geographical coordinates. Geographic region.* Māhele 'āina.

geologic See *geology.* ~ *change.* Loli honua. ~ *depression, as Death Valley.* 'Āpoho 'āina. ~ *fault, as San Andreas Fault.* Hakinahe'e. ~ *trench, as Aleutian Trench.* 'Auwaha. ~*al site.* Kahua hulihonua.

geologist Kanaka hulihonua.

geology Hulihonua. See *geologic, geologist, geophysics.*

geometric ~ *cone.* 'Ōpa'a. ~ *curve.* Uma. ~ *figure.* Kinona. ~ *solid.* Pa'a. See *plane figure, space figure.*

geometrid moth 'Ō'aki.

geometry Anahonua, moleanahonua.

geophysics Kālaihonua. See *geology.*

Georgia *Also Georgian.* Keokia.

geothermal electricity Uila māhu pele. See *electricity.*

geranium Laniuma.

gerbil 'Iole kepila, 'iole kebira.

germ Mūhune. See *pathogen.*

German cockroach *Blattella germanica.* 'Elelū la'aloa.

Germany *Also German.* Kelemānia.

germinate *To sprout.* Ilo. *To cause to ~ or sprout.* Ho'oilo.

gesture *Hand ~; also to ~ with the hands, to use sign language.* Kuhi lima. See *sign language.*

geyser Waipelekī.

Ghana *Also Ghanaian, Ghanian.* Gāna.

Giant Red Spot *A huge gaseous feature on Jupiter.* 'Ōnohi 'Ula Kūāhewa.

giant sloth Melalemu pilikua.

gift certificate Palapala makana.

gifted education *As a school program.* Ho'ona'auao haumāna lololo.

giga- *A prefix meaning billion (G).* Pāpiliona. *Abb.* pp. See entries below and *deca-, hecto-, kilo-, mega-, tera-.*

gigabyte 'Ai pāpiliona. *Abb.* PP. See *byte.*

gigajoule *A unit of energy.* Kule pāpiliona. See *joule.*

gills *Of a fish.* Pihapiha.

gingerbread 'Awakeke.

gingham Kinamu.

give and go *To ~, in basketball.* Hā'awiaholo.

given *As in a math problem.* Hō'ike 'ia.

gizmo *Device, doohickey, gadget, thingamajig.* Hāme'a. See *apparatus, instrument, tool.*

glaciation Ka haunene'e 'ana.

glacier Haunene'e.

Glacier National Park Pāka Aupuni 'o Haunene'e.

gland Lōku'u. *Endocrine ~.* Lōku'u ku'uloko. *Exocrine ~.* Lōku'u ku'uwaho. *Lymph ~.* Lōku'u 'anapu'u. *Salivary ~.* Lōku'u hā'ae. *Thyroid ~.* Lōku'u ho'okonukonu pūnao.

glass ball *A Japanese fishing float.* Pōpō aniani.

glasses *Safety ~.* Makaaniani kaupale. *Sun~.* Makaaniani kala, makaaniani lā.

glass wool Hulu aniani.

glaucoma Kaukoma.

glaucus Hīhīkai.

glib *Also smooth talk, smooth talker.* Waha wali.

glide *In linguistics.* 'Ōlali.

glider *Hang ~.* Lupekau.

glitter Hune hulili.

global warming *Greenhouse effect.* Ho'omehana Honua.

globe *Also sphere.* Poepoe. *~ of Earth.* Poepoe Honua.

glossary Papa wehewehe 'ōlelo. See *dictionary.*

glove *Baseball ~ or mitt.* Mikilima pōhili.

glowing *As in the dark; fluorescent, phosphorescent.* Hāweo.

glucose Monakō. See *fructose. Blood ~.* Monakō koko.

glue Tuko. See *paste, rubber cement.*

glycine Galaisine.

GNP *Gross national product, i.e. the total monetary value of all goods and services produced in a country in a year.* Kumuloa'a kā'oko'a.

goal Pahuhopu, pahuhopu laulā. See *objective. Field ~, in football.* 'Ai peku.

goblin 'E'epa pau'aka.

go for it *Also go for broke, geevum.* Lawe pīlahi. See *do with all one's might or strength.*

go freely *To ~, i.e. to have freedom to go wherever one pleases, to "have the run of the place."* Hele lanakila.

goggles *Diving ~ or mask.* Makaaniani lu'u kai, makaaniani lu'u. *Protective ~.* Makaaniani kaupale.

golden rectangle *A rectangle in which the ratio of the width to the length is the same as that of the length to the sum of the width plus the length.* Huinahā lō'ihi kula.

golf Kolepa. *~ club.* 'Ūhili kolepa. *Municipal ~ course.* Kahua pā'ani kolepa kiwikā.

good *Common ~, as the well-being of all members of society.* Pono o ka lehulehu.

good night *Sleep well.* E hiamoe pono 'oe, e hiamoe maika'i 'oe, a hui hou i kakahiaka.

gooseneck barnacle Pī'oe 'ōhā kai.

goto *As in a computer program.* E lele i.

government Aupuni. *Two-party system of ~.* Aupuni 'ao'ao 'elua.

gradient *Or band, as of colors.* 'Auina. *Color ~.* 'Auina kala.

graduate *~ level, as of a student in a university who has already achieved an undergraduate degree.* Muli puka. See *undergraduate. ~ student.* Haumāna muli puka.

graduated cylinder Hano ana.

graduation card Kāleka puka kula, kāleka hemo kula.

graffiti Kahakaha kolohe.

graft Pākuʻi. *~ing wax.* Pīlali pākuʻi. *To grow by ~ing.* Hoʻoulu pākuʻi.

grain Napoe. *Pigment ~, in biology.* Huna kaukala.

gram Kalame. *Abb.* kal.

grammar Pilinaʻōlelo. See *pattern.* *~ lesson, a lesson related to sentence structure.* Haʻawina pilinaʻōlelo. *~ or sentence-structure skill.* Mākau pilinaʻōlelo.

grammatical sentence *Or clause.* Pepeke. See *clause, sentence.*

Grand Canyon Hakaʻama, ke awāwa kūhōhō nui ʻo Hakaʻama. See *Colorado River.*

grand total Huinanui pau loa. See *total.*

granule *Solar ~, gigantic waves of gas which roll across the surface of the sun.* ʻAle ahi lā. See *solar, sunspot.*

grapefruit ʻĀlani pomelo. See *pomelo.*

grapevine *The plant.* Kumu waina.

graph *Also chart, in math.* Pakuhi. *Bar ~.* Pakuhi ʻaukā. *Double bar ~.* Pakuhi paʻa ʻaukā. *Box and whiskers ~.* Pakuhi pahu me ka ʻumiʻumi. *Circle ~.* Pakuhi pōʻai. *Cross-tab ~.* Pakuhi huina ʻikepili. *Line ~.* Pakuhi lākiō. *~ origin.* Piko pakuhi. *~ paper.* Pepa makaʻaha. *To ~ or chart.* Kākuhi. See *graphing calculator. To ~ the point.* Kākuhi i ke kiko.

graphics Kiʻi. See *bitmap.* *~ technician, as for movie or video production.* Mea ʻenehana kiʻi.

graphing calculator Mīkini kākuhi. See *graph.*

graphite Kalapaike.

grass *General term.* Mauʻu, mahiki. *California ~.* Mauʻu Kaleponi. *Nut~.* Mauʻu pīneki.

grasshopper ʻŪhini.

grassland ʻĀina mauʻu.

gravel Hakuʻili.

gravity ʻUmekaumaha. See *micro-gravity. Anti~ machine.* Mīkini hoʻopau ʻumekaumaha. *Center of ~.* Piko ʻumekaumaha. *Specific or relative ~.* Lākiō paʻapū wai. *Zero ~.* ʻUmekaumaha ʻole.

grazer *An animal that eats grass.* Hamulau mauʻu. See *browser.*

grease *As used in machines or for tools with moving parts.* Hinukele.

greater than *In math.* Nui aʻe, ʻoi aku ka nui. See *less than.*

greatest *~ decrease, in math.* Emi haʻahaʻa loa. *~ increase.* Piʻi kiʻekiʻe loa.

greatest possible error *In math.* Palena ʻāluna o ka hewa. *Abb.* PʻĀH.

great horned owl Pueo kiwi hulu.

Greece *Also Greek, Grecian.* Helene.

greenhouse Hale hoʻoulu meakanu. *~ effect, global warming.* Hoʻomehana Honua.

Greenland Sea Ke kai ʻo ʻĀinaʻōmaʻomaʻo.

green onion *Having a white bulb with purple inside.* Lina. *With a purple bulb becoming white close to the tip.* ʻOʻa.

green sea turtle Honu lūʻau, honu.

greensword *Maui ~.* ʻĀhinahina ʻōmaʻomaʻo.

greeting card Kāleka aloha.

grid Makaʻaha. See entry below and *graph paper, spreadsheet.*

grid paper *In math.* Pepa makaʻaha. *Base-ten ~.* Pepa makaʻaha kumu hoʻohui pāʻumi.

grind *To ~ one's teeth.* Nau kuai i ka niho.

grip *Stagehand, as for movie or video production.* Mea kūkulu kahua. *Key ~, stage manager.* Luna kūkulu kahua.

groove *On a finger as appears in a fingerprint.* Māioio manamana lima. See *fingerprint.*

grosbeak finch *Chloridops kona.* Hona. See *finch.*

gross national product *The total monetary value of all goods and services produced in a country in a year; GNP.* Kumuloaʻa kāʻokoʻa.

ground cover Kapauli.

groundhog *Also marmot.* Māmota.

ground layer *Of vegetation.* Papa kū honua. See *vegetation layers.*

groundnut *Also peanut or any edible nut.* Pīneki, pineki, pīnaki.

groundwater Wai honua.

ground zero *As in field mapping.* Papahonua.

group Pūʻulu. See *food group. To form or break into ~s; also to ~, in math.* Hoʻopūʻulu. *~ing property.* ʻAnopili hoʻopūʻulu (*preceded by* ke).

grow *See entry below and* hydroponics. *To ~ by grafting.* Hoʻoulu pākuʻi. *To ~ wild, as weeds.* Ulu wale. *To ~ wild and lush.* Uluāhewa.

grow *To ~, as in a computer program.* Ulu. *To ~ vertically.* Ulu papakū. *To ~ horizontally.* Ulu papamoe. *~ limit.* Palena ulu.

Guam *Also Guamanian.* Guama.

guarantee *An assurance of quality or length of use with promise of reimbursement.* Palapala hoʻohiki. See *warranty.*

guard *See entry below and* mud guard. *Coast ~.* Pūʻali pale kapa kai. *King's ~.* Pūʻali kiaʻi mōʻī. *Security ~.* Kiaʻi, kiaʻi pō, mākaʻi kiaʻi (pō).

guard *In football.* Kūkahi. *Left ~.* Kūkahi hema. *Right ~.* Kūkahi ʻākau. *Defensive middle ~, nose ~, or nose tackle.* Haunaku. *Point ~ or one man, in basketball.* Kūkahi. *Shooting ~ or two man.* Kūlua.

Guatemala *Also Guatemalan.* Kuakemala.

guava Kūawa.

Guernsey Kunesi. *~ Island.* Ka mokupuni ʻo Kunesi.

guess *Also estimate; to ~, estimate.* Koho. See *estimate. ~ing bag.* Pūʻolo kohokoho.

guest room Lumi moe malihini.

Guiana Kiana. *French ~.* Kiana Palani.

guide *Page ~, as in a computer document or dictionary.* Kuhi lihi. *Teacher's ~ or manual.* Puke alakaʻi.

guided imagery *To utilize ~.* Hoʻohele moeā.

guilty See *convict.*

Guinea Kini. See *Papua New Guinea. Equatorial Guinea.* Kini ʻEkuakolia.

Guinea-Bissau Kinibisau.

guinea pig ʻIole kawia.

guitar Kīkā. *For parts, see* ʻukulele.

guppy Iʻa kapi.

guyot Mauna kai pālahalaha. See *seamount.*

gym *Jungle ~, as playground equipment.* Hao pīnana. See *gymnasium, monkey bars.*

gymnasium Hale haʻuki. See *athletic club.*

gymnastics *Also gymnast.* Kaʻalehia.

H

habitat Kaianoho.

hair *To style ~, as for a play, movie, or video production.* Hoʻoponopono lauoho. *~ stylist.* Mea hoʻoponopono lauoho.

hairband Apo poʻo.

hairclip *Barrette.* Pine lauoho. *Folding ~ with teeth.* Kahi ʻūmiʻi lauoho.

hair gel *Also Dep.* Palaholo lauoho.

hairline *As in a computer program.* Laina lahilahi.

hairs See *root hairs.*

Haiti *Also Haitian.* Heiti.

half Hapalua. *~ dollar.* Hapalua kālā, hapalua. *~ gallon.* Hapalua kālani. *One-~ part.* Māhele hapalua.

halfback *In football.* ʻĀhaʻi.

half-court line *On a basketball court.* Laina kūwaena. See *line, as on a basketball court.*

half-court press *In basketball.* Lulumi hapa. See *press.*

half note *In music.* Hua mele hapalua. *Dotted ~.* Hua mele hapalua kiko.

half-rectangle principle Kulehana huinahā lōʻihi hapalua.

half rest *In music.* Hoʻomaha hapalua.

halftime *In sports or games.* Hoʻomaha hapalua.

half-turn image *In math.* Kinona like wili hapalua. See *turn image.*

hall *Residence ~, as at a school.* Hale noho haumāna. See *hallway.*

Halley Hēli. *~'s comet.* Ka hōkū puhipaka ʻo Hēli.

Halloween Heleuī, lā hoʻomākaʻukaʻu.

hallucination *To cause ~.* Hōʻolalau manaʻo. See *hallucinogen.*

hallucinogen Lāʻau hōʻolalau manaʻo.

hallway Holoē, holo.

Hampshire See *New Hampshire.*

hand *As opposed to arm.* Peʻahi lima. See *gesture, hand-held. As of an analog clock or watch.* Lima kuhikuhi. *Minute ~.* Lima kuhikuhi minuke. *Hour ~.* Lima kuhikuhi hola.

hand *As a single round in a game of cards.* Puni. See *lap, round.*

handcuffs ʻŪpiki lima.

hand cultivator Kīkoʻu paʻa lima.

hand-held Paʻa lima. See *hand mirror, pocket compass.*

handle *For lifting, as of a bucket or suitcase.* Kākai. *Knob-style ~.* Pōheo, pōheoheo. *As of a bureau drawer, faucet, frying pan, toilet, etc.* ʻAu (*preceded by* ke).

handlebars *On a bicycle.* ʻAu paikikala (*preceded by* ke), kalaiwa paikikala.

hand lens *Magnifying glass.* Aniani hoʻonui ʻike.

hand mirror Aniani paʻa lima.

hand off *To ~ (the ball), in football.* Hoʻoili.

handshake *As in a computer program.* Hoʻolauna.

handstand *Also to do a ~.* Kū lima. See *headstand.*

hang *Flexed-arm ~.* Paʻaalewa. See *hung.*

hanger Uea kau lole, lāʻau kau lole, mea kau lole, ʻea kau lole.

hang glider Lupekau.

happy face spider Nananana makakiʻi, nanana makakiʻi.

harassment *Sexual ~; also to subject to sexual ~.* Kekohala.

hard disk *As in a computer.* Pā paʻaloko (*prededed by* ke). *Removable ~.* Pā paʻaloko wehe.

hard drive *On a computer.* Kakena paʻaloko.

hardening of the arteries *Also arteriosclerosis or artherosclerosis, in medicine.* Aʻalāʻau. See *arteriolosclerosis.*

hardware *As for a computer.* Lako paʻa. See *software. As tools made of metal.* Lako hao. *~ store.* Hale kūʻai lako hao.

harmonica Pila puhipuhi.

harmonize Hoʻokūlauna. See *harmony.*

harmony *In music.* Kūlauna. See *harmonize. To sing in ~.* Hīmeni kūlauna like.

harp *The musical instrument.* Hāpa. See *autoharp, Jew's harp.*

hash-brown potatoes ʻUala kahiki kolikoli, ʻuala kolikoli.

hatch *To incubate eggs.* Hoʻomoe.

hatch *Explosive escape ~, as in a spaceship.* ʻĪpuka pakele pahū.

hatred *Of males, misandry.* Hoʻokae kāne. *Of mankind, misanthropy.* Hoʻokae kanaka. *Of women, misogyny.* Hoʻokae wahine.

hauled See *close hauled.*

haunted Lapu. ~ *house, not Hallow-*
een variety. Hale lapu.

Hawai'i *Also Hawaiian.* Hawai'i. *See*
entries below. ~ *State Department of*
Finance. 'Oihana Kālā o ka Moku'āina 'o
Hawai'i. ~ *State Department of*
Planning and Economic Development.
'Oihana Ho'olālā a me ka Ho'omohala
Waiwai o ka Moku'āina 'o Hawai'i.

Hawai'i Volcanoes National Park
Pāka Aupuni 'o Kīlauea.

Hawaiian *See entries below and* Office
of Hawaiian Affairs.

Hawaiian Islands National
Wildlife Refuge 'Āina Ho'omalu
Holoholona Lōhiu o Hawai'i.

Hawaiian medium Kaiapuni Hawai'i.
~ *class.* Papa kaiapuni Hawai'i. ~
school. Kula kaiapuni Hawai'i.

Hawaiian monk seal Sila Hawai'i.

Hawaiian studies department *A s*
at a university or community college.
Māhele ha'awina Hawai'i.

hawthorne Haukona. ~ *berry.* Pī'ai
haukona.

head ~ *or foot of trail.* Nuku. *See pass,*
shower head. As of an 'ukulele or
guitar. Papa kī. ~ *nut.* Nī'au li'ili'i. *See*
'ukulele.

headboard *Of a bed.* Kūmoe. *See*
bedframe.

header *As in computer documents.*
Kau luna. *See footer.* ~ *information or*
file prefix, as codes at the beginning of
each computer file. Po'o pā'ālua
(*preceded by* ke).

heading *Also subheading, as in a*
story. Po'omana'o.

headlight Kukuipo'o, kukuipo'o o
mua.

headphone *Headset.* Apo lohe. *See*
earphone.

heads *As in coin toss.* Po'o (*preceded*
by ke), 'ao'ao po'o. *See flip, tails.*

headset *Headphone.* Apo lohe. *See*
earphone.

headstand *Also to do a handstand.* Kū
po'o. *See handstand.*

healing *Total* ~ *environment.*
Kaiapuni ho'ōla piha.

health Olakino. *See healthy.* ~ *food.*
Mea'ai hā'ehuola. ~ *status.* Kūlana
olakino. *Allied* ~ *professional.* Kāko'o
'oihana olakino. *Community-based* ~
system. 'Ōnaehana olakino kaiaulu.

healthy *Also healthful, wholesome,*
i.e. promoting physical health.
Hā'ehuola. *See health, vigor.*

hearing *Sense of* ~. Lonoa pepeiao. *A*
time for presenting official testimony or
argument. Hālāwai ho'olohe, 'aha
ho'olohe.

hearing aid Pihi ho'onui lohe
(*preceded by* ke).

heart *Shape.* Haka. *See atrium,*
chamber, valve, ventricle. ~ *rate, pulse*
rate. Helu pana pu'uwai. *Transplanted*
~. Pu'uwai ili. *To transplant a* ~. Ho'oili
pu'uwai.

heartworm Ko'e pu'uwai.

heat *Medium* ~. Wela lōpū. *Specific*
~, *in physics.* Ana pi'i wela.

heater *Water* ~. Kula ho'owela wai,
pahu ho'owela wai.

heating lamp Kukui ho'omehana.

hectare *A metric unit of land*
measurement. Hekekale, heketare.
Abb. ht.

hecto- *A prefix meaning hundred (h).*
Pāhaneli. *Abb.* ph. *Also* heko-. *See*
entries below and deca-, kilo-, mega-,
giga-, tera-.

hectogram Hekokalame. *Abb.* hkkal.

hectoliter Hekolika. *Abb.* hkl.

hectometer Hekomika. *Abb.* hkm.

height Ki'eki'e, ana ki'eki'e. *Abb.* ki'e.
See length, width. ~ *or depth, in math.*
Hohonu. ~ *of a wave.* Ki'eki'ena nalu,
ki'eki'ena 'ale, ki'eki'ena. *See*
wavelength.

helicopter Helekopa. *Also* mokulele
helekopa.

helium Hiliuma.

helmet Paleupoʻo.

hem *As of a dress.* Pelu. *Of a net.* Pelu ʻupena.

hemisphere Poepoe hapa. See *sphere*.
Eastern ~. Poepoe hapa hikina.
Northern ~. Poepoe hapa ʻākau.
Southern ~. Poepoe hapa hema.
Western ~. Poepoe hapa komohana.

hemlock Hemalaka.

hemoglobin ʻAwehā.

heptagon *A seven-sided polygon.*
Huinahiku.

her *Also hers, his, its.* Kōna, kona.

herb *As basil, thyme, etc.* Lauʻala.

herbicide Lāʻau make nāhelehele.

herbivore *Also herbivorous.* Hamulau. See *browser, grazer*.

heredity Kumu welo. See *gene*.
Hereditary trait. Welo.

Hermes *Pearl and* ~ *reef.* Holoikauaua.

heroin Heroina.

heron *General term.* ʻAlekea. See
egret.

herringbone weave Maka puhi,
iwipuhi.

Herzogovina Hesegowina. *Bosnia
and* ~. Bosenia me Hesegowina.

hexagon Huinaono.

hexahedron *A space figure with six
faces, in math.* Paʻaʻiliono. See *cube*.

hex nut Pihi wili ono.

hibernate *Also hibernation.* Moekau.

hibernation *Also to hibernate.*
Moekau.

hieroglyph *Also hieroglyphics.*
Lalinoka.

high-fat food Meaʻai ʻailakele nui,
meaʻai nui o ka ʻailakele. See *low-fat
food*.

high jump *A track event.* Lele kiʻekiʻe.

highlight *To block text, as in a
computer program.* Kahiāuli. See
shade.

high post *In basketball.* Kūliu waho.
See *low post*.

high-pressure system *In
meteorology.* ʻŌnaehana mīkā piʻi. See
low-pressure system.

highrise *As a building.* Nuʻuoʻa. See
lowrise, skyscraper.

high vowel *In linguistics.* Woela
kiʻekiʻe. See *vowel*.

hike *Also to go on a* ~. Hekehi. See
entry below and *stroll*. *Hiker.* Mea
hekehi. *Hiking shoe.* Kāmaʻa hekehi.
Hiking trail. Ala hekehi.

hike *To* ~ *(the ball), in football.* Huki
pōpō, huki i ka pōpō, huki i ke kinipōpō.
See *center*.

hilly *Also small cliffs.* Kīpāpali.

hinge ʻAmi. *Door* ~. ʻAmi puka, ʻami
ʻīpuka.

hint ʻŌlelo hoʻohani. *To* ~ *at, give a* ~.
Hoʻohani.

hip bone *Pelvis.* Iwi kā. See *ilium,
ischium*.

hippopotamus Hipopōkamu.

his *Also her, hers, its.* Kōna, kona.

histogram *A bar graph showing
frequencies, in math.* Pakuhi ʻaukā
alapine.

historical fiction Hakupuni
mōʻaukala.

history Mōʻaukala. See *historical
fiction*.

hit *To* ~ *with a racket.* Kīpehi. *To* ~
forehand. Kīpehi pohoalo. *To* ~
backhand. Kīpehi pohokua. *To* ~ *or
fake, in volleyball.* Hana kolohe, mīʻoi
wale. ~*ter.* Mea pākī, pākī. See *spike*.

HIV *Human immunodeficiency virus.*
Mū hōlapu pale ʻea pau. See *AIDS*.

hockey Hōkē. *Street* ~. Hōkē alanui.

hoe Koʻi kālai, hō, ʻōʻō kālai. *To* ~.
Kālai, hō.

holder *Cassette* ~, *tape case.* Pāiki lola.
Toothbrush ~. Kauna palaki niho.

holding *Insect ~ jar.* ʻŌmole mālama ʻelala.

hole *Sound ~, as on an ʻukulele or guitar.* Puka kani.

hole punch *For paper.* Pāniki pepa.

hollow tile Paomeki.

home appliance Mīkini home. See *appliance store.*

home economics *As a course at school.* Mākau nohona home.

homemade Hana ʻia ma kauhale.

home plate *In baseball.* Pahu eo.

home rule *Self-government or limited autonomy, as in a city or county.* Home lula.

home run *In baseball.* ʻAi puni.

home screen *In a computer program.* Kahua paʻa.

homework Haʻawina hoʻihoʻi.

homonym Huaʻōlelo puana like. See *synonym, antonym.*

Honduras *Also Honduran.* Honodurasa.

honeycreeper *General term.* Manu mūkīkī.

honeydew *A sweet juice secreted by aphids.* Meli ʻeleao.

honey locust bean Pāpapa ʻūhinihone.

honored Laehano. See *honor roll.*

honor roll *As in elementary through high school.* Papa laehano.

honors *With ~, also with distinction, cum laude, as in academics.* Me ke kau i ka hano, me ka hanohano, me ka hoʻomaikaʻi. *With high ~, magna cum laude.* Me ke kau i ka hano hoʻonani, me ka hoʻomaikaʻi nui. *With highest ~, summa cum laude.* Me ke kau i ka hano hāweo.

hood *As of a car or truck.* Pani ʻenekini (*preceded by* ke). *As an exhaust ~ above a stove.* Kaupokupoku omo, kaupoku-poku.

hoof Maiʻao.

Hoʻohokuikalani *Daughter of Wākea and Papa.* Hoʻohokuikalani.

hook *As for hanging things.* Lou. *Clothes ~.* Lou kau lole.

hook pass *In basketball; to throw such a pass.* Kīloi ʻaoʻao. See *hook shot.*

hook shot *In basketball; to make such a shot.* Kī piʻo. See *hook pass, lob pass.*

hopper Kānuku. *~ car, as on a train.* Kaʻa kānuku.

horizontal Papamoe. See entry below and *grow, vertical.* *To grow ~ly, as in a computer program.* Ulu papamoe.

horizontal lines *As written above and below a word or words to indicate that they should be written or printed straight, in proofreading.* Kaha hoʻolālani. See *musical staff.*

hormone Hōmona. See *endocrine system.* *Rooting ~.* Hōmona hoʻāʻa.

horn *A musical instrument.* Pū, pū hoʻokani. *As on a car or bicycle.* ʻŌlea, ʻōlē.

horror Hoʻokauweli. *~ movie.* Kiʻiʻoniʻoni hoʻokauweli. *~ story.* Moʻolelo hoʻokauweli.

horse *Rocking ~.* Lio paipai. See *brumby.*

horticulture Kālaikanu. *Horticulturist.* Mea kālaikanu.

host *As of a parasite.* Kauomolia. See *parasite.*

hot chocolate See *chocolate.*

hot dog Naʻaukake ʻAmelika.

hot key *As on a computer keyboard.* Pihi wiki (*preceded by* ke). *~s.* Nā pihi wiki.

hotline Helu wawe. *Conservation ~.* Helu wawe maluō.

hot plate Kapuahi papakau. See *burner.*

hot spot *In geology.* Piko pele.

hour Hola. *Abb.* hl. *~ hand.* Lima kuhikuhi hola.

House *As a legislative assembly; also short for ~ of Representatives.* Hale.

household product *Any of a variety of products used for cleaning floors, sinks, etc.* Lāʻau hoʻomaʻemaʻe hale.

housing development *Also subdivision.* Kaiahale.

how *Also what, as in asking about any kind of measurement.* ʻEhia, he aha. *~ many to each, to a group.* Pāhia.

Howland Island Ulukou ʻAilana.

Hubble Hāpela. *~ space telescope.* Ka ʻohenānā lewa lipo ʻo Hāpela.

hull See *port, starboard.*

hum *To ~ a tune.* Nūnū.

Humane Society ʻAhahui Makaʻala Holoholona.

human immunodeficiency virus *HIV.* Mū hōlapu pale ʻea pau. See *AIDS.*

humerus *The long bone of the upper arm.* Iwi uluna.

humidity Kawaūea. See *hygrometer. Relative ~.* Pā kawaūea.

hummingbird Manu hū.

humorous Hoʻomakeʻaka. *~ book.* Puke hoʻomakeʻaka.

humpback whale Koholā kuapiʻo.

humus ʻElepopo.

hundred Haneli. See entries below and centi-, hecto-. *One ~.* Hoʻokahi haneli.

hundreds *Place value, in math.* Kūana haneli.

hundredths Hapa haneli. *~ square.* Moena helu hapa haneli. See *ten-strip board, tenth strip.*

hung *To be ~, as a network system in a computer program.* Pupū.

Hungary *Also Hungarian.* Hunakalia, Hunagaria.

hunting spider *No-eyed big-eyed ~.* Nananana maka ʻole, nanana maka ʻole.

hurricane Makani pāhili. *~ watch.* Kūkala makaʻala makani pāhili. *~ warning.* Kūkala pōʻino makani pāhili.

hydrant See *fire hydrant.*

hydrochloric Haidorokoloriku. *~ acid.* ʻAkika haidorokoloriku.

hydrocortisone Kokikone wai. See *cortisone.*

hydroelectric *Also hydroelectricity.* Uila wai kahe. See *electricity. ~ power.* Ikehu uila wai kahe.

hydrogen Haikokene. *~ peroxide (H_2O_2).* Haikokene lua ʻokikene lua. See *peroxide.*

hydrology Kālaiwai. *Hydrologist.* Kanaka kālaiwai, mea kālaiwai.

hydrolysis Ka hoʻokāwaihia ʻana.

hydrolyze Hoʻokāwaihia. *See hydrolysis.*

hydrometer Ana kaumaha wai. See *hygrometer.*

hydroponics *The growing of plants in a nutrient solution.* Kāmāhuaola. *Hydroponic solution.* Māʻōʻāna kāmāhuaola. *To grow hydroponically in water.* Hoʻoulu kāmāhuaola wai. *In sand.* Hoʻoulu kāmāhuaola one. *In vermiculite.* Hoʻoulu kāmāhuaola hunehune ʻūpī.

hydrosphere Waiapuni.

hygrometer Ana kawaūea. See *hydrometer, psychrometer. Wet-and-dry bulb ~.* Ana kawaūea ʻōpuʻu pulu a maloʻo.

hygroscopic Kīpuni. *~ water.* Wai kīpuni.

Hyperion *A moon of Saturn.* Haipeliona.

hypertension *Abnormally high arterial blood pressure.* Pākela koko piʻi.

hyphen *Also to hyphenate.* Kaha moe. See *dash.*

hypodermic needle Kui mōpina.

hypotenuse Lala kūpono.

hypothesis Kuhiakau.

hypothetical ʻInāʻinā.

I

Iapetus *A moon of Saturn.* Iapetusa.

I-bar *Also cursor or insertion point in a computer program.* Kahaʻimo. *See mouse arrow.*

ibis *A flightless bird in prehistoric Hawaiʻi.* Manu ʻīpiki.

-ic *Suffix in chemical compounds and terms.* -iku.

ice age Au paʻahau.

iceberg Mokuhaulana.

icecap ʻOmohau.

ice cream ʻAikalima. *~ cone.* Kone ʻaikalima. *~ topping.* Pāhina.

ice skate Kāmaʻa holo hau. *To skate with ~s.* Holo hau.

icicle Kuluna hau, kulu hau paʻa.

icon *As in a computer program.* Kiʻiona.

icosahedron *A space figure with twenty faces, in math.* Paʻaʻili iwakālua.

Idaho *Also Idahoan.* ʻIkahō.

-ide *Suffix in chemical compounds and terms.* -side.

idea *Main ~ or thought, as of a paragraph or story.* Manaʻo nui. *Supporting ~, as in a composition.* Manaʻo kākoʻo. *To sequence ~s, as in a composition.* Hoʻokaʻina manaʻo.

ideal result *In math.* Hopena kaukonu.

identical ʻĀlike. *~ parts.* Nā hapa ʻālike.

idiophone *A musical instrument whose sound is dependant upon the nature of the material from which it is made.* Olokino. *See Hawaiian entries beginning with olo-.*

igneous rock *Rock formed by the solidification of molten magma.* Pōhaku pelemaka.

ignorance *To feign ~.* Hoʻohūpō, hoʻopalō.

iguana ʻIkuana.

iliac artery Aʻa puʻuwai kā. *See Hawaiian entries under aʻa puʻuwai.*

iliac vein Aʻa kino kā. *See Hawaiian entries under aʻa kino.*

ilium *The upper portion of the pelvis.* Iwi kā o luna. *See ischium, pelvis.*

illegal *To outlaw, make something ~.* Pāpā kānāwai. *See entries below.*

illegal alien *Also to arrive as an ~.* Pae malū. *See legal alien.*

illegal screen *In basketball.* ʻĀkeʻa neʻe. *See blocking foul.*

Illinois *Also Illinoisan.* ʻIlinoe.

illusion *Magic trick, sleight of hand.* Pāhaʻohuna. *Optical ~.* Kuhi hewa o ka maka.

image *In math.* Kinona like. *Turn ~.* Kinona like wili. *Half-turn ~.* Kinona like wili hapalua. *Quarter-turn ~.* Kinona like wili hapahā. *Reflection ~.* Kinona aka like o kekahi ʻaoʻao. *Rotation ~.* Kinona like o kekahi ʻaoʻao. *Translation ~.* Kinona like kau.

imagery *See guided imagery.*

imaginary Moeā. *See imagine. ~ line.* Laina moeā. *~ number.* Helu moeā. *See real number.*

imagination *Creative ~; also to use one's ~.* Makakū. *See imagine.*

imagine *To ~ oneself to be something or someone.* Moeā. *To ~ deliberately.* Hoʻomoeā. *See imaginary.*

imitation Hoʻopilipili. *~ milk.* Waiū hoʻopilipili.

immersion *See medium.*

immigrate Komoneʻe. *See emigrate.*

immune system *As in mammals.* ʻŌnaehana pale ʻea. *See AIDS, HIV.*

impact *Environmental ~ Statement (EIS).* Palapala Hōʻike Hopena Kaiapuni.

impartial *See justice.*

impatiens ʻŌlepe.

impeach *To formally accuse (a public official) of misconduct in office.* Hoʻāhewa. *See recall.*

imply Hoʻohuʻu. See *infer*.

import *To ~, also as in a computer program.* Kākomo. See *export*.

impregnate *Also to breed.* Hoʻopiʻi.

impression *General appearance or ~.* Hiʻona. See *feature*.

impromptu *Spontaneous.* Ulu wale.

improper *In math.* Lapa. *~ fraction.* Hakina lapa.

improve Holomua. *Suggested ~ments.* He mau manaʻo e holomua ai ka hana.

impulse *The change in momentum produced by a force, in physics.* Loli uluō. See *momentum*.

imu *To set an ~.* Kuʻi i ka imu. *To open an ~.* Huaʻi i ka imu.

inalienable rights *Rights that people are born with and that a government should not attempt to deny; also natural rights.* Kuleana hānau.

inappropriate ʻAʻohe launa. See *incompatible*.

inbound pass *In basketball; to throw such a pass.* Kīloi ulele.

incandescent light Kukui ʻuiki ʻā. See *filament*.

inch ʻĪniha. *Abb.* ʻīn.

incidence *Angle of ~, i.e. the angle made between a wave striking a barrier and the normal to the surface.* Huina papā. See *angle of reflection*.

included Komo pū. *Tax ~.* ʻAuhau komo pū.

incompatible *As of computer programs.* Launa ʻole. See *compatible, inappropriate*.

increase *Greatest ~, in math.* Piʻi kiʻekiʻe loa. See *decrease*.

increment *One of a series of additions in groups or quantity.* ʻĀpanakahi.

incubate *To hatch (eggs).* Hoʻomoe.

incubator *For eggs.* Mīkini hoʻomoe hua.

incumbent *The holder of a political office.* Luna noho.

indent *To ~, as the first line of a paragraph.* Kīpoʻo. See *tab*.

independent variable Kumuloli kūʻokoʻa. See *dependent variable*.

index Papa kuhikuhi kikoʻī. See *table of contents*. *~ card.* Kāleka pahu. *~ finger.* Manamana kuhikuhi, manamana miki.

India *Also Indian, i.e. referring to India and its peoples.* ʻĪnia. See *Indian Ocean*.

Indiana *Also Indianian.* ʻInikiana, ʻInidiana.

Indian Ocean Moana ʻIniana. See *India*.

indicator *Also to indicate.* Kuhikuhi. *Ninhydrin ~.* Ninahaidirina kuhikuhi.

indict See *indictment*.

indictment *Also to indict.* Hoʻopiʻi kūhelu.

indigenous *Native.* ʻŌiwi. *~ plant.* Meakanu ʻōiwi.

indigo bunting Manu ʻinikō.

Indo- ʻĪnio-. *See entry below.*

Indo-Australian ʻĪnionūhōlani. *~-Plate.* Ka Una Honua ʻĪnionūhōlani.

Indonesia *Also Indonesian.* ʻInidonesia.

indoor Maluhale. *~ concert.* ʻAha mele maluhale. *~ market.* Mākeke maluhale. *~ sport.* Haʻuki maluhale.

inductive reasoning *Generalizing from examples, as in math.* Hoʻoholo pili laʻana.

industrialize Hōʻoiʻenehana. See *industry*.

industry *Especially that with a highly technological structure of production or service; industrialized.* ʻOiʻenehana. See *industrialize, technology. Construction ~.* ʻOiʻenehana kūkulu. *Manufacturing ~.* ʻOihana kāpili, ʻoiʻenehana kāpili. *Service ~.* ʻOihana lawelawe.

inequality *In math.* Kaulike 'ole. ~ *statement.* 'Ōlelo no ke kaulike 'ole.

inertia Ehuō.

infection *Also infected.* Palahēhē.

infer Hu'u. See *imply.*

inferior vena cava Wenakawa o lalo. See *vena cava.*

infield *Baseball diamond.* Kaimana pōhili. See *baseball field.*

infiltrate *To pass through by filtering or permeating, in science.* Kānono.

infinity *In math.* Pau 'ole.

infix Pāku'ina kau loko. See *affix.*

inflammable *Also inflammability, flammable, flammability.* Pē'āhia.

inflate *To fill with air.* Ho'opūhalalū, puhi a piha.

informal Pōnolu.

information 'Ike. See *header information.* ~ *book.* Puke kumuhana. *For your* ~. I mea e maopopo ai 'oe, i maopopo iā 'oe, he mea ho'omaopopo kēia.

initial Hua inoa. See *abbreviation, signature. To* ~. Pūlima hua.

initialize *To format, as a computer disk.* Ho'āla. See *disk.*

initiate Ho'okomo pae. See *initiation.*

initiation *Passage, as into a group.* Komo pae. See *initiate. Rite of passage.* Hana komo pae.

initiative *The procedure enabling citizens to propose a law and submit it to the legislature for approval.* Hāpai kānāwai. *Constitutional* ~, *a process by which one can propose an amendment by gathering signatures on a petition.* Palapala noi ho'ololi kānāwai.

inning Pale. *Baseball* ~. Pale pōhili.

input *As in a computer program.* Huakomo. See *output.* ~ *device.* Hāme'a huakomo. *To* ~. Kāhuakomo. *To* ~ *data.* Kāhuakomo 'ikepili.

in-school detention *As punishment at school.* Ho'opa'i 'au'a i ka wā kula. See *after-school detention.*

insect *Also bug.* 'Elala. ~ *mounting; also to mount* ~*s.* Pine 'elala. ~ *net.* 'Upena 'elala. ~ *bag net.* 'Upena 'elala 'eke. ~ *fixed net.* 'Upena 'elala ho'olewalewa. ~ *sweep net.* 'Upena 'elala kā'e'e. ~ *holding jar.* 'Ōmole mālama 'elala. ~ *killing jar.* 'Ōmole pepehi 'elala. ~ *sucker.* Mea omo 'elala.

insecticide See *aldrin, dieldrin, systemic insecticide.*

insectivore *Also insectivorous.* Hamu'elala.

insert *To put in, as a disk into a computer.* Ho'okomo.

insert *Caret* (^), *an editing mark used to show where something is to be* ~*ed, in proofreading.* Kaha ho'okomo. *A circle around a period, colon, or semicolon to show that it has been* ~*ed.* Lina ho'okomo.

insertion point *Also cursor or I-bar in a computer program.* Kaha'imo. See *mouse arrow.*

inservice teacher training Ho'oikaika kumu. See *preservice teacher training.*

inside out Lolea. See *upside down.*

install *To* ~, *as computer software; also to load, as a program onto a computer.* Ho'ouka. See *download.*

instinctive behavior Lawena 'ike hānau. See *learned behavior.*

instrument *As a specialized tool for a particular occupation.* Mauha'a. See entry below and *apparatus, device, tool. Any musical* ~, *but especially string* ~*s.* Pila. *See Hawaiian entries beginning with* olo-. *Brass* ~. Pū keleawe. *Woodwind* ~. Pū 'o'ohe.

instrument *A prefix indicating the* ~ *or cause of a particular action.* 'Ū-. *Bonding* ~. 'Ūlou. *See Hawaiian entry* 'ū- *and* bond.

insulate Hōʻīpale. See *insulation*.

insulation ʻĪpale. See *insulate*.

insurance ʻInikua. ~ *premium*. Uku ʻinikua. *Medical* ~. ʻInikua olakino. See *medical coverage number*.

integer *Whole number, in math*. Helu piha. *Positive* ~. Helu piha ʻiʻo. *Negative* ~. Helu piha ʻiʻo ʻole.

integrate *To incorporate (parts) into a whole*. Hoʻononiakahi. *Integrated*. Noniakahi.

integumentary system *In biology*. ʻŌnaehana ʻili.

intelligible *Clear, plain*. Mōakāka.

intentional *To commit an* ~ *foul, in team sports such as basketball*. Hoʻokuʻia ahuwale. See *foul*.

interactive *As computer programs*. Kūkaʻipā.

intercept *In math*. Huina pā. *X-intercept*. Huina pā X.

intercept *To* ~ *(the ball), in football*. ʻApo lilo. See *receive*.

intercommunication *Also two-way communication*. Kaʻaʻike pānaʻi.

interdependence *Also interdependent*. Kūkaukaʻi.

interest *On principal, as a charge for borrowing money*. Uku paneʻe. See *principal*. *Rate of* ~. Pākēneka uku paneʻe.

integrated *As computer software*. Huikuʻi.

interim release *Also maintenance release, as of a computer program*. Hoʻopuka hoʻoponopono ʻia. See *update*.

interisland call *Also to make such a call*. Kelepona piliʻāina. *See Hawaiian entries under* kelepona.

intermediate directions *On a compass, in geography*. Nā kūkulu o waena. See *primary directions*.

intermediate level Pae waena.

intermedius See *vastus intermedius*.

intermission Hoʻomaha. See *halftime*.

in terms of *In math*. Ma o. *In terms of X*. Ma o ke X.

intern *One who works as an apprentice*. Huʻeaʻo.

internal Kūloko. See entries below and external. ~ *drive, as on a computer*. Kakena kūloko. ~ *memorandum, as in telecommunication*. Memo kūloko.

internal abdominus oblique muscle Mākala kū hiō o loko.

internal mail *As in an office or school*. Leka kūloko. See *campus mail, office mail*.

international Kauʻāina. *See entries below*.

international call *Also to make such a call*. Kelepona ʻāina ʻē. *See Hawaiian entries under* kelepona.

international date line Laina helu lā.

Internet See *World Wide Web*.

interrogate Ninaninau. See *interview, questionnaire*.

intersect *As lines on a grid, in math*. Hui. See *intersection*. *The intersection of two or more lines, all of which go through the intersection point; to* ~ *thus*. Hui kaupeʻa. *The intersection of two lines wherein one or both lines do not continue beyond the point of intersection; to* ~ *thus*. Hui poʻo. ~*ing lines*. Nā kaha huina.

intersection *An* ~ *of two lines on a grid, in math*. Huina keʻa, huina. See *dot, intersect*.

intertropical convergent zone ITCZ. Kāʻei kuʻina kopikala. *Abb*. KKK.

interval *The number of units between spaces on a graph's scale, in math*. Wā.

interview Nīnauele. See *interrogate*.

in the long run I ka hikiāloa.

intonation Kiʻina leo.

intricate Lāliʻi.

introduce *To ~, as plants and animals to a particular place.* Lawekahiki. *See borrow. Introduced.* Lawekahiki 'ia, malihini.

introduction *As in a book.* 'Ōlelo ho'ākāka. *See foreword, preamble.*

introductory level *Also beginning level.* Pae ho'omaka.

invent Ho'ohakuhia. *~ed.* Hakuhia.

inventory Mo'olako.

inverse *In math.* Huli hope. *~ operation.* Hana ho'omākalakala huli hope.

invertebrate Iwi kuamo'o 'ole. *See vertebrate. ~ animal.* Holoholona iwi kuamo'o 'ole.

invest Ho'opukapuka. *~ment.* Mea ho'opukapuka kālā, ho'opukapuka.

investigation *Also to investigate, in math.* Noi'i.

invisible Kūnalohia. *See visible.*

inward Ha'aloko.

iodide 'Iodiside. *Potassium ~.* Potasiuma 'iodiside.

iodine 'Iokine.

iodize Hō'iokine.

ion 'Iona.

Iowa *Also Iowan.* 'Aioā, 'Ioa.

Iran *Also Iranian.* 'Ilana, 'Irana.

Iraq *Also Iraqi.* 'Ilaka, 'Iraka.

Ireland *Also Irish.* 'Ilelani, 'Irelani. *See Irish.*

iris *Also fleur-de-lis.* Puapalani.

Irish 'Ailiki. *See Ireland.*

iron *The element.* Meki.

ironwood Paina luhe, paina.

irrational number *In math.* Helu pu'unaue koena. *See rational number.*

irregular *As in shape.* Laukua. *See regular. ~ shape.* Kinona laukua.

irrigate Ho'okahe wai.

ischium *The lower portion of the pelvis.* Iwi kā o lalo. *See ilium, pelvis.*

island *See archipelago. Aleutian ~s.* Ka pae 'āina 'o 'Aleuta. *Kure ~.* Moku-pāpapa. *Laysan ~.* Kauō. *Lisianski ~.* Papa'āpoho. *Midway ~.* Pihemanu. *Necker ~.* Mokumanamana. *Palmyra ~.* Honuaiākea.

island arc Pae moku hoaka.

isle *See Hawaiian entry* pae moku.

Isle of Man 'Ailana Kanaka.

-ism *A suffix meaning devotion or adherence to something; in Hawaiian, a prefix meaning to laud, encourage.* Pai-. *See Hawaiian entries beginning with* pai-.

isn't that so *Also right, yeah; used only at the end of a sentence or phrase.* Ē. *See Hawaiian entry.*

isolationism Paikū ka'awale.

isometric Analike. *~ dot paper.* Pepa kiko analike.

isosceles *In math.* 'Elua 'ao'ao like. *~ triangle.* Huinakolu 'elua 'ao'ao like.

isostacy *The equilibrium of the earth's crust, in geology.* Mīkā anakonu. *See equilibrium.*

Israel *Also Israeli.* 'Isera'ela.

issue *A matter in dispute between two or more parties.* Nīnau.

italic Hiō, hua hiō. *See italicize.*

italicize Ho'ohiō. *See italic.*

Italy *Also Italian.* 'Īkālia, 'Ītālia.

ITCZ *Intertropical convergent zone.* Kā'ei ku'ina kopikala. *Abb.* KKK.

-ite *Suffix in chemical compounds and terms.* -hite.

item *Also entry, object.* 'Ikamu.

I told you so *Also don't you forget it, you dummy, you should know, used only at the end of a sentence or phrase.* Ā. *See Hawaiian entry.*

its *Also his, her, hers.* Kōna, kona.

Ivory Coast *Also Ivorian.* Kapa Kai Palaoa.

ivy Lau hihi pā, 'aiwi.

J

jab *To ~ with fingertips, in volleyball.* Koʻu.

jabong *A type of citrus.* Iāpona. See *pomelo.*

jacket Lākeke. See *blouse.*

jackfruit ʻAnanaka.

jack-in-the-box Keakapahu.

jack-in-the-pulpit *A kind of flower.* Keakaikaʻāwai.

jack-oʻ-lantern Palaʻai heleuī, pū heleuī.

jacks *The game.* Kimo. *A jack.* Hōkūkimo.

jade *Also jadeite.* Pounamu. *~ plant.* Nukukikiwi.

jalousie Pukaaniani ʻōlepe, pukaaniani ʻōlepelepe.

jam Kele pahē.

Jamaica *Also Jamaican.* Iāmaika, Iāmeka.

January Ianuali. *Abb.* Ian.

Japan Iāpana. *Sea of ~.* Ke kai ʻo Iāpana.

Japanese lucky welcome cat Manekineko.

jar ʻŌmole. *Battery ~.* ʻŌmole iho uila. *Dustfall ~, as for scientific experiments.* ʻŌmole ʻapo hunahuna. *Gallon ~ or jug.* ʻŌmole kālani. *Insect holding ~.* ʻŌmole mālama ʻelala. *Insect killing ~.* ʻŌmole pepehi ʻelala.

Java Iawa. *~ Sea.* Ke kai ʻo Iawa.

jawbone *Mandible.* Iwi ā.

jay See *blue jay.*

Jell-O Kielo.

jelly bean Pāpapa kele.

jellyfish Pololia. See *blue-button, by-the-wind-sailor, Portuguese man-of-war.*

jeopardy *Double ~, to be tried in court twice for the same offense.* ʻAlo hoʻopiʻi ʻelua.

Jersey Ierese. See *New Jersey.* *~ Island.* Ka mokupuni ʻo Ierese.

jess *A leg strap for falcons.* ʻIli kalapu wāwae.

jet Hēkī. *~ airplane.* Mokulele hēkī. *~ stream.* Au makani kikī.

jewelry Lako kāhiko, lako hoʻonani.

Jew's harp Nīʻaukani.

jigsaw puzzle Nane ʻāpana.

jobs *As for movie or video production.* Nā māhele hana. See *call sheet.*

jog *Also jogging.* Holo peki.

join *A curved line (or lines) linking two letters or words to indicate that the letters or words should be ~ed, in proofreading.* Kaha hoʻokuʻi.

Jordan *Also Jordanian.* Ioredāne.

joule *A unit of energy.* Kule *Giga~.* Kule pāpiliona.

journal *Also diary.* Puke moʻomanaʻo.

journalism ʻOihana haʻilono.

Jovian *In astronomy.* Iowiana. *~ planet.* Hōkūhele Iowiana.

Juan De Nova Huanadenowa. *~ Island.* Ka mokupuni ʻo Huanadenowa.

judicial branch *As of a government.* Māhele ʻaha hoʻokolokolo. See *branch.*

judo Kulo. See *sidewinder serve.*

jug See *gallon jar.*

juggle Hoʻoleialewa.

jugular vein Aʻa kino ʻāʻī. *See Hawaiian entries under* aʻa kino.

July Iulai. *Abb.* Iul.

jumble *To mix up the order.* Hoʻokake kaʻina.

jump *Vertical ~.* Lele haʻaluna. *~ rope.* Kaula lele. *To ~ rope.* Lele kaula. *Running under the rope.* Luʻu nalu poʻi. See *high jump, long jump, rock the boat.*

jump ball *In basketball.* Lele paʻi.

jump shot *In basketball; to make such a shot.* Kī lele.

junco *A kind of bird.* Kunuko, manu kunuko.

June Iune. *Abb.* Iun.

jungle gym *A kind of playground equipment.* Hao pīnana. *See monkey bars.*

junior varsity *As a league of sports at school.* Pae 'ōpio. *See varsity.*

juniper Iunipela.

Jupiter *The planet.* Ka'āwela.

jurisdiction *Appellate ~, a court's authority to hear an appeal of a decision made by another court.* Mana ho'okolokolo. *See appeal. Original ~.* Mana ho'okolokolo maka mua.

jury of peers *As in court trials.* Kiule hoa kupa.

just *Fair, equitable, balanced.* Kaulike.

justice *The quality of being impartial or fair.* Pono kaulike.

justified *As type in printing.* Kaulihi. *See justify. Left ~.* Kaulihi hema. *Right ~.* Kaulihi 'ākau. *Full ~.* Kaulihi like. *Two vertical lines written to the left of lines of print to indicate that the left margin should be ~, in proofreading.* Kaha ho'okaulihi.

justify *To ~, as type in printing.* Ho'okaulihi. *See center, justified. To center ~.* Ho'okauwaena. *To full ~.* Ho'okaulihi like. *To left ~.* Ho'okaulihi hema. *To right ~.* Ho'okaulihi 'ākau.

juvenile delinquency Lawehala 'ōpiopio. *See juvenile delinquent.*

juvenile delinquent Keiki lawehala. *See juvenile delinquency.*

K

K *Kilobyte, in computer terminology.* PK ('ai pākaukani).

kamaboko *Fish cake.* Kamapoko.

Kamehameha butterfly Pulelehua Kamehameha.

Kansas *Also Kansan.* Kanesasa.

kayak Wa'a kaiaka.

Kazakhstan Kasakana.

Kelvin Kelewine. *Zero degrees K (Kelvin); absolute zero, a hypothetical temperature characterized by complete absence of heat.* 'Ole Kelewine.

kennel *A crate for transporting animals.* Pene halihali. *A shelter for a dog.* Pene 'īlio. *An establishment for boarding or breeding dogs.* Hale mālama 'īlio.

Kentucky *Also Kentuckian.* Kenekuke, Kenetuke.

Kenya *Also Kenyan.* Kenia.

key *In music.* Kī. *See entries below and note, pitch.*

key *Dichotomous ~.* 'Āmana koho.

key *Also keyhole, as on a basketball court.* Pukakī. *Side line of the ~.* Laina iwi kī. *Top of the ~.* Uma kī, uma, pōheo.

key *As on a typewriter or computer keyboard.* Pihi *(preceded by* ke). *See Hawaiian entries under* pihi *and* escape, memory, option, tab, space bar, *etc. Name of ~.* Inoa o ke pihi. *Arrow ~.* Pihi nahau. *Caps lock ~.* Pihi laka ma'aka, pihi laka, laka ma'aka. *Control ~.* Pihi ho'oholo. *Hot ~s.* Nā pihi wiki. *Return ~.* Pihi kāho'i. *Shift ~.* Pihi kake.

keyboard *As on a typewriter or computer.* Papa pihi. *Computer ~.* Papa pihi kamepiula. *~ layout.* 'Ōkuene papa pihi. *~ mapping.* Ka'akuene papa pihi.

key caps *On a computer program.* Hō'ike hua pihi.

key code *The order to press keys on a calculator to find an answer.* Pā'ālua ka'ina hana.

keyhole *Also key, as on a basketball court.* Pukakī.

kidney Haku'ala.

kill *In volleyball.* Kinipōpō hele wale.

killing *Insect ~ jar.* 'Ōmole pepehi 'elala.

kilo- *A prefix meaning thousand (k).* Pākaukani. *Abb.* pk. *See entries below and* deca-, hecto-, mega-, giga-, tera-.

kilo Kilo. *Abb.* kl.

kilobyte *K, in computer terminology.* 'Ai pākaukani. *Abb.* PK. See *byte.*

kilocalorie Ikehu'ā pākaukani. *Abb.* ikpk

kilogram Kilokalame. *Abb.* klkal.

kiloliter Kilolika. *Abb.* kll.

kilometer Kilomika. *Abb.* klm.

kilowatt Kilouate. *Abb.* klt. See *watt.*

kindergarten Mālaa'o.

kinesthetic-based learning *Also performance-based learning.* A'o kahua lawena. *See Hawaiian entries beginning with* a'o kahua.

kinetic energy Ikehu ne'e.

kingdom *In Egyptology.* Au Pala'o. See entry below and *United Kingdom. Old ~ (2780-2280 BC).* Au Pala'o Kūkahiko. *Middle ~ (2133-1780 BC).* Au Pala'o Kūwaena. *New ~ (1574-1085 BC).* Au Pala'o Kūhou.

Kingdom of Tonga Aupuni Mō'ī 'o Tonga.

kingfisher Pakūka'ā.

King Kong finch *Chloridops regiskongi.* Nuku 'ekue.

Kingman Reef Nalukākala.

king's guard Pū'ali kia'i mō'ī.

Kiribati Kilipaki. *Republic of ~.* Lepupalika 'o Kilipaki.

kit *As of equipment needed for a particular activity.* Hōkeo. *Standard soil-testing ~.* Hōkeo kūmau ho'ā'o lepo.

kit *First aid ~.* Kini lapa'au, poho lā'au pōulia. *Repair ~ for tires.* Kini poho ea.

kitchen Lumi kuke.

kiwi fruit Hua'ai kiwi, lahomāpū.

knapsack *Backpack.* Pāiki hā'awe, pāisi hā'awe, 'awe.

knife See *putty knife.*

knit Kā pāaniani. See *yarn.*

knob Pōheo, pōheoheo. *Door~.* Pōheo puka, pōheoheo puka. *Drawer ~.* Pōheo 'ume.

knot Hīpu'u. See *bow.*

knowledge *Traditional ~.* 'Ike ku'una. *Traditional ~-based learning.* A'o kahua 'ike ku'una. *See Hawaiian entries beginning with* a'o kahua.

Komephoros *A star.* Luku'āina.

Korea *Also Korean.* Kōlea, Kōrea. *North ~.* Kōlea 'Ākau, Kōrea 'Ākau. *South ~.* Kōlea Hema, Kōrea Hema.

kumquat Kamakūaka.

Kure *The island; formerly Ocean 'Ailana.* Mokupāpapa.

Kuwait *Also Kuwaiti.* Kuete.

kw *Kilowatt.* Klt (kilouate). See *watt.*

Kyrgyzstan Kaikikana.

L
---

la *The sixth note on the musical scale.* Lā. *See Hawaiian entry* pākōlī.

label *Tag; also to ~.* Lepili. *Food ~, as for giving product information on a package of food.* Lepili māhuaola.

labial *In linguistics.* Lehelehe.

labor *To contract ~.* Kepa.

laboratory Ke'ena ho'okolohua.

Labrador Labaradora. *~ Sea.* Ke kai 'o Labaradora.

labroides Phthirophegus *Cleaner wrasse, a kind of fish.* Hīnālea nā'uke.

lacquer Waniki.

ladle Puna kī'o'e, puna ukuhi. *To ~, scoop.* Kī'o'e, 'o'e. See *skim.*

ladybug Ponumomi.

lake *Also large pond.* Māluawai.

laminate Lamineka.

lamp *Floor ~.* Kukui kū, kukui kū hale. *Table ~.* Kukui kū pākaukau. *~shade.* Pale kukui.

lamp *Heating ~.* Kukui ho'omehana.

land *To ~, as an airplane or bird.* Ku'u.

land *Private ~.* 'Alokio, 'alodio. *Public ~.* 'Āina no ka lehulehu. *Department of ~ and Natural Resources (DLNR).* 'Oihana Kumuwaiwai 'Āina.

land court 'Aha ho'onā 'āina. See *land registration system, settle.*

land division *Also division, piece, portion, department, category, part; to divide, apportion.* Māhele.

land feature *As mountains, valleys, etc., in geography.* Hiʻona ʻāina. *See water feature.*

landing *Staircase ~.* Paepae alapiʻi.

land registration system ʻŌnaehana hoʻonā ʻāina. *See land court, settle.*

landscape Hiʻonaina. *See feature. To ~, as a yard.* Kāhiʻonaina.

landscape orientation *As of a page in a computer program.* Kuana moe. *See portrait orientation.*

landslide *Also avalanche.* ʻĀholo.

land use *In geography.* Hoʻohana ʻāina. *State ~ Commission.* Komikina Hoʻohana ʻĀina o ka Mokuʻāina.

lane *As on a highway or in a bowling alley.* Ala.

language *See sign language.*

language arts Mākau ʻōlelo.

language awareness Makakau ʻōlelo.

language-based learning Aʻo kahua ʻōlelo. *See Hawaiian entries beginning with aʻo kahua.*

lantern *Hanging ~, as Japanese type.* Kukui lākene.

Laos *Also Laotian.* Laosa.

lap *Complete circuit.* Puni. *To run or take a ~.* Holo puni.

La Pérouse Rock Kuamanō.

Laptev Lapatewe. *~ Sea.* Ke kai ʻo Lapatewe.

laptop computer Kamepiula lawelima, lolouila lawelima.

larder beetle *Dermestid.* Ponu ʻili.

large *As shirt or drink size.* Nui. *See small, medium. ~ soda.* Koloaka nui. *Extra ~ (XL), as shirt size.* Nui keu. *Double-extra ~ (XXL).* Nui keu pālua. *Triple-extra ~ (XXXL).* Nui keu pākolu.

lark Manu lāke.

larva Piohē. *Of damselfly and other dragonflies.* Lohaloha, lohelohe.

larvae *See post-larvae.*

laryngopharynx *The lower part of the pharynx adjacent to the larynx, in anatomy.* Haka moni o lalo. *See pharynx.*

larynx Kaniʻāʻī, paipu hanu o luna. *See epiglottis, trachea.*

laser Wanaʻā. *~ beam.* Kukuna wanaʻā.

latch *Sliding ~.* Laka uai.

late *As registration for a conference.* Hiki hope. *~ registration.* Kāinoa hiki hope.

lateral *In linguistics.* Lālelo.

lateralis *See vastus lateralis.*

lateral line *A linear series of sensory pores and tubes along the side of a fish, in biology.* Kahana lonoa.

latex Lekesa.

Latin America *Also Latin American, Central America, Central American.* ʻAmelika Waena.

latitude Lakikū, latitū. *See longitude, parallel.*

Latvia Lakawia.

laud *A prefix meaning to ~, encourage; -ism, a suffix in English meaning devotion or adherence to something.* Pai-. *See Hawaiian entries beginning with pai-.*

launch *Also to cause to blast off.* Hoʻōlapa. *See lift off. ~ pad.* Kahua hoʻōlapa.

lava cricket ʻŪhini nēnē pele.

lava lizard Moʻo pōhaku pele.

lava tube Ana kahe pele.

lavender *Both flower and plant.* Poniʻala.

law Kānāwai. *See Hawaiian entries following kānāwai and ordinance, statute. To break the ~.* Haʻihaʻi kānāwai, aʻe kānāwai. *See outlaw. Boyle's ~, i.e. decreasing the volume of a gas will increase the pressure the gas exerts if the temperature remains constant.* Ke kānāwai a Poila. *Charles' ~, i.e. the* *volume of a gas increases as its temperature increases if the pressure remains constant.* Ke kānāwai a Kale. *Civil ~.* Kānāwai kīwila, kānāwai sīwila. *Common ~.* Kānāwai kumu.

lawn *To mow the ~.* 'Oki i ka mau'u, 'oki i ka mahiki. See *grass.*

lax *As articulation in linguistics.* 'Alu. *~ vowel.* Woela 'alu. See *tense, vowel.*

lay away *To accumulate, store away.* Ho'āhu.

layer *As of skin or tissue beneath the skin.* Papa. See *vegetation layer.*

layout *As of a computer keyboard.* 'Ōkuene. *Keyboard ~.* 'Ōkuene papa pihi. See *keyboard mapping.*

Laysan *The island.* Kauō. *~ finch, telespiza cantanc.* 'Ainohu Kauō.

lay-up *In basketball; to make such a shot.* Kī kīko'o, kī pai.

LDEF *Long Duration Exposure Facility, a kind of experimentation satellite placed in orbit by a space shuttle.* Poelele ho'okolohua wā loa.

leach *To ~, the action of liquid percolating through layers of soil thus removing nutrients from the soil.* He'eaholo. *To ~, subject to the action of percolating liquid.* Ho'ohe'eaholo.

lead *Also leaden.* Kēpau.

leader See *floor leader.*

leading question Nīnau pākākā.

lead pass *In basketball; to throw such a pass.* Kīloi ulele kikī, kīloi kaha. See *fast break.*

leaf Lau. *Newly opened ~.* Liko. *Bud of a ~.* Mu'o. *Node, where a ~ is connected to the stem.* Piko. *Base of a ~, as* hala. Po'o (*preceded by* ke).

leaf miner Mū pao lau.

league *In sports.* Ku'ikahi. See *conference. American Baseball ~.* Ku'ikahi Pōhili 'Amelika. *National Baseball ~.* Ku'ikahi Pōhili Aupuni. *National Football ~ (NFL).* Ku'ikahi Pōpeku Aupuni.

lean *As meat.* Pākā. *Extra ~.* Pākā loa.

lean-to shelter Hale kāpi'o.

learned behavior Lawena 'apo. See *instinctive behavior.*

learning center Kauno'o.

learning environment See *environment.*

learning process See *domain.*

learning styles *See Hawaiian entries beginning with* a'o kahua.

leash Kaula ka'i.

least common denominator *In math.* Kinopiha ha'aha'a loa.

leave as is *To make no change, as in a computer program.* Waiho.

Lebanon *Also Lebanese.* Lepanona, Lebanona.

Leeward Community College Kulanui Kaiaulu o 'Ewa.

left guard *In football.* Kūkahi hema.

left justified *As type in printing.* Kaulihi hema.

left margin Lihi hema. See *justify, margin.*

left tackle *In football.* Kūlua hema. See *tackle.*

leg *Also side, of a triangle.* 'Ao'ao. See *base, ray. Corresponding ~.* 'Ao'ao launa. *Adjacent ~, of a right triangle.* 'Ao'ao pili. *Opposite ~, of a right triangle.* 'Ao'ao huli alo.

leg *Chair ~.* Wāwae noho. *Table ~.* Wāwae pākaukau.

legal Kū kānāwai. *See entries below.*

legal alien *Also to arrive as a ~.* Pae kānāwai. See *illegal alien.*

legal-size paper Pepa loio. See *letter-size paper, tabloid paper.*

legislation *In politics.* Kānāwai. *See Hawaiian entry.*

legislative *Division of a ~ bill, larger than a section or article.* Mokuna. *See Hawaiian entries under* kānāwai *and* title. *~ branch, as of a government.* Māhele 'aha'ōlelo. See *branch. ~*

powers. Mana kau kānāwai.

legume Lekeuma.

lemonade Wai lemi.

lemur Lāmia.

lend *Not to borrow.* 'Ae. *See sample sentence under Hawaiian entry 'ae and borrow, loan. To ~, as money lent at interest.* Ho'olako 'ai'ē.

length *In math.* Lō'ihi. *Abb.* lō. *Also* ana lō'ihi; loa (*no abb.*), ana loa. See *lengthwise, height, width.*

length *Of a wave, wave~.* Kōā nalu, kōā 'ale, kōā. See *height, wave.*

lengthwise Lau loa.

lens *As for a camera or microscope.* Aniani kaulona. *Concave ~.* Aniani kaulona 'e'ele. *Convex ~.* Aniani kaulona 'e'emu. *Water ~, in geology.* Papa wai kau luna.

lentil Lenekila.

leptospirosis Lepopiloki.

Lesotho Lesoto.

lesson *A catalog listing or sequence of ~s of a curriculum.* Mo'oha'awina.

less than *In math.* Emi iho, 'oi aku ke emi. See *greater than.*

let *To assign a value or power, as in math problems.* Ho'āmana.

letter *Of the alphabet.* Huapalapala. See *case sensitive, correspondence. Lower case (small) ~.* Hua na'ina'i. *Upper case (capital) ~.* Hua ma'aka. *Cover ~.* Leka wehewehe.

letterhead Po'o kuni (*preceded by* ke). *~ design.* Lau po'o kuni.

letter-size paper Pepa leka. See *legal-size paper, tabloid paper.*

leukemia Lūkīmia.

level *Of difficulty; also stage of development.* Pae. See entry below and *sea level. Novice ~.* Pae 'akahi akahi. *Beginning or introductory ~.* Pae ho'omaka. *Intermediate ~.* Pae waena. *Advanced ~.* Pae holomua.

level *Carpenter's ~.* 'Iliwai.

lever *Also to pry, as with a ~.* Une.

Liberia *Also Liberian.* Lipelia, Liberia.

liberty *Also freedom.* Kūnoa, kūkā'oko'a. *Statue of ~.* Kūkā'oko'a Kiaho'omana'o, ke kiaho'omana'o 'o Kūkā'oko'a, Kūkā'oko'a.

Libra *A constellation.* Iloano.

library *A temporary buffer for storage of codes or information in a computer program.* Hōkeo ho'āhu.

Libya *Also Libyan.* Libia.

lichen *General term.* Nahi.

lid *As for a jar; also cap, as for a toothpaste tube.* Pani (*preceded by* ke).

Liechtenstein Likenekaina.

life See *pro-life.*

life cycle Pō'aiapuni ola.

life-long Hikiāpuaaneane.

lifesaving skills Mākau ho'opakele ola.

life span Kāwā ola.

lift *To ~ or make a double hit, in volleyball.* Hāpai. See *carrying violation. As a ski ~.* Noho pi'i mauna.

lift-off *As of a rocket or missile; also blast off.* 'Ōlapa. See *launch.*

lift weights Amo hao, hāpai hao.

ligament Oloolonā.

light Kukui, kuikui. *~ bulb.* 'Ōpu'u kukui. *~ switch.* Kuiki kukui, pana kukui. *Filament in a ~ bulb.* 'Uiki 'ā. *Incandescent ~.* Kukui 'uiki 'ā. *Fluorescent ~.* Kukui hāweo. *~ controls, as for stage productions.* Une kukui. *Traffic ~.* Kukui ho'okū.

light *To ~, as a set for a movie or video production.* Ho'omālamalama. *~ing director.* Luna ho'omālamalama.

light *Speed of ~.* Māmā kukuna lā, māmā holo o ke kukuna lā. *~ year.* Makahiki holo kukuna lā.

light *Coherent ~, i.e. light in which all the waves vibrate in a single plane with the crests and troughs all aligned.* Mālamalama aukahi.

light To "see the ~" after not under-standing or after being in opposition to an idea. Makili ka no'ono'o.

like Also as if, as though. Me he.

like term In math. Hoa like. See constant term, term.

Lili'u 'ukulele 'Ukulele Lili'u.

lima bean Pāpapa laima.

lime Laimi.

limit Grow ~, as in a computer program. Palena ulu. See grow.

limousine Ka'a limo.

line In math. Kaha, kaha laina, laina. See entries below. Imaginary ~. Laina moeā. ~ segment. 'Āpana kaha. Num-ber ~. Laina helu. Intersecting ~s. Nā kaha huina. Parallel ~s. Nā kaha pilipā. Perpendicular ~s. Nā kaha kūpono. Sight ~. Laina 'ike. Skew ~. Laina pāweo. ~ graph. Pakuhi lākiō. ~ of symmetry. Kaha 'ālikelike.

line As on a basketball court or in sports. Laina. Base or end ~. Laina hīna'i, laina hupa, laina kumu, laina po'o. Half-court ~. Laina kūwaena. Side ~. Laina iwi, laina 'ao'ao. Free throw ~. Laina kī noa. Defensive ~, in football. Laina kūpale, laina pale. Offensive ~. Laina kūlele. Scrimmage ~. Laina ho'ouka. Over the ~, in volleyball. Ka'ahi hewa, 'ke'ehi hewa. Three-meter ~. Laina 'ekolu mika. Ten-foot ~. Laina 'umi kapua'i. Starting ~, as in a race. Laina pahukū. Finish ~. Laina pahuhope.

line Lateral ~, a linear series of sensory pores and tubes along the side of a fish, in biology. Kahana lonoa. Safety ~, as in a spacecraft. Kaula piko.

line Horizontal ~ on a musical staff. Laina o ke kōkua hua mele, laina o ke kōkua. See musical staff.

linear equation Ha'ihelu lālani.

linear function In math. Hahaina lālani.

linear scale In geography. Pālākiō lālani.

linear unit paper In math. Pepa anakuhi lālani.

linebacker Defensive ~, in football. Mahikua.

line note In music. Hua mele laina. See note.

line of sight Also sight line. Laina lena, laina 'ike.

line out To strike through, as on a typewriter or computer; also used to indicate that the letters or words lined out are to be deleted and replaced by those written above, in proofreading. Kahawaena. A series of dots written under a word or words which have been lined out to show that no change should be made from the original; stet. Kaha waiho.

liner Eye ~. Mahaka maka. For a fish tank, in aquaculture. Pale'eke. See fish tank.

line spike In volleyball. Hili laina. See spike.

line up To ~ vertically. Ho'okolamu.

linguistics Kālai'ōlelo.

link To ~, as in a computer program. Loulou. File ~. Loulou waihona. Data ~. Loulou 'ikepili. A curved line (or lines) ~ing two letters or words to indicate that the letters or words should be joined, in proofreading. Kaha ho'oku'i.

linoleum Also linoleum flooring. Linoleuma, moena 'ili. See floor tile.

lion Sea ~. Liona kai.

lipliner Peni pena waha, peni pena lehelehe. See lipstick.

lipstick Pena waha, pena lehelehe. See lipliner. To put on ~. Hana i ka pena waha.

liquid As opposed to solid or gas. Kinowai.

Lisianski The island. Papa'āpoho.

list Papa. ~ *of computer commands.* Papa kauoha kamepiula. *Mailing* ~. Papa helu wahi.

list editor screen *In a computer program.* Pukaaniani kolamu ʻikepili.

litchi *Also lychee.* Laikī.

liter Lika. *Abb.* l.

literature *General term.* Moʻokalaleo. *See tale. Creation* ~. Moʻokalaleo kumu honua. *Oral* ~. Moʻokalaleo haʻi waha. *Traditional* ~. Moʻokalaleo kuʻuna. *Written* ~. Moʻokalaleo palapala.

literature response log *As a student's journal for recording reactions to literature.* Puke moʻomanaʻo moʻokalaleo.

lithified Paʻa pōhaku.

lithium Likiuma.

lithograph Kiʻi māio.

Lithuania Lituania.

litmus paper *For measuring pH.* Pepa ana ʻakika.

little finger Manamana iki, manamana liʻiliʻi.

liver Ake. ~ *fluke.* Koʻelau ake.

living room Lumi hoʻokipa.

lizard *Lava* ~. Moʻo pōhaku pele.

load *To install, as programs onto a computer.* Hoʻouka. *See download.*

loafer *Slip-on style shoe.* Kāmaʻa pohopū.

loam ʻElemakua.

loan *As money lent at interest; also to have a* ~. Lako ʻaiʻē, ʻaiʻē. *See lend, borrow.*

lobar bronchus *Also secondary bronchus, in anatomy.* ʻĀmanapuʻu kualua.

lobby *To conduct activities aimed at influencing public officials or legislation.* Hoʻopaipai. ~*ist.* Mea hoʻopaipai.

lobe *Ear* ~. Lepe pepeiao.

lob pass *In basketball; to throw such a pass.* Kīloi piʻo. *See hook shot.*

lobster *Maine* ~. ʻŌmā. *Slipper* ~. Ula pāpapa, ula ʻāpapapa.

local call *Also to make such a call.* Kelepona kūloko. *See Hawaiian entries under kelepona.*

location *Absolute* ~, *in geography.* Kuhikuhina. *Relative* ~. Pilina henua.

lock *Also to* ~. Laka. *See entries below. Combination* ~. Laka helu. *Combination, as for a* ~. Helu laka.

lock *Caps* ~, *as on a typewriter or computer keyboard.* Laka maʻaka. *Caps* ~ *key.* Pihi laka maʻaka, pihi laka (*preceded by* ke).

locker Waihona pāiki, pahu laka.

locket Pihipoho (*preceded by* ke).

locust *Honey* ~ *bean.* Pāpapa ʻūhinihone.

log *Literature response* ~, *as a student's journal for recording reactions to literature.* Puke moʻomanaʻo moʻokalaleo.

logic *Also logical.* Kūpili. ~ *error, as a message on a calculator display that shows an operation is not logical.* Hewa kūpili. ~*al thinking.* Noʻonoʻo kūpili.

log in *See log on.*

logo Lōkō.

log off *Or to log out, as of a network or other computer system.* Lele. *See log on.*

log on *Or to log in, as of a network or other computer system.* ʻEʻe. *See log off.*

log out *See log off.*

lollipop *Also sucker.* Kanakē ʻau, kō omōmo.

long Loa. *See length.*

long bean *A common Filipino dish.* Pāpapa loloa.

long-distance call *Also to make such a call.* Kelepona kūwaho. *See Hawaiian entries under kelepona.*

Long Duration Exposure Facility
LDEF, a kind of experimentation satellite placed in orbit by a space shuttle. Poelele hoʻokolohua wā loa.

longitude Lonikū, lonitū. See *latitude.*

long jump *Standing ~.* Lele loloa. *Running ~.* Holo a lele loloa.

long-range *Also long-term.* Hikiāloa. See *short-range, medium-range. ~ plan.* Papa hoʻolālā hikiāloa.

long run *In the ~.* I ka hikiāloa.

long-term See *long-range.*

lookout *Scenic viewpoint.* ʻImaka.

loop *As in a computer program.* Pīnaʻiapuni. *Belt ~, as on a pair of pants.* Apo ʻili kuapo.

lose Eo, hāʻule. See *Hawaiian entries.*

loss Kumulilo. See *profit.*

lottery Pili helu laki.

lotus Kalo Pākē, līkao.

Louisiana *Also Louisianan, Louisianian.* Luikiana, Luisiana.

lousewort Pekikulali.

lower case *Small, as a letter of the alphabet.* Naʻinaʻi. See *letter. To change (a letter of the alphabet) from capital to ~.* Hoʻonaʻinaʻi. See *capitalize. A line drawn diagonally through a capital letter to indicate that the letter is to be written in ~, in proofreading.* Kaha hoʻonaʻinaʻi.

lower division *As a course at a college or university.* Heluhaʻa. See *upper division. ~ course.* Papa heluhaʻa.

lowest *~ terms of a fraction, in math.* Palena haʻahaʻa loa. *~-terms fraction.* Hakina palena haʻahaʻa loa.

low-fat food Meaʻai ʻailakele iki, meaʻai liʻiliʻi o ka ʻailakele. See *high-fat food.*

low post *In basketball.* Kūliu loko. See *high post.*

low-pressure system *In meteorology.* ʻŌnaehana mīkā emi. See *high-pressure system.*

lowrise *As a building.* Nuʻuhaʻa. See *highrise.*

low vowel *In linguistics.* Woela haʻahaʻa. See *vowel.*

lucky *Japanese ~ welcome cat.* Manekineko.

lumber Papa. *Four-by-four ~.* Papa hā hā. *Two-by-four ~.* Papa lua hā.

lunar rover Kaʻa holo mahina.

lunch pail Kini ʻaiō, kini ʻai.

lung Akemāmā.

Luxembourg Lukemapuka.

lychee *Also litchi.* Laikī.

lye ʻĀkililehu.

lymph ʻAnapuʻu. See *lymphoma. ~ gland or node.* Lōkuʻu ʻanapuʻu.

lymphoma Maʻi ʻaʻai ʻanapuʻu.

Lyra *A constellation.* Kehoʻoea.

M

MA *Master's, Master of Arts, as a degree at a university.* MA (*pronounced* mū ʻā). See *Master's, MS.*

macadamia Makakema, makeima, makekemia.

Macao Makao.

macaroni Makaloni.

machine See *Hawaiian entries under* mīkini. *Compound ~.* Kaumīkini.

macro- Mānui. See *macronutrient.*

macro *As in a computer program.* Kōmi ʻōkuhi.

macronutrient Māhuaola mānui. See *micronutrient.*

Madagascar *Also Madagascan.* Madagaseka.

magazine Makakina, makasina.

magenta ʻUla mākuʻe.

maggot Ilo. *Onion ~.* Ilo ʻakaʻakai.

magic *As supernatural or enchanted.* Hoʻokalakupua. *~ trick, illusion, sleight of hand.* Pāhaʻohuna.

magma Pelemaka. *~ chamber.* Nupa pelemaka.

magna cum laude *Also with high honors, as in academics.* Me ke kau i ka hano hoʻonani, me ka hoʻomaikaʻi nui. See *cum laude, summa cum laude.*

magnesium Makanekiuma.

magnet Mākēneki.

magnetism ʻUme mākēneki.

magnifying glass *Hand lens.* Aniani hoʻonui ʻike.

magnitude *Order of ~, in math.* Kūlana pāhoʻonui.

mahogany *The wood.* Mahakonia.

maidenhair fern ʻIwaʻiwa.

mail See entries below and *air mail, E-mail. Internal ~, as in an office or school.* Leka kūloko. *Campus ~.* Leka kūloko kula. *Office ~.* Leka kūloko keʻena.

mailing list Papa helu wahi.

mail merge *As in a computer program.* Hoʻokuʻi helu wahi.

main clause *In grammar.* Pepeke haku.

main dictionary *As in a computer program.* Papa huaʻōlelo kūmau. See *user dictionary.*

Maine Maine, Meine. *~ lobster.* ʻŌmā.

main idea *Also main thought, as of a paragraph or story.* Manaʻo nui.

main menu *As in a computer program.* Papa kuhikuhi kahua paʻa.

maintenance release *Also interim release, as of a computer program.* Hoʻopuka hoʻoponopono ʻia. See *update.*

major *As an academic field of specialization.* Mēkia. See *minor.*

majority party *In politics.* ʻAoʻao hapa nui. See *minority party, political party.*

make *To ~, as a test.* Haku. See *take.*

makeup Pena maka. *To put on ~.* Hoʻouʻiuʻi, hoʻonaninani, pena maka. *~ artist, as for a play, movie, or video production.* Mea pena maka.

malaria Malaria. *Avian ~.* Malaria manu.

malathion Malationa.

Malawi *Also Malawian.* Malaui.

Malaysia *Also Malaysian.* Malaisia.

Maldives Maladiwa.

males *Hatred of ~; misandry.* Hoʻokae kāne. See *misanthropy, misogyny.*

Mali *Also Malian.* Māli.

mall *Shopping center.* Kikowaena kūʻai.

mallee bird *Of Australia.* Mālī, manu mālī.

Malta Malata. *~ Island.* Ka mokupuni ʻo Malata.

mammal Holoholona ʻai waiū, māmela. *Marine ~ Commission.* Komikina Māmela Kai. *Marine ~s Act.* Kānāwai Māmela Kai.

mammoth *Woolly ~.* ʻElepani pūhuluhulu.

Man *Isle of ~.* ʻAilana Kanaka.

management *Fish and game ~; also to manage fish and game.* Hoʻomalu lawaiʻa a me ka hahai holoholona. *Western Pacific Fishery ~ Council.* ʻAha Hoʻomalu Lawaiʻa o ka Pākīpika Komohana.

manager Manakia. *Product ~.* Luna huahana. *Production ~, as for a movie or video production.* Manakia ʻenehana.

mandible *Jawbone.* Iwi ā.

maneuvering engine *As for a spacecraft.* ʻEnekini kīkaha.

maneuvering unit See *Manned Maneuvering Unit.*

manganese Manakanika.

mangrove Kukunaokalā.

manhole cover *As for a sewer.* Pani paipu lawe ʻino (*preceded by* ke). See *sewer pipe.*

maniacal delirium Maʻi hehena.

manipulator arm *Remote ~, space crane.* Lima kia pihi.

mankind *Hatred of ~; misanthropy.* Hoʻokae kanaka. See *misandry, misogyny.*

man-made topographical feature Hiʻona na ke kanaka. *See Hawaiian entries hiʻona wai, hiʻona ʻāina.*

Manned Maneuvering Unit *As for a space flight.* Ahikao hāʻawe.

manned space flight Lele lewa lipo kanaka.

mannequin Kanaka ʻea.

man offense *Offense for attacking face defense, in basketball.* Kūlele alo.

man-of-war *Portuguese ~, Physalia.* Paʻi, paʻimalau. See *blue-button, by-the-wind-sailor.*

mantis *Praying ~.* ʻŪhinipule.

mantle *Earth's ~.* ʻAhu honua. See *core, crust.*

man-to-man defense *As in basketball; to execute such a play.* Pale alo.

manual *Teacher's ~ or guide.* Puke alakaʻi.

manufacture Hana kāpili. See entry below and *build. Manufacturer.* Hui hana kāpili, kanaka hana kāpili.

manufacturing industry ʻOihana kāpili, ʻoiʻenehana kāpili.

many See *how many, multi-.*

map *Rainfall ~.* Palapala ʻāina ua. *Site ~.* Palapala ʻāina kahua. *To field ~ a site.* Kaha palapala ʻāina. *Space ~.* Palapala lewa lipo. *Thematic ~.* Palapala ʻāina kumuhana. *Topographic ~.* Palapala hiʻona ʻāina.

map *To ~, as a computer keyboard.* Kaʻakuene. *Keyboard ~ping.* Kaʻakuene papa pihi.

maple Mēpala.

marathon Malakona.

March Malaki. *Abb.* Mal.

margarine *Also oleomargarine.* Makalina.

margin *As on a printed page.* Lihi. *Left ~.* Lihi hema. *Right ~.* Lihi ʻākau. *Top ~.* Lihi o luna. *Bottom ~.* Lihi o lalo. *To set the ~s.* Hoʻopaʻa i nā lihi. *Two vertical lines written to the left of lines of print to indicate that the left ~ should be justified, in proofreading.* Kaha hoʻokaulihi.

marguerite *Daisy.* Makalike.

maria *A crater-free plain on the surface of the moon.* Maria.

marine Kai. *Fish or any ~ animal.* Iʻa, iʻa kai. See entries below and *fish.* *~ sediment.* Koʻana kai. *National ~ Fisheries Service.* ʻOihana Lawaiʻa Kai Pekelala.

marine corps Pūʻali hoʻouka kaua.

Marine Mammal Commission Komikina Māmela Kai.

Marine Mammals Act Kānāwai Māmela Kai.

Marineris Malineli. *Valles ~, a valley on Mars.* Ke awāwa ʻo Malineli.

marionette Pāpeka kaula, pāpeta kaula.

market *Indoor ~.* Mākeke maluhale. *Outdoor ~.* Mākeke kaupokulani. *To ~ something, i.e. to make available and promote the sale of a product.* Hokona. *~ value.* Waiwai kūʻai.

markup *As in the price of an article.* Pākēneka hoʻopiʻi.

marmot *Also groundhog.* Māmota.

Maro Reef Koʻanakoʻa.

marquisette *A kind of curtain.* Pākū makaliʻi.

Mars *The planet.* Hōkūʻulapīnaʻau, Hōkūʻula.

marsh *With salt or brackish water and no trees.* Ālialia. See *bog, swamp.* *Fresh-water ~.* Ālialia wai maoli.

Marshall Islands *Also Marshallese.* Mākala, Mākala ʻAilana, Ka pae moku ʻo Mākala.

marshmallow Mahamelo, masamelo.

marsh pen Peni kuni.

marshy Nenelu.

Maryland *Also Marylander.* Melelana, Merelana.

mascara Pena lihilihi maka. *To put on ~.* Hana i ka pena lihilihi maka.

mask *Diving goggles.* Makaaniani lu'u kai, makaaniani lu'u. *Gas ~, as used during World War II.* Pūnuku ea make.

masking tape *Freezer tape.* Leki pahu.

mass *Bulk.* Nuipa'a. *Air ~.* Ahu ea. *Atomic ~.* Nuipa'a 'ātoma. See *atomic mass.*

Massachusetts Makakukeka, Masakuseta.

masseter *The muscle that closes the jaw.* Mākala 'ūpā.

master See *props master.*

master bedroom Lumi moe haku.

master copy *Also original, a master used for making additional copies.* Kope kumu.

Master's *As a degree at a university.* Laeo'o, MA (*pronounced* mū'ā), MS (*pronounced* mūsā). See *bachelor's, doctorate, undergraduate, graduate. ~ degree.* Kēkelē laeo'o, palapala laeo'o, kēkelē MA, kēkelē MS.

mat See *counting mat, water slide.*

match *To ~, as in the game of concentration.* Ho'olikelike. *As one thing to its counterpart by drawing a line.* Ho'opili.

matching *Identical.* 'Ālike.

material *Cloth.* 'Īalole. *See entry below. Bolt of ~.* 'Āpā lole.

material *A general term but not relating to cloth.* Makelia, memea. *Raw ~.* Makelia kūlohelohe, memea kūlohelohe.

math sentence *Also number sentence.* Hopunahelu. See *mental math.*

matrix *A rectangular array of numbers, symbols, or functions which are often added or multiplied according to certain rules.* Ha'imaulia.

matter *Physical substance.* Meakino.

mattress *Also bed.* Pela, pela moe. *Air ~.* Pela ho'olana. *~ cover.* 'Eke pela (*preceded by* ke).

Maui *Name of the island.* Maui. See entries below.

Māui *Name of the demigod.* Māui. See *Maui.*

Maui greensword 'Āhinahina 'ōma'oma'o.

Maui parrotbill *Pseudonestor xanthophrys.* Kīkēkoa.

Mauritania *Also Mauritanian.* Mauritania.

Mauritius Mauritiusa *~ Island.* Ka mokupuni 'o Mauritiusa.

maximum Palena nui. See *minimum. The ~ weight.* Ka palena nui o ke kaumaha.

May Mei. *No abbreviation.*

mayonnaise Meoneki.

Mayotte Maiota. *~ Island.* Ka mokupuni 'o Maiota.

maytansine *A chemical compound once investigated for therapeutic uses but later found to be too toxic for human use.* Maikeni.

meadow *Also grassy field.* Kula mau'u.

mealworm Ane ko'e.

mealy bug Ane 'uku.

mean *In math.* 'Awelike.

measles 'Ulāli'i.

measure *To ~ depth, as in the ocean.* Ho'opapā hohonu. See entries below and *accent unit.*

measurement *Also used when referring to dimensions.* Ana. See *height, length, width; how, what, measure. Unit of ~.* Anakahi. *Metric unit of ~.* Anakahi mekalika. *US standard or customary unit of ~.* Anakahi 'Amelika.

measuring cup Kī'aha ana. See *cup.*

meat meal 'I'o wiliwili. See *bonemeal.*

mechanical *Also mechanics.*
Kūmikini. *~ engineer.* 'Enekinia mīkini.

mechanism *Apparatus or device, ordinarily including some mechanical part or parts.* Maomeka. *See device, instrument, tool. Balancing ~, in biology.* 'Ōnaehana ho'okauapono.

medaka *Mosquito fish.* I'a makika.

media *As radio, TV, etc.* Pāpaho.

medialis *See vastus medialis.*

median Kūwaena. *~ number, in math.* Helu kūwaena.

medical *~ insurance.* 'Inikua olakino. *~ coverage number.* Helu 'inikua olakino.

medication *Also medicine, medicinal drug.* Lā'au. *See medicine. Prescription ~.* Lā'au kuhikuhi. *Prescription for ~ or medicinal drugs.* Kuhikuhi lā'au. *Over-the-counter ~.* Lā'au kū'ai wale.

medicine *Also medication, medicinal drug.* Lā'au. *See medication. ~ cabinet.* Waihona lā'au lapa'au. *To take ~.* Inu i ka lā'au, 'ai i ka lā'au.

Mediterranean Sea Ke Kai Waena Honua.

medium *A means of affecting or conveying something.* Kaiapuni. *See entries below. Hawaiian-~ class.* Papa kaiapuni Hawai'i. *Hawaiian-~ school.* Kula kaiapuni Hawai'i.

medium *As drink size.* Lōpū. *Abb.* lō. See entries below and *small, large. ~ heat.* Wela lōpū. *~ soda.* Koloaka lōpū.

medium-range *Also medium-term.* Hikiālōpū. *See short-range, long-range. ~ plan.* Papa ho'olālā hikiālōpū.

medium rare *As meat.* Hapa mo'a, mo'a hapa.

medium shot *As of a photograph or in movie or video production.* Pa'i lōpū *(preceded by ke). See close-up, wide shot. To take a ~.* Pa'i a lōpū.

medium-term *See medium-range.*

Meeker burner Kapuahi Mika. *See burner.*

meeting *See convergent.*

Meg *Megabyte, in computer terminology.* PM ('ai pāmiliona).

mega- *A prefix meaning million (M).* Pāmiliona. *Abb.* pm. *See entry below and deca-, hecto-, kilo-, giga-, tera-.*

megabyte *In computer terminology.* 'Ai pāmiliona. *Abb.* PM. *See byte.*

Megalagrion spp *See damselfly.*

mejiro Manu peleita.

melodeon Melokiana.

melody *Also tune.* Leo, 'ea. *One who sings the ~ of a song.* Leo alaka'i.

melon Meleni, ipu. *See cantaloupe.*

melt Hehe'e. *See melting point.*

melting point Kēkelē hehe'e. *See boiling point, freezing point.*

member *As of an organization.* Lālā. *Board ~s.* Nā lālā o ka papa.

membrane Niniki.

membranophone *A musical instrument whose sound is produced by striking a membrane or skin of the instrument.* Olo'ili. *See Hawaiian entries beginning with olo-.*

memo *Or note for conveying a message to someone; message.* Memo. *See memorandum, note. To write a ~ or take a message.* Kākau i memo.

memorandum *Also memo.* Memo. *See memo. Internal ~, as in telecommunication.* Memo kūloko.

memory *As in a computer program.* Waihona 'ike. *Built-in ~.* Waihona 'ike pa'aloko. *Expanded ~.* Waihona 'ike māhuahua. *Extended ~.* Waihona 'ike keu. *Virtual ~.* Hope waihona 'ike. *~ key, as on a calculator keyboard.* Pihi ho'omana'o *(preceded by ke).*

mental math Helu na'au, makemakika na'au.

menu *As in a computer program.* Papa kuhikuhi. *Main ~.* Papa kuhikuhi kahua pa'a. *Pop-up ~.* Papa 'ō'ili. *~ bar.* Papa koho.

merchandise Mea kū'ai.

mercury *The metallic element in chemistry.* Melekulia. *The planet.* Ukalialiʻi.

merge *To ~, as in a computer program.* Hoʻokuʻi pū. *Mail ~.* Hoʻokuʻi helu wahi.

meridian *Prime ~, in geography.* Kumu lonikū, kumu lonitū.

Mesolithic *In anthropology.* Haku kā nahau. *~ age, period.* Ke au haku kā nahau.

mesophilic *Midtemperature-loving.* Ola mehana. See *thermophilic. ~ bacteria.* Koʻohune ola mehana.

message *A memo or note for conveying a ~ to someone.* Memo. See *note. To take a ~ or write a memo.* Kākau i memo.

metabolism Pūnao.

metal Mekala, metala. See *alkali metal, alkaline earth metal, alloy.*

metamorphosis Kūaloli. *Morphological ~.* Kūaloli kino.

metatarsus *The bone of the foot between the phalanges and the tarsus.* Iwi poli wāwae.

metathesis *Transposition of letters, syllables, or sounds in a word.* Panoko.

meteor Koli.

meteorology Kālaianilā. See *wind.*

meter *The unit of measurement.* Mika. *Abb. m.* See *metric. In music.* Lauana wā.

meter *An instrument that automatically measures and registers quantity.* Mīka. *~ box.* Pahu mīka. *Parking ~.* Mīka kāki. *~ed parking or any parking for which there is a charge.* Kū kāki.

methane Mēkene, mētene.

methanol Metanola.

method *Also technique.* Kiʻina hana, kiʻina. *Sampling ~s.* Nā kiʻina ʻohi hāpana.

methyl Meto.

metric Mekalika. *~ unit of measure.* Anakahi mekalika. *~ system.* ʻŌnaehana mekalika. *~ conversion chart.* Pakuhi hoʻololi makalika.

Mexico *Also Mexican.* Mekiko. *New ~.* Nūmekiko.

mi *The third note on the musical scale.* Lī. See *Hawaiian entry* pākōlī.

Miaplacidus *A star in the constellation Carina.* Makawela.

Michigan *Also Michigander, Michiganite.* Mikikana.

micro- *Also microscopic.* Māiki. *A prefix meaning one millionth (u).* Hapa miliona. *Abb.* hml. See entries below and *deci-, centi-, milli-, nano-, pico-.*

microbiology Kālaimeaolahune. See *biology.*

microclimate Aniau hāiki.

microgram Māikikalame.

microgravity ʻUmekaumaha māiki. See *gravity.*

micron *0.0001 centimeter.* Maikolona.

Micronesia Maikonesia. *Federated States of ~.* Nā Mokuʻāina Hoʻohui ʻia o Maikonesia.

micronutrient Māhuaola māiki. See *macronutrient.*

microorganism Meaola māiki.

microphone Ipuleo, mea hoʻolele leo.

microscope ʻOhe hoʻonui ʻike. *~ slide.* Aniani kaupaneʻe, *usu.* aniani. *~ stage.* Paepae aniani kaupaneʻe.

microscopic Māiki.

microsecond *In math.* Hapa miliona kekona.

microwave oven ʻOmawawe.

middle *Used only in special terminology.* Kūwaena. See entries below and *dermis, new, old. ~ Kingdom, in Egyptology.* Au Palaʻo Kūwaena.

Middle East *Also Middle Eastern.* Hikina Waena.

middle finger Manamana loa, manamana waena.

midge fly Nalo wiʻu.

midocean Waena moana. *~ ridge.* Kualapa waena moana.

midpoint *In math.* Kiko kauwaena.

Midway *The island.* Pihemanu.

might *To do with all one's ~ or strength.* Kuʻupau. See *geevum.*

migrate *Also migration, migratory.* Neʻekau.

mild *As a solution.* ʻŪpalu.

mile Mile. *Abb.* mil. *~s per hour.* Mile o ka hola. *Abb.* mil/hl.

military base Kahua pūʻali koa.

military service *Also army.* Pūʻali koa.

military transport aircraft Mokulele hali koa.

militia Pūʻali koa kūikawā.

milk Waiū. See *chocolate, dairy product. Imitation ~.* Waiū hoʻopilipili. *Powdered ~.* Waiū ehu, waiū pauka. *Skim ~.* Waiū heʻe. *Whole ~.* Waiū piha. *~ carton.* Pahu waiū. *~ shake.* Waiū luliluli. *Residue of ~ after beating.* Kale ʻai.

milli- Mili-. *A prefix meaning one thousandth (m).* Hapa kaukani. *Abb.* hkk. See entries below and *deci-, centi-, micro-, nano-, pico-.*

milligram Milikalame. *Abb.* mkal.

milliliter Mililika. *Abb.* ml.

millimeter Milimika. *Abb.* mm.

million See *mega-, micro-.*

millisecond *In math.* Hapa kaukani kekona.

Mimas *A moon very near to Saturn.* Mima.

mineral Minelala, minerala.

mineral water *Also sparkling water.* Wai piʻipiʻi.

minimum Palena iki. See *maximum. The ~ weight.* Ka palena iki o ke kaumaha.

Minnesota *Also Minnesotan.* Minekoka.

minor *As a ~ academic field of study.* Māina. See *major.*

minority party *In politics.* ʻAoʻao hapa ʻuʻuku. See *majority party, political party.*

Mintaka *A star.* Kaʻawili.

minus Lawe. *~ sign.* Kaha hoʻolawe.

minute *Time.* Minuke. *Abb.* min. *Revolutions per ~ (rpm).* Puni o ka minuke. *Abb.* p/min. *~ hand.* Lima kuhikuhi minuke.

Mira *A star.* Lanihou.

Mirach *A star.* Kōkoʻolua.

Mirphack *A star.* Hānaipono.

mirror Aniani, aniani nānā, aniani kilohi, aniani kilo. *Bicycle ~.* Aniani kilohi paikikala, aniani kilo paikikala, aniani paikikala. *Concave ~.* Aniani ʻeʻele. *Convex ~.* Aniani ʻeʻemu. *Full-length ~.* Aniani kū. *Hand ~.* Aniani paʻa lima, aniani lima. *Rear-view ~ for a car.* Aniani kilohi kaʻa, aniani kaʻa. *Small ~ to keep in a purse.* Aniani pāiki, aniani liʻiliʻi.

misandry *Hatred of males.* Hoʻokae kāne. See *misanthropy, misogyny.*

misanthropy *Hatred of mankind.* Hoʻokae kanaka. See *misandry, misogyny.*

misogyny *Hatred of women.* Hoʻokae wahine. See *misandry, misanthropy.*

missed shot *Also air ball, in basketball; to make such a shot.* Kī halahī, kī halahū.

missile Kao lele. *~ bomb.* Kao lele pahū.

mission *As in the ~ statement of an organization.* Ala nuʻukia. See *vision. ~ statement.* ʻŌlelo ala nuʻukia.

Mississippi *Also Mississippian.* Mikikipi, Misisipi.

Missouri *Also Missourian.* Mikouli, Misouri.

misspelled word A circle around a ~ with the letters ph (pela hewa) written above the word, in proofreading. Kaha pela hewa.

mitogen Any substance or agent that stimulates mitotic cell division. Mikokene.

mitt Baseball glove. Mikilima pōhili.

mix To ~ or dilute, as a drink. Pa'ipa'i. See dilute.

mixed Also combined, in math and science. 'Ō'ā. See alloy, whole number. Chemically combined. 'Ō'ā kemikala 'ia. ~ decimal. Kekimala 'ō'ā. ~ number. Helu 'ō'ā.

mixture Also combination. Huihuina.

mix up To jumble the order. Ho'okake ka'ina.

mobile A piece of artwork which dangles and moves in the wind. Māhielewa.

mobility In geography. Pēne'e.

mochi Mōchī. ~ rice. Laiki mōchī, lāisi mōchī.

mode As the number or numbers that occur most often in a set, in math. Lauika. As in a computer program. Pē'ano. ~ of transportation. Alakau.

model Example, as of behavior. Kumu ho'ohālike. Usually miniature. Kūkohu. ~ boat. Kūkohu moku. To ~, i.e. to mold or shape, as clay. Hō'omo'omo. See clay.

modem Mōkema.

moderator As of a panel. Luna ho'omalu.

modern Kaila hou.

modernize To ~ a written document using modern spelling and punctuation standards. Hō'ano hou. See adapt.

modulation See amplitude modulation, frequency modulation.

moist Damp or ~ with fog or dew, wet from cold. Kawaū.

mold Punahelu. To ~, i.e. model or shape as clay. Hō'omo'omo.

molding As around windows or doors. Mōlina. See frame.

Moldova Molodowa.

mole The animal. Mio'awi.

molecule Lātoma. See structure.

Molluca Moluka. ~ Sea. Ke kai 'o Moluka.

mollusk Hakuika.

molly I'a moli.

molt To ~, as a crab its shell. Ho'omalule. As a snake its skin. Māunu.

molybdate Molaibadahate. Ammonium ~. 'Amoniuma molaibadahate.

molybdenum Molaibedenuma.

momentum Uluō. See impulse.

Monaco Monako.

monarch butterfly Pulelehua pua kalaunu.

Monday Po'akahi. Abb. P1.

monetary denomination Kūana kālā.

money Kālā. ~ order. Pila 'oka kālā. To draw ~ from the bank. Kīko'o.

Mongolia Also Mongolian. Monokolia, Monogolia.

monitor As for a computer or in movie or video production. Pahu papakaumaka. See screen. Computer ~. Pahu papakaumaka kamepiula. TV ~. Pahu papakaumaka kīwī.

monkey Owl ~. Keko pueo. Rhesus ~. Keko lekuka.

monkey bars A kind of playground equipment. Hao keko. See jungle gym.

monkfish Mōnekakai.

monk seal Hawaiian ~. Sila Hawai'i.

monocotyledon Lau 'īnana kahi. See cotyledon.

monofilament Aho 'ea.

monolith Pōhakukūkahi.

monopoly Exclusive possession or control of a commodity or service in a market. Ka'alilo. A business or company which has a ~. Pā'oihana ka'alilo.

monotheism *Also monotheistic.* Akua kahi. See *polytheism.*

monoxide Monokesaside. *Carbon ~.* Karabona monokesaside.

monstera Lāʻape.

Montana *Also Montanan.* Monakana, Monekana.

montane area Wao kuahiwi. *Lower ~.* Wao kuahiwi haʻahaʻa. *Upper ~.* Wao kuahiwi kiʻekiʻe. *Vegetation area at the base of a mountain.* Wao kumu kuahiwi.

month Mahina, māhina. *Abb.* mhn.

monument Kiahoʻomanaʻo. *National ~.* Pāka kiahoʻomanaʻo aupuni.

mood *As in music.* Au.

moose ʻEleka.

mop *Also to ~.* Māpa. *~ head.* Hulu māpa.

moraine Puʻu neʻena hau.

Morocco *Also Moroccan.* Moloko, Moroko.

morphine Mōpine.

morphological metamorphosis Kūaloli kino.

mosquito fish *Medaka.* Iʻa makika.

mosquito netting Pākū makika.

moss *General term.* Mākōpiʻi. See *sphagnum. Peat ~.* Mākōpiʻi ʻelenahu.

moth *Geometrid ~.* ʻŌʻaki.

mothball Pōpō pale mū.

motion *Brownian ~, in chemistry.* Lelekē Palaunu.

mount *kik* Mauna. *See entries below.*

mount *Slide ~.* Mōlina kiʻiaka. *To ~ insects; also insect ~ing.* Pine ʻelala.

mountain *~ range.* Pae kuahiwi. *~ pass.* Nuku. *Volcanic ~.* Kuapele. See *montane, passageway, seamount.*

mountain beaver Peawa kuahiwi.

mountain bike Paikikala holo kuahiwi.

Mount Everest Mauna ʻEweleka.

Mount Olympus Mauna ʻOlumepika.

Mount Saint Helens Mauna Kana Helena, Mauna Sana Helena.

mouse ʻIole. *Deer ~.* ʻIole kia. *White-footed ~.* ʻIole wāwae kea.

mouse *As for a computer.* ʻIole. *~ arrow; also pointer or cursor.* Nahau ʻiole, nahau.

moustache ʻUmiʻumi lehelehe. See *beard.*

mouth *River ~.* See *estuary.*

move *A circle around a word or words with an arrow going from the words to the place where they are to be ~d, in proofreading.* Kaha hoʻoneʻe. *As in a sports play.* ʻOnina. *To ~, as files in a computer program.* Hoʻoneʻe.

movement Neʻena. *Video camera ~.* Neʻena pahu paʻi wikiō. *Film ~, as in a movie or video camera.* Holo lola. *As of body parts.* ʻOnina.

movements *As in dancing.* Kiʻina. *Hand ~.* Kiʻina lima. *Foot ~.* Kiʻina wāwae.

movie Kiʻiʻoniʻoni. See entry below and *action movie, three-dimensional movie. ~ projector.* Mīkini hoʻolele kiʻiʻoniʻoni, mīkini kiʻiʻoniʻoni. *~ screen.* Pākū hoʻolele kiʻi. *To shoot a ~ film.* Paʻi kiʻiʻoniʻoni *(preceded by ke).*

movie studio *The building where movies are made.* Hale hana kiʻiʻoniʻoni. *The company responsible for making movies.* Keʻena hana kiʻiʻoniʻoni.

mow *To ~ the lawn.* ʻOki i ka mauʻu, ʻoki i ka mahiki.

Mozambique *Also Mozambican.* Mozamabika.

MS *Master's, Master of Science, as a degree at a university.* MS *(pronounced* mūsā). See *Master's, MA.*

mud ʻŪkele, lepo pohō. *Pond ~.* Pohō. *~ guard.* Pale lepo. *Bicycle ~ guard.* Pale lepo paikikala.

muffin Māpina. *Bran ~.* Māpina pelene.

muffler *As on a car.* Kini paipu ahi. See *exhaust pipe.*

multi- *Also many.* Lau-. ~*engined spaceships.* Nā moku ahikao lau'enekini.

multiple *In math.* Helu māhua, māhua. *Common* ~. Helu māhua like, māhua like. *Least common* ~. Helu māhua ha'aha'a loa, māhua ha'aha'a loa.

multiple-choice Kohokoho, pane kohokoho. ~ *question.* Nīnau kohokoho. ~ *book.* Puke pane kohokoho.

multiplication *In math.* Ho'onui. See *multiply.* ~ *sign.* Kaha ho'onui. ~ *tables.* Papa 'ālualua. *Zero property of* ~. 'Anopili 'ole o ka ho'onui.

multiply Ho'onui. See *multiplication.* ~ *through.* Ho'onui paukū pākahi.

mumps Pēheu.

mung bean Pāpapa munukō.

municipal *Note that in Hawai'i most things are county rather than municipal.* Kiwikā. ~ *golf course.* Kahua pā'ani kolepa kiwikā. ~ *watershed.* 'Āina kumu wai kiwikā.

municipality *A city or town having its own incorporated government for local affairs.* Aupuni kiwikā. See *ordinance.*

muscle Mākala. See *Hawaiian entries under* mākala.

muscular system *In biology.* 'Ōnaehana mākala.

mush *Hawaiian-style* ~, *made of flour and water.* Palaoa lūlū.

mushroom Melehune, kūkaelio. *Puffball, a kind of* ~. Melehune pōpōehu.

mushy *As rice cooked with too much water.* Palahē.

music Puolo. See *entries below.* ~ *box.* Pohokuikilani. *To arrange* ~; *also* ~ *arranger.* Kūkulu puolo.

musical instrument *Especially string instruments.* Pila. See *Hawaiian entries beginning with* olo-.

musical note Hua mele. See *note.*

musical scale Alapi'i mele, pākōlī. See *Hawaiian entries.*

musical staff Kōkua hua mele, ko'oko'o, kumu 'ākōlī. *Horizontal line on a* ~. Laina o ke kōkua hua mele, laina o ke kōkua. *Space between horizontal lines on a* ~. Wā o ke kōkua hua mele, wā o ke kōkua.

musician *General term.* Mea puolo. *Particularly one who plays Hawaiian music.* Mea ho'okani pila.

musicology Kālaipuolo. *Ethno*~. Kālaipuolo lāhui. *Musicologist.* Mea kālaipuolo, kanaka kālaipuolo.

musk-ox Pipi 'Ālika.

mustang Makekana, masetana.

mustard Masakeke.

musubi *Rice ball.* Musubī, pōpō laiki, pōpō lāisi.

mutate See *mutation.*

mutation *Also to mutate.* 'Āhuli.

mystery *As a story or movie.* Pōliu. ~ *novel.* Nōwela pōliu.

N

name *As of a file in a computer program.* Inoa. See *document.* ~ *of key.* Inoa o ke pihi.

Namibia *Also Namibian.* Namibia.

nano- *A prefix meaning one billionth (n).* Hapa piliona. *Abb.* hpl. See *deci-, centi-, milli-, micro-, pico-.*

narcissus Kuikina. See *daffodil.*

narcotic drug Lā'au 'ona.

narrate *To* ~ *orally, as in a speech.* Kūhaha'i. See *narrative speech.*

narration *As in movie or video production.* Mo'olelo ha'i waha. *Traditional elements of Hawaiian poetry, story telling, oratory, and* ~. Meiwi.

narrative speech Ha'i'ōlelo kūhaha'i. See *speech.*

NARS *Natural Areas Reserves System.* 'Ōnaehana Ho'omalu 'Āina Kūlohelohe.

nasal *In linguistics.* Manā. *~ cavity.* Haka ihu.

nasopharynx *The portion of the pharynx behind the nasal cavity and above the soft palate, in anatomy.* Haka moni o luna. *See pharynx.*

nation *Also country, national.* Kaumokuʻāina.

national Aupuni, kaumokuʻāina. *See entries below and federal.* *~ organization.* ʻAhahui kaumokuʻāina. *~ monument.* Pāka kiahoʻomanaʻo aupuni.

National Baseball League Kuʻikahi Pōhili Aupuni.

National Football Conference *NFC.* Hui Pōpeku Aupuni.

National Football League *NFL.* Kuʻikahi Pōpeku Aupuni.

nationalism *Also patriotism.* Aloha ʻāina.

National Marine Fisheries Service ʻOihana Lawaiʻa Kai Pekelala.

national park Pāka aupuni. *See entry below. Glacier ~.* Pāka Aupuni ʻo Hauneneʻe. *Hawaiʻi Volcanoes ~.* Pāka Aupuni ʻo Kīlauea. *Yosemite ~.* Pāka Aupuni ʻo ʻIosemite.

National Park Service ʻOihana Pāka Aupuni.

national product *Gross ~, GNP.* Kumuloaʻa kāʻokoʻa.

native *Indigenous.* ʻŌiwi. *~ bird.* Manu ʻōiwi.

natural *Lacking human intervention or contamination.* Kūlohelohe. *See entries below and nature, raw.* *~ biological community.* Kaiameaola kūlohelohe. *~ food.* Meaʻai kūlohelohe. *~ force.* Manehu kūlohelohe. *~ resource.* Kumuwaiwai kūlohelohe.

Natural Areas Reserves System *NARS.* ʻŌnaehana Hoʻomalu ʻĀina Kūlohelohe.

naturalist Puni ao kūlohelohe, kanaka puni ao kūlohelohe.

naturalization Ka hoʻomakaʻāinana ʻana. *See naturalize.*

naturalize *To admit to citizenship of a country.* Hoʻomakaʻāinana. *See naturalization.*

naturally occurring *~ weak acid.* ʻAkika ʻūpalu kūlohelohe.

natural resources *Department of Land and ~ (DLNR).* ʻOihana Kumuwaiwai ʻĀina.

natural rights *Rights that people are born with and that a government should not attempt to deny; also inalienable rights.* Kuleana hānau.

natural vegetation Lau nahele ʻōiwi.

nature Ao kūlohelohe. *See natural.* *~ reserve.* ʻĀina hoʻomalu ao kūlohelohe.

Navaho *Also Navajo.* Nawahō.

navy Pūʻali kaua moana, ʻau moku kaua, ʻoihana moku. *~ base.* Kahua pūʻali kaua moana.

Nazca Naseka. *~ Plate.* Ka Una Honua Naseka.

near *Close.* Kokoke.

Nebraska *Also Nebraskan.* Nepalaka, Nebaraka.

neck *As of an ʻukulele, guitar, etc.* ʻAu. *See ʻukulele.*

Necker *The island.* Mokumanamana.

neck stretches *A warm-up exercise for sports such as volleyball; also to do this exercise.* Hoʻomālō ʻāʻī.

necktie Lei ʻāʻī, lei ʻāʻī kalawake, lei kalawake. *See bow tie, cravat.*

necropsy *Also autopsy.* Kālaikupapaʻu.

nectar *Sweet liquid secreted by the nectaries of a plant.* Wai pua.

needle *Hypodermic ~.* Kui mōpina.

negative *Photo ~.* Akakiʻi.

negative *As of an electrical charge or south pole of a magnet.* ʻIne. *See electron, neutral, positive.* *~ number, in math.* Helu ʻiʻo ʻole. *~ integer.* Helu piha ʻiʻo ʻole. *~ sign, in math (-).* Kaha ʻiʻo ʻole. *See minus sign.*

neighbor *Not necessarily next door.* Hoa kaiahome. See *neighborhood.*

neighborhood Kaiahome.

nematode Koʻe ʻelemuku.

Neolithic *In anthropology.* Haku ʻānai. *~ age, period.* Ke au haku ʻānai.

neon Nīane.

Nepal *Also Nepalese.* Nepala.

Neptune Nepekune.

nerve Aʻalolo.

nervous system ʻŌnaehana lolokū.

nest Pūnana. *To ~.* Hoʻopūnana. *~ing season.* Kau hoʻopūnana.

net ʻUpena. *See entry below. Hem of a ~.* Pelu ʻupena. *Insect ~.* ʻUpena ʻelala. *Insect bag ~.* ʻUpena ʻelala ʻeke. *Insect fixed ~.* ʻUpena ʻelala hoʻolewalewa. *Insect sweep ~.* ʻUpena ʻelala kāʻeʻe.

net *As of a basket on a basketball court, or a volleyball ~.* ʻUpena. *Basketball ~.* Hīnaʻi. *Into the ~, in volleyball.* Kala. *~ ball.* Ua ʻupena ke kinipōpō. *~ violation.* ʻAʻena ʻupena. *Volleyball ~.* ʻUpena pōpaʻipaʻi.

Netherlands *The ~; also Netherlander, Netherlandian.* Nekelana.

netting *Mosquito ~.* Pākū makika.

network Pūnaewele. *~ controller or administrator, as for computers.* Kahu pūnaewele. *~ server, as for a computer ~.* Kikowaena pūnaewele. *~ station.* Poʻopoʻo pūnaewele. *~ system.* ʻŌnaehana pūnaewele.

neutral *As particles in an atom.* Hohoki. See *charge, positive, negative, neutron.* *~ electric charge.* Ikehu uila hohoki, ikehu hohoki. *As neither base nor acid on a pH scale.* Kūpapa.

neutral *Not taking sides, as in a dispute; neutrality.* Kūkonu. *To take a ~ position.* Hoʻokūkonu.

neutrality See *neutral.*

neutron Huna hohoki. See *proton, electron.*

Nevada *Also Nevadan.* Newaka, Newada.

new *Brand ~.* Hou loa. *Used only in special terminology.* Kūhou. See *middle, old.* *~ Kingdom, in Egyptology.* Au Palaʻo Kūhou.

New Caledonia Nūkaledonia.

New Guinea *Also New Guinean.* Nūkini. See *Papua New Guinea.*

New Hampshire *Also New Hampshirite, New Hampshireman.* Nūhamekia, Nūhamesia.

New Jersey *Also New Jerseyite.* Nūierese, Nūkelese.

New Mexico *Also New Mexican.* Nūmekiko.

New York *Also New Yorker.* Nūioka.

New Zealand Aotearoa. *Also New Zealander.* Nukilani.

Nicaragua *Also Nicaraguan.* Nikalakua, Nikarakua.

nichrome Nikoroma. *~ wire.* Uea nikoroma.

nickel *Five cents.* Hapaʻumi. *The metallic element.* Nikala.

nicotine Nikotina.

Niger *Also Nigerien.* Naigera.

Nigeria *Also Nigerian.* Naigeria.

nightgown *Pajamas.* Lole moe pō.

nightstand *Bedside table.* Pākaukau moe.

Nīhoa *The island.* Nīhoa. *~ finch (Telespiza ultima).* ʻAinohu Nīhoa.

ninhydrin indicator Ninahaidirina kuhikuhi.

nitrate Nitarahate.

nitric Nikiriku. See *nitrogen.* *~ acid.* ʻAkika nikiriku, ʻakika naikokene.

nitrite Nitarahite.

nitrogen *Also nitric.* Naikokene. See *azobacter, nitric.* *Free ~ compound.* Pūhui naikokene kaʻawale. *~ dioxide.* Naikokene diokesaside, naikokene ʻokikene lua. *~ cycle.* Pōʻaiapuni naikokene.

nocturnal Ala pō. See *crepuscular, diurnal.*

node *Where a leaf is connected to the stem.* Piko. *Lymph ~.* Lōku'u 'anapu'u.

nodule *As on a leguminous plant.* Pu'upu'u.

no-eyed big-eyed hunting spider Nananana maka 'ole, nanana maka 'ole.

no-look pass *Also blind pass, in basketball; to throw such a pass.* Kīloi ho'opalai.

nomad Kīhoe.

nominate Hāpai inoa, waiho inoa.

nonagon *A nine-sided polygon.* Huinaiwa.

nonfiction Hakule'i. *See fiction. ~ book.* Puke hakule'i.

non-point source pollution Kumu ho'ohaumia 'ike 'ole 'ia. *See point source pollution.*

nonstandard *As in units of measurement.* Kūhelu 'ole.

noodle Nulu. *See pasta.*

nook *Inside corner.* Kū'ono, po'opo'o.

normal *In math and science.* Haiakonu. *See deviation. ~ distribution.* Ili haiakonu.

Norse *See Norway.*

north 'Ākau. *Abb.* 'Āk. *See entries below. ~ pole.* Wēlau 'ākau.

North America *Also North American.* 'Amelika 'Ākau. *See opossum.*

North Carolina *Also North Carolinean.* Kalolaina 'Ākau.

North Dakota *Also North Dakotan.* Kakoka 'Ākau, Dakota 'Ākau.

Northern Equatorial Current *In oceanography.* Kūkahikahi. *See Southern Equatorial Current, Equatorial Countercurrent.*

northern hemisphere Poepoe hapa 'ākau. *See hemisphere.*

northern lights *Aurora borealis.* 'Olili'ula.

North Korea *Also North Korean.* Kōlea 'Ākau, Kōrea 'Ākau.

North Sea Ke Kai 'Ākau.

North Yemen *Also North Yemenite, North Yemeni.* Iemene 'Ākau. *See South Yemen.*

Norway *Also Norwegian, Norse.* Nolewai.

Norwegian *Also Norway, Norse.* Nolewai. *~ Sea.* Ke kai 'o Nolewai.

nose guard *In football; also defensive middle guard, nose tackle.* Haunaku.

nose tackle *See nose guard.*

notation *In math and science.* Kauhelu. *Exponential ~.* Kauhelu pāho'onui. *Scientific ~.* Kauhelu 'epekema.

note *Or memo for conveying a message to someone; message.* Memo. *See notes. To make a ~ of something.* Kakaha. *As in a book or research paper.* Kuhia. *See endnote, footnote.*

note *On music staff, musical ~.* Hua mele. *See key. Line ~.* Hua mele laina. *Whole ~.* Hua mele 'oko'a. *Half ~.* Hua mele hapalua. *Dotted half ~.* Hua mele hapalua kiko. *Quarter ~.* Hua mele hapahā. *Dotted quarter ~.* Hua mele hapahā kiko. *Eighth ~.* Hua mele hapawalu. *Sixteenth ~.* Hua mele hapa 'umikūmāono.

notebook *Tablet.* Kālana kākau. *See binder.*

notes *As taken during a lecture, etc.; to take such ~.* Kakaha. *See memo, note.*

novel *As a work of literature.* Nōwela. *Biographical ~.* Nōwela piliolana. *Mystery ~.* Nōwela pōliu. *~ette.* Nōwela pōkole.

November Nowemapa. *Abb.* Now.

novice level Pae 'akahi akahi.

nozzle Nuku. *Bellows ~.* Nuku 'ūpā makani.

nuclear Nukelea. *See nucleus. ~ energy.* Ikehu nukelea. *~ fusion.* Ku'i nukeliu. *~ radiation.* Pāhawewe nukelea.

nucleus *As in an atom.* Nukeliu. *Of a syllable in linguistics.* Iho.

null *In math.* Kuhiakau kūpapa.

number *In math.* Helu. *See entries below and integer, numeral. See also atomic number. Figure (the character) or numeral.* Huahelu. *Counting ~, in math.* Hua helu kumu. *Complex ~.* Helu hapa moeā. *Double ~.* Helu māhoe. *Even ~.* Helu kaulike. *Odd ~.* Helu kauʻewa. *Cardinal ~.* Helu heluna. *Imaginary ~.* Helu moeā. *Mixed ~.* Helu ʻōʻā. *Ordinal ~.* Helu kaʻina. *Transcendental ~.* Helu kohu pai. *Whole ~.* Helu piha.

number *Positive ~.* Helu ʻiʻo. *Negative ~.* Helu ʻiʻo ʻole. *Rational ~.* Helu puʻunaue koena ʻole. *Irrational ~.* Helu puʻunaue koena. *Composite ~.* Helu puʻunaue lua. *~ line.* Laina helu. *~ pair.* Paʻa helu. *~ pattern.* Lauana helu. *~ property.* ʻAnopili helu (*preceded by* ke).

number *Prime ~.* Helu kumu. *Relatively prime ~s, i.e. numbers which share one factor between them, and that factor is 1.* Hoa helu hoʻonui like kahi. *Twin primes.* Helu kumu kūlua. *~ or math sentence.* Hopunahelu. *~ puzzle.* Nane huahelu.

numeral *The character.* Huahelu. *Expanded ~.* Helu unuhi kūana. *Roman ~.* Helu Loma.

numerator *In math.* Kinohapa. *See denominator.*

numerical problem Haʻihelu.

numerical value *In math.* Waiwai helu.

nut *As on an ʻukulele or guitar.* Nīʻau. *See ʻukulele. Head ~.* Nīʻau liʻiliʻi. *As in ~s and bolts.* Pihi, pihi wili. *See bolt. Hex ~.* Pihi wili ono. *Wing ~.* Pihi wili ʻēheu.

nut *Pea~ or any edible ~.* Pīneki, pineki, pīnaki.

nutgrass Mauʻu pīneki.

nuthatch *A kind of bird.* Manu nūhata.

nutmeg ʻAlameka.

nutrient Māhuaola. *~ culture.* ʻOulu māhuaola. *~ salts, the deposits that remain after a liquid has been removed.* Paʻamāhuaola.

nutrition Kūlana ʻaiaola. *See nutritious.*

nutritious Paiola. *To eat ~ food.* ʻAiaola.

nutritive value Waiwai ʻaiaola.

nylon Naelona.

O

oaktag *A strong cardboard used for posters; also called tagboard.* Pepa papa ʻoka.

oatmeal ʻOkamila. *~ flake.* Ulahi ʻokamila.

object *Also entry, item.* ʻIkamu. *Reference ~, as in science.* Kiko kuhia. *See referent.*

objective Pahuhopu hāiki. *See goal.*

oblique *See abdominus oblique muscle.*

observatory Hale kilo hōkū. *See planetarium.*

obsidian Mākā.

obtuse *In math.* Peleleu. *~ angle.* Huina peleleu. *~ triangle.* Huinakolu peleleu.

occupation *Also career.* ʻOihana. *See business.*

ocean *Also oceanic.* Moana. *~ crust.* Pāpaʻa moana. *Pacific ~.* Moana Pākīpika.

Ocean ʻAilana *See Mokupāpapa.*

ocotillo *A kind of cactus.* Pānini ʻokotio.

octagon Huinawalu.

octahedron *A space figure with eight faces, in math.* Paʻaʻiliwalu.

octane ʻOkatene.

October ʻOkakopa. *Abb.* ʻOk.

octopus *Haole definition; squid (local definition).* He'e. See *cuttlefish.*

odd number Helu kau'ewa.

of Kō, ko.

offense *As in sporting events; to play* ~. Kūlele. See entries below. *Man* ~, *i.e.* ~ *for attacking face defense, in basketball.* Kūlele alo. *Zone* ~. Kūlele kā'ei.

offensive foul *In team sports such as basketball.* Ku'ia kūlele. See *foul.*

offensive line *In football.* Laina kūlele.

office *Also department.* Ke'ena, 'oihana. See entries below and *division.*

office appliance Mīkini ke'ena.

office mail Leka kūloko ke'ena. See *campus mail, internal mail.*

Office of Hawaiian Affairs *OHA.* Ke'ena Kuleana Hawai'i.

Office of Instructional Services *OIS.* Ke'ena Ho'onohonoho Ha'awina.

official *As an* ~ *representative or language.* Kūhelu. See *unofficial.*

off-line *Describing the state of an electronic device not ready to receive data, or not connected to a computer or computer network.* Pahemo. See *on-line. To take* ~, *as a computer system.* Ho'opahemo.

off-road vehicle *General term, as for ATV, dirt bike, 4x4, etc.* Ka'a holo 'āpu'upu'u, ka'a 'āpu'u. See *all-terrain vehicle.*

offsides *In football.* Mī'oi. See *encroachment.* ~ *on the offense.* Mī'oi na ke kūlele.

OHA *Office of Hawaiian Affairs.* Ke'ena Kuleana Hawai'i.

Ohio *Also Ohioan.* 'Ohaio.

ohm *A unit of resistance in electricity.* 'Ome. See *ohmmeter, volt.*

ohmmeter Ana 'ome. See *ohm.*

Ohta-san 'ukulele 'Ukulele Ohta-san.

oil *Vegetable* ~. 'Aila meakanu.

oil rig *For drilling oil on either land or sea.* Wili 'aila.

OIS *Office of Instructional Services.* Ke'ena Ho'onohonoho Ha'awina.

Okhostk 'Okosoka. *Sea of* ~. Ke kai 'o 'Okosoka.

'okina *Printer's symbol for single open quote.* Kaha puana'ī pākahi wehe.

Oklahoma *Also Oklahoman.* 'Okalahoma.

old *Also olden, used only in special terminology.* See *middle, new.* ~ *Kingdom, in Egyptology.* Au Pala'o Kūkahiko.

olden See *old.*

oleomargarine *Also margarine.* Makalina.

Oliarus tamehameha *Planthopper.* 'Ūmi'ilau.

olivine 'Ōma'ohaku.

-ology *Scientific study of something.* Kālai-. *Scientific study of something with no specific intent to influence change.* Huli-.

olympic *Also Olympics.* 'Olumepika. See *Olympus.* ~ *Winter Games.* Nā Pā'ani 'Olumepika Ho'oilo.

Olympus 'Olumepika. See *olympic. Mount* ~; ~ *Mons, a volcano on Mars.* Mauna 'Olumepika.

Oman *Also Omani.* 'Omana.

omnivore *Also omnivorous.* Hamu'ako'a.

one-and-one free throw *In basketball.* Kī noa kī hou.

one and one-half space *As on a typed document.* Koana pākahi me ka hapalua.

one cell *Also one-celled; single cell, single-celled.* Hunaola kahi.

one man *Also point guard, in basketball.* Kūkahi. See *guard.*

one property *In multiplication.* 'Anopili 'ekahi (*preceded by* ke).

ones *Place value, in math.* Kūana 'ekahi.

one-way *As a street or trip.* Holokahi. See *round trip.*

onion *Green ~ with a purple bulb becoming white close to the tip.* 'O'a. *Having a white bulb with purple inside.* Lina.

onion maggot Ilo 'aka'akai.

on-line *Describing the state of an electronic device ready to receive data, connected to a computer network, or accessible by means of a computer or computer network.* Pa'e'e. See *off-line.* *To bring ~, as a computer system.* Ho'opa'e'e.

onset *Of a syllable, in linguistics.* Ka'i.

on time I ka hola kūpono.

opaque A'ia'i hau'oki. See *transparent.*

open *As for business; unlocked; ajar.* Hemo. See entries below and *bracket, imu, leaf, parenthesis. Spread ~; also blossoming, blooming, as a flower.* Mohala. *Wide ~.* Hāmama. *~ reel, as for fishing.* Wiliaho hāmama. *To ~ an imu.* Hua'i i ka imu.

open *As a primary election.* Kūākea. See *closed. ~ primary.* Wae moho kūākea.

open *To complete, as an electric circuit.* Ho'oku'i. See *break.*

open *As a frame in a computer program.* Ka'aka'a. See *close, closed. ~ frame.* Mōlina ka'aka'a. *To ~, as a file.* Wehe.

open *To be ~, as for a play in basketball.* Hemo. *To get oneself ~.* Ho'ohemo.

open-ended question Nīnau ho'omohala mana'o.

opener *Can ~.* Mea wehe kini.

opening *As of a story.* Ho'omaka. See *body, closing, topic sentence. ~ ceremonies.* Wehena papahana.

operand *As a digit in a computer mathematical operation.* Pākō. See *operator.*

operating system *As for a computer program.* Pae 'ōnaehana.

operation *In math.* Hana ho'omākalakala. *Order of ~s in math problems.* Ka'ina ho'omākalakala. *Inverse ~.* Hana ho'omākalakala huli hope.

operator *As a sign in a computer mathematical operation.* Ha'i ho'okō. See *operand.*

opinion survey Anamana'o.

opossum 'Opakuma. *North American ~.* 'Opakuma 'Amelika 'Ākau.

opponent *As in a sporting event.* Hoa paio.

opposite 'Eko'a. See *side, of a triangle.* *To be the ~ of.* 'Eko'a me.

opposites property *In math.* 'Anopili o ka 'ēko'a (*preceded by* ke).

optical illusion Kuhi hewa o ka maka.

option *As on a computer keyboard.* Koho. *~ key.* Pihi koho (*preceded by* ke).

oral Ha'i waha. See *paraphrase, written. ~ communication.* Ka'a'ike ha'i waha, ka'a'ike waha. *~ literature.* Mo'okalaleo ha'i waha. *~ report.* Hō'ike ha'i waha, 'ōlelo hō'ike. *~ report, presented as a speech.* Ha'i'ōlelo hō'ike.

oral cavity *In linguistics.* Haka waha.

oral reprimand *Also to scold.* Nuku.

orange tree frog Poloka kau lā'au 'ālani.

oratory *Traditional elements of Hawaiian poetry, story telling, ~, and narration.* Meiwi.

orbicularis oris *The muscles surrounding the mouth and lips.* Mākala nuku.

orbit Ala pō'ai. *To ~.* Pō'ai.

order *Money ~.* Pila 'oka kālā. *~ form.* Palapala 'oka. *Purchase ~ (PO).* Palapala 'oka kū'ai.

order *Also sequence.* Ka'ina. *Alphabetical ~.* Ka'ina pī'āpā. *~ of operations in math problems.* Ka'ina ho'omākalakala. *To put in ~ or sequence.* Ho'oka'ina. *To coordinate or put in ~.* Ho'olauka'i.

ordered pair *Two numbers used to give the location of a point on a graph, in math.* Pa'a helu kuhikuhina.

order of magnitude *In math.* Kūlana pāho'onui.

ordinal number Helu ka'ina. *See cardinal number.*

ordinance *A municipal regulation.* Kānāwai kūloko. *See law, statute.*

ore 'Ōha'i.

Oregon *Also Oregonian.* 'Olekona, 'Oregona.

organ *As of an animal.* Lōkino. *~ system.* 'Ōnaehana lōkino.

organic *Relating to the branch of chemistry concerning the carbon compounds of living things.* Pa'upopo.

organism Meaola. *Micro~.* Meaola māiki.

organophosphate 'Oraganoposopahate.

organ pipe cactus Pānini 'okana.

orientation *As of a page in a computer program.* Kuana pepa. *Landscape ~.* Kuana moe. *Portrait ~.* Kuana kū.

origin *Of the world; creation.* Kumu honua. *See creation. Of a graph.* Piko pakuhi, piko. *Root, source, or derivation, as the etymology of a word.* Molekumu.

original *Also master copy, a master used for making additional copies.* Kope kumu.

original jurisdiction *In law.* Mana ho'okolokolo maka mua.

oriole Manu 'oliō.

oris *See orbicularis oris.*

ornament Wehi. *Christmas tree ~.* Wehi lā'au Kalikimaka. *See Christmas ball.*

orographic *Dealing with mountains.* Pili pali. *~ rainfall.* Ua pili pali.

oropharynx *The lower part of the pharynx contiguous to the mouth, in anatomy.* Haka moni o waena. *See pharynx.*

orthodontist Kauka ho'opololei niho.

osteopathy *Also to practice osteopathy.* Ha'iha'i iwi. *Osteopath.* Kauka ha'iha'i iwi.

ostracod *A tiny crustacean having a shrimplike body enclosed in a hinged bivalve shell.* 'Oliliko.

otter 'Ota.

ounce 'Auneki. *Abb.* 'an. *Fluid ~.* 'Auneki wai. *Abb.* 'an w.

out *In baseball.* 'Auka. *To tag or strike ~.* Hō'auka. *In volleyball.* Hala akula i waho. *Side ~.* Hā'awi i ke kinipōpō i kekahi 'ao'ao. *Time ~, in team sports such as volleyball.* Manawa ho'omaha.

outcome *A possible result in a probability experiment, in math.* Hopena. *Equally likely ~s.* Like ka papaha o nā mea e loa'a ana.

outdoor Kaupokulani. *See indoor. ~ concert.* 'Aha mele kaupokulani. *~ market.* Mākeke kaupokulani. *~ sport.* Ha'uki kaupokulani.

outer planet Hōkūhele o waho loa.

outlaw Mea pale kānāwai. *To break laws, act as an ~.* Pale Kānāwai. *To make something illegal.* Pāpā kānāwai.

outlet *Electrical ~.* Puka uila. *See plug.*

outline *A summary using letters and numbers in headings to indicate topics and subtopics.* 'Oloke'a. *See Hawaiian entry 'oloke'a. Document ~, as in a computer program.* 'Oloke'a palapala. *To ~.* Hō'oloke'a.

outline *As a line marking the outer limits of an object or figure.* Mahaka. *To ~, as type on a computer or in typesetting.* Hoʻomeheu. *Outlined.* Meheu.

output *As in a computer program.* Huapuka. *See input. To ~.* Kāhuapuka. *To ~ data.* Kāhuapuka ʻikepili. *~ device.* Hāmeʻa huapuka.

outside set *To make an ~, in volleyball.* Hānai lōʻihi.

outward Haʻawaho.

oval Pōʻai lōʻihi, ʻololaha. *See ellipse.*

ovary Lōkino huaʻine. *See ovulate, ovum.*

oven *Broiler ~.* ʻOma kōʻala. *Microwave ~.* ʻOmawawe.

overalls *Coveralls.* Lole wāwae kāʻawe, lole wāwae ʻepane.

overdose *To ~ on drugs.* Pākela ʻai lāʻau.

overestimate Kohoʻoi. *See underestimate.*

overflow error *As on a calculator display.* Hū.

overlap *As shingles on a roof.* ʻUnuʻunu. *See flush.*

override *To ~, as in a computer program.* Mauʻaʻe.

over-the-counter Kūʻai wale. *See prescription. ~ drug or medication.* Lāʻau kūʻai wale.

over the line *In volleyball.* Kaʻahi hewa, keʻehi hewa.

overtime Kaulele. *~ pay.* Uku kaulele. *~ hours.* Hola kaulele. *~ work.* Hana kaulele.

ovipositor ʻŌ hāʻule hua.

ovoid Paʻaʻololaha.

ovulate Hoʻokuʻu huaʻine. *See ovary, ovum.*

ovum *In biology.* Huaʻine. *See ovary, ovulate, sperm.*

owl *Elf ~.* Pueo peke. *Great horned ~.* Pueo kiwi hulu. *~ monkey.* Keko pueo.

Oxford *Saddle shoe.* Kāmaʻa ʻili helei.

oxide ʻOkesaside. *Cupric ~.* Kupuriku ʻokesaside. *Ferric ~.* Feriku ʻokesaside. *Ferrosoferric ~.* Ferosoferiku ʻokesaside. *Ferrous ~.* Ferousa ʻokesaside.

oxidize *Also oxidized.* Kāʻokikene.

oxilate *Calcium ~.* Kalipuna ʻokesailihate.

oxygen ʻOkikene. *~ tank.* Kini ʻokikene. *~-carbon dioxide cycle.* Pōʻaiapuni ʻokikene kalapona ʻokikene lua.

oyster *Edible ~.* Kupekio. *Pearl ~.* Pipi.

ozone ʻOkikene kolu. *~-sensitive fabric.* Lole ana ʻokikene kolu.

P

Pacific *Western ~ Fishery Management Council.* ʻAha Hoʻomalu Lawaiʻa o ka Pākīpika Komohana.

Pacific Ocean Moana Pākīpika.

pack *To ~, as a suitcase.* ʻŪlū.

pack *For items other than drinks, as gum, baseball cards, or cigarettes.* ʻOpe. *See case, six-pack, twelve-pack. Four-~.* ʻOpe hā. *Six-~.* ʻOpe ono.

pack saddle Noho ʻāmana.

pad *Brake ~.* Pale peleki. *See launch pad.*

page ʻAoʻao. *Abb.* ʻao. *Cover ~, as in a computer document.* ʻAoʻao hoʻākāka. *~ break.* Hoʻokaʻawale ʻaoʻao. *~ guide.* Kuhi lihi. *~ setup.* Hoʻokuene ʻaoʻao.

pail Pākeke liʻiliʻi. *Lunch ~.* Kini ʻaiō, kini ʻai.

paint *Also the area within the key below the free throw line on a basketball court.* Pena. *See spray paint. ~ brush.* Hulu pena. *~ roller.* Lola pena. *To ~ with a roller.* Pena lola. *Tempera ~.* Pena pelaha. *Water-base ~.* Pena kuapapa wai.

pair *Number ~, in math.* Paʻa helu. *See action-reaction pair. Ordered ~.* Paʻa helu kuhikuhina. *To ~ off.* Hoʻokūlua.

pajamas *Nightgown.* Lole moe pō.

Pakistan *Also Pakistani.* Pakitana.

palaʻai Pumpkin. See *squash.*

palate *In linguistics.* Palaku. *Hard ~.* Palaku iwi. *Soft ~.* Palaku kīleo.

Paleolithic *In anthropology.* Haku kā pahi. *~ age, period.* Ke au haku kā pahi.

paleontology Hulimōʻalihaku. *Paleontologist.* Kanaka hulimōʻalihaku, mea hulimōʻalihaku.

palette *As in a computer program.* Papa pena.

palindrome Huaaka.

palm *To carry or ~ (the ball), in basketball.* Poholuna.

Palmyra island Honuaiākea.

pamphlet *Also brochure, flyer.* Pepelu.

pan *Baking ~.* Pā ʻoma *(preceded by* ke*).* *Frying ~.* Pā palai *(preceded by* ke*).* *Sauce ~.* Ipuhao hana kai. See *handle.*

pan *To ~, as with a movie or video camera.* Paʻi kāhela *(preceded by* ke*).*

Panama *Also Panamanian.* Panamā.

pancake *Unleavened ~.* Palaoa linalina. *~ turner, spatula.* ʻŪlau.

pancake dig *In volleyball.* ʻAli ʻūlau.

panda Pea Kina. See *teddy bear.*

panel Pānela. See *paneling. Control ~, on a computer.* Papa hoʻoholo. *Solar ~.* ʻŪomo ikehu lā.

paneling Papa pānela. *Wood ~.* Papa pānela lāʻau.

pant *To ~, as a dog.* Haha.

papain *An enzyme found in papayas and used as a meat tenderizer.* Papaina.

paper Pepa. See entries below and *posterboard. Butcher ~.* Pepa lole pipi. *Carbon ~.* Pepa ʻōpaʻu. *Construction ~.* Pepaānue. *Corrugated ~.* Pepa pahu. *~ bag.* Pūʻolo pepa. *~ clip.* Pine pepa. *~ tape.* Leki pepa. *~ towel dispenser.* ʻŪhōloʻa kāwele pepa.

paper *Legal-size ~.* Pepa loio. *Letter-size ~.* Pepa leka. *Tabloid ~.* Pepa 11" X 17" *(pronounced* pepa ʻumikūmākahi ʻīniha i ka ʻumikūmāhiku ʻīniha). *~ tray or cassette in a computer printer.* Poho pepa. *~ tray slot.* ʻĀpoʻo poho pepa.

paper *Graph ~, grid ~.* Pepa makaʻaha. *Base-ten grid ~.* Pepa makaʻaha kumu hoʻohui pāʻumi. *Isometric dot ~.* Pepa kiko analike. *Linear unit ~.* Pepa anakuhi lālani. *Litmus ~, for measuring pH.* Pepa ana ʻakika. See *chromatography.*

paper shell *Foraminiferans.* Unahione.

paperweight Hekau pepa.

papier mâché Pepa paluhē.

Papua New Guinea *Also Papua New Guinean.* Pāpua Nūkini.

papyrus Kaluhā.

parabola *Also parabolic.* Palapola. See *directrix. Parabolic curve.* Uma palapola.

parachute Haʻupoho.

paradise *Bird of ~, the bird.* Manu palekaiko. *The flower.* Pua manu.

paraffin Uepa ihoiho.

paragraph Paukū. See *phrase. ~ symbol (¶).* Poʻo hou *(preceded by* ke*). A line written from the end of one ~ to the beginning of the next ~ to indicate that the two ~s should be combined, in proofreading.* Kaha hopu. *To ~, as in written compositions.* Paukūkū.

Paraguay *Also Paraguayan.* Palakuae, Paraguae.

parakeet Pālokeʻiʻi.

parallel Pilipā. See entries below and *balance beam. ~ lines.* Nā kaha pilipā. *~ bars.* Lāʻau kaulua. *Even ~ bars.* Lāʻau kaulua kaulike. *Uneven ~ bars.* Lāʻau kaulua kaulike ʻole.

parallel *An imaginary circle on the earth's surface ~ to the equator and designated in degrees of latitude.* Laina lakikū, laina latitū.

parallel *As of a computer port.* Ala pilipā. *~ port.* Awa ala pilipā.

parallelogram Huinahā pilipā.

paraphrase *To ~ orally.* Haʻi hou ma kekahi ʻano. *In writing.* Kākau hou ma kekahi ʻano.

parasite *Also to live as a parasite.* Omoola. See *host.*

parasitic worm *General term.* Koʻe omoola. See *heartworm, nematode, roundworm, tapeworm, etc.*

parenthesis Kahaapo. See *bracket. Open ~.* Kahaapo wehe. *Close ~.* Kahaapo pani.

parenthood *Planned ~; also family planning, population control.* Kaupalena hānau. See *pro-choice, pro-life.*

parent rock *Rocks in upper surface of the earth which break down to form rocks, sand, dirt, etc.* Pōhaku makua.

park *Amusement ~.* Pāka kāniwala. *Department of ~s and Recreation.* ʻOihana o nā Pāka a me nā Hana Hoʻonanea. *National ~.* Pāka aupuni. *National ~ Service.* ʻOihana Pāka Aupuni. *Glacier National ~.* Pāka Aupuni ʻo Hauneneʻe. *Hawaiʻi Volcanoes National ~.* Pāka Aupuni ʻo Kīlauea. *Yosemite National ~.* Pāka Aupuni ʻo ʻIosemite. *State ~.* Pāka mokuʻāina. *~ keeper.* Kahu pāka.

parking meter Mīka kāki. *Metered parking or any parking for which there is a charge.* Kū kāki.

Parmesan Pamesana. *~ cheese.* Waiūpaʻa pamesana.

parrot Pāloke, manu pāloke.

parrotbill *Maui ~, pseudonestor xanthophrys.* Kīkēkoa.

parsley Pakalī.

part *Also division, piece, portion, department, category, land division; to divide, apportion.* Māhele. *Fractional ~.* Māhele hapa. *One-half ~.* Māhele hapalua.

particle *As in an atom.* Huna. See *proton, electron, neutron. Alpha ~, a positively charged particle made up of two protons and two neutrons.* Huna ʻālepa. *Beta ~, a negatively charged electron moving at high speed.* Huna beta. *Visible airborne ~s, as from a spray can.* Ehu kīkina. See *substance.*

partitioning *Disk ~, in a computer hard drive.* Māhele pā.

party *Majority ~, in politics.* ʻAoʻao hapa nui. *Minority ~.* ʻAoʻao hapa ʻuʻuku. *Political ~.* ʻAoʻao kālaiʻāina. *Two-~ system of government.* Aupuni ʻaoʻao ʻelua.

party favor Alelomoʻo.

pass *In mountains.* Nuku. See entry below and *passageway, trail.*

pass *To ~, in basketball.* Kīloi. *Back-door ~.* Kīloi palemo. *Behind-the-back ~.* Kīloi kua. *Blind ~, no-look ~.* Kīloi hoʻopalai. *Bounce ~.* Kīloi papahele. *Chest ~.* Kīloi umauma. *Hook ~.* Kīloi ʻaoʻao. *Inbound ~.* Kīloi ulele. *Lead ~.* Kīloi ulele kikī, kīloi kaha. *Lob ~.* Kīloi piʻo. *Tip ~.* Kīloi papaʻi. *Touch ~.* Hoʻopāhiʻa. See *baseball pass. First ~, in volleyball; also to receive a serve.* Kiʻi. *~ through the block.* Hala ka pālulu.

passage *Initiation, as into a group.* Komo pae. See *initiate. Rite of ~.* Hana komo pae.

passageway *Narrow ~, as in a canyon.* Hānuku.

pass out See *deal.*

passport Palapala holo ʻāina ʻē.

pasta Nulu ʻĪkālia. See *noodle.*

paste Tuko keʻokeʻo. See *glue, rubber cement.*

pathogen *A disease-producing agent.* Mūhune ʻino. See *antibiotic.*

patriotism *Also nationalism.* Aloha ʻāina.

patron Mea mahalo pānaʻi. See *patronage.*

patronage *A political system in which party leaders do favors for loyal supporters.* Mahalo pānaʻi. See *patron.*

pattern *Repeating series.* Lauana. *Number* ~. Lauana helu. *As a word or sentence* ~ *in Hawaiian grammar.* Analula. ~ *book, as for teaching grammatical* ~s *in reading.* Puke aʻo analula. *Settlement* ~, *in geography.* Lauana hoʻokahua.

pave *To* ~ *with asphalt.* Hoʻūnukā. See *asphalt.*

payload bay *The part of a spacecraft where scientific instruments and passengers are carried.* ʻOneki hana.

payment *For services; also to compensate, i.e. to make amends for loss or damage.* Uku pānaʻi.

pea Pāpapa poepoe.

peanut *Also groundnut or any edible nut.* Pīneki, pineki, pīnaki. ~ *brittle.* Pakē pīneki. ~ *butter.* Pīnekipaka.

pear *Usually Bartlett* ~. Pea pakeleke. See *avocado.*

Pearl and Hermes Reef Holoikauaua.

pearl oyster Pipi. See *oyster.*

peat ʻElenahu.

peck *A unit of measurement.* Peka.

pectoralis major *A muscle of the upper chest.* Mākala uma nui.

pectoralis minor *A muscle of the upper chest.* Mākala uma iki.

pedagogy *The art of teaching.* Kiʻina aʻo.

pedal Mea hehi wāwae.

pedicab Kalaikikala lawe ʻōhua.

pedometer Ana hele wāwae.

peel *To* ~, *as an orange or taro.* Ihi. *As a banana; to strip.* Uhole. *Easy to* ~, *as small corms of cooked taro.* Pohole.

peeling *To be* ~, *as skin from sunburn.* ʻAkaʻakaʻa.

peer *To look narrowly or searchingly at something.* Kiʻei, ʻōwī.

peers *Jury of* ~, *as in court trials.* Kiule hoa kupa.

peewee *Wood* ~, *a kind of bird.* Manu pīuīlāʻau.

peg *As for tuning stringed instruments.* Kī. *Wooden* ~. Kui lāʻau.

pelvis *Hip bone.* Iwi kā. See *ilium, ischium.*

pen Peni, peni ʻīnika. *Fine point* ~. Peni makakui. *Fountain* ~. Peni pāuma. *Marsh or felt* ~. Peni kuni. ~ *cap.* Poʻi peni (*preceded by* ke).

pencil See *eyebrow pencil. Colored* ~. Penikala kala.

pendulum Uleʻo. See *amplitude, bob, swing. Period of a* ~. Wā ʻukē.

penis See *baculum.*

Pennsylvania *Also Pennsylvanian.* Penekelewinia, Peneselevinia.

pennyroyal *A kind of flower.* Penialiʻi.

pension Uku hoʻomau. *To draw or take a* ~. Lawe i ka uku hoʻomau.

pentagon Huinalima.

pentathalon ʻĀlapakonalima. See *decathalon, triathalon.*

pentomino *In math.* Penatomino.

pepperoni Pepaloni.

percent *Also percentage.* Pākēneka. See entry below and *markup, rate.*

Percent Daily Value *Formerly known as percentage of US Recommended Daily Allowances (USRDA).* Pākēneka o ka papaʻai.

percolate *To* ~, *as water passing through a porous substance.* Manono.

per diem *A daily allowance for living expenses while traveling in connection with one's work.* Uku ola lā, ola lā.

Peregrine falcon Palekona kāluʻu.

performance-based learning *Also kinesthetic-based learning.* Aʻo kahua lawena. *See Hawaiian entries beginning with* aʻo kahua.

performing art Pāhiahia.

perimeter *In math.* Anapuni. *Abb.* anp.

period *In punctuation.* Kiko pau. *Each set of three numerals, in math.* Poke. *Of a pendulum.* Wā ʻukē.

period *Also age, epoch, era, as in athropology.* Au. *See Eolithic, Paleolithic, Mesolithic, Neolithic, Aeneolithic.*

periosteum *The tough membrane adhering tightly to a bone.* Niniki wahī iwi.

peripherals *Or accessories, as for a computer.* Lakolako.

Periplaneta ~ *americana, American cockroach.* ʻElelū kīkēkē. ~ *australasiae, Australian cockroach.* ʻElelū Nūhōlani.

permanent resident *As an alien residing in one country over an extended period of time.* Malihini noho loa.

permeable *Also permeability.* Nono.

permutation *A selection of objects from a set in a particular order, in math; also to permute.* Kake kaʻina. *See entry below.*

permutatorial coefficient *In math.* Haʻi kake kaʻina. *See coefficient.*

peroxide Perokesaside. *Hydrogen* ~ *(H₂O₂).* Haikokene lua ʻokikene lua.

perpendicular *In math.* Kūpono. ~ *bisector.* Kaha ʻoki hapalua kūpono. ~ *lines.* Nā kaha kūpono.

Perseus *A constellation.* Ānui.

personal foul *In team sports such as basketball.* Kuʻia pilikino. *See foul.*

person-to-person call *Also to make such a call.* Kelepona inoa. *See Hawaiian entries under kelepona.*

perspective Kuanaʻike.

persuade *To induce change of opinion.* Hoʻohuli manaʻo. *See persuasive speech.*

persuasive speech Haʻiʻōlelo hoʻohuli manaʻo. *See speech.*

Peru *Also Peruvian.* Pelū, Perū.

pest *Any plant or animal detrimental to humans or their interests.* Haipilikia. *See pesticide.*

pesticide Lāʻau make haipilikia, lāʻau haipilikia.

pet Hānaiahuhu. ~ *shop.* Hale kūʻai hānaiahuhu.

petri dish Pā piki *(preceded by ke).*

petrolatum *Vaseline.* Kele hoʻopaheʻe.

petroleum ʻAila kā, ʻaila tā.

petting zoo Kahua hamohamo holoholona.

petty cash Kālā kini.

petunia Pekunia.

phalanx *One of the bones of the fingers.* Iwi manamana lima. *One of the bones of the toes.* Iwi manamana wāwae.

Pharaoh Palaʻo. *See kingdom.*

pharynx *In anatomy.* Haka moni. *Laryngo~, i.e. the lower part of the ~ adjacent to the larynx.* Haka moni o lalo. *Naso~, i.e. the portion of the ~ behind the nasal cavity and above the soft palate.* Haka moni o luna. *Oro~, i.e. the lower part of the ~ contiguous to the mouth.* Haka moni o waena.

phase ʻEpaki. ~ *of the moon (Western concept).* ʻEpaki mahina.

Philippines ʻĀina Pilipino, ʻĀina Pinopino. *See Filipino.*

Philippine Sea Ke Kai Pilipino.

philodendron ʻAʻapehihi lau liʻi. *See pothos.*

philosophy Kālaimanaʻo.

phloem Kikiʻuʻai. *See xylem.*

Phobos *A moon of Mars.* Popoka.

Phoebe *The most distant moon of Saturn.* Poepe.

phone *In linguistics.* Puanaleo. *See Hawaiian entries under kelepona.*

phoneme *In linguistics.* Hualeo.

phonics ʻApo kani kākau.

phonology *In linguistics.* Kālaileo.

phosphate Posapahate.

phosphorescent *Also fluorescent.* Hāweo.

phosphorus Posoporusa.

photograph Ki'i pa'i. *Negative of a ~.* Akaki'i. *To take, shoot, or snap a picture, either still or motion.* Pa'i ki'i. *~er.* Mea pa'i ki'i.

photolysis Kā'amawāhiwai. See *photosynthesis.*

photosynthesis Kā'ama'ai.

phrase *In grammar.* Lālā. See *paragraph. In literary or general use.* Māmala'ōlelo. *To ~, as in speaking or reading orally.* Puana māmala. *As in written compositions.* Kūkulu māmala.

physalia *Portuguese man-of-war.* Pa'i, pa'imalau. See *blue-button, by-the-wind sailor.*

physical *As a scientific term relating to ~ matter.* Paku. *~ properties.* Nā 'anopili paku. *~ science.* Kālaiaopaku

physical education Mākau kino.

physical therapy *To provide ~.* Pākōlea. *Physical therapist.* Mea pākōlea, kanaka pākōlea.

physician *Coordinated ~ referral system.* 'Ōnaehana kauka no ka lapa'au like 'ana.

physics Kālaikūlohea.

pi π, *in math.* Pai.

piccolo Pikolō.

pick *Dentist's probe.* 'Ōhiki kauka niho. *To ~, as an 'ukulele or guitar.* Hiku, panapana.

pick and roll *In basketball; to make such a play.* 'Āke'a 'ūniu.

pico- *A prefix meaning one trillionth (p).* Hapa kiliona. *Abb.* hkl. See *deci-, centi-, milli-, micro-, nano-.*

pictogram *Also pictograph, as in a computer program.* Pakuhi ki'i.

pictograph *Also pictogram, as in a computer program.* Pakuhi ki'i.

picture frame Mōlina ki'i.

pie *Pot ~.* Kinipai.

piece *Also division, portion, department, category, part, land division; to divide, apportion.* Māhele.

pie chart *As for showing statistics.* Pakuhi pai.

pier block *In construction.* Palaka kimeki. See *termite block.*

piggy bank Panakō hale.

pigment Kaukala. *~ grain, in biology.* Huna kaukala.

pill *To take a ~.* Inu i ka huaale, 'ai i ka huaale.

pillow Uluna. *~case.* Pale uluna.

pin *Bowling ~.* Pine maika. *Safety ~.* Pine kaiapa.

piñata Piniaka, piniata.

pinch clamp 'Ūmi'i pani.

pin cushion Pulu kui.

pine *Conifer or any tree which resembles a ~.* Paina, paina lau kukuna, paina tidara. See *cypress, ironwood. Cook ~.* Kumu paina Kuke, paina Kuke.

pineapple Hala kahiki, paina'āpala. See *polyethylene. ~ crown.* 'Ēlau hala kahiki, 'ēlau paina'āpala.

ping-pong *Table tennis.* Kenika pākaukau.

Pinnacles *Gardner ~.* Pūhāhonu.

pinniped *Any of the suborder of aquatic mammals including the seal and walrus.* 'Ohana sila.

pint Paina. *Abb.* pin.

pinwheel *A toy.* Pelahū.

pipe *Used to hold up clear plastic sheeting over an aquaculture tank.* Paipu ko'o. See *Hawaiian entries under* paipu *and* plumber, tap water.

pipe cement *Plastic ~.* Tuko paipu 'ea, tuko paipu. See *primer.*

pipe fitting Ku'i paipu.

pipette Paipuli'i. *Capillary ~.* Paipuli'i 'umelauoho.

pipe wrench Kala paipu.

pitch Kēpau kā. See entries below and *asphalt compound.*

pitch *To make a ~, as a sales ~, or to "sell" an idea.* Paialou.

pitch *In linguistics and music.* Ki'eleo. See *capo.* *High ~.* Ki'eleo ki'eki'e. *Low ~.* Ki'eleo ha'aha'a.

pivot *As a position in basketball; also ~ point.* Kū 'ūniu. *To ~.* 'Ūniu.

pizza Pai pika, pika.

place *~ value, usually in compound terms.* Kūana. *~ value of a number.* Kūana helu. *Ones.* Kūana 'ekahi. *Tens.* Kūana 'umi. *Hundreds.* Kūana haneli. *Decimal ~.* Kūana kekimala.

plain *An expanse of flat land.* Kula laulaha, 'āina kula laulaha. See *plateau.*

plain *Clear, intelligible.* Mōakāka.

plaintiff Mea ho'opi'i. See entry below and *prosecution, prosecutor.*

plaintiff attorney *Also prosecutor, prosecuting attorney.* Loio ho'opi'i. See *defense attorney, plaintiff.*

plaiting *Twill ~.* Maka pūalu, 'o'eno.

plan Papa hana. *Particularly one which involves thought and decision-making.* Papa ho'olālā. See *short-range, medium-range, long-range.*

planaria Ko'e pāki'i.

plane *Coordinate ~, in math.* Papa kuhikuhina.

plane figure *A figure that lies on a flat surface, in math.* Kinona papa. See *geometric figure, space figure.*

planet Hōkūhele. *Jovian ~.* Hōkūhele Iowiana. *Outer ~.* Hōkūhele o waho loa.

planetarium Hale a'o kilo hōkū. See *observatory.*

plankton 'Ōulaula

planned parenthood *Also family planning, population control.* Kaupalena hānau. See *pro-choice, pro-life.*

planning *County ~ Department.* Ke'ena Ho'olālā o ke Kalana. *Hawai'i State Department of ~ and Economic Development.* 'Oihana Ho'olālā a me ka Ho'omohala Waiwai o ka Moku'āina 'o Hawai'i. *~ skill.* Mākau ho'olālā.

plant Meakanu. See *crop.* *Flowering ~.* Meakanu pua.

planter *As for growing plants.* Pahu ho'oulu meakanu.

planthopper *Oliarus tamehameha.* 'Ūmi'ilau.

planting medium 'Elekanu. See *potting soil.*

plaque *A commemorative tablet.* Pāhai. See *trophy.*

plasma Palasema, wai koko.

plaster of Paris Puna Pālisa.

plastic 'Ea. *~ bag.* 'Eke 'ea (*preceded by* ke). *Any ~ film for wrapping food, as Saran Wrap.* Wahī 'ea. *~ sheeting, general term.* Hāli'i 'ea. See *polyethyline.*

plastic pipe cement Tuko paipu 'ea, tuko paipu. See *primer.*

plastid *Tiny structures inside plant cells that contain pigment as well as chlorophyll.* Palasika.

plate *Geologic ~.* Una honua. See *base (in baseball).* *Cocos ~.* Ka Una Honua Kokosa. *Eurasian ~.* Ka Una Honua 'Eulāsia. *Indo-Australian ~.* Ka Una Honua 'Inionūhōlani. *Nazca ~.* Ka Una Honua Naseka.

plateau *High level land.* Nu'u laulaha. See *plain.*

platelet Pāhune (*preceded by* ke).

plate techtonics *In geology.* Ku'ina una honua. See *boundary, convergent, divergent, transform.*

platform *A declaration of principles and policies adopted by a political party or candidate.* Kahua kālai'āina.

platform *As DOS, UNIX, Macintosh, etc., for a computer program.* Pae. See *operating system.*

platinum Palakiniuma.

play *As a particular maneuver in a sporting event; to execute a ~.* Ka'ane'e.

play *Dramatic* ~. Hana keaka paiwa.

Play-Doh Palēkō. See *clay*.

player *Record* ~. Mīkini hoʻokani pāleo, mīkini pāleo. See *recorder*. *Cassette* ~. Mīkini hoʻokani lola, mīkini lola. *Reel-to-reel tape* ~. Mīkini hoʻokani pōkaʻa, mīkini pōkaʻa leo.

playoff *As in sporting events.* Hoʻokūkū moho.

plea bargain *As in the negotiation of an agreement between a prosecutor and a defendant.* Kūkā hoʻēmiemi.

plexiglass Aniani ʻea. See *fiberglass*.

pliers Palaea, palaea huki.

plot *Chart or graph, in math.* Pakuhi. See *Hawaiian entries under* pakuhi *and* chart, graph. *To* ~ *or chart.* Kākuhi. *Stem and leaf* ~. Pakuhi ʻau me ka lau.

plug Palaka. See *outlet, prong, spark plug. Electrical* ~. Palaka uila. *Two-pronged* ~. Palaka niho lua. *Three-pronged* ~. Palaka niho kolu.

plug-in *As in a computer program.* Kuʻina koʻo.

plumber Kanaka hoʻomoe paipu, wilipaipu.

plunge pool Kiʻo wai wailele.

plunger *As for cleaning clogged drains.* Pāuma lua. *Syringe* ~. ʻŪkaomi hano kui, ʻūkaomi, ʻūkōmi hano kui, ʻūkōmi.

plus sign Kaha hui.

Pluto *The planet.* ʻIlioki.

plywood Papa ʻililahi. *For building boats.* Papawai.

p.m. *Post meridium.* P.m. (*pronounced* pīmū). See *a.m.*

pneumonia Nūmōnia.

PO *Purchase order.* Palapala ʻoka kūʻai.

pocket compass Pānānā paʻa lima.

pocket veto *A way in which the President can veto a bill by holding onto the bill for ten days, during which time Congress ends its session.* Kīpoʻi.

pod *Seed* ~. Wahī ʻanoʻano.

podium Pākau, pākau haʻiʻōlelo.

poem *Also poetry, general term.* Mele (*preceded by* ke).

poetry *Also poem.* Mele (*preceded by* ke). *Traditional elements of Hawaiian* ~, *story telling, oratory, and narration.* Meiwi.

pogo stick Aeʻolele.

poi *Residue of* ~ *after pounding.* Kale ʻai. *To take up* ~ *with the fingers.* Miki.

poinsettia Pua Kalikimaka.

point *As in a game or sporting event.* ʻAi. See *entries below and basket, pivot, score, touchback, touchdown.* ~ *for Mea.* Lilo ka ʻai iā Mea. ~ *after touchdown, in football.* ʻAi manuahi. ~ *after by passing or running.* ʻAi manuahi holo. ~ *after by kicking.* ʻAi manuahi peku. ~ *from block, dink, or spike, in volleyball.* ʻAi hele wale.

point *In math; also a unit of measurement for type size.* Kiko. See *decimal, referent. To graph the* ~. Kākuhi i ke kiko. *Reference* ~. Kiko kuhia.

point *Boiling* ~. Kēkelē paila. *Freezing* ~. Kēkelē paʻahau. *Melting* ~. Kēkelē heheʻe. *Fine* ~, *fine line, as of a pen* ~. Makakui. *To* ~, *as a mouse arrow in a computer program.* Kuhikuhi. See *pointer*.

pointer *Also mouse arrow or cursor, as in a computer program.* Nahau ʻiole, nahau. *As used in a classroom.* Lāʻau kuhikuhi.

point guard *Also one man, in basketball.* Kūkahi. See *guard*.

points *The four cardinal* ~, *or four primary directions of the compass, in geography.* Nā kūkulu ʻehā.

point source pollution Kumu hoʻohaumia ʻike ʻia. *Non-*~. Kumu hoʻohaumia ʻike ʻole ʻia.

poison Lāʻau make. See *aldrin, curare, dieldrin, fumigant, systemic insecticide.* *Contact ~.* Lāʻau make pā ʻili. *Stomach ~.* Lāʻau make ʻai.

poka *Banana ~.* Poka maiʻa.

pokeweed Pīʻai poku.

Poland *Also Pole, Polish.* Pōlani.

polar bear Pea ʻĀlika.

pole Wēlau. *North ~.* Wēlau ʻākau. *South ~.* Wēlau hema. *Elevation ~, as for surveying.* Lāʻau ana kiʻekiʻena. See *sighter. Range ~, surveying rod.* Lāʻau ana ʻāina.

pole vault Koʻo lele. *To ~.* Lele koʻo.

police badge Pihi mākaʻi *(preceded by* ke).

policy Kulekele. *Domestic ~.* Kulekele kūloko. *Foreign ~.* Kulekele ʻāina ʻē.

polio Poliō.

polish *A substance used to give smoothness or shine.* Mea hoʻohinuhinu. See *wax.*

political party ʻAoʻao kālaiʻāina. See *majority party, minority party.*

poll *Also to take a ~.* Anamanaʻo.

pollen Ehu. See *pollinate. Flower ~.* Ehu pua.

pollinate Hoʻēhu pua. See *pollen. Cross-~.* Hoʻēhu pua kaʻakepa.

polliwog *Tadpole.* Polewao.

pollution Haumia. *Air ~.* Haumia ea. *Source ~.* Kumu hoʻohaumia. *Point source ~.* Kumu hoʻohaumia ʻike ʻia. *Non-point source ~.* Kumu hoʻohaumia ʻike ʻole ʻia.

poly- *A prefix for chemical terms.* Polai-. *See entries below.*

polychaete worm *A kind of worm found underneath stream rocks.* Moeʻalā, koʻe moeʻalā.

polyethylene ʻEa painaʻāpala. See *plastic sheeting.*

polygon Huinalehulehu. *Regular ~.* Huinalehulehu analahi.

polyhedron *A space figure with many faces, in math.* Paʻaʻili lehulehu, paʻaʻili.

Polynesia *French ~.* Polenekia Palani.

polyphosphate Polaiposapahate.

polytheism *Also polytheistic.* Akua lehulehu. See *monotheism.*

polyunsaturated fat ʻAilakele laupaʻahapa. See *fat.*

pomace fly *Family Drosophilidae.* Pōnalo.

pomelo Pomelo. See *grapefruit, jabong.*

pompom Pōpō kīlepalepa, kīlepelepa.

pond *Large ~, lake.* Māluawai. *~ mud.* Pohō.

pony Lio pone.

pool *Of water, as in a stream.* Kiʻo wai. *Plunge ~.* Kiʻo wai wailele. *Anchialine ~.* Ālialia nono. *Side ~, as in a stream.* Wai wiliau. *Swimming ~.* Pūnāwai ʻauʻau.

pool cue Kiu pahupahu.

popover Palaoa pūhaʻuhaʻu.

pop-pops *Fireworks that explode on impact.* Lūpahū.

poppy *California ~.* Papi. *~ flower.* Pua papi.

popsicle. ʻAikalima ʻau.

population *As in biology.* Pūʻuo. *~ density, for humans only.* Paʻapū pūʻuo kanaka. *~ distribution, in geography.* Ili pūʻuo, ili pūʻuo kanaka.

population control *Also planned parenthood, family planning.* Kaupalena hānau. See *pro-choice, pro-life.*

pop-up book *As for children's stories.* Puke kiʻi kū.

pop-up menu *As in a computer program.* Papa ʻōʻili.

porcupine Kīpoka.

pore Pukapakī.

port *As in a computer.* Awa. *Parallel ~.* Awa ala pilipā. *Serial ~.* Awa ala pūkaʻina.

port *Left or ~ side of a double-hulled canoe or a ship when looking forward.* Ama. See *starboard*.

portable Lawelima. See *laptop computer*.

portion *Also division, piece, department, category, part, land division; to divide, apportion.* Māhele.

portrait orientation *As of a page in a computer program.* Kuana kū. See *landscape orientation*.

Portugal Pokukala, Potugala.

Portuguese cypress Paina Pukikī, paina tireza.

Portuguese man-of-war *Physalia.* Paʻi, paʻimalau. See *blue-button, by-the-wind-sailor*.

portulaca ʻĀkulikuli kula.

positive *As of an electrical charge or north pole of a magnet.* ʻĀne. See *negative, neutral. ~ number, in math.* Helu ʻiʻo. *~ integer.* Helu piha ʻiʻo.

possibility See *chance*.

possum See *opossum*.

post- *After-.* Muli. See *after, postcolonial, posttest*.

post *High ~, in basketball.* Kūliu waho. *Low ~.* Kūliu loko.

postage Uku leka.

postcard Kāleka poʻoleka.

postcolonial Muli panalāʻau. *~ country.* Kaumokuʻāina muli panalāʻau, ʻāina muli panalāʻau.

poster Pelaha.

posterboard Pepa mānoanoa.

posterior *In biology.* Lauhope. See *anterior, dorsal, ventral. ~ dorsal fin, of a fish.* Kualā lauhope.

post-larvae Pua.

post meridium *P.m.* P.m. *(pronounced* pīmū). See *ante meridium*.

posttest Hōʻike muli aʻo. See *pretest*.

pot See *flower pot*.

potash *Potassium carbonate or potassium insoluble compounds.* Pokala.

potassium Potasiuma. *~ cyanide.* Potasiuma kaianaside. *~ iodide.* Potasiuma ʻiodiside.

potato chip Kipi ʻuala kahiki.

potatoes *Hash-brown ~.* ʻUala kahiki kolikoli, ʻuala kolikoli. *Scalloped ~.* ʻUala kahiki pepeiao, ʻuala pepeiao.

potential Palena papaha. *~ energy.* Ikehu noho.

pothos ʻAʻapehihi. See *philodendron*.

pot pie Kinipai.

potting soil Lepo kanu meakanu. See *planting medium*.

Poughkeepsie Pakipi.

pound *Unit of weight.* Paona. *Abb.* pon.

pound sign *A sign (#) used in proofreading to indicate that a space should be inserted; a superscript number written next to the symbol indicates the number of spaces if more than one (#²).* Kaha kaʻahua. See *caret*.

powder *Face ~.* Pauka helehelena. *To put on face ~.* Hana i ka pauka helehelena, kau i ka pauka helehelena.

powdered milk Waiū ehu, waiū pauka.

power Ikehu. See *entries below and energy. Hydroelectric ~.* Ikehu uila wai kahe. *Solar ~.* Manehu lā. *Thermo-electric ~.* Ikehu uila puhi wāwahie.

power *A product in which each factor is the same, in math.* Pāhoʻonui. See *exponent*.

power *Concurrent ~, as powers shared by federal and state governments.* Mana ʻālike. *Delegated ~s, as of Congress.* Mana ʻākuleana.

power forward *Also four man, in basketball.* Kūhā.

powers *Legislative ~.* Mana kau kānāwai.

pox *Chicken ~.* Puʻupuʻu moa.

practical life skill Mākau ola.

practice Ho‘oma‘ama‘a. ~ *book*. Puke ho‘oma‘ama‘a ha‘awina, puke ho‘oma‘ama‘a.

prairie dog Kokei‘a.

praise Ho‘omaika‘i. See *honors*.

prank *Trick; to play a ~, usually with malicious intent*. Kēpuka. See *trick*.

prawn *Tahitian ~*. ‘Ōpae Polapola.

praying mantis ‘Ūhinipule.

pre- *Early, beforehand*. Hiki mua. See entries below and *late*. *~registration*. Kāinoa hiki mua.

preamble ‘Ōlelo mua, ‘ōlelo ha‘i mua. See *introduction, preface*.

precedent *Something done or said that may act as an example to justify it being done again*. Kumu alaka‘i.

precipitate *A substance separated from a solution or suspension by chemical or physical change*. Ko‘ako‘ana.

precipitation Kimu.

precision *Also precise*. ‘Aulili‘i. *In math*. Pololei. *As high-quality print resolution on a computer printer*. Miomio. *~ bitmapping*. Kākiko miomio.

predator *Also predatory, to prey*. Po‘ii‘a. *Victim of a ~*. Luapo‘i.

predictable *As the ending of a story*. Hopena ahuwale. *~ story*. Mo‘olelo hopena ahuwale.

prediction *Also to predict, as in a scientific experiment*. Wānana. *~ skill*. Mākau wānana.

preface *Also foreword, as in a book*. ‘Ōlelo ha‘i mua, ‘ōlelo mua. See *introduction, preamble*.

preference Makemake. *~s, as in a computer program*. Nā makemake.

prefix Pāku‘ina kau mua. See *affix*. *A ~ indicating a process*. Kā-. *A ~ meaning one one-hundredth (1/100)*. Keni-. *File ~ or header information, as codes at the beginning of each computer file*. Po‘o pā‘ālua (*preceded by* ke).

prehistoric Kuamanawa.

prejudice *Also discrimination; to discriminate or be prejudiced against*. Ho‘okae. See *racism*.

premium *Insurance ~*. Uku ‘inikua.

preschool Kula kamali‘i.

prescription *For drug or medication; also to prescribe*. Kuhikuhi lā‘au. See *over-the-counter*. *~ drug or medication*. Lā‘au kuhikuhi.

preservice teacher training Ho‘omākaukau kumu. See *inservice teacher training*.

president *As of a college or university*. Pelekikena. See *chancellor, provost*.

press *To click or depress, as in a computer program*. Kōmi, kaomi.

press *To ~, in basketball*. Lulumi. See *press defense*. *Half-court ~*. Lulumi hapa. *Three-quarter-court ~*. Lulumi ‘ekolu hapahā. *Full-court ~*. Lulumi piha.

press defense *As in basketball; to execute such a play*. Pale lulumi. See *press*.

pressure Mīkā. *Air ~, as in a tire*. Mīkā ea. *Blood ~*. Mīkā koko. *High-~ system, in meteorology*. ‘Ōnaehana mīkā pi‘i. *Low-~ system*. ‘Ōnaehana mīkā emi. *~ receptor*. A‘alonoa mīkā. See *receptor*.

pressure *To ~, in basketball*. ‘Umi.

pressurize Ho‘omīkā. *Pressurized*. Ho‘omīkā ‘ia.

pretest Hō‘ike mua a‘o. See *posttest*.

pretzel Pelena pe‘a.

preview Nāmua. See *view*. *Print ~, as in a computer program*. Nāmua pa‘i.

prewrite *To ~, as part of the writing process, i.e. introducing the topic through brainstorming, discussion, presentations, etc*. Hō‘ike mana‘o. See *conference*.

prey *To ~; also predator, predatory*. Po‘ii‘a. *Victim of a predator*. Luapo‘i.

price *Also cost.* Kumukū'ai, kāki.
Estimated ~. Kumukū'ai koho.
Reasonable ~. Kumukū'ai kūpono.
Retail ~. Kumukū'ai hale kū'ai. *Sale ~.*
Kāki kū'aiemi. *Unit ~.* Kumukū'ai
anakahi. *Wholesale ~.* Kumukū'ai
kālepa.

prickly pear cactus Pānini, pānini
maoli, pāpipi. See *cactus*.

primary *As first in time, order, or
importance.* Kuamua. See entries below
and *secondary, tertiary, terminal. ~
bronchus, in anatomy.* 'Āmanapu'u
kuamua. *~ shield volcano.* Lua pele
kuahene kuamua. *~ volcanic activity.*
Hū pele kuamua.

primary *Also ~ election, a
preliminary election to nominate
candidates for office.* Koho pāloka wae
moho, wae moho. *Closed ~.* Wae moho
kūloko. *Open ~.* Wae moho kūākea.

primary directions *The four ~, or
four cardinal points of the compass, in
geography.* Nā kūkulu 'ehā. See
intermediate directions.

primate *An order of animals
including man, apes, and monkeys.*
Māpūnaka.

prime *~ number, in math.* Helu kumu.
*Relatively ~ numbers, i.e. numbers
which share one factor between them,
and that factor is 1.* Hoa helu ho'onui
like kahi. *~ factorization.* Huli helu
ho'onui kumu. *Twin ~s.* Helu kumu
kūlua.

prime meridian *In geography.* Kumu
lonikū, kumu lonitū.

primer *For PVC pipe cement.* Pena
holoi. See *plastic pipe cement*.

primitive Makakumu.

principal *Money loaned, usually at a
given interest rate and for a specified
time.* Kumupa'a, kālā kumupa'a. See
interest.

Principe Panikipe. *Sao Tome and ~
Island.* Ka mokupuni 'o Saotome me
Panikipe.

principle *As an accepted rule of
action.* Kulehana, kahua hana.
*Archimedes' ~, i.e. the buoyant force on
an object submerged in a fluid is equal
to the weight of the fluid displaced by
that object, in science.* Ke kulehana a
'Akimika. *Bernoulli's ~.* Ke kulehana a
Penuli. *Basic counting ~, in math.*
Kulehana no ka helu 'ana. *Half-
rectangle ~.* Kulehana huinahā lō'ihi
hapalua.

print *As in handwriting.*
Limahakahaka. *Also to ~.* Kākau
pākahikahi. See entry below and
*resolution, script. To ~, as on a
computer.* Pa'i (*preceded by ke*). *~ style
or attribute, as italic or bold.* Kaila hua.
~ preview. Nāmua pa'i.

print *To impress or stamp something
in or on something else.* Kāpala. *As
something impressed or stamped with a
~.* Lau kāpala.

printer *As for a computer.* Mīkini pa'i.
~ effects. Hi'ohi'ona pa'i.

prioritize *To ~, set priorities.*
Ho'oka'ina makakoho. See *priority*.

priority Makakoho. See *prioritize. To
make something a ~.* Ho'omakakoho.

prism 'Ōpaka. *Rectangular ~.* 'Ōpaka
huinahā lō'ihi.

private land 'Alokio, 'alodio. See
public land.

privilege *Or rights, as in a computer
network.* Kuleana. *Executive ~, the
right of the President to withhold
information about his activities from
the legislature or judiciary.* Kuleana
lau'au'a.

probability Pahiki. See *chance. High
~.* Pahiki nui. *Low ~.* Pahiki li'ili'i.
Experimental ~. Pahiki ho'okolohua.
Mathematical ~. Pahiki makemakika.

probation *In law.* Wā ho'omalu. *~
officer.* Luna wā ho'omalu.

probe *Dentist's pick.* 'Ōhiki kauka niho.
To ~. 'Akiu. *Space ~.* 'Akiu lewa lipo.

problem *In math.* Polopolema. See *equation, solve. Numerical* ~. Haʻihelu.

problem *Also difficulty, as in the plot of a story.* Hihia. See *resolution.*

proboscis *As of a butterfly.* Nūkihu.

procedure *Process to follow.* Kaʻina hana.

process Haʻaliu. See *due process, procedure.* ~*(ed) cheese.* Waiūpaʻa i haʻaliu ʻia. *A prefix indicating a* ~. Kā-.

processor *As in computer hardware.* Unu lawelawe. See *chip. Word* ~, *as a computer program.* Polokalamu kikokiko palapala.

pro-choice *Advocating legalized abortion.* Paikoho. See *family planning, pro-life.*

produce *To* ~, *as a movie or video production.* Hoʻopuka. See *entry below* and *production. Producer.* Luna hoʻopuka. *Project* ~*r.* Luna hoʻopuka papahana.

producer *An organism that can make its own food, such as green plants.* Kāpuka ʻai.

product *In multiplication.* Hualoaʻa. *Cross* ~. Hualoaʻa kaupeʻa.

product *Something that has been produced or manufactured.* Huahana. See *household product, input.* ~ *manager.* Luna huahana. *Dairy* ~. Meaʻai waiū. *Gross national* ~, *GNP.* Kumuloaʻa kāʻokoʻa.

production ~ *manager, as for a movie or video* ~. Manakia ʻenehana. See *produce.* ~ *engineer.* Luna ʻenehana. *Assistant* ~ *engineer.* Hope luna ʻenehana. *Video* ~ *crew.* Nā limahana paʻi wikiō. *Factors of* ~, *in economics.* Lako hoʻopuka.

productive-thinking skill Mākau hoʻomohala manaʻo.

professional *Also professionally.* ʻOihana. *Allied health* ~. Kākoʻo ʻoihana olakino. ~ *dancer.* Mea hulahula ʻoihana. ~*ly printed.* Paʻi ʻoihana ʻia.

professional diploma *For teaching.* Palapala ʻoihana aʻo.

profit Kumuloaʻa. See *loss.*

program *As for a computer; also application, as in a computer program; also as on TV.* Polokalamu. See *spreadsheet. Database* ~. Polokalamu hōkeo ʻikepili. ~ *disk.* Pā polokalamu *(preceded by ke).* ~ *title, as for a TV* ~. Poʻo inoa polokalamu *(preceded by ke). Space* ~. Polokalamu lewa lipo. *To write a computer* ~. Haku polokalamu.

project *As for a class.* Pāhana. *As in a curriculum program.* Papahana. *ʻŌhiʻa* ~. Papahana ʻŌhiʻa.

projector *Slide* ~. Mīkini hoʻolele kiʻiaka, mīkini kiʻiaka. See *transparency. Movie* ~. Mīkini hoʻolele kiʻiʻoniʻoni, mīkini kiʻiʻoniʻoni.

pro-life *Opposed to abortion; also right to life.* Paihānau. See *family planning, pro-choice.*

prominences *Solar* ~, *puffs of gas which gently drift above the surface of the sun.* Puapuaʻi lā.

prompt *On time.* (I ka) hola kūpono.

prong *Of electrical plug.* Niho palaka. *Two-*~*ed plug.* Palaka niho lua. *Three-*~*ed plug.* Palaka niho kolu.

pronunciation Puana.

proof *In math.* Kūkulu hōʻoia. See *verify.*

proofread Loihape. See *Hawaiian entries under* kaha *for proofreading symbols.*

propaganda Kalapepelo.

propagate *To* ~ *plants or breed animals.* Haʻakipu. See *breed.*

propane Pōpene.

property *Distinctive attribute, as of a number, in math.* ʻAnopili *(preceded by ke). Associative* ~. ʻAnopili hoʻolike. *Chemical* ~. ʻAnopili kemikala. *Commutative* ~. ʻAnopili kaʻina hoʻi hope. *Distributive* ~. 'Anopili ho'oili. *Equality* ~. 'Anopili kaulike. *Grouping* ~. 'Anopili ho'opū'ulu. *Number* ~. 'Anopili helu. *One* ~. 'Anopili 'ekahi. *Opposites* ~. 'Anopili o ka 'ēko'a. *Zero* ~. 'Anopili 'ole. *Zero* ~ *of multiplication.* 'Anopili 'ole o ka ho'onui.

proportion *Also proportional, in math.* Lākiō like. *Constant of* ~*ality.* Lākiō anapuni.

props *As for a play, movie, or video production.* Pono kahua. ~ *master.* Luna pono kahua. ~ *needed.* Nā pono kahua e pono ai.

prosecuting attorney *Also prosecutor, plaintiff attorney.* Loio ho'opi'i. See *defense attorney, plaintiff.*

prosecution *The prosecuting party in a court case.* 'Ao'ao ho'opi'i. See *defense, prosecutor*

prosecutor *Also prosecuting attorney, plaintiff attorney.* Loio ho'opi'i. See *defense attorney.*

protected *Write* ~, *as a computer file or disk.* Ho'opale kākau 'ia.

protective ~ *glasses or goggles.* Makaaniani kaupale.

protein Kumu'i'o, polokina.

pro tem *Also pro tempore.* No ka manawa. *President* ~. Pelekikena no ka manawa.

protocol *In a computer system.* Leaka'a'ike.

proton Huna 'āne. See *electron, neutron.*

protozoa Porotozoa.

protractor Ana huina. *Right-angle* ~. Ana huina kūpono.

prove *To check, verify.* Hō'oia.

provost *As of a college or university.* Luna kulanui. See *chancellor, president.*

pry *Also lever; to* ~, *as with a lever.* Une.

pseudonestor xanthophrys *Maui parrotbill.* Kīkēkoa.

psychomotor domain *As relating to the learning process.* Pō'ai 'onina kino. See *domain.*

psychrometer Ana kawaūea kūlua. See *hygrometer. Sling* ~. Ma'a ana kawaūea kūlua.

publicist Mea ho'olaulaha. See *publicize.*

publicize Ho'olaulaha. See *publicist.*

public land 'Āina no ka lehulehu. See *private land.*

publish *As in a computer program.* Ho'opuka. See *release, update.*

puddle Hālokoloko.

Puerto Rico *Also Puerto Rican.* Pokoliko.

puffball *A kind of mushroom.* Melehune pōpōehu.

puffin Pupē, manu pupē.

pull-up Hukialewa, hukialewa pohoalo. See *chin-up.*

pulmonary artery A'a pu'uwai akemāmā. *See Hawaiian entries under* a'a pu'uwai.

pulmonary vein A'a kino akemāmā. *See Hawaiian entries under* a'a kino.

pulse Pana. See *beat.* ~ *rate, heart rate.* Helu pana pu'uwai.

pump *Also to* ~, *as air or water.* Pāuma. See *valve. Air* ~, *as for tires.* Pāuma ea, pāuma paikikala.

punch *Hole* ~, *as for paper.* Pāniki pepa.

punctuate *Also punctuation mark.* Kaha kiko.

pungent *Also sharp, as the smell of ammonia or vinegar.* Wi'u.

pupa *Also pupal.* Pupa. *To pupate.* Moeapupa.

puppet Pāpeka, pāpeta, ki'i lima. See *marionette.*

purchase order *PO.* Palapala 'oka kū'ai.

purse *Also suitcase.* Pāiki, pāisi. *Coin* ~. 'Eke kenikeni (*preceded by* ke).

push Pahu, pohu. ~*cart.* Ka'a pahu.

pushup *Also to do ~s.* Koʻo lima.

put away *To ~, as in a computer program.* Hoʻokaʻawale. See *cancel, undo.*

put in *To insert, as a disk into a computer.* Hoʻokomo. *To ~ order or sequence.* Hoʻokaʻina. See *alphabetize.*

put on *To ~ makeup.* Hoʻouʻiuʻi, hoʻonaninani.

putrefaction *Aerobic ~ or decomposition.* Ka hoʻohāpopopo eaea ʻana. See *putrefied. Anaerobic ~ or decomposition.* Ka hoʻohāpopopo eaea ʻole ʻana.

putrefied *Decomposed.* Hāpopopo. See *putrefaction. To decompose or putrefy something.* Hoʻohāpopopo.

put together *To ~, as a model.* Kāpili. See *manufacture. To ~ a model airplane.* Kāpili kūkohu mokulele.

putty Pake. *~ knife.* Pahi pake.

puzzle Nane. *Crossword ~.* Nane huaʻōlelo. *Jigsaw ~.* Nane ʻāpana. *Number ~.* Nane huahelu.

pyramid *~ shape.* Pelamika. *Energy ~.* Pelamika ikehu. *As in Egypt.* Puʻu pelamika.

Pyrex Paileki. *~ test tube.* Hano hoʻokolohua paileki.

pyrogallol Pairogalola.

Pythagorean *Also Pythagoras.* Paekakoleo. *~ theorum, in math.* Manaʻohaʻi o Paekakoleo.

Q

Qatar Katala.

Q-tip *Cotton swab.* Lāʻau pulupulu.

quadrant ʻĀpana hapahā.

quadrat *A rectangular plot used for ecological or population studies.* ʻĀpana noiʻi.

quadratic Pāhoʻonui lua. *~ equation.* Haʻihelu pāhoʻonui lua. *~ function.* Hahaina pāhoʻonui lua.

quadriceps femoris *Any muscle in the group of muscles that extend the leg.* Mākala ʻūhā. See *rectus femoris, vastus.*

quadrilateral Huinahā. *See Hawaiian entries under* huinahā.

quality See *resolution, service, vowel.*

quarantine Hoʻomalu maʻi. *~ station.* Hale hoʻomalu maʻi.

quart Kuaka. *Abb.* kk.

quarter *The coin.* Hapahā. *To ~, as an animal.* Pākā hapahā. See *skin.*

quarterback *In football.* ʻAlihikūlele, ʻalihi.

quarter note *In music.* Hua mele hapahā. *Dotted ~.* Hua mele hapahā kiko.

quarter rest *In music.* Hoʻomaha hapahā.

quarter-turn image *In math.* Kinona like wili hapahā, kinona like wili 1/4.

question *Bonus or extra credit ~.* Nīnau hoʻopiʻi kaha, nīnau ʻai keu. *Leading ~.* Nīnau pākākā. *Multiple-choice ~.* Nīnau kohokoho. *Open-ended ~.* Nīnau hoʻomohala manaʻo. *~ mark.* Kiko nīnau.

questionnaire Palapala ninaninau. See *interrogate.*

quilt Kapa kuiki.

quinine Kinikona.

quit *To ~, as a computer program.* Haʻalele.

quota Kuanaki.

quotation *Also to quote.* Puanaʻī. *~ mark.* Kaha puanaʻī. *Single open quote; printer's symbol for* ʻokina. Kaha puanaʻī pākahi wehe. *Double close quote.* Kaha puanaʻī pālua pani.

quote Puanaʻī. See *quotation. A stated price, as for merchandise.* Kumukūʻai.

quotient Helu puka.

R

rabbit Lāpaki, lāpiki, 'iole lāpiki. *Cottontail ~.* Lāpaki huelo pulupulu, lāpiki huelo pulupulu, 'iole lāpiki huelo pulupulu. *Chinchilla ~.* Lāpaki kinikila, lāpiki kinikila, 'iole lāpiki kinikila.

raccoon Lakuna.

race *Relay ~.* Heihei ho'oili, kūkini ho'oili. See *baton.*

racism *Adhering to a belief that one's own race is superior to another race.* Paiha'akei 'ili, paiha'akei lāhui. See *prejudice.*

rack *For clothes, as on wheels in a clothing store.* Hao kau lole, haka lole. *For drying dishes.* Haka kaula'i pā. *Towel ~.* Kaola kāwele.

racket *Also bat, club.* 'Ūhili. See *hit.*

radiate See *radiation.*

radiation *Also to radiate.* Malele. *Adaptive ~, in biology.* Malele ho'oliliuwelo. *Also to radiate, as in the form of waves.* Pāhawewe. *Atomic ~.* Pāhawewe 'atoma. *Nuclear ~.* Pāhawewe nukelea. *Solar ~.* Pāhawewe lā.

radio Lēkiō, pahu ho'olele leo.

radioactivity Pāhawewe ikehu.

radiocarbon date *Also carbon dating.* Helu makahiki kalapona.

radio-wave signal See *carrier.*

radish Lakika.

radius *Of a circle.* Kahahānai. *Abb.* khh. *The shorter and thicker of the two bones of the forearm on the same side as the thumb.* Iwi pili lima. See *fibula, ulna.*

radius *The shorter and thicker of the two bones of the forearm on the same side as the thumb.* Iwi pili lima. See *fibula, ulna.*

raffia *The fiber of the ~ palm of Madagascar.* Pā'ā pāma.

raft Lāpa. *Rubber ~.* Lāpa laholio. *Wooden ~.* Lāpa lā'au.

raid *Also attack.* Ho'ouka. See *counterattack.*

rail *Flightless ~.* Moho lele 'ole.

railing *Ballustrade.* Paehumu. *~ support, balluster.* 'Ūlili, hūlili.

rain *In a small area while sun is shining, sometimes considered an omen of misfortune.* Kualā, ua kualā. *~ distribution.* Ka ili o ka ua. *~fall.* Ua. *Orographic ~ distribution.* Ua pili pali. *~ forest.* Nahele ma'ukele. *~ map.* Palapala 'āina ua. *~ shadow.* Lulu 'alaneo. *~ water.* Wai ua. *Rainy side, as of a mountain.* Alo ua.

raisin Hua waina malo'o.

rake *As for leaves.* Kope 'ōpala. *Garden ~.* Hao kope. *To ~.* Kope, kopekope, pūlumi.

ramp Alahiō. *As for skateboarding.* He'ena. *Skateboard ~.* He'ena papa huila.

random Pono koho. *~ sample.* Hāpana pono koho.

range *As a series of mountains.* Pae. See *chain, series. Mountain ~.* Pae kuahiwi. *The difference between the largest and smallest number or value.* Laulā, laulā loa.

range pole *Also surveying rod.* Lā'au ana 'āina. See *elevation pole, sighter.*

ranger Lanakia. *~ watchtower, especially for watching for forest fires.* Hale kia'i ululā'au.

rank *As position or social standing.* Kūlana. *As in an orderly arrangement.* Pae. *To ~, as from small to large.* Ho'oka'ina pae.

rap *~ music; also to ~.* Pāleoleo.

rapid *In ~ succession.* 'Āma'amau.

rapids *As in a river.* Wai hālo'alo'a.

rare *As meat.* Koko, kokoko. *Medium ~.* Hapa mo'a, mo'a hapa.

rarefaction *The least dense concentration of wave particles in a compressional wave.* Wele. See *compression.*

rarely *Also few, sparse; seldom.* Kāka'ikahi.

Rasalhague *A star.* Hopuhopu.

rasp *The tool.* Apuapu.

rat 'Iole. *Roof* ~. 'Iole kaupoku.

rate *Also percent, percentage rate.* Pākēneka. *See ratio, repeat rate. Tax* ~. Pākēneka 'auhau. ~ *of interest.* Pākēneka uku pane'e. *A ratio that compares different kinds of units; quantity, amount, or degree of something measured per unit of something else, as of time.* Lākiō. *Rating response.* Pane pālākiō. *To* ~, *as on a scale.* Loipālākiō.

ratification Ka 'āpono 'ana. *See ratify.*

ratify *As a legislative bill or a treaty.* 'Āpono. *See ratification.*

ratio Lākiō. *See proportion, rate. Equal* ~. Lākiō like.

rational number *In math.* Helu pu'unaue koena 'ole. *See irrational number.*

rattan Pāma hihi.

rattle *Baby* ~. 'Ulīkeke. *See tambourine.*

raw *Unprocessed, as* ~ *materials.* Kūlohelohe. *See entries below and natural.* ~ *material.* Makelia kūlohelohe, memea kūlohelohe.

raw footage *As of video tape.* Līpine pa'i maka. *See footage.*

raw sewage Kaekene maka. *See treat (chemically).*

ray *As in geometry.* Kukuna, wāwae, 'ao'ao. *Cathode-~ tube (CRT).* 'Ohe kīwī. *Cosmic* ~. Kukuna lewa lipo. *Ultraviolet* ~. Kukuna kuawehi. *One of the bony spines supporting the membrane of a fish's fin.* Nī'au lā.

re *The second note on the musical scale.* Kō. *See Hawaiian entry* pākōlī.

reach *See beam reach, broad reach.*

react *Also reaction, as chemical compounds.* Mō'aui. *See reactant, reactor.*

reactant *Also reagent.* 'Ūmō'aui. *See reaction, reactor.*

reaction *Also to react, as chemical compounds.* Mō'aui. *See action-reaction pair, reactant, reactor. Allergic* ~. Hopena pāheu. *See allergy.*

reactor Mea mō'aui. *See reactant, reaction.*

read *Speed* ~. Heluwawe. *See skim read, speed write. Speed* ~*ing.* Ka heluwawe 'ana.

reader *Storybook.* Puke heluhelu.

reagent *Also reactant.* 'Ūmō'aui. *See reaction, reactor.*

realistic Kohu 'oia'i'o. ~ *fiction.* Hakupuni kohu 'oia'i'o.

real number *In math.* Helu maoli. *See imaginary number.*

real time *As in a computer program.* Manawa 'ānō.

reasonable Kūpono. ~ *price.* Kumukū'ai kūpono.

reasoning *Inductive* ~, *i.e. generalizing from examples, as in math.* Ho'oholo pili la'ana.

rebound *To* ~, *in basketball.* 'Āpō.

recall *The right or procedure by which an elected official may be removed from office.* Kīpaku luna kālai'āina, kīpeku luna kālai'āina. *See impeach.*

receive *To* ~, *in football; reception.* 'Apo. *See intercept. Receiver.* Mea 'apo. *To* ~ *a serve, in volleyball; also first pass.* Ki'i.

receiver *Telephone* ~. 'Apo kelepona.

reception *See receive.*

receptor *As of nerve endings in the body, in biology.* A'alonoa. *Pressure* ~. A'alonoa mīkā. *Taste* ~. A'alonoa 'ono.

recess *As during school.* Wā pā'ani.

recession *A period of reduced economic activity.* Au emi.

recipe Lekapī.

reciprocal *In math.* Pālike.

Recommended Daily Allowances *USRDA; now known as Percent Daily Value.* Pākēneka o ka papaʻai.

record *A quantity of facts treated as a unit.* Moʻokūʻikena. *As a list of facts about achievements or tasks accomplished; also résumé, vita, curriculum vitae.* Moʻomōʻali. *Greatest achievement or performance to date.* Kūhoʻe. *To set the* ~. Mākia i ke kūhoʻe.

record *Also* ~ *album, as for a* ~ *player.* Pāleo, pāʻōlelo. ~ *album cover.* Wahī pāleo. ~ *player.* Mīkini hoʻokani pāleo, mīkini pāleo. *To* ~, *as on a cassette.* Hoʻopaʻa, ʻoki. ~*ing tape.* Līpine. *See recorder.*

recorder *Tape* ~. Mīkini hoʻopaʻa leo. *See player. Cassette* ~. Mīkini hoʻopaʻa lola, mīkini lola. *Reel-to-reel tape* ~. Mīkini hoʻopaʻa pōkaʻa, mīkini pōkaʻa leo.

recovery *See Seal Recovery Program.*

recreation *Department of Parks and* ~. ʻOihana o nā Pāka a me nā Hana Hoʻonanea.

rectangle Huinahā lōʻihi. *See entry below and half-rectangle principle. Golden* ~, *a* ~ *in which the ratio of the width to the length is the same as that of the length to the sum of the width plus the length.* Huinahā lōʻihi kula.

rectangular *See rectangle.* ~ *array, in math.* Lau huinahā lōʻihi. ~ *prism.* ʻŌpaka huinahā lōʻihi.

rectus abdominus *A muscle of the anterior torso.* Mākala keʻahaka.

rectus femoris *One of the group of muscles that extend the leg.* Mākala alo ʻūhā. *See quadriceps femoris, vastus.*

recycle Hoʻopōʻaiapuni. *See cycle.*

red blood cell Hunaola koko ʻulaʻula.

red-eyed vireo *A kind of bird.* Manu wiliō mākole.

Red Sea Ke Kai ʻUla.

Red Spot *Giant* ~, *a huge gaseous feature on Jupiter.* ʻŌnohi ʻUla Kūāhewa.

reduce *To diet.* Hoʻēmi kino.

reduction *Vowel* ~, *in linguistics.* Hoʻēmi woela. *See vowel. Reduced vowel.* Woela emi.

reed Mauʻu ʻohe.

reef ʻĀpapapa. *See slipper lobster. Artificial* ~. Umukoʻa. *Kingman* ~. Nalukākala. *Maro* ~. Koʻanakoʻa. *Pearl and Hermes* ~. Holoikauaua.

reel *For recording tape.* Pōkaʻa līpine. *See player, recorder, tape.* ~*-to-*~ *tape.* Līpine pōkaʻa.

reel *As for fishing.* Wiliaho. *Open* ~. Wiliaho hāmama. *Bait-casting* ~. Wiliaho hekau maunu.

referee *Also umpire; also to* ~. ʻUao, ʻuao haʻuki. *In volleyball.* Kanaka makaʻala ʻupena.

reference *Source, as a dictionary or other* ~ *material.* Kūmole. *See resource.*

reference *Also coordinate, in math.* Kuhikuhina. *See coordinate, ordered pair, referent.* ~ *object.* Kuhia. ~ *point.* Kiko kuhia.

referent *In math.* Kuhia (O-class).

referral *Coordinated physician* ~ *system.* ʻŌnaehana kauka no ka lapaʻau like ʻana.

reflect *To* ~, *as light, heat, or sound.* Kūpī, hoʻokūpī.

reflection *In math.* Aka aniani. *See angle of incidence. Angle of* ~, *i.e. the angle between a reflected wave and the normal to the barrier from which it is reflected.* Huina kūpī. ~ *image.* Kinona aka like o kekahi ʻaoʻao. ~ *symmetry.* ʻĀlikelike aka.

reflector ʻOwakawaka, kukui ʻowakawaka.

reformat *To* ~, *as a computer disk.* Hoʻāla hou. *See format.*

refresh *As a computer screen.* Hōʻano hou.

refuge *Hawaiian Islands National Wildlife ~.* ʻĀina Hoʻomalu Holoholona Lōhiu o Hawaiʻi.

region *A specific area, in math.* Wahi. *Geographic ~; also regional.* Māhele ʻāina.

register *Cash ~.* Mīkini ʻohi kālā. *See cashier. Check ~.* Moʻo pila kīkoʻo. *To ~ or check in, as at a conference or hotel.* Kāinoa komo, kāinoa. *See check out, registration. To ~ (someone for something).* Hoʻokāinoa. *To ~ voters for an election.* Hoʻokāinoa poʻe koho pāloka.

registration Kāinoa. *See check out, register. Early ~, pre~.* Kāinoa hiki mua. *Late ~.* Kāinoa hiki hope. *~ form.* Palapala kāinoa.

registration system *Of land.* ʻŌnaehana hoʻonā ʻāina. *See land court, settle.*

regular *As in shape.* Analahi. *See irregular. ~ polygon.* Huinalehulehu analahi. *~ shape.* Kinona analahi.

regulate *To fix the time, amount, degree, or rate of something by making adjustments.* Hoʻokonukonu.

related species *In biology.* Pili lāhulu.

relative gravity *Also specific gravity.* Lākiō paʻapū wai.

relative humidity Pā kawaūea.

relative location *In geography.* Pilina henua. *See absolute location.*

relatively prime numbers *Numbers which share one factor between them, and that factor is 1, in math.* Hoa helu hoʻonui like kahi.

relay race Heihei hoʻoili, kūkini hoʻoili. *See baton, shuttle run.*

release *Interim or maintenance ~, as of a computer program.* Hoʻopuka hoʻoponopono ʻia. *See update.*

remainder *Difference, in math.* Koena. *Abb.* K.

remote control *Also to control by ~.* Kia pihi. *See remote manipulator arm.*

remote manipulator arm *Also space crane.* Lima kia pihi.

removable hard disk *As in a computer.* Pā paʻaloko wehe (*preceded by* ke).

remove Wehe. *Staple ~r.* Mea wehe ʻūmiʻi. *To ~, as an ʻopihi from its shell.* Kuaʻi, poke, poʻe. *To ~ food from one's mouth and eat it again, as gum.* ʻAi hemo.

renal artery Aʻa puʻwai hakuʻala. *See Hawaiian entries under aʻa puʻuwai.*

renal vein Aʻa kino hakuʻala. *See Hawaiian entries under aʻa kino.*

rename *To ~, in math.* Hoʻonoho kūana helu.

repair kit *For tires.* Kini poho ea.

repeat *To ~, as the action of a computer key when held down.* Pīnaʻi. *See turbo button. ~ rate.* Māmā pīnaʻi.

repeating decimal Kekimala pīnaʻi.

repel *To ~, as like charges in a magnet.* ʻĀpahupahu.

replace *To change or ~, as in search-and-~ feature in a computer program.* Kuapo. *To find and change, search and ~.* Huli a kuapo.

report Hōʻike. *Oral ~.* Hōʻike haʻi waha, ʻōlelo hōʻike. *Oral ~, presented as a speech.* Haʻiʻōlelo hōʻike. *Written ~.* Hōʻike palapala.

reprimand *Oral ~; also to scold.* Nuku.

reproductive system *In biology.* ʻŌnaehana hoʻohua.

reptile Moʻohana.

republic *Central African ~.* Lepupalika ʻApelika Waena. *Democratic ~ of the Congo.* Lepupalika Kemokalaka ʻo Konokō. *Czech ~.* Lepupalika ʻo Tieka. *Dominican ~.* Lepupalika Kominika. *~ of Kiribati.* Lepupalika ʻo Kilipaki. *United ~ of Tanzania.* Lepupalika Hui Pū ʻia ʻo Tanazania.

required *Also requirement.* Koina. See *elective.* ~ *class, course, as in school.* Papa koina. ~ *credit.* ʻAi koina. ~ *coursework, curriculum.* Papa haʻawina koina.

requirement See *required.*

research Noiʻi. ~*er.* Kanaka noiʻi. *Scientific* ~*er.* Kanaka noiʻi ʻepekema.

reserpine *An alkaloid used as a tranquilizer.* Resepine.

reservation See *reserve.*

reserve *A reservation or tract of land set apart.* ʻĀina hoʻomalu. *Forest* ~. ʻĀina hoʻomalu ululāʻau. *Nature* ~. ʻĀina hoʻomalu ao kūlohelohe. *Natural Areas* ~*s System (NARS).* ʻŌnaehana Hoʻomalu ʻĀina Kūlohelohe.

residence Hale noho, wahi noho. ~ *hall or dormitory, as at a school.* Hale noho haumāna.

resident *Permanent* ~, *as an alien residing in one country over an extended period of time.* Malihini noho loa.

residue *Of* poi *after pounding, or of* milk *after beating.* Kale ʻai.

resin *For musical instrument strings.* Hūkaʻa.

resist *To* ~, *as water on corrosive things.* ʻAʻalo. See *Teflon, waterproof.*

resistance *Opposition to the flow of electricity, or any opposition that slows down or prevents movement of electrons through a conductor.* Āohiohi. *Air* ~. Āohiohi ea. ~ *arm, i.e. the distance from the fulcrum to the resistance force in a lever.* Lima āohiohi. ~ *force.* Manehu āohiohi.

resolution *Low-quality print* ~, *as on a computer printer.* Kalakala. *Precision or high-quality print* ~. Miomio.

resolution *Also solution, as of a problem in a story.* Hopena holo. See *problem.*

resource *Or reference book, as an encyclopedia.* Puke noiʻi. See *reference.*

resource *A source of supply.* Kumuwaiwai. *Division of Aquatic* ~*s.* Māhele Kumuwaiwai Kai. *Natural* ~. Kumuwaiwai kūlohelohe.

respiration *Also respiratory.* Hanu. See *respiratory system.* *Also to respire.* Kōpiaʻā.

respiratory system ʻŌnaehana hanu.

response *As to a stimulus.* Hāpane.

response log *Literature* ~, *as a student's journal for recording reactions to literature.* Puke moʻomanaʻo moʻokalaleo.

response rating *In math.* Pane pālākiō.

rest *In music.* Hoʻomaha. *Whole* ~. Hoʻomaha ʻokoʻa. *Half* ~. Hoʻomaha hapalua. *Quarter* ~. Hoʻomaha hapahā. *Eighth* ~. Hoʻomaha hapawalu. *Sixteenth* ~. Hoʻomaha hapa ʻumikūmāono. *Thirty-second* ~. Hoʻomaha hapa kanakolukūmālua.

restaurant Hale ʻaina. *Fast-food* ~. Hale ʻaina meaʻai hikiwawe.

result *Ideal* ~, *in math.* Hopena kaukonu.

résumé *Also vita, curriculum vitae.* Moʻomōʻali.

retail price Kumukūʻai hale kūʻai. See *wholesale price.*

retardant *Flame* ~. Pale ahi.

reteaching book Puke aʻo hou.

retire Līkaia, rītaia, hoʻomaha loa.

return *To use the enter or* ~ *key on a computer or typewriter keyboard in order to return the cursor or carriage to the left margin on a new line; enter or* ~, *as the key just above the shift key on a computer keyboard.* Kāhoʻi. See *enter.* ~ *key.* Pihi kāhoʻi (*preceded by* ke).

Reunion Leuniona. ~ *Island.* Ka mokupuni ʻo Leuniona.

reverse *A curved line written over a word or letter and then under the adjoining word or letter to indicate that the order of the words or letters should be ~d, in proofreading.* Kaha kuapo.

revert *To ~, as in a computer program.* Hoʻi. *To ~ to previous save.* Hoʻi i ka mālama. *See save.*

review *Checkpoint.* Nāʻana.

revolution *Puni.* *~s per minute (rpm).* Puni o ka minuke. *Abb.* p/min.

revolution *As against a government.* Hoʻokahuli aupuni. *~ary war.* Kaua hoʻokahuli aupuni.

rewind *To ~, as a film or audio tape.* Wili i hope. *See fast forward.*

Rhea *The second largest moon of Saturn.* Rea.

rhesus monkey Keko lekuka.

rhizome ʻAuaʻa.

Rhode Island *Also Rhode Islander.* Loke ʻAilana, Rode ʻAilana.

rhododendron Pua wīkōlia.

rhombus Huinahā hiō like.

rhythm *In linguistics.* Aupana. *In music.* Papana.

rice Laiki, lāisi. *Brown ~.* Laiki mākuʻe, lāisi mākuʻe. *White ~.* Laiki keʻokeʻo, lāisi keʻokeʻo. *Mōchī ~.* Laiki mōchī, lāisi mōchī. *~ ball, musubi.* Pōpō laiki, pōpō lāisi, musubī.

Richter scale Pālākiō ikehu ōlaʻi.

ride *As at a carnival or amusement park.* Hololeʻa.

ridge *Midocean ~.* Kualapa waena moana.

riffle *As in a stream.* Kahena hulili.

rift Māwae. *~ valley.* Awāwa māwae. *Series of ~ valleys.* Pae awāwa māwae. *~ zone.* Kāʻei māwae.

rig *Oil ~, for drilling oil on either land or sea.* Wili ʻaila.

right *Also yeah, isn't that so; used only at the end of a sentence or phrase.* Ē. *See Hawaiian entry.*

right angle *In math.* Huina kūpono. *~ protractor.* Ana huina kūpono.

right guard *In football.* Kūkahi ʻākau.

right justified *As type in printing.* Kaulihi ʻākau.

right margin Lihi ʻākau. *See justify, margin.*

rights *Or privilege, as in a computer network.* Kuleana. *See natural rights. Bill of ~.* Palapala pono kanaka.

right tackle *In football.* Kūlua ʻākau. *See tackle.*

right to life *Opposed to abortion; also pro-life.* Paihānau. *See family planning, pro-choice.*

rim *Of basket, in basketball.* Hao, kuku. *See basket. Of a wheel.* Kuapo hao.

rimless *Also swish, i.e. to make a basket without touching the rim, in basketball.* Kuhō. *See shot.*

ring Komo. *~ finger.* Manamana komo, manamana pili. *As in a ~ binder.* Lina kui. *~ binder.* Puke lina kui. *Six-pack ~, i.e. the plastic ~ which holds the cans together.* ʻEa ʻekeʻeke. *Six-pack beer ~.* ʻEa ʻekeʻeke pia. *Six-pack soda ~.* ʻEa ʻekeʻeke koloaka.

ring of fire *In geology.* Lei o Pele.

ring stand *As for a test tube.* Kū hano hoʻokolohua.

rite of passage *Also initiation.* Hana komo pae.

river *See delta, estuary. ~ tributary.* ʻAumana muliwai.

riverbed Papakū, papakū muliwai.

robot Lopako.

rock *Black, porous, light ~ used to scrape the interior of gourds.* Kūnānahu. *See calcarious rock, igneous rock. Parent ~, i.e. rocks in upper surface of the earth which break down to form rocks, sand, dirt, etc.* Pōhaku makua.

Rock *La Pérouse ~.* Kuamanō.

rocket *As space or fireworks.* Ahikao. See *Manned Maneuvering Unit.* *~ ship.* Moku ahikao. *Solid ~ booster.* Kao wāwahie kinopaʻa, kao wāwahie paʻa.

rocking horse Lio paipai.

rock the boat *A jump rope game of jumping and bouncing a ball at the same time.* ʻOni a ka moku. See *jump rope.*

rod *Surveying ~.* Lāʻau ana ʻāina. See *counting rod, elevation pole, sighter.*

rodeo Hoʻokūkū hana paniolo.

roe deer Kia lō.

role *As in a play or movie.* Hāmeʻe.

roll *As of film.* ʻŌwili. See entries below and *pick and roll.* *~ of film.* ʻŌwili kiʻi.

roller *Paint ~.* Lola pena. *To paint with a ~.* Pena lola. *Steam~.* Kimalola.

rollerblade Kāmaʻa lapa huila. *To skate with ~s.* Holo lapa huila.

roller coaster Kaʻa lola.

roller skate Kāmaʻa huila. *To skate with ~s.* Holo kāmaʻa huila.

rolling pin Lola palaoa.

Roman candle Ihoihokī.

Romania *Also Romanian.* Romānia.

Roman numeral Helu Loma.

roof *To ~ (a shot), in basketball.* Paku ʻino. See *block.* *~ rat.* ʻIole kaupoku.

room *See Hawaiian entries under* lumi. *~ temperature.* Mehana ea, mehana lumi.

root *Source, derivation, or origin, as the etymology of a word.* Molekumu. See *square root.* *Of tongue.* Mole alelo.

root *To enable to develop ~s.* Hoʻāʻa, hoʻoaʻa. *~ing hormone.* Hōmona hoʻāʻa, hōmona hoʻoaʻa. *~ hairs.* Huluhulu aʻa.

rope See *jump rope.*

rose *Wood ~.* Loke lāʻau.

rosette Pākaʻapohe.

rotary tiller *Also rotary cultivator, Rototiller.* Mīkini kipikipi lepo. See *cultivator.*

rotate *To ~, in volleyball; also to switch sides.* Kuapo.

rotational symmetry *In math.* ʻĀlikelike wili.

rotation image *In math.* Kinona like o kekahi ʻaoʻao.

rotenone *A chemical compound.* Lokeni.

Rototiller See *rotary tiller.*

rouge *Also blush, as makeup.* Hehelo pāpālina.

round *To ~ off, in math.* Kolikoli. *To ~ down.* Kolikoli haʻalalo. *To ~ up.* Kolikoli haʻaluna.

round *As in boxing.* Puni. See *hand, lap.*

rounded *In linguistics.* Mōkio. See *vowel.* *~ vowel.* Woela mōkio.

round-robin *As in sports.* Hoʻokūkū pā puni.

round trip Holopuni. See *one-way.*

roundworm Koʻe poepoe.

routine Moʻokiʻina.

rover *Lunar ~.* Kaʻa holo mahina.

rowboat *Also skiff.* ʻŌpā.

rpm See *revolutions per minute.*

rub *To ~, as one's eyes.* ʻĀnai. *To ~ repeatedly.* ʻAnaʻanai.

rubber *~ band.* Apo laholio. *~ boot.* Lapa puki, laba puki, puki lapa. *~ cement.* Tuko laholio. See *glue, paste.*

rubbing *To make a ~, as of petroglyphs.* Kāmahaka.

rug *For any large room.* Hāliʻi papahele, moena. See *carpet. Small ~, as in a bathroom or beside a bed.* Pale papahele, pale wāwae.

rule *Function ~, in math.* Lula hahaina. *Exception to a ~.* Kūʻē lula. *Home ~, in government.* Home lula.

ruler *Measuring device.* Lula. See *tape measure. Wooden ~.* Lula lāʻau.

run Holo. See *lap, long jump, shuttle run. Three-hundred yard ~.* Holo ʻekolu haneli ʻiā. *As in a stream.* Wai kōʻieʻie.

runner-up *Also second place.* Kūlana 'elua.

running back *General term, in football.* Mea holo.

runoff *As water running from the land into the sea.* Holo kele wai.

runway Ala ku'u mokulele.

Russia *Also Russian.* Lūkia, Rūsia.

rustle *To ~, as leaves or the sea.* Nehe.

Rwanda *Also Rwandan.* Ruanada.

S

saddle *Pack ~.* Noho 'āmana.

saddle shoe *Oxford.* Kāma'a 'ili helei.

Sadr *A star.* Hikiwawe.

safe sex *Also to practice ~.* Ai palekana. See *unprotected sex.*

safety *In football.* 'Āwa'a. *Strong ~.* 'Āwa'a muku. *Weak ~.* Āwa'a lala.

safety glasses *Also protective glasses.* Makaaniani kaupale.

safety line *As in a spacecraft.* Kaula piko.

safety pin Pine kaiapa.

Sahara *Western ~, Western Saharan.* Sahara Komohana.

sail *To ~ directly downwind.* Kele ka'alalo. See *beam reach, broad reach, close hauled.*

saimin Kaimine.

Saint Helens *Mount ~.* Mauna Kana Helena, Mauna Sana Helena.

salamander Kalamena, salamena. *Red-backed ~.* Kalamena kua'ula.

sale *Also to be or put on ~.* Kū'aiemi. *~ price.* Kāki kū'aiemi.

sales pitch *To make a pitch, as a ~, or to "sell" an idea.* Paialou.

sales tax 'Auhau kumukū'ai.

saliva *Also salivary.* Hā'ae. See *salivary gland.*

salivary gland Lōku'u hā'ae.

salt *Epsom ~.* Pa'akai 'epesoma. *Nutrient ~s, the deposits that remain after a liquid has been removed.* Pa'amāhuaola.

salty water Wai kai. *To desalinate/ desalinize ~.* Ho'omānalo wai kai.

Salvador *El ~, Salvadoran, Salvadorian.* 'Ela Salavadora.

Sāmoa *Also Sāmoan.* Kāmoa, Ha'amoa. *American ~, American ~n.* Kāmoa 'Amelika, Ha'amoa 'Amelika.

sample *As a small part of a larger whole.* Hāpana. *Composite ~.* Hāpana huihuina. *Random ~.* Hāpana pono koho. *Sampling methods.* Nā ki'ina 'ohi hāpana.

sample space *The set of all possible outcomes of an experiment, in math.* 'Ōpa'a hopena.

sand culture 'Oulu one.

sandstone Pōhāone.

sandwich Kanauika. See *filling.*

sanitary pad *Ni'ihau usage.* Palema'i. See *underpants.*

Sao Tome and Principe Saotome me Panikipe. *~ Island.* Ka mokupuni 'o Saotome me Panikipe.

sap Kohu.

sapling Kumulā'au 'ōpiopio.

Saran Wrap *Any plastic film for wrapping food.* Wahī 'ea.

sartorius *A muscle crossing the anterior portion of the upper leg.* Mākala ka'akepa 'ūhā.

sassafras Sasapalasa.

satellite Ukali, poelele. See *Long Duration Exposure Facility.* *~ star.* Hōkū ukali.

saturated fat 'Ailakele pa'apū. See *fat.*

Saturday Po'aono. *Abb.* P6.

Saturn *The planet.* Makulu.

sauce pan Ipuhao hana kai.

saucer See *flying saucer.*

Saudi Arabia *Also Saudi.* Saudi 'Alapia, Saudi 'Arabia.

savanna *A tropical or subtropical grassland containing scattered trees.* Sawana.

save *To ~, in basketball.* Ki'ilou. *In volleyball.* Ho'iho'i, lou.

save *To ~, as in a computer program.* Mālama. *To ~ as.* Mālama ma ka inoa 'o. *To revert to previous ~.* Ho'i i ka mālama.

savings *As money saved on a sale item.* Kālā mālama. *~ account, as in a bank.* Waihona ho'āhu kālā. *See account.*

sawdust Oka lā'au.

saxophone Kakopone, pū kakopone.

scab Piele.

scale *In math.* Pālākiō. *See entries below. Conversion ~.* Papa pālākiō. *~ drawing.* Ki'i pālākiō. *To rate, as on a ~.* Loipālākiō.

scale *Linear ~, in geography.* Pālākiō lālani. *Richter ~.* Pālākiō ikehu ōla'i.

scale *Musical ~.* Alapi'i mele, pākōlī. *See Hawaiian entries.*

scalene *In math.* 'Ao'ao like 'ole. *~ triangle.* Huinakolu 'ao'ao like 'ole.

scales *For weighing something.* Anapaona. *See adjuster. Bathroom ~.* Anapaona home, *usu.* anapaona. *Balance ~.* Anapaona kaulike. *Spring ~.* Anapaona pilina. *Balancing tray for ~.* Pā ana (*preceded by* ke). *Weight for ~.* Koihā.

scale selection *As in a computer program.* Koho pālākiō.

scalloped potatoes 'Uala kahiki pepeiao, 'uala pepeiao.

scan *To ~ or scroll, as in a computer program.* Lolelole. *To ~ forward.* Lolelole i mua. *To ~ backward.* Lolelole i hope. *To ~ search, as with audio or video equipment.* Huli lolelole.

Scandanavia *Also Scandanavian.* Kanakawia.

scanner *As for a computer program.* Mīkini ho'oili ki'i.

scar Ninanina, 'ālina (*preceded by* ke).

scarecrow Ki'i ho'omaka'u manu.

scarf Kā'ei 'ā'ī.

scattergram *In math.* Pakuhi kikokiko.

scattergraph *In math.* Pakuhi lū.

scavenger *Also to scavenge.* Hamupela.

scene *Also scenery, as for a stage production.* Nānaina. *Forest ~.* Nānaina ululā'au.

scenery *See scene.*

scenic viewpoint *Lookout.* 'Īmaka.

Scheat *A star.* Mākahi.

schematic drawing *Also diagram.* Ki'ikuhi.

schizophrenia Ma'i huohuoi. *Schizophrenic convulsion.* Ma'i huki huohuoi.

scholarship Ha'awina kālā hele kula, ha'awina kālā. *Athletic ~.* Ha'awina kālā 'ālapa.

school *See campus mail. Large ~ of fish such as akule or aku.* Kumu i'a. *Small ~ of reef fish such as manini.* Naho i'a, naha i'a.

schoolbox Pahu pono ha'awina. *See school supplies.*

school supplies Pono ha'awina. *See schoolbox.*

science 'Epekema, akeakamai. *Physical ~.* Kālaiaopaku. *~ fair.* Hō'ike'ike 'epekema.

science fiction Mōhihi'o. *~ movie.* Ki'i'oni'oni mōhihi'o.

scientific *~ notation.* Kauhelu 'epekema. *~ researcher.* Kanaka noi'i 'epekema.

scientist Kanaka 'epekema, kanaka akeakamai.

scion Weli.

scold *Also oral reprimand.* Nuku.

scoop *To ladle, skim.* Kī'o'e, 'o'e. *See ladle.*

scooter *Child's* ~. Peke, ka'a peke.

score *In sports or games.* Helu'ai. See *point.*

scoreboard *As for sports.* Papa helu'ai.

scorpion Kopiana. *See other entries in dictionary.*

Scotch tape *Also transparent tape.* Leki 'ea.

Scotland *Also Scot, Scots, Scottish.* Kekokia, Sekotia.

scowl Pūtē. See *frown.*

scrapbook *As in a computer program.* Puke hunahuna.

scratch *To* ~, *as an itch.* Wa'u, wa'uwa'u. *To* ~ *with claws, as a cat.* Walu.

screen *As for windows.* Uea makika, maka'aha. ~ *door.* Pani puka uea makika, pani puka maka'aha (*preceded by* ke). *For projecting slides or movies.* Pākū ho'olele ki'i.

screen *As on a TV or computer monitor.* Papakaumaka. See *monitor. Calculator display* ~. Papakaumaka mīkini helu. *Computer monitor* ~. Papakaumaka kamepiula. *Edit* ~, *in a computer program.* Pukaaniani ho'oponopono. *Home* ~. Kahua pa'a. *TV* ~. Papakaumaka kīwī. *List editor* ~. Pukaaniani kolamu 'ikepili.

screen *Also to block out, in basketball.* 'Āke'a. See *blocking foul. Illegal* ~. 'Āke'a ne'e.

screenplay Mo'olelo ki'i'oni'oni. See *screenwriter. To write a* ~. Kākau mo'olelo ki'ioni'oni, kākau mo'olelo.

screenwriter Mea kākau mo'olelo ki'i'oni'oni, mea kākau ki'i'oni'oni. See *screenplay.*

screw Kui nao.

screwdriver Kolūkalaiwa.

scribe *Also secretary.* Kākau 'ōlelo.

scrimmage *As for sports.* Ho'okūkū kio. See *championship, tournament.* ~ *line, in football.* Laina ho'ouka.

script *As in handwriting.* Limahiō. *Also to write in* ~. Kākau maoli. See entries below and *print.*

script *As for a play or movie.* Mo'olelo hana keaka, mo'olelo. See *screenplay.* ~*writer.* Mea kakau mo'olelo. ~ *supervisor.* Luna kākau mo'olelo.

script *A set of computer codes programmed to run consecutively in a computer system.* Kōmi 'ōkuhi. *To write a (computer)* ~; *scripting.* Haku kōmi 'ōkuhi.

scripting See *script.*

scroll *To* ~ *or scan, as in a computer program.* Lolelole. *To* ~ *forward.* Lolelole i mua. *To* ~ *backward.* Lolelole i hope.

scroll *Oriental-style* ~, *usually decorative.* Kiuna.

scrutinize *To look over critically.* Loi. See *critical thinking.*

scuba *To* ~ *dive;* ~ *diving.* Lu'u kini ea. ~ *diver.* Kanaka lu'u kai. ~ *tank.* Kini ea lu'u kai, kini ea.

sculpture Ki'i ku'ikepa.

sea *At* ~, *asea.* I waena moana. See *midocean.*

sea anemone 'Ōkala, 'ōkole.

seagull Kalapuna.

sea horse Mo'olio.

seal Sila. See *pinniped. Fur* ~. Sila pūhuluhulu. *Hawaiian monk* ~. Sila Hawai'i.

sea level 'Ilikai.

sea lion Liona kai.

seal-of-Solomon *A kind of flower.* Kilaokolomona.

Seal Recovery Program Papa Hana Ho'opakele Sila.

seamount Mauna kai. See *guyot. Chain of* ~*s.* Pae mauna kai. *Emperor* ~*s.* Ka pae mauna kai 'o 'Emepela.

search *To find or* ~ *(for), as in a computer program.* Huli. See *scan search. To find and change,* ~ *and replace.* Huli a kuapo.

season Kau. *Nesting* ~. Kau ho'opūnana.

seasonal Kū kau, kū i ke kau.

seat *Bicycle* ~. Noho paikikala. *Toilet* ~. Noho lua. ~ *back.* Kua noho.

sea turtle *Green* ~. Honu lū'au, honu.

sea vent Puale kai.

seaweed See *agar.*

secant *A line which intersects a circle at two points, in math.* Kaha 'oki pō'ai. See *tangent.*

second *Unit of time.* Kekona. *Abb.* kkn.

secondary *As second in time, order, or importance.* Kualua. See *primary, tertiary, terminal.* ~ *activity, of a volcano.* 'Ā kualua. ~ *or lobar bronchus, in anatomy.* 'Āmanapu'u kualua.

second base *In baseball.* Pahu 'elua. See *base.*

second-hand *Used.* Pāmia. ~ *car.* Ka'a pāmia.

second place *Also runner-up.* Kūlana 'elua.

secretary *Also scribe.* Kākau 'ōlelo.

section *Cross* ~, *in math.* Hi'ona kaha.

security guard Kia'i, kia'i pō, māka'i kia'i (pō).

sediment Ko'ana. *Marine* ~. Ko'ana kai. *Stream* ~. Ko'ana kahawai.

seed 'Ano'ano. ~ *pod.* Wahī 'ano'ano.

seedling *As of* 'ilima *plants.* Hehu. See *shoot.*

seesaw Papa hulei. *To* ~. Hulehulei.

see the light *To* "~" *after not understanding or after being in opposition to an idea.* Makili ka no'ono'o.

Segin *A star.* Laniholo'oko'a.

segment *Line* ~, *in math.* 'Āpana kaha. *Sound* ~, *in linguistics.* Hua.

segmental bronchus *Also tertiary bronchus, in anatomy.* 'Āmanapu'u kuakolu.

segregate Ho'oka'awale.

seismograph Mīkini ana ōla'i, ana ōla'i.

seldom *Also few, sparse; rarely.* Kāka'ikahi.

selection *Scale* ~, *as in a computer program.* Koho pālākiō.

selective solubility Pēmā'ō'ā wae 'ano.

self- *Or auto- (prefix).* Hika-.

semicircle Pō'ai hapalua.

semicolon Hapa kolona. See *colon.*

semilunar valve *Of the heart.* Pepeiao 'a'apu. See *valve.*

seminar Seminā.

Senegal Senekala.

sense Lonoa. ~ *of hearing.* Lonoa pepeiao. ~ *of sight.* Lonoa maka. ~ *of smell.* Lonoa ihu. ~ *of taste.* Lonoa alelo. ~ *of touch.* Lonoa 'ili.

sense *Common* ~; *also to use common* ~. No'ono'o kanaka.

sensitive *Case* ~, *as in a computer program.* Maka'ala ma'aka.

sentence *A grammatical unit.* Hopuna'ōlelo, pepeke. See *clause.* *Math or number* ~. Hopunahelu. *Topic* ~, *as of a paragraph.* Hopuna'ōlelo wehe kumuhana.

separate Ho'oka'awale. See *buffer.* *To* ~ *easily, as a nut from its shell.* 'Ēkaka'a.

separated *A "straight" Z-shaped line written to indicate where two words written as one should be* ~, *in proofreading.* Kaha ho'okōā, kaha ho'oka'ahua.

September Kepakemapa. *Abb.* Kep.

sequence Ka'ina. See *alphabetize.* *In math.* Lauka'ina. *In* ~, *consecutive.* Moekahi. *To put in order.* Ho'oka'ina. *To* ~ *ideas, as in a compositon.* Ho'oka'ina mana'o.

serendipity *Making a fortunate discovery by accident.* Ūlialia pōmaika'i. See *coincidence.*

serial *As of a computer port.* Ala
pūkaʻina. *~ port.* Awa ala pūkaʻina.

series Pūkaʻina. *See alkane, alkene,
alkyne, chain, range.* *~ of volcanic
eruptions.* Pūkaʻina hū pele. *TV ~.*
Pūkaʻina polokalamu kīwī. *~ of
geological features.* Pae. *See Hawaiian
entries under* pae.

serious *To act or "get ~."* Hoʻokūoʻo.

serve *To ~, in volleyball.* Hānai, paʻi
ulele. *See service, set.* *To ~ underhand.*
Hānai puʻupuʻu. *To make a sidewinder
~.* Paʻi kulo. *To receive a ~; also first
pass.* Kiʻi.

server *Network ~, as for a computer
network.* Kikowaena pūnaewele. *See
network station.*

service Lawelawe. *See entry below and
Bulletin Board Service, weather service.
High-quality ~.* Lawelawe poʻokela. *~
industry.* ʻOihana lawelawe. *Military ~;
also army.* Pūʻali koa. *National Marine
Fisheries ~.* ʻOihana Lawaiʻa Kai Pekelala.
National Park ~. ʻOihana Pāka Aupuni.
US Fish and Wildlife ~. ʻOihana Iʻa me
ka Holoholona Lōhiu o ʻAmelika.

service *In volleyball; also to serve (the
ball).* Paʻi ulele. *See serve, side out.* *~
violation.* ʻAʻena paʻi ulele.

serving *Of food.* Haʻawina ʻai.

session *A period of time spent in an
application of a computer program.* Wā
hoʻohana.

set *A collection of like items or
elements.* Huikaina. *See entries below.
As of golf clubs or silverware.* ʻŌpaʻa.
To ~, as a record. Mākia. *To ~, as the
sun.* Napoʻo, anapoʻo. *To ~ an imu.* Kuʻi
i ka imu. *To ~ a deadline.* Kaupalena.
See deadline.

set *To ~, as margins or tabs on a
computer file or typewriter.* Hoʻopaʻa.
*See margin, set up, setup, spacing, tab.
To ~ the margins.* Hoʻopaʻa i nā lihi. *To
~ the tabs.* Hoʻopaʻa i nā kāwāholo. *To
~ spacing.* Hoʻokoana.

set *As for movie or video production.*
Kahua. *To decorate ~s.* Hoʻoponopono
kahua. *~ decorator.* Mea hoʻoponopono
kahua. *To design ~s.* Hakulau kahua.
~ designer. Mea hakulau kahua.

set *To ~ or ~ up (the ball), in volleyball.*
Hānai, hāʻawi. *To make a back ~.* Hānai i
hope, hānai kīkala. *To make an outside
~.* Hānai lōʻihi. *To make a short ~.*
Hānai pōkole. *~ter.* Mea hānai, hānai.

set shot *In basketball; to make such a
shot.* Kī kū.

settle *To ~, as a claim.* Hoʻonā. *See
land court, land registration system.*

settlement pattern *In geography.*
Lauana hoʻokahua.

set type *To ~, as for video captions.*
Ulele hua. *See character operator.*

set up *To ~, as printer specifications
for a computer.* Hoʻonoho. *See setup.*

setup *Also to set up, as in a computer
program.* Hoʻokuene. *See set up.* *Page
~.* Hoʻokuene ʻaoʻao.

sewage *~ sludge.* Kaekene. *Raw ~.*
Kaekene maka. *Treated ~.* Ke kaekene i
kāemikala ʻia.

sewer pipe Paipu lawe ʻino. *See
manhole cover.*

sex *Safe ~; to practice safe ~.* Ai
palekana. *Unprotected ~; to practice
unprotected ~.* Ai palekana ʻole.

sexism Hoʻokae keka.

sextant Ana kilo lani.

sexual harassment *Also to subject to
~.* Kekohala.

sexually transmitted disease *STD.*
Maʻi lele ai.

Seychelles Sekele. *~ Islands.* Ka pae
moku ʻo Sekele.

shade *For a lamp.* Pale kukui. *To ~, as
with a pencil.* Kahiāuli. *See highlight.*

shadow *As on a computer or in
typesetting.* Hoʻāka. *See eye shadow.*
~ed. Aka. *Rain ~.* Lulu ʻalaneo.

shake *Milk ~.* Waiū luliluli.

shallow *As a dish.* Pānainai.

shampoo Kopa lauoho. See *soap.*

shape *Geometric figure, in math.* Kinona. *Regular ~.* Kinona analahi.

shape *To model or mold, as clay.* Hōʻomoʻomo.

sharp *Pungent, as the smell of ammonia or vinegar.* Wiʻu.

shave ice *Snow cone.* Haukōhi.

shavings *Wood ~.* Hānā.

shaving soap Kopa kahi ʻumiʻumi, *usu.* kopa ʻumiʻumi.

shawl *Also light blanket.* Kīhei, kīhei pili.

sheet *As of stamps.* Laulahi. *~ of stamps.* Laulahi poʻoleka. See *bedsheet, call sheet.*

sheet feeder *As for a computer printer.* Poho pepa. *Additional ~.* Poho pākuʻi.

sheeting *Plastic ~, general term.* Hāliʻi ʻea. See *polyethyline.*

shelf Haka kau. *Book~.* Haka kau puke. See *continental shelf.*

shelter Wahi hoʻomalu. *Lean-to ~.* Hale kāpiʻo.

shield *As for battle.* Pale kaua. *As in volcanoes.* Kuahene. *~ building; to build a shield (volcano).* Hoʻāhua kuahene. *~ cone.* Puʻu kuahene. *~ volcano.* Lua pele kuahene. *Primary ~ volcano.* Lua pele kuahene kuamua. *To ~ or cover, as one's mouth.* Pale.

shift *To ~, as on a computer or typewriter keyboard.* Kake. *~ key.* Pihi kake *(preceded by* ke*).*

shifting cultivation *In geography.* Mahi ʻai mahakea.

shirt *With short or long sleeves.* Palaka, pālule. *Aloha ~.* Palaka aloha. *T-~.* Palaʻili, paleʻili. *Any pullover style shirt.* Palaʻili.

Shoals *French Frigate ~.* Kānemilohaʻi.

shock *To give an electric ~.* Omo, miki. *To give a severe electric ~.* ʻŪmiʻi.

shock therapy Lapaʻau hoʻomiki uila.

shoe *Hiking ~.* Kāmaʻa hekehi. See *hike. Saddle ~, Oxford.* Kāmaʻa ʻili helei. *Snow ~.* Kāmaʻa hele hau.

shoot *To ~, as a photograph.* Paʻi *(preceded by* ke*).* See *shot, take. To ~ a movie film.* Paʻi kiʻiʻoniʻoni. *To ~ a video.* Paʻi wikiō.

shoot *From the root of a plant.* Kauwowo, kawowo, kā, ʻelia, ilo. See *seedling.*

shooting forward *Also swing man or three man, in basketball.* Kūkolu.

shooting guard *Also two man, in basketball.* Kūlua.

shooting star Hōkū welowelo. See *comet.*

shopping cart Kaʻa mākeke.

shopping center Kikowaena kūʻai.

shortcut *Also to take a ~.* ʻOki pōkole.

short-range *Also short-term.* Hikiāpoko. See *medium-range, long-range. ~ plan.* Papa hoʻolālā hikiāpoko.

short set *To make a ~, in volleyball.* Hānai pōkole.

short-term See *short-range.*

shot *Photograph.* Kiʻi paʻi. See *close-up, medium shot, wide shot. As of a photograph or in movie or video production.* Paʻi *(preceded by* ke*). Types of ~s.* Nā ʻano paʻi.

shot *Also to shoot, as in basketball.* Kī. See *basket, missed shot. Bank ~.* Kī papa. *Hook ~.* Kī papaʻi. *Jump ~.* Kī lele. *Lay-up.* Kī kīkoʻo, kī pai. *Set ~.* Kī kū. *Slam dunk.* Pākī. *Swish, rimless ~.* Kuhō. *Three-point ~.* Kī ʻai kolu. *Tip-in.* Kī papaʻi.

shovel Kopalā. See *trowel, spade. Steam ~.* Kewe kopalā.

show *To demonstrate, as how a math problem is solved.* Kuhikuhi.

show and tell *As in a preschool or elementary school class.* Hōʻikeʻike.

shower *For bathing.* Kililau. *To take a ~, bathe by ~ing.* ʻAuʻau kililau. *Handheld ~.* Kililau lima. *~ cap.* Pāpale kililau. *~ curtain.* Pale kililau. *~ stall.* Keʻena kililau. *~ head.* Poʻo kililau (*preceded by* ke).

shoyu *Soy sauce.* Koiū. See *soybean.*

shrimp *Brine ~.* Pokipoki ālia.

shrink-wrapping *Also to shrink-wrap.* Wahī mimiki.

shrivelled *As grass or leaves.* Pīʻaʻaka.

shrub *Bush.* Laʻalāʻau. *Alpine ~land.* Wao laʻalāʻau.

shuffle *To ~, as cards.* Kakekake. See *deal.*

shuttle Kaʻa halihali. *Space ~.* Mokuhali lewa lipo.

shuttle run *In track.* Holo hoʻoili.

shy *Also wild, general term.* ʻĀhiu. See *wild.*

Siberia *Also Siberian.* Siberia. *East Siberian Sea.* Ke kai ʻo Siberia Hikina.

side *Also leg, of a triangle.* ʻAoʻao. See *base, ray. Corresponding ~.* ʻAoʻao launa. *Adjacent ~, of a right triangle.* ʻAoʻao pili. *Opposite ~, of a right triangle.* ʻAoʻao huli alo.

side *Of a sporting field or court.* Iwi, ʻaoʻao. *See entries below and* end, line (*as on a basketball court*). *~ line.* Laina iwi, laina ʻaoʻao. *~ line of the key on a basketball court.* Laina iwi kī.

side out *In volleyball.* Hāʻawi i ke kinipōpō i kekahi ʻaoʻao; kaʻa paʻi ulele, kaʻa. See *service.*

side pool *As in a stream.* Wai wiliau.

side stroke *Also to swim the ~.* ʻAu ʻaoʻao. See *stroke.*

sidewalk Alapīpā.

sideward Haʻaaʻe.

sidewinder serve *To make a ~, in volleyball.* Paʻi kulo.

Sierra Leone Sielaleone.

sight *Sense of ~.* Lonoa maka. *~ line.* Laina lena, laina ʻike.

sighter *As for surveying.* Lena māka. See *elevation pole, surveying rod. ~ arm.* Lima lena māka.

sight line *Also line of sight.* Laina lena, laina ʻike.

sign *As political or business, etc.* Papa hoʻolaha, hōʻailona. *See Hawaiian entries under* kaha *and* signature, symbol. *Cent ~.* Kaha kēneka. *Dollar ~.* Kaha kālā.

signal baton *As used by a marching bandleader.* ʻAukaʻi pāna.

signature *Also to sign one's name.* Pūlima. See *initial.*

sign language ʻŌlelo kuhi lima. *To use ~.* Kuhi lima. *American ~ (ASL).* ʻŌlelo Kuhi Lima ʻAmelika.

silence *A command for ~ on the set of a film, play, or video production.* Hāmau, e hāmau kō ke kahua.

silica Silaka. *~ gel g, a powder used as the sorbent layer in thin-layer chromatography.* Palaholo silaka g (*pronounced* palaholo silaka gā).

silicon Silikone.

silicone *Used as an adhesive.* Tuko pīlali.

sill *Window ~.* Paepae pukaaniani.

silt ʻElehune.

silver dollar Kālā keʻokeʻo.

similar *In math.* ʻAno like. *~ figure.* Kinona ʻano like.

simple *Basic, uncomplicated.* Nōhie. See *complex.*

simplify *As in a math problem.* Hoʻomaʻalahi.

simulate Hoʻokūkohukohu. See *simulation.*

simulation *In math.* Hoʻomeamea.

sing *To ~ in harmony.* Hīmeni kūlauna like.

Singapore Sinapoa.

singer Puʻukani.

single cell *Also single-celled; one cell, one-celled.* Hunaola kahi.

single space See *spacing*.

sink *As in a bathroom or kitchen.* Kinika.

sink *To make a basket, in basketball.* Hoʻokomo i ke kinipōpō.

site Kahua. *Archaeological ~.* Kahua hulikoehana. *Geological ~.* Kahua hulihonua. *~ map.* Palapala ʻāina kahua.

situp *Also to do ~s.* Pelu ʻōpū.

six inches *A warm-up exercise for sports such as volleyball.* ʻEono ʻīniha.

six man *Also first off the bench, i.e. first alternate or substitute player, in basketball.* Kūono.

six-pack *As of drinks.* ʻEkeʻeke. See *case, pack, twelve-pack. ~ of soda.* ʻEkeʻeke koloaka. *~ of beer.* ʻEkeʻeke pia. *~ ring, the plastic ring which holds the cans together.* ʻEa ʻekeʻeke. *Six-pack beer ring.* ʻEa ʻekeʻeke pia. *Six-pack soda ring.* ʻEa ʻekeʻeke koloaka.

sixteenth note *In music.* Hua mele hapa ʻumikūmāono.

sixteenth rest *In music.* Hoʻomaha hapa ʻumikūmāono.

size *As of clothes.* Helu. *Small, as of clothes or drinks.* Liʻiliʻi. *Abb.* liʻi. *Medium.* Lōpū. *Abb.* lō. *Large.* Nui. See *extra large*.

skate *Ice ~.* Kāmaʻa holo hau. *To ~ with ice ~s.* Holo hau. *Roller ~.* Kāmaʻa huila. *To ~ with roller ~s.* Holo kāmaʻa huila. *Rollerblade.* Kāmaʻa lapa huila. *To ~ with rollerblades.* Holo lapa huila.

skateboard Papa huila. *~ ramp.* Heʻena papa huila.

skeleton Kinanahiwi. *As for Halloween.* Kanaka iwi, kelekona. See *dragon*.

skew *To ~, as a deviation from a straight line, in math.* Pāweo. *~ line.* Laina pāweo.

ski *To ~, in snow.* Heʻe hau. See *lift. To cross-country ~.* Heʻe hau peʻa ʻāina. *To water ~.* Heʻe wai. *~ boot.* Kāmaʻa

puki heʻe hau. *~ cap, stocking cap.* Pāpale kapuhau.

skid *To ~, as a car; to slip.* Pakika.

skiff *Also rowboat.* ʻŌpā.

skill Mākau. See *language arts, physical education. Communication ~.* Mākau hoʻokaʻaʻike. *Decision-making ~.* Mākau hoʻoholo manaʻo. *Grammar or sentence structure ~.* Mākau pilinaʻōlelo. *Life-saving ~.* Mākau hoʻopakele ola. *Planning ~.* Mākau hoʻolālā. *Practical life ~.* Mākau ola. *Prediction ~.* Mākau wānana. *Productive-thinking ~.* Mākau hoʻomohala manaʻo. *Thinking ~.* Mākau noʻonoʻo. *Building thinking ~s book.* Puke mākau noʻonoʻo. *Word ~.* Mākau huaʻōlelo.

skim *To ~, as milk.* Heʻe. *~ milk.* Waiū heʻe. *To ~, as oil from the top of stew.* Kīʻoʻe, ʻoʻe. See *ladle*.

skim read Heluhelu pākākā. *~ing.* Ka heluhelu pākākā ʻana.

skin ʻIli, ʻaluʻalu. See *dermis, epidermis, subcutus. To ~, as a pig or sheep.* Pākā. See *quarter*.

skip count *In math.* Helu lele.

skull Iwi poʻo.

skunk Ponī. *~ cabbage.* Kāpiki ponī.

sky dive Luʻu lewa. *Sky diver.* Mea luʻu lewa.

skyscraper Kiʻenaoʻa. See *highrise*.

slalom course Ala heihei kīkeʻekeʻe.

slam dunk *In basketball.* Pākī. See *shoot*.

slang Palaualea.

slash *In printing (/).* Kaha hiō, kaha hiō piʻi. *Back~ (\).* Kaha hiō iho.

slash and burn *A method of land cultivation.* Kā makawela.

slat Leka.

slaw See *cole slaw*.

sled *For snow.* Hōlua hau.

sleek *Also streamlined.* Mio. See *sports car*.

sleep ~*ing bag.* 'Eke moe, 'eke hiamoe (*preceded by ke*). *To be* ~*ing or snoring, as a response when asked where someone is.* Kula'i hāpu'u. ~ *well.* Hiamoe pono, hiamoe maika'i. See *good night.*

sleight of hand *Magic trick, illusion.* Pāha'ohuna.

slice *To* ~ *off.* 'Okikaha.

slide *Photographic transparency.* Ki'iaka. *See entries below.* ~ *mount.* Mōlina ki'iaka. ~ *projector.* Mīkini ho'olele ki'iaka, mīkini ki'iaka. *Movie or* ~ *screen.* Pākū ho'olele ki'i.

slide *As for a microscope.* Aniani kaupane'e, *usu.* aniani. See *microscope stage.*

slide *To move a geometric figure without flipping or turning, in math.* Ho'one'e. See *flip.*

slide *To* ~, *as a door.* Uai. *Sliding door.* Puka uai, 'īpuka uai. *Sliding latch.* Laka uai.

slide *To execute a defensive* ~, *in basketball.* Pāpa'i.

slide *Water* ~, *as Slip 'n' Slide; to go on a water* ~. Pahe'e wai. *Water-*~ *mat.* Moena pahe'e wai.

sliding See *transform.*

sling psychrometer Ma'a ana kawaūea kūlua. See *hygrometer, psychrometer.*

slip *To* ~, *as on a wet sidewalk; to skid.* Pakika.

Slip 'n' Slide See *water slide.*

slipper lobster Ula pāpapa, ula 'āpapapa.

sliver *Also splinter.* Māmalamala.

slope *Continental* ~. Hene mokuhonua. See *continental shelf.*

slot *Paper tray* ~, *as for a computer printer.* 'Āpo'o poho pepa.

sloth *The animal.* Melalemu. *Giant* ~. Melalemu pilikua.

Slovakia Solowakia.

Slovenia Solowenia.

slow down *To* ~, *as in a fast break, in basketball; also to bring back out.* Kuemi, kuemi iki.

sludge *Sewage* ~. Kaekene.

slug *A gastropod closely related to land snails.* Kamaloli.

slurry *A viscous solution of liquid and a solid.* Kaluli.

small *As drink size.* Li'ili'i. See *medium, large. Abb.* li'i. ~ *soda.* Koloaka li'ili'i.

small *Lower case.* Na'ina'i. See *letter.* ~ *letter.* Hua na'ina'i.

small-claims court *Also small-debts court.* 'Aha koi pohō 'u'uku.

small-debts court See *small-claims court.*

smell *Sense of* ~. Lonoa ihu.

smoke *To* ~, *as meat or fish.* Ho'ouahi.

smoke alarm Oeoe uahi.

smokestack *As for a factory.* Pū'o'a uahi.

smooth *To* ~, *as in a computer program.* Ho'olaumania. See *unsmooth.*

smooth muscle Mākala kū'oko'a.

smooth talk *Also smooth talker, to talk smooth; glib.* Waha wali.

smut *A kind of plant disease or the fungus which causes it.* Kalina pa'u. *Corn* ~. Kalina pa'u kūlina.

snail *Land* ~. Homeka. *Cannibal* ~. Homeka hamuhika.

snakeweed Nāhelehesa.

snap *Fastener.* Pihi 'ūmi'i (*preceded by ke*), 'ūmi'i. ~ *cube.* Palaka kepa.

snap *To* ~, *as a photograph.* Pa'i (*preceded by ke*). See *take.*

snapdragon Pualāpaki.

sneaker *Tennis shoe.* Kāma'a lole.

snoring *To be* ~ *or sleeping, as a response when asked where someone is.* Kūla'i hāpu'u.

snorkel Paipu hanu. *To* ~. 'Au'au paipu hanu.

snow ~ *avalanche.* 'Āholo hau. *See entries below.* ~ *cone, shave ice.* Haukōhi. ~ *shoe.* Kāma'a hele hau.

snowflake Ulahi hau.

snowman Kanaka hau.

snowmobile Ka'a hau.

so *The fifth note on the musical scale.* Nō. *See Hawaiian entry pākōlī.*

soap Kopa. *See shampoo. Dishwasher* ~. Kopa mīkini holoi pā. *Shaving* ~. Kopa kahi 'umi'umi, *usu.* kopa 'umi'umi. ~ *dish.* Pā kopa (*preceded by* ke). ~ *dispenser.* 'Ūhōlo'a kopa.

soccer Pōwāwae. ~ *ball.* Kinipōpō pōwāwae.

socialization *See socialize.*

socialize *To fit or train (someone) for a social environment or to associate sociably with others; also socialization.* A'o launa kanaka.

social services Lawelawe kōkua.

social studies Pilikanaka.

society *An enduring social group.* Kaiapili. *Humane* ~. 'Ahahui Maka'ala Holoholona.

sociology Kālailauna kanaka.

soda Koloaka. *See baking soda. Six-pack of* ~. 'Eke'eke koloaka. *Twelve-pack of* ~. Pū'olo koloaka. *Case of* ~. Pahu koloaka. ~ *can tab.* Une kini koloaka.

sodium Sodiuma. ~ *bisulfate.* Sodiuma bisulafahate. ~ *citrate.* Sodiuma kitarahate.

software *As for a computer.* Lako polokalamu. *See hardware.*

soil Lepo. *See planting medium. Alluvial* ~. Lepo makaili. *Potting* ~. Lepo kanu meakanu. *Standard* ~ *testing kit.* Hōkeo kūmau ho'ā'o lepo.

solar Lā. *See sunspot.* ~ *constant.* Kā'ei kau lā. ~ *energy wave.* Hawewe ikehu lā. ~ *flare.* Lapa ahi lā. ~ *granule, gigantic waves of gas which roll across the surface of the sun.* 'Ale ahi lā. ~

prominences, i.e. puffs of gas which gently drift above the surface of the sun. Puapua'i lā. ~ *panel.* 'Ūomo ikehu lā. ~ *power.* Manehu lā. ~ *radiation.* Pāhawewe lā. ~ *system.* Poe lā.

solid *As opposed to liquid or gas.* Kinopa'a, pa'a. *See solid rocket booster. Geometric* ~. Pa'a. ~ *figure.* Kinona pa'a.

solid rocket booster Kao wāwahie kinopa'a, kao wāwahie pa'a.

solstice Māuiki'iki'i. *See equinox. Summer* ~. Ka māuiki'iki'i o ke kauwela. *Winter* ~. Ka māuiki'iki'i o ka ho'oilo.

solubility *Also soluble.* Pēmā'ō'ā. *See solution. Selective* ~. Pēmā'ō'ā wae 'ano.

solute Mea hehe'e. *See solvent.*

solution *To a problem.* Hā'ina. *See entry below and problem, solve. Also resolution, as of a problem in a story.* Hopena holo.

solution *A homogeneous mixture.* Mā'ō'āna. *See solubility, suspension. Aqueous* ~. Mā'ō'āna 'ūhehe'e wai. *Chemical* ~. Mā'ō'āna kemikala. *Hydroponic* ~. Mā'ō'āna kāmāhuaola. *See hydroponics. To be in* ~. Mā'ō'ā.

solve Hana a loa'a ka hā'ina. *To resolve difficulties.* Ho'oponopono pilikia. *To look for a solution.* Huli hā'ina, huli i ka hā'ina, 'imi hā'ina. *To* ~ *a problem.* Ho'omākalakala i ka polopolema. *Decoded,* ~*d.* Mākalakala.

solvent 'Ūhehe'e. *See solute.* ~ *front, i.e. the leading edge of a moving* ~ *as in a developing chromatogram.* 'Ae omowaho.

Somalia *Also Somalian.* Somalia.

soprano Leo 'ekahi. ~ *'ukulele.* 'Ukulele leo 'ekahi.

sorbent *An absorbent material such as used in chromatography.* 'Ūomo. *See absorb.*

sound ~ *barrier.* Palena holo kani. *Speed of* ~. Māmā kani, māmā holo o ke kani. *See entries below.*

sound *Also ~ effects, as on a computer.* Kani. See *beep*. *~ effects, as for a play, movie, or video production.* Kani keaka. *~ editor.* Luna hoʻoponopono kani. *~ effects coordinator.* Luna kani keaka. *~ technician.* Mea ʻenehana kani.

sound *~ segment, in linguistics.* Hua. *Epenthetic ~.* Hua komo.

sound hole *As on an ʻukulele or guitar.* Puka kani.

sound wavelength Kōā hawewe kani. See *amplitude, sound waves*.

sound waves *As used in measuring ocean depths.* Hawewe kani. See *sound wavelength*.

source *Reference material, as a dictionary.* Kūmole. See entry below and *resource*. *Root, derivation, or origin, as the etymology of a word.* Molekumu.

source pollution Kumu hoʻohaumia. *Point ~.* Kumu hoʻohaumia ʻike ʻia. *Non-point ~.* Kumu hoʻohaumia ʻike ʻole ʻia.

south Hema. *Abb. Hm. See entries below.* *~ pole.* Wēlau hema.

South Africa *Also South African.* ʻApelika Hema, ʻAferika Hema.

South America *Also South American.* ʻAmelika Hema.

South Carolina *Also South Carolinean.* Kalolaina Hema.

South China Sea Ke kai ʻo Kina Hema.

South Dakota *Also South Dakotan.* Kakoka Hema, Dakota Hema.

Southern Equatorial Current *In oceanography.* Kalekale. See *Northern Equatorial Current, Equatorial Counter-current*.

southern hemisphere Poepoe hapa hema. See *hemisphere*.

South Korea *Also South Korean.* Kōlea Hema, Kōrea Hema.

South Yemen *Also South Yemenite, South Yemeni.* Iemene Hema. See *North Yemen*.

sow bug Pokipoki.

soybean *Also soya bean.* Pāpapa koiū.

soy sauce *Shoyu.* Koiū.

space *As a crack between fence boards.* Kōā. See entries below and *crack*. *As on a game board such as Monopoly.* Kuea. *Chance ~ (in Monopoly).* Kuea huki pepa. *Between horizontal lines on a musical staff.* Wā o ke kōkua hua mele, wā o ke kōkua. See *musical staff*.

space *As between words when typing on a computer or typewriter.* Kaʻahua. See *tab, spacing*. *~ bar.* Pihi hoʻokōā, pihi kaʻahua (*preceded by* ke). *As in tab settings on a computer or typewriter.* Kāwā. *Disk ~, as on a computer hard drive or floppy disk.* Hakahaka pā.

space *A pound sign (#) used in proofreading to indicate that a ~ should be inserted, in proofreading; a superscript number written next to the symbol indicates the number of ~s if more than one (#^{2}).* Kaha kaʻahua.

space Lewa. See entries below and *atmosphere*. *Outer ~.* Lewa lipo. *~ alien, extraterrestrial.* Mea ao ʻē. *~ map.* Palapala lewa lipo. *~ walk.* Hele lewa lipo. *~ capsule.* Kelena moku ahikao.

spacecraft *Also spaceship.* Moku ahikao.

space crane *Also remote manipulator arm.* Lima kia pihi.

space figure *In math.* Kinona pihanahaka. See *geometric figure, plane figure*.

space flight Lele lewa lipo. *Manned ~.* Lele lewa lipo kanaka.

space probe ʻAkiu lewa lipo.

space program Polokalamu lewa lipo.

spaceship *Also spacecraft.* Moku ahikao.

space shuttle Mokuhali lewa lipo.

space station Oʻioʻina lewa lipo.

space suit Paʻalole hele lewa.

spacing *As lines in a printed document.* Koana. *See* space. *Single space, single-line* ~. Koana pākahi. *One and one-half space, one and one-half-line* ~. Koana pākahi hapalua. *Double space, double-line* ~. Koana pālua. *To set* ~. Ho'okoana.

spade *Small* ~, *as a garden tool.* Kopalā li'ili'i.

spading fork 'Ō 'eli (*preceded by* ke).

spaghetti Pakeki.

Spain Kepania, Sepania.

span *Life* ~. Kāwā ola.

sparkler *Fireworks.* Hōkūpa'alima.

sparkling water *Also mineral water.* Wai pi'ipi'i.

spark plug 'Ōpu'uahi.

sparrow Manu kālā.

sparse *Also few; seldom, rarely.* Kāka'ikahi.

spatter cone *In geology.* Pu'u pōhāhā. *See* ejecta.

spatula *Also pancake turner.* 'Ūlau. *Rubber* ~. 'Ūlau kahi.

speaker *As for a stereo.* Pahu leo. *See* amplifier.

special effects Hi'ohi'ona na'iau. *To have* ~. Na'iau. *To add* ~. Ho'ona'iau (i ka hi'ohi'ona). ~ *coordinator, as for movie or video production.* Luna hi'ohi'ona na'iau.

specialist Laekahi.

species *In biology.* Lāhulu, lāhui. *See* endangered. *Depleted* ~. Lāhulu emi, lāhui emi. *Endangered* ~ *Act.* Kānāwai Lāhulu 'Ane Halapohe. *Related* ~. Pili lāhulu.

specific Kiko'ī. *See entries below and* document specific.

specifications *Also specs, to specify.* Kuhi'ī.

specific gravity *Also relative gravity.* Lākiō pa'apū wai.

specific heat *In physics.* Ana pi'i wela.

specify *See* specifications.

specimen La'ana.

speech Ha'i'ōlelo. *See* oral report. *Expressive* ~; ~ *to entertain.* Ha'i'ōlelo mikolololehua. *Narrative* ~. Ha'i'ōlelo kūhaha'i. *Persuasive* ~. Ha'i'ōlelo ho'ohuli mana'o.

speed Māmā holo. *See entries below and* accelerate, decelerate. *Average* ~. 'Awelike māmā holo. ~ *of light.* Māmā kukuna lā, māmā holo o ke kukuna lā. ~ *of sound.* Māmā kani, māmā holo o ke kani.

speed bump *As on a road or in a parking lot.* Pu'u ha'apupū.

speed read *To* ~. Heluwawe. ~*ing.* Ka heluwawe 'ana. *See* speed write.

speed write *To* ~; *also any document which has been written using speed writing.* Kāwawe. *See* speed read.

spell *See* misspelled word.

spell checker *As of a computer document; also to spell check.* Loipela. *See* proofread.

spending *Deficit* ~. Ho'olilo pākeu.

sperm *Also spermatozoon, in biology.* Hua'āne. *See* ovum.

sphagnum Hulupō'e'ē, mākōpi'i hulupō'e'ē. *See* moss.

sphere Poepoe. *See* globe, hemisphere. *In math.* Pa'apoepoe.

sphincter *An annular muscle surrounding and able to contract or close a bodily opening or channel.* Mākala 'amo.

sphinx *A mythological monster with the head of a woman and the body of a lion.* Kanaka kino liona. *See entry below.*

Sphinx *The huge sphinx found near the pyramids at Giza in Egypt.* Sapenika Liona.

spider Nananana, nanana. *See* tarantula. *Black widow* ~. Nananana hese 'ele'ele, nanana hese 'ele'ele. *Happy face* ~. Nananana makaki'i, nanana makaki'i. *No-eyed big-eyed hunting spider.* Nananana maka 'ole, nanana maka 'ole.

spike *To ~ (the ball), in volleyball.* Hili, pākī. See *hitter*. *To ~ with closed fist.* Ku'i pu'upu'u. *To ~ with open hand.* Pa'i pālahalaha. *To make a fake ~, an off-speed shot.* Pākī 'epa. *Angle ~.* Hili 'ao'ao. *Line ~.* Hili laina. *Point from ~.* 'Ai hele wale.

spinach Lū'au Haole.

spine *Backbone.* Iwi kuamo'o. See *vertebra*.

spinner *As in board games.* Pāniniu *(preceded by ke)*.

spiralateral *In math.* Pāka'awili. *To draw a ~.* Kaha pāka'awili.

spiritually-based learning A'o kahua 'uhane. *See Hawaiian entries beginning with a'o kahua.*

spleen Akeloa.

splice *To ~, as film or video segments for movie or video production.* Ho'oku'iku'i. See *assemble editor*.

splinter *Also sliver.* Māmalamala.

split *As in a sidewalk; also to ~.* 'Oā. See *crack*.

split end *In football.* Lala. See *tight end, safety*.

spoke *As on a bicycle wheel.* Kukuna. *Bicycle ~.* Kukuna huila paikikala.

sponge *The aquatic animal.* Hu'akai.

spongy *As leaves of the pānini.* 'Ūpī'ū. See *coconut*.

sponsor *A legislator who presents and/or assumes responsibility for the passing of a bill.* Mea hāpai pila.

spontaneous *Impromptu.* Ulu wale.

sport Ha'uki. *Indoor ~.* Ha'uki maluhale. *Outdoor ~.* Ha'uki kaupokulani. *Coach for ~s.* Ka'i 'ālapa. *~s trainer.* Ka'i ha'uki.

sports car Ka'a mio.

spout *To ~, as a whale.* Pūhāhā.

sprained 'Unu.

spray Kīkī. See *substance*. *~ paint.* Pena kīkina. *~ wax.* Kīkina ho'ohinuhinu.

spread *As data on a graph, in math.* Waiho. *Data ~.* Ka waiho o ka 'ikepili.

spreading See *divergent*.

spread open *Also blossoming, blooming, as a flower.* Mohala.

spreadsheet *As in a computer program.* Pakuhi maka'aha. *~ program.* Polokalamu pakuhi maka'aha.

spring Kupulau. See *vernal equinox*.

spring beauty *A kind of flower.* Nanikupulau.

sprint *Dash.* Holo kikī.

sprout Kawowo. See *coconut*. *Alfalfa ~.* Kawowo 'alapapa. *Bean ~.* Kawowo pāpapa. *To germinate.* Ilo. *To cause to ~.* Ho'oilo.

spur *Also to ~; to gore with a tusk.* Kepa, kēpā. See *boar's tusk*.

square *In math.* Pāho'onui lua. See entries below and *cubed, hundredths square*. *The ~ of the number.* Ka pāho'onui lua o ka helu. *Geometric shape.* Huinahā like.

square foot *In math.* Kapua'i pāho'onui lua. *Abb. kp ph^2. Lay term.* Kapua'i kuea.

square root *In math.* Kumu pāho'onui lua.

squash *General term.* Ipu. See *pumpkin. An edible variety.* Pipinola.

squid *As per Haole definition; cuttlefish as per local definition.* Mūhe'e. *As per local definition; octopus as per Haole definition.* He'e.

squirrel Kiulela. See *chipmonk. Arctic ground ~.* Kiulela 'Alika.

Sri Lanka Sililanaka.

stable Hale lio.

stack *To ~, as windows in a computer program.* Ho'okūpa'i. *To ~ windows.* Ho'okūpa'i pukaaniani.

staff *Musical ~.* Kōkua hua mele, ko'oko'o, kumu 'ākōlī.

stage *As of a microscope.* Paepae aniani kaupane‘e. *See slide (microscope). As level of development or difficulty.* Pae. *See level.*

stagehand *Or grip, as for movie or video production.* Mea kūkulu kahua. *See stage manager.*

stage manager *Or key grip, as for movie or video production.* Luna kūkulu kahua. *See stagehand.*

stair ‘Anu‘u. *See step.*

staircase landing Paepae alapi‘i.

stake *Tent ~.* Pine halepe‘a.

stalactite Kuluna.

stalagmite Kulalo.

stall *Shower ~.* Ke‘ena kililau.

stamp *Airmail ~.* Po‘oleka halilele. *Sheet of ~s.* Laulahi po‘oleka.

stance *Defensive ~, as in basketball.* Kūlana pale.

stand Kū. *See tripod, easel. Ring ~, as for a test tube.* Kū hano ho‘okolohua.

standard Ma‘amau, kūmau. *See entries below and deluxe. ~ room, as in a hotel.* Lumi ma‘amau. *~ soil- testing kit.* Hōkeo kūmau ho‘ā‘o lepo. *An established model or example.* Ana ho‘ohālike. *To set the ~.* Ho‘opa‘a i ke ana ho‘ohālike.

standard *US or customary unit of measurement.* Anakahi ‘Amelika. *~ form, as for numbers.* Kino huahelu.

standard *As in deviation, in math.* Kūmau. *See normal. ~ deviation.* Haiahū kūmau.

stand for *To ~, as in a math problem.* Kūhō‘ailona.

stand-in *As for an actor in a movie or video production.* Pani hakahaka, pani (*preceded by* ke).

standing long jump *In track.* Lele loloa.

stannous chloride Satanousa koloriside.

staple *For paper.* Kui ‘ūmi‘i pepa. *To ~.* ‘Ūmi‘i. *Stapler.* Mea ‘ūmi‘i pepa. *~ remover.* Mea wehe ‘ūmi‘i.

star *Shooting ~.* Hōkū welowelo. *The ~ in the center of the constellation Carina.* Mākoi.

starboard *Right or ~ side of a single-hulled canoe when looking forward.* Muku. *See port. ~ hull of a double-hulled canoe or right side of a ship when looking forward.* ‘Ākea.

starch *A white, tasteless, solid carbohydrate found in plants.* Pia‘ai.

starfish Hōkū kai.

starfruit Hua hōkū.

start *To ~, as a computer program.* Ho‘omaka. *See quit. To ~, as a machine; also to play, as a film or tape.* Ho‘oholo.

starting *~ point, as in a race.* Pahukū. *~ line.* Laina pahukū. *See finish.*

startup disk *As in a computer program.* Pā ho‘omaka (*preceded by* ke).

state *As one of the United States.* Moku‘āina. *See entries below. ~ fair.* Hō‘ike‘ike moku‘āina. *~ park.* Pāka moku‘āina.

State Department of Agriculture ‘Oihana Mahi ‘Ai o ka Moku‘āina.

statehood act *Also admission act.* Kānāwai ho‘olilo moku‘āina.

State Land Use Commission Komikina Ho‘ohana ‘Āina o ka Moku‘āina.

statement ‘Ōlelo. *Exclamatory ~; also to make such a statement.* ‘Ōlelo ho‘ōho. *Inequality ~, in math.* ‘Ōlelo no ke kaulike ‘ole. *Mission ~.* ‘Ōlelo ala nu‘ukia. *Vision ~.* ‘Ōlelo nu‘ukia.

state wildlife official Luna ho‘omalu holoholona lōhiu, ho‘omalu holoholona lōhiu.

station *As for a computer network.* Po‘opo‘o. *See network server. Network ~.* Po‘opo‘o pūnaewele. *Also channel, as on radio or television.* Kānela.

station *Field ~, as used when mapping a certain area.* Kikowaena pānānā. *See* subway. *Quarantine ~.* Hale hoʻomalu maʻi.

stationary front *As of weather.* Kuʻina paʻa. *See* front.

station-to-station call *Also to make such a call.* Kelepona kahua. *See Hawaiian entries under* kelepona.

statistics *Numerical facts or data, as in math.* ʻIkepili helu. *See* pie chart, table.

Statue of Liberty Kūkāʻokoʻa Kiahoʻomanaʻo, ke kiahoʻomanaʻo ʻo Kūkāʻokoʻa, Kūkāʻokoʻa.

status Kūlana. *Health ~.* Kūlana olakino.

statute *A law enacted by the legislative branch of a government.* Kānāwai ʻahaʻōlelo. *See* law, ordinance.

stay tuned *"To be continued," as during a TV program.* ʻAʻole i pau.

STD *Sexually transmitted disease.* Maʻi lele ai.

steal *To ~, in basketball.* ʻAihue.

steamed milk *(Hot) chocolate with ~.* Kokoleka me ka waiū māhu.

steamroller Kimalola.

steam shovel Kewe kopalā.

steel wool *Wire gauze.* Pulupulu uea.

stem and leaf plot *In math.* Pakuhi ʻau me ka lau. *See* chart.

stencil Anakuhi mahaka.

step *Also stair.* ʻAnuʻu. *As in problem solving.* ʻAnuʻu hana, ʻanuʻu.

steps *As in a dance or routine.* Kaʻina wāwae.

stereo *See* record player.

sternocleido-mastoid *The muscles between the sternum and the base of the ear.* Mākala luli poʻo.

steroid Pūhōmona.

stet *A series of dots written under a word or words which have been lined out to show that no change should be made from the original, in proof-*
reading. Kaha waiho.

stethoscope ʻIli hoʻolohe puʻuwai, kiupe hoʻolohe.

steward(ess) *Flight attendant.* Kuene mokulele.

stick *Small ~, twig.* ʻAulaʻo *(preceded by* ke). *Fish ~.* Manamana iʻa.

sticker Pepili.

stilt *Either the bird or the toy.* Kūkuluaeʻo.

stimulant Lāʻau haʻinole. *See* depressant.

stimulate *Also stimulus.* Kūlale. *See* response, stimulant. *To ~, as with a drug.* Haʻinole.

stock *As in the ~ market.* Kea hoʻopukapuka, kea. *See* invest.

stocking cap Pāpale kapuhau.

stoma Pukahanu.

stomach poison Lāʻau make ʻai.

stone *Air ~, the porous rock in an aquarium that creates tiny bubbles at the surface of the water to facilitate the exchange of gases.* Pōhaku puka ea.

stool *Without a back.* Noho kū.

stop *In linguistics.* Pohā. *To ~ or break, as an electric circuit.* ʻOki. *See* open.

stoplight Kukui hoʻokū.

stop sign Hōʻailona hoʻokū.

stopwatch Uaki helu manawa, uāki helu manawa.

storage cabinet Waihona hoʻāhu. *See* storeroom.

store Hale kūʻai. *Garden ~, gardening ~.* Hale kūʻai mahi māla.

store away *Also to accumulate, lay away.* Hoʻāhu.

storeroom Lumi hoʻāhu. *See* storage cabinet.

storm *See* gale.

story *Floor, as in a building.* Papahele. *See entries below and* tale. *Predictable ~, in literature.* Moʻolelo hopena ahuwale.

storyboard *As in movie or video production.* Moʻolelo kaha. *~ artist.* Lima kaha moʻolelo. *~ terms.* Huaʻōlelo kaha moʻolelo.

storybook *Reader.* Puke heluhelu.

story telling *Traditional elements of Hawaiian poetry, ~, oratory, and narration.* Meiwi.

straight *Horizontal lines written above and below a word or words to indicate that they should be written or printed ~, in proofreading.* Kaha hoʻolālani.

straight angle *An angle that has a measure of 180°, in math.* Huina kaha.

straightedge Kaʻe pololei.

strap Kāʻawe. *See coveralls, tank top. Slipper ~.* Kāʻawe kalipa. *Metal ~ or band, as for banding around metal boxes, water tanks, etc.* Kalapu hao, kuapo hao. *See banding tool.*

strapping tape *Also filament tape.* Leki aʻa.

strategy *Or approach, as in solving a math problem.* Kaʻakālai.

stratus cloud Ao loa. *See cloud.*

straw *Drinking ~.* Meaomōmo. *Grain stalk.* Pua huika.

stream Kahawai. *See data stream. ~ current, in oceanography.* Au kikī. *Jet ~.* Au makani kikī. *~ sediment.* Koʻana kahawai.

streambed Papakū, papakū kahawai, kahena wai.

stream current *In oceanography.* Au kikī.

streamlined *Also sleek.* Mio. *See sports car.*

stream tributary ʻAumana kahawai.

stress *Emotional ~.* ʻAloʻahia. *Also accent, in linguistics.* Kālele.

stretch *To ~, as for warming up before exercise.* Hoʻomālō. *See neck stretches.*

striated muscle Mākala kū kōkua.

stride Kaʻi wāwae.

strike *To tag or ~ out, in baseball.* Hōʻauka. *To ~, as a match.* Koe.

strike through *To line out, as on a typewriter or computer; also used to indicate that the letters or words lined out are to be replaced by those written above, in proofreading.* Kahawaena.

string *As on an ʻukulele or guitar.* Kaula. *See ʻukulele. Names of ~s on an ʻukulele:* ke kaula o luna loa *(G),* ke kaula ʻelua *(C),* ke kaula ʻekolu *(E),* ke kaula ʻehā *(A). Eight-~ ʻukulele.* ʻUkulele ʻewalu kaula.

string bass *Also bass viol.* Pila kū nui, pila nui.

string bean Pāpapa hihi.

string instrument Pila.

string of firecrackers Kālī pahūpahū.

strip *As in a ~mat counting system, in math.* ʻAulahi *(preceded by* ke*). See counting strip, hundredths square, ten-strip board. Tenth ~.* ʻAukā helu hapa ʻumi.

stripmat *See counting mat.*

stroke *Breast ~; to swim the breast ~.* ʻAu umauma. *Back ~; to swim the back ~.* ʻAu kua. *Side ~; to swim the side ~.* ʻAu ʻaoʻao. *Butterfly ~; to swim the butterfly ~.* ʻAu mālolo. *See crawl, dog paddle.*

stroll *Also to go for a ~.* Holoholo wāwae. *See hike.*

strong *As wind; large branches in motion and whistling heard in wires between utility poles, in meteorology.* Ulūlu. *See wind.*

strong safety *In football.* ʻĀwaʻa muku. *See weak safety.*

strontium Solonokiuma.

structure *As of a molecule.* Hakakino.

strum *To ~, as an ʻukulele or guitar.* Koekoe.

strut *To act cocky, ~ about looking for a fight.* Hoʻonanā.

student assessment Loiloi holomua haumāna.

student teacher *Also to student teach.* A'oākumu. *~ field service supervisor.* Luna a'oākumu.

studies *See Hawaiian studies department.*

studio *The building where movies are made.* Hale hana ki'i'oni'oni. *The company responsible for making movies.* Ke'ena hana ki'i'oni'oni. *~ teacher.* Kumu ke'ena hana ki'i'oni'oni.

study *To examine, observe something.* Kilo. *Scientific ~.* Kālai-. *With no specific intent to influence change.* Huli-.

stunt *A feat which requires unusual daring or skill, as in movie or video production; to do or perform a ~.* Pāha'oweli. *~person.* Kanaka pāha'oweli. *~ coordinator.* Luna pāha'oweli.

style *Also attribute, as italic or bold in printing or a computer program.* Kaila hua. *See code style, font.*

style *To ~ hair, as for a play, movie, or video production.* Ho'oponopono lauoho. *Hair stylist.* Mea ho'oponopono lauoho.

styles *Learning ~; see Hawaiian entries beginning with* a'o kahua.

styrofoam Panua, 'ūpīhu'a.

sub- *Also under-.* Lalo. *See entries below and* under-.

subalpine Lalo 'alapaina. *See alpine. ~ forest.* Ululā'au lalo 'alapaina.

subconference *In telecommunications.* Hālāwai malū.

subcutus *In biology.* 'Ili kūloko.

subdivision *Also housing development.* Kaiahale.

subfield *As in a computer program.* Hope kahua. *See field.*

subheading *Also heading, as in a story.* Po'omana'o.

subject *General ~ or topic, as in literature.* Kumuhana.

submarine *Also submerged, undersea.* Lalo kai. *See submerged.*

submerged *Also submarine, undersea.* Lalo kai. *~ volcano.* Lua pele lalo kai.

subsand Lalo one.

subscribe *As in a computer program.* Loulou ki'i.

subscript *As in a computer program or printing.* Kauha'a. *See superscript.*

subsoil Lalo lepo. *See topsoil.*

substance 'Akano. *See compound, element, matter, particles, spray paint. Amorphous ~.* 'Akano laukua. *As sprayed from an aerosol can.* Kīkina.

substitute *As in sports; also to ~.* Pani, pani hakahaka *(preceded by ke). First ~ player or alternate, in basketball; also called first off the bench or six man.* Kūono.

substrate *As in a stream.* Papa o lalo.

subsummary *As in a computer program.* Hope hō'ulu'ulu palapala. *See summary.*

subtitle Lepe unuhi. *See caption.*

subtotal Huinanui hapa. *See grand total.*

subtract *Also subtraction.* Ho'olawe.

subtribe *Also clan.* Hapū. *See tribe.*

subtropical Lalo kopikala.

suburb Kaona ukali.

subway *~ train.* Ka'akōnelo. *~ tunnel.* Ala ka'akōnelo. *~ station.* Kahua ka'akōnelo.

subzone Kā'ei iki.

succession Mo'ona. *In rapid ~.* 'Āma'amau.

sucker *Also lollipop.* Kanakē 'au, kō omōmo.

sucker *Insect ~, an instrument for drawing an insect into a tube by suction.* Mea omo 'elala.

suction cup fin *As beneath the stomach of an* 'o'opu. Halo 'āpikapika.

Sudan *Also Sudanese.* Sudana.

suffix Pāku'ina kau hope. *See affix.*

suffocate *To experience a suffocating sensation.* Kenakena.

suffrage *The right to vote.* Kuleana koho pāloka.

suit *Space ~.* Pa'alole hele lewa. See *warm-up suit.*

suit *As in a deck of playing cards.* Pa'a likelike.

suitcase *Also purse.* Pāiki, pāisi.

sulfate Sulafahate. *Cupric ~.* Kupuriku sulafahate. *Ferrous ~.* Ferousa sulafahate.

sulfide Sulafaside. *Cupric ~.* Kupuriku sulafaside. *Ferrous ~.* Ferousa sulafaside.

sulfur dioxide Sulufura diokesaside, kūkaepele 'okikene lua.

sulfuric Sulufuriku. *~ acid.* 'Akika sulufuriku.

Sulu Sulu. *~ Sea.* Ke kai 'o Sulu.

sum *Total.* Huinanui. See *total.*

summa cum laude *Also with highest honors, as in academics.* Me ke kau i ka hano hāweo. See *cum laude, magna cum laude.*

summary *Also to summarize.* Hō'ulu'ulu mana'o. See *subsummary.* *Document ~, as in a computer program.* Hō'ulu'ulu palapala.

summer Kauwela. *~ solstice.* Ka māuiki'iki'i o ke kauwela.

summit *A conference of highest-level officials, as heads of government.* 'Aha kūkā po'o aupuni.

Sunday Lāpule. *Abb.* Lp.

sunglasses Makaaniani kala, makaaniani lā.

sunscreen *The lotion.* 'Aila pale lā. See *suntan lotion.*

sunspot Kiko lā. See *solar flare, solar granule, solar prominences.*

suntan lotion 'Aila 'ōlala. See *sunscreen.*

superior vena cava Wenakawa o luna. See *vena cava.*

superphosphate Superoposapahate.

superscript *As in a computer program or printing.* Kaupi'i. See *subscript.*

supervisor *Script ~, as in movie or video production.* Luna kākau mo'olelo. *Student teacher field service ~.* Luna a'oākumu. See *student teacher.*

supplement *To ~, as angles, in math.* Ho'opiha kaha. See *complement, supplementary angles.*

supplementary *~ book or text; also any book which supplements a primary text.* Puke kāko'o.

supplementary angles *Two angles whose measures have a sum of 180°, in math.* Nā huina ho'opiha kaha. See *complementary angles.*

supply and demand *In economics.* Ho'olako me ka heluna makemake.

support *Education ~ staff.* Kāko'o ho'ona'auao. See *allied health professional.*

supporting idea *As in a composition.* Mana'o kāko'o.

surf *To ~, as the Internet.* Kele. See *browse.*

surface area *In math.* 'Ili alo.

surface water Wai 'ili honua, wai 'ili.

surf break *Where a wave breaks.* Po'ina nalu (*preceded by* ke).

Surinam Suliname.

surplus *As a quantity or amount over and above what is needed.* Loa'a pākeu. See *deficit.*

survey *Opinion ~; also to conduct an opinion ~.* Anamana'o.

surveying rod *Also range pole.* Lā'au ana 'āina. See *elevation pole, sighter.*

susceptible *Also vulnerable.* Pā wale. *Fragile, ~ to change.* Pāloli. *To be ~ or vulnerable to disease.* Pāma'i.

suspend See *suspension.*

suspension *Also to suspend, as from school.* Ho'oku'u no ka manawa. See *detention.*

suspension *A mixture in which the particles are mixed but not dissolved in fluid, solid, or gas.* Pūaina. *See* solution. *To be suspended.* Pūai.

sustained Pa'a mau. *~ yield, as in crop production.* Loa'a pa'a mau.

swab *Cotton ~, Q-tip.* Lā'au pulupulu.

swamp 'Olokele. *See* bog, marsh.

Swaziland Suazilana.

sweat duct Puka kikī hou.

sweatshirt Kueka ha'uki. *See* warm-up suit.

Sweden *Also Swede, Swedish.* Kuekene.

sweep net *See* insect sweep net.

swim *~ cap.* Pāpale 'au. *~ styles. See* stroke.

swimming *~ pool.* Pūnāwai 'au'au. *~ tube.* Lina ho'olana.

swing *Free ~, as a single rope hanging from a tree branch.* Lele koali. *Fixed ~, as with two or more ropes or chains.* Paiō. *To ~, as a pendulum.* 'Ukē. *See* pendulum.

swing man *Also shooting forward or three man, in basketball.* Kūkolu.

swish *Also rimless, i.e. to make a basket without touching the rim, in basketball.* Kuhō. *See* shot.

Swiss cheese Waiūpa'a Kuikilani.

switch *Light ~.* Kuiki kukui, pana kukui. *As on radio, TV set, etc.* Pihi *(preceded by* ke*)*.

switch sides *To ~, in volleyball; also to rotate.* Kuapo.

Switzerland *Also Swiss.* Kuikilani, Kuikilana.

syllabary *In linguistics.* Hakalama. *~ symbol.* Huahakalama.

syllable Kāpana. *Nucleus of a ~, in linguistics.* Iho. *Onset of a ~.* Ka'i. *Coda of a ~.* Muli.

syllabus *As for a college course.* 'Oloke'a koina papa.

symbol *Also to symbolize, stand for.* Hō'ailona.

symmetry *Also symmetric, symmetrical, in math.* 'Ālikelike. *Line of ~, a line on which a figure can be folded so the two parts fit exactly.* Kaha 'ālikelike. *Reflection ~.* 'Ālikelike aka. *Rotational ~.* 'Ālikelike wili. *Symmetric figure.* Kinona 'ālikelike. *Translation ~.* 'Ālikelike kau.

synchronic *In linguistics.* Kikowā. *See* diachronic. *~ rule.* Lula kikowā.

synonym Hua'ōlelo mana'o like. *See* antonym, homonym.

synthesize *To ~, as compounds; also synthetic.* Hakuahua. *~d compounds.* Nā pūhui i hakuahua 'ia.

Syria *Also Syrian.* Suria.

syringe Hano kui. *~ plunger.* 'Ūkōmi hano kui, 'ūkōmi, 'ūkaomi hano kui, 'ūkaomi.

syrup Hone, malakeke.

system 'Ōnaehana. *See entries below. Community-based health ~.* 'Ōnaehana olakino kaiaulu. *Coordinated physician referral ~.* 'Ōnaehana kauka no ka lapa'au like 'ana. *Land registration ~.* 'Ōnaehana ho'onā 'āina. *See* land court, settle. *Natural Areas Reserves ~ (NARS).* 'Ōnaehana Ho'omalu 'Āina Kūlohelohe. *Two-party ~ of government.* Aupuni 'ao'ao 'elua.

system *Decimal ~.* 'Ōnaehana kekimala. *Metric ~.* 'Ōnaehana mekalika. *Solar ~.* Poe lā. *High-pressure ~, in meteorology.* 'Ōnaehana mīkā pi'i. *Low-pressure ~.* 'Ōnaehana mīkā emi.

system *In biology: Circulatory ~.* 'Ōnaehana mānowai. *Digestive ~.* 'Ōnaehana ho'ohehe'e mea'ai. *Endocrine ~.* 'Ōnaehana hōmona. *Immune ~, as in mammals.* 'Ōnaehana pale 'ea. *Integumentary ~.* 'Ōnaehana 'ili. *Muscular ~.* 'Ōnaehana mākala. *Nervous ~.* 'Ōnaehana lolokū. *Organ*

~. 'Ōnaehana lōkino. *Reproductive ~.*
'Ōnaehana ho'ohua. *Respiratory ~.*
'Ōnaehana hanu.

system *Network ~, as for a computer program.* 'Ōnaehana pūnaewele. *Operating ~.* Pae 'ōnaehana.

systemic insecticide Lā'au make laoa. See *poison.*

T

tab *As on an audio cassette which can be removed to prevent erasing of what has been recorded, or an index ~ on a notebook divider page.* Lepe. *See entry below. As on soda cans.* Une kini. *Soda can ~.* Une kini koloaka.

tab *As on a computer or typewriter.* Kāwāholo. See *indent, space, shift. ~ key.* Pihi kāwāholo *(preceded by* ke). *To set ~s.* Ho'opa'a i nā kāwāholo. *To ~.* Ho'okāwāholo.

table *Bedside ~, nightstand.* Pākaukau moe *(also preceded by* ke). See *water table. ~ leg.* Wāwae pākaukau. *~ lamp.* Kukui kū pākaukau.

table *As of statistics, etc.* Pakuhi papa. See *multiplication tables.*

table of contents Papa kuhikuhi. See *index.*

tablespoon *A unit of measurement.* Puna pākaukau *(preceded by* ke). *Abb.* pup.

tablet *Notebook.* Kālana kākau. See *binder.*

table tennis *Ping-pong.* Kenika pākaukau.

tabloid paper Pepa 11" X 17" *(pronounced* pepa 'umikūmākahi 'īniha i ka 'umikūmāhiku 'īniha). See *paper.*

tackle *The act of seizing and throwing down an opposing player with the ball, in football; to ~ (someone).* Kula'i, ho'ohina. See *block and tackle, nose tackle. Either an offensive or defensive player.* Kūlua. *Left ~.* Kūlua hema. *Right ~.* Kūlua 'ākau.

tadpole *Polliwog.* Polewao.

tag *Label; to label.* Lepili. *To ~ or strike out, in baseball.* Hō'auka.

tagboard *A strong cardboard used for posters; also called oaktag.* Pepa papa 'oka.

tag file See *cookie.*

Tahitian prawn 'Ōpae Polapola.

taiga Taika.

tailbone *The terminus of the spinal column; coccyx.* Iwi ku'e 'amo, ku'e 'amo.

tails *As in coin toss.* Hi'u, 'ao'ao hi'u. See *flip, heads.*

Taiwan *Also Taiwanese.* Taiuana.

Tajikistan Takisitana.

take *To ~ a class.* Aia i loko o ka papa, komo i loko o ka papa, komo i ka papa. *To ~ a test.* Hana i ka hō'ike, kākau i ka hō'ike. See *make.*

take *To ~, as a photograph.* Pa'i *(preceded by* ke). See *close-up, shoot. To photograph or ~ a picture, either still or motion.* Pa'i ki'i. *A ~, i.e. a successful shot in movie or video production.* He 'āpona!

take *To ~, as medicine or a pill.* Inu, 'ai. *To ~ a pill.* Inu i ka huaale, 'ai i ka huaale. *To ~ medicine.* Inu i ka lā'au, 'ai i ka lā'au.

take off *To ~, as a bird or plane taking flight.* Ulele.

take time *To take the time, as to do something.* Ho'oka'awale i ka manawa, ho'olilo i ka manawa.

take turns Māhele manawa.

takuwan Kakuana.

tale *A folk~ or traditional ~, especially one relating to a particular culture.* Ka'ao, mo'oka'ao. See *Hawaiian entries under ka'ao.*

talk *To ~ smooth; also smooth ~er; glib.* Waha wali.

talkathon 'Ōlelokona.

tally Helu kaha.

tambourine Lina 'ulīkeke. See *baby rattle.*

tampon Pani wai 'ula (*preceded by* ke).

tangent *A line which touches a circle at one point, in math.* Kaha pā lihi. See *secant.*

tank *Oxygen* ~. Kini 'okikene. *Scuba* ~. Kini ea lu'u kai, kini ea.

tank top Pala'ili kā'awe, pale'ili kā'awe. See *T-shirt.*

tannic Tanika. ~ *acid.* 'Akika tanika.

Tanzania *Also Tanzanian.* Tanazania. *United Republic of* ~. Lepupalika Hui Pū 'ia 'o Tanazania.

tapa *Bark cloth.* Pa'ūpa'ū.

tape Leki. See *entries below. Electrician's* ~. Leki uea. *Masking* ~. Leki pahu. *Paper* ~. Leki pepa. *Strapping* ~. Leki a'a. *Teflon* ~, *for use in plumbing.* Leki nao. *Transparent* ~. Leki 'ea.

tape *Recording* ~. Līpine. See *cassette, player, recorder. Reel-to-reel* ~. Līpine pōka'a. ~ *case, cassette holder.* Pāiki lola.

tape measure *As a tailor's or for track events, etc.* Līpine ana. See *ruler. Carpenter's* ~. Lula poho.

tap water Wai paipu. *Hot* ~. Wai wela paipu.

tar Kā, tā.

tarantula Kalanakula, nananana kalanakula, nanana kalanakula. See *spider.*

target Māka.

taro See *corm.* ~ *chip.* Kipi kalo.

taste *Sense of* ~. Lonoa alelo. ~ *receptor.* A'alonoa 'ono. See *receptor.*

tasty *To flavor, make* ~. Hō'ono'ono. See *flavoring.*

tax 'Auhau. *Sales* ~. 'Auhau kumukū'ai. ~ *included.* 'Auhau komo pū. ~ *rate.* Pākēneka 'auhau. ~*payer.* Mea uku 'auhau.

taxonomy *The science of classifying plants and animals.* Kālaikapa inoa.

teaberry Pī'ai kī.

teacher *Student* ~; *also to student teach.* A'oākumu. *Student* ~ *field service supervisor.* Luna a'oākumu.

teacher's guide *Also* teacher's manual. Puke alaka'i.

teacher training *Inservice* ~. Ho'oikaika kumu. *Preservice* ~. Ho'omākaukau kumu.

teaching See *pedagogy.*

teaching certificate Palapala 'oihana a'o.

teak *A kind of wood.* Kiaka.

team *Of draft animals.* Pūkolo.

team foul *In team sports such as basketball.* Ku'ia kime. See *foul.*

teaspoon *A unit of measurement.* Puna kī (*preceded by* ke). *Abb.* puk.

technical foul *In team sports such as basketball.* Ku'ia kūhelu. See *foul.*

technician Mea 'enehana. *Graphics* ~. Mea 'enehana ki'i. *Sound* ~. Mea 'enehana kani.

technique Ki'ina hana. See *method.*

technology 'Enehana. See *industry.*

techtonics *Plate* ~, *in geology.* Ku'ina una honua. See *boundary, convergent, divergent, transform.*

teddy bear Pea ki'i, pea pā'ani. See *panda.*

teetertotter Papa hulei. *To* ~. Hulehulei.

Teflon 'A'alo pili. See *resist, waterproof.* ~ *tape, for use in plumbing.* Leki nao.

telecommunication Keleka'a'ike.

telephone See *Hawaiian entries under* kelepona. ~ *receiver.* 'Apo kelepona.

telescope 'Ohenānā.

telespiza ~ *cantanc, Laysan finch.* 'Ainohu Kauō. ~ *ultima, Nīhoa finch.* 'Ainohu Nīhoa.

telethon Kīwīkona.

television Kelewikiona. *TV.* Kīwī, kelewī.

tell time Helu uaki, helu uāki. See *time.*

tempera paint Pena pelaha.

temperate Kemepale. See *tropical.* ~ *forest.* Nahele kemepale.

temperature *When weather considered cold.* Anu. *When weather considered warm.* Mahana, mehana. *When weather considered hot.* Wela. See *Hawaiian entries. Room ~.* Mehana ea, mehana lumi. *To take the ~ of.* Ana wela.

template Anakuhi.

tempo *In music.* Māmā.

temporalis *The muscle of the side of the head.* Mākala maha.

ten See *deci-, deca-. Base-~ grid paper.* Pepa maka'aha kumu ho'ohui pā'umi. *~-dollar bill.* Pepa pā'umi.

tenderizer See *papain.*

tendon Uaua, lohi.

ten-foot line *In volleyball.* Laina 'umi kapua'i. See *three-meter line.* ~ *violation.* 'A'ena 'umi kapua'i.

Tennessee *Also Tennessean.* Kenekī, Tenesī.

tennis shoe *Sneaker.* Kāma'a lole.

tenor Leo 'ekolu. ~ *'ukulele.* 'Ukulele leo 'ekolu.

tens *Place value, in math.* Kūana 'umi.

tense *As articulation, in linguistics.* Mālō. See *lax, vowel. ~ vowel.* Woela mālō.

ten-second violation *In basketball.* 'A'ena 'umi kekona. See *violation.*

ten-strip board *In math.* Papa 'aukā helu. See *hundredths square, tenth strip.*

tent Halepe'a. ~ *stake.* Pine halepe'a.

tentacle 'Awe'awe.

tenths Hapa 'umi.

tenth strip *In math.* 'Aukā helu hapa 'umi. See *hundredths square, ten-strip board.*

tera- *A prefix meaning trillion (T).* Pākiliona. *Abb.* pkl. See *deca-, hecto-, kilo-, mega-, giga-.*

term *In math.* Paukū. See *terms. Constant ~.* Hua pa'a. *Like ~.* Hoa like.

terminal *A computer device which is connected to a network system.* Po'ohana.

terminal *Final, as last in time, order, or importance.* Kuahope. See *primary, secondary, tertiary. ~ bronchiole, in anatomy.* 'Āmanapu'u kuahope.

terminating decimal Kekimala pani.

termite block *In construction.* Palaka kimeki pale mū. See *pier block.*

terms ~ *of a fraction, in math.* Palena. *Lowest ~.* Palena ha'aha'a loa. *In ~ of.* Ma o. *In ~ of X.* Ma o ke X.

terrace *Underwater ~.* Papa 'anu'u lalo kai.

terrarium Pahuhonuaea.

terrier Kēlia, 'īlio kēlia.

terrorize Ho'oweliweli.

tertiary *As third in time, order, or importance.* Kuakolu. See *primary, secondary, terminal. ~ or segmental bronchus, in anatomy.* 'Āmanapu'u kuakolu.

tesselation *In math.* Makalau.

test *To make a ~.* Haku i ka hō'ike. *To take a ~.* Hana i ka hō'ike, kākau i ka hō'ike. *To ~ for something, as in a scientific experiment.* Ho'ā'o. See *trial.*

tester *As a battery ~, when the ~ is a machine.* Mīkini ho'ā'o. *Battery ~ (a machine).* Mīkini ho'ā'o iho. *Battery ~ (not a machine).* Hāme'e ho'ā'o iho.

testimony See *hearing.*

test tube Hano ho'okolohua. See *collection tube, cylinder, ring stand. Pyrex ~.* Hano ho'okolohua paileki. ~ *clamp.* 'Ūmi'i hano ho'okolohua.

Tethys *A moon of Saturn.* Tetisa.

tetrahedron *A space figure with four faces, in math.* Paʻaʻilihā.

Texas *Also Texan.* Kekeka, Tekasa, Teseta.

text *Of a document, as in a computer program.* Kikokikona. See *text wrap.*

textbook Puke haʻawina. See *supplementary text.*

texture Hiʻonapāʻili.

text wrap *As in a word-processing document.* Kikokikona kīpuni.

T-fitting *For putting pipes together.* ʻŌmaka T. See *universal fitting.*

Thailand Tailani.

thematic map Palapala ʻāina kumuhana.

theorum *In math.* Manaʻohaʻi. *Pythagorean ~.* Manaʻohaʻi o Paekakoleo.

therapy *To provide physical ~.* Pākōlea. *Physical therapist.* Kanaka pākōlea, mea pākōlea. *Shock ~.* Lapaʻau hoʻomiki uila.

thermal energy *The total energy of all the particles in an object.* Ikehu kāʻokoʻa. See *calorimeter.*

thermoelectric *Also thermoelectricity.* Uila puhi wāwahie. See *electricity.* *~ power.* Ikehu uila puhi wāwahie.

thermometer Ana wela. See *temperature.*

thermophilic *Heat-loving.* Ola wela. *~ bacteria.* Koʻohune ola wela.

thermos Hano.

thesaurus Puke manaʻo laulike. *As in a computer program.* Papa manaʻo laulike. *~ entry.* Manaʻo laulike.

thick Mānoanoa, mānoʻanoʻa.

thigh *Chicken ~.* ʻŪhā moa. See *drumstick.*

thigh bone See *femur.*

thigmotactic ʻOnipā.

thin *To ~, as plants when gardening.* Waewaele.

thingamajig *Device, doohickey, gadget, gizmo.* Hāmeʻa. See *apparatus, instrument, tool.*

thinking *Critical ~.* Noʻonoʻo loi. *Logical ~.* Noʻonoʻo kūpili. *~ skills.* Mākau noʻonoʻo. *Building ~ skills book.* Puke mākau noʻonoʻo. *Productive-~ skill.* Mākau hoʻomohala manaʻo.

third base *In baseball.* Pahu ʻekolu. See *base.*

third-party call *Also to make such a call.* Kelepona kāki iā haʻi. See *Hawaiian entries under* kelepona.

Third World Country ʻĀina hōʻoiʻenehana. See *developing, First World Country.*

thirty-second rest *In music.* Hoʻomaha hapa kanakolukūmālua.

-thon *Suffix.* -kona. See *-athalon, dance-a-thon, marathon, walkathon, etc.*

thorax Paukū kino, paukū.

thousand See *kilo-, milli-.*

thrasher *A bird related to the thrush.* Manu kelaka.

threat See *triple-threat position.*

threatened *As rare plants or animals.* Hopo halapohe, hopo make loa, hopo nalowale loa. See *endangered, extinct.*

three-dimensional *In math.* Paʻa. See *two-dimensional.* *~ figure.* Kinona paʻa. *Also 3D, as a picture or movie.* Kohu paʻa. *~ movie.* Kiʻiʻoniʻoni kohu paʻa.

three man *Also swing man or shooting forward, in basketball.* Kūkolu.

three-meter line *In volleyball.* Laina ʻekolu mika. See *ten-foot line.* *~ violation.* ʻAʻena ʻekolu mika.

three-point arc *In basketball.* Hoaka kīkolu.

three-point shot *In basketball; to attempt such a shot.* Kī ʻai kolu. *A successful ~.* ʻAi kolu.

three-quarter-court press *In basketball.* Lulumi ʻekolu hapahā. See *press.*

three-second violation *In basketball.* 'A'ena 'ekolu kekona. See *violation.*

threshold *Of a door.* Paepae puka.

thrips *A kind of insect.* Pīnalonalo.

throat Pu'u.

through Puka ma kekahi 'ao'ao (o). *Multiply ~, in math.* Ho'onui paukū pākahi.

throw *To ~ overhand.* Nou. *To ~ underhand.* Kiola. See *discus.*

throw away *To ~ (the ball), in basketball.* Kīloi pa'ewa.

thrush Keluka, manu keluka. *Wood ~.* Manu keluka ululā'au.

thumb Manamana nui. See *finger, scroll. To ~ through, as a magazine.* Lolelole.

thumbtack Kui pahu.

thunderbird Manu hekili.

Thursday Po'ahā. *Abb.* P4.

thyroid gland Lōku'u ho'okonukonu pūnao.

ti *The seventh note on the musical scale.* Mī. See *Hawaiian entry* pākōlī.

tibia *The inner bone of the lower leg.* Iwi kū wāwae. See *fibula, ulna.*

tibial artery A'a pu'uwai kū wāwae. *See Hawaiian entries under* a'a pu'uwai.

tibialis *The muscle of the lower leg and foot region.* Mākala pelu mua.

tibial vein A'a kino kū wāwae. *See Hawaiian entries under* a'a kino.

tick *To ~, as a clock.* Kani ko'ele.

tickle Ho'omāne'one'o.

tic-tac-toe Kesa'ō.

tide Hoehoena o ke kai. See *fluctuate.*

tie *Bow ~.* Lei 'ā'ī pewa.

tight end *In football.* Muku. See *split end, safety.*

tilapia Talapia.

tile Kile. *Ceramic ~.* Kile lāmeka. *Floor ~.* Kile papahele, kile 'ili, moena 'ili 'āpanapana. *Hollow ~.* Paomeki.

tile windows *As in a computer program.* Kīpapa pukaaniani.

tiller See *rotary tiller.*

tilt *To ~ or tip, as a glass containing water.* Ho'ohiō. *To cause to ~, as the camera when filming a movie or video production.* Ho'okīki'i.

tilth *The nature of soil with porous texture and well-aggregated crumb structure.* Mā'elenono. See *crumb.*

timbre *In music.* Pualeo.

time Manawa. See *on time, time zone. Real ~, as in a computer program.* Manawa 'anō. *Recorded duration.* Helu manawa. *To ~, as speed, duration, etc.* Helu manawa; uaki, uāki. *To tell ~.* Helu uaki, helu uāki. *To take the ~, as to do something.* Ho'oka'awale i ka manawa, ho'olilo i ka manawa.

time line Laina manawa.

time out *In team sports such as volleyball.* Manawa ho'omaha.

time zone *As Pacific or Rocky Mountain ~.* Kā'ei hola.

tinder *Powdery ~.* 'Āhia.

tin foil Pepa kini.

tint *As of a television screen.* Laulā kala. See *color gradient.*

tip *To ~ or tilt, as a glass containing water.* Ho'ohiō.

tip *Of a leaf.* Hi'u, welelau. *Bulb ~.* 'Ōmaka hua kanu. *Of the tongue.* Wēlau alelo.

tip-in *As a basket in basketball; to make such a shot.* Kī papa'i. See *tip pass.*

tiple *A musical instrument with ten strings.* Kipola.

tip pass *In basketball; to throw such a pass.* Kīloi papa'i. See *tip-in.*

tire Kaea, taea. *Bicycle ~.* Kaea paikikala.

tissue *As structural material of a plant or animal.* 'A'a'a hunaola. See *cell. Adipose ~, i.e. animal ~ in which fat is stored.* 'A'a'a hunaola 'ailakele.

Titan *A moon of Saturn.* Kaikana.

title *As of a book or story.* Inoa; po'o inoa (*preceded by* ke). *As at the beginning of a movie or video production.* Po'o inoa. *Program ~, as for a TV program.* Po'o inoa polokalamu. *The heading which names a legislative act or statute.* Po'o kānāwai. *See Hawaiian entries under* kānāwai *and* bill.

to *Also and, when, until, etc.* A.

toe bone *See* phalanx.

tofu *Also bean curd.* Tōfū.

Togo Tōkō.

toilet Lua. *~ bowl.* Ipu lua. *~ handle.* 'Au ho'oku'u wai o ka lua, 'au ho'oku'u (*preceded by* ke). *~ seat.* Noho lua. *To flush the ~.* Ho'oku'u i ka wai o ka lua, ho'oholo i ka wai.

toll free Kāki 'ole. *~ number.* Helu kelepona kāki 'ole.

tomorrow 'Āpōpō.

ton Kana. *Abb.* k.

tone *In music.* Huakani. *In linguistics, as relating to Chinese or Navaho languages.* Nioe. *As of a literary work.* Au mana'o.

toner *As for a computer printer.* Pauka 'īnika.

Tonga *Kingdom of ~.* Aupuni Mō'ī 'o Tonga.

tongue Alelo. *Back of the ~.* Kū'au alelo. *Blade of the ~.* Lau alelo. *Central portion of the ~.* Waena alelo. *Root of the ~.* Mole alelo. *Tip of the ~.* Wēlau alelo.

tool *As a shovel, crowbar, etc.* Mea hana. *See* apparatus, device, instrument. *As a specialized instrument for a particular occupation.* Mauha'a.

tooth Niho. *See* drill, filling, grind, orthodontist, pick.

toothbrush *~ container, usually made of plastic.* Poho palaka niho. *~ holder.* Kauna palaki niho.

toothpaste Pauka niho. *See* cap. *~ tube.* Poho pauka niho.

top *Clothing.* Lole o luna. *See* bottom, tank top.

topic *General ~ or subject, as in literature.* Kumuhana. *~ sentence, as of a paragraph.* Hopuna'ōlelo wehe kumuhana.

top margin Lihi o luna. *See* margin.

top of the key *On a basketball court.* Uma kī, uma, pōheo.

topographic *Also topography.* Hi'ona 'āina. *See Hawaiian entries* hi'ona wai, hi'ona 'āina. *~ map.* Palapala hi'ona 'āina. *Man-made ~al feature.* Hi'ona na ke kanaka.

topping *As for ice cream.* Pāhina.

topsoil Lepo uhi. *See* subsoil.

tornado Makani ka'awiliwili.

tortilla Tōtia.

total *Sum.* Huinanui. *Grand ~.* Huinanui pau loa. *Sub~.* Huinanui hapa.

totem pole Pou 'aumakua 'Ilikini.

toucan Tūkana.

touch *Sense of ~.* Lonoa 'ili.

touchback *In football.* 'Ai hopu. *See* point, touchdown.

touchdown *In football.* 'Ai holo. *See* point, touchback.

touch pass *In basketball; to make such a pass.* Ho'opāhi'a.

tournament *In sports.* Ho'okūkū, ho'okūkū moho. *See* championship, scrimmage. *Volleyball ~.* Ho'okūkū pōpa'ipa'i.

tow Kauō. *~ truck.* Kalaka kauō.

towel rack Kaola kāwele. *See* paper towel dispenser.

town Kūlanakauhale. *See* city. *Down~.* Kaona.

toxic 'Awahia.

toy box *Also toy chest.* Pahu mea pā'ani, waihona mea pā'ani.

trace *A small amount.* 'Āwe'awe'a. *~ element.* Kumumea 'āwe'awe'a. *To ~, as a picture, etc.* Ho'omahaka.

trachea *Also windpipe, in anatomy.* Paipu hanu. See *epiglottis, esophagus, larynx.*

track and field Ha'uki Helene. ~ *events.* Nā ha'uki Helene. *Course for running events in* ~. Lina poepoe holo wāwae.

tractor Ka'a huki palau, ka'a palau.

trade *To* ~, *in math.* Kuapo.

trademark Kunikia.

traditional Ku'una. ~ *knowledge.* 'Ike ku'una. *See entry below.* ~ *literature.* Mo'okalaleo ku'una. ~ *tale, i.e. a folktale, especially one relating to a particular culture.* Ka'ao, mo'oka'ao. *See Hawaiian entries under* ka'ao.

traditional knowledge-based learning A'o kahua 'ike ku'una. *See Hawaiian entries beginning with* a'o kahua.

traffic *Especially the movement of* ~. Kaheaholo. *Highway* ~. Kaheaholo ka'a. *Air* ~. Kaheaholo mokulele. ~ *light.* Kukui ho'okū. ~ *sign.* Hō'ailona. *See stop sign, yield sign.*

trail *Head or foot of* ~. Nuku. *Hiking* ~. Ala hekehi. See *hike.*

trailer Kaleila. *Flatbed* ~. Pākihuila.

train *Elevated* ~, *as the Japan monorail.* Ka'aahi kau lewa.

train *To* ~ (*someone*), *as for sports.* Ka'i. *Sports* ~*er.* Ka'i ha'uki.

training See *teacher training.*

trait *Hereditary* ~. Welo. See *gene.*

trampoline Ke'elelena.

transcendental number *In math.* Helu kohu pai.

transcription Palapala leo. *To transcribe.* Palapala.

transect *A sample area, as of vegetation, usually in the form of a long strip.* Laina kālailai.

transfer *As funds in a bank account.* Ho'oili.

transform *Sliding in plate techtonics, in geology.* Kākele. See *convergent, divergent.* ~ *boundary.* Palena kākele.

transition area *An area where natural topography changes from one land feature to another.* 'Āina loliloli.

translation image *In math.* Kinona like kau.

translation symmetry *In math.* 'Ālikelike kau.

transparency *As for an overhead projector.* Māliko.

transparent A'ia'i. See *opaque.*

transparent tape *Scotch tape.* Leki 'ea.

transpiration *Also to transpire.* Pi'ikū. See *evapotranspiration.*

transplant Ho'oili. *To* ~ *a heart.* Ho'oili pu'uwai. ~*ed.* Ili. ~*ed heart.* Pu'uwai ili.

transport *Military* ~ *aircraft.* Mokulele hali koa.

transportation *Mode of* ~. Alakau.

transversal *A line that intersects two given lines, in math.* Kaha 'oki'oki.

transverse wave *A wave in which matter vibrates at right angles to the direction in which the wave moves.* Hawewe 'ale'ale. See *compressional wave.*

trap *In basketball; to make such a play.* 'Ūpiki. *Deadfall, a kind of animal* ~. Hā'uleāpa'a.

trapeze Koali lelepinao. *To use a* ~. Lelepinao.

trapezoid Huinahā pa'a pilipā.

trash *To empty* ~, *as in a computer program.* Kīloi.

travel *To* ~, *in basketball; also* ~*ing.* Holoholo.

traveler's check Pila kīko'o huaka'i.

tray Pā halihali (*preceded by* ke). *See entry below. Balancing* ~ *for scales.* Pā ana. *Chalk* ~. Paepae poho.

tray *Paper ~, as for a computer printer.* Poho pepa. *Paper ~ slot.* 'Āpo'o poho pepa.

tread *As on a tire.* Nihoniho. See *bald.*

treasure chest Pahu waihona waiwai.

treat *To ~ chemically, as sewage.* Kāemikala. *~ed sewage.* Ke kaekene i kāemikala 'ia.

treble clef *In music.* Hō'ailona mele leo wahine, leo wahine. See *bass clef.*

tree diagram *In math.* Ki'ikuhi pahiki.

tree frog Poloka kau lā'au. *Orange ~.* Poloka kau lā'au 'ālani.

treehouse Hale kau lā'au.

treetop *Top of a tree or plant.* Ēulu.

tremor *As of an earthquake; to ~.* Manunu.

trench *Geologic ~.* 'Auwaha. *Aleutian ~.* Ka 'auwaha 'o 'Aleuta.

trend Kū i ke au, mea kū i ke au.

trial *A test as in a probability experiment, in math.* Ho'ā'oamaka. See *test.*

trial and error *Also to do something by ~.* Ho'ā'oa'o.

triangle Huinakolu. *Acute~.* Huinakolu 'oi. *Congruent ~.* Huinakolu komolike. *Equilateral ~.* Huinakolu like. *Isosceles ~.* Huinakolu 'elua 'ao'ao like. *Obtuse ~.* Huinakolu peleleu. *Scalene ~.* Huinakolu 'ao'ao like 'ole. *Base of a ~.* 'Ao'ao kau.

triathalon 'Ālapakonakolu. See *decathalon, pentathalon.*

tribe *People in a district who have intermarried, specifically referring to Hawai'i.* 'Alaea. See *clan. Of people outside of Hawai'i.* Nāki.

tributary 'Aumana. *River ~.* 'Aumana muliwai. *Stream ~.* 'Aumana kahawai.

triceps *The muscle of the back of the upper arm.* Mākala kumukolu.

trick *As a dog's ~.* Nalea. *Magic ~ or illusion, sleight of hand.* Pāha'ohuna. *Prank; to play a ~, usually with malicious intent.* Kēpuka.

trick or treat Kiliki o lapu.

tricuspid valve *Of the heart.* Pepeiao pākolu. See *valve.*

tricycle Kalaikikala.

trident 'Ō maka kolu (*preceded by* ke).

trillion See *pico-, tera-.*

triple-extra large *XXXL, as shirt size.* Nui keu pākolu. See *large.*

triple-threat position *In basketball; also to execute such a position.* Kūliukolu.

tripod Kū ko'okolu.

Triton *A moon of Neptune.* Kalaikona.

trivia Hunahuna 'ike.

trombone Pū puhi uai.

trophy Kiahai. See *plaque.*

tropical *Also tropic.* Kopikala. See *temperate. ~ storm.* 'Ino kopikala. *The tropics.* Kā'ei kopikala.

troposphere Lewalaniha'a.

trough *Of a wave.* Honua, honua o ka nalu, honua o ka 'ale. See *crest, wave.*

trout I'a punakea.

trowel *As used for digging.* Hāpale. *Garden ~.* Kopalā lima.

trumpet Pū pihi. See *bugle, cornet.*

T-shirt Pala'ili, pale'ili. See *tank-top. Any pullover-style shirt.* Pala'ili.

tube Kiupe. See *cap, cathode-ray tube, collection tube, lava tube, toothpaste. Swimming ~.* Lina ho'olana. *Toothpaste ~.* Poho pauka niho.

tuber Huaa'a.

tubifex Ko'e 'ula.

Tuesday Po'alua. *Abb.* P2.

tuff *A rock composed of finer kinds of detritus, usually more or less stratified and in various states of consolidation, in geology.* Hakuhune. *~ cone.* Pu'u hakuhune.

tulip Puahōlani.

tuna Tuna. *Can of ~.* Kini tuna.

tundra Nakilinaka.

tune *Also melody.* Leo, 'ea. *To ~, as a stringed instrument; to ~ up, as an engine.* Kī.

tuning fork Hao ho'okani, 'ō ho'okani (*preceded by* ke).

Tunisia *Also Tunisian.* Tunisia.

tunnel Kōnelo. See *subway.*

turbo button *As in Nintendo games.* Pihi pīna'i (*preceded by* ke). See *warp zone.*

Turkey *Also Turk, Turkish.* Kuleke, Tureke.

Turkmenistan Tukemenikana.

turn *Or curve, as in a road or on a trail.* Uake'e. *Banked ~.* Uake'e hiō. *To ~, as a figure in math.* Wili. *~ center.* Kikowaena wili. *~ image.* Kinona like wili. *Half-~ image.* Kinona like wili hapalua.

turn off *To ~, as a light, radio, TV, etc.* Ho'opio. *To ~ the water.* Ho'opa'a i ke kī wai. See *faucet.*

turn on *To ~, as a light, radio, TV, etc.* Ho'ā. *To ~ the water.* Wehe i ke kī wai.

turnover *In basketball.* Lilo.

turns *To take ~.* Māhele manawa.

turquoise *The mineral.* Hakukuleke.

turtle *Box ~.* Honu pahu. *Green sea ~.* Honu lū'au, honu.

turtle shell 'ukulele 'Ukulele 'ea honu.

tusk *Boar's ~.* Niho kepa.

TV Kīwī, kelewī. See *television.* *~ screen.* Papakaumaka kīwī. *~ monitor.* Pahu papakaumaka kīwī. *~ series.* Pūka'ina polokalamu kīwī.

twelve-pack *As of drinks.* Pū'olo. See *six-pack, case, pack.* *~ of soda.* Pū'olo koloaka. *~ of beer.* Pū'olo pia.

twig *Small stick.* 'Aula'o (*preceded by* ke).

twill plaiting Maka pūalu, 'o'eno.

twin *In math.* Kūlua. See *double number, prime number.* *~ primes.* Helu kumu kūlua.

twirl *To ~, as a baton.* Wili.

twist tie *As used with plastic bags.* Uea nāki'i.

two-by-four Lua hā. *~ board or lumber.* Papa lua hā.

two-dimensional *In math.* Papa. *~ figure.* Kinona papa. See *three-dimensional.*

two man *Also shooting guard, in basketball.* Kūlua.

two-party system *Of government.* Aupuni 'ao'ao 'elua.

type *Blood ~.* Hulu koko. *See entry below.*

type *To ~, as on a typewriter.* Kikokiko, pa'i hakahaka. *~ style or attribute, as italic or bold.* Kaila hua. *~face or font.* Kinona hua. See *font, style.* *To set ~, as for video captions.* Ulele hua. See *character operator.*

U

Ukraine 'Ukelena.

'ukulele 'Ukulele. For kinds, see *baritone, cigar-box, coconut shell, cutaway, double-hole, eight-string, Lili'u, Ohta-san, soprano, tenor, turtle shell.* For parts, see *body, bridge, fret, head, neck, nut, string.*

ulna *The longer and thinner of the two bones of the forearm on the side opposite the thumb.* Iwi kū lima. See *radius, tibia.*

ultraviolet Kuawehi. *~ ray.* Kukuna kuawehi.

umpire *Also referee.* 'Uao ha'uki, 'uao.

UN *United Nations.* 'Aha Aupuni Hui Pū 'ia.

unailienable rights See *inalienable rights.*

uncomplicated *Basic, simple.* Nōhie. See *complex.*

under- *Also sub-.* Lalo. See entries below and *sub-.*

underestimate Kohoemi. See *overestimate.*

undergraduate ~ *level, as of a student in a college or university.* Mua puka. See *graduate.* ~ *student.* Haumāna mua puka.

underground Lalo honua.

underhand *To serve ~, in volleyball.* Hānai puʻupuʻu. See *spike.*

underline Kahalalo.

underpants Palemaʻi, lole wāwae palaʻili. See *sanitary pad.*

undersea *Also submarine, submerged.* Lalo kai.

understory ~ *layer of vegetation, as low trees and shrubs.* Papa hapamalu. See *vegetation layers.*

underwater *Referring only to sea water.* Lalo kai. ~ *terrace.* Papa ʻanuʻu lalo kai.

undo *To ~, in math.* Hoʻomakala. See *build. To ~, as in a computer program.* Hoʻihoʻi mai. See *cancel, put away.*

unencrypt *As a code or computer data.* Hoʻokala pāʻālua. See *code, encrypt.*

uneven See *parallel bars.*

unfolded *As a flower.* Mohala.

union ʻUniona. See *collective bargaining. As of states or countries into one political entity.* Hui ʻāina.

unit *Of measurement.* Anakahi. See *accent unit, CPU, place value. Metric ~ of measure.* Anakahi mekalika. *US standard or customary ~ of measure.* Anakahi ʻAmelika. *Of counting.* Kūana helu. ~ *fraction.* Hakina anakahi. ~ *price.* Kumukūʻai anakahi.

united Hui pū ʻia. See *entries below.*

United Arab Emirates Aupuni ʻEmira ʻAlapia Hui Pū ʻia.

United Kingdom Aupuni Mōʻī Hui Pū ʻia.

United Nations *UN.* ʻAha Aupuni Hui Pū ʻia.

United Republic of Tanzania Lepupalika Hui Pū ʻia ʻo Tanazania.

United States of America *Also American.* ʻAmelika Hui Pū ʻia. See *America.*

unitize *To ~, in math.* Hoʻānakahi.

universal fitting *For putting pipes together.* ʻŌmaka kau peʻa. See *T-fitting.*

universe *As a scientific term only.* ʻŌnaeao.

unleavened pancake Palaoa linalina.

unlocked *Also open, as for business; ajar.* Hemo.

unofficial *Also nonstandard, as in units of measurement.* Kūhelu ʻole. See *official.*

unprocessed *As raw materials.* Kūlohelohe. See *raw.*

unprotected sex *Also to practice ~.* Ai palekana ʻole. See *safe sex.*

unrest *Civil ~.* Haunaele kūloko.

unsaturated fat ʻAilakele paʻahapa. See *fat.*

unsmooth *To ~, as in a computer program.* Hoʻokalakala. See *smooth.*

until *Also and, when, to, etc.* A.

update *An ~, as of a computer program.* Hoʻopuka hou loa. See *release. To ~, as a computer program.* Hōʻano hou.

upper case *Capital, as a letter of the alphabet.* Maʻaka. See *letter.*

upper division *As a course at a college or university.* Helukiʻe. See *lower division.* ~ *course.* Papa helukiʻe.

upside down Hulihia. See *inside out.*

up to bat *Also up, at bat, in baseball.* Manawa hili.

upward Haʻaluna. See *round off.*

Uranus Heleʻekela.

urban ~ *area.* Kiwikā. See *city. To ~ize.* Hoʻokiwikā.

urea 'Ulea.

urinal Ipu mimi, mīana. See *bedpan, toilet bowl.*

Uruguay *Also Uruguayan.* 'Ulukuae, 'Uruguae.

use *Land ~.* Ho'ohana 'āina. *State Land ~ Commission.* Komikina Ho'ohana 'Āina o ka Moku'āina.

used *Second-hand.* Pāmia. *~ car.* Ka'a pāmia.

useful Makehana.

user *End ~, as of computer programs.* Mea ho'ohana. *~ dictionary.* Papa hua'ōlelo pāku'i. See *main dictionary.* *~ friendly.* Hana ma'alahi.

US Fish and Wildlife Service 'Oihana I'a me ka Holoholona Lōhiu o 'Amelika.

u-shaped valley Awāwa uma.

USRDA *Percentage of US Recommended Daily Allowances; now known as Percent Daily Value.* Pākēneka o ka papa'ai.

Utah *Also Utahan, Utahn.* 'Ūtā, Mauna Pōhaku.

utilities *As electricity, gas, etc.* Mikaō.

utility clamp 'Ūmi'i ho'opa'a. See *forceps.*

Uzbekistan 'Usepekikana.

V

vaccine Lā'au ko'oko'o.

vacuum *Also to ~.* Wākiuma.

vain attempt *"Missed out."* Pohō.

Valles Marineris *A valley on Mars.* Ke awāwa 'o Malineli.

valley *Rift ~.* Awāwa māwae. *Series of ~s.* Pae awāwa. *U-shaped ~.* Awāwa uma.

value Waiwai. See *nutritive value, Percent Daily Value, place value.* *Absolute ~.* Waiwai 'i'o. *Expected ~.* Waiwai wānana. *Face ~.* Waiwai kū'ike. *Market ~.* Waiwai kū'ai. *Numerical ~, in math.* Waiwai helu.

valve *Air ~, as on a tire.* Pihi pāuma ea *(preceded by* ke).

valve *Of the heart.* Pepeiao. *Bicuspid ~.* Pepeiao pālua. *Tricuspid ~.* Pepeiao pākolu. *Semilunar ~.* Pepeiao 'a'apu.

vamp *To ~, as in hula or singing.* Ki'ipā.

vane *Weather or wind ~.* Kuhimakani.

vanilin *A crystalline solid used chiefly as a flavoring agent and in perfumery.* Wanilina.

vapor Māhuea.

variable *As in a scientific experiment.* Kumuloli. *Dependent ~.* Kumuloli kauka'i. *Independent ~.* Kumuloli kū'oko'a. *A symbol that can stand for any quantitative value, in math.* Hualau. *~ width, as in a computer program.* Laulā loli.

varsity *As a league of sports at school.* Pae o'o. *Junior ~.* Pae 'ōpio.

vase *Flower ~.* Pika pua.

vaseline *Petrolatum.* Kele ho'opahe'e.

vastus *Any of the group of muscles that extend the leg, including: ~ intermedius.* Mākala hope alo 'ūhā. *~ lateralis.* Mākala ku'i 'ūhā. *~ medialis.* Mākala kumu 'ūhā. See *quadriceps femoris, rectus femoris.*

vault *Pole ~.* Ko'o lele. *To pole ~.* Lele ko'o.

vegetable Lau'ai. *~ oil.* 'Aila meakanu.

vegetation *Natural ~.* Lau nahele 'ōiwi. *~ layer.* Papa meakanu. *~ area at the base of a mountain.* Wao kumu kuahiwi. See *montane* and separate layers: *ground, understory, canopy, emergent.* *~ zonation sheet.* Palapala kā'ei meakanu.

vehicle *Ground ~ with wheels or runners.* Ka'a. *General term for off-road ~s, as ATV, dirt bike, 4x4, etc.* Ka'a holo 'āpu'upu'u, ka'a 'āpu'u. See *all-terrain vehicle.*

vein Aʻa koko kino, aʻa kino. *See Hawaiian entries under* aʻa kino *and* artery.

Velcro Loupili. *~ fastener.* Mea hoʻopaʻa loupili.

velocity Māmā holo.

vena cava *Any of the large veins by which the blood is returned to the right atrium of the heart.* Wenakawa, aʻa kino wenakawa. *Inferior ~.* Wenakawa o lalo. *Superior ~.* Wenakawa o luna.

veneer ʻIliwehi.

Venetian blinds Pale pukaaniani ʻōlepelepe.

Venezuela Wenezuela.

Venn diagram *A diagram using overlapping circles to show relationship of data, in math.* Kiʻikuhi Wene.

vent *Air ~.* Puka ea. *Sea ~.* Puale kai.

ventral *In biology.* Laualo. *See anterior, dorsal, posterior.*

ventricle *Of the mammalian heart.* ʻŌpū puʻuwai, ʻōpū. *See chamber.*

Venus *The planet.* Hōkūloa. *The name.* Wenuke, Wenuse.

Venus flytrap ʻŪmiʻinalo.

Verde *See Cape Verde.*

verify *To check, give proof, as for a math problem.* Hōʻoia.

vermiculite Hunehune ʻūpī. *See hydroponics.*

Vermont *Also Vermonter.* Welemoneka, Veremona, Veremoneta.

vernal equinox Ka māuiili o ke kupulau. *See equinox.*

version *As of a computer program, network, etc.* Mana.

vertebra *A segment of the backbone.* Paukū iwi kuamoʻo. *See spine.*

vertebrate Iwi kuamoʻo. *See invertebrate. ~ animal.* Holoholona iwi kuamoʻo.

vertex *In math.* Kihiʻaki.

vertical Papakū. *See entry below and grow, horizontal. To make ~.* Hoʻopapakū. *To grow ~, as in a computer program.* Ulu papakū. *~ jump.* Lele haʻaluna. *To line up ~ly, place in columns.* Hoʻokolamu.

vertical line *Two ~s written to the left of lines of print to indicate that the left margin should be justified, in proofreading.* Kaha hoʻokaulihi.

veto *Pocket ~, a way in which the President can veto a bill by holding onto the bill for ten days, during which time Congress ends its session.* Kīpoʻi.

vial ʻŌmoleliʻi.

vibrate Kuekueni.

vice versa Kaʻina ʻēkoʻa, kaʻina ʻokoʻa.

victim *Of a predator.* Luapoʻi. *See predator.*

video Wikiō. *~ cassette.* Lola wikiō. *~ camera, camcorder.* Pahu paʻi wikiō. *~ camera movement.* Neʻena pahu paʻi wikiō. *~ equipment.* Pono hana wikiō. *To shoot a ~.* Paʻi wikiō (*preceded by* ke). *~ production crew.* Nā limahana paʻi wikiō.

Vietnam *Also Vietnamese.* Wiekanama.

view *As in a computer program.* Nānaina. *See preview.*

viewpoint *Scenic ~, lookout.* ʻĪmaka.

vigor Ehuola. *See healthy.*

Viking Wīkini.

vincristine *An alkaloid derived from the periwinkle.* Winikilikini.

vinyl Wainola.

viol *Bass ~, string bass.* Pila kū nui, pila nui.

violation *As in basketball.* ʻAʻena. *See entry below. Backcourt ~.* ʻAʻena laina kūwaena. *Ten-second ~.* ʻAʻena ʻumi kekona. *Three-second ~.* ʻAʻena ʻekolu kekona.

violation *As in volleyball.* 'A'ena. *See entry above. Antenna ~.* 'A'ena kukuna. *Carrying ~.* 'A'ena hāpai. *Double-hit ~.* 'A'ena pa'i lua. *Net ~.* 'A'ena 'upena. *Service ~.* 'A'ena pa'i ulele. *Ten-foot line ~.* 'A'ena 'umi kapua'i. *Three-meter line ~.* 'A'ena 'ekolu mika.

violent *Also animated.* Ehuehu. *See action movie.*

violet *Dog's tooth ~, a kind of flower.* Waioleka niho'īlio.

violin *Also fiddle.* Waiolina.

vireo *A kind of bird.* Manu wiliō. *Red-eyed ~.* Manu wiliō mākole.

Virginia *Also Virginian.* Wilikinia. *West ~, West ~n.* Wilikinia Komohana.

virtual memory *As in a computer program.* Hope waihona 'ike.

virus *As in a computer program.* Mū hōlapu.

visa *An endorsement made on a passport by proper authorities denoting it has been examined and that the bearer may proceed.* Wisa.

visible Kūmaka. *See invisible.*

vision *As in the ~ statement of an organization.* Nu'ukia. *See mission. ~ statement.* 'Ōlelo nu'ukia.

vita *Also curriculum vitae, résumé.* Mo'omō'ali.

vitamin Wikamina, witamina. *B-complex ~.* Kauwikamina B.

vitriol Wikiola, witiola.

vivarium Pahumeaolaea.

vocal coach Ka'i pu'ukani.

vog Polalauahi.

voice *As in linguistics.* Leo.

volcanic Pele. *See volcano. ~ cinder.* One 'ā. *~ cone.* Pu'u pele. *~ ejecta.* Pōhāhā. *~ mountain.* Kuapele. *Primary ~ activity.* Hū pele kuamua. *Series of ~ eruptions.* Pūka'ina hū pele.

volcano Luapele, pele. *See caldera, hot spot, spatter cone, volcanic. Active ~.* Lua pele 'ā. *Hawai'i ~es National Park.* Pāka Aupuni 'o Kīlauea. *Shield ~.* Lua pele kuahene. *Primary shield ~.* Lua pele kuahene kuamua. *Submerged ~.* Lua pele lalo kai.

volley *To keep the ball in play, in volleyball.* Pa'i manamana, pohu. *To ~, as a volleyball.* Lelekīkē.

volleyball *The sport.* Pōpa'ipa'i. *The ball.* Kinipōpō pōpa'ipa'i. *~ antenna.* Kukuna pōpa'ipa'i. *See antenna. ~ court.* Kahua pōpa'ipa'i, pahu. *~ net.* 'Upena pōpa'ipa'i. *~ tournament.* Ho'okūkū pōpa'ipa'i.

volt *In electricity.* Anakahi uila. *See ohm.*

volume Pihanahaka. *Abb.* phk. *See capacity, space figure.*

vowel *In linguistics.* Woela. *Back ~.* Woela kauhope. *Central ~.* Woela kauwaena. *Front ~.* Woela kaumua. *High ~.* Woela ki'eki'e. *Low ~.* Woela ha'aha'a. *Rounded ~.* Woela mōkio. *Tense ~.* Woela mālō. *Lax ~.* Woela 'alu. *Reduced ~.* Woela emi. *~ quality.* Pua woela. *~ reduction.* Ho'ēmi woela.

vulnerable *Also susceptible.* Pā wale. *To be susceptible or ~ to disease.* Pāma'i.

W

waffle Palaoa kīpo'opo'o.

wagon *Child's ~.* Ka'a'auhuki

waiting room Lumi ho'olulu.

Wake Island Uēki 'Ailana.

walkathon Helekona.

walkie-talkie Pahu kāhea.

wallpaper Pepa paia.

walrus Pala'o, 'elepani o ke kai. *See pinniped.*

wand *Bubble, ~ for blowing bubbles.* Lina puhi hu'ahu'a.

war Cold ~, i.e. intense rivalry between nations but without military combat. Kaua koʻekoʻe. Revolutionary ~. Kaua hoʻokahuli aupuni.

warbler A kind of bird. Manu kūolokū.

wardrobe As stage costumes for a play, movie, or video production. Nā ʻaʻahu hana keaka, nā ʻaʻahu.

warm Mahana, mehana. See entries below and temperature.

warm-blooded As an animal. Koko mehana. See cold-blooded.

warm front As of weather. Kuʻina mehana. See front.

warming Global ~, greenhouse effect. Hoʻomehana Honua.

warm-up suit As for sports. Lole kueka haʻuki. See sweatshirt.

warning As in a weather report. Kūkala pōʻino. See watch. Flood ~. Kūkala pōʻino wai hālana. Hurricane ~. Kūkala pōʻino makani pāhili.

warp As in Nintendo games, not as wood. Kaʻakepa. See turbo button. ~ zone. Kāʻei kaʻakepa.

warrant Also arrest ~, ~ for arrest, as a document issued by a magistrate authorizing an officer to make an arrest. Palapala hopu.

warranty A written guarantee of integrity of a product with promise to repair or replace. Palapala hoʻokō. See guarantee.

washer As used in plumbing. Hoʻopiha; pihi hoʻopiha, pihipihi (preceded by ke).

Washington Also Wahingtonian. Wakinekona.

waste As of plants and animals. Moka.

watch As in a weather report. Kūkala makaʻala. See warning, clock. Flood ~. Kūkala makaʻala wai hālana. Hurricane ~. Kūkala makaʻala makani pāhili.

watchtower Ranger station, especially for watching for forest fires. Hale kiaʻi ululāʻau. See ranger.

water Wai. See entries below. To turn on the ~. Wehe i ke kī wai. To turn off the ~. Hoʻopaʻa i ke kī wai. Tap ~. Wai paipu. Hot tap ~. Wai wela paipu.

water ~ing can. Kini hoʻopulu meakanu. ~ dish. Pā wai (preceded by ke). ~ heater. Kula hoʻowela wai, pahu hoʻowela wai. ~ table, as used in preschools. Pākaukau wai (also preceded by ke).

water Body of ~. Hiʻona wai. See water feature. Ground~. Wai honua. Mineral or sparkling ~. Wai piʻipiʻi. Rain ~. Wai ua. Surface ~. Wai ʻili honua, wai ʻili. ~ displacement. Pohupani wai. ~ lens, in geology. Papa wai kau luna. ~ table, in geology. Papa wai.

water-base Kuapapa wai. ~ paint. Pena kuapapa wai.

water code State ~. Papa kānāwai wai o ka mokuʻāina.

watercolor Pena wai.

water commission Komikina wai.

water dispenser As in a bird cage. Kāhāinu. See feeder.

water feature Also water form, as a lake, pond, river, etc., in geography. Hiʻona wai. See land feature.

water filter For a fish tank, in aquaculture. Kulamakaloa. See fish tank.

waterproof See water-resistant.

water-resistant Also waterproof. ʻAʻalo wai. See resist. ~ watch. Uaki ʻaʻalo wai, uāki ʻaʻalo wai.

watershed An area from which water drains. ʻĀina kumu wai. Municipal ~. ʻĀina kumu wai kiwikā.

water ski Heʻe wai. See ski.

water slide Slip ʻnʻ Slide; also to go on a ~. Paheʻe wai. ~ mat. Moena paheʻe wai.

watt Uate. Abb. uat. See kilowatt.

wave *As surf near the land.* Nalu. *As a swell in the open ocean.* 'Ale. *Height of a ~.* Ki'eki'ena nalu, ki'eki'ena 'ale, ki'eki'ena. *Length of a ~, ~length.* Kōā nalu, kōā 'ale, kōā. *Crest of a ~.* Hokua o ka nalu, hokua o ka 'ale, hokua. *Trough of a ~.* Honua, honua o ka nalu, honua o ka 'ale. *Where a ~ breaks, surfbreak.* Po'ina nalu (*preceded by* ke). *Sound ~, as used in measuring ocean depths.* Hawewe kani. *~-cut cliff.* Pali 'a'aianalu. *See erode, weathered.*

wave *To ~ something.* Ho'āni.

wave *Scientific usage.* Hawewe. *See amplify, amplitude, carrier, compressional wave, solar energy wave, sound wave, transverse wave, wavelength.*

wavelength *Sound ~.* Kōā hawewe kani.

wax Uepa, pīlali. *See paraffin. ~ paper.* Pepa pīlali, pepa 'aila. *As for polishing a car.* 'Aila ho'ohinuhinu. *Grafting ~.* Pīlali pāku'i. *Spray ~.* Kīkina ho'ohinuhinu. *Waxy, as in texture.* 'Ōihoiho.

wayfinding *Also to wayfind.* Ho'okele wa'a, kele moana.

weak acid *Naturally occurring ~.* 'Akika 'ūpalu kūlohelohe.

weak safety *In football.* 'Āwa'a lala. *See strong safety.*

weather Anilā. *See climate, erode, temperature. ~ service.* 'Oihana anilā. *~ station.* Kikowaena kilo anilā. *~ vane, wind vane.* Kuhimakani. *~ed.* 'A'aianilā.

weave *To ~, as on a loom.* Kālino. *Herringbone ~.* Maka puhi, iwipuhi.

web *See World Wide Web. Food ~.* Pūnaewele mea'ai.

webbed *As a duck's feet.* Pepewa.

Weddell Wedele. *~ Sea.* Ke kai 'o Wedele.

wedelia *A ground cover.* Wekelia.

Wednesday Po'akolu. *Abb.* P3.

weed Nāhelehele, nā'ele'ele.

week Pule. *Abb.* pl.

weight *In math.* Kaumaha. *For scales.* Koihā.

weightless *As when in outer space.* Lewalana. *See zero gravity.*

weight lifting *Also to lift weights.* Amo hao, hāpai hao.

welcome *Japanese lucky ~ cat.* Manekineko.

welcome banquet 'Aha'aina ho'okipa.

weld Ku'ihao.

welfare *Public financial assistance for needy persons.* Kōkua nele.

well done *As meat.* Mo'a loa.

west Komohana. *Abb.* Km. *See entries below.*

Western Europe *Also Western European.* 'Eulopa Komohana.

western hemisphere Poepoe hapa komohana. *See hemisphere.*

Western Pacific Fishery Management Council 'Aha Ho'omalu Lawai'a o ka Pākīpika Komohana.

Western Sahara *Also Western Saharan.* Sahara Komohana.

West Virginia *Also West Virginian.* Wilikinia Komohana.

wet *~ from cold, damp or moist with fog or dew.* Kawaū.

whale *Humpback ~.* Koholā kuapi'o.

what *As in asking about any kind of measurement; also how.* 'Ehia, he aha.

wheat Huika. *See straw and Hawaiian entries under palaoa. ~ bread.* Palaoa huika. *Whole ~.* Huika piha. *Whole ~ bread.* Palaoa huika piha. *Whole ~ flour.* Palaoa maka huika piha.

wheel Huila. *Bicycle ~.* Huila paikikala. *~ rim.* Kuapo hao.

when *Also and, until, to, etc.* A.

whipped cream Kalima huipa. *(Hot) chocolate with ~.* Kokoleka me ke kalima huipa.

whippoorwill Uipouila, manu uipouila.

whistle *As a referee's ~.* 'Ūlili.

white *Egg ~.* Kauō ke'oke'o, kauō. *See entries below and yolk.*

white blood cell Hunaola koko ke'oke'o.

white board *Also dry erase board.* Papa ke'oke'o, papa peni kuni.

white bread Palaoa ke'oke'o.

whitecap 'Ale kuakea. *To have ~s.* Niho.

whitefish I'akea.

white-footed mouse 'Iole wāwae kea.

white rice Laiki ke'oke'o, lāisi ke'oke'o.

whole milk Waiū piha.

whole note *In music.* Hua mele 'oko'a.

whole number *In math.* Helu piha. *See integer, mixed number.*

whole rest *In music.* Ho'omaha 'oko'a.

wholesale price Kumukū'ai kālepa. *See retail price.*

wholesome *Also healthful, healthy, i.e. promoting physical health.* Hā'ehuola. *See health food.*

whole wheat Huika piha. *~ bread.* Palaoa huika piha. *~ flour.* Palaoa maka huika piha.

wide open Hāmama. *See open.*

wide shot *As of a photograph or in movie or video production.* Pa'i laulā *(preceded by* ke*).* *See close-up, medium shot.* *To take a ~.* Pa'i a laulā. *Extreme ~.* Pa'i laulā loa. *To take an extreme ~.* Pa'i a laulā loa.

width *Also breadth, in math.* Ākea, ana ākea, laulā *(abb.* ll*)*, ana laulā. *See height, length.* *Variable ~, as in a computer program.* Laulā loli.

wild *General term; also shy.* 'Āhiu. *See wildlife. Naturally wild, as tiger,* 'i'iwi, 'a'ali'i, *etc.* Lōhiu. *Overactive, as an unruly child.* Lapa. *To grow ~ and lush.* Ulu wale, uluāhewa.

wildcat Pōpoki lōhiu.

wildlife Holoholona lōhiu. *~ expert.* Loea holoholona lōhiu. *Hawaiian*

Islands National ~ Refuge. 'Āina Ho'omalu Holoholona Lōhiu o Hawai'i. *State ~ official.* Luna ho'omalu holoholona lōhiu, ho'omalu holoholona lōhiu. *US Fish and ~ Service.* 'Oihana I'a me ka Holoholona Lōhiu o 'Amelika.

win *See Hawaiian entry* eo.

wind *See Hawaiian entries* pohu, kolonahe, aheahe, ho'oholunape, ulūlu, 'ena makani.

windbreaker *A kind of jacket.* Kuka makani.

wind-generated electricity Uila huila makani. *See electricity.*

windmill Huila makani.

window Pukaaniani. *See jalousie.* *~ curtain.* Pale pukaaniani. *~ frame or molding.* Mōlina pukaaniani. *~ sill.* Paepae pukaaniani.

windows *See stack, tile windows.*

windpipe *Also trachea, in anatomy.* Paipu hanu. *See epiglottis, esophagus, larynx.*

windsurf Holo papa pe'a. *Board for ~ing.* Papa pe'a.

wind vane *Also weather vane.* Kuhimakani.

wing nut Pihi wili 'ēheu.

wingspan Anana 'ēheu.

winner *As in the consolation bracket of a sports tournament.* Mea puka. *~'s bracket.* Māhele lanakila.

winter Ho'oilo. *See equinox.* *~ solstice.* Ka māuiki'iki'i o ka ho'oilo.

winterberry Pī'ai ho'oilo.

wintergreen Pailola.

wipe *See dust.*

wiped out *An exclamation used by the winner in a card game to the loser meaning "you got ~."* Palaina puna, *also* pāpa'a piele.

wire *Nichrome ~.* Uea nikoroma.

wire gauze *Steel wool.* Pulupulu uea.

Wisconsin *Also Wisconsinite.* Wikonekina, Wikonesina.

witch Hese. See *black widow*.

withdraw *To ~ money from the bank.* Kīkoʻo.

witty *Funny.* Hoʻomakeʻaka.

women *Hatred of ~; misogyny.* Hoʻokae wahine. See *misandry, misanthropy*.

wood Lāʻau. See entries below and *peg*. *~ paneling.* Papa pānela lāʻau.

woodpecker Manu pao lāʻau.

woodpecker finch Ōpuhe pao lāʻau.

wood peewee *A kind of bird.* Manu pīuīlāʻau.

wood rose Loke lāʻau.

wood shavings Hānā.

wood thrush Manu keluka ululāʻau.

woodwind instrument Pū ʻoʻohe.

wool Hulu. See *blanket*. *Glass ~.* Hulu aniani. *Steel ~.* Pulupulu uea.

woolly mammoth ʻElepani pūhuluhulu.

word Huaʻōlelo. *~ skill.* Mākau huaʻōlelo.

word processor *As a computer program.* Polokalamu kikokiko palapala.

workbook Puke hoʻomaʻamaʻa haʻawina, puke hoʻomaʻamaʻa.

workshop Hālāwai hoʻonaʻauao.

World Wide Web *Also www, as on the Internet.* Pūnaewele Puni Honua.

worm *See Hawaiian entries under* koʻe. *Polychaete ~, a kind of ~ found underneath stream rocks.* Moeʻalā.

wrap See *text wrap*.

wraparound *As a window or eyeglasses.* Kewe. *~ window.* Pukaaniani kewe.

wrasse *Cleaner ~, labroides Phthirophegus, a kind of fish.* Hīnālea nāʻuke.

wrench *Pipe ~.* Kala paipu.

wrinkled frog Poloka mimino.

wrist bone See *carpal bone*.

wrist brace Kāliki pūlima.

write *To ~, as a computer program.* Haku. See *speed write, writing*.

write protect *To ~, as a computer file or disk.* Hoʻopale kākau. *~ed.* Hoʻopale kākau ʻia.

writing *Creative ~.* Kākau makakū. *Extemporaneous ~; also to freewrite, as writing about anything one chooses.* Kākau ulu wale.

written Palapala. *~ literature.* Moʻokalaleo palapala. *~ report.* Hōʻike palapala.

www *World Wide Web, as on the Internet.* Pūnaewele Puni Honua.

Wyoming *Also Wyomingite.* Waiomina.

X

XL *Extra large, as shirt size.* Nui keu.

XXL *Double-extra large.* Nui keu pālua.

XXXL *Triple-extra large.* Nui keu pākolu.

xylem Kikiʻuwai. See *phloem*.

Y

yard *Unit of measurement.* ʻĪā. *No abbreviation. Cubic ~.* ʻĪā paʻaʻiliono.

yarn Pāaniani. See *knit*.

yeah *Also isn't that so, right; used only at the end of a sentence or phrase.* Ē. *See Hawaiian entry.*

year Makahiki. *Abb.* MH. *Light ~.* Makahiki holo kukuna lā.

yearbook *Annual.* Puke hoʻohaliʻa makahiki.

yeast Hū.

Yellow Sea Ke Kai Melemele.

Yemen *South ~; also South ~ite, South Yemeni.* Iemene Hema. *North ~; also North ~ite, North Yemeni.* Iemene ʻĀkau.

yield *To ~, as in traffic.* Hōʻae. *~ sign.* Hōʻailona hōʻae.

yield *Sustained ~, as in crop production.* Loaʻa paʻa mau.

yogurt Waiūtepe. *Frozen ~.* Hauwaiūtepe.

yolk *Egg ~.* Kauō melemele, kauō. See *white.*

York See *New York.*

Yosemite Iosemite. See *national park.* *~ National Park.* Pāka Aupuni 'o Iosemite.

you dummy *Also I told you so, don't you forget it, you should know; used only at the end of a sentence or phrase.* Ā. See *Hawaiian entry.*

you should know See *you dummy.*

yoyo Ioio.

Yugoslavia *Also Yugoslavian.* Iugosolawia.

Z

Zaire *Also Zairian.* Zāire.

Zambia *Also Zambian.* Zamibia.

Zealand See *New Zealand.*

zebrina *A kind of flower.* Pua kepela, kepela.

zero *Ground ~, as in field mapping.* Papahonua. *~ degrees K (Kelvin); absolute zero, a hypothetical temperature characterized by complete absence of heat.* 'Ole Kelewine.

zero gravity 'Umekaumaha 'ole.

zero property *In math.* 'Anopili 'ole (*preceded by* ke). *~ of multiplication.* 'Anopili 'ole o ka ho'onui.

Zimbabwe *Also Zimbabwean.* Zimababue.

zinc Kiniki.

zip code Helu kuhi.

zipper Huka.

zonation sheet *Vegetation ~.* Palapala kā'ei meakanu.

zone Kā'ei. See entry below and *intertropical convergent zone, tropics.* *Rift ~.* Kā'ei māwae. *Time ~, as Pacific or Rocky Mountain.* Kā'ei hola. *Warp ~, as in Nintendo games.* Kā'ei ka'akepa.

zone *End ~, on a football field.* Pahu 'ai holo. *~ defense, as in basketball; to execute such a play.* Pale kā'ei. *~ offense.* Kūlele kā'ei.

zoo *Petting ~.* Kahua hamohamo holoholona.

zoom *To ~ in, as with a movie or video camera.* Ho'okokoke. *To ~ out.* Ho'olaulā.

Z-shaped line *A "straight" ~ written to indicate where two words written as one should be separated, in proofreading.* Kaha ho'oka'ahua, kaha ho'okōā.

Zuben Elgenubi *A star.* Hauhoa.

Zuben Elschamali *A star.* Nāki'iki'i.

zucchini Sūkini.

Hale Kuamoʻo

Kākoʻo a paipai ka Hale Kuamoʻo–Kikowaena ʻŌlelo Hawaiʻi i ka hoʻokumu ʻana i ka ʻōlelo Hawaiʻi, ʻo ia ka ʻōlelo kaiapuni o nā kula, o ke aupuni, o nā ʻoihana like ʻole, i lohe ʻia mai hoʻi ka ʻōlelo Hawaiʻi mai ʻō a ʻō o Hawaiʻi Pae ʻĀina. Na ka Hale Kuamoʻo e hoʻomohala nei i nā haʻawina e pono ai ka holomua o ka ʻōlelo Hawaiʻi ʻana ma nā ʻano pōʻaiapili like ʻole e like hoʻi me ka haʻawina ʻōlelo Hawaiʻi no nā kula ʻōlelo Hawaiʻi, nā papahana kākoʻo kumu, ka nūpepa ʻo *Nā Maka O Kana*, a me kēia puke wehewehe ʻōlelo nei ʻo *Māmaka Kaiao*.

Ua hoʻokumu ʻia ka Hale Kuamoʻo e ka ʻAhaʻōlelo o ka Mokuʻāina ʻo Hawaiʻi i ka makahiki 1989. ʻO ka Hale Kuamoʻo ke keʻena Mokuʻāina ʻōlelo Hawaiʻi mua loa a puni ʻo Hawaiʻi. Inā makemake ʻoe e kākoʻo i nā pahuhopu a me nā hana o ka Hale Kuamoʻo ma ka lūlū mai i ke kālā hāʻawi manawaleʻa, e hoʻouna mai i ka University of Hawaiʻi Foundation–Hale Kuamoʻo ma ka helu wahi i hōʻike ʻia ma lalo iho nei.

The Hale Kuamoʻo–Hawaiian Language Center supports and encourages expansion of Hawaiian language as the medium of education, business, government, and other contexts of social life in Hawaiʻi. The Center provides professional and material resources necessary to address this goal including educational support in the development of curriculum materials for Hawaiian medium education, teacher training, Nā Maka O Kana *Hawaiian language newspaper, and* Māmaka Kaiao: A Modern Hawaiian Vocabulary.

Established and funded by the State Legislature in 1989, the Hale Kuamoʻo is the first example of a State office conducting its business in Hawaiian. If you wish to contribute to the goals and activities of the Hale Kuamoʻo, please send your donation to the University of Hawaiʻi Foundation–Hale Kuamoʻo at the address below.

Hale Kuamoʻo
University of Hawaiʻi at Hilo
200 West Kāwili Street
Hilo, Hawaiʻi 96720-4091

Kelepona (*Phone*): (808) 974-7339 • Kelepaʻi (*Fax*): (808) 974-7686
Leka Uila (*E-mail*): hale_kuamoo@leoki.uhh.hawaii.edu

Kahua Paʻa (*Web Site*): www.olelo.hawaii.edu

'Aha Pūnana Leo

He 'ahahui ho'ona'auao 'ōiwi Hawai'i 'auhau 'ole ka 'Aha Pūnana Leo ('APL) i ho'okumu 'ia i ka makahiki 1983. Ua ulu mai ke aukahi Pūnana Leo mai loko mai o ka 'i'ini e ho'okumu pa'a 'ia a puni 'o Hawai'i nei ke kūlana mana o ka 'ōlelo Hawai'i ola o kēlā me kēia lā. 'O ka 'Aha Pūnana Leo kekahi o nā alaka'i o ke ao ma ia hana he ho'ōla 'ōlelo 'ane halapohe. A he kūpa'a pono ma hope o kona mākia e kia mau nei, 'o ia ho'i "E Ola Ka 'Ōlelo Hawai'i."

I kēia wā, he 'umikumamālua kula kamali'i a ka 'APL e ho'okele nei, a ke mālama alu like nei ka 'APL i papahana kula ho'okolohua 'ōlelo Hawai'i mai ka mālaa'o a i ka papa 12. Kaulana ka 'APL i ka mālama 'ana i ko nā kula ona, ko nā Kula Kaiapuni Hawai'i, nā 'ohana 'ōlelo Hawai'i, a me ka lehulehu ākea ma kāna papahana ho'opuka a ho'omalele lako a'o 'ōlelo Hawai'i. He mau ha'awina palapala kēia me ka palapala 'ole (kīwī, wikiō, lēkiō, a pēlā aku) i noi'i 'ia, hakulau 'ia, a ho'opuka 'ia me ka nui no'eau a me ka helu 'ekahi o ka nani. Ma lalo pū o ka 'APL he papahana ho'olako kālā hele kulanui a me kekahi mau papahana 'ē a'e e kūlia ana i ke ola o ka 'ōlelo Hawai'i a me ka ho'ona'auao 'ōlelo Hawai'i.

'Aha Pūnana Leo, Inc. ('APL), established in 1983, is a nonprofit native Hawaiian educational organization which grew out of a dream that the indigenous language of Hawai'i be reestablished as a daily living language. 'APL is an internationally known leader in language revitalization. Its vision remains clear and focused: E Ola Ka 'Ōlelo Hawai'i ("The Hawaiian language shall live").

Currently, 'APL administers twelve preschools and coadministers a K-12 model program in Hawaiian language medium education. 'APL is widely respected for researching, designing, publishing, and distributing the highest quality print and nonprint curriculum materials for use by the Pūnana Leo preschools, the Kula Kaiapuni Hawai'i immersion sites, 'APL families, and the general public. 'APL also manages a postsecondary scholarship program and other support activities for Hawaiian language education and revitalization.

'Aha Pūnana Leo, Inc.
1744 Kino'ole Street
Hilo, Hawai'i 96720-5245

Kelepona (*Phone*): (808) 959-4979 • Kelepa'i (*Fax*): (808) 959-4725
Leka Uila (*E-mail*): namaka@leoki.uhh.hawaii.edu

Kahua Pa'a (*Web Site*): www.ahapunanaleo.org